The American Years

The American Years

CHRONOLOGIES OF AMERICAN HISTORY AND EXPERIENCE

SECOND EDITION

2

1901 to 2002

ERNIE GROSS, ROBERT D. JOHNSTON, RUSSELL LAWSON, AND PAUL ROSIER

CHARLES SCRIBNER'S SONS®

New York • Detroit • San Diego • San Francisco • Cleveland • New Haven, Conn. • Waterville, Maine • London • Munich

The American Years, Second Edition

Ernie Gross, Robert D. Johnston, Russell Lawson, and Paul Rosier

For more information, contact
Charles Scribner's Sons
An imprint of The Gale Group
300 Park Avenue South, 9th Floor
New York, NY 10010
Or you can visit our Internet site at
http://www.gale.com

LIBRARY OF CONGRESS CATALOGING-IN-PUBLICATION DATA

The American years: a chronology of United States history /
Ernie Gross ... [et al.]. — 2nd ed.
p. cm.
Includes bibliographical references and index.
Contents: v. 1. The colonial era to 1900 — v. 2. 1901 to 2002.
ISBN 0-684-31254-9 (set : alk. paper) — ISBN 0-684-31255-7
(v. 1 : alk paper) — ISBN 0-684-31256-5 (v. 2 : alk. paper)
1. United States—History—Chronology. I. Gross, Ernie.
E174.5.G753 2003
973 ' .02 ' 02—dc21

2002010006

ISBNs
Set: 0-684-31254-9
Volume 1: 0-684-31255-7
Volume 2: 0-684-31256-5

Printed in the United States of America
10 9 8 7 6 5 4 3 2

Contents

The locations of overview essays are highlighted below. The bold headings indicate new sections. See separate index for primary source documents.

Abbreviations

AAFC	All-American Football Conference
AAU	American Athletic Union
AEC	Atomic Energy Commission
AFB	Air Force Base
AFL	American Federation of Labor
AFL	American Football League
AIAW	Association of Intercollegiate Athletics for Women
ATT	American Telephone & Telegraph Co.
BAA	Basketball Association of America
CBS	Columbia Broadcasting System
FBI	Federal Bureau of Investigation
FCC	Federal Communications Commission
IBM	International Business Machines Corp.
ICC	Interstate Commerce Commission
IC4A	Intercollegiate Association of Amateur Athletes of America
ITT	International Telephone & Telegraph Co.
LPGA	Ladies Professional Golf Association
MIT	Massachusetts Institute of Technology
NAACP	National Association for the Advancement of Colored People
NASA	National Aeronautics and Space Administration
NASCAR	National Association for Stock Car Auto Racing
NBC	National Broadcasting Co.
NBA	National Basketball Association
NCAA	National Collegiate Athletic Association
NFL	National Football League
NHL	National Hockey League
NIT	National Invitational Tournament (basketball)
PBA	Professional Bowlers Association
PGA	Professional Golfers Association
TVA	Tennessee Valley Authority
UCLA	University of California, Los Angeles
UN	United Nations
UNLV	University of Nevada, Las Vegas
USFL	United States Football League
USLTA	U.S. Lawn Tennis Association
USO	United Service Organization
VFW	Veterans of Foreign Wars

The American Years: Chronology and Context (continued)

1901

INTERNATIONAL

Second Hay-Pauncefote Treaty is signed (November 18), gives U.S. right to build, operate an isthmian (Panama) canal open to all shipping; is ratified (December 16).

American troops capture Filipino revolt leader, Emilio Aguinaldo (March 23); military government in Philippines ends, civil government is established (July 4) with William Howard Taft governor general.

Cuba sets up provisional independent government (June 12).

NATIONAL

President William McKinley is shot at Pan-American Exposition in Buffalo, New York, by an anarchist, Leon Czolgosz (September 6), dies eight days later; Vice President Theodore Roosevelt becomes president; Czolgosz is tried, convicted (September 23), electrocuted (October 29).

President Roosevelt, in first annual message, calls on Congress to consider safeguards against industrial combinations.

Bureau of Standards, Weights, and Measures is created as a separate office (July 1), becomes National Bureau of Standards (1913); permanent Census Bureau is created.

Army War College is established with Tasker H. Bliss president (November 27); first class held (1903).

Louisiana and Alabama adopt new constitutions.

American Hall of Fame at New York University dedicated (May 30).

Carry Nation, temperance crusader, makes first hatchet attack on a saloon (Wichita, Kansas, January 21); she continues as do other temperance workers elsewhere.

Galveston, Texas, adopts commission form of government.

DEATHS Former President Benjamin Harrison (1889–1893); Hiram R. Revels, first black elected to Senate (Mississippi, 1870); Union Gen. Daniel Butterfield, composer of bugle call "Taps."

BUSINESS/INDUSTRY/INVENTIONS

Texas oil boom begins with Spindletop well near Beaumont; first important commercial oil well is drilled in Oklahoma.

U.S. Steel Corp., first billion dollar company, incorporates with Charles M. Schwab as president.

New companies formed include Gillette Safety Razor Co., Monsanto Chemical Co., Victor Talking Machine Co.; Guggenheim Exploration Co. takes over American Smelting & Refining Co., Quaker Oats Co. replaces American Cereal Co.

Peter Cooper Hewitt patents mercury vapor lamp; Reginald Fessenden, an improved wireless transmitter.

Ellsworth Statler builds his first hotel, a temporary building of 2,100 rooms for the Pan-American Exposition in Buffalo, New York.

TRANSPORTATION

New York State requires license plates on automobiles.

Booker T. Washington Dines at the White House

Famed for his ideas on educational reform and his role in founding the Tuskegee Institute in Alabama, Booker T. Washington (1856–1915) considered economic equality central to the progress of African Americans in U.S. society. A popular national figure, Washington dined at the White House on October 16, 1901 on invitation from President Theodore Roosevelt. The two men discussed southern politics, with Roosevelt seeking Washington's advice on federal appointments in the region. Not intended to provoke controversy, the dinner nonetheless outraged some white southerners, who accused Roosevelt of interfering with issues of racial and social hierarchy. One Memphis newspaper declared Roosevelt's invite "the most damnable outrage ever committed by any citizen of the United States," while Senator Benjamin Tillman of South Carolina railed, "The action of President Roosevelt in entertaining that nigger will necessitate our killing a thousand niggers in the South before they will learn their place again." The president politely responded by noting his right to invite whomever he wanted for dinner, and in private letters he expressed his admiration for Washington, whom he considered "a good citizen and good American."

Hendee Manufacturing Co. markets the "Indian" motorcycle with built-in gas engine; Sinclair Oil Co. is founded.

Railroad engineer Casey Jones crashes his Cannonball Express into a stopped freight train near Vaughn, Mississippi.

DEATHS Aaron French, inventor of coil elliptical springs that revolutionized railroad industry; Clement Studebaker, wagon and auto manufacturer.

SCIENCE/MEDICINE

Army Nurses Corps is established (February 2); Army Dental Corps is authorized.

Rockefeller Institute of Medical Research (now Rockefeller University) is founded.

Scripps Institution for Biological Research (later Oceanography) is established.

Miller R. Hutchinson produces the Acousticon, an electrical hearing aid.

Chemist Jokichi Takamine isolates adrenaline.

EDUCATION

Francis W. Parker founds University of Chicago School of Education.

Chemist Ira Remsen becomes president of Johns Hopkins University.

Andrew Carnegie gives New York City $5.2 million for 65 branch libraries.

Grambling State (Louisiana) University and Idaho State University are founded.

Union catalog, combining books alphabetically in many catalogs and libraries, begins at Library of Congress.

RELIGION

Mother Alphonsa (Rose Hawthorne) founds Servants of Relief for Incurable Cancer, which she heads for 27 years.

Joseph Fielding Smith becomes president of Mormon church, succeeding Lorenzo Snow.

ART/MUSIC

George W. Chadwick writes lyric drama *Judith.*

Museum of Art in Toledo is founded.

Alfred H. Maurer completes the painting *An Arrangement;* Thomas Moran, *Grand Canyon of the Yellowstone.*

SONGS (POPULAR): "Just a-Wearyin' for You," "I Love You Truly," "Mighty Lak a Rose," "Hiawatha."

DEATH Ethelbert W. Nevin, composer ("The Rosary," "Mighty Lak a Rose").

LITERATURE/JOURNALISM

Munsey newspaper chain is founded when Frank A. Munsey buys *Washington Times* and the *New York News.*

Clarence W. Barron buys Dow Jones & Co., becomes publisher of the *Wall Street Journal.*

Edgar Guest writes poems that are syndicated by *Detroit Free Press.*

BOOKS *Graustark* by George B. McCutcheon, *Mrs. Wiggs of the Cabbage Patch* by Alice Hegan Rice, *The Crisis* by Winston Churchill, *The Octopus* by Frank Norris, *The Making of an American* by Jacob A. Riis.

Leon Czolgosz, an anarchist, shoots President William McKinley at the Pan-American Exposition reception on September 6, 1901. Vice President Theodore Roosevelt assumes the presidency after McKinley dies eight days later. THE LIBRARY OF CONGRESS

ENTERTAINMENT

Manhattan Theater in New York City opens.

PLAYS David Warfield stars in *The Auctioneer,* Richard Mansfield in *Beaucaire,* Ethel Barrymore in *Capt. Jinks of the Horse Marines,* Mrs. Leslie Carter in *DuBarry,* E. H. Sothern in *If I Were King,* William Collier in *On the Quiet,* Julia Marlowe in *When Knighthood Was in Flower,* Lillian Russell in *Hoity Toity,* Anna Held in *The Little Duchess.*

SPORTS

First American League baseball game is played in Chicago (April 24), first doubleheader (July 15) split by Washington and Baltimore; Cy Young of Boston Red Sox wins his 300th game; Connie Mack becomes manager and part-owner of Philadelphia Athletics; National Association of Professional Baseball Leagues is organized in Chicago (September 5).

First American Bowling Congress sponsors tournament in Chicago; 41 teams from 17 cities compete for $1,592 in prize money.

WINNERS *Automobile racing*—David W. Bishop, 500-mile Buffalo–New York race; *Boxing*—Jim Jeffries, heavyweight; Joe Gans, lightweight; *Horse racing*—His Eminence, Kentucky Derby; The Parader, Preakness Stakes; Commando, Belmont Stakes; *Yachting*—U.S. boat *Columbia* retains America's Cup.

MISCELLANEOUS

Anna Edson Taylor goes over Niagara Falls in a barrel.

President Roosevelt causes uproar in South when he invites Booker T. Washington to White House (October 16).

Fire in Jacksonville, Florida, destroys 1,700 buildings, causes $11 million damage, leaves 10,000 homeless.

1902

INTERNATIONAL

Isthmian Act provides $40 million to purchase property and rights of the new Panama Canal Co., calls on Colombia to grant U.S. perpetual control of the canal right-of-way (June 28).

Territorial government forms in Philippines (July 1).

U.S. withdraws from Cuba (May 20).

NATIONAL

President Theodore Roosevelt asks attorney general to

A boy reads the playbill poster outside of Havlin's Theatre in St. Louis, Missouri. The first U.S. movie theater, Los Angeles's Electric Theater, opens in 1901. CORBIS-BETTMANN

bring first antitrust suit to dissolve Northern Securities Co., a railroad holding company (March 10).

National Reclamation Act sets aside proceeds from public-land sales in 16 states to finance, maintain irrigation projects; U.S. Reclamation Service begins (January 7).

Carnegie Institution in Washington, D.C., is founded (January 28).

U.S. Army uniform changes from blue to olive drab.

Juliette G. Low founds first troop of Girls Guides (later Girl Scouts) in Savannah, Georgia.

Woman Suffrage Alliance is founded.

Crater Lake (Oregon) National Park is established.

DEATHS Former First Lady Julia D. Grant (1869–1877); cartoonist Thomas Nast, who created political party symbols; Elizabeth Cady Stanton, women's rights leader.

BUSINESS/INDUSTRY/INVENTIONS

Maryland adopts first state workmen's compensation law, later found unconstitutional.

United Mine Workers call strike against anthracite coal mines; federal mediation ends strike.

Horn & Hardart opens first automatic food-vending restaurant in U.S. at 818 Chestnut St., Philadelphia, Pennsylvania.

Merger of McCormick and Deering companies forms International Harvester Co.

PATENTS for rayon to Arthur D. Little, William H. Walker, and Harry S. York; to David D. Kenney for a vacuum cleaner.

Newt Graham founds National Farmers Union.

DuPont Co. establishes explosives laboratory at Gibbstown, New Jersey.

Chemist Herman Frasch begins American sulphur industry when he develops method for extracting sulphur from deep deposits in Louisiana.

DEATHS Levi Strauss, developer of pants ("Levi's") made of canvas; Potter Palmer, founder of store that became Marshall Field's.

TRANSPORTATION

American Automobile Assn. is founded (March 4).

Glenn H. Curtiss, motorcycle racer, develops an engine and establishes motorcycle plant.

Packard Motor Co. is founded.

Vermont passes ordinance requiring that a mature individual carrying a red flag precede every moving automobile.

SCIENCE/MEDICINE

New York City is first in U.S. to appoint a school nurse.

Dr. Charles W. Stiles discovers the hookworm, a widespread southern parasite.

DEATH Walter Reed, military surgeon who headed study of yellow fever.

EDUCATION

John D. Rockefeller endows General Education Board.

Simmons College in Boston opens.

University of Michigan Department of Forestry is established.

Nicholas Murray Butler becomes president of Columbia University; Woodrow Wilson, president of Princeton University.

DEATH Francis W. Parker, a founder of progressive elementary education.

RELIGION

Catholic Bishop John M. Farley becomes archbishop of New York City.

William James completes book *The Varieties of Religious Experience.*

DEATH Patrick A. Feehan, first Catholic archbishop of Chicago (1880–1902).

ART/MUSIC

Alfred Stieglitz founds Photo-Secession, an organization to promote photography as an art form.

Edward A. MacDowell composes his *New England Idylls.*

Robert Henri completes the painting *Young Woman in Black;* Arthur B. Davies, *Dancing Children;* Everett Shinn, *The Hippodrome.*

SONGS (POPULAR): "In the Good Old Summertime," "Bill Bailey, Won't You Please Come Home?" "In the Sweet Bye and Bye," "On a Sunday Afternoon," "Under the Bamboo Tree," "Because."

DEATH Albert Bierstadt, painter of Western scenes.

LITERATURE/JOURNALISM

Edward W. Scripps founds Newspaper Enterprise Assn. (NEA), a feature syndicate.

Richard Outcault draws "Buster Brown" comic strip in *New York Herald.*

BOOKS *The Virginian* by Owen Wister, *Ranson's Folly* by Richard Harding Davis, *Captain Craig* (poetry) by Edwin Arlington Robinson, *The Valley of Decision* by Edith Wharton, *The Wings of the Dove* by Henry James.

ENTERTAINMENT

Thomas L. Tally establishes first movie theater in U.S., Electric Theater, in Los Angeles.

PLAYS May Robson stars in *The Billionaire,* Marie Dressler in *The Hall of Fame,* Lillian Russell in *Twirly Whirly;* other plays are *The Sultan of Sulu* by George Ade, *The Girl with the Green Eyes* by Clyde Fitch, *The Darling of the Gods* by David Belasco.

SPORTS

John J. McGraw, manager of the Baltimore baseball club, becomes manager of New York Giants.

WINNERS *Boxing*—Jim Jeffries, heavyweight; *Football*—Michigan in first Rose Bowl 49–0 over Stanford; *Horse racing*—Alan-a-Dale, Kentucky Derby; Old England, Preakness Stakes; Masterman, Belmont Stakes; *Tennis*—U.S., Davis Cup.

MISCELLANEOUS

Fire in a Birmingham church causes 115 deaths.

Two mine disasters occur: Coal Creek, Tennessee, 184 die, and Johnstown, Pennsylvania, 112 die.

1903

INTERNATIONAL

Hay-Herran Treaty with Colombia provides for 100-year lease of 10-mile-wide strip across Isthmus of Panama for $10 million and annual payments of $250,000 (January 22); Hay-Buneau-Varilla Treaty (November 18) with Panama reaffirms earlier treaty.

U.S. and Great Britain agree to arbitrate Alaska-Canada boundary; final line excludes Canada from ocean inlets of southern Alaska.

Marine Corps formally occupies Guantanamo Bay, Cuba.

NATIONAL

Department of Commerce and Labor is established (February 14) with George B. Cortelyou secretary.

Supreme Court in *Champion* v. *Ames* upholds federal law that prohibits sending lottery tickets through the mails, establishes federal-law police power; Congress passes law giving antitrust suits precedence on court dockets.

Wisconsin adopts direct primary elections.

Elkins Act strengthens Interstate Commerce Commission, eliminates rebates, defines unfair discrimination.

Army General Staff Corps is established.

First national bird reservation is established on Pelican Island near Sebastian, Florida.

BUSINESS/INDUSTRY/INVENTIONS

Cable across Pacific Ocean (San Francisco to Honolulu) available for public use (January 1); cable from Honolulu to Manila is completed (July 3).

Miners strike Colorado Fuel & Iron Co.; some return in few weeks, rest come back six months later; coal mine mediation commission awards miners who struck in 1902 a 10% increase.

Oregon passes 10-hour workday for women in industry.

DEATHS Frederick Law Olmsted, pioneer landscape architect; Gordon McKay, inventor of shoe-making machinery; Ebenezer Butterick, inventor of paper patterns for shirts, suits, dresses; Luther C. Crowell, inventor of square-bottom paper bag; Gustavus F. Swift, founder of meatpacking firm.

Orville Wright pilots the first motor-propelled flight on December 17, 1903. His brother Wilbur watches from the ground. **THE LIBRARY OF CONGRESS**

TRANSPORTATION

Wilbur and Orville Wright demonstrate first motor-driven airplane at Kitty Hawk, North Carolina (December 17); Wilbur flies 120 feet in 12 seconds, then Orville flies 852 feet in 59 seconds; nine days earlier, the *New York Times* criticizes Samuel P. Langley for "wasting" money trying to build a plane, states man would not fly for a thousand years.

First cross country–auto trip begins in San Francisco (May 23), ends in New York City (August 31); Boston YMCA opens an automobile school; New York Police Department issues "Rules for Driving" to help regulate traffic; Barney Oldfield becomes first to drive a car at a mile a minute (June 15).

Henry Ford founds Ford Motor Co.; Firestone Tire & Rubber Co. produces tires.

Clyde J. Coleman patents automobile electric self-starter.

Williamsburg Bridge over East River, New York City, is completed.

SCIENCE/MEDICINE

Vermont passes law that requires annual eye examinations of schoolchildren.

DEATH Josiah Willard Gibbs, considered U.S.'s greatest theoretical scientist.

EDUCATION

General Education Board incorporates to promote education.

Andrew Carnegie gives Cleveland $250,000 to build branch libraries.

DEATH Charles A. Cutter, father of library dictionary catalog.

RELIGION

Catholic Bishop John J. Glennon becomes archbishop of St. Louis, Missouri.

Bishop Daniel S. Tuttle becomes presiding Episcopal bishop.

ART/MUSIC

Victor Herbert produces his operetta *Babes in Toyland.*

Dallas (Texas) Museum of Fine Arts and Berkshire Museum, Pittsfield, Massachusetts, are founded.

SONGS (POPULAR): "Toyland," "Sweet Adeline," "Kashmiri Love Song," "Ida, Sweet as Apple Cider," "Goodbye, Eliza Jane," "Bedelia," "The Eyes of Texas."

LITERATURE/JOURNALISM

Joseph Pulitzer gives $1 million to found Columbia University School of Journalism.

An overhead view of the first World Series game. **AP/WIDE WORLD PHOTOS**

Ida M. Tarbell writes exposé of Standard Oil Co. in *McClure's.*

John T. McCutcheon begins 42 years as cartoonist for *Chicago Tribune.*

BOOKS *The Little Shepherd of Kingdom Come* by John Fox Jr., *Rebecca of Sunnybrook Farm* by Kate Douglas Wiggin, *The Call of the Wild* by Jack London, *The Pit* by Frank Norris, *The Ambassadors* by Henry James, *Children of the Tenements* by Jacob Riis.

DEATH Charles B. Smith, humorist writing as Bill Arp.

ENTERTAINMENT

John Barrymore makes stage debut in *Magda* in Chicago.

New Amsterdam Theater in New York City opens; Majestic Theater, also in New York, hires women ushers.

Warner Brothers opens first movie theater in U.S. (New Castle, Pennsylvania) that is called a "nickelodeon" because admission is 5 cents.

Edwin S. Porter produces movie *The Great Train Robbery.*

Dreamland amusement park costs $2 million, opens at Coney Island in Brooklyn, New York.

PLAYS Maxine Elliott stars in *Her Own Way,* Bert Williams in *In Dahomey,* Lionel Barrymore in *The Other Girl,* Henrietta Crosman in *Sweet Kitty Bellaire,* Lillian Russell in *Whoop-dee-do,* Eddie Foy in *Mr. Bluebeard.*

SPORTS

National (baseball) League recognizes American League as an equal; Harry C. Pulliam becomes National League president; Frank Ferrell and Bill Devery purchase Baltimore baseball franchise for $18,000, move it to New York.

Jamaica Racetrack on Long Island (New York) opens.

Lou Dillon, driven by Millard Sanders, is first trotter to run mile in less than 2 minutes (1 min, 58 1/2 sec.).

American Power Boat Assn. is formed.

WINNERS *Baseball*—Boston Red Sox beat Pittsburgh Pirates in first World Series; *Bicycling*—Iver Lawson, world professional sprint riding; *Boxing*—Jim Jeffries, heavyweight; Bob Fitzsimmons, light heavyweight; Frankie Neal, bantamweight; *Football*—Dartmouth (opening of Harvard Stadium); *Golf*—Willie Anderson, U.S. Open; *Horse racing*—Judge Himes, Kentucky Derby; Flocarline, Preakness

OVERVIEW

The Progressive Era, 1900–1920

ROBERT D. JOHNSTON, YALE UNIVERSITY

The first two decades of the twentieth century have become known as the Progressive Era. At that time American reformers believed that they could make progress on all kinds of troubling issues. Crusaders thought that the often naked grasp for economic gain might be overcome, along with the struggles between business and workers, and the conflicts between ethnic and racial groups that had characterized much of the late nineteenth century.

An Era of Political Reforms

During the Progressive Era many Americans turned to above all the political process to solve social ills. Native-born Protestants feared that heavily Catholic and immigrant "machines" in the big cities paid illiterates to vote, preventing good, clean government. They also believed that large corporations and other special interests bribed their way to political influence in city halls, state legislatures, and even the halls of Congress. Helped by journalist "muckrakers," these reformers mounted major campaigns against corruption.

Much of what the reformers did was democratic, resulting in more power for the people. Campaign finance laws, direct primaries that allowed ordinary voters to nominate candidates, and the election of U.S. senators by the people—instead of by state legislatures—were great accomplishments. At the same time, tightened election regulations, such as registration and the secret ballot, had the generally unintentional consequence of making it much harder for the poor and illiterate to vote. Prohibition, which outlawed the production, sale, and distribution of alcohol, had the support of the majority of citizens in most areas. However, it also became an offensive against immigrants and Catholics. And in the South, an all-out assault on the voting rights of blacks, and many poor whites, solidified the control of racist white elites.

A New Corporate Economy

Much of what concerned political reformers was the increasing power of big business. Corporations began to take control of critical areas of the American economy. Increasingly, Americans worked in factories controlled by United States Steel, had their oil refined by John D. Rockefeller's Standard Oil, and even bought their food from supermarkets instead of the local Mom and Pop grocery store. The "robber barons" who controlled these new enterprises proudly spoke about the great prosperity that the new technology, such as electricity and the automobile, brought to the masses. In contrast, individuals such as future Supreme Court Justice Louis Brandeis upheld the virtues of small business and advocated vigorous antitrust actions against big business.

Roosevelt, Taft, and Wilson

The differences over how to handle large corporations dominated the age's politics. These conflicts can be discerned most easily in the different approaches of the era's three presidents. Theodore Roosevelt, who became president after an anarchist assassinated William McKinley in 1901, in many ways had the most radical and modern of solutions to the "trust" problem. TR, who came from an aristocratic New York family, wanted to grant the federal government extensive powers to regulate big companies. His vice president, William Howard Taft, became president in 1909. Taft took a more conservative position on economic questions. Although he supported many Justice Department lawsuits to disband monopolies, Taft did not envision a fundamentally new relationship between the government and big business. Finally, Woodrow Wilson, president from 1913 to 1921, sympathized with small business and believed that American freedoms were dependent on "busting up" big corporations.

Stakes; Africander, Belmont Stakes; *Motor cycling*—Glenn H. Curtiss, Riverdale hill climb; *Tennis*—Great Britain, Davis Cup; *Wrestling*—Tom Jenkins, heavyweight; *Yachting*—U.S.'s *Reliance* retains America's Cup.

DEATH Ed Delehanty, baseball player, falls through ties of railroad bridge into Niagara River.

MISCELLANEOUS

Fire in Iroquois Theater, Chicago, kills 602 persons; mine disaster at Hanna, Wyoming, kills 169.

Martha Washington Hotel, exclusively for women, opens in New York City.

Forerunner of Big Brother movement is established in Cincinnati, Ohio.

The economic philosophies of these three leaders, along with those of socialist Eugene Victor Debs, came to a head in the 1912 presidential election. This was one of the classic elections of the modern era, as significant as the races in 1932, 1968, and 2000. TR decided to come out of retirement to seek the Republican nomination, but party regulars gave the nod to Taft. Roosevelt then formed a new party, the Progressive Party, to advance his candidacy. The Progressive Party also supported a number of innovative democratic reforms, such as initiative and referendum voting (by which citizens voted on, and decided, specific legislative and constitutional issues) and even the popular recall of judicial decisions. Wilson, the former president of Princeton University and governor of New Jersey, garnered the Democratic nomination. Many Americans believed that the problems of the country were so great that the very survival of the republic depended on the outcome of the election. TR declared: "We stand at Armageddon, and we battle for the Lord." Indeed, the American crisis was so deep that the socialist Debs received nearly a million votes. In the end, Wilson took advantage of the split in Republican ranks, becoming the first post–Civil War southern president.

Race: Washington vs. Du Bois

Woodrow Wilson was considered an anticorporate progressive on economic matters, but on issues of race he was decidedly reactionary. Roosevelt had opened the political door, at least slightly, to African Americans. He invited Booker T. Washington, the most visible and powerful black leader of the time, to the White House. He sought black votes and distributed patronage jobs to African Americans. However Wilson reversed these tentative advances. He segregated the civil service and gave active support to racist spokesmen. Wilson's actions came within the context of a horrible epidemic of lynching and the erosion of African-American political liberties in the South.

How should African Americans respond to this mounting oppression? Booker T. Washington and W. E. B. Du Bois were the spokesmen for the chief points of view. Washington argued for accommodation; Du Bois for resistance.

Washington, born into slavery, had through hard work become president of Tuskegee Institute, which under Washington's leadership was transformed into one of the premiere African-American colleges in America. In political matters, Washington urged the acceptance of the existing racial power structure. Once blacks had become economically successful, then they might be in a position to press white America for their deserved rights.

Du Bois would have none of this gradualist approach. Du Bois demanded full equality for African Americans, and he wanted it immediately. Born in Massachusetts, Du Bois was a Harvard-educated and European-trained scholar. He helped found the National Association for the Advancement of Colored People (NAACP) which became, during the course of the twentieth century, the most effective champion for African-American political rights.

Women as Progressives

It would be decades before African Americans won basic political and legal equality. In the meantime, black women took on the task of upholding the pride and dignity of their race. Even at the height of Jim Crow segregation, they served as teachers, public health officials, and social workers. In these capacities, they also served as progressive political reformers. Many African-American women, such as anti-lynching activist Ida B. Wells, also demanded women's suffrage, full voting rights for women.

The Nineteenth Amendment, granting women the right to vote, was the most expansive democratic reform of the Progressive Era. Ratified in 1920, it was the culmination of a movement that had commenced before the Civil War. Women in several, mainly western, states had gained the right to vote in the previous three decades. But, the vast majority of women remained formally excluded from the political system until Woodrow Wilson promised his support of suffrage in return for their support of American involve-

Richard Stieff designs "teddy" bear, named for President Theodore Roosevelt.

Flooding Kansas, Missouri, and Des Moines rivers drown 200, leave 8,000 homeless, cause about $4 million in damage.

DEATHS "Judge" Roy Bean, the "law west of the Pecos;" Calamity Jane (Martha Jane Burke), frontierswoman companion of Wild Bill Hickok.

1904

INTERNATIONAL

President Theodore Roosevelt issues a corollary to Monroe Doctrine, defends U.S. intervention in Latin America to stop European aggression (December 2).

ment in World War I. Critical to this outcome were the joint efforts of Carrie Chapman Catt, who organized the campaign for a federal amendment as president of the moderate National American Woman Suffrage Association, and Alice Paul, the head of the considerably more militant National Women's Party.

World War I and the End of Reform

World War I began in Europe in 1914 as a dispute between the continent's great powers. The main antagonists were Britain and France (the Allies) versus Germany. Most of the American population, with the exception of some German and Irish Americans, supported the Allies. Still, the great majority of Americans wished to stay out of the deadly conflict. Woodrow Wilson was, in fact, reelected as president in November 1916 on the basis of his pledge to maintain America's neutral status.

Just months later, however, Wilson became convinced that German attacks on American merchant shipping required the United States to enter the war on the side of the Allies. American soldiers did not arrive in Europe in large numbers until nearly a year later. They then played an important role in pushing Germany out of France and, ultimately, ending the war in November 1918.

The war was fought at home as well as abroad. Wilson's government sought out and prosecuted supposedly disloyal citizens, such as German Americans. Political newspapers or journals expressing disagreement with the government were shut down. This repression continued after the end of the war, culminating in the Red Scare of 1919. Although 52,000 American soldiers died in combat or from disease in World War I, some commentators claimed that the biggest casualty of the war was free speech.

War can sometimes be a quite effective stimulus for reform. Political leaders may realize that in order to win the support of the masses for a war effort, they must try to bring about greater fairness, justice, and equality. This formula did not, however, hold for World War I. Historians often debate when the formal end to the Progressive Era actually occurred. Much of the reform impulse continued into the 1920s and the decade beyond that. Still, the great hopes for democracy and an openness to new ideals that filled the air before 1914 were effectively extinguished once America decided to enter the conflict. A more "modern," and in many ways much less hopeful, age followed.

BIBLIOGRAPHY

The best overviews of this period may be found in Richard Hofstadter, *The Age of Reform: From Bryan to FDR* (1955); Robert H. Wiebe, *The Search for Order, 1877–1920* (1967); Arthur S. Link and Richard L. McCormick, *Progressivism* (1983); Nell Irvin Painter, *Standing at Armageddon: The United States, 1877–1919* (1987); and Steven J. Diner, *A Very Different Age: Americans of the Progressive Era* (1998). On the era's politics, see John Milton Cooper Jr., *The Warrior and the Priest: Woodrow Wilson and Theodore Roosevelt* (1983). For a biography of the most important socialist of the age, Eugene Debs, see Nick Salvatore, *Eugene V. Debs: Citizen and Socialist* (1982). Louis R. Harlan, *Booker T. Washington: Wizard of Tuskegee, 1901–1915* (1983), and David Levering Lewis, *W. E. B. Du Bois: Biography of a Race, 1868–1919* (1993), provide perspectives on these legendary African-American political enemies. J. Morgan Kousser, *The Shaping of Southern Politics: Suffrage Restriction and the Establishment of the One-Party South, 1880–1910* (1974), explores southern politics as does Glenda Elizabeth Gilmore, *Gender and Jim Crow: Women and the Politics of White Supremacy in North Carolina, 1896–1920* (1996). For a controversial but influential interpretation of economic reform, see Gabriel Kolko, *The Triumph of Conservatism: A Reinterpretation of American History* (1963); newer and more positive views of economic and social reform are available in Daniel T. Rodgers, *Atlantic Crossings: Social Politics in a Progressive Age* (1998), and Elizabeth Sanders, *Roots of Reform: Farmers, Workers, and the American State, 1877–1917* (1999).

SEE PRIMARY DOCUMENT Theodore Roosevelt's Annual Message to Congress

U.S. formally acquires Panama Canal Zone (February 26).

NATIONAL

President Theodore Roosevelt, Republican, is elected to full term over Judge Alton B. Parker, Democrat, by popular vote of 7,628,834 and 336 electoral votes to 5,084,401 and 140.

Supreme Court in *Northern Securities* v. *United States* rules that a holding company created solely to eliminate competition is an illegal combination in restraint of trade, a violation of antitrust laws.

William Howard Taft becomes Secretary of War.

Oregon adopts direct primaries for party nominations.

Louisiana Purchase Exposition, also called the World's Fair, is held in St. Louis, Missouri.

BUSINESS/INDUSTRY/INVENTIONS

A. P. Giannini founds Bank of America as the Bank of Italy.

Political cartoon shows President Theodore Roosevelt wielding the "big stick" of American power in the Caribbean region.
CORBIS-BETTMANN

Lane Bryant stores are established.

Oil field is brought in near Bartlesville, Oklahoma.

Roger Babson establishes Babson Business Statistical Organization to provide summaries, analysis of business conditions for investors.

Long, bitter strike of 25,000 textile workers occurs in Fall River, Massachusetts.

The Interior Decorator magazine begins publication.

Thorstein B. Veblen writes *The Theory of Business Enterprise.*

TRANSPORTATION

First section of New York City subway operates from City Hall to 145th Street; first municipally owned transit line opens in Seattle, with a fare of 2½ cents.

East River Tunnel in New York City is built.

New York Travelers Aid Society is organized.

New York State is first in U.S. to adopt automobile speed limits: 10 miles per hour in cities, 15 in small towns, 20 in the country.

Harry D. Weed patents an automobile tire chain.

DEATH William R. Grace, shipping company founder.

SCIENCE/MEDICINE

National Tuberculosis Assn. is organized in Atlantic City, New Jersey.

EDUCATION

Mary M. Bethune opens Daytona (Florida) Normal & Industrial Institute for Negro Girls; vocational high school for girls opens as summer experiment in Boston.

Western University of Pennsylvania moves to Pittsburgh, becomes part of University of Pittsburgh.

DEATH Francis Wayland, dean, Yale Law School (1873–1903).

RELIGION

Buddhist Temple is established in Los Angeles.

Catholic Bishop Henry Moeller becomes archbishop of Cincinnati, Ohio.

ART/MUSIC

Chicago's Orchestra Hall opens.

Robert Henri completes the painting *Willie Gee;* William J. Glackens, *Luxembourg Gardens.*

St. Louis City Art Museum and Hispanic Museum in New York City open.

SONGS (POPULAR): "Fascination," "Give My Regards to Broadway," "Goodbye, My Lady Love," "Meet Me in St. Louis, Louis," "Teasing."

LITERATURE/JOURNALISM

Color comic books first appear in New York City, reprinting cartoons from newspapers.

Amerikai Magyar Nepszava, Hungarian daily paper, begins publication in New York City.

Bibliographical Society of America is organized.

BOOKS *The Shame of the Cities* by Lincoln Steffens, *The Sea Wolf* by Jack London, *Freckles* by Gene Stratton Porter, *Cabbages and Kings* by O. Henry (William S. Porter), *The Tar Baby* by Joel Chandler Harris, *The Crossing* by Winston Churchill, *The Golden Bowl* by Henry James.

DEATHS Prentiss Ingraham, author of about 700 "dime" novels; Mary E. M. Dodge, author *(Hans Brinker),* editor *(St. Nicholas Magazine);* Lafcadio Hearn, author.

ENTERTAINMENT

George P. Baker teaches "47 Workshop" class for playwrights at Harvard University.

Emile Berliner develops flat phonograph record.

PLAYS Mrs. Minnie Maddern Fiske stars in George Ade's *The College Widow,* George M. Cohan in *Little Johnny Jones,* David Warfield in *The Music Master,* Dustin Farnum in *The Virginian.*

SPORTS

Baseball leagues cannot agree on arrangements for World Series, which is not held.

First Olympic Games in U.S. are held in St. Louis, Missouri; U.S. wins 21 track and field events, 10 in gymnastics.

Norman Dole first to surpass 12 feet (12 ft. 1¼ in.) in pole vault.

Coach Amos Alonzo Stagg of University of Chicago organizes first lettermen's club.

First Vanderbilt Cup auto race is run on 10-lap course at Hicksville, New York.

National Ski Assn. is organized.

Tennis & Racquet Club is built in Boston.

WINNERS *Bicycling*—Robert Waltheur, world professional motor-paced riding; *Boxing*—Jim Jeffries, heavyweight; Tommy Sullivan, featherweight; Joe Bowker, bantamweight; *Golf*—Willie Anderson, U.S. Open; *Horse racing*—Elwood, Kentucky Derby; Bryn Mawr, Preakness Stakes; Delhi, Belmont Stakes; *Motorboating—Standard,* piloted by C. C. Riotte, first race under organized rules; *Wrestling*—Frank Gotch, heavyweight.

MISCELLANEOUS

Fire destroys most of Baltimore's business district.

Steamer *General Slocum* burns in New York City's East River, 1,021 die; train wreck at Eden, Colorado, kills 96.

American Academy of Arts & Letters is founded.

Carnegie Hero Fund Commission is established.

St. Louis Police Department begins fingerprinting persons arrested on serious charges.

Evangeline Booth, daughter of founder, heads Salvation Army in U.S.; serves until 1934 when she becomes world leader.

PRIMARY SOURCE DOCUMENT

Theodore Roosevelt's Annual Message to Congress, December 6, 1904

INTRODUCTION Theodore Roosevelt (1858–1919), the twenty-sixth president of the United States, assumed the presidency after William McKinley (1843–1901) was assassinated in 1901. In November 1904 he was elected by a wide margin over Democrat Alton B. Parker. As president, Roosevelt continued to build on America's expansion overseas that began in 1898 with the Spanish-American War, in which he served with a volunteer force known as the Rough Riders. A former secretary of the United States Navy, Roosevelt initiated the expansion of American naval forces to enable the United States to compete on the world stage. Sir William White, the great British designer of warships, toured the United States in 1904 and discovered that fourteen battleships and thirteen armored cruisers were being built simultaneously, representing an extraordinary rate of production. In 1907 Roosevelt sent what was called the "great white fleet" of U.S. warships around the world to signify American naval strength. In 1890 the United States spent \$22 million on naval construction, representing 6.9 percent of federal spending; by 1914, it was spending $139 million, or 19 percent of all federal spending. And by 1914 it boasted the third largest navy in the world.

Roosevelt also aggressively expanded American influence in the Western Hemisphere by securing the rights to build a trans-isthmian canal through Panama and by revising the Monroe Doctrine to assert American dominance in that region. The Roosevelt Corollary to the Monroe Doctrine was conceived in response to European military and economic activity in Latin America. Roosevelt and other American leaders feared that Latin American states would incur debts which European countries would later use to gain political power; serious economic crises in Venezuela in 1902 and the Dominican Republic in 1904 alarmed Roosevelt. The Roosevelt Corollary justified military intervention in the event of "chronic wrongdoing" on the part of Latin American leaders to preserve political stability and to protect Americans' considerable investments. American capital investment in Latin America was about $250 million in 1890, but after the Spanish-American War it rose to $1.6 billion by 1904. Historians have noted that referring to Roosevelt's policy as a corollary to the Monroe Doctrine is largely ironic since the original Monroe Doctrine was designed to prevent European colonialism in the Americas; the Roosevelt Corollary in fact helped to underwrite U.S. dominance in the region.

The Roosevelt Corollary established the practice of installing dictators friendly to American interests; led to a series of military interventions by the U.S. Marines in Cuba, Nicaragua, the Dominican Republic, Haiti, and Mexico; and created bitterness on the part of many Latin Americans opposed to what they regarded as "Yankee" imperialism. Teddy Roosevelt's policy of interventionism would last until 1934, when President Franklin D. Roosevelt abandoned it in favor of a "good neighbor policy."

To the Senate and House of Representatives:

The Nation continues to enjoy noteworthy prosperity. Such prosperity is of course primarily due to the high individual average of our citizenship, taken together with our great natural resources; but an important factor therein is the working of our long-continued governmental policies. The people have emphatically expressed their approval of the principles underlying these policies, and their desire that these principles be kept substantially unchanged, although of course applied in a progressive spirit to meet changing conditions.

Foreign Policy

In treating of our foreign policy and of the attitude that this great Nation should assume in the world at large, it is absolutely necessary to consider the Army and the Navy, and the Congress, through which the thought of the Nation finds its expression, should keep ever vividly in mind the fundamental fact that it is impossible to treat our foreign policy, whether this policy takes shape in the effort to secure justice for others or justice for ourselves, save as conditioned upon the attitude we are willing to take toward our Army, and especially toward our Navy. It is not merely unwise, it is contemptible, for a nation, as for an individual, to use high-sounding language to proclaim its purposes, or to take positions which are ridiculous if unsupported by potential force, and then to refuse to provide this force. If there is no intention of providing and keeping the force necessary to back up a strong attitude, then it is far better not to assume such an attitude.

The steady aim of this Nation, as of all enlightened nations, should be to strive to bring ever nearer the day when there shall prevail throughout the world the peace of justice. There are kinds of peace which are highly undesirable, which are in the long run as destructive as any war. Tyrants and oppressors have many times made a wilderness and called it peace. Many times peoples who were slothful or timid or shortsighted, who had been enervated by ease or by luxury, or misled by false teachings, have shrunk in unmanly fashion from doing duty that was stern and that needed self-sacrifice, and have sought to hide from their own minds their shortcomings, their ignoble motives, by calling them love of peace. The peace of tyrannous terror, the peace of craven weakness, the peace of injustice, all these should be shunned as we shun unrighteous war. The goal to set before us as a nation, the goal which should be set before all mankind, is the attainment of the peace of justice, of the peace which comes when each nation is not merely safe-guarded in its own rights, but scrupulously recognizes and performs its duty toward others. Generally peace tells for righteousness; but if there is conflict between the two, then our fealty is due first to the cause of righteousness. Unrighteous wars are common, and unrighteous peace is rare; but both should be shunned. The right of freedom and the responsibility for the exercise of that right can not be divorced. One of our great poets has well and finely said that freedom is not a gift that tarries long in the hands of cowards. Neither does it tarry long in the hands of those too slothful, too dishonest, or too unintelligent to exercise it. The eternal vigilance which is the price of liberty must be exercised, sometimes to guard against outside foes; although of course far more often to guard against our own selfish or thoughtless shortcomings.

If these self-evident truths are kept before us, and only if they are so kept before us, we shall have a clear idea of what our foreign policy in its larger aspects should be. It is our duty to remember that a nation has no more right to do injustice to another nation, strong or weak, than an individual has to do injustice to another individual; that the same moral law applies in one case as in the other. But we must also remember that it is as much the duty of the Nation to guard its own rights and its own interests as it is the duty of the individual so to do. Within the Nation the individual has now delegated this right to the State, that is, to the representative of all the individuals, and it is a maxim of the law that for every wrong there is a remedy. But in international law we have not advanced by any means as far as we have advanced in municipal law. There is as yet no judicial way of enforcing a right in international law. When one nation wrongs another or wrongs many others, there is no tribunal before which the wrongdoer can be brought. Either it is necessary supinely to acquiesce in the wrong, and thus put a premium upon brutality and aggression, or else it is necessary for the aggrieved nation valiantly to stand up for its rights. Until some method is devised by which there shall be a degree of international control over offending nations, it would be a wicked thing for the most civilized powers, for those with most sense of international obligations and with keenest and most generous appreciation of the difference between right and wrong, to disarm. If the great civilized nations of the present day should completely disarm, the result would mean an immediate recrudescence of barbarism in one form or another. Under any circumstances a sufficient armament would have to be kept up to serve the purposes of international police; and until international cohesion and the sense of international duties and rights are far more advanced than at present, a nation desirous both of securing respect for itself and of doing good to others must have a force adequate for the work which it feels is allotted to it as its part of the general world duty. Therefore it follows that a self-respecting, just, and far-seeing nation should on the one hand endeavor by every means to aid in the development of the various movements which tend to provide substitutes for war, which tend to render nations in their actions toward one another, and indeed toward their own peoples, more responsive to the general sentiment of humane and civilized mankind; and on the other hand that it should keep prepared, while scrupulously avoiding wrongdoing itself, to repel any wrong, and in exceptional cases to take action which in a more advanced stage of international relations would come under the head of the exercise of the international police. A great free people owes it to itself and to all mankind not to sink into helplessness before the powers of evil.

Policy Toward Other Nations of the Western Hemisphere

It is not true that the United States feels any land hunger or entertains any projects as regards the other nations of the Western Hemisphere save such as are for their welfare. All that this country desires is to see the neighboring countries stable, orderly, and prosperous. Any country whose people conduct themselves well can count upon our hearty friendship. If a nation shows that it knows how to act with reasonable efficiency and decency in social and political matters, if it keeps order and pays its obligations, it need fear no interference from the United States. Chronic wrongdoing, or an impotence which results in a general loosening of the ties of civilized society, may in America, as elsewhere, ultimately require intervention by some civilized nation, and in the Western Hemisphere the adherence of the United States to the Monroe Doctrine may force the United States, however reluctantly, in flagrant cases of such wrongdoing or impotence, to the exercise of an international police power. If every country washed by the Caribbean Sea would show the progress in stable and just civilization which with the aid of the Platt Amendment Cuba has shown since our troops left the island, and which so many of the republics in both Americas are constantly and brilliantly showing, all question of interference by this Nation with their affairs would be at an end. Our interests and those of our southern neighbors are in reality identical. They have great natural riches, and if within their borders the reign of law and justice obtains, prosperity is sure to come to them. While they thus obey the primary laws of civilized society they may rest assured that they will be treated by us in a spirit of cordial and helpful sympathy. We would interfere with them only in the last resort, and then only if it became evident that their inability or unwillingness to do justice at home and abroad had violated the rights of the United States or had invited foreign aggression to the detriment of the entire body of American nations. It is a mere truism to say that every nation, whether in America or anywhere else, which desires to maintain its freedom, its independence, must ultimately realize that the right of such independence can not be separated from the responsibility of making good use of it.

In asserting the Monroe Doctrine, in taking such steps as we have taken in regard to Cuba, Venezuela, and Panama, and in endeavoring to circumscribe the theater of war in the Far East, and to secure the open door in China, we have acted in our own interest as well as in the interest of humanity at large. There are, however, cases in which, while our own interests are not greatly involved, strong appeal is made to our sympathies. Ordinarily it is very much wiser and more useful for us to concern ourselves with striving for our own moral and material betterment here at home than to concern ourselves with trying to better the condition of things in other nations. We have plenty of sins of our own to war against, and under ordinary circumstances we can do more for the general uplifting of humanity by striving with heart and soul to put a stop to civic corruption, to brutal lawlessness and violent race prejudices here at home than by passing resolutions and wrongdoing elsewhere. Nevertheless there are occasional crimes committed on so vast a scale and of such peculiar horror as to make us doubt whether it is not our manifest duty to endeavor at least to show our disapproval of the deed and our sympathy with those who have suffered by it. The cases must be extreme in which such a course is justifiable. There must be no effort made to remove the mote from our brother's eye if we refuse to remove the beam from our own. But in extreme cases action may be justifiable and proper. What form the action shall take must depend upon the circumstances of the case; that is, upon the degree of the atrocity and upon our power to remedy it. The cases in which we could interfere by force of arms as we interfered to put a stop to intolerable conditions in Cuba are necessarily very few. Yet it is not to be expected

In addition to being a lucrative venture for big business at the turn of the century, mining allows individual entrepreneurs to strike it rich. This group of prospectors is photographed around 1905. **HULTON ARCHIVE/GETTY IMAGES**

that a people like ours, which in spite of certain very obvious shortcomings, nevertheless as a whole shows by its consistent practice its belief in the principles of civil and religious liberty and of orderly freedom, a people among whom even the worst crime, like the crime of lynching, is never more than sporadic, so that individuals and not classes are molested in their fundamental rights—it is inevitable that such a nation should desire eagerly to give expression to its horror on an occasion like that of the massacre of the Jews in Kishenef, or when it witnesses such systematic and long-extended cruelty and oppression as the cruelty and oppression of which the Armenians have been the victims, and which have won for them the indignant pity of the civilized world.

Theodore Roosevelt

SOURCE: Theodore Roosevelt's Annual Message to Congress, December 6, 1904. From James D. Richardson, ed., *Messages and Papers of the Presidents,* 1905.

1905

INTERNATIONAL

President Theodore Roosevelt invites warring Japan and Russia to a peace conference in U.S. (June 8); representatives meet in Portsmouth (New Hampshire) Navy Yard (August 9); sign peace treaty a month later (September 5).

Panama Canal Engineering Commission recommends construction of a $250 million sea-level canal.

U.S. signs extradition treaty with Norway and Sweden.

NATIONAL

Forest Service is established.

Annual immigration to U.S. reaches 1,026,499.

Paul P. Harris founds Rotary International in Chicago.

Oris P. and Mantis Van Sweringen develop Shaker Heights, a Cleveland suburb; build streetcar line connecting it to Cleveland.

Lewis & Clark Exposition is held in Portland, Oregon.

BUSINESS/INDUSTRY/INVENTIONS

Burroughs Adding Machine Co. is established; Statler Hotels chain is founded.

First air-conditioned factory is built for Gray Manufacturing Co. in Gastonia, North Carolina.

Sarah Breedlove Walker, who calls herself "Madame C. J. Walker," produces and distributes haircare products for African-American women. Her company grows to become the biggest corporation run by an African American at the time, and she becomes one of the first U.S. women millionaires. **THE GRANGER COLLECTION, NEW YORK**

Pyrene Manufacturing Co. introduces fire extinguisher with vaporized chemical; Portland (Oregon) Manufacturing Co. produces Douglas-fir plywood.

Supreme Court orders meat packers to stop making agreements on bidding, price fixing, blacklists; upholds lower court order to break up "beef trust."

Merger of Western Federation of Miners and American Labor Union forms Industrial Workers of the World.

National Boot & Shoe Manufacturers Assn. is founded.

U.S. sues Standard Oil (New Jersey) under antitrust law.

DEATHS Meyer Guggenheim, founder of worldwide copper company; Charles T. Yerkes, Chicago street railway owner; Jay Cooke, financier.

TRANSPORTATION

Ferryboat service between Staten Island and Manhattan (New York) begins.

William C. Durant founds Buick Motor Co.

Chicago & Northwestern Railroad are first to install electric lamps in trains.

Aerial ferry operates between Duluth and Minnesota Point.

Number of registered automobiles rises to 77,988.

SCIENCE/MEDICINE

Yellow fever epidemic begins in New Orleans, Louisiana (July 23); ends in October with about 3,000 cases, 400 deaths.

Supreme Court rules that states have power to enact compulsory vaccination laws.

Samuel Hopkins Adams writes *The Great American Fraud,* an exposé of patent medicines that leads to passage of Pure Food & Drug Act.

Dr. Albert Einhorn produces "procaine" (Novocain).

EDUCATION

Carnegie Foundation for the Advancement of Teaching is established.

RELIGION

Russian Orthodox church moves episcopal see (area headquarters) from San Francisco to New York City.

DEATH Placide L. Chappelle, Catholic archbishop (1894–1905), Santa Fe, New Mexico, New Orleans.

ART/MUSIC

Edward J. Steichen and other photographers open famed 291 Gallery in New York City to win recognition of photography as art form.

Juilliard School of Music in New York City is founded.

Houston's Museum of Fine Arts opens.

Childe Hassam completes the painting *Southwest Wind;* William J. Glackens, *Chez Mouquin;* Jerome Myers, *The Tambourine;* Paul W. Bartlett completes the frieze figures in New York Public Library.

Henry F. B. Gilbert composes *Comedy Overture on Negro Themes.*

Victor Herbert's operetta *The Red Mill* opens; featured song is "Kiss Me Again."

SONGS (POPULAR): "In My Merry Oldsmobile," "In the Shade of the Old Apple Tree," "My Gal Sal," "Wait Till the Sun Shines, Nellie," "I Don't Care," "Mary's a Grand Old Name."

LITERATURE/JOURNALISM

Chicago Defender, African-American newspaper, begins publication.

BOOKS *The House of Mirth* by Edith Wharton, *The Clansman* by Thomas Dixon, *Isidro* by Mary Austin, *The Life of Reason* by George Santayana.

DEATHS Union Gen. Lew Wallace, author *(Ben-Hur);* John Bartlett, compiler of *Familiar Quotations.*

ENTERTAINMENT

Sime Silverman founds *Variety,* entertainment journal.

Hippodrome Theater in New York City opens.

PLAYS Mrs. Leslie Carter stars in *Adrea,* Blanche Bates in David Belasco's *The Girl of the Golden West,* George M. Cohan in *Forty-Five Minutes from Broadway,* Maude Adams in *Peter Pan,* William Faversham in *The Squaw Man,* Margaret Anglin in *Zira,* Julia Sanderson and Douglas Fairbanks in *Fantana.*

Harry Davis opens a nickelodeon theater in Pittsburgh, Pennsylvania.

DEATHS Two noted actors, Joseph Jefferson and Maurice Barrymore.

SPORTS

Intercollegiate Athletic Association of U.S. is founded by 62 institutions; later becomes National Collegiate Athletic Assn. (NCAA); five colleges form Intercollegiate Association Football League.

J. Scott Leary becomes first American to swim 100 yards in 60 seconds.

Touring English team introduces soccer to American public.

WINNERS *Baseball*—New York Giants, World Series; *Boxing*—Marvin Hart, heavyweight; Jack O'Brien, light heavyweight; *Golf*—Willie Anderson, U.S. Open; *Horse racing*—Agile, Kentucky Derby (in which only three horses run); Cairngorm, Preakness Stakes; Tanya, Belmont Stakes; *Tennis*—Great Britain, Davis Cup; *Wrestling*—Tom Jenkins, heavyweight; Yale, first intercollegiate title.

MISCELLANEOUS

Sarah B. Walker devises treatment to straighten tightly curled hair; becomes one of first U.S. women millionaires.

Mine disaster at Virginia City, Alabama, kills 112.

American Sociological Society is organized.

San Francisco Earthquake

At 5:31 A.M. April 18, 1906, an earthquake measuring between 7.8 and 8.0 on the Richter scale hit northern California. A rupture along the San Andreas Fault led to a spate of shockwaves, with severe property damage at Santa Rosa resulting in the loss of fifty lives. At Point Reyes, the ground shifted 6.4 meters. In the center of San Francisco, streetcar tracks buckled and buildings collapsed. Thomas Jefferson Chase, a ticket clerk, described the scene: "I heard a low distant rumble. It was coming from the west. Louder and louder. I stopped and listened. Then it hit. Power and trolley lines snapped like threads. The ends of the power lines dropped to the pavement not ten feet from where I stood, writhing and hissing like reptiles. Brick and glass showered about me. Buildings along First Street from Howard to Market crumbled like card houses. One was brick. Not a soul escaped. Clouds of that obliterated the scene of destruction. The dust hung low over the rubble in the street." With gas pipes broken, multiple fires ensued. For three days flames engulfed the city while firemen struggled to locate reliable water supplies. The San Francisco earthquake and fire destroyed 28,000 buildings, with 250,000 people left homeless. The National Guard and U.S. Army patrolled city streets to deter looters while aiding in the distribution of food supplies and emergency tents. Relief came by ferry and railroad from Los Angeles, Oakland, and other U.S. cities. More than 700 people died, with some estimates of the final death toll as high as 3,000.

1906

NATIONAL

President Theodore Roosevelt wins Nobel Peace Prize for leadership in settling Russo-Japanese war; leaves for Panama inspection trip, first president to leave country while in office.

Alice Lee Roosevelt, president's daughter, and Rep. Nicholas Longworth (later Speaker) marry in the White House.

Alaska is authorized to have delegate in Congress; Wisconsin holds first statewide primary election.

Mesa Verde (Colorado) National Park is established; President Roosevelt dedicates first national monument, Devils Tower, Wyoming.

The aftermath of the 1906 San Francisco earthquake. The view is from Pioneer Hall north to the St. Francis Hotel.

National Recreation Assn. is founded as Playground Association of America.

Congress authorizes plans for a lock canal in Panama.

DEATH Susan B. Anthony, women's rights leader.

BUSINESS/INDUSTRY/INVENTIONS

Pure Food and Drug, and Meat Inspection acts pass (June 30), the latter due in part to Upton Sinclair's book on meatpacking *(The Jungle)*.

Lee De Forest invents triode electron tube, which leads to rapid growth in communications, electronics; Ernst F. W. Alexanderson develops alternator that is able to produce continuous radio waves.

President Roosevelt extends eight-hour day to all government workers; California enacts first law in U.S. to set minimum wage, $2 per day for almost all public employees.

W. K. Kellogg Co. (Battle Creek, Michigan), cereal maker, is established; Commonwealth Edison Co. in Chicago is organized; Alfred C. Fuller founds Capitol (later Fuller) Brush Co.

Hart-Parr Co. introduces first commercially successful machine, the "tractor."

Oil fields are discovered in Kansas and Oklahoma.

DEATH Joseph F. Glidden, barbed-wire inventor.

TRANSPORTATION

First double-decker bus, imported from France, is put into service on Fifth Avenue, New York City.

Hepburn Act strengthens Interstate Commerce Commission, gives it authority to fix maximum railroad rates, to prescribe uniform accounting methods; jurisdiction extends to express and sleeping car companies, oil pipelines, terminals, and ferries.

SCIENCE/MEDICINE

Mt. Wilson (California) Observatory opens.

Dr. Howard T. Ricketts determines that Rocky Mountain spotted fever is spread by cattle ticks.

DEATH Samuel P. Langley, astronomer and aeronautical pioneer.

EDUCATION

Rand School of Social Science in New York City is founded.

Phillips University in Enid, Oklahoma, is chartered as Oklahoma Christian University.

DEATH Christopher C. Langdell, Harvard Law School dean (1870–1895), introduced case method of teaching.

RELIGION

Christian Science Cathedral in Boston is dedicated.

ART/MUSIC

Louis M. Eilshemius completes the painting *Figures in Landscape;* Childe Hassam, *Church at Old Lyme.*

John Herron Art Institute in Indianapolis, Indiana, is founded.

Soprano Geraldine Farrar begins 16 years with Metropolitan Opera.

SONGS (POPULAR): "At Dawning," "I Love You Truly," "You're a Grand Old Flag," "Because You're You," "Anchors Aweigh," "I Love a Lassie," "Love Me and the World Is Mine," "Waltz Me Around Again, Willie."

DEATH Eastman Johnson, painter.

LITERATURE/JOURNALISM

Fontaine Fox draws "Toonerville Trolley" cartoon.

BOOKS *The Spirit of the Border* by Zane Grey, *The Devil's Dictionary* by Ambrose Bierce, *The Four Million* by O. Henry, *Uncle Remus and Br'er Rabbit* by Joel Chandler Harris, *The Spoilers* by Rex Beach.

ENTERTAINMENT

Reginald Fessenden makes first radio broadcast of voice and music from Brant Rock, Massachusetts (December 24).

Bill (Bojangles) Robinson, dancer, and Sophie Tucker, singer, begin careers.

Vitagraph Studios releases the first animated movie cartoon, James S. Blackton's "Humorous Phases of Funny Faces."

Belasco Theater in New York City is built.

PLAYS Margaret Anglin stars in *The Great Divide,* Minnie Maddern Fiske in *The New York Idea,* William Collier in *Caught in the Rain,* Grace George in *Clothes,* Anna Held in *A Parisian Model.*

SPORTS

Charles M. Daniels sets swimming record of 56 seconds for 100 yards.

Willie Hoppe, 18, wins his first (of many) billiards championship.

Consecutive game pitching streak of Jack Taylor, Chicago Cubs, St. Louis Cardinals, ends at 188; pitches 1,727 innings without relief.

National Coursing Assn. (now National Greyhound Assn.) is formed to govern greyhound racing.

Football forward pass is legalized; flying wedge is outlawed.

National Association of Scientific Angling Clubs is organized.

WINNERS *Baseball*—Chicago White Sox, World Series; *Boxing*—Tommy Burns, heavyweight; *Golf*—Alex Smith, U.S. Open; *Horse racing*—Sir Huon, Kentucky Derby; Whimsical, Preakness Stakes; Burgomaster, Belmont Stakes; *Tennis*—Great Britain, Davis Cup; *Wrestling*—Frank Gotch, heavyweight; *Yachting*—*Tamerlane,* first Bermuda race; *Lurline,* first transpacific race.

MISCELLANEOUS

Stanford White, prominent architect, is shot to death by Harry K. Thaw, jealous of White's earlier friendship with Mrs. Thaw.

Young Women's Christian Assn. (YWCA) is organized.

1907

INTERNATIONAL

Fleet of U.S. warships leaves Hampton Roads, Virginia (December 16), on a round-the-world goodwill trip; returns in 1909.

President Theodore Roosevelt and environmentalist John Muir together on Glacier Point, Yosemite Valley, California. Muir helps lead the fight to make Yosemite a national park, and TR is the first conservationist president. ARCHIVE/CORBIS-BETTMANN

American representatives attend second Hague Conference, which again fails to agree on disarmament.

First elections are held in Philippine Islands; first legislature convenes.

U.S. Marines land in Honduras to protect U.S. lives and property.

NATIONAL

Gen. George W. Goethals is named chief engineer for construction of Panama Canal.

Corrupt Election Practices Law is enacted, prohibits corporations from contributing funds in national elections.

Oklahoma's constitution is adopted, ratified; Oklahoma is admitted as 46th state (November 16).

Army War College in Washington opens; Army organizes aeronautical unit in Signal Corps.

New York City holds first U.S. night court.

Food and Drug Administration begins operation.

Effort to unseat Senator Reed Smoot of Utah because of his Mormon church membership fails; his election is confirmed (42–28).

Immigrant children are checked for diseases at Ellis Island.
CORBIS-BETTMANN

Tercentenary Exposition is held in Jamestown, Virginia.

More than a million immigrants arrive at Ellis Island, New York, in year.

DEATH Former First Lady Ida S. McKinley (1897–1901).

BUSINESS/INDUSTRY/INVENTIONS

Drop in stock market, followed by business failures, touches off Panic of 1907 (March 13); Knickerbocker Trust Co., New York City, fails (October 22).

Federal government files antitrust suit against American Tobacco Co.

U.S. Steel Co. acquires Tennessee Coal & Iron Co.; Bell & Howell Co. and United Parcel Service (UPS) are founded.

George F. Baker founds First Security Corp. in New York City.

Hurley Machine Co. markets a complete self-contained electric washing machine (the Thor); Maytag Co. produces its first washing machines; Hoover Co. introduces rolling vacuum cleaner with handle and dust bag.

J. C. Penney buys store in Kemperer, Wyoming, starts his chain of stores.

DEATH William L. Jenney, pioneer architect.

TRANSPORTATION

First Hudson River tunnel connects New York and New Jersey (February 25).

Bendix Co., pioneer auto parts company, is formed; John N. Willys, bicycle maker, buys Overland Automobile Co., renames it Willys-Overland.

First taxicabs in U.S. appear in New York City when a fleet of "taximeter cabs" arrives from Paris.

Philadelphia's first subway operates.

SCIENCE/MEDICINE

Albert A. Michelson becomes first American to win a Nobel Prize in physics; award is given for optical measuring instruments and work in meteorology and spectroscopy.

Columbia University names Mary A. Nutting first full-time U.S. professor of nursing.

American Telephone & Telegraph Co. opens research laboratory in New York City (later moves to Murray Hill, New Jersey).

William H. Taggart develops casting process that makes gold inlay fillings possible in dentistry.

DEATH Wilbur O. Atwater, founder of agricultural extension stations.

EDUCATION

Alain L. Locke, a Harvard graduate, is first black awarded a Rhodes scholarship.

RELIGION

Cornerstone is laid for St. Paul (Minnesota) Cathedral (Catholic).

William H. O'Connell becomes Catholic archbishop of Boston.

Cleland K. Nelson becomes first Episcopal bishop of Atlanta, Georgia.

Stephen S. Wise founds Free Synagogue in New York City.

DEATH John A. Dowie, founder of Christian Catholic Apostolic church.

ART/MUSIC

Mary Garden makes Metropolitan Opera debut in Massenet's *Thaïs.*

Irving Berlin's first song, "Marie of Sunny Italy," is published.

George W. Bellows completes the painting *Stag at Sharkey's;* John F. Sloan, *Wake of Ferry;* George B. Luks, *The Little Madonna.*

SONGS (POPULAR): "Glow-Worm," "Merry Widow Waltz," "On the Road to Mandalay," "Harrigan," "School Days," "I Wish I Had a Girl."

LITERATURE/JOURNALISM

United Press, a wire service, begins.

H. C. (Bud) Fisher draws first daily comic strip, "Mutt and Jeff," in *San Francisco Chronicle.*

BOOKS *Sister Carrie* by Theodore Dreiser, *The Shepherd of the Hills* by Harold Bell Wright, *Sonnets to Duse* (poetry) by Sara Teasdale, *The Education of Henry Adams* by Henry Adams (privately printed).

DEATH William T. Adams, who wrote more than 125 books, 1,000 stories under name of Oliver Optic among others.

ENTERTAINMENT

Lee De Forest transmits Rossini's *William Tell Overture* from Telharmonic Hall in New York City to Brooklyn in first musical program radio broadcast (March 5).

Ringling Bros. buy Barnum & Bailey's to become nation's leading circus.

Florenz Ziegfeld stages *Follies of 1907,* the first American "revue."

PLAYS George M. Cohan writes and produces *The Talk of New York,* David Warfield stars in *Grand Army Man,* Augustus Thomas writes *The Witching Hour.*

The two-step becomes a popular dance.

DEATH Richard Mansfield, actor.

SPORTS

Committee is named to study origin of baseball; Chairman A. G. Mills, former National League president, reports (personally) (December 30) that game began with New York Knickerbocker Base Ball Club (1845).

WINNERS *Baseball*—Chicago Cubs, World Series; *Boxing*—Tommy Burns, heavyweight; *Cross-country*—Asario Autio, first national race; *Golf*—Alex Ross, U.S. Open; *Horse racing*—Pink Star, Kentucky Derby; Don Enrique, Preakness Stakes; Peter Pan, Belmont Stakes.

MISCELLANEOUS

Emily P. Bissell designs first Christmas seals; initial drive to aid tubercular children is held.

Russell Sage Foundation to improve social and living conditions is created with $10 million endowment.

Frank Lloyd Wright completes Robie House in Chicago.

Coal-mine explosion in Monongah, West Virginia, results in 361 deaths; another at Jacob's Creek, Pennsylvania, kills 239.

1908

INTERNATIONAL

Root-Takahira agreement provides for Japanese confirmation of the Open Door policy in China (November 30).

NATIONAL

William Howard Taft, Republican, is elected president over William Jennings Bryan, Democrat; Taft receives 7,679,006 popular and 321 electoral votes to Bryan's 6,409,106 and 162.

Supreme Court in *Adair* v. *United States* strikes down a provision of the 1898 Erdman Act that requires railroad workers to sign promise not to join the union, terming it an unreasonable violation of freedom of contract and property rights; in *Loew* v. *Lawler* (the Danbury [Connecticut] hatters' case), the Court rules that a secondary boycott is a violation of the antitrust act; *Muller* v. *Oregon* upholds the state law that sets maximum working hours for women.

Federal Bureau of Investigation (FBI) begins as Bureau of Investigation (July 26).

President Theodore Roosevelt calls a meeting on conservation, results in creation of National Conservation Commission with Gifford Pinchot chairman (June 8).

The motto "In God We Trust," first used briefly in 1860s, is restored on U.S. coins.

Aldrich-Vreeland Act establishes National Monetary Commission to study existing monetary and banking systems, eventually leads to creation of Federal Reserve System.

Charles E. Ashburner becomes first-named city manager; post is in Staunton, Virginia.

North Carolina and Mississippi establish statewide prohibition.

The 47-story Singer Building in New York City is completed.

U.S. Army buys first aircraft, a dirigible; only its inventor, T. S. Baldwin, can fly the craft.

DEATHS Former President Grover Cleveland (1885–

Ford Motor Company advertisement for the Model T Torpedo.
UPI/CORBIS-BETTMANN

1889, 1893–1897); Ainsworth R. Spofford, Librarian of Congress (1864–1897).

BUSINESS/INDUSTRY/INVENTIONS

U.S. Circuit Court of Appeals finds American Tobacco Co. guilty of restraining trade and violating antitrust law.

Federal workmen's compensation law goes into effect (August 1).

Racine (Wisconsin) Confectioner's Machinery Corp. develops machine to make lollipops; John H. Breck Co., maker of hair-care products, is founded.

General Electric patents electric iron and electric toaster.

William D. Coolidge develops method of making fine tungsten wire for light bulbs, radio tubes.

TRANSPORTATION

East River Tunnel from Battery to Brooklyn (New York) and the first railroad tunnel under the Hudson River are completed.

Henry Ford introduces the Model T, price $850; with higher production, price continuously drops ($310 by 1926).

Fisher Body Co. is founded; General Motors incorporates.

SCIENCE/MEDICINE

First child-hygiene bureau is established in New York City; International Children's Welfare Congress meets in Washington.

Louisville (Kentucky) extends its health services into surrounding Jefferson County.

University of Minnesota establishes School of Nursing.

A 60-inch reflecting telescope goes into service at Mt. Wilson (California) Observatory.

Richard Tolman and Gilbert N. Lewis deliver first U.S. paper on theory of relativity.

Henry Fairfield Osborn, vertebrate paleontology curator, becomes president of American Museum of Natural History.

Clifford W. Beers launches Connecticut Society for Mental Hygiene, first such organization in world.

EDUCATION

New York City provides school lunches, establishes first Division of School Hygiene.

DEATH Daniel C. Gilman, first president, Johns Hopkins University (1875–1901).

RELIGION

Federal Council of Churches of Christ is organized.

Andover Theological Seminary moves to Cambridge, Massachusetts, affiliates with Harvard University.

Merger of several small religious groups forms Church of the Nazarene.

Methodist Conference of New England lifts ban on dancing, card playing, theatergoing.

Gideons place their first Bible in a hotel room (Superior, Montana).

ART/MUSIC

Young American artists who revolted against conservatism of National Academy hold first "Ashcan School" art exhibit.

Arturo Toscanini arrives from Milan to conduct Metropolitan Opera orchestra.

PAINTINGS George W. Bellows, *Up the Hudson;* Frederic Remington, *The Scout, Friends or Enemies;* Joseph Stella, *Pittsburgh Winter.*

SONGS (POPULAR): "Cuddle Up a Little Closer," "Take Me Out to the Ball Game," "Smarty," "Sweet Violets," "Shine On, Harvest Moon."

DEATH Edward A. MacDowell, composer *(Indian Suite, Woodland Sketches)*.

LITERATURE/JOURNALISM

First issue of *Christian Science Monitor* is published; replaces *Christian Science Sentinel.*

School of Journalism is created at University of Missouri.

Julia Ward Howe, author of "Battle Hymn of the Republic," is first woman elected to American Academy of Arts & Letters.

BOOKS *The Trail of the Lonesome Pine* by John Fox Jr., *The Circular Staircase* by Mary Roberts Rinehart, *The Vermilion Pencil* by Homer Lea, *The Last of the Plainsmen* by Zane Grey, *Get-Rich-Quick Wallingford* by George R. Chester.

ENTERTAINMENT

Modern Electrics, first radio magazine, begins publication.

PLAYS Henry J. Miller stars in *The Servant in the House,* Mrs. Minnie Maddern Fiske in *Salvation Nell,* Douglas Fairbanks in *The Gentleman from Mississippi,* Anna Held in *Miss Innocence.*

DEATH Tony Pastor, theater operator.

SPORTS

Automobile race from New York to Paris by way of Seattle and Yokohama begins in New York City (February 12); race takes 170 days; car built by Thomas Motor Co., Buffalo, New York, wins.

Olympic Games are held in London; U.S. wins 15 of 28 events; Ray Ewry wins standing high jump for fourth time; John J. Hayes, the marathon.

Football game between University of Pittsburgh and Washington & Jefferson College is first where numbers are sewn on the back of jerseys.

Forbes Field baseball stadium in Pittsburgh opens (June 30).

First steel ski jump in U.S. is built at Chippewa Falls, Wisconsin.

WINNERS *Archery*—Will H. Thompson, national title; *Baseball*—Chicago White Sox, World Series; *Boxing*—Tommy Burns (until December 26), then Jack Johnson, heavyweight; Stanley Ketchel, middleweight; Abe Attell, featherweight; *Cross country*—Cornell, first intercollegiate race; *Golf*—Fred McLeod, U.S. Open; *Harness racing*—Allen Winter, first U.S. Trotting Derby; *Horse racing*—Stone Street, Kentucky Derby; Royal Tourist, Preakness Stakes; Colin, Belmont Stakes; *Tennis*—Australia, Davis Cup; *Wrestling*—Frank Gotch, heavyweight.

MISCELLANEOUS

Glenn H. Curtiss wins his first aeronautical trophy flying his "June Bug" at 40 miles per hour at Hammondsport, New York; first aviation casualty in world occurs at Ft. Myer, Virginia, when plane goes out of control, killing the pilot, Lt. Thomas Selfridge; Orville Wright is seriously injured.

Four disasters occur: fire in Rhoads Theater, Boyertown, Pennsylvania, kills 170; fire in Collinwood, Ohio, school claims 176 lives; mine accident at Marianna, Pennsylvania, kills 154; fire destroys Chelsea, Massachusetts, leaves 10,000 homeless.

New York City makes smoking in public by women illegal.

American Home Economics Assn. is founded.

Alpha Kappa Alpha, first black sorority, is founded at Howard University, Washington, D.C.

Permanent wave for hair is introduced to U.S. from England.

Very narrow skirts without petticoats are in style for women; also huge hats and dotted veils, boned collars and "fishnet" stockings.

1909

INTERNATIONAL

U.S. and Great Britain agree to submit continuing controversy over North Atlantic fisheries to arbitration (January 27).

U.S. and Canada create an international joint commission to settle disputes, set limits on water diversion at Niagara Falls (January 11).

Fleet of 16 U.S. battleships complete 15-month around-the-world cruise.

NATIONAL

Robert E. Peary and his assistant, Matthew Henson, accompanied by four Inuit, reach the North Pole (April 6).

Robert Edwin Peary, the first American Arctic explorer. **CORBIS-BETTMANN**

Congress passes the Sixteenth Amendment to permit a federal income tax (June 12); submits to states for ratification.

Payne-Aldrich Tariff reduces duties to about 38%.

Salary of President increases from $50,000 to $75,000, Vice President to $12,000.

Lincoln penny is first issued (August 2).

First White House Conference on Children recommends creation of a federal children's bureau.

National Conference on the Negro is held, leads to creation of National Association for the Advancement of Colored People (NAACP).

Tennessee enacts statewide prohibition.

First report of National Conservation Commission provides an inventory of U.S. natural resources.

Hudson-Fulton Celebration in New York commemorates 300th anniversary of Henry Hudson's arrival and 100th of Robert Fulton's steamboat.

Alaska-Yukon-Pacific Exposition is held in Seattle.

DEATHS Geronimo, Apache chief; Carroll D. Wright, first labor commissioner (1885–1905); William M. Stewart, Nevada senator, author of Fifteenth Amendment.

BUSINESS/INDUSTRY/INVENTIONS

U.S. Circuit Court holds that Standard Oil Co. is an illegal monopoly, orders its dissolution.

Henry E. Warren invents an electric clock.

Kansas enacts law that gives state insurance commissioner power over rates charged by fire insurance companies.

DeVilbiss Co. produces a paint sprayer; Murphy Door Bed Co. manufactures "in-a-door" beds; Kraft Foods begins as S. L. Kraft Co.

Patents are granted to Leo H. Baekeland for thermosetting plastic (Bakelite) and Adon J. Hoffman for steam-operated pressing machine.

Caddo oil pool in Louisiana is discovered.

DEATHS Edwin Reynolds, developer of Corliss-Reynolds engine; Joseph Wharton, benefactor of Wharton School of Finance.

TRANSPORTATION

Annual production of automobiles reaches 123,900; Roy D. Chapin and Howard E. Coffin found Hudson Motor Car Co.

Queensborough and Manhattan suspension bridges over East River in New York City open.

Chicago, Milwaukee & St. Paul Railroad is completed to Pacific coast.

DEATH Albert A. Pope, founder of U.S. bicycle industry.

SCIENCE/MEDICINE

Walter Reed Hospital in Washington, D.C., opens.

Robert A. Millikan of University of Chicago demonstrates that all electrons are identically charged particles.

Navy Nurses Corps is created.

Clifford W. Beers founds National Commission for Mental Hygiene.

EDUCATION

A. Lawrence Lowell begins 24 years as president of Harvard University; Harvard offers course in city planning.

Berkeley (California) opens first U.S. junior high school.

Arkansas State University founded.

DEATHS Arthur Gilman, developer of Radcliffe College; Sheldon Jackson, supervisor of public instruction in Alaska.

RELIGION

Cyrus I. Scofield publishes Scofield Reference Bible.

ART/MUSIC

Leopold Stokowski becomes principal conductor of Cincinnati Symphony.

Henry K. Hadley composes opera *Safie.*

Rockwell Kent completes the painting *Road Roller.*

SONGS (POPULAR): "By the Light of the Silvery Moon," "From the Land of the Sky Blue Water," "Put On Your Old Grey Bonnet," "I Wonder Who's Kissing Her Now," "I've Got Rings on My Fingers," "My Pony Boy."

DEATH Frederic Remington, painter and sculptor.

LITERATURE/JOURNALISM

Harvard Classics, "five-foot shelf" of books, begin to appear.

BOOKS *A Girl of the Limberlost* by Gene Stratton Porter, *The Calling of Dan Matthews* by Harold Bell Wright, *The Valor of Ignorance* by Homer Lea, *The Man in Lower Ten* by Mary Roberts Rinehart, *Martin Eden* by Jack London.

DEATHS Martha F. Finley, author (Elsie Dinsmore books); Sarah Orne Jewett, author.

ENTERTAINMENT

First color motion pictures are exhibited at Madison Square Garden, New York City.

National Board of Censorship (later Review) of Motion Pictures is established.

PLAYS John Barrymore stars in *The Fortune Hunter,* Florence Reed in *Seven Days,* Grace George in *A Woman's Way,* Walter Hampden in *The City.*

SPORTS

Benjamn F. Shibe invents cork-center baseball.

Ole Evinrude develops first commercially successful outboard motor.

Eastern Canada Hockey League and Federal League merge to form National Hockey Assn., predecessor of National Hockey League.

Present Indianapolis (Indiana) Speedway opens as dirt track for auto testing.

Shortstop Neal Ball of Cleveland Indians completes baseball's first unassisted triple play.

John A. Heydler is named president of National (baseball) League, serves only five months, is renamed in 1918 for 16 years.

Ralph Rose is first to throw shot more than 50 feet.

Matthew Henson, American Arctic explorer and Peary's assistant. The two reach the North Pole on April 6, 1909.
CORBIS-BETTMANN

WINNERS *Auto racing*—Bert W. Scott and C. James Smith, first transcontinental race; *Baseball*—Pittsburgh Pirates, World Series; *Bicycling*—Georges Parent, world professional motor-paced riding; *Boxing*—Jack Johnson, heavyweight; *Chess*—Frank Marshall, U.S. champion; *Golf*—George Sargent, U.S. Open; *Horse racing*—Wintergreen, Kentucky Derby; Effendi, Preakness Stakes; Joe Madden, Belmont Stakes; *Tennis*—Australia, Davis Cup.

MISCELLANEOUS

Carlisle (Pennsylvania) Trust Co. begins first Christmas Club account.

Mine disaster at Cherry, Illinois, kills 259 miners.

1910

INTERNATIONAL

International Court of Arbitration settles long-running dispute between U.S. and Great Britain over Newfoundland fishing rights.

A woman marches in New York for the right to vote. **CORBIS-BETTMANN**

NATIONAL

Postal savings bank system is established (June 25).

Thirteenth census reports population of 92,228,496.

Supreme Court Chief Justice Melville W. Fuller dies; Justice Edward D. White succeeds him.

Washington amends its state constitution to provide women's suffrage; women march down Fifth Avenue, New York City, demanding right to vote; New Mexico holds its constitutional convention.

First domestic relations court is established in Buffalo, New York.

Forest Service Chief Gifford Pinchot accuses Interior Secretary Richard A. Ballinger of hurting conservation by aiding corporations; President William Howard Taft dismisses Pinchot for making the dispute public.

Speaker Joseph G. Cannon's power to appoint powerful House Rules Committee is taken from him; Committee, in which the Speaker could not serve, is to be named by House vote.

Congress requires statements of financial contributions in House elections.

U.S. Bureau of Mines is established.

Rockefeller Foundation is founded.

Glacier (Montana) National Park is created.

Benjamin D. Foulois establishes Air Force.

Franklin D. Roosevelt is elected to New York Senate; Woodrow Wilson is elected governor of New Jersey.

State governors hold first national meeting.

Victor L. Berger of Wisconsin is elected to House of Representatives, first Socialist to serve in Congress.

National debt stands at $1.1 billion; Gross National Product is $30.4 billion.

About 8.7 million immigrants have arrived in U.S. since 1900.

BUSINESS/INDUSTRY/INVENTIONS

Eastman Kodak produces a copying machine (photostat); American Viscose Co. makes rayon; George Hughes builds first electric range.

Charles R. Walgreen founds drug-store chain (Walgreen Co.); Joyce C. Hall establishes forerunner of Hallmark Cards Inc.; Elizabeth Arden begins cosmetics career as partner in a beauty salon.

Mann-Elkins Act gives Interstate Commerce Commission power over telephone, telegraph, cable, and wireless companies; creates Court of Commerce to hear appeals from rate decisions.

Julius Rosenwald begins 15-year career as president of Sears Roebuck; then becomes chairman.

Newly formed Sperry Gyroscope Co. installs first gyrocompass on battleship *Delaware.*

DEATH Octave Chanute, pioneer aviator, designer of biplane glider.

TRANSPORTATION

First auto show is held in Madison Square Garden, New York City, with 31 exhibitors of cars, 20 of accessories; more than 460,000 cars are sold in last decade.

Charles Kettering and Edward A. Deeds found Dayton Engineering Co., which becomes Delco; Henry L. Doherty establishes Cities Service Co.

Installment buying of automobiles begins.

Trackless trolley system is installed between Laurel Canyon and Los Angeles (California).

SCIENCE/MEDICINE

Abraham Flexner does major study that results in modern medical education.

Moses Gomberg discovers trivalent carbon.

Immigrants land at Ellis Island. **THE LIBRARY OF CONGRESS**

Columbia University offers courses in optics and optometry.

New York School of Chiropody is organized.

Halley's Comet passes the Sun without incident.

Dr. Peyton Rous is first to isolate a cancer-causing virus.

EDUCATION

Women's College of Baltimore becomes Goucher College.

Harvard University names first climatology professor, Robert D. Ward.

RELIGION

St. Patrick's Cathedral in New York City is dedicated.

DEATH Mary Baker Eddy, founder of Christian Science Church.

ART/MUSIC

Metropolitan Opera House presents first American opera, *The Pipe of Desire* by Frederick S. Converse; Giacomo Puccini's *The Girl of the Golden West* premieres there, too, conducted by Toscanini (see 1905) and starring Enrico Caruso.

Victor Herbert presents his operetta *Naughty Marietta*, featuring song "Ah, Sweet Mystery of Life."

Ballerina Anna Pavlova makes New York debut.

Arthur B. Davies completes the painting *Crescendo;* Childe Hassam, *Against the Light;* Maurice Prendergast, *Seashore.*

SONGS (POPULAR): "Come, Josephine, in My Flying Machine," "Down by the Old Mill Stream," "Let Me Call You Sweetheart," "Mother Machree," "A Perfect Day," "Some of These Days," "Put Your Arms Around Me, Honey."

DEATHS Winslow Homer, painter of seascapes; John Q. A. Ward, first U.S.-trained sculptor; John La Farge, painter.

LITERATURE/JOURNALISM

Yale University Press is founded.

Loeb Classical Library of Greek and Latin literature is founded.

Pittsburgh Courier begins publication.

"Krazy Kat" cartoon by George Herriman first appears.

Doubleday Co., publishers, is founded.

BOOKS *Twenty Years at Hull-House* by Jane Addams, *The Town Down the River* (poetry) by Edwin Arlington Robinson.

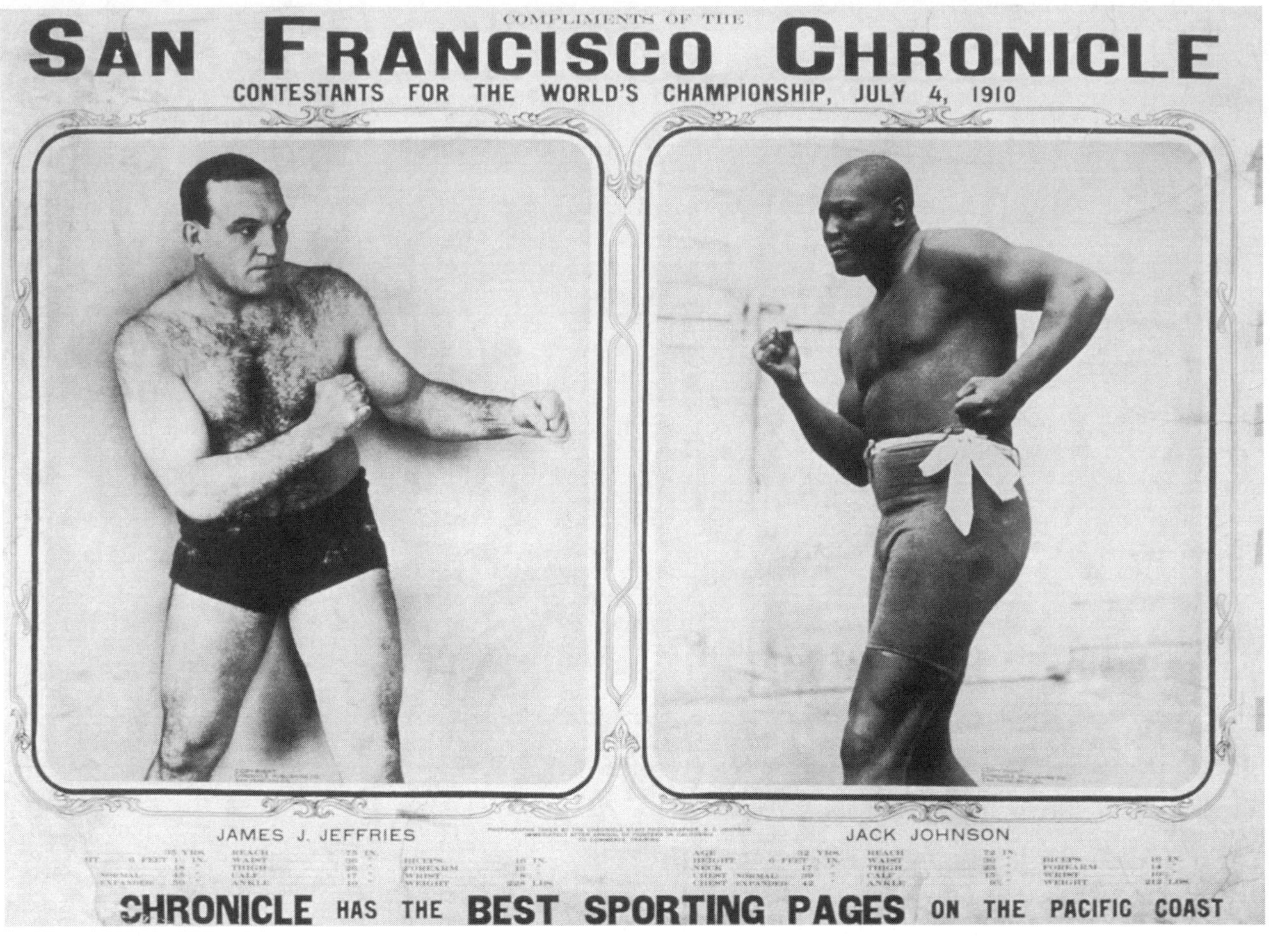

Jack Johnson's victory over James Jeffries, the "Great White Hope," in the July 4, 1910, world heavyweight boxing championship fight triggers racial violence that leaves scores of African Americans dead and wounded and leads to African-American boxers being banned from championship competition until the 1930s. **CORBIS-BETTMANN**

ENTERTAINMENT

Fanny Brice debuts on Broadway in Ziegfeld Follies.

Pathe News shows first screen newsreels in world, and the first animated movie cartoon, "Little Nemo," is shown.

PLAYS George M. Cohan's *Get-Rich-Quick-Wallingford* is produced; H. B. Warner stars in *Alias Jimmy Valentine,* Lina Abarbanell in *Madame Sherry,* Blanche Bates in *Nobody's Widow,* Julia Sanderson in *The Arcadians.*

SPORTS

First aviation meet is held in Los Angeles; first international air races in U.S. are held at Belmont Park, California.

President Taft begins tradition of chief executive throwing out first ball to start the baseball season.

Thomas J. Lynch becomes president of National (baseball) League.

League Park, home of Cleveland Indians, and White Sox (later Comiskey) Park in Chicago open.

Barney Oldfield sets automobile land speed record of 131.7 miles per hour.

Patent is issued to Arthur F. Knight for golf club with steel shaft.

Cy Young of Cleveland Indians pitches 500th victory.

John Flanagan sets hammer-throw record of 184 feet, 4 inches.

First Pendleton (Oregon) Round-Up is held.

Stanley Ketchel, middleweight boxing champion, is shot and killed in Springfield, Ohio.

WINNERS *Baseball*—Philadelphia Athletics, World Series; *Boxing*—Jack Johnson, heavyweight; Ad Wolgast, lightweight; *Golf*—Alex Smith, U.S. Open; *Horse racing*—Donan, Kentucky Derby; Layminster, Preakness Stakes; Sweep, Belmont Stakes; *Tennis*—William Larned, U.S. Open.

MISCELLANEOUS

Boy Scouts of America incorporate; Luther H. and Charlotte V. Gulick found Camp Fire Girls.

Explosion in *Los Angeles Times* building kills 41 people.

Eugene B. Ely becomes first pilot to land on a ship, the cruiser *Philadelphia* (January 18); is first to take off from a ship (cruiser *Birmingham,* November 10).

Spokane (Washington) Ministerial Assn. and YMCA launch observance of Father's Day.

Carnegie Endowment for International Peace is founded.

Rose C. O'Neill produces Kewpie dolls.

1911

INTERNATIONAL

U.S. and Canada sign agreement to reduce or eliminate duties on Canadian farm goods and U.S. manufactured products (January 26).

U.S., Great Britain, and Japan sign treaty to abolish seal hunting in North Pacific waters for 15 years.

NATIONAL

California adopts women's suffrage; Illinois passes law that provides assistance to women with dependent children.

Postal savings service begins at 48 second-class post offices (January 3).

Arizona adopts state constitution; President William Howard Taft vetoes joint resolution to admit Arizona to statehood because its constitution permits recall of judges.

National Urban League is founded as National League on Urban Conditions.

Insurgent Republicans, led by Wisconsin Sen. Robert M. La Follette, are organized as National Progressive Republican League.

Roosevelt Dam in Arizona is dedicated.

DEATHS Norman J. Colman, first Agricultural Secretary (1885–1889); Carry A. Nation, axe-wielding temperance crusader.

BUSINESS/INDUSTRY/INVENTIONS

Supreme Court orders dissolution of Standard Oil Co. as a monopoly (May 1); similar order is issued on the "tobacco trust" (American Tobacco Co.) (May 29) and DuPont Co. (June 21); each Standard Oil Co. subsidiary assumes control of its own operations, becomes independent (November 30).

Triangle Shirtwaist Co. factory in New York City burns, killing 146 workers (March 25); leads to stringent building codes, revision of state labor laws.

First workmen's compensation law goes into effect in New Jersey (July 4); ten other states quickly follow; Equitable Life Insurance Co. issues first group insurance policy for employees of a company.

Merger of three companies forms Computing-Tabulating Recording Co.; Jay R. Monroe founds Monroe Calculating Machine Co.

James McCurdy demonstrates feasibility of two-way radio contact between air and ground.

Broome County (New York) Farm Bureau, first of its kind, is established.

Willis S. Farnsworth patents a coin-operated locker; John M. Browning invents automatic pistol.

Procter & Gamble introduces a shortening, Crisco.

Herman Hollerith and others form the C-T-R Company, later to be known as International Business Machines.

DEATHS Franklin H. King, inventor of cylindrical silo; Tom L. Johnson, inventor of coin farebox; John D. Archbold, Standard Oil executive; Milton Bradley, founder of games company; John M. Carrere, architect; Seaman A. Knapp, developer of Louisiana rice growing.

TRANSPORTATION

Galbraith M. Rogers makes first transcontinental flight, takes 68 hops in 49 days with flying time of 82 hours.

Glenn Curtiss, inventor, flies first successful hydroplane.

Charles F. Kettering perfects automobile electric self-starter.

First Chevrolet motor car is produced.

SCIENCE/MEDICINE

Arnold L. Gesell founds Yale Clinic of Child Development.

Greensboro, North Carolina, turns its health department into a county unit; typhoid epidemic in Yakima, Washington, leads to appointment of full-time county health worker.

EDUCATION

Philander P. Claxton becomes U.S. Education Commissioner.

Memorial parade for the 146 workers who died in the Triangle Shirtwaist fire. **THE LIBRARY OF CONGRESS**

Carnegie Corporation of New York is created to support educational projects.

Southern Methodist University, Dallas, is founded.

RELIGION

Completed portion of the Cathedral of St. John the Divine in New York City is dedicated.

Catholic Bishop James J. Keane becomes archbishop of Dubuque (Iowa).

Rev John G. Murray is named Episcopal bishop of Maryland; Rev. James DeWolf Perry Jr. becomes Episcopal bishop of Rhode Island.

ART/MUSIC

Los Angeles County Museum and Isaac Delgado Museum of Art in New Orleans, Louisiana, are founded.

Victor Herbert presents his opera *Natoma* in Philadelphia; Scott Joplin's ragtime opera, *Treemonisha,* is produced.

Leon Kroll completes the painting *The Bridge.*

SONGS (POPULAR): "Goodnight, Ladies," "Oh, You Beautiful Doll," "I Want a Girl Just Like the Girl," "The Whiffenpoof Song," "Alexander's Ragtime Band," "Memphis Blues."

DEATH Thomas Bell, sculptor (equestrian Washington in Boston Public Gardens); James A. Bland, minstrel musician and composer.

LITERATURE/JOURNALISM

BOOKS *Mother* by Kathleen Norris, *The Harvester* by Gene Stratton Porter, *The Winning of Barbara Worth* by Harold Bell Wright, *Ethan Frome* by Edith Wharton, *Jennie Gerhardt* by Theodore Dreiser, *Mother Carey's Chickens* by Kate Douglas Wiggin.

DEATHS Joseph Pulitzer, publisher *(St. Louis Post-Dispatch, New York World);* Howard Pyle, author and illustrator of children's books.

ENTERTAINMENT

Sophie Tucker first sings "Some of These Days," which becomes her trademark.

Winter Garden Theater in New York City opens.

PLAYS David Warfield stars in *The Return of Peter Grimm,* Mrs. Minnie Maddern Fiske in *Mrs. Bumpstead-Leigh,* Ina Claire in *The Quaker Girl,* George M. Cohan in *The Little Millionaire,* Otis Skinner in *Kismet.*

SPORTS

WINNERS *Auto racing*—Ray Harroun, first Indianapolis 500 race; *Baseball*—Philadelphia Athletics, World Series; *Golf*—John J. McDermott, first U.S.-born winner of U.S. Open; *Horse racing*—Meridian, Kentucky Derby; Watervale, Preakness Stakes; Belmont Stakes not run; *Squash*—Dr. Alfred Stillman 2d, first national tournament; *Tennis*—Australia, Davis Cup; William Larned, U.S. Open.

MISCELLANEOUS

Harriet Quimby is licensed as first American woman pilot; Earl L. Ovington is sworn in as first airmail pilot.

First uniformed Boy Scout troop is organized in Troy, New York; *Boys' Life* magazine, official Boy Scout magazine, begins publication.

Mine disaster at Littleton, Alabama, kills 128.

Dartmouth College stages first collegiate ice festival.

1912

INTERNATIONAL

U.S. Marines land in Nicaragua to protect U.S. interest (August 14); a small contingent remains until 1925.

American Institute of International Law is founded.

NATIONAL

Woodrow Wilson, Democrat, is elected president, defeating former President Theodore Roosevelt, who runs on the Progressive ticket, and Republican President William Howard Taft; Wilson receives 6,286,214 popular and 435 electoral votes to 4,126,020 and 88 for Roosevelt and 3,483,922 and 8 for Taft.

Elihu Root, Secretary of State (1905–1909), is awarded Nobel Peace Prize for work on various treaties.

New Mexico is admitted as 47th state (January 6); Arizona is admitted as 48th state (February 14) after removing a judicial-recall provision in its constitution (see 1911); Territory of Alaska is established (August 24).

Ohio voters ratify new constitution; an amendment to permit women's suffrage is turned down; Arizona, Kansas, and Oregon approve women's suffrage.

Parcel post service is authorized.

United States Chamber of Commerce is founded in Washington, D.C.

National Monetary Commission proposes various legislative steps on banking and financial matters that lead to creation of Federal Reserve System.

Panama Canal Act exempts U.S. coastwise traffic from tolls; this is rescinded after British protest.

Juliette G. Low establishes Girl Scouts (see 1902).

First Japanese cherry trees are planted at Tidal Basin in Washington, D.C.

"All the News That's Fit to Print."

The New York Times.

TITANIC SINKS FOUR HOURS AFTER HITTING ICEBERG; 866 RESCUED BY CARPATHIA, PROBABLY 1250 PERISH; ISMAY SAFE, MRS. ASTOR MAYBE, NOTED NAMES MISSING

Col. Astor and Bride, Isidor Straus and Wife, and Maj. Butt Aboard.

"RULE OF SEA" FOLLOWED

PICKED UP AFTER 8 HOURS

FRANKLIN HOPEFUL ALL DAY

HEAD OF THE LINE ABOARD

Biggest Liner Plunges to the Bottom at 2:20 A.M.

RESCUERS THERE TOO LATE

WOMEN AND CHILDREN FIRST

SEA SEARCH FOR OTHERS

OLYMPIC SENDS THE NEWS

The Lost Titanic Being Towed Out of Belfast Harbor.

PARTIAL LIST OF THE SAVED.

CAPT. E. J. SMITH.

New York Times front page coverage of the *Titanic*, which sinks in the North Atlantic after striking an iceberg. **CORBIS-BETTMANN**

Children's Bureau is created in Labor Department.

First National Safety Congress meets in Milwaukee, Wisconsin.

Mt. Katmai in Alaska erupts, forms Valley of the Ten Thousand Smokes.

Former President Theodore Roosevelt, while campaigning for president, is shot and slightly wounded.

Plant quarantine legislation goes into effect.

DEATH Vice President James S. Sherman (1909–1912).

BUSINESS/INDUSTRY/INVENTIONS

Montgomery Ward & Co. signs contract with Equitable Life Insurance Society for health insurance for its 3,000 employees, the first important group policy.

Massachusetts enacts minimum-wage law for women and minors; eight-hour day is authorized for all workers under federal contracts.

Alfred C. Gilbert produces Erector Set, a new type of toy.

Textile workers strike in Lawrence, Massachusetts.

Bradley A. Fiske patents an airplane torpedo.

Fred M. Kirby chain of five-and-ten-cent stores merge with Woolworth chain.

DEATH Daniel H. Burnham, architect, supervised construction of 1893 World's Fair.

TRANSPORTATION

Steamer *Titanic* sinks on maiden voyage in Atlantic Ocean with 1,513 of its 2,340 passengers, including many Americans, lost.

First U.S. dirigible, *Akron,* explodes in midair over Atlantic City, New Jersey.

Supreme Court dissolves merger of Union Pacific and Southern Pacific railroads, calls it a combination in restraint of trade.

Staten Island to Brooklyn to Manhattan (New York) ferry begins to operate.

Vincent Bendix develops automobile starter drive.

William Burton introduces thermal process for refining petroleum.

SCIENCE/MEDICINE

Navy Dental Corps is authorized.

Dr. Alexis Carrel of Rockefeller Institute is awarded Nobel Prize in physiology/medicine for research on vascular suture and transplants of blood vessels and organs.

Casimir Funk announces isolation of thiamine in brown rice, which is used to cure beriberi.

University of California establishes Scripps Institution for Biological Research.

American College of Surgeons is incorporated.

National Organization for Public Health Nursing is founded.

U.S. Public Health Service is established.

EDUCATION

William M. Rice endows Rice University in Houston; Memphis State University and Loyola University of New Orleans are established.

RELIGION

Richard Wolfe organizes Liberal Church of America, which has no creed, dogma, or theology.

ART/MUSIC

Gaston Lachaise completes massive bronze statue *Standing Woman.*

PAINTINGS Lyonel Feininger, *Bicycle Riders;* John Sloan, *McSorley's Bar* and *Sunday, Women Drying Their Hair;* Paul Burlin, *Figure of a Woman.*

Leopold Stokowski begins 24 years as conductor of the Philadelphia Orchestra.

Rudolf Friml writes the operetta *The Firefly.*

SONGS (POPULAR): "In the Evening by the Moonlight," "It's a Long Way to Tipperary," "My Melancholy Baby," "Sweetheart of Sigma Chi," "Ragtime Cowboy Joe," "Row, Row, Row Your Boat," "When Irish Eyes Are Smiling," "You Can't Stop Me from Loving You."

LITERATURE/JOURNALISM

Columbia School (now Graduate School) of Journalism opens, is endowed by Joseph Pulitzer.

Harriet Monroe founds *Poetry* magazine.

Authors League of America is created.

BOOKS *Riders of the Purple Sage* by Zane Grey, *The Financier* by Theodore Dreiser, *A Dome of Many-Colored Glass* (poetry) by Amy Lowell, *Lee, the American* by Gamaliel Bradford.

DEATH Whitelaw Reid, editor, *New York Tribune* (1877–1905).

ENTERTAINMENT

PLAYS Jerome Kern writes the musical *The Red Petticoat;* Lewis Stone stars in *The Bird of Paradise,* Laurette Taylor in *Peg o' My Heart,* Jane Cowl in *Within the Law,* Elsie Janis in *The Lady of the Slipper.*

Carl Laemmle founds Universal Pictures Corp.; Mack Sennett founds the Keystone Co.; Actors Equity Assn. is founded.

Ragtime music brings out such dances as the fox trot, turkey trot, and bunny hug.

SPORTS

Fenway Park in Boston, Massachusetts, and Tiger Stadium in Detroit, Michigan, open.

Olympic Games are held in Stockholm; U.S. wins 23 events, including Jim Thorpe's victories in the decathlon and pentathlon.

George Horine, using the "western roll," highjumps 6 feet, 7 inches; James Duncan becomes first to surpass 150 feet (156 ft., 1¼ in.) in discus throw; Robert Gardner becomes first to pole vault higher than 13 feet (13 ft., ¾ in.).

Duke Kahanamoku sets 100-meter freestyle swimming record of 61.6 seconds.

Football double-wing formation is first used in Carlisle Indian School's 27–6 win over Army.

WINNERS *Auto racing*—Joe Dawson, Indianapolis 500; *Baseball*—Boston Red Sox, World Series; *Bicycling*—George Wiley, world motor-paced riding; Frank Kramer, sprint riding; *Boxing*—Willie Ritchie, lightweight; Johnny Kilbane, featherweight; *Golf*—John McDermott, U.S. Open; *Horse racing*—Worth, Kentucky Derby; Colonel Holloway, Preakness Stakes; Belmont Stakes not run; *Tennis*—Maurice McLaughlin, U.S. Open.

MISCELLANEOUS

George E. Haynes becomes first African-American to receive Ph.D. degree at Columbia University.

Glenn L. Martin makes first overwater plane flight, flies one of his own planes from Los Angeles to Catalina Island; Capt. Albert Lewis makes first U.S. parachute jump.

Uncle Sam collects taxes from famous millionaires, who weep bitter tears over having to write checks to the government for the first time. The Sixteenth Amendment is ratified on February 25, 1913. **CORBIS-BETTMANN**

1913

INTERNATIONAL

New Chinese Republic is recognized.

U.S. blockades Mexico in support of revolutionaries.

NATIONAL

States ratify Sixteenth Amendment, authorizing a federal income tax (February 25), also ratify Seventeenth Amendment, calling for popular election of senators (May 31).

Department of Commerce and Labor divide into two departments, Commerce headed by William C. Redfield, Labor headed by William B. Wilson (March 4).

President Woodrow Wilson appears before Congress (April 8), first president to do so since John Adams (1800), calls for tariff revision; the Underwood Tariff Act lowers duties to about 30%, with iron, steel, and raw wool on free list (October 3).

Congress, over President William Howard Taft's veto, prohibits shipment of liquor into states that forbid its sale.

Cleveland Municipal Court establishes small claims court, Kansas authorizes small debtor's court; Los Angeles County creates public defender's office.

Newlands Act creates Board of Mediation and Conciliation.

Parcel Post Service begins (January 1).

First regular White House news conference is held.

Alice Paul and others found Congressional Union for Woman Suffrage; Illinois allows women to vote in local elections.

Keokuk Dam across the Mississippi River is completed.

National Safety Council is organized.

Franklin D. Roosevelt is named Assistant Secretary of the Navy.

Growing number of immigrants in U.S. is reflected in fact that there are 538 newspapers printed in 29 foreign languages.

DEATH Harriet Tubman, organizer of Underground Railroad to help fleeing slaves.

SEE PRIMARY DOCUMENT Excerpt from *The New Freedom: A Call for the Emancipation of the Generous Energies of a People* by Woodrow Wilson

BUSINESS/INDUSTRY/INVENTIONS

Armstrong Cork Co. introduces insulating brick; Hood Rubber Co. manufactures synthetic rubber.

Sheaffer Pen Co. is established.

Textile workers in Paterson, New Jersey, strike; miners strike Colorado Fuel & Iron Co. for second time; 150,000 garment workers win shorter hours, wage increase after short strike.

Mellon Institute of Industrial Research is founded.

Suffragettes in automobile, 1913. Their campaign to win the vote for American women intensifies during World War I and succeeds in 1920. © UNDERWOOD & UNDERWOOD/CORBIS-BETTMANN

Sale of "hump" hairpins, bobbie-pin predecessor, begins.

Gideon Sundback patents zipper.

Federal Reserve System is established with 12 district banks and a Federal Reserve Board to set rediscount rates (December 23).

Sixty-story Woolworth Building and 50-story Metropolitan Tower in New York City are completed.

TRANSPORTATION

Gulf Oil in Pittsburgh, Pennsylvania, opens first drive-in gasoline station.

Grand Central Terminal in New York City opens.

Interstate Commerce Commission is empowered to establish railroad costs and physical valuations as basis for rate making.

Ford Motor Co. introduces conveyor-belt assembly-line production of cars.

Stutz Car Co., maker of Stutz Bearcat, is founded; Hudson Motors produces first auto sedan.

Lincoln Highway Assn. forms to promote transcontinental highway; work begins in 1914.

Igor I. Sikorsky flies first multi-motor airplane.

Passenger car registrations reach 1,258,062.

SCIENCE/MEDICINE

Dr. Bela Schick devises a skin test for diphtheria.

American Association of Immunologists is organized.

Biochemist Elmer McCollum isolates vitamins A and B.

John B. Watson founds behaviorist school of psychology.

DEATH Daniel D. Palmer, pioneer chiropractor.

EDUCATION

Massachusetts Institute of Technology offers first aeronautical engineering course.

RELIGION

Solomon Schechter founds United Synagogue of America.

ART/MUSIC

Armory Show in New York City introduces European and new American works.

Metropolitan Opera presents Walter Damrosch's opera *Cyrano de Bergerac;* Victor Herbert's operetta *Sweethearts* and Rudolf Friml's *High Jinks* open.

Sculptor Alexander Archipenko completes *Geometric Statue;* Arthur B. Davies completes the painting *Dances;* George W. Bellows, *Cliff Dwellers;* Robert Henri, *Himself and Herself;* Lyonel Feininger, *Sidewheeler.*

SONGS (POPULAR): "Danny Boy," "Peg o' My Heart," "You Made Me Love You," "Sweethearts," "Brighten the Corner Where You Are," "There's a Long, Long Trail."

LITERATURE/JOURNALISM

Franklin P. Adams (FPA) writes column "The Conning Tower" and Don(ald) Marquis writes daily humorous column "The Sun Dial," in which characters Archy and Mehitabel appear.

Vachel Lindsay's poem "General William Booth Enters Into Heaven" is published in *Poetry.*

New York Times Index begins.

Ogden Mills Reid edits and publishes *New York Tribune* succeeding his father, Whitelaw Reid.

Masses, a magazine of art, literature, and socialism, begins publication.

BOOKS *Pollyanna* by Eleanor H. Porter, *Laddie* by Gene Stratton Porter, *O Pioneers!* by Willa Cather, *A Preface to Politics* by Walter Lippmann, *Seven Keys to Baldpate* by Earl Derr Biggers, *Merchants from Cathay* (poetry) by William Rose Benet.

ENTERTAINMENT

Cecil B. DeMille, Jesse Lasky, and Samuel Goldwyn form movie company; *The Squaw Man* is the first full-length movie; the movie *The Perils of Pauline* is also produced.

PLAYS Vernon and Irene Castle make their dancing debut in *The Sunshine Girl,* in which Julia Sanderson stars; other plays: Emily Stevens stars in *Today,* Al Jolson in *The Honeymoon Express,* and Montagu Glass writes *Potash and Perlmutter.*

New York's Palace Theater begins 20 years' reign as outstanding U.S. vaudeville house.

The dance "ballin-the-jack" becomes popular.

SPORTS

John K. Tener is named National (baseball) League president.

International Olympic Committee strips Jim Thorpe of his 1912 victories and medals because he played professional baseball before the Olympics (action reversed in 1982).

At the time it is erected, the Woolworth Building in New York City is the tallest building in America. The skyscraper is also notable for its use of Gothic architectural elements. © MUSEUM OF THE CITY OF NEW YORK/CORBIS-BETTMANN

New York State Athletic Commission bans fights between black and Caucasian boxers.

Present-day game of shuffleboard begins in Daytona Beach, Florida.

Ebbets (baseball) Field in Brooklyn, New York, opens.

Merger of American Football Assn. and American Amateur Football Assn. forms U.S. Soccer Football Assn.

Patrick Ryan sets hammer-throw record of 189 feet, 6½ inches.

WINNERS *Auto racing*—Jules Goux, Indianapolis 500; *Baseball*—Philadelphia Athletics, World Series; *Golf*—Francis Ouimet, U.S. Open; *Horse racing*—Donerail (91–1 longshot), Kentucky Derby; Buskin, Preakness Stakes; Prince Eugene, Belmont Stakes; *Tennis*—U.S., Davis Cup; Maurice McLaughlin, U.S. Open.

MISCELLANEOUS

Four major disasters occur: a dynamite explosion in Baltimore Harbor kills 55, a mine accident at Finleyville, Pennsylvania, kills 96, a similar accident at Dawson, New Mexico, takes 263 lives, and three days of flooding in March in Ohio and Indiana cause 732 deaths.

Veterans of Foreign Wars (VFW) is founded.

Monument by Mahouri Young to honor sea gulls is unveiled in Salt Lake City; gulls had consumed an army of grasshoppers that were destroying the 1848 wheat crop.

Arthur Wynne prepares first crossword puzzle; is published in *New York World.*

PRIMARY SOURCE DOCUMENT

Excerpt from *The New Freedom: A Call for the Emancipation of the Generous Energies of a People* by Woodrow Wilson

INTRODUCTION Thomas Woodrow Wilson (1856–1924), the twenty-eighth president of the United States, grew up in the South during the Civil War and Reconstruction. He graduated from Princeton University in 1879, earned a law degree from the University of Virginia and obtained a Ph.D. in history and political science from Johns Hopkins University in Baltimore. After teaching at Bryn Mawr College and Wesleyan University, he returned to Princeton in 1890, becoming its president in 1902.

Wilson first articulated his vision of an activist president in his dissertation at Johns Hopkins, later published as *Congressional Government* in 1885. In his inaugural address at Princeton, Wilson had said, "We are not put into this world to sit still and know. We are put into it to act." At Princeton he instituted a number of reforms that caught the attention of New Jersey's Democratic Party organization, who helped to secure his election as governor of New Jersey in 1910. Wilson combined his knowledge of politics and history with this passion for political action. Influenced by nearly a decade of political activity by *progressives*, Americans intent on reforming virtually all aspects of society, Gov. Wilson pushed his state legislature to enact changes that many states had already implemented.

During the 1912 presidential campaign, Wilson ran against former president Theodore Roosevelt, who had left the Republican Party to form the Progressive (or Bull Moose) Party, and the incumbent President, Republican William Henry Taft. The race narrowed to Wilson and Roosevelt, both of whom articulated a progressive vision to address the destructive impact of corporate power on labor relations, politics, and society in general, as well as to head off more radical reform embraced by American socialists. Roosevelt offered his New Nationalism agenda, influenced by the ideas contained in Herbert Croly's book *The Promise of American Life.* Although Wilson accepted one of Croly's axioms, that the state of the American political economy demanded an activist central government, his New Freedom program emphasized aggressive antitrust activity to encourage business competition rather than coercive governmental regulation of corporations, as Roosevelt's plan urged. At the heart of Wilson's New Freedom program, featured in the document here, is the idea that the federal government had to achieve a power commensurate with that of Big Business in order to limit corporate influence in politics and to restore fair competition in the American economy.

With the Republican Party split between Roosevelt's and Taft's supporters, Wilson won a resounding victory claiming 435 of 531 electoral votes. Wilson took office along with Democratic majorities in the Senate and the House. Over the next few years Wilson helped to push through a receptive Congress a series of economic reforms, including the Federal Reserve Act, the Clayton Anti-Trust Act, the Federal Trade Commission, the Sixteenth Amendment that created a federal income tax, and tariff reductions, although some of these reforms were later weakened by conservative elements in Congress. Pressured by more progressive Democrats, Wilson eventually signed off on social issues: child labor and legislation addressing specific credit for farmers.

I. The Old Order Changeth

There is one great basic fact which underlies all the questions that are discussed on the political platform at the present moment. That singular fact is that nothing is done in this country as it was done twenty years ago.

We are in the presence of a new organization of society. Our life has broken away from the past. The life of America is not the life that it was twenty years ago; it is not the life that it was ten years ago. We have changed our economic conditions, absolutely, from top to bottom; and, with our economic society, the organization of our life. The old political formulas do not fit the present problems; they read now like documents taken out of a forgotten age. The older cries sound as if they belonged to a past age which men have almost forgotten. Things which used to be put into the party platforms ten years ago would sound antiquated if put into a platform now. We are facing the necessity of fitting a new social organization, as we did once fit the old organization, to the happiness and prosperity of the great body of citizens; for we are conscious that the new order of society has not been made to fit and provide the convenience or prosperity of the average man. The life of the nation has grown infinitely varied. It does not centre now upon questions of the very structure and operation of society itself, of which government is only the instrument. Our development has run so fast and so far along the lines sketched in the earlier day of constitutional definition, has crossed and interlaced those lines, has piled upon them such novel structures of trust and combination, has elaborated within them a life so manifold, so full of forces which transcend the boundaries of the country itself and fill the eyes of the world, that a new nation seems to have been created which the old formulas do not fit or afford a vital interpretation of.

We have come upon a very different age from any that preceded us. We have come upon an age when we do not do business in the way in which we used to do business,—when we do not carry on any of the operations of manufacture, sale, transportation, or communication as men used to carry them on. There is a sense in which in our day the individual has been submerged. In most parts of our country men work, not for themselves, not as partners in the old way in which they used to work, but generally as employees,—in a higher or lower grade,—of great corporations. There was a time when corporations played a very minor part in our business affairs, but now they play a chief part, and most men are the servants of corporations.

You know what happens when you are the servant of a corporation. You have in no instance access to men who are really determining the policy of the corporation. If the corporation is doing the things that it ought not to do, you really have no voice in the matter and must obey the orders, and you have oftentimes with deep mortification to co-operate in the doing of things which you know are against the public interest. Your individuality is swallowed up in the individuality and purpose of a great organization.

It is true that, while most men are thus submerged in the corporation, a few, a very few, are exalted to a power which as individuals they could never have wielded. Through the great organizations of which they are the heads, a few are enabled to play a part unprecedented by anything in history in the control of the business operations of the country and in the determination of the happiness of great numbers of people.

Yesterday, and ever since history began, men were related to one another as individuals. To be sure there were the family, the Church, and the State, institutions which associated men in certain wide circles of relationship. But in the ordinary concerns of life, in the ordinary work, in the daily round, men dealt freely and directly with one another. To-day, the everyday relationships of men are largely with great impersonal concerns, with organizations, not with other individual men....

In this new age we find, for instance, that our laws with regard to the relations of employer and employee are in many respects wholly antiquated and impossible. They were framed for another age, which nobody now living remembers, which is, indeed, so remote from our life that it would be difficult for many of us to understand it if it were described to us. The employer is now generally a corporation or a huge company of some kind; the employee is one of hundreds or thousands brought together, not by individual masters whom they know and with whom they have personal relations, but by agents of one sort or another. Workingmen are marshaled in great numbers for the performance of a multitude of particular tasks under a common discipline. They generally use dangerous and powerful machinery, over whose repair and renewal they have no control. New rules must be devised with regard to their obligations and their rights, their obligations to their employers and their responsibilities to one another. Rules must be devised for their protection, for their compensation when injured, for their support when disabled.

There is something very new and very big and very complex about these new relations of capital and labor. A new economic society has sprung up, and we must effect a new set of adjustments. We must not pit power against weakness. The employer is generally, in our day, as I said, not an individual, but a powerful group; and yet the workingman when dealing with his employer is still, under out existing law, an individual....

So what we have to discuss is, not wrongs which individuals intentionally do,—I do not believe there are a great many of those,—but the wrongs of a system. I want to record my protest against any discussion of this matter which would seem to indicate that there are bodies of our fellow-citizens who are trying to grind us down and do us injustice. There are some men of that sort. I don't know how they sleep o' nights, but there are men of that kind. Thank God, they are not numerous. The truth is, we are all caught in a great economic system which is heartless....

Since I entered politics, I have chiefly had men's views confided to me privately. Some of the biggest men in the United States, in the field of commerce and manufacture, are afraid of somebody, are afraid of something. They know that there is a power somewhere so organized, so subtle, so watchful, so interlocked, so complete, so pervasive, that they had better not speak above their breath when they speak in condemnation of it.

They know that America is not a place of which it can be said, as it used to be, that a man may choose his own calling and pursue it just as far as his abilities enable him to pursue it; because to-day, if he enters certain fields, there are organizations which will use means against him that will prevent his building up a business which they do not want to have built up; organizations what will see to it that the ground is cut from under him and the markets shut against him. For if he begins to sell to certain retail dealers, the monopoly will refuse to sell to those dealers, and those dealers, afraid, will not buy the new man's wares.

And this is the country which has lifted to the admiration of the world its ideals of absolutely free opportunity, where no man is supposed to be under any limitation except the limitations of his character and of his mind; where there is supposed to be no distinction of class, no distinction of blood, no distinction of social status, but where men win or lose on their merits.

I lay it very close to my own conscience as a public man whether we can any longer stand at our doors and welcome all newcomers upon those terms. American industry is not free, as once it was free; American enterprise is not free; the man with only a little capital is finding it harder to get into the field, more and more impossible to compete with the big fellow. Why? Because the laws of this country do not prevent the strong from crushing the weak. That is the reason, and because the strong have crushed the weak the strong dominate the industry and the economic life of this country. No man can deny that the lines of endeavor have more and more narrowed and stiffened; no man who knows anything about the development of industry in this country can have failed to observe that the larger kinds of credit are more and more difficult to obtain, unless you obtain them upon terms of uniting your efforts with those who already control the industries of the country; and nobody can fail to observe that any man who tries to set himself up in competition with any process of manufacture which has been taken under the control of large combinations of capital will presently find himself either squeezed out or obliged to sell and allow himself to be absorbed....

What this country needs above everything else is a body of laws which will look after the men who are on the make rather than the men who are already made. Because the men who are already made are not going to live indefinitely, and they are not always kind enough to leave sons as able and as honest as they are.

The originative part of America, the part of America that makes new enterprises, the part into which the ambitious and gifted workingman makes his way up, the class that saves, that plans, that organize, that presently spreads its enterprises until they have a national scope and character,—that middle class is being more and more squeezed out by the processes which we have been taught to call processes of prosperity. Its members are sharing prosperity, no doubt; but what alarms me is that they are not *originating* prosperity. No country can afford to have its prosperity originated by a small controlling class. The treasure of America does not lie in the brains of the small body of men now in control of the great enterprises that have been concentrated under the direction of a very small number of persons. The treasury of America lies in those ambitions, those energies, that cannot be restricted to a special favored class....

There has come over the land that un-American set of conditions which enables a small number of men who control the government to get favors from the government; by those favors to exclude their fellows from equal business opportunity; by those favors to extend a network of control that will presently dominate every industry in the country....

We used to think in the old-fashioned days when life was very simple that all that government had to do was put on a policeman's uniform and say, "Now don't anybody hurt anybody else." We used to say that the ideal of government was for every man to be left alone and not interfered with, except when he interfered with somebody else; and that the best government was the government that did as little governing as possible. That as the idea that obtained in Jefferson's time. But we are coming now to realize that life is so complicated that we are not dealing with the old conditions, and that the law has to step in and create new conditions under which we may live, the conditions which will make it tolerable for us to live....

We are in a new world, struggling under old laws. As we go inspecting our lives to-day, surveying this new scene of centralized and complex society, we shall find many more things out of joint.

One of the most alarming phenomena of the time,—or rather it would be alarming if the nation had not awakened to it and shown its determination to control it,—one of the most significant signs of the new social era is the degree to which the government has become associated with business. I speak, for the moment, of the control over the government exercised by Big Business. Behind the whole subject, of course, is the truth that, in the new order, government and business must be associated closely. But that association is at present of a nature absolutely intolerable; the precedence is wrong, the association is upside down. Our government has been for the past few years under the control of heads of great allied corporations with special interests. It has not controlled these interests and assigned them a proper place in the whole system of business; it has submitted itself to their control. As a result, there have grown up vicious systems and schemes of governmental favoritism (the most obvious being the extravagant tariff), far-reaching in effect upon the whole fabric of life, touching to his injury every inhabitant of the land, laying unfair and impossible handicaps upon competitors, imposing taxes in every direction, stifling everywhere the free spirit of American enterprise.

Now this has come about naturally; as we go on we shall see how very naturally. It is no use denouncing anybody, or anything, except human nature. Nevertheless, it is an intolerable thing that the government of the republic should have got so far out of the hands of the people; should have been captured by the interests which are special and not general. In the train of this capture follow the troops of scandals, wrongs, indecencies, with which our politics swarm.

There are cities in America of whose governments we are ashamed. There are cities everywhere, in every part of the land, in which we feel that, not the interests of the public, but the interests of special privileges, of selfish men, are served; where contracts take precedence over public interest. Not only in big cities is this the case. Have you not noticed the growth of socialistic sentiment in the smaller towns?...

All over the Union people are coming to feel that they have no control over the course of affairs. I live in one of the greatest States in the union, which was at one time in slavery. Until two years ago we had witnessed with increasing concern the growth in New Jersey of a spirit of almost cynical despair. Men said: "We vote; we are offered the platform we want; we elect the men who stand on that platform, and we get absolutely nothing." So they began to ask: "What is the use of voting? We know that the machine of both parties are subsidized by the same persons, and therefore it is useless to turn in either directions."

This is not confined to some of the state governments and those of some of the towns and cities. We know that something intervenes between the people of the United States and the control of their own affairs at Washington. It is not the people who have been ruling there of late.

Why are we in the presence, why are we at the threshold, of a revolution? Because we are profoundly disturbed by the influences which we see reigning in the determination of our public life and our public policy. There was a time when America was lithe with self-confidence. She boasted that she, and she alone, knew the processes of popular government; but now she sees her sky overcast; she sees that there are at work forces which she did not dream of in her hopeful youth....

The old order changeth—changeth under our very eyes, not quietly and equably, but swiftly and with the noise and heat and tumult of reconstruction....

I doubt if any age was ever more conscious of its task or more unanimously desirous of radical and extended changes in its economic and political practice.

We stand in the presence of a revolution,—not a bloody revolution; America is not given to the spilling of blood,—but a silent revolution, whereby America will insist upon recovering in practice those ideals which she has always professed, upon securing a government devoted to the general interest and not to special interests.

We are upon the eve of a great reconstruction. It calls for creative statesmanship as no age has done since that great age in which we set up the government under which we live, that government which was the admiration of the world until it suffered wrongs to grow up under it which have made many of our own compatriots question the freedom of our institutions and preach revolution against them. I do not fear revolution. I have unshaken faith in the power of America to keep its self-possession. Revolution will come in peaceful guise, as it came when we put aside the crude government of the Confederation and created the great Federal Union which governs individuals, not States, and which has been these hundred and thirty years our vehicle of progress. Some radical changes we must make in our law and practice. Some reconstructions we must push forward, which a new age and new circumstances impose upon us. But we can do it all in calm and sober fashion, like statesmen and patriots.

I do not speak of these things in apprehension, because all is open and above-board. This is not a day which great forces rally in secret. The whole stupendous program must be publicly planned and canvassed. Good temper, the wisdom that comes of sober counsel, the energy of thoughtful and unselfish men, the habit of cooperation and of compromise which has been bred in us by long years of free government, in which reason rather than passion has been made to prevail by the sheer virtue of candid and universal debate, will enable us to win through to still another great age without violence.

SOURCE: Woodrow Wilson, *The New Freedom: A Call for the Emancipation of the Generous Energies of a People,* (New York: Garden City, Doubleday, Page & Company, 1913).

1914

INTERNATIONAL

President Woodrow Wilson issues neutrality proclamation when war breaks out in Europe.

U.S. sailors buying supplies in Tampico, Mexico, are arrested, released a short time later (April 9); Congress grants President Wilson right to use force if needed to uphold U.S. rights.

U.S. Marines land in Veracruz, Mexico (April 22), to prevent landing of German munitions; Mexico breaks off relations with U.S.; the ABC powers (Argentina, Brazil, Chile) meet in Niagara Falls, New York (July 2), resolve the U.S.-Mexico dispute.

Convention signed with Panama defines boundaries of the Panama Canal Zone (September 2); George W. Goethals becomes first governor of the zone.

Bryan-Chamorro Treaty gives U.S. exclusive right to build an interoceanic canal across Nicaragua.

NATIONAL

Clayton Anti-Trust Act passes to strengthen Sherman Act; Food and Fuel Control Act passes.

Margaret Sanger publishes *The Woman Rebel,* a feminist monthly that advocates the use of birth control.

Dayton, Ohio, becomes first large U.S. city to adopt commission—city manager form of government (January 1).

Air Service of U.S. Army is established in Signal Corps.

Margaret Sanger (left), founder of American birth control movement, and Lillian Fassett going to court. In 1914 Sanger champions the use of contraception in the monthly publication *The Woman Rebel.* UPI/CORBIS-BETTMANN

Women march on the Capitol, demand the right to vote.

Prohibition goes into effect in Tennessee and West Virginia; Nevada and Montana approve women's suffrage.

Congress establishes second Sunday in May as Mother's Day.

DEATHS First Lady Ellen Wilson; former Vice President Adlai E. Stevenson (1893–1897); Samuel W. Allerton, a builder of modern Chicago.

BUSINESS/INDUSTRY/INVENTIONS

Federal Trade Commission is established (September 26), replaces Bureau of Corporations; is designed to guard against unfair competition in interstate commerce.

Port of Houston is opened to international commerce.

Merrill Lynch brokerage firm is founded.

Thomas J. Watson becomes president of Computing-Tabulating Recording Co., which becomes IBM in 1924.

Sidney Hillman begins 32 years as first president of Amalgamated Clothing Workers union.

Robert H. Goddard patents a liquid fuel rocket.

Grossinger's resort in the Catskills (New York) opens.

DEATHS John P. Holland, submarine developer; Charles W. Post, cereal maker; Frederick Weyerhaeuser, lumber "king"; Joseph Fels, founder of Fels-Naphtha (soaps); Herman Frasch, developer of smelting process that led to sulphur industry; Richard W. Sears, a founder of Sears Roebuck.

TRANSPORTATION

A self-propelled crane boat makes first passage of Panama Canal (January 7); commercial traffic begins (August 15).

Ford Motor Co. assembly line production cuts time for assembling a car from 12½ hours to 93 minutes; company raises basic wage from $2.40 for nine-hour day to $5 for eight hours.

First electric traffic signals in U.S. are installed (Euclid Avenue and 105th Street, Cleveland, Ohio).

First eight-cylinder automobile motor is developed; Charles Lawrence develops first successful air-cooled airplane engine.

Seasonal commercial air passenger service begins between Tampa and St. Augustine, Florida.

SCIENCE/MEDICINE

Theodore W. Richards is awarded Nobel Prize in chemistry for determination of atomic weight of chemical elements.

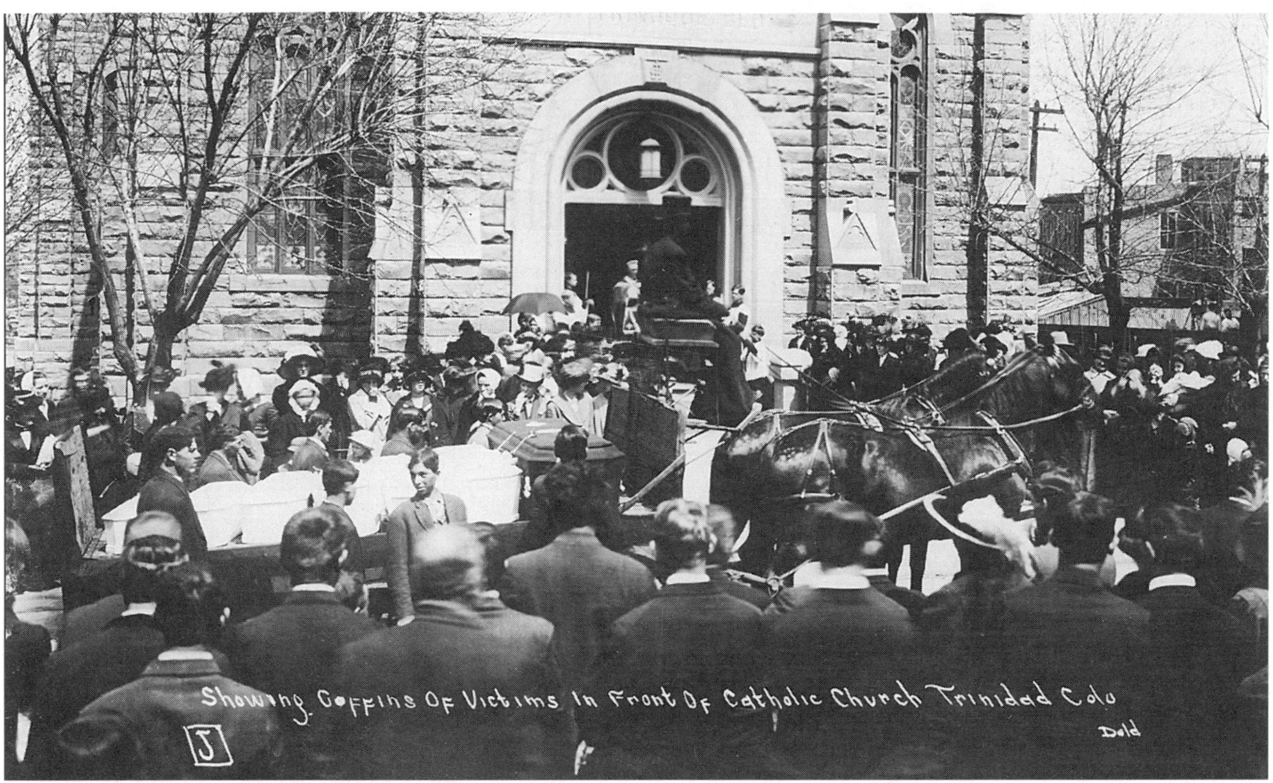

Showing Coffins Of Victims In Front Of Catholic Church Trinidad Colo
Dold

Funeral procession for victims of the Ludlow Massacre. Sixty-six men, women, and children were killed when Colorado state militia and company police attacked and burned a tent colony set up by striking coal miners, April 20, 1914. CORBIS-BETTMANN

Dr. Simon Flexner announces successful isolation of infantile paralysis virus.

Astronomer Seth B. Nicholson discovers ninth moon of Jupiter, discovers three more by 1952; Walter S. Adams develops method of calculating distances of faraway stars.

Museum of Science and Industry in New York City is established as Museum of Peaceful Arts.

RELIGION

Assemblies of God church is organized (April 2).

DEATH Joseph Smith, son of Mormon Church founder and head of Reorganized Latter Day Saints church (1860–1914).

ART/MUSIC

ASCAP (American Society of Composers, Authors, and Publishers) forms in New York City.

Metropolitan Opera presents Victor Herbert's opera *Madeline.*

John Sloan completes the painting *Backyards, Greenwich Village;* Lyonel Feininger, *Allée;* William J. Glackens, *Washington Square.*

Margaret Anderson founds *Little Review,* a magazine of the arts.

Original Dixieland Jazz Band forms in Chicago.

SONGS (POPULAR): "St. Louis Blues," "That's A-Plenty," "They Didn't Believe Me," "When You Wore a Tulip," "By the Beautiful Sea," "Love's Old Sweet Song," "Missouri Waltz," "Twelfth Street Rag."

DEATH Rudolph Wurlitzer, musical instrument maker.

LITERATURE/JOURNALISM

Carl Sandburg's poems "Fog" and "I Am the People" and Joyce Kilmer's poem "Trees" appear in *Poetry* magazine.

Association of American Advertisers organizes Audit Bureau of Circulation.

First newspaper rotogravure sections appear in seven papers.

Herbert D. Croly founds *New Republic* magazine.

H. L. Mencken edits *The Smart Set* magazine.

BOOKS *Tarzan of the Apes* by Edgar Rice Burroughs, *Penrod* by Booth Tarkington, *The Eyes of the World* by Harold Bell Wright, *The Titan* by Theodore Dreiser, *The Congo and Other Poems* by Vachel Lindsay, *North of Boston* (poetry) by Robert Frost.

ENTERTAINMENT

Louella Parsons writes movie column for *Chicago*

A Ford assembly line becomes operational in Detroit, Michigan, pushing thousands of automobiles onto American roads.
NATIONAL ARCHIVES AND RECORDS ADMINISTRATION, RECORDS OF THE BUREAU OF PUBLIC ROADS

Record-Herald; Alexander Woollcott begins eight years as the *New York Times* drama critic.

MOVIES *Tillie's Punctured Romance* with Charlie Chaplin and Marie Dressler is produced, the first American feature-length movie comedy; Theda Bara stars in *A Fool There Was.*

PLAYS Al Jolson stars in *Dancing Around,* Vernon and Irene Castle in *Watch Your Step,* Ruth Chatterton in *Daddy Long-Legs,* John Barrymore in *Kick In,* Douglas Fairbanks in *The Show Shop,* Frank Craven in *Too Many Crooks.*

The waltz and two-step are the fashionable society dance steps; other popular dances are the grizzly bear, bunny hug, turkey trot, and fox-trot.

DEATHS Benjamin F. Keith, vaudeville circuit founder; George C. Tilyou, amusement rides inventor and developer of Coney Island (Brooklyn, New York).

SPORTS

U.S. Power Squadrons are formed.

Southwest Intercollegiate Athletic Conference is established.

Honus Wagner of Pittsburgh Pirates and Nap Lajoie of Cleveland Indians each get their 3,000th base hits.

Grand League of American Horseshoe Players is organized.

WINNERS *Auto racing*—Rene Thomas, Indianapolis 500; *Baseball*—Boston Braves, World Series; *Boxing*—Jack Johnson, heavyweight; Kid Williams, bantamweight; *Figure skating*—Theresa Weld, women's international title; Norman Scott, men's; *Golf*—Walter Hagen, U.S. Open; *Horse racing*—Old Rosebud, Kentucky Derby; Holiday, Preakness Stakes; Luke McLuke, Belmont Stakes; *Motorcycling*—Glenn R. Boyd, first race (300 miles); *Rowing*—Harvard, first U.S. winner of Henley Grand Challenge Cup; *Tennis*—Australia, Davis Cup; Richard Williams, U.S. Open.

MISCELLANEOUS

Mine disaster at Eccles, West Virginia, kills 181.

Women give up tight corsets, but fashionable skirts are so tight that they impede walking; skirts are shorter, and women wear high-buttoned shoes.

1915

INTERNATIONAL

World War I

German submarine sinks wheat-laden U.S. vessel *William Frye* (January 28). Germany announces area around British Isles is a war zone, enemy merchant ships will be destroyed beginning February 18; German mines sink U.S. steamers *Evelyn* (February 19) and *Carib* (February 23); German torpedoes sink tanker *Gulflight.* Germany warns that U.S. vessels entering war zone do so at their own peril.

British steamer *Lusitania* sunk (May 7) off Ireland, taking 1,198 lives, including 128 Americans (author Elbert Hubbard, producer Charles Frohmann, Alfred G. Vanderbilt). U.S. steamers *Nebraskan* (May 25) and *Leelanaw* (July 25) are sunk.

War-related activities at home include opening of military training camp at Plattsburgh, New York (August 10); an explosion in DuPont plant (Wilmington, Delaware), believed due to sabotage, kills 31; Henry Ford and a peace delegation travel to Europe (December 4) to end war; Ford leaves the group (December 22), returns to U.S.; President Woodrow Wilson outlines comprehensive national defense program (December 7).

Other International Events

U.S. Marines land at Santo Domingo, Dominican Republic, to begin occupation (May 5); Marines land in Haiti (July 29), following a revolution; new government signs treaty making Haiti a virtual U.S. protectorate for 10 years.

NATIONAL

Secretary of State William Jennings Bryan resigns in disagreement with presidential policy on *Lusitania* sinking.

Bomb is placed by Eric Muenter, German instructor, explodes in Senate reception room (July 2); no one is injured; the next day, Muenter slightly wounds J. P. Morgan, war contract agent for British; Muenter commits suicide three days later.

Combining Life Saving and Revenue Cutter services creates Coast Guard (January 28).

William J. Simmons of Atlanta revives Ku Klux Klan (November 25).

Young Men's Progressive Civic Assn. (later Junior Chamber of Commerce) is organized.

Prohibition goes into effect in Alabama, Arizona, Idaho; and South Carolina, Oregon, and Colorado pass prohibition laws.

National Committee for Aeronautics is created, forerunner of National Aeronautics and Space Administration (NASA) (March 3).

Widowed President Wilson marries a widow, Mrs. Edith B. Galt.

Warren G. Harding begins term as senator from Ohio; Herbert Hoover is named chairman of Commission for Relief in Belgium.

Alexander Graham Bell in New York and his assistant, Thomas A. Watson, in San Francisco hold first transcontinental telephone conversation; costs $20.70 for first three minutes (January 25).

San Diego hosts Panama-California Exposition.

Rocky Mountain (Colorado) National Park is established.

DEATHS Anthony Comstock, reformer; John A. Holmes, first director, Bureau of Mines (1910–1915), who popularized phrase, "Safety first."

SEE PRIMARY DOCUMENT "Do You Know?" by Carrie Chapman Catt

BUSINESS/INDUSTRY/INVENTIONS

John T. Thompson invents submachine gun; David Sarnoff, a radio set.

La Follette Seamen's Act regulates employment conditions of maritime workers.

Willis H. Carrier founds Carrier Corp.

Oil is discovered at El Dorado, Kansas.

American Association of Engineers is founded.

DEATHS Frank W. Taylor, industrial engineer, father of scientific management; W. Atlee Burpee, plant-seed merchant; John McTammany, inventor.

Charlie Chaplin in his classic tramp costume. The character will be Chaplin's on-screen persona for most of his movies. **THE LIBRARY OF CONGRESS**

TRANSPORTATION

One-millionth Ford comes off assembly line; Chevrolet Motor Co. is founded.

First automobile finance company is Bankers Commercial Corp., New York City; Guarantee Securities Co. is organized to buy consumers' installment notes from Willys-Overland dealers.

DEATHS Lorenzo S. Coffin, led successful campaign for railroad automatic coupling.

SCIENCE/MEDICINE

Mayo Clinic in Rochester, Minnesota, opens.

Dinosaur National Monument in Utah and Colorado is established to preserve paleontological finds.

Zoological Society of America is founded.

DEATHS Greene V. Black, pioneer dentist; Francis Delafield, founder, Association of American Physicians.

EDUCATION

Xavier University in New Orleans, Louisiana, opens.

American Association of University Professors is founded.

DEATH Booker T. Washington, founder, head of Tuskegee (Alabama) Institute.

RELIGION

Catholic Bishop George W. Mundelein becomes archbishop of Chicago; Bishop Edward J. Hanna archbishop of San Francisco.

DEATH Frances J. Crosby, blind Protestant hymn writer ("Blessed Assurance," "Sweet Hour of Prayer").

ART/MUSIC

Ruth St. Denis and Ted Shawn establish Denishawn School of Dance.

Arthur G. Dove completes the painting *Plant Forms;* John F. Kensett, *Lake George;* Max Weber, *Chinese Restaurant.*

SONGS (POPULAR): "Auf Wiedersehen," "The Magic Melody," "The Old Gray Mare," "Pack Up Your Troubles in Your Old Kit Bag," "Fascination," "Jelly Roll Blues," "Keep the Home Fires Burning," "Memories," "Song of the Islands."

DEATH John W. Alexander, muralist (*Evolution of the Book* in Library of Congress).

LITERATURE/JOURNALISM

Alfred A. Knopf establishes publishing company.

BOOKS *The Harbor* by Ernest Poole, *Spoon River Anthology* by Edgar Lee Masters, *The Bent Twig* by Dorothy Canfield Fisher, *Ruggles of Red Gap* by Harry L. Wilson, *Rivers to the Sea* (poetry) by Sara Teasdale, *Old Judge Priest* by Irvin S. Cobb, *The Song of the Lark* by Willa Cather.

ENTERTAINMENT

MOVIES Movies of the year include Charles Chaplin in *The Tramp,* and D. W. Griffith's *The Birth of a Nation.*

W. C. Fields begins six-year run in the Ziegfeld Follies.

PLAYS Ralph Morgan stars in *Fair and Warmer,* Alice Brady in *Sinners;* two musicals are produced: *Alone at Last* with music by Franz Lehar and *Princess Pat* with music by Victor Herbert.

Neighborhood Playhouse and Washington Square Players begin in New York City; Provincetown (Massachusetts) Players organized; moves to New York in 1916.

SPORTS

Jacob Ruppert and T. L. Huston buy New York Yankees for $460,000.

Babe Ruth, then a Boston Red Sox pitcher, hits his first home run.

Federal League ends legal battle with National and American leagues, folds as its players sign with other teams.

American Lawn Bowling Assn. is formed.

Pacific Coast Intercollegiate Athletic Conference is founded.

WINNERS *Auto racing*—Ralph DePalma, Indianapolis 500; *Baseball*—Boston Red Sox, World Series; *Boxing*—Jess Willard, heavyweight; Ted Lewis, welterweight; *Golf*—Jerome Travers, U.S. Open; *Horse racing*—Regret, first filly to win Kentucky Derby; Rhine Maiden, Preakness Stakes; The Finn, Belmont Stakes; *Tennis*—William Johnston, U.S. Open.

MISCELLANEOUS

Submarine F-4 sinks outside Honolulu Harbor with loss of 21 men.

Lewisohn Stadium in New York City is dedicated.

Kiwanis International is founded in Detroit.

Four major disasters occur: Excursion steamer *Eastland* capsizes in Chicago River, kills 812; floods in Galveston, Texas, cause 275 deaths; gasoline tank car explodes in Ardmore, Oklahoma, kills 47; mine accident at Layland, West Virginia, kills 46.

Dancer Irene Castle popularizes bobbed hair.

DEATH Fannie Farmer, cooking expert.

PRIMARY SOURCE DOCUMENT

"Do You Know?" by Carrie Chapman Catt

INTRODUCTION One of America's great political activists, Carrie Chapman Catt (1859–1947) was a driving force behind the passage of the Nineteenth Amendment, which extended suffrage to women in 1920, and a founder of the League of Women Voters. She was born in Ripon, Wisconsin, but her family moved to Iowa when she was seven. In 1880 she was the only woman to graduate from the Iowa Agricultural College and Model Farm (now called Iowa State University). Three years later she joined the ranks of a handful of American women who served as superintendents of the nation's schools. After a brief stint as San Francisco's first female newspaper reporter, she began her long and influential political career by joining the Iowa Woman Suffrage Association in 1887.

As Catt quickly rose through the ranks of this state-wide organization, she also began to work for the National American Woman Suffrage Association (NAWSA), attracting the attention of its president, Susan B. Anthony, whom she succeeded in 1900. Catt enlarged the scope of her suffrage activity in 1902, helping to organize the International Woman Suffrage Alliance (IWSA), which soon became active in thirty-two nations. Grief-stricken from the deaths of her husband, brother, mother, and mentor

Susan B. Anthony, over a two-year period, Catt nonetheless devoted considerable time and effort to the causes of the IWSA between 1907 and 1915. She then returned to the United States to help unify the struggling NAWSA, rebuilding the organization's infrastructure and energizing its membership with her Winning Plan to gain women's suffrage. Catt, a brilliant strategist, organizer, and communicator, placed enormous pressure on both federal and state legislators to support women's right to vote, slowly building enough interest to secure congressional support and the votes necessary for the ratification of a new constitutional amendment to that effect by the states.

The heroic efforts of Catt and others who had worked tirelessly for decades to secure a woman's right to vote paid off on August 26, 1920, when the U.S. Constitution was amended to guarantee women's suffrage. Determined to help women make effective use of their new found voting rights, Catt established the League of Women Voters, which remains an important organization dedicated to American democratic practices. The essay "Do You Know?" excerpted here, is an example of her effective use of publicity to highlight her cause, outlining the ways in which American society was backward, during a progressive age, in denying women a fundamental right of citizenship.

DO YOU KNOW that the question of votes for women is one which is commanding the attention of the whole civilized world; that woman suffrage organizations of representative men and women exist in twenty-seven different countries; that in this country alone there are more than 1,000 woman suffrage organizations; that there is an International and a National Men's League for Woman Suffrage and numbers of local men's leagues; that the number of women who are asking for the vote in this country is larger than the number of men who have ever asked for anything in its entire history; that more and larger petitions asking for votes for women have been sent to legislative bodies than for any other one measure; that the press of this country is giving more space to woman suffrage than to any other one public question; that the legislatures of twenty-eight states in year 1914 entertained woman suffrage measures; and that a bill for a woman suffrage amendment to the United States Constitution is now before Congress?

DO YOU KNOW that the women of New Zealand and the women of Australia possess all the political rights accorded to men?

DO YOU KNOW that in Norway all women have the full Parliamentary vote, and that in 1910 one woman sat in the Norwegian Parliament, and that numbers of women are serving as members and alternates to city councils?

DO YOU KNOW that in England, Ireland, Scotland and Wales women vote in all elections except for members of Parliament; that they are eligible and have been elected to office as mayors and members of city and county councils and that on the Isle of Man women who pay rent or taxes can vote for member of the Manx Parliament?

DO YOU KNOW that in eight of the provinces of Canada—Ontario, New Brunswick, Manitoba, Prince Edward Island, Quebec, British Columbia, Alberta and Saskatchewan—tax-paying widows and spinsters have the municipal vote, while in Nova Scotia married women whose husbands are not voters are included also?

DO YOU KNOW that women have the municipal vote in Rangoon, the capital of Burmah; in Belize, the capital of British Honduras; and in the cities of Baroda and Bombay in British India; and that in certain provinces of Austria, Hungary and Russia they have limited communal franchise rights?

DO YOU KNOW that in our own country women have been voting on the same terms as men in Wyoming since 1860, in Colorado since 1893, in Utah and Idaho since 1896; that in 1910, the state of Washington voted three to one to extend the full suffrage to women; that in 1911, California doubled the number of voting women in this country by giving the full suffrage to more than half a million women citizens; that in 1912, the men of Kansas, Oregon, and Arizona voted to give votes to their women; that in 1913, the legislature of the State of Illinois passed a measure giving to women all the voting rights within the power of the legislature to bestow, including presidential electors, all municipal officers and some county and some state officers; and that the territorial legislature of Alaska granted full suffrage to women, and that in 1914 Nevada and Montana gave full suffrage to women?

DO YOU KNOW that wherever women have got the vote they have used it in large numbers—larger, frequently, than the men of the same city, state or country;...that in the equal suffrage states of our own country from seventy to ninety per cent of the women vote, whereas in most states of the Union only sixty to sixty-five per cent of the qualified men voters actually cast their ballots....

DO YOU KNOW that, on the other hand, large numbers of men are utterly indifferent to their rights as voters; that in the presidential election of 1912, the total vote cast was only 14,720,1038, while the number of men eligible to vote was 24,335,000: that in the presidential election of 1909 the total vote cast was only 14,888,442, while the number of men eligible to vote was fully 22,000,000; that in the presidential election of 1904 the total vote was only 13,961,560 while the total number of men eligible to vote was 21,000,000?

DO YOU KNOW, moreover, that in every state and country where the franchise has been extended to women, the vote of the men has steadily risen?...

DO YOU KNOW that extending the franchise to women actually increases the proportion of intelligent voters; that there is now and has been for years, according to the report of the Commissioner of Education, one-third more girls in the high schools of the country than boys; and that, according to the last census, the illiterate men of the country greatly outnumbered the illiterate women?

DO YOU KNOW that extending the suffrage to women increases the moral vote; that in all states and countries that have adopted equal suffrage the vote of the disreputable women is practically negligible, the slum wards of cities invariably having the lightest woman vote and respectable residence wards the heaviest; that only one out of every twenty criminals are women; that women constitute a minority of drunkards and petty miscreants;

DO YOU KNOW that extending the suffrage to women increases the number of native-born voters; that for every one hundred foreign white women immigrants coming to this country there are 129 men, while among Asiatic immigrants the men outnumber the women two to one, according to the figures of the census of 1910?

DO YOU KNOW that there are in the United States about 8,000,000 women in gainful occupations outside the home who need the protection of the ballot to regulate the conditions under which they must labor; and that the efforts of working women to regulate these conditions without the ballot have been practically unavailing?

DO YOU KNOW that wherever women, the traditional housekeepers of the world, have been given a voice in the government, public housekeeping, has been materially improved by an increased attention to questions of pure food, pure water supply, sanitation, housing, public health and morals, child welfare and education?

DO YOU KNOW that the movement for woman suffrage is just a part of the eternal forward march of the human race toward a complete democracy; that in the American colonies only a very small proportion of the men could vote; that even after the Revolution only property-holders could vote; that it was only by slow and hard-fought stages that all men finally won the right to vote; and that in most foreign countries the franchise for men is still heavily loaded with restrictions?

DO YOU KNOW…that in all the places where women vote, the opponents, thus far, have not been able to find a dozen respectable men to assert, over their own names and addresses, that it has had any bad results; that more than five hundred organizations—state, national and international other than woman suffrage associations—aggregating approximately a membership of over 50,000,000, have officially endorsed woman suffrage?

DO YOU KNOW one single sound, logical reason why the intelligence and individuality of women should not entitle them to the rights and privileges of self-government?

DO YOU KNOW that the women in twelve states and in Alaska will vote for President in 1916?

SOURCE: From Frances M. Borkman and Annie G. Poritt, eds., *Woman Suffrage: History, Arguments, And Results* (New York: National Woman Suffrage Publishing, 1915), 151–160.

1916

INTERNATIONAL

World War I

President Woodrow Wilson tours nationally to urge preparedness (January 27); Congress votes to increase army to 175,000 men, then to 223,000 at end of five years (June 3); authorizes 450,000-man National Guard, establishes Officers Reserve Training Corps.

Fire and explosion in munitions plant at Black Tom Island, New Jersey, causes $22 million damage (July 30), is attributed to sabotage.

National Research Council organizes to promote wartime research (September 20); Council of National Defense is organized (October 11) with six cabinet members, headed by War Secretary Newton D. Baker, and an Advisory Commission.

Germany announces (February 10) that enemy-armed merchant ships will be treated as war vessels; U.S. steamer *Lanso* (October 28) and steamer *Columbian* (November 7) are sunk by German submarines; Germany announces its willingness to discuss peace (December 12); Allies turn it down because no peace terms are disclosed; President Wilson calls on both sides to disclose peace terms (December 18).

Other International Events

Pancho Villa leads 1,500 Mexicans in setting Columbus, New Mexico, on fire, killing 19 Americans (March 9); President Wilson orders U.S. troops into Mexico to capture Villa (March 10); 4,000 troops led by Gen. John J. Pershing conduct nine-month fruitless chase.

U.S. and Great Britain (for Canada) sign migratory bird treaty.

U.S. and Haiti sign treaty for U.S. control of the island (May 3).

U.S. buys Virgin Islands (Danish West Indies) from Denmark for $25 million (August 4); is ratified by Senate (September 7).

NATIONAL

President Wilson, Democrat, is reelected over Supreme Court Justice Charles Evans Hughes, Republican;

General John J. Pershing on a horse, crossing a river into Mexico in pursuit of Pancho Villa. **NATIONAL ARCHIVES AND RECORDS ADMINISTRATION**

receives 9,129,606 popular and 277 electoral votes to Hughes's 8,538,221 and 254.

Supreme Court upholds constitutionality of federal income tax; Louis D. Brandeis is confirmed as first Jewish Supreme Court justice.

U.S. Shipping Board is created to acquire vessels through an Emergency Fleet Corp. (September 7).

Bomb explodes during Preparedness Day parade in San Francisco, kills nine (July 22); two men later are found guilty.

National Park Service is established; Lassen (California) National Park is created.

Margaret Sanger and others open birth-control clinic at 46 Amboy Street, Brooklyn, New York.

Farm Loan Act gives farmers long-term credit facilities similar to those for industry and commerce; creates Federal Farm Loan Board and 12 district banks.

Statewide prohibition begins in Arkansas, Iowa, Virginia; is enacted in Utah.

Jeanette Rankin of Montana is first woman elected to House of Representatives.

Tariff Commission is established.

Calvin Coolidge becomes lieutenant governor of Massachusetts.

BUSINESS/INDUSTRY/INVENTIONS

Adamson Act passes, reduces railroad workers' day from 10 to 8 hours without reducing pay.

William G. Mennen founds toiletries company; A. C. Gilbert Co., toymaker, is established; Hall Brothers produces Hallmark greeting cards; Clarence Saunders opens Piggly Wiggly grocery chain, features self-service.

Nearly 2,100 strikes and lockouts occur in first six months of year.

DEATHS Hetty (Henrietta H.) Green, financier, reputedly richest woman of era; William Stanley, inventor of electrical transformer, generator; James J. Hill, financier and railroad president; Hiram S. Maxim, machine-gun inventor.

TRANSPORTATION

Nash Motor Co. and Fruehauf Trailer Co. are founded.

More than 1 million (1,525,578) automobiles are manufactured.

Boeing Airplane Co., Sinclair Oil & Refining Co., and Getty Oil Co. are founded.

Aviation and Aeronautical Engineering magazine begins publication, later becomes *Aviation* magazine.

Woodrow Wilson throwing out a pitch on opening day. Baseball's immense popularity will be severely tested three years later in the "Black Sox" World Series scandal. **THE LIBRARY OF CONGRESS**

SCIENCE/MEDICINE

Gilbert N. Lewis sets forth new theory on structure of atom.

Severe polio epidemic strikes country.

Lewis M. Terman, psychologist, coins term *IQ (intelligence quotient)* in widely used test for measuring intelligence.

EDUCATION

John Dewey's *Democracy and Education* is published.

RELIGION

Mordecai Kaplan founds Jewish Center in New York City.

DEATHS Charles Taze Russell, founder of Jehovah's Witnesses; Samuel D. Ferguson, first black Episcopal bishop.

ART/MUSIC

Saturday Evening Post accepts Norman Rockwell's first cover painting.

Baltimore Symphony Orchestra gives its first concert.

Cleveland (Ohio) Museum of Art opens.

Rudolf Friml's operetta *Katinka* is published.

Louis M. Eilshemius completes the painting *The Funeral;* Naum Gabo completes the sculpture *Head of a Woman.*

Player-piano music rolls are introduced.

SONGS (POPULAR): "Bugle Call Rag," "If You Were the Only Girl in the World," "Nola," "Poor Butterfly," "Roses of Picardy," "Beale Street Blues," "I Ain't Got Nobody," "Pretty Baby."

LITERATURE/JOURNALISM

McGraw-Hill Publishing Co. is founded.

Journal of Negro History begins publication.

BOOKS *A Heap o' Livin'* (poetry) by Edgar A. Guest, *When a Man's a Man* by Harold Bell Wright, *Mountain Interval* (poetry) by Robert Frost, *Sea Garden* (poetry) by Hilda Doolittle, *You Know Me, Al* by Ring Lardner, *Chicago Poems* by Carl Sandburg, *Seventeen* by Booth Tarkington, *Tish* by Mary Roberts Rinehart.

ENTERTAINMENT

Ernst F. W. Alexanderson invents modern radio-tuning device.

Theater Arts Magazine begins publication as a quarterly.

PLAYS The musical *Have a Heart* by Jerome Kern and P. G. Wodehouse is produced; Marjorie Rambeau stars in *Cheating Cheaters,* Walter Hampden in *Good Gracious, Annabelle,* William Collier in *Nothing But the Truth,* Elsie Janis in *The Century Girl.*

MOVIES Mary Pickford stars in *Daddy Long Legs,* William S. Hart in *The Aryan,* Enid Markey in *Civilization,* Lillian Gish in *Intolerance.*

SPORTS

Ed "Strangler" Lewis and Joe Stecher wrestle 5½ hours to a draw.

Professional Golfers Assn. (PGA) is organized.

Women's National Bowling Assn. (now Women's International Bowling Congress) is organized; AAU holds its first national women's swimming competition; Grand American Handicap awards prizes for first time to women trapshooters.

Weeghman Park (later Wrigley Field), home of baseball's Chicago Cubs, opens.

Dan Patch, all-time great harness race horse, dies.

WINNERS *Auto racing*—Dario Resta, Indianapolis 500; *Baseball*—Boston Red Sox, World Series; *Golf*—Chick Evans, U.S. Open; Jim Barnes, first PGA tournament; *Football*—Washington State, first annual Rose Bowl; Georgia Tech, in most one-sided game (220–0 over Cumberland, of Lebanon, Tennessee); *Horse racing*—George Smith, Kentucky Derby; Damrosch, Preakness Stakes; Friar Rock, Belmont Stakes; *Tennis*—Richard Johnson, U.S. Open.

MISCELLANEOUS

Fire in Paris, Texas, burns 1,400 buildings, does $11 million damage.

First Mother's Day is observed in Philadelphia and in Grafton, West Virginia.

Henrietta Szold founds Hadassah, American women's Zionist organization.

1917

INTERNATIONAL

World War I

President Woodrow Wilson issues a program for peace settlement, calls for an international organization to keep the peace (January 22); Germany notifies U.S. that unrestricted submarine warfare will be resumed February 1; President Wilson announces breaking relations with Germany (February 3); U.S. arms merchant vessels (March 12); the president calls a special session of Congress, asks for a war declaration against Germany; Congress approves (April 6).

U.S. steamer *Magnolia* fires first U.S. shots of war beating off a submarine attack; first U.S. destroyers arrive in Ireland (May 3); President Wilson sends one army division to France (May 18), arrives June 26; Gen. John J. Pershing, head of American Expeditionary Force, arrives (June 14).

First regular U.S. convoy of merchant ships sails for Europe (July 2). German subs that earlier sank the *Heraldton* killing 20 (March 21) and the *Aztec* step up their attacks: oil steamer *Montano* (July 31), sinks transport *Minnehaha* with loss of 48 (September 7), destroyer *Cassin* (October 15), sinks transport *Antilles* with 70 lost (October 17), and sinks destroyer *Jacob Jones* (December 6).

Rainbow Division arrives in France (November 30).

Congress declares war on Austria-Hungary.

Other National Events

U.S. takes possession of Virgin Islands (March 31), which were purchased from Denmark (see 1916); Puerto Rico becomes U.S. territory, its residents U.S. citizens (March 2).

NATIONAL

World War I

At home, war-related activities include: President Wilson calls up National Guard from Eastern states (March 25), extends the call nationwide (July 3); Selective Service Act is signed (May 18), calls for registration of 21–30-year-old men; is amended to include men 18 to 45 (August 31); more than 9 million register for the draft (June 5); executive order calls 678,000 men into service (July 13); drawing is held (July 20) to determine order of entry into service; National Guard is absorbed into army (August 5).

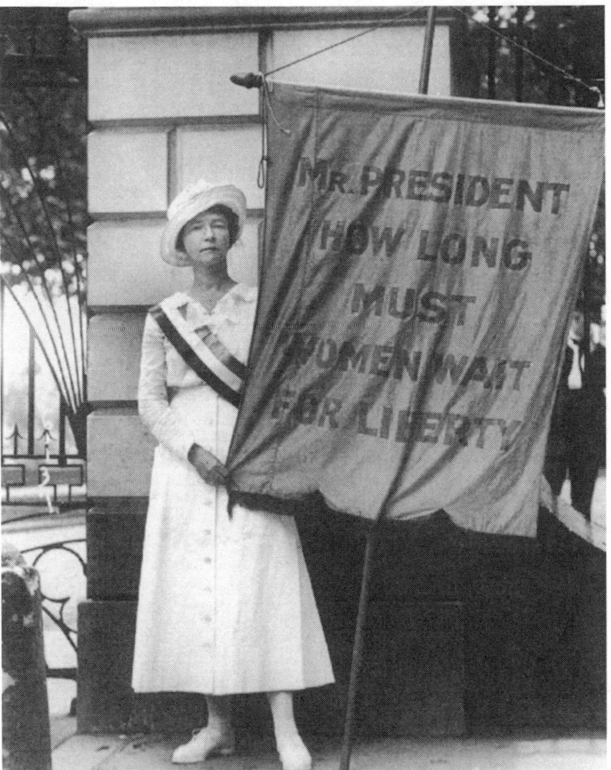

A woman pickets the White House for the right to vote.
UPI/CORBIS-BETTMANN

First government aviation training field opens at Rantoul, Illinois (July 4); Army Balloon School is established (April 6).

General Munitions Board is created (March 31) to coordinate procurement of war materials (becomes War Industries Board) (July 28); Committee on Public Information is created (April 14); President is given power (August 10) to regulate production and distribution of food and fuel, names Herbert Hoover food administrator, Harry Garfield, fuel administrator.

Law passes that forbids trading with enemy (October 6), creates Alien Property Custodian to handle U.S. property owned by enemy aliens; President issues proclamation (November 16) requiring registration of enemy aliens.

To help finance the war, first Liberty Loan drive begins (May 2); 4 million subscribe more than $2 billion in first drive; another drive in November results in $3.8 billion. War Revenue Act (October 3) sets up gradu-

A crowd sees off soldiers departing to fight in World War I. CORBIS-BETTMANN

ated income and excess profits taxes, increases excise taxes.

President Wilson issues proclamation placing all railroads under federal control (December 26); railroads return to private owners in 1920.

Two explosions, thought to be caused by sabotage, occur at Kingsland (New Jersey) car and foundry plant (January 11) and Eddystone (Pennsylvania) munitions plant, where 133 die (April 10).

Congress submits Eighteenth (Prohibition) Amendment to states for ratification (December 18).

Supreme Court in *Wilson* v. *New* upholds constitutionality of act that sets eight-hour day on interstate railways.

Congressional Union for Woman Suffrage pickets White House; a number of states enact women's suffrage statutes: North Dakota, Ohio, Indiana, Texas, Rhode Island, Michigan, Nebraska.

More than 100 blacks are killed or wounded in two-day riot in East St. Louis, Illinois (July 2).

Immigration Act is passed, which requires literacy tests; bill passes over president's veto. Similar bill was vetoed 20 years earlier.

Julius Rosenwald Foundation is created with $40 million endowment to be used for the "welfare of mankind."

First class postage increases a penny to 3 cents an ounce.

National Travelers Aid Society is formed.

American Friends Service Committee is created.

Mt. McKinley (now Denali) National Park is established in Alaska.

DEATH Stephen B. Luce, founder of Naval War College.

BUSINESS/INDUSTRY/INVENTIONS

Mary Lathrop is first woman lawyer admitted to American Bar Assn.

Otto Y. Schnering founds what is now Curtiss Candy Co.

DEATHS Irving W. Colburn, invented process for making continuous sheets of flat glass; James B. (Diamond Jim) Brady, financier; George H. Hartford, developer of Atlantic-Pacific food chain.

TRANSPORTATION

Robert Manley develops an automobile-wrecking crane.

Chance M. Vought founds company to design and build military aircraft.

Hell Gate Bridge in New York City opens.

Phillips Petroleum and Humble Oil companies are founded.

Registered cars in U.S. reach 4.8 million.

SCIENCE/MEDICINE

Harlow Shapley measures distances in the Milky Way.

Hundred-inch telescope at Mt. Wilson (California) Observatory is completed.

DEATH Andrew T. Still, founder of osteopathy.

EDUCATION

Alaska territorial legislature appropriates $60,000 to start University of Alaska at Fairbanks.

ART/MUSIC

Violinist Jascha Heifetz makes American debut at Carnegie Hall.

Society for Independent Artists is organized.

Sigmund Romberg's operetta *Maytime* opens; Reginald De Koven composes the opera *The Canterbury Pilgrims.*

University of Kansas Museum of Art opens.

PAINTINGS Charles Burchfield, *Church Bells Ringing* and *Rainy Winter Nights;* George Grosz, *Memories of New York;* Marsden Hartley, *Movement No. 10.*

SONGS (POPULAR): "The Bells of St. Mary's," "Darktown Strutters Ball," "For Me and My Gal," "Back Home Again in Indiana," "McNamara's Band," "Over There," "Oh, Johnny, Oh, Johnny, Oh!"

DEATHS Scott Joplin, composer; Albert P. Ryder, painter.

LITERATURE/JOURNALISM

Boni & Liveright, publishers, is founded.

Columbia University confers first Pulitzer Prize awards: Herbert B. Swope for reporting, *New York Tribune* for editorial writing, J. J. Jusserand for U.S. history, Laura E. Richards and Maude H. Elliot for biography.

Arthur Brisbane writes editorial column "Today," which is syndicated to more than 1,000 daily and weekly newspapers.

BOOKS *His Family* by Ernest Poole, *Three Black Pennies* by Joseph Hergesheimer, *Love Songs* (poetry) by Sara Teasdale, *A Son of the Middle Border* by Hamlin Garland, *The Amazing Interlude* by Mary Roberts Rinehart, *King Coal* by Upton Sinclair, *Just Folks* (poetry) by Edgar A. Guest, *Renascence and Other Poems* by Edna St. Vincent Millay.

DEATHS Robert T. S. Lowell, poet and translator; Edward Cary, editor, the *New York Times* (1871–1917); Harrison G. Otis, publisher, *Los Angeles Times* (1886–1917).

ENTERTAINMENT

PLAYS Fred and Adele Astaire make Broadway debut in *Over the Top;* Ina Claire stars in *Polly with a Past,* Lenore Ulric in *Tiger Rose,* Majorie Rambeau in *Eyes of Youth,* Leo Carrillo in *Lombardi Ltd.,* Nat Wills in *Cheer Up,* Frank Craven in *Going Up,* Lionel Barrymore in *Peter Ibbetson,* Helen Hayes in *Pollyanna.*

MOVIES Charles Chaplin stars in both *The Adventurer* and *The Immigrant.*

DEATHS Vernon Castle, dancer, in plane crash; Buffalo Bill (William Cody), hunter and showman.

SPORTS

Jim Vaughn of Chicago Cubs and Fred Toney of Cincinnati Reds pitch nine-inning no-hit games against each other; Cincinnati wins 1–0 in tenth on a hit and two errors (May 2); Toney also pitches both games in a doubleheader (July 20), allowing only three hits in each game.

National Hockey League (NHL) is organized (November 22); first game is played in Toronto (December 19).

First baseball game in New York City's Polo Grounds results in arrest of Managers John McGraw and Christy Mathewson for playing on Sunday (August 19).

WINNERS *Baseball*—Chicago White Sox, World Series; *Boxing*—Benny Leonard, lightweight; Pete Herman, bantamweight; *Football*—Oregon, Rose Bowl; *Horse racing*—Omar Khayyam, Kentucky Derby; Kalitan, Preakness Stakes; Hourless, Belmont Stakes; *Tennis*—Richard Murray, U.S. Open.

MISCELLANEOUS

Lions Clubs form Lions International.

Father Edward J. Flanagan founds Boys Town, near Omaha, as Home for Boys.

American Girl magazine, official Girl Scout publication, is founded.

Three mine disasters occur: Hastings, Colorado, 121 die; Butte, Montana, 163; and Clay, Kentucky, 62.

Fire destroys about 2,000 buildings in Atlanta.

1918

INTERNATIONAL

World War I

President Woodrow Wilson outlines his 14 points for a peace program, including creation of an international peace-keeping organization (January 8).

Street cleaners wearing white uniforms and masks for protection against the influenza virus. CORBIS-BETTMANN

U.S. Army air squadron sees its first action in France when it is attacked while on reconnaissance flight (April 12); U.S. planes make first air raid, bomb railroad station near Metz (June 11); Capt. Eddie Rickenbacker is credited with shooting down 22 enemy planes and four balloons between April and October.

U.S. troops capture Cantigny (May 28), take Vaux, Bouresches, and Belleau Wood, play large role in Battle of the Marne. First U.S. troops land in Italy (May 30). U.S. and French troops turn back German attack on Champagne (July 15); second Battle of Marne begins (July 18); German offensive ends (August 6).

First independent U.S. army is formed, fights with Allies in Oise-Aisne and Ypres-Lys offensives; plays major role in St. Mihiel fighting in the Meuse-Argonne offensive.

Germans, followed the next day by Austria, ask President Wilson for an armistice (October 6).

Allies are reluctant to accept Wilson's 14-point formula and armistice; Kaiser Wilhelm abdicates (November 9) and German Republic is formed; armistice is signed at 5 A.M., November 11; firing stops at 11 A.M.

Activity at sea is minimal, though submarine sinks British ship *Tuscania* carrying 2,000 U.S. troops off Irish coast; 210 men are lost.

First issue of *Stars and Stripes*, official Army weekly, is published.

First American troops return from Europe (December 1).

NATIONAL

World War I

War-related activities at home include third Liberty Loan drive in May, which raises $4.2 billion, another in October for $6 billion; War Finance Corp. is created (April 5) to finance war industries.

Government takes over operation of nation's railroads (January 1), telephone and telegraph systems (August 1).

Supreme Court in *Arver* v. *United States* upholds constitutionality of Selective Service Act; executive order exempts conscientious objectors from military service.

Americans are asked to observe "wheatless" Mondays and Wednesdays, "meatless" Tuesdays, "porkless" Thursdays and Saturdays, and are urged to eat Victory bread (January 10); sugar rationing goes into effect (July 1); Herbert Hoover is named to represent U.S. on European food-relief organization.

Bernard M. Baruch heads War Industries Board; War Labor Board is created with Frank P. Walsh and former President Taft cochairmen; U.S. shipyards launch 98 vessels in one day (July 4).

Troops contending with poisonous gas wear masks while advancing across the field in France on May 20, 1918. CORBIS-BETTMANN

Sedition Act enlarges 1917 Espionage Act to include acts of antiwar and pacifist proponents.

Government orders baseball to end its season September 1; allows playing of World Series.

Chemical Warfare Service is created in the Army.

Other National Events

Daylight saving time begins March 30; is repealed in August 1919.

U.S. Employment Service is created in Labor Department.

First experimental airmail route is flown from Washington, D.C., to New York via Philadelphia (May 15); regular service is established August 12; first airmail stamp (24 cents) is issued.

Mississippi becomes first state to ratify Eighteenth Amendment (January 8); several states enact statewide prohibition: Indiana, Texas, Colorado, Nevada, Montana.

Annette A. Adams becomes first woman U.S. district attorney (North California District).

Laura Spelman Rockefeller Memorial Foundation is endowed.

Calvin Coolidge is elected governor of Massachusetts.

DEATHS Former First Lady Lucretia P. Garfield (1881); former Vice President Charles W. Fairbanks (1905–1909); Margaret Olivia Sage, founder of foundation to improve U.S. social and living conditions; Luther H. Gulick, cofounder of Camp Fire Girls.

BUSINESS/INDUSTRY/INVENTIONS

Construction of Muscle Shoals Dam on Tennessee River is ordered.

American Express Co. absorbs Adams Express Co. and several others.

Elmer A. Sperry invents arc searchlight; Henry E. Warren invents electric clock that only has to be plugged into an electric circuit, needs no timekeeping elements.

Brinks, Inc., in Chicago puts first armored car into use.

TRANSPORTATION

Glenn L. Martin Co. builds first successful twin-engine plane; William W. Stout builds U.S.'s first commercial monoplane.

Charles R. Wittemann builds first automatic pilot system.

SCIENCE/MEDICINE

Army School of Nursing is authorized.

President Wilson signs order that perpetuates wartime National Research Council.

Influenza epidemic spreads from Europe to U.S.; sweeps through nation, kills about 500,000 by 1919.

Edwin H. Armstrong invents superheterodyne circuit, basis for most modern radio, television, and radar reception.

EDUCATION

Smith-Hughes Act provides federal grants to be matched by states for agricultural and vocational instruction.

RELIGION

Merging three branches of denomination forms United Lutheran Church; Native American church, composed of many members, incorporates in Oklahoma.

Heber J. Grant becomes president of Mormon church.

Catholic Bishop Dennis J. Dougherty becomes archbishop of Philadelphia.

Aimee Semple McPherson, evangelist, founds International Church of the Four-Square Gospel in Los Angeles.

DEATHS Washington Gladden, Congregational minister considered founder of American Social Gospel movement; Walter Rauschenbusch, Baptist theologian who founded Brotherhood of the Kingdom; John Ireland, Catholic archbishop of St. Paul (1888–1918).

ART/MUSIC

Cleveland Symphony Orchestra is formed; Summer concerts begin in Lewisohn Stadium, New York.

George Gershwin writes "Swanee," Irving Berlin writes show *Yip, Yip, Yaphank,* which includes song "Oh, How I Hate to Get Up in the Morning."

Phillips Collection (art) opens in Washington.

SONGS (POPULAR): "I'm Always Chasing Rainbows," "A Good Man Is Hard to Find," "Somebody Stole My Gal," "After You've Gone," "Hinky Dinky Parley Voo," "K-K-K-Katy," "Till We Meet Again."

LITERATURE/JOURNALISM

Little Review serializes James Joyce's *Ulysses;* issues are seized by postal authorities during three-year serialization; court upholds obscenity charges.

Robert L. Ripley, cartoonist, develops "Believe It or Not" syndicated feature.

BOOKS *Dere Mabel* by Edward Streeter, *The U.P. Trail* by Zane Grey, *My Antonía* by Willa Cather, *The Magnificent Ambersons* by Booth Tarkington, *Corn Huskers* (poetry) by Carl Sandburg.

DEATHS Henry Adams, author; James Gordon Bennett, editor *New York Herald;* Joyce Kilmer, poet ("Trees").

ENTERTAINMENT

Louis B. Mayer founds motion picture company.

PLAYS Helen Hayes stars in *Penrod,* Lionel Barrymore in *The Copperhead,* Helen Menken in *Three Wise Fools,* Richard Bennett in *The Unknown Purple,* Conrad Nagel in *Forever After,* DeWolf Hopper in *Everything,* Al Jolson in *Sinbad,* Ed Wynn and Mae West in *Sometime.*

MOVIE Charles Chaplin stars in *A Dog's Life.*

SPORTS

John A. Heydler becomes president of American (baseball) League.

Casey Stengel's return to Brooklyn's Ebbets Field is memorable: he steps to the plate and takes off his cap, and a bird flies out.

WINNERS *Baseball*—Boston Red Sox, World Series; *Horse racing*—Exterminator, Kentucky Derby; War Cloud and Jack Hare Jr. (dead heat), Preakness Stakes; Johnson, Belmont Stakes; *Horseshoe pitching*—Fred Burst, first world championship; *Tennis*—Richard Murray, U.S. Open.

DEATH John L. Sullivan, world heavyweight boxing champion (1882–1892).

MISCELLANEOUS

Numerous disasters occur: forest fire in Cloquet, Minnesota, area (October 12) kills 400; 600 others perish in fires in adjoining Minnesota, Wisconsin areas; excursion steamer *Columbia* sinks in Illinois River with loss of 200 lives; earthquake destroys San Jacinto and Hemet, California; explosions destroy chemical plant in Oakdale, Pennsylvania (193 die), and a shell-loading plant in Morgan, New Jersey (90 die); three railroad accidents take 266 lives (Nashville, Tennessee, Brooklyn, New York, and Ivanhoe, Indiana).

1919

INTERNATIONAL

Peace negotiations begin in Versailles, France (January 18); Allies agree to include League of Nations creation in peace settlement (January 25); President

The national park that contains the Grand Canyon is established in 1919. **NATIONAL PARK SERVICE**

Woodrow Wilson returns to U.S. to find Republican-controlled Congress opposed to League until after peace; President goes back to France with proposed changes.

Germany signs peace treaty (June 28); it calls for Germany to admit guilt, give up Alsace-Lorraine, Saar basin, Posen, parts of Schleswig and Silesia; reparations are sought (set at $56 billion later); League of Nations covenant is attached.

Herbert Hoover is named head of international relief efforts.

International Labor Organization (ILO) holds first meeting (October 29).

NATIONAL

President Wilson presents peace treaty to Senate (July 10); committee adds 45 amendments, four reservations; President tries to get public support, makes 9,500-mile western tour with 37 speeches in 29 cities.

President collapses in Pueblo, Colorado (September 25), is rushed back to Washington, suffers stroke (October 2), virtually incapacitating him for remainder of his term.

Nebraska becomes 36th state to ratify Eighteenth Amendment (January 16); to become effective January 16, 1920.

Congress passes joint resolution approving the Nineteenth Amendment, granting women's suffrage (June 5); is sent to states for ratification; League of Women Voters is organized.

President Wilson is awarded Nobel Peace Prize for founding the League of Nations.

Supreme Court in *Schenck* v. *United States* upholds 1917 Espionage Act, finds that free speech can be restrained in wartime; also upholds 1918 Sedition Act.

Telephone and telegraph lines return to private owners after year of government operation.

National debt increases because of World War I to $25.2 billion; Victory Loan bond sale raises $4.5 billion.

Boston police strike; riots and disorders follow; Gov. Calvin Coolidge orders state militia to restore order; strike ends.

Grand Canyon (Arizona) and Zion (Utah) national parks are established.

First daily airmail service begins between New York City and Chicago (July 1); price of first-class postage stamp is reduced to 2 cents from 3.

Communist Party of America and Communist Labor Party organize; U.S. transport *Buford* with 249 deported "agitators" sails for Russia.

Women rivet heaters and passers on ship construction work in the Navy Yard at Puget Sound, Seattle, Washington. **HULTON ARCHIVE/GETTY IMAGES**

DEATH Former President Theodore Roosevelt (1901–1909).

BUSINESS/INDUSTRY/INVENTIONS

Reynolds Aluminum Co. is founded as U.S. Foil Co.

Owen D. Young organizes Radio Corporation of America (RCA), with David Sarnoff as president.

First American general strike occurs in Seattle to protest elimination of western cost-of-living differential by U.S. Shipping Board; lasts six days.

Bruce Barton and two partners found advertising agency, which later becomes a giant in the industry (Batton, Barton, Durstine & Osborne).

First U.S.-built fighter plane, the Thomas-Morse MB-1 Scout, is unveiled; Glenn L. Martin develops a bomber.

DEATHS Josiah C. Cady, architect (Original Metropolitan Opera); William C. W. Sabine, founder of architectural acoustics.

TRANSPORTATION

Oregon becomes first state to pass gasoline tax (1 cent per gallon); two other states (Colorado, New Mexico) follow.

Henry Ford turns over presidency of Ford Motor Co. to his son, Edsel.

First municipally owned airport opens in Tucson, Arizona.

SCIENCE/MEDICINE

American Association for the Hard of Hearing is founded.

DEATHS Jane Delano, organizer of World War I Red Cross nursing service; Dr. Abraham Jacobi, founder of American pediatrics; Edward C. Pickering, director, Harvard Observatory (1876–1919).

EDUCATION

New School of Social Research is founded in New York City.

Roger Babson founds Babson Park near Boston and Babson Institute, a two-year business school.

James H. Breasted founds Oriental Institute at University of Chicago with grant from John D. Rockefeller Jr.

RELIGION

Two U.S. Catholic bishops are elevated to archbishop: Patrick J. Hayes of New York and Albert A. Daeger of Santa Fe, New Mexico.

Soldiers of the 369th Infantry returning home from Europe after World War I. The soldiers of the African-American regiment are heroes in France and nicknamed the "Harlem Hellfighters." The soldiers wear the Croix de Guerre (Cross of War), awarded for bravery in battle. **HULTON/ARCHIVE**

Archbishop Edward J. Hannon becomes first chair of National Catholic Welfare Council.

ART/MUSIC

Fritz Kreisler's operetta *Apple Blossoms* is produced.

Eastman School of Music is founded in Rochester, New York.

Paul Whiteman organizes his band.

Stuart Davis completes the painting *Yellow Hills;* George B. Luks, *Otis Skinner as Colonel Bridan;* Joseph Stella, *Orange Bars;* Rockwell Kent, *North Wind;* Georgia O'Keeffe, *Lake George, Coat and Red.*

SONGS (POPULAR): "Alice Blue Gown," "Baby, Won't You Please Come Home," "Dardanella," "I'm Forever Blowing Bubbles," "Irene," "A Pretty Girl Is Like a Melody," "The World Is Waiting for the Sunrise," "How Ya Gonna Keep Them Down on the Farm."

DEATHS Augustus D. Juilliard, benefactor of music school; Oscar Hammerstein I, founder of what later became Metropolitan Opera.

LITERATURE/JOURNALISM

Illustrated Daily News begins publication in New York City.

True Story magazine is founded.

BOOKS *Jurgen* by James Branch Cabell, *Java Head* by Joseph Hergesheimer, *Winesburg, Ohio* by Sherwood Anderson, *Prejudices* (first of six volumes) and *The American Language* by H. L. Mencken, *Ten Days That Shook the World* by John Reed, *Lad, A Dog* by Albert Payson Terhune, *Humoresque* by Fannie Hurst, *Banners* (poetry) by Babette Deutsch.

Harcourt, Brace, publishers, is founded.

Arthur ("Bugs") Baer syndicates his column in *New York American.*

Emanuel Haldeman-Julius publishes Little Blue Books, which sell for 10 cents.

Frank King syndicates his comic strip "Gasoline Alley" (Uncle Walt and Skeezix); Elzie C. Segar draws "Thimble Theater," a cartoon featuring Olive Oyl and (later) Popeye.

DEATHS Ella Wheeler Wilcox, popular syndicated poet; Henry M. Alden, editor, *Harper's Magazine* (1863–1919); L. Frank Baum, author *(The Wonderful Wizard of Oz).*

ENTERTAINMENT

United Artists motion picture company is founded.

John Murray Anderson stages first *Greenwich Village Follies.*

PLAYS Alfred Lunt stars in *Clarence,* Ethel Barrymore in *Déclassée,* Ina Claire in *The Gold Diggers,* Edith Day in *Irene,* Peggy Wood in *Buddies;* Theatre Guild stages its first production, Jacinto Benavente's *The Bonds of Interest.*

MOVIE Lillian Gish stars in *Broken Blossoms.*

SPORTS

Branch W. Rickey, president of St. Louis Cardinals baseball team, inaugurates farm system for developing players.

Baseball outlaws the spitball and shineball and the use of foreign substances on a ball.

National League of Horseshoe and Quoit Pitchers is formed.

WINNERS *Auto racing*—Howdy Wilcox, Indianapolis 500; *Baseball*—Cincinnati Reds, World Series; *Boxing*—Jack Dempsey, heavyweight; Jack Britton, welterweight; *Golf*—Walter Hagen, U.S. Open; *Horse racing*—Sir Barton becomes first Triple Crown winner, takes Kentucky Derby, Preakness Stakes, and Belmont Stakes; *Tennis*—William Johnston, U.S. Open.

MISCELLANEOUS

Lena M. Phillips founds National Federation of Business & Professional Women's Clubs.

American Legion is organized in Paris, is incorporated by Congress.

Order of DeMolay, related to Masonic Order, is founded for young men.

Women's International League for Peace & Freedom is organized.

Dirigible crashes into downtown Chicago building; 12 die.

1920

INTERNATIONAL

Supreme Court in *Missouri* v. *Holland* upholds constitutionality of 1918 Migratory Bird Treaty.

NATIONAL

Warren G. Harding, Republican, is elected president over Democrat James M. Cox with a popular vote of 16,152,200 and 404 electoral votes to Cox's 9,147,353 popular and 127 electoral votes; election returns are broadcast on radio (Station KDKA, Pittsburgh) for the first time.

Nineteenth Amendment gives women the right to vote (August 26); Eighteenth Amendment (Prohibition) goes into effect (January 16).

Senate fails to get required two-thirds (49–35) to ratify League of Nations Covenant and Versailles Peace Treaty (March 19).

Fourteenth census reports national population of 106,021,537.

End of World War I brings increase in immigration to U.S. (430,001).

Post Office approves use of postage meters; transcontinental airmail service is established between New York City and San Francisco.

Helen H. Gardener is sworn in as first woman member of Civil Service Commission; Women's Bureau is created in Labor Department.

American Civil Liberties Union is founded; Rev. Harry F. Ward is president.

Nation's railroads return to private ownership after two years of government operation.

Junior Chamber of Commerce holds first national convention.

First pension for Civil War service is granted.

National debt is reported at $24.2 billion; Gross National Product is $71.6 billion.

DEATH Former Vice President Levi Morton (1889–1893).

BUSINESS/INDUSTRY/INVENTIONS

Federal Power Commission is established (June 10); Railroad Labor Board is created (February 28).

Strike for union recognition at Gary (Indiana) U.S. Steel plant fails.

John L. Lewis begins 40-year presidency of United Mine Workers Union.

Navy Department constructs helium plant at Ft. Worth, Texas.

American Farm Bureau Federation is established.

National Bureau of Economic Research is founded.

Sosthenes Behn founds International Telephone & Telegraph Co. (ITT).

DEATHS John W. Hyatt, discovered fundamental principles for making celluloid; Theodore N. Vail, first president, ATT (1885–1897, 1907–1919).

Federal agents pour whiskey down the sewer during the days of Prohibition. The Eighteenth Amendment makes it illegal to manufacture, sell, and transport alcohol. But as this photo indicates, drinking alcohol remains a popular pastime. CORBIS-BETTMANN

TRANSPORTATION

Douglas Aircraft Co. is founded.

Americans buy 10 million automobiles in the decade.

SCIENCE/MEDICINE

Langley Research Center at Hampton, Virginia, opens as the Langley Memorial Aeronautical Laboratory.

Karl A. Menninger founds Menninger Clinic for psychiatric research and therapy.

Andrew E. Douglass develops dendrochronology, dating wood from tree rings.

Edward W. Scripps founds Science Service, a newspaper feature syndicate.

DEATH William C. Gorgas, Surgeon General who led effort to eliminate yellow fever in Cuba, Panama.

EDUCATION

Scholastic Magazine is founded.

RELIGION

Arthur W. Moulton becomes Episcopal bishop of Utah.

DEATH John H. Vincent, Methodist bishop and cofounder, Chautauqua Movement.

ART/MUSIC

Guy Lombardo organizes nine-man band; Joseph ("King") Oliver forms jazz band.

Chicago Opera Assn. presents Reginald De Koven's opera *Rip Van Winkle;* Henry K. Hadley composes opera *Cleopatra's Night.*

Sculptor Lorado Taft completes *Fountain of Time* in Chicago; Alexander Archipenko, the statue *Standing Figure.*

Charles Burchfield completes the painting *February Thaw;* George Grosz, *Cafe Neptune;* Rockwell Kent, *Wilderness;* Lyonel Feininger, *Viaduct.*

Freer Art Gallery in Washington, D.C., opens.

SONGS (POPULAR): "Avalon," "Margie," "Whispering," "Hold Me," "I Never Knew I Could Love Anybody," "When My Baby Smiles at Me."

LITERATURE/JOURNALISM

Station WWJ, Detroit, makes first radio news broadcasts (August 31).

BOOKS *The Americanization of Edward Bok* by Edward Bok, *Main Street* by Sinclair Lewis, *The Age of Innocence* by Edith Wharton, *This Side of Paradise* by F. Scott Fitzgerald, *The Domesday Book* (poetry) by

F. Scott Fitzgerald, his wife, Zelda, and daughter, Scottie (b. 1921) heading for Europe. Fitzgerald publishes his first novel, *This Side of Paradise*, in 1920. **AP/WIDE WORLD PHOTOS**

Edgar Lee Masters, *Smoke and Steel* (poetry) by Carl Sandburg, *Flame and Shadow* (poetry) by Sara Teasdale, *The Story of Dr. Dolittle* by Hugh Lofting, *Poor White* by Sherwood Anderson.

DEATH John Reed, radical journalist, only American buried in the Kremlin in Moscow.

ENTERTAINMENT

Public radio begins to broadcast at Station KDKA, Pittsburgh, Pennsylvania (November 2).

MOVIES Douglas Fairbanks marries movie star Mary Pickford, makes movie *The Mark of Zorro;* Lillian Gish stars in *Way Down East.*

PLAYS Milton Berle makes stage debut in *Floradora;* Ed Wynn presents his *Carnival;* Marilyn Miller stars in musical *Sally,* Fred Stone in *Tip Top,* Eva Le Gallienne in *Not So Long Ago,* Richard Bennett in Eugene O'Neill's *Beyond the Horizon,* Arnold Daly in *The Tavern.*

SPORTS

Chicago grand jury indicts eight Chicago White Sox players accused of "throwing" the 1919 World Series; the "Black Sox" scandal results in election of Judge Kenesaw M. Landis as the first baseball commissioner (November 2).

American Professional Football Assn., forerunner of National Football League, forms (September 17) with 11 clubs; Jim Thorpe is elected president.

Ray Chapman of Cleveland Indians dies (August 17) from being struck in the head by a pitch from Carl Mays of New York Yankees the previous day.

Radio broadcasts of sports begin: first college football game (November 25) (Texas vs. Texas A&M); first prizefight (September 6) (Jack Dempsey vs. Billy Miske).

Olympic Games are held in Antwerp; U.S. wins 39 gold medals; Olympic flag with five interlocking rings flies for first time.

John B. Kelly of Philadelphia's Vespers Boat Club is barred from the Henley Regatta in England; Kelly and club are barred because of alleged amateur violations.

Walter Johnson of Washington Senators pitches 300th winning game.

First dog racetrack is built in Emeryville, California.

WINNERS *Auto racing*—Gaston Chevrolet, Indianapolis 500; *Baseball*—Cleveland Indians, World Series; *Boxing*—Jack Dempsey, heavyweight; Georges Carpentier, light heavyweight; Joe Lynch, bantamweight; *Football*—Harvard, Rose Bowl; *Golf*—Edward Ray, U.S. Open; *Handball*—William Ranft, first AAU senior title; *Horse racing*—Paul Jones, Kentucky Derby; Man o' War, Preakness Stakes and Belmont Stakes; *Tennis*—U.S. Davis Cup; Bill Tilden, U.S. Open; *Yachting*—U.S. boat *Resolute* retains America's Cup.

MISCELLANEOUS

Anarchists Nicola Sacco and Bartolomeo Vanzetti are arrested for alleged murder of two men in a payroll holdup at a shoe factory in South Braintree, Massachusetts.

Floods of Arkansas River nearly destroy Pueblo, Colorado.

Bomb explodes on Wall Street, New York City; kills 35, injures 100.

1921

INTERNATIONAL

Congress, by joint resolution, terminates war with Germany and Austria-Hungary (July 21); ratifies separate treaties with them (October 18).

Treaty with Colombia is ratified; Colombia receives $25 million for loss of Panama and is provided free access to canal.

Conference on Limitation of Armaments is held in Washington, D.C.; nine nations are represented.

NATIONAL

Johnson Act is passed by Congress, limiting the number of aliens admitted annually to 3% of the number of that foreign-born nationality already in the U.S.; total is about 358,000 (May 10).

Monument to the Unknown Soldier in Arlington (Virginia) National Cemetery is unveiled on first observance of Armistice Day (November 11).

U.S. Budget Bureau is created (June 10) with Charles G. Dawes as first director; Comptroller General's office is established (June 21); U.S. Veterans Bureau is founded (August 9).

Andrew Mellon begins 11 years as Secretary of the Treasury; Herbert Hoover becomes Secretary of Commerce.

Former President Taft is named Chief Justice of the Supreme Court.

Nevada is first state to authorize capital punishment by lethal gas.

West Virginia levies first state sales tax (July 1); Iowa enacts first state tax on cigarettes (April 11).

Rep. Alice Robertson of Oklahoma presides over House for 30 minutes, first woman to do so (June 20).

Infantile paralysis strikes Franklin D. Roosevelt.

Hot Springs (Arkansas) National Park is established.

Emergency tariff act raises rates on agricultural products.

National unemployment rate is 5.7%.

DEATH Philander C. Knox, Secretary of State (1909–1913) who started "dollar diplomacy."

BUSINESS/INDUSTRY/INVENTIONS

Congress passes the Packers and Stockyards Act and Grain Futures Act to prevent unfair and discriminatory practices or price manipulation.

Crosley Radio Corp. and Seiberling Rubber Co. are founded.

John A. Larson invents polygraph (lie detector).

John Robert Powers agency (modeling) opens.

DEATHS Francis B. Parker, instrumental in setting U.S. electrical standards; William Robinson, inventor of automatic electric signaling system; Samuel S. Laws, inventor of stock ticker.

TRANSPORTATION

Port Authority of New York and New Jersey is established.

SCIENCE/MEDICINE

Dr. George W. Crile and others found Cleveland Clinic Hospital.

Ernest O. Lawrence, University of California physicist, founds what will become the Lawrence Radiation Laboratory.

Harlow Shapley begins 31 years as director of the Harvard Observatory.

University of Rochester (New York) School of Medicine and Dentistry is founded.

EDUCATION

John J. Tigert IV becomes U.S. Education Commissioner.

Lafayette College in Easton, Pennsylvania, establishes civil rights chair; Graduate School of Geography opens at Clark University, Worcester, Massachusetts.

RELIGION

First religious service broadcast on radio is that of Calvary Episcopal Church in Pittsburgh, Pennsylvania (January 2).

International Missionary Council forms with John R. Mott chairman.

First general synod of African Orthodox Church meets in New York City with George McGuire as first bishop.

Dennis J. Dougherty, Catholic archbishop of Philadelphia, is elevated to cardinal.

William T. Manning becomes Episcopal bishop of New York.

DEATH Antoinette L. B. Blackwell, first woman ordained as a minister (Congregational).

ART/MUSIC

Sigmund Romberg's operetta *Blossom Time* is produced.

Stuart Davis completes the paintings *Lucky Strike* and *Cigarette Papers;* Samuel Halpert, *Her First Book of Lessons.*

SONGS (POPULAR): "Ain't We Got Fun," "April Showers," "Look for the Silver Lining," "My Man," "Sally," "Second-Hand Rose," "Wabash Blues," "Ma, He's

Nicola Sacco and Bartolomeo Vanzetti, Italian immigrants and anarchists, are found guilty of killing two men during a robbery. The trial focuses on their political beliefs, and despite a lack of concrete evidence, they are convicted and executed. **ARCHIVE PHOTOS, INC.**

Making Eyes at Me," "There'll Be Some Changes Made," "Kitten on the Keys."

DEATH Enrico Caruso, opera tenor.

LITERATURE/JOURNALISM

Barron's Weekly begins publication; Newhouse newspaper chain is founded.

Little Review, arts magazine that serialized James Joyce's *Ulysses* and was found guilty of obscenity, moves from New York to Paris.

Heywood Broun writes column "It Seems to Me" in *New York World.*

United Press becomes a major news service.

BOOKS *A Daughter of the Middle Border* by Hamlin Garland, *The Brimming Cup* by Dorothy Canfield Fisher, *Alice Adams* by Booth Tarkington, *Erik Dorn* by Ben Hecht, *Three Soldiers* by John Dos Passos, *Scaramouche* by Rafael Sabatini, first edition of Emily Post's *Etiquette, Poems* by Marianne Moore.

ENTERTAINMENT

PLAYS Eva Le Gallienne stars in *Liliom,* Ed Wynn in *The Perfect Fool,* Otis Skinner in *Blood and Sand,* Lynn Fontanne in *Dulcy,* Pauline Lord in *Anna Christie,* Al Jolson in *Bombo;* Katharine Cornell debuts in *Nice People.*

MOVIES John Barrymore stars in *Dr. Jekyll and Mr. Hyde,* Lillian Gish in *Orphans of the Storm,* Charles Chaplin in *The Kid,* Douglas Fairbanks in *The Three Musketeers,* Rudolph Valentino in *The Sheik.*

SPORTS

Eight Chicago White Sox baseball players who were accused of "throwing" the 1919 World Series are acquitted on a technicality (August 3); Baseball Commissioner Kenesaw M. Landis bars the players from baseball for life.

Radio broadcasts of baseball games air (August 25); first radio coverage of World Series begins with play-by-play bulletins.

Joe E. Carr is named president of the National Football League.

American Soccer League forms; National Horseshoe Pitching Assn. incorporates.

Babe Ruth becomes all-time home run leader when he hits 120th; Ty Cobb of Detroit Tigers gets his 3,000th hit.

Edwin Gourdin becomes first to surpass 25 feet (25 ft., 3 in.) in the long jump.

Southern Intercollegiate Conference is formed; becomes Southeastern Conference.

WINNERS *Auto racing*—Tommy Milton, Indianapolis 500; *Baseball*—New York Giants, World Series; *Boxing*—Jack Dempsey, heavyweight; Johnny Wilson, middleweight; Johnny Buff, bantamweight; *Fencing*—U.S., first international competition; *Football*—California, Rose Bowl; *Golf*—Jim Barnes, U.S. Open; *Horse racing*—Behave Yourself, Kentucky Derby; Broomspun, Preakness Stakes, Grey Lag, Belmont Stakes; *Tennis*—U.S., Davis Cup; Bill Tilden, U.S. Open; *Track*—Illinois, first NCAA championship; *Wrestling*—Ed "Strangler" Lewis, heavyweight.

MISCELLANEOUS

Nicola Sacco and Bartolomeo Vanzetti are found guilty of murdering two men in a South Braintree, Massachusetts, payroll robbery.

Floods in San Antonio cause 250 deaths.

St. Louis Zoo opens.

Christian K. Nelson invents the Eskimo Pie.

Race riots in Tulsa, Oklahoma, result in death of 25 white and 60 black persons.

Women's fashion feature cloche hats, silk stockings, knee-length skirts, and fake jewelry; men wear their hair slicked down and parted in the middle, wear snappy hats and saddle shoes. Smoking increases and doubles sales of tobacco products during the decade.

1922

INTERNATIONAL

Washington Armament Conference of nine nations ends (February 6) with the signing of both treaties that set naval strength and restrict use of submarines, and an agreement on Pacific operations.

Second Central American conference meets in Washington.

NATIONAL

Supreme Court upholds constitutionality of Nineteenth Amendment, which gives women the vote.

Interior Secretary Albert B. Fall secretly leases naval oil reserve lands to oil operator Harry F. Sinclair; Edward L. Doheny leases California lands.

Seven states sign Colorado River Compact to regulate river's water.

A cartoon regarding the Teapot Dome scandal, which involves the secret leasing of naval oil reserve lands to private companies. CORBIS-BETTMANN

First U.S. aircraft carrier, *Langley,* is converted from the collier *Jupiter.*

Florence E. Allen is first woman justice of a state (Ohio) Supreme Court, later (1934) becomes first woman justice of Circuit Court of Appeals; Rebecca Felton of Georgia is first woman U.S. senator, serving from October 3 to November 22.

President Warren G. Harding dedicates Francis Scott Key Memorial in Baltimore, Maryland, in first presidential radio broadcast.

Fordney-McCumber Tariff raises rates generally.

BUSINESS/INDUSTRY/INVENTIONS

Herrin (Illinois) massacre occurs during coal-mine strike when union miners and nonunion men clash; 20 nonunion men die.

American Rolling Mill Co. builds continuous-sheet steel mill at Ashland, Kentucky.

Raytheon Manufacturing Co. begins as American Appliance Corp.

Bradley A. Fiske patents microfilm reading device; a sonic depth finder is introduced.

First mechanical telephone switchboard is installed in New York City.

DEATH Alexander Graham Bell, inventor of telephone.

TRANSPORTATION

Ford Motor Co. acquires Lincoln Motor Co.

U.S. dirigible *Roma* explodes over Hampton, Virginia; 34 are killed.

Glenn L. Martin Co. builds first U.S. metal monoplane; Henry A. Berliner demonstrates a helicopter for government officials.

DEATH George B. Selden, inventor of gasoline motor.

SCIENCE/MEDICINE

DEATH George W. Gould, inventor of bifocal lens glasses.

EDUCATION

Cornell University opens School of Hotel Administration.

Texas Tech University, Lubbock, opens.

DEATH John F. Goucher, benefactor and president of what became Goucher College.

RELIGION

Harry Emerson Fosdick resigns from Presbyterian church over differences between liberal and traditional doctrine.

American Episcopal church deletes word *obey* from marriage service.

Alfred Haatanen begins 28 years as president of American Finnish Lutheran Evangelical church.

Stephen S. Wise founds Jewish Institute of Religion.

ART/MUSIC

Edwin Franko Goldman band begins 33 years of open-air concerts in New York City's Central Park.

Seated statue of Abraham Lincoln by Daniel C. French in Lincoln Memorial is dedicated.

Childe Hassam completes the painting *Montauk.*

Museum of the American Indian in New York City opens.

SONGS (POPULAR): "Goin' Home," "My Buddy," "Toot, Toot Tootsie," "Way Down Yonder in New Orleans," "Carolina in the Morning," "Chicago," "Limehouse Blues," "Hot Lips."

LITERATURE/JOURNALISM

DeWitt Wallace and his wife, Lila Bell, launch *Reader's Digest.*

Scripps-Howard newspaper chain is established.

Will Rogers writes weekly column in the *New York Times.*

BOOKS *Babbitt* by Sinclair Lewis, *One of Ours* by Willa Cather, *Ballad of the Harp Weavers* (poetry) by Edna St. Vincent Millay, *The Breaking Point* by Mary Roberts Rinehart, *Under the Tree* (poetry) by Elizabeth M. Roberts, *Merton of the Movies* by Harry L. Wilson, *The Covered Wagon* by Emerson Hough.

ENTERTAINMENT

Will R. Hays begins 23 years as "movie czar" (president, Motion Picture Producers & Distributors).

Herbert T. Kalmus develops Technicolor process.

Ed Wynn produces *The Perfect Fool,* first radio broadcast of a Broadway show and the first broadcast with a studio audience (June 12).

Robert Benchley delivers classic monologue "The Treasurer's Report," which is later produced as one of the first movie "shorts."

PLAYS *Abie's Irish Rose* begins its record 2,327 performances; Helen Hayes stars in *To the Ladies,* Florence Eldridge in *The Cat and the Canary,* Jeanne Eagels in *Rain,* Helen Menken in *Seventh Heaven,* Eddie Dowling in *Sally, Irene and Mary.*

MOVIES *Blood and Sand* with Rudolph Valentino, *Robin Hood* with Douglas Fairbanks, *Cops* with Buster Keaton.

DEATHS Lillian Russell, actress and feminine ideal of her time; Marcus Loew, movie industy pioneer.

SPORTS

Jacob Ruppert is sole owner of New York Yankees baseball team.

Johnny Weissmuller breaks four swimming records: 300 and 400 meters, 440 and 500 yards.

Eddie Collins of Philadelphia Athletics steals six bases in a game, setting American League and major leagues baseball record; duplicates feat 11 days later.

U.S. Field Hockey Assn. and International Star Class Yacht Racing Assn. are established.

WINNERS *Auto racing*—Jimmy Murphy, Indianapolis 500; *Baseball*—New York Giants, World Series; *Boxing*—Gene Tunney, light heavyweight; Mickey Walker, welterweight; Joe Lynch, bantamweight; *Football*—Washington—Jefferson and California (tie), Rose Bowl; *Golf*—U.S., first Walker Cup matches with England; Gene Sarazen, U.S. Open and PGA; *Horse racing*—Morvich, Kentucky Derby; Pillory, Preakness Stakes and Belmont Stakes; *Polo*—

Princeton, first indoor intercollegiate title; *Tennis*—U.S., Davis Cup; Bill Tilden, U.S. Open; *Track*—Cornell, first indoor IC4A meet; *Volleyball*—Pittsburgh YMCA, first national tournament; *Wrestling*—Ed "Strangler" Lewis, heavyweight.

MISCELLANEOUS

Two-day snowstorm in Washington, D.C., results in collapse of Knickerbocker Theater roof, killing 100.

Ten days of hurricanes in Florida and Alabama kill 243.

Ancient Chinese game of mah-jongg is introduced in U.S., becomes a craze.

1923

INTERNATIONAL

Treaty signed by U.S., Great Britain, France, and Japan covers handling of Pacific possessions (December 13).

Central American conference ends with a neutrality treaty, limitation of armaments, and a Central American court of justice (February 7).

U.S. and Turkey sign treaty of friendship and commerce.

NATIONAL

President Warren G. Harding dies in San Francisco during his return trip from Alaska (August 2); Vice President Calvin Coolidge is sworn in as president (August 3).

First equal rights amendent is introduced in Congress, does not pass.

Montana and Nevada are first states to enact an old-age pension.

Congress passes over president's veto a veteran's bonus of $1.25 per day for overseas duty, $1 a day for U.S. service; bonus given in form of 20-year endowment policy.

The *Baltimore Sun* and *New York Times* print exposés of Ku Klux Klan activities; articles lead to decline in membership.

President Coolidge gives first presidential message specifically for radio (December 6).

DEATH Henry Cabot Lodge, senator who led successful fight against League of Nations.

BUSINESS/INDUSTRY/INVENTIONS

U.S. Steel Co. adopts an eight-hour day, reducing it from 12 hours.

Dancer Bee Jackson performs the Charleston on stage. A champion dancer, Jackson helps popularize the dance that becomes a hit during the 1920s. **CORBIS-BETTMANN/HULTON-DEUTSCH COLLECTION**

Zenith Radio Corp. and Burlington Industries are founded.

Young & Rubicam advertising agency is founded.

Intermediate Credit Act makes it easier to get crop financing loans.

DEATHS Francis W. Ayer, pioneer advertising executive; Charles P. Steinmetz, electrical inventor who helped make alternating current commercially feasible; John Davey, tree-care specialist; William Holabird, architect who established skeleton method of skyscraper building.

TRANSPORTATION

First ethyl gasoline is marketed in Dayton, Ohio (February 2).

Firestone Tire & Rubber Co. produces balloon tires.

First transcontinental nonstop plane flight (New York City to San Diego) is completed in 26 hours, 50 minutes.

Registered automobiles total about 13.3 million.

DEATH Alexander McDougall, designer of Great Lakes "whaleback" freighter.

During better times President Calvin Coolidge is visited by members of the Investment Bankers Association. Bankers' fortunes and those of many Americans will take a turn for the worse in 1929. **THE LIBRARY OF CONGRESS**

SCIENCE/MEDICINE

Robert A. Millikan is awarded Nobel Prize in physics for work on the elementary charge of electricity and on the photoelectric effect.

Physicist Arthur H. Compton discovers the photon, a particle unit of light.

Naval Research Laboratory opens in Washington, D.C.

New York Cancer Institute on Welfare Island is dedicated.

George and Gladys Dick isolate the scarlet fever toxin, develop an effective antitoxin.

EDUCATION

Merger of Daytona Normal and Cookman Institute forms Bethune-Cookman College; Mary M. Bethune is first president.

John D. Rockefeller Jr. endows International Education Board.

RELIGION

Edgar J. Goodspeed prepares *New Testament: An American Translation.*

DEATH Daniel S. Tuttle, presiding American Episcopal bishop (1903–1923).

ART/MUSIC

Bessie Smith, blues singer, records "Down Hearted Blues," the first phonograph record to sell more than 2 million copies.

Martha Graham makes solo debut as a ballerina in the *Greenwich Village Follies.*

George W. Bellows completes the painting *Emma and Her Children;* Charles Sheeler, *Bucks County Barn;* George Grosz, *Ecce Homo;* Naum Gabo completes the sculpture *Column.*

Denver (Colorado) Art Museum is founded.

Roger Sessions composes orchestral suite *The Black Maskers.*

SONGS (POPULAR): "Barney Google," "It Ain't Gonna Rain No Mo'," "Linger Awhile," "That Old Gang of Mine," "Who's Sorry Now?," "Yes, We Have No Bananas," "Bugle Call Rag," "Mexicali Rose," "Charleston."

DEATH Edward C. Potter, sculptor of animals (lions at entrance to New York Public Library).

LITERATURE/JOURNALISM

Henry R. Luce and Briton Hadden launch *Time* magazine (March 3).

College Humor magazine and *Kiplinger Washington Newsletter* begin publication.

BOOKS *New Hampshire* (poetry) by Robert Frost, *Cane* by Jean Toomer, *Black Oxen* by Gertrude Atherton, *A Lost Lady* by Willa Cather, *Tulips and Chimneys* (poetry) by E. E. Cummings.

ENTERTAINMENT

Warner Bros. Pictures Inc. is established.

Lee De Forest shows first sound-on-film motion picture, *Phonofilm.*

PLAYS Eddie Cantor stars in *Kid Boots,* Walter Hampden in *Cyrano de Bergerac,* W. C. Fields in *Poppy,* George M. Cohan in *The Song and Dance Man,* Edna May Oliver in *Icebound,* H. B. Warner in *You and I.*

MOVIES *Safety Last* with Harold Lloyd, *The Hunchback of Notre Dame* with Lon Chaney, *The Pilgrim* with Charlie Chaplin, *The Ten Commandments* with Theodore Roberts, *The Covered Wagon* with Ernest Torrence.

Dance marathons become popular and new dance, the Charleston, sweeps country.

SPORTS

Henry F. Sullivan of Lowell, Massachusetts, becomes first American to swim English Channel, does it in 27 hours, 23 minutes.

Yankee Stadium in New York City opens (April 18); before 72,400 spectators, Babe Ruth hits three home runs.

WINNERS *Auto racing*—Tommy Milton, Indianapolis 500; *Baseball*—New York Yankees, World Series; *Boxing*—Jack Dempsey, heavyweight; Mike McTigue, light heavyweight; Harry Greb, middleweight; Johnny Dundee, featherweight; *Fencing*—Army, three-weapon intercollegiate title; *Football*—Southern California, Rose Bowl; *Golf*—U.S., Walker Cup; Bobby Jones, U.S. Open; Gene Sarazen, PGA; *Horse racing*—Zev, Kentucky Derby and Belmont Stakes; Vigil, Preakness Stakes; *Tennis*—U.S., Davis Cup; Bill Tilden, U.S. Open (men); Helen Wills, USLTA (women); *Track*—Prudential, AAU women's meet.

MISCELLANEOUS

Mine disaster at Dawson, New Mexico, kills 120.

1924

INTERNATIONAL

Dawes Plan on German reparations calls for stabilizing German currency, setting up a five-year schedule of payments (April 9); plan is adopted.

U.S. Marines withdraw from Nicaragua, only to return nine months later.

George Gershwin, composer, debuts *Rhapsody in Blue* in 1924. The orchestration incorporates jazz for a distinctly American sound, bringing both fame and fortune to Gershwin.

NATIONAL

President Calvin Coolidge, Republican, is elected to first full term, defeats Democrat John W. Davis; Coolidge receives 15,725,016 popular and 382 electoral votes to Davis's 8,385,586 popular and 136 electoral votes; Progressive Party candidate Robert M. La Follette receives 4,822,586 popular and 13 electoral votes.

Charles G. Dawes shares Nobel Peace Prize with Sir J. Austen Chamberlain of England for developing German reparations plan.

Former Interior Secretary Albert B. Fall is indicted in Teapot Dome scandal, later is convicted and sentenced to one year, $100,000 fine; Oilmen Harry F. Sinclair and Edward L. Doheny are also indicted but later are acquitted.

Annual admissions quota for immigrants is reduced to 2% of the number of that foreign-born nationality in U.S.; new law also requires that immigrants obtain visas, which is a complicated and lengthy process.

Foreign Service Act is reorganized, consolidates U.S. diplomatic and consular service.

Indian Citizenship Act makes all U.S.-born Native Americans U.S. citizens.

Nellie Tayloe Ross becomes first woman state governor (Wyoming) when elected to complete unexpired term of her husband.

Two U.S. Army planes complete 26,103 mile flight around the world from Seattle in 35 days, 1 hour, 11 minutes.

First wilderness area is set aside in the Gila (New Mexico) National Forest.

J. Edgar Hoover becomes acting head of Federal Bureau of Investigation (May 10), begins 48 years' service as director December 10.

DEATHS Former President Woodrow Wilson (1913–1923); former First Lady Florence Harding (1921–1923).

BUSINESS/INDUSTRY/INVENTIONS

William Green assumes AFL presidency on the death of Samuel Gompers.

Howard Johnson enters food business in Wollaston, Massachusetts (see 1929).

DuPont plant in Buffalo, New York, first produces cellophane.

Calvin Coolidge attends the World Series with his wife, shortly before his election in 1924. **AP WIDE WORLD PHOTOS**

Ernst F. W. Alexanderson transmits first transatlantic facsimile message.

J. C. Penney opens 500th store in Hamilton, Missouri, where he first worked as a clerk in 1904 for $2.27 a month.

Jacob Schick introduces first successful electric shaver.

DEATHS Samuel Gompers, president of AFL (1886–1924); Louis H. Sullivan, father of modernist architecture; Henry Bacon, architect who designed Lincoln Memorial.

TRANSPORTATION

Chrysler Motors is founded, introduces first six-cylinder car.

National Association of Finance Companies adopts minimum standards of one-third down payment for a new car, two-thirds for a used car.

Midland Transit Co. of West Virginia, which later becomes Atlantic Greyhound Co., is founded.

Regular transcontinental air service begins.

Big Lake oil field in western Texas is discovered.

Diesel electric locomotive is put into service.

Bear Mountain Bridge across Hudson River opens.

DEATH Clifford M. Holland, New York tunnel builder.

SCIENCE/MEDICINE

Morris Fishbein begins 25-year editorship of *AMA Journal* (American Medical Assn.).

Western Electric Co. demonstrates new electrical portable stethoscope.

Dr. George R. Minot develops liver treatment for pernicious anemia.

DEATH T. Mitchell Prudden, pathologist, first American to make diphtheria antitoxin.

EDUCATION

National Congress of Parents and Teachers is established.

Trinity College (Durham, North Carolina) is renamed Duke University in honor of school's benefactors.

RELIGION

Methodist General Conference lifts traditional ban on dancing and theatergoing.

Rev. Harry Emerson Fosdick is cleared of heresy charges by New York Presbytery.

Two Catholic archbishops, Patrick J. Hayes of New York and George W. Mundelein of Chicago, elevated to cardinal.

Edward L. Parsons becomes Episcopal bishop of California.

ART/MUSIC

Howard H. Hanson begins 40 years as director of Eastman School of Music.

The operettas *Rose Marie* by Rudolf Friml and *The Student Prince* by Sigmund Romberg are presented.

Serge Koussevitsky arrives from Russia to begin 25 years as conductor of the Boston Symphony Orchestra.

Paul Whiteman and his orchestra give first formal jazz concert at Aeolian Hall, New York City; features George Gershwin at the piano playing his *Rhapsody in Blue* (February 12).

Charles Burchfield completes the painting *House of Mystery;* Preston Dickinson, *Factory.*

Pierpont Morgan Library (art) in New York City opens.

SONGS (POPULAR): "All Alone," "Fascinating Rhythm," "I Wonder What's Become of Sally," "I'll See You in My Dreams," "Tea for Two," "Indian Love Call," "Shine," "Amapola," "It Had to Be You," "Rose-Marie," "California, Here I Come."

DEATH Victor Herbert, composer.

LITERATURE/JOURNALISM

Saturday Review of Literature begins publication; George Jean Nathan and H. L. Mencken found *The American Mercury.*

New York City tabloid *Daily Mirror* begins publication; Ogden Mills Reid purchases *New York Herald* and combines it with *New York Tribune.*

Walter Winchell begins 49 years of writing show-business gossip column in *New York Graphic* (later in the *Mirror*).

Simon & Schuster, publishers, is founded.

Harold L. Gray draws the cartoon strip "Little Orphan Annie" in *Chicago Tribune.*

BOOKS *So Big* by Edna Ferber, *The Old Maid* by Edith Wharton, *Arrowsmith* by Sinclair Lewis, *Tamar and Other Poems* by Robinson Jeffers, *Israfel* by Hervey Allen, *Sunrise Trumpets* (poetry) by Joseph Auslander.

DEATH Frances H. Burnett, author *(Little Lord Fauntleroy).*

ENTERTAINMENT

First coast-to-coast radio hookup is used successfully.

Combining the Metro, Mayer, and Goldwyn companies creates Metro-Goldwyn-Mayer; Harry Cohn founds Columbia Pictures.

American own 2.5 million radios compared to 5,000 in 1920.

PLAYS Alfred Lunt and Lynn Fontanne star in *The Guardsman,* Paul Robeson in *The Emperor Jones,* Helen Hayes in *Dancing Mothers,* Walter Huston in *Desire Under the Elms,* Fred and Adele Astaire in *Lady Be Good* (music by George Gershwin), Roland Young in *Beggar on Horseback.*

MOVIES *Beau Brummel* with John Barrymore, *Forbidden Paradise* with Pola Negri, *Janice Meredith* with Marion Davies, *The Thief of Bagdad* with Douglas Fairbanks.

DEATH Lew Dockstader, minstrel and entertainer.

SPORTS

First Winter Olympics are held in Chamonix, France; U.S. wins one gold medal; Summer Olympics are held in Paris; U.S. wins 48 golds, with William Hubbard winning the long jump, the first African-American to win a gold medal.

Frank Caruna of Buffalo becomes first bowler to roll two consecutive 300 games; rolls 274 in third game.

Jim Bottomley of St. Louis Cardinals sets National League record, driving in 12 runs in a game.

Newly formed American Motorcyclist Assn. holds three-day rally.

WINNERS *Auto racing*—L. L. Corum and Joe Boyer, Indianapolis 500; *Baseball*—Washington Senators, World Series; *Boxing*—Joe Goldstein, bantamweight; *Football*—Navy—Washington (tie), Rose Bowl; *Golf*—U.S., Walker Cup; Cyril Walker, U.S. Open; Walter Hagen, PGA; *Horse racing*—Black Gold, Kentucky Derby; Nellie Morse, Preakness Stakes; Mad Play, Belmont Stakes; *Tennis*—U.S., Davis Cup; Bill Tilden, U.S. Open (men).

MISCELLANEOUS

Two mine disasters occur; Castle Gate, Utah (171 are killed), and Benwood, West Virginia (119 deaths).

First crossword puzzle book is published.

First national cornhusking championship is held near Alleman, Iowa.

Tornadoes destroy 35 towns in Midwest, killing 800.

Shipwreck Kelly begins career of flagpole sitting.

1925

INTERNATIONAL

U.S. and Canada agree to improve St. Lawrence River between Montreal and Lake Ontario.

NATIONAL

Supreme Court in *Gitlow* v. *New York* rules that the First Amendment prohibition against governmental abridgment of free speech applies to both federal and state governments.

Court-martial finds Col. Billy Mitchell, outspoken critic of U.S. air power, guilty of conduct prejudicial to good order and military discipline; he later resigns from army.

National Aircraft Board is named to investigate government's role in aviation; Dwight W. Morrow is chairman.

Guggenheim Foundation is established.

U.S. Chamber of Commerce headquarters in Washington, D.C., is dedicated.

DEATHS Former Vice President Thomas R. Marshall (1913–1921), remembered for quote: "What this country needs is a really good five-cent cigar"; William Jennings Bryan, former Secretary of State (1912–1915), three-time Democratic presidential candidate; Robert M. La Follette, Wisconsin governor and senator.

BUSINESS/INDUSTRY/INVENTIONS

Bell Telephone Laboratories organize as nonprofit corporation.

Wilson Dam on Tennessee River in Alabama is completed.

Dry ice is first produced commercially; A. A. Walter Co. erects plant in Albany to produce potato chips.

Armstrong Cork & Insulation Co. introduces embossed inlaid linoleum.

A. Philip Randolph organizes Brotherhood of Sleeping Car Porters, becomes strong civil rights leader.

DEATHS Frank S. Baldwin, inventor of what became Monroe calculator; Charles F. Chandler, inventor of flushing toilet water closet, who refused to patent it in the public interest; James B. Duke, American Tobacco Co. president.

TRANSPORTATION

Ford Motor Co. introduces eight-hour day, five-day workweek.

National Air Transport Inc., which later becomes United Air Lines, is founded.

Merger of GM Laboratories and Delco forms General Motors Research Corp.; Charles Kettering is first president.

DEATH Elwood Haynes, pioneer automobile manufacturer, patented stainless steel process.

SCIENCE/MEDICINE

John T. Scopes, high school teacher, is arrested in Dayton, Tennessee, for violating state law that makes it illegal to teach any theory that denies the story of "the Divine creation of man" in any public school; Clarence Darrow is defense lawyer, William Jennings Bryan is part of prosecution team; Scopes is found guilty, is fined $100.

Robert A. Millikan announces discovery of a cosmic ray.

Annie Jump Cannon, astronomer, becomes first woman to receive honorary doctorate (Oxford).

Battelle Memorial Institute in Columbus, Ohio, incorporates to conduct research.

EDUCATION

Yale University Aeronautics School receives $500,000 endowment from Daniel Guggenheim.

RELIGION

Rev. Harry Emerson Fosdick leaves Presbyterian church, refuses to accept General Assembly requirements for his continued stay (see 1924).

Episcopal Bishop William M. Brown of Arkansas is deposed for heresy; author of *Communism and Christianity.*

Catholic Bishop John T. McNichols becomes Archbishop of Cincinnati.

ART/MUSIC

The operetta *The Vagabond King* by Rudolf Friml is presented.

Edward Hopper completes the paintings *House by the Railroad* and *Model Reading;* Robert Laurent, *Wave;* Arthur G. Dove, *Portrait of A.S.;* Jacques Lipchitz completes the sculpture *Bather.*

Herbert Elwell composes the ballet *The Happy Hypocrite.*

SONGS (POPULAR): "Always," "Dinah," "Drifting and Dreaming," "Sleepy Time Gal," "Sweet Georgia Brown," "Who?," "Yes, Sir, That's My Baby," "Clap Hands, Here Comes Charlie," "Jalousie," "Show Me the Way to Go Home," "I'm Sittin' on Top of the World."

DEATHS John Singer Sargent, portrait painter; Willard L. Metcalf, artist of New England scenes.

LITERATURE/JOURNALISM

Harold W. Ross founds *The New Yorker,* features Helen Hokinson's cartoons of middle-aged matrons and Peter Arno's work.

Clarence S. Darrow (left), prominent defense attorney, sits next to William Jennings Bryan, prosecuting attorney, at the John Scopes trial. Scopes, a 24-year-old educator, is charged with teaching evolution to his biology class instead of "Divine creation." **AP/WIDE WORLD PHOTOS**

Viking Press is founded.

Robert R. McCormick becomes editor, publisher of *Chicago Tribune;* Westbrook Pegler writes his column in the *Tribune.*

BOOKS *Gentlemen Prefer Blondes* by Anita Loos, *The Man Nobody Knew* by Bruce Barton, *The Great Gatsby* by F. Scott Fitzgerald, *An American Tragedy* by Theodore Dreiser, *Porgy* by DuBose Hayward, *Roan Stallion* (poetry) by Robinson Jeffers, *Barren Ground* by Ellen Glasgow, *Collected Poems* by Hilda Doolittle.

DEATHS Amy Lowell, poet; Frank Munsey, magazine and newspaper publisher.

ENTERTAINMENT

PLAYS Marilyn Miller stars in *Sunny,* Charles Winninger in *No, No, Nanette,* George Jessel in *The Jazz Singer,* Fay Bainter and Walter Abel in *The Enemy.*

MOVIES *The Freshman* with Harold Lloyd, *The Phantom of the Opera* with Lon Chaney, *The Gold Rush* with Charlie Chaplin, *The Merry Widow* with Marion Davies, *The Big Parade* with John Gilbert.

The "Grand Ole Opry" broadcasts locally on radio.

Brooks Atkinson begins 35 years as the *New York Times* drama critic.

SPORTS

Lou Gehrig enters baseball as a pinch hitter and first baseman for New York Yankees (June 1), starts a 2,130-consecutive-game streak; Everett Scott, New York Yankees shortstop, ends his consecutive-game streak at 1,307 (May 6).

Tris Speaker of Cleveland Indians and Eddie Collins of Chicago White Sox each get their 3,000th base hits.

American (basketball) League is organized.

First contract-bridge game is played aboard a steamer waiting to enter Panama Canal (November 1); players are Harold S. Vanderbilt, game's inventor, and friends.

St. Petersburg (Florida) Kennel Club opens greyhound racing track.

First East-West Shrine football game is played.

New Madison Square Garden opens.

Tim Mara buys New York Giants football franchise for $500.

WINNERS *Auto racing*—Peter DePaolo, Indianapolis 500; *Baseball*—Pittsburgh Pirates, World Series; *Boxing*—Paul Berlenbach, light heavyweight; Rocky

Kansas, lightweight; Fidel La Barba, flyweight; *Football*—Notre Dame, Rose Bowl; *Golf*—Willie MacFarlane, U.S. Open; Walter Hagen, PGA; *Gymnastics*—Alfred Jochim, AAU all-around title; *Horse racing*—Flying Ebony, Kentucky Derby; Coventry, Preakness Stakes; American Flag, Belmont Stakes; *Tennis*—U.S., Davis Cup; Bill Tilden, U.S. Open (men); *Wrestling*—Ed "Strangler" Lewis, heavyweight.

DEATH Christy Mathewson, Hall of Fame baseball pitcher.

MISCELLANEOUS

Tornadoes in Missouri, Illinois, and Indiana claim 689 lives (March 18).

Earthquake destroys downtown Santa Barbara, California.

Louisville Courier-Journal inaugurates national spelling bee.

The flapper dress, featuring a drop waist, is introduced.

1926

INTERNATIONAL

Senate ratifies World War I debt-funding agreements with European countries.

U.S. fails to join Permanent Court of International Justice and Arbitration.

NATIONAL

Philadelphia Sesquicentennial Exposition is held.

Army Air Corps is created (July 2).

Personal income and inheritance taxes are reduced; some excise taxes are abolished.

DEATHS Sanford B. Dole, first governor, Territory of Hawaii; Eugene V. Debs, radical labor leader and Social Democratic Party presidential candidate.

BUSINESS/INDUSTRY/INVENTIONS

American Arbitration Assn. is founded.

Railroad Labor Board replaces an independent Board of Mediation.

Dr. Colin G. Fink patents chromium-plating process.

McGraw Electric Co. markets electric toaster (Toastmaster); Electrolux unveils gas household refrigerator.

Neiman Marcus inaugurates department-store fashion shows.

George F. Doriot begins 40 years of teaching manufacturing at Harvard University; is credited with creating American professional managers.

DEATHS John M. Browning, machine gun and automatic gun inventor; Leonidas Merritt, discoverer of Mesabi iron-ore deposits; Luther Burbank, plant breeder; Washington A. Roebling, builder of Brooklyn Bridge.

TRANSPORTATION

Air Commerce Act places civil aviation under the Commerce Department.

The *Governor Moore,* a ferryboat built exclusively to carry cars, is placed in service between New York City and New Jersey.

Richard E. Byrd and Floyd Bennett fly over North Pole (May 9).

Carl E. Wickman founds what later becomes Greyhound Corp.

Benjamin Franklin Bridge over Delaware River in Philadelphia opens.

SCIENCE/MEDICINE

Robert H. Goddard successfully demonstrates a liquid fuel rocket in flight of 184 feet in 22 seconds at Auburn, Massachusetts.

Paul de Kruif writes *Microbe Hunters,* and Thomas H. Morgan *The Theory of the Gene.*

EDUCATION

University of California, Los Angeles (UCLA), is dedicated.

DEATH Charles W. Eliot, Harvard University president (1869–1909).

RELIGION

International Eucharistic Congress holds first U.S. meeting in Chicago suburb.

Henry Sloane Coffin becomes president of Union Theological Seminary.

Rev. Andrew J. Brennan becomes Catholic bishop of Richmond, Virginia.

Charles M. (Daddy) Grace, evangelist, founds House of Prayer for All People.

ART/MUSIC

National Broadcasting Co. broadcasts its first major orchestra, carries a Boston Symphony concert.

John A. Carpenter composes the ballets *The Birthday of the Infanta* and *Skyscrapers;* Sigmund Romberg's operetta *The Desert Song* is presented.

Georgia O'Keeffe completes the painting *Black Iris;* Lyonel Feininger, *Church of the Minorities;* William J. Glackens, *Promenade;* Kenneth H. Davis, *Day Dream;* Preston Dickinson, *Plums on a Plate;* Alexander Calder completes wire sculpture *Josephine Baker.*

Louis Armstrong (Satchmo) forms band.

SONGS (POPULAR): "Baby Face," "Birth of the Blues," "Bye, Bye, Blackbird," "In a Little Spanish Town," "When Day Is Done," "Charmaine," "Tip Toe Through the Tulips," "One Alone," "Someone to Watch Over Me."

DEATHS Rida Young, librettist *(Naughty Marietta);* Carl E. Akeley, sculptor who made large habitat animal groups; Mary Cassatt, impressionist painter.

LITERATURE/JOURNALISM

Book of the Month Club issues its first selection, *Lolly Willowes* by Sylvia Townsend Warner; Harold K. Guinzburg founds Literary Guild.

BOOKS *Elmer Gantry* by Sinclair Lewis, *The Story of Philosophy* by Will Durant, *The Sun Also Rises* by Ernest Hemingway, *Show Boat* by Edna Ferber, *Enough Rope* (poetry) by Dorothy Parker, *Dark of the Moon* by Sara Teasdale, *Soldier's Pay* by William Faulkner.

DEATH Edward W. Scripps, newspaper publisher.

ENTERTAINMENT

First talking moving picture, a series of short features, is shown at Warner Theater, New York City (August 5); Warner Bros.' *Don Juan* is first movie with sound accompaniment (August 26).

National Broadcasting Co. (NBC) goes on air with 24 radio stations (November 25), first major radio network.

Edgar Bergen begins act with a dummy, Charlie McCarthy, in vaudeville.

Civic Repertory Theatre, led by Eva Le Gallienne, stages its first production.

Cities Service radio concerts start 20-year run on the air.

PLAYS Gertrude Lawrence stars in *Oh, Kay,* with music by George Gershwin; Eddie Dowling in *Honeymoon Lane,* Charles Ruggles in *Queen High,* Helen Morgan in *Americana,* Lee Tracy in *Broadway,* Mae West in *Sex,* the Marx Brothers in *Coconuts.*

MOVIES *Ben-Hur* with Ramon Novarro, *The Black Pirate* with Douglas Fairbanks, *Beau Geste* with Ronald Colman, *Don Juan* with John Barrymore, *The Scarlet Letter* with Lillian Gish, *The General* with Buster Keaton.

DEATH Harry Houdini, escape artist; Rudolph Valentino, silent screen idol.

Route 66

In 1921 the Federal Highway Act was revised in anticipation of a system of interstate highways. Oklahoman Cyrus Stevens Avery, a member of several highway associations, rose to prominence in the planning of the network. Called "the father of Route 66," Avery helped organize a route linking Chicago to Los Angeles, crossing eight separate states on the way. On November 11, 1926, federal and state highway officials approved a national network, including Route 66. While 800 miles of Route 66 was already paved, 1,648 required upgrading to meet the requirements of everyday road traffic (a process that took until 1937 to complete). Dubbed the "Main Street of America" since 1927, Route 66 became a tourist hub from the 1940s through the 1960s as the postwar leisure industry peaked. With its car-friendly motels, gas stations, and roadside diners, Route 66 marked the full splendor of the asphalt adventure. The route inspired countless authors including Jack Kerouac and John Steinbeck (who called it America's "Mother Road") as well as popular songs, notably Bobby Troup's paean to the open highway, "Get Your Kicks on Route 66," released in 1948.

SPORTS

Gertrude Ederle becomes first woman to swim English Channel (August 6), takes 14 hours, 34 minutes.

Eddie Rickenbacker, World War I ace, buys controlling interest in Indianapolis Speedway.

Charles C. Pyle promotes national tennis tour for Suzanne Lenglen and Vinnie Richards.

International Greyhound Racing Assn. is established.

Lillian Copeland becomes first woman to throw javelin farther than 110 feet (112 ft., 5½ in.).

WINNERS *Auto racing*—Frank Lockhart, Indianapolis 500; *Baseball*—St. Louis Cardinals, World Series;

Lillian Gish, as Hester Prynne, and Lars Hanson, as Rev. Arthur Dimmesdale, in the silent film *The Scarlet Letter.* THE KOBAL COLLECTION

Boxing—Gene Tunney, heavyweight; Pete Latzo, welterweight; Mickey Walker, middleweight; Sammy Mandell, lightweight; *Football*—Alabama, Rose Bowl; *Golf*—U.S., Walker Cup; Bobby Jones, U.S. Open; Walter Hagen, PGA; *Harness racing*—Guy McKinney, first Hambletonian; *Horse racing*—Bubbling Over, Kentucky Derby; Display, Preakness Stakes; Crusader, Belmont Stakes; *Tennis*—U.S., Davis Cup; Rene Lacoste, U.S. Open (men); Molla Mallory, U.S. Open (women).

MISCELLANEOUS

Hurricane near Miami causes 370 deaths, thousands of injuries.

DEATH Annie Oakley, frontierswoman.

1927

INTERNATIONAL

Naval conference is held in Geneva with no concrete results.

About 1,000 marines land in China to protect property in civil war.

NATIONAL

President Calvin Coolidge announces he will not run for president in 1928 (August 2).

Supreme Court invalidates Elks Hill lease of oil lands involved in Teapot Dome scandal.

Merger of three organizations establishes Brookings Institution in Washington, D.C.

Food & Drug Administration is created as the Food, Drug and Insecticide Administration; Congress creates Bureau of Customs and a Bureau of Prohibition in Treasury Department.

Drive-up mailboxes for motorists are first installed in Houston, Texas.

BUSINESS/INDUSTRY/INVENTIONS

Commercial transatlantic telephone service is established between New York and London.

John D. and Mack D. Rust invent mechanical cotton picker.

Buckminster Fuller builds first luxury house using Dymaxion principle, is designed to achieve maximum output with a minimum of material and energy.

TRANSPORTATION

Spectacular airplane flights: Charles A. Lindbergh flies solo across the Atlantic, lands in Paris 33 hours, 29 minutes, 30 seconds after leaving Long Island, New York (May 20); Richard E. Byrd lands off French coast in transatlantic plane flight; Clarence D. Chamberlin flies nonstop from New York City to Germany; two Army Air Corps pilots (Lester J. Maitland and Albert F. Hegenberger) make first successful San Francisco—Honolulu flight (June 28).

Massachusetts becomes first state to impose compulsory auto insurance; requires $5,000/$10,000 liability coverage.

Lockheed Aircraft Corp. is founded; Clyde V. Cessna builds first cantilever plane; Juan Trippe founds Pan American Airways.

Production of Model T Ford discontinues after 15 millionth car.

Holland Tunnel under Hudson River at New York City opens.

International Peace Bridge across Niagara River at Buffalo opens.

American Express and airlines establish air express.

SCIENCE/MEDICINE

Albert A. Compton shares Nobel Prize in physics with Charles T. R. Wilson of England for discovery of the Compton effects, the scattering of X rays by matter.

Philip Drinker and Louis A. Shaw invent the iron lung (respirator).

EDUCATION

Second Maimonides College opens in New York City.

DEATH Elizabeth Harrison, a leader in kindergarten movement.

RELIGION

Henry S. Tucker becomes Episcopal bishop of Virginia.

ART/MUSIC

Metropolitan Opera presents *The King's Henchmen* by Deems Taylor and Edna St. Vincent Millay.

Victor Talking Machine Co. introduces phonograph with automatic record changer.

Lawrence Welk and Duke Ellington form bands.

First regular series of opera broadcasts begins from Chicago Civic Opera; regular concert broadcasts from Boston and New York symphonies follow.

Paul Whiteman hires Bing Crosby, Al Rinker, and Harry Barris to form successful Rhythm Boys.

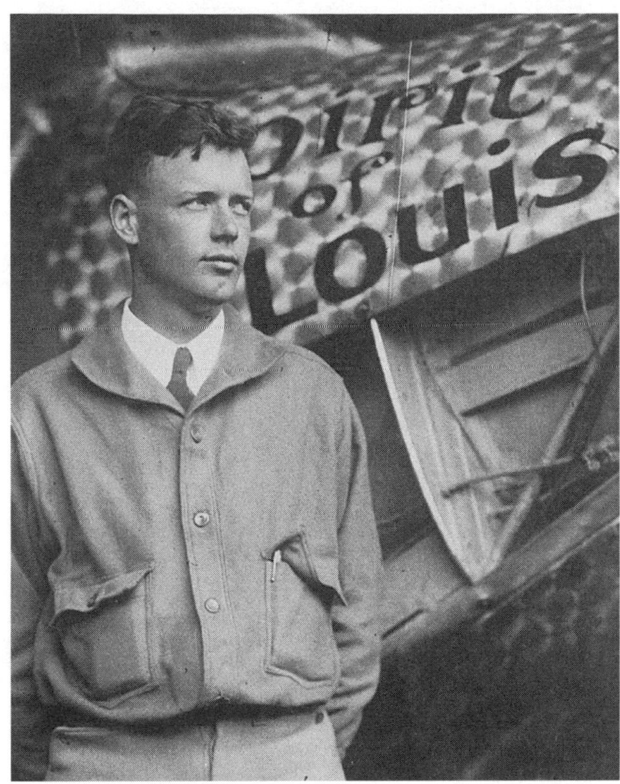

Charles Lindbergh with his monoplane *Spirit of St. Louis*, in which he is the first to fly alone across the Atlantic. THE LIBRARY OF CONGRESS

Gaston Lachaise completes the sculpture *Standing Woman;* Preston Dickinson completes the painting *Old Quarter, Quebec;* Glenn O. Coleman, *The Mirror.*

Detroit Institute of Arts, Philadelphia Museum of Art, and Fogg Art Museum in Cambridge, Massachusetts, open.

George Antheil composes *Ballet Mecanique.*

SONGS (POPULAR): "Ain't She Sweet," "Among My Souvenirs," "The Best Things in Life Are Free," "Chloe," "I'm Looking Over a Four-Leaf Clover," "My Blue Heaven" (Gene Austin's record sells 1 million copies), "The Song Is Ended," "Varsity Drag," "Ol' Man River," "Let a Smile Be Your Umbrella."

DEATH Isadora Duncan, a founder of modern expressive dancing.

LITERATURE/JOURNALISM

Random House and Doubleday Doran & Co., publishers, are founded.

Roy W. Howard purchases *New York Telegram.*

BOOKS *Death Comes for the Archbishop* by Willa Cather, *The Bridge of San Luis Rey* by Thornton Wilder,

Black April by Julia Peterkin, *Tristram* (poetry) by Edwin Arlington Robinson, *Oil* by Upton Sinclair, *Copper Sun* (poetry) by Countee Cullen.

ENTERTAINMENT

Television is demonstrated for first time (April 7).

Federal Radio Commission is created.

Columbia Broadcasting System (CBS) is organized with William S. Paley president.

Academy of Motion Picture Arts and Sciences is founded; awards first Oscars: best actor, Emil Jannings *(The Way of All Flesh);* best actress, Janet Gaynor *(Seventh Heaven);* best picture, *Wings.*

Ziegfeld Theater in New York City opens.

PLAYS Fred and Adele Astaire star in Gershwin's *Funny Face,* Charles Winninger in *Show Boat,* Ethel Waters in *Africana,* Helen Hayes in *Coquette,* Marx Brothers in *Animal Crackers,* Barbara Stanwyck in *Burlesque,* Ruth Gordon in *Saturday's Children,* Ann Harding in *The Trial of Mary Dugan.*

MOVIES *The King of Kings* with H. B. Warner, *Seventh Heaven* with Janet Gaynor, *The Jazz Singer* with Al Jolson, *Wings* with Gary Cooper, *Dracula* with Bela Lugosi, *The Divine Woman* with Greta Garbo, *It* with Clara Bow, *My Best Girl* with Mary Pickford.

SPORTS

Babe Ruth of New York Yankees hits 60th home run to set new season major-league record; Ty Cobb of Detroit Tigers gets 4,000th base hit.

Ben Johnson, president of American (baseball) League for 26 years, resigns because of poor health; Ernest S. Barnard succeeds him.

Harlem Globetrotters play their first basketball game.

Sabin Carr becomes first to pole vault 14 feet.

Major H. O. Seagrave drives his car at 203.79 miles per hour at Daytona Beach, Florida.

First Golden Gloves boxing matches are held.

WINNERS *Auto racing*—George Souders, Indianapolis 500; *Baseball*—New York Yankees, World Series; *Boxing*—Gene Tunney, heavyweight; Tommy Loughran, light heavyweight; Joe Dundee, welterweight; *Football*—Alabama—Stanford (tie), Rose Bowl; *Golf*—U.S., Ryder Cup; Tommy Armour, U.S. Open; Walter Hagen, PGA; *Hockey*—Ottawa, Stanley Cup; *Horse racing*—Whiskery, Kentucky Derby; Bostonian, Preakness Stakes; Chance Shot, Belmont Stakes; *Rowing*—Yale, first Blackwell Cup race; *Tennis*—France, Davis Cup; Rene Lacoste, U.S. Open (men); Helen Wills, U.S. Open (women).

MISCELLANEOUS

Tornadoes in Arkansas and Poplar Bluffs, Missouri, kill 92; in St. Louis 90; floods in lower Mississippi Valley bring death to 313, $300 million in damage.

Nicola Sacco and Bartolomeo Vanzetti are executed for payroll holdup slaying of two (1920).

Submarine S-4 sinks after colliding with Coast Guard destroyer off Provincetown, Massachusetts, 40 men are lost.

1928

INTERNATIONAL

Fourteen nations sign Kellogg-Briand Treaty to outlaw war (August 27); eventually 62 nations sign; the Senate later ratifies the pact.

NATIONAL

Herbert Hoover, Republican, is elected president, receives 21,392,190 popular and 444 electoral votes to 15,016,443 popular and 87 electoral votes for Democrat Alfred E. Smith.

Flood Control Act is signed (May 15), provides $325 million for a 10-year flood control program in the Mississippi Valley.

Harry F. Sinclair is acquitted of charges involving his role in Teapot Dome scandal.

Airmail postage rate is set at 5 cents per ounce.

The "Motogram" flashes election returns on the New York Times building for the first time (November 6).

Franklin D. Roosevelt is elected governor of New York.

Bryce Canyon (Utah) National Park is established.

DEATH George W. Goethals, directed construction of Panama Canal.

BUSINESS/INDUSTRY/INVENTIONS

Transamerica Corp. is founded.

DuPont Co. in Wilmington, Delaware, establishes new research laboratory.

Milan Building in San Antonio, Texas, first air-conditioned building in U.S. opens.

Vannevar Bush develops differential analyzer, an early analog computer.

Commercial Cable Co. and Postal Telegraph merge into International Telephone & Telegraph Co.

First training school for fashion models, L'Ecole des Mannequins, opens in Chicago.

Marriott hotel and restaurant chain is founded.

Sears Roebuck opens its first retail store.

DEATH Sara A. M. Conroy, first woman named to national labor post (Secretary-Treasurer, United Textile Workers).

TRANSPORTATION

Merchant Marine Act provides $250 million loan program for ship rebuilding, construction.

Three bridges open: Arthur Kill Cantilever Bridge connects Staten Island and New Jersey; James River Bridge in Virginia, world's longest highway bridge; and Goethals Bridge connects Staten Island and Elizabeth, New Jersey.

Yellow Bus Line begins transcontinental bus service; trip takes 5 days, 14 hours.

Chrysler Corp. acquires Dodge Brothers firm.

First autogiro (helicopter) flies at Pitcairn Field, Willow Grove, Pennsylvania.

Graf Zeppelin flies from Germany to U.S. with 20 passengers.

Amelia Earhart, a passenger, becomes first woman to fly over Atlantic Ocean.

Newark Airport is completed.

SCIENCE/MEDICINE

Dr. George N. Papanicolau develops pap smear test for early detection of cervical cancer.

Dr. Willis R. Whitney constructs diathermy machine for medical use.

Iron lung is used for treatment of polio.

Dr. William H. Park of New York City Health Department develops tuberculosis vaccine.

Mead, Johnson & Co. markets vitamin D.

Clifford W. Beers founds American Foundation for Mental Hygiene.

DEATH Dr. Robert Abbe, first American to use radium in cancer treatment.

EDUCATION

Yeshiva College in New York City is chartered.

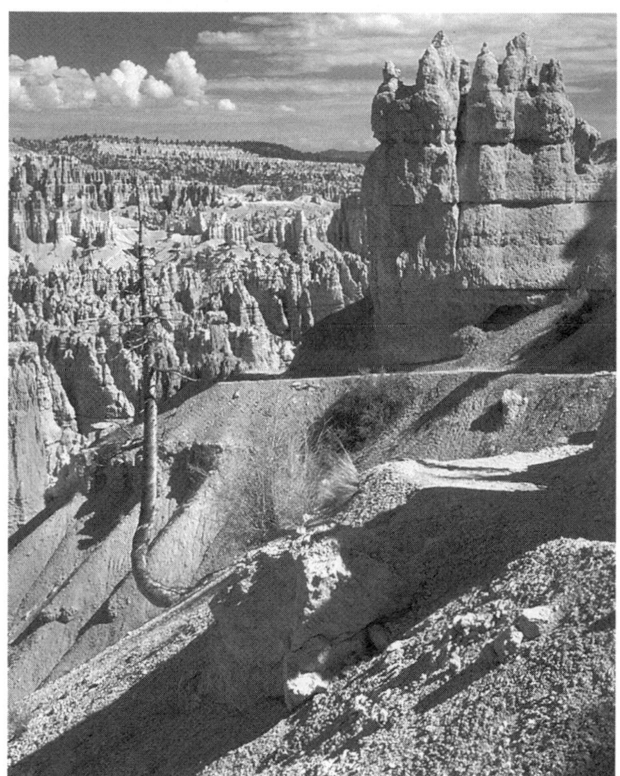

Bryce Canyon, with its unique rock formations, becomes a national park in 1928. © ROBERT J. HUFFMAN/FIELD MARK PUBLICATIONS

RELIGION

Samuel F. Cadman, president, Federal Council of Churches of Christ, becomes first U.S. radio minister.

ART/MUSIC

Arturo Toscanini conducts New York Philharmonic Symphony Orchestra; merger of the Symphony Society and Philharmonic forms this ensemble.

Boston Symphony performs Walter Piston's Symphonic Piece for first time in U.S.

Doris Humphrey and Charles Weidman form ballet company.

Sigmund Romberg's operetta *The New Moon* and Rudolf Friml's *The Three Musketeers* open.

Rudy Vallee forms band.

Thomas Hart Benton completes the painting *Baptism in Kansas.*

SONGS (POPULAR): "Coquette," "I Can't Give You Anything But Love," "I'll Get By," "Lover Come Back to Me," "Marie," "Sonny Boy," "Sweet Sue," "Button Up Your Overcoat," "Sweethearts on Parade," "There's a Rainbow 'Round My Shoulder," "Jeanine, I Dream of Lilac Time."

DEATHS Nora Bayes, singer and actress who was co-author of "Shine On, Harvest Moon"; Henry Gilbert, first composer to rely primarily on American folk music.

LITERATURE/JOURNALISM

President Coolidge dedicates National Press Club in Washington.

BOOKS *Scarlet Sister Mary* by Julia Peterkin, *John Brown's Body* (poetry) by Stephen Vincent Benét, *Coming of Age in Samoa* by Margaret Mead, *Cawdor* (poetry) by Robinson Jeffers, *A Lantern in Her Hand* by Bess Streeter Aldrich, *Good Morning, America* (poetry) by Carl Sandburg.

DEATHS Clarence W. Barron, owner of Dow Jones, founder of *Barron's Weekly;* Edwin T. Meredith, founder and publisher, *Better Homes and Gardens.*

ENTERTAINMENT

Walt Disney releases first cartoon, "Plane Crazy."

First radio broadcast of *Amos 'n Andy* show is aired, is broadcast nationwide in 1929.

March of Time and *Voice of Firestone* radio progams begin.

PLAYS Lynn Fontanne stars in *Strange Interlude,* Lee Tracy in *The Front Page,* Ethel Barrymore in *Kingdom of God,* Eddie Cantor in *Whoopee,* Paul Robeson in *Porgy,* Bert Lahr in *Hold Everything,* Alfred Lunt in *Marco Millions,* Marilyn Miller in *Rosalie,* Will Rogers in *Three Cheers.*

MOVIES *The Actress* with Norma Shearer, *My Man* with Fanny Brice, *Our Dancing Daughters* with Joan Crawford, *The Singing Fool* with Al Jolson.

DEATH Eddy Foy, musical entertainer.

SPORTS

Winter Olympics are held in St. Moritz, Switzerland; U.S. wins two gold medals; Summer Games are held in Amsterdam; U.S. wins 22 gold medals, Peter Desjardins scores two perfect 10s in springboard diving; women's track events are included for first time.

First organized men's field hockey match is played at Germantown (Pennsylvania) Cricket Club.

U.S. Volleyball Assn. is formed.

WINNERS *Auto racing*—Louis Meyer, Indianapolis 500; *Baseball*—New York Yankees, World Series; *Boxing*—Gene Tunney, heavyweight; Andre Routis, featherweight; *Football*—Stanford, Rose Bowl; *Golf*—U.S., Walker Cup; John Farrell, U.S. Open; Leo Diegel, PGA; *Hockey*—New York Rangers, Stanley Cup; *Horse racing*—Reigh Count, Kentucky Derby; Victorian, Preakness Stakes; Vito, Belmont Stakes; *Lawn bowling*—David White, first U.S. singles; *Skeet shooting*—Yale, first college tournament; *Tennis*—France, Davis Cup; Henri Cochet, U.S. Open (men), Helen Wills, U.S. Open (women); *Wrestling*—Ed "Strangler" Lewis, heavyweight.

MISCELLANEOUS

St. Francis Dam at Saugus, California, bursts, floods cause 950 deaths; hurricane moves from Caribbean islands to Florida, causes 4,000 deaths, 1,800 in Florida.

Two-day frog-jumping contest is held for first time in Calaveras County, California.

Jean Lassier goes over Niagara Falls in a rubber ball.

Detroit Zoological Park opens.

1929

INTERNATIONAL

German reparations are reduced to $8.04 billion, payable over 58½ years at 5½% interest; Bank for International Settlements is created.

Canada and U.S. sign convention (agreement) to preserve Niagara Falls (January 2).

NATIONAL

Frank B. Kellogg, Secretary of State (1925–1929), awarded 1929 Nobel Peace Prize for working out the Kellogg-Briand Peace Pact.

Supreme Court upholds presidential pocket veto.

Fire in White House destroys a portion of the executive offices; official papers are saved.

Albert B. Fall, former Interior Secretary, is found guilty of accepting a bribe to grant valuable oil leases in Teapot Dome scandal; is sentenced to a year in prison.

New smaller dollar bills are issued.

Grand Teton (Wyoming) National Park is established.

DEATHS Wyatt Earp, frontier lawman; Francis E. Warren, Wyoming senator known as the father of reclamation.

BUSINESS/INDUSTRY/INVENTIONS

Stock market begins crash (October 29) when 13 million shares are traded, continues for several days; stocks lose $30 million in market value by mid-November; touches off worst depression in U.S. history.

Federal Farm Board is created to promote marketing of farm commodities through cooperatives and stabilization boards (June 15).

Since 1920, installment buying quintuples to $6 billion a year, accounts for 90% of all piano, sewing and washing machine sales; 80% of vacuum, radio, and refrigerator sales; 70% of furniture sales, 60% of auto sales.

Republic Steel Co., R. G. LeTourneau Inc. (heavy equipment maker), and Levitt & Sons, Inc. (home builder) are founded.

Benton & Bowles advertising agency is created.

Business Week magazine begins publication.

First Howard Johnson restaurant opens in Massachusetts.

Indiana enacts tax on chain stores.

Frances Perkins is named New York State Industrial Commissioner.

Violence occurs when police raid a union strike meeting in Gastonia, North Carolina; the Gastonia police chief and seven strikers are killed.

Ford Motor Co. raises daily pay from $6 to $7.

DEATHS Herman Hollerith, inventor of punchcard tabulating system; Minor C. Keith, founder of United Fruit Co.

TRANSPORTATION

Grumman Aircraft Engineering Corp. and Bendix Aviation Corp. are founded.

Several bridges are completed: Brockport Bridge in Paducah (Kentucky); Lake Champlain Bridge, connecting Vermont and New York; Ambassador Bridge at Detroit; Mt. Hope Bridge in Rhode Island.

Richard E. Byrd and Bernt Balchen become first to fly over the South Pole (October 28).

SCIENCE/MEDICINE

Baylor University Hospital inaugurates group hospitalization insurance plan.

Journal of Allergy is published.

Edwin G. Boring writes *History of Experimental Psychology*, major contribution to the field.

DEATHS Joseph Goldberger, physician whose work on pellagra led to its virtual elimination; Robert Ridgway, U.S. National Museum bird curator (1880–1929).

Harlem Jazz

First heard in New Orleans in the early 1900s, jazz became popular in Chicago and New York in the 1920s. In Harlem, the Cotton Club and the enormous Savoy Ballroom dominated the final years of the decade. Louis Armstrong, who helped define jazz as a stage for the solo artist with his impressive performances, played in Harlem. Between 1927 and 1932 the Ellington Band, headed by eminent composer Duke Ellington, resided at the Cotton Club. Although the Cotton Club entertained a whites-only audience and resembled a southern plantation in decor, African-American jazz fans excluded from the famous "supper club" found solace in house-rent parties fashionable during the period. In order to pay the monthly dues, tenants held their own jazz parties, charging a small fee for admission and refreshments. Thursdays and Saturdays proved most popular with dancers and musicians alike. The Savoy meanwhile, boasted a 200 feet by 50 feet dance floor and two bandstands, which became the stage for a regular "Battle of Jazz" feature. Along with a rising interest in black literature and art, jazz became part of the Harlem Renaissance and played a key role in the cultural emancipation of African Americans in 1920s America.

EDUCATION

Morehouse and Spelman colleges merge with Atlanta University to form Atlanta University System.

Robert M. Hutchins becomes president of University of Chicago, the youngest (30) major university president.

DEATHS Charles H. Cooley, founder of U.S. sociology; Willam F. Warren, cofounder and first president, Boston University (1873–1903).

RELIGION

DEATH Charles H. Brent, chief of World War I chaplains in Europe.

ART/MUSIC

New York Philharmonic inaugurates regular Sunday broadcasts.

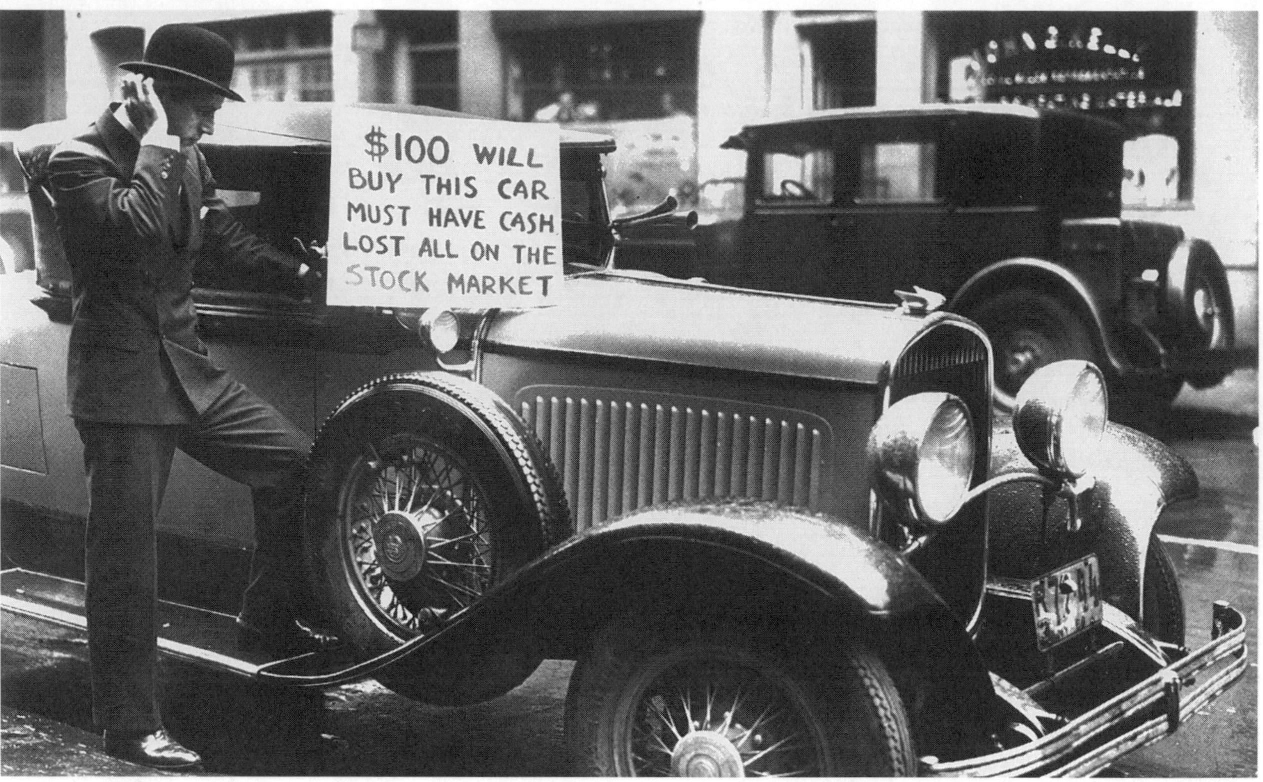

"$100 will buy this car. Must have cash. Lost all on the stock market." Following the stock-market crash of 1929, a dapper young man contemplates his sudden change in circumstances. UPI/CORBIS-BETTMANN

Edgard Varèse founds the Symphony Orchestra in New York City.

Grant Wood completes the painting *Woman with Plants;* Charles Sheeler, *Upper Deck;* Arthur G. Dove, *Fog Horns.*

Baltimore Museum of Art opens.

SONGS (POPULAR): "Ain't Misbehavin'," "Am I Blue?," "Honeysuckle Rose," "Mean to Me," "Pagan Love Song," "Singin' in the Rain," "With a Song in My Heart," "Love, Your Magic Spell Is Everywhere," "More Than You Know," "Basin Street Blues," "Stardust."

DEATH Robert Henri, artist and teacher who influenced American art.

LITERATURE/JOURNALISM

H. V. Kaltenborn becomes chief news commentator for Columbia Broadcasting System.

Ellery Queen, a pseudonym of Frederic Dannay and Manfred B. Lee, begins to write with *The Roman Hat Mystery.*

The Embassy, a newsreel theater, opens in New York City.

BOOKS *Magnificent Obsession* by Lloyd C. Douglas, *A Farewell to Arms* by Ernest Hemingway, *Laughing Boy* by Oliver La Farge, *Selected Poems* by Conrad Aiken, *Dodsworth* by Sinclair Lewis, *Look Homeward, Angel* by Thomas Wolfe, *The Sound and the Fury* by William Faulkner, *Blue Juniata* by Malcolm Cowley, *Rome Haul* by Walter D. Edmonds.

ENTERTAINMENT

Bell Telephone Laboratories demonstrate color television.

Alexander Woollcott hosts his weekly *Town Crier* radio show; *The Goldbergs* radio show airs.

Gypsy Rose Lee begins her burlesque career.

PLAYS Leslie Howard stars in *Berkeley Square,* Jack Haley in *Follow Through,* Humphrey Bogart in *It's a Wise Child,* Helen Morgan in *Sweet Adeline,* Marc Connelly's *The Green Pastures* is produced.

MOVIES *Disraeli* with George Arliss, *Sunny Side Up* with Janet Gaynor, *The Virginian* with Gary Cooper, *The Vagabond Lover* with Rudy Vallee, *The Iron Mask* with Douglas Fairbanks.

SPORTS

Babe Ruth hits 500th home run.

Ernie Nevers of Chicago Cardinals rushes for record six touchdowns, adds four extra points.

Ely Culbertson publishes magazine, *Bridge World.*

Dr. William E. Code invents codeball, combination of golf and soccer.

WINNERS *Auto racing*—Ray Keech, Indianapolis 500; *Baseball*—Philadelphia Athletics, World Series; *Boxing*—Chris (Battling) Battalino, featherweight; *Football*—Georgia Tech, Rose Bowl; Green Bay, first NFL title; *Golf*—Great Britain, Ryder Cup; Bobby Jones, U.S. Open; Leo Diegel, PGA; *Hockey*—Boston, Stanley Cup; *Horse racing*—Clyde Van Dusen, Kentucky Derby; Dr. Freeland, Preakness Stakes; Blue Larkspur, Belmont Stakes; *Tennis*—France, Davis Cup; Bill Tilden, U.S. Open (men); Helen Wills, U.S. Open (women); *Wrestling*—Gus Sonnenberg, heavyweight.

DEATH Tex Rickard, boxing promoter.

MISCELLANEOUS

St. Valentine's Day massacre occurs in Chicago when a rival gang executes seven gangsters in a garage.

Poisonous fumes from burning X-ray film kill 125 in Crile Hospital, Cleveland, Ohio.

Chrysler Building in New York City, then world's tallest, is completed.

The Seeing Eye, for training guide dogs, is incorporated.

Mine disaster at Mather, Pennsylvania, kills 195.

1930

INTERNATIONAL

London Naval Conference results in agreement among U.S., Great Britain, and Japan on cruiser limitations, ratios for all vessels (April 22); Senate ratifies (July 21).

NATIONAL

President Herbert Hoover asks for, receives $116 million for emergency construction projects to aid the unemployed, $45 million for drought relief; unemployment reaches 4.5 million.

Former President Taft resigns as Supreme Court Chief Justice (February 3) because of poor health; Charles Evans Hughes succeeds him; Taft dies March 8.

Fifteenth census reports population at 123,202,624.

Annual immigration to U.S. totals 241,700; it drops to under 100,000 until after World War II.

National debt is reduced to $16.1 billion.

Veterans Administration is created (July 3); Bureau of Prisons is established.

Construction of Boulder (later Hoover) Dam begins.

USS *Constitution* ("Old Ironsides"), reconditioned by public subscription, is relaunched.

Carlsbad (New Mexico) National Park is established.

Streamlined submarine *Nautilus* is commissioned.

DEATHS Irving Hale, founder of Veterans of Foreign Wars (VFW); Tasker H. Bliss, World War I Army chief of staff; Stephen T. Maher, first National Park Service director.

BUSINESS/INDUSTRY/INVENTIONS

Thomas Midgley of General Motors announces development of refrigerant Freon.

Butler Consolidated Coal Co., Wildwood (Pennsylvania) plant, opens with 100% mechanical operation.

Use of reflector seismograph results in discovery of Edwards (Oklahoma) oil field; East Texas oil field is tapped for first time.

Bank of the United States (New York City) closes; about 1,300 banks close between late 1929 and summer of 1930; 827 more close in September and October.

David Sarnoff begins 17 years as president of RCA.

DEATHS Dorr E. Felt, inventor of first wholly key-operated calculator; Henry E. House, inventor of buttonholing machine; Henry C. Folger, oil company executive, endower of Shakespeare library; Daniel Guggenheim, industrialist who created philanthropic and aeronautics foundations; Elmer A. Sperry, inventor of gyrocompass.

TRANSPORTATION

Maritime Administration is established.

Braniff Airlines and Greyhound Corp. are established.

Thomas Edison runs first electric passenger train experimentally from Hoboken to Montclair, New Jersey.

Motor Car Transport Co. is founded; later becomes Commercial Carriers Inc.

Jimmy Doolittle, military aviator, makes first successful test of a blind, instrument-controlled landing.

Passenger-car registrations total 26,545,281.

First airline stewardess, Ellen Church, flies on United Airlines from San Francisco to Cheyenne, Wyoming.

Detroit-Windsor Tunnel under the Detroit River opens.

Mid-Hudson Bridge at Poughkeepsie, New York, and Longview (Washington) Bridge over Columbia River open.

Unemployed people try to sell apples for 5 cents during the Great Depression. AP/WIDE WORLD PHOTOS

SCIENCE/MEDICINE

Karl Landsteiner is awarded Nobel Prize for physiology/medicine for work on blood groups.

DuPont Co. produces sulfanilamide.

Clyde W. Tombaugh of Lowell Observatory (Flagstaff, Arizona) discovers the planet Pluto (February 18); astronomers make first photograph of the planet.

Woods Hole (Massachusetts) Oceanographical Institute is established.

Ernest O. Lawrence constructs first cyclotron.

Adler Planetarium in Chicago opens.

Radar is first used to detect airplanes.

Drs. Fred Allison and Edgar J. Murphy discover element 87, francium.

Mental Hygiene International Congress meets in Washington, D.C., 3,000 from 53 countries attending.

DEATH Samuel Theobald, ophthalmologist who introduced use of boric acid for eye diseases.

EDUCATION

Abraham Flexner, organizer of Institute for Advanced Study at Princeton University, is named its first director.

Robert G. Sproul becomes president of University of California; Karl T. Compton of MIT.

DEATH Arthur T. Hadley, president of Yale University (1899–1921).

RELIGION

Merger of Buffalo Lutheran and Iowa and Ohio Evangelical Lutheran synods forms American Lutheran church; *International Lutheran Hour* broadcasts on 36-station radio network, Dr. Walter A. Maier is speaker.

Sarah E. Dickson of Milwaukee becomes first woman Presbyterian elder.

Jesse E. Bader begins 33 years as president and general secretary of World Convention of Churches of Christ (Disciples).

Rev. Fulton Sheen preaches regularly on NBC radio's *Catholic Hour.*

Rev. Henry K. Sherrill becomes Episcopal bishop of Massachusetts.

ART/MUSIC

Sculptor Gutzon Borglum unveils the first of four 60-foot-high heads of presidents (Washington) carved out of rock in Mt. Rushmore in Black Hills (South Dakota).

An American family tunes in to a radio program during the 1930s. **AP/WIDE WORLD PHOTOS**

Arthur Fiedler founds Boston Pops Orchestra.

Walter Piston composes Suite for Orchestra; Aaron Copland, Piano Variations.

Grant Wood completes his most famous painting, *American Gothic;* George B. Luks, *Mrs. Gamely;* Sculptor George G. Bernard finishes the marble *Refugee.*

SONGS (POPULAR): "Beyond the Blue Horizon," "Body and Soul," "Little White Lies," "Three Little Words," "I've Got Rhythm," "Old Rockin' Chair," "Ten Cents a Dance," "Georgia on My Mind," "Bidin' My Time," "On the Sunny Side of the Street."

Ringling Museum of Art in Sarasota, Florida, opens.

DEATH Preston Dickinson, modern art pioneer.

LITERATURE/JOURNALISM

Sinclair Lewis becomes first U.S. writer to win Nobel Prize for literature for his novels.

Henry B. Luce founds *Fortune,* monthly magazine.

Lowell Thomas newscasts for CBS, serves more than 40 years.

Chic Young draws comic strip "Blondie."

BOOKS *Cimarron* by Edna Ferber, *Years of Grace* by Margaret Ayer Barnes, *Collected Poems* by Robert Frost, *The Deepening Stream* by Dorothy Canfield Fisher, *Arundel* by Kenneth Roberts, *The Maltese Falcon* by Dashiell Hammett, *N by E* by Rockwell Kent, *New Found Land* (poetry) by Archibald MacLeish, *The Woman of Andros* by Thornton Wilder, *Flowering Judas* by Katherine Anne Porter.

DEATHS Clare A. Briggs, cartoonist ("When a Feller Needs a Friend"); Edward Stratemeyer, author *(Rover Boys, Tom Swift, Bobbsey Twins)* under various pseudonyms; George P. Putnam, founder and head of family publishing firm (1872–1930).

ENTERTAINMENT

Americans own 13 million radio sets.

Arthur Godfrey announces on radio in Washington; Walter Winchell begins his radio gossip program.

PLAYS Alfred Lunt and Lynn Fontanne star in *Elizabeth the Queen,* Ethel Merman in *Girl Crazy* by the Gershwins, Ethel Waters in *Blackbirds,* Bert Lahr in *Flying High,* Spencer Tracy in *The Last Mile.*

MOVIES *Abraham Lincoln* with Walter Huston, *The Green Goddess* with George Arliss, *Min and Bill* with Marie Dressler and Wallace Beery, *Whoopee* with Eddie Cantor, *Morocco* with Marlene Dietrich and Gary Cooper, *Hell's Angels* with Jean Harlow, *Little Caesar* with Edward G. Robinson, *Cimarron* with

Richard Dix, *All Quiet on the Western Front* with Lew Ayres. Donald Duck makes his screen debut.

New radio programs include *Rin Tin Tin, Ripley's Believe It or Not, Death Valley Days,* and Kate Smith's show.

DEATH Lon Chaney, screen actor ("the man of a thousand faces").

SPORTS

Bobby Jones wins U.S. amateur golf tournament, becomes first (and only) golfer to win U.S. and British Opens, U.S. and British amateur titles in same year; is awarded first Sullivan Medal as year's outstanding amateur athlete.

Stella Walsh becomes first woman to run 100 yards in less than 11 seconds (10.8 sec.)

WINNERS *Auto racing*—Billy Arnold, Indianapolis 500; *Baseball*—Philadelphia Athletics, World Series; *Boxing*—Max Schmeling, heavyweight; Maxie Rosenbloom, light heavyweight; Tony Canzoneri, lightweight; Baby Arizmendi, featherweight; *Football*—Southern California, Rose Bowl; Green Bay, NFL title; *Golf*—U.S., Walker Cup; Bobby Jones, U.S. Open; Tommy Armour, PGA; *Harness racing*—Hanover's Bertha, Hambletonian; *Hockey*—Montreal, Stanley Cup; *Horse racing*—Gallant Fox wins Kentucky Derby, Preakness Stakes, and Belmont Stakes to become second Triple Crown winner; *Marathon*—Clarence De Mar, Boston Marathon for seventh time; *Tennis*—France, Davis Cup; John Doeg, U.S. Open (men); Betty Nuttall, U.S. Open (women); *Yachting*—U.S. boat *Enterprise* retains America's Cup.

MISCELLANEOUS

Fire in Ohio Penitentiary in Columbus kills 320.

Judge Joseph F. Crater of New York State Supreme Court vanishes mysteriously; no trace of him is ever found.

Empire State Building, then the world's tallest, is completed.

In & Outdoor Games Co. of Chicago manufactures pinball game machine.

1931

INTERNATIONAL

President Herbert Hoover calls for a one-year moratorium on interallied debts and reparations because of universal economic crisis (June 20); is generally accepted.

NATIONAL

Congress designates "Star-Spangled Banner" as the national anthem (March 3).

President Hoover sends Congress the Wickersham Report on prohibition; calls for revisions of law but opposes repeal of Eighteenth Amendment; Supreme Court upholds constitutionality of the amendment.

Overriding a presidential veto, Congress authorizes improvement of veterans' bonus benefits.

Smoot-Hawley Tariff raises rates on agricultural raw materials from 38% to 49%, other commodities from 31% to 34%, gives special protection to sugar and textiles.

Jane Addams of Chicago's Hull House and Dr. Nicholas Murray Butler, president of Columbia University, share Nobel Peace Prize for their work toward international peace.

Civil government is established in the Virgin Islands.

Gangster Al Capone is found guilty of tax evasion, is sentenced to 11 years.

Representative Maria Norton of New Jersey becomes first woman chair of a congressional committee.

The keel is laid for first aircraft carrier, the *Ranger.*

BUSINESS/INDUSTRY/INVENTIONS

Vladimir K. Zworykin, RCA research head, invents the iconoscope, which makes all-electronic television possible.

DuPont Co. manufactures synthetic rubber (neoprene); fiberglass is introduced.

Wilcox's Pier Restaurant, West Haven, Connecticut, installs a "magic eye" (photoelectric cell) to operate a door.

Robert Van de Graaff builds first electrostatic generator.

Caterpillar Tractor Co. produces first diesel-powered tractor.

Schick, Inc. produces electric dry shavers.

Sears, Roebuck founds All-State Insurance Co.

ATT begins commercial teletype service.

Henry J. Kaiser organizes group of contractors, the Six Companies, to build Boulder (Hoover) Dam; it is completed in 1936, two years ahead of schedule.

Unemployment is estimated between 4 and 5 million.

DEATHS Thomas A. Edison, inventor; Edward G. Acheson, discoverer of silicon carbide (carborundum); Isaac Gimbel, department store cofounder; George Eastman, camera and film developer.

As the Depression continues, people gather outside a bank where their money has been lost. **CORBIS-BETTMANN/HULTON-DEUTSCH COLLECTION**

TRANSPORTATION

Wiley Post and Harold Getty complete round-the-world flight in 8 days, 16 hours; Clyde Pangborn and Hugh Herndon Jr. complete first nonstop flight across Pacific Ocean.

First transcontinental helicopter flight begins May 14 in Philadelphia; is completed May 28 in San Diego.

Piper Cub airplane is introduced.

Four bridges are completed: George Washington over Hudson River at New York City; St. John's at Portland, Oregon; Maysville (Kentucky) over the Ohio River; and Bayonne, New Jersey, over the Kill van Kull.

SCIENCE/MEDICINE

Harold C. Urey announces discovery of heavy hydrogen, a hydrogen atom of double weight (deuterium) (December 29).

Langley (Virginia) Research Center of National Advisory Committee for Aeronautics places full-scale wind tunnel in operation.

Elk City, Oklahoma, dedicates first community hospital (August 13).

DEATHS George A. Dorsey, anthropologist and author *(Why We Behave Like Human Beings);* Albert A. Michelson, first American to win Nobel Prize in physics.

EDUCATION

Municipal College for Negroes opens as part of University of Louisville (Kentucky).

Pitrim A. Sorokin begins 25 years as first chair of Harvard University sociology department.

DEATHS Melvil Dewey, librarian who originated decimal classification system; John W. Burgess, father of U.S. political science.

RELIGION

Merger of Christian and Congregational denominations forms General Council of Congregational and Christian Churches.

Park Ave. Baptist Church (New York City) becomes the interdenominational Riverside Church; Harry Emerson Fosdick is pastor.

Jehovah's Witnesses becomes new name of Adventist sect known as Russellites or International Bible Students.

First Baha'i house of worship opens in Wilmette, Illinois.

The films of the Marx Brothers—Groucho, Zeppo, Chico, and Harpo—are wildly popular during the 1930s. **THE KOBAL COLLECTION**

ART/MUSIC

Metropolitan Opera presents Deems Taylor's opera *Peter Ibbetson;* broadcasts full performance of *Hansel and Gretel* for the first time.

Ferde Grofé completes the *Grand Canyon* Suite; Robert Russell Bennett the symphony *Abraham Lincoln.*

Ruth St. Denis founds the Society of Spiritual Arts, which attempts to demonstrate the potential of dance as a form of worship.

Lily Pons joins Metropolitan Opera Co.

Walt Kuhn completes the painting *Blue Clown;* Georgia O'Keeffe, *Cow's Skull: Red, White and Blue;* Alexander Calder completes the mobile *Dancing Torpedo Shape.*

Whitney Museum of American Art (New York City) and Joslyn Art Museum (Omaha, Nebraska) open.

SONGS (POPULAR): "All of Me," "Dancing in the Dark," "Goodnight, Sweetheart," "I Surrender, Dear," "Lazy River," "Love Letters in the Sand," "Minnie the Moocher," "Mood Indigo," "Wrap Your Troubles in Dreams," "Got a Date with an Angel."

DEATHS Leon ("Bix") Beiderbecke, jazz cornetist; Buddy Bolden, legendary creator of New Orleans jazz; Daniel C. French, sculptor (seated Lincoln in Memorial); Henry O. Tanner, painter of biblical scenes.

LITERATURE/JOURNALISM

Roy Howard buys *New York World,* merges it with *Telegram* to form *World-Telegram.*

Walter Lippmann writes syndicated newspaper column "Today and Tomorrow"; Emily Post writes her column on etiquette.

Chester Gould draws comic strip "Dick Tracy" in *Chicago Tribune.*

Story, a monthly magazine, begins publication.

BOOKS *The Good Earth* by Pearl Buck, *Shadows on the Rock* by Willa Cather, *Sanctuary* by William Faulkner, *John Henry* by Roark Bradford, *Back Street* by Fannie Hurst, *Guys and Dolls* by Damon Runyon, *Grand Hotel* by Vicki Baum.

DEATHS William L. McLean, publisher, *Philadelphia Bulletin* (1895–1931); Edward Channing, historian; Vachel Lindsay, poet.

ENTERTAINMENT

PLAYS Fred and Adele Astaire star in *The Band Wagon,* Katharine Cornell in *The Barretts of Wimpole Street,* Paul Muni in *Counsellor-at-Law,* Paul Robeson in *The Hairy Ape,* Alfred Lunt and Lynn Fontanne in *Reunion in Vienna,* Ethel Waters in *Rhapsody in Black.*

Easy Aces radio program debuts; Emmett Kelly begins his career as the clown Weary Willie.

MOVIES *City Lights* with Charles Chaplin, *The Champ* with Wallace Beery, *The Sin of Madelon Claudet* with Helen Hayes, *Dr. Jekyll and Mr. Hyde* with Fredric March, *Mata Hari* with Greta Garbo, *Street Scene* with Sylvia Sidney, *Dracula* with Bela Lugosi, *Monkey Business* with the Marx Brothers.

DEATH David Belasco, playwright and producer.

SPORTS

Will Harridge, American (baseball) League secretary-treasurer since 1911, is named president.

Ely Culbertson and partner win bridge battle of century, defeat Sidney Lenz and partner, 77 rubbers to 73.

WINNERS *Auto racing*—Louis Schneider, Indianapolis 500; *Baseball*—St. Louis Cardinals, World Series; *Boxing*—Max Schmeling, heavyweight; Lou Brouillard, welterweight; *Football*—Alabama, Rose Bowl; Green Bay, NFL title; *Golf*—U.S., Ryder Cup; William Burke, U.S. Open; Tom Creavy, PGA; *Gymnastics*—Roberta C. Rauck, first national woman's all-round title; *Hockey*—Montreal, Stanley Cup; *Horse racing*—Twenty Grand, Kentucky Derby and Belmont Stakes; Mate, Preakness Stakes; *Table tennis*—Marcus Schussheim, first national title; *Tennis*—Ellsworth Vines, U.S. Open (men); Helen Wills (Moody), U.S. Open (women).

DEATHS Knute Rockne, Notre Dame football coach, in plane crash; Charles A. Comiskey, baseball player and owner, Chicago White Sox (1900–1931); first two presidents of baseball's American League, Byron (Ban) Johnson and Ernest S. Barnard.

MISCELLANEOUS

Original mosque of Temple of Islam (Black Muslims) opens in Detroit; Elijah Muhammad becomes movement's leader.

1932

INTERNATIONAL

Scheduled Lausanne Conference to discuss remaining German reparations is cancelled.

NATIONAL

Depression reaches new low with monthly wages 60% below 1929 average; more than 5,000 banks close; business losses are reported at $6 billion; average monthly unemployment is 12 million.

After becoming the first woman to fly across the Atlantic Ocean as a passenger in 1928, Amelia Earhart sets her own transatlantic record in 1932. U.S. INFORMATION AGENCY

Reconstruction Finance Corp. (RFC) is created (January 22) to provide emergency financing for various businesses; Charles G. Dawes is director; RFC is liberalized (July 21) to include agriculture; Federal Home Loan Bank Board is established (July 22).

Franklin D. Roosevelt, Democrat, is elected president by 22,809,638 popular and 472 electoral votes to President Herbert Hoover's 15,758,901 popular and 59 electoral votes; Roosevelt breaks tradition by appearing in person to accept Democratic nomination; the term *New Deal* is first used in that speech. He said, "I pledge you, I pledge myself, to a New Deal for the American people."

Twentieth Amendment is submitted to states for ratification; provides for Congress to convene January 3, presidential inauguration January 20; both traditionally in March.

About 1,000 veterans arrive in Washington (May 29) to urge cash payment of their bonus; "bonus army" grows to 17,000; a bonus bill fails to pass, but money is provided to pay vets for trip home; 2,000 elect to stay until forced out by police and army (July 28).

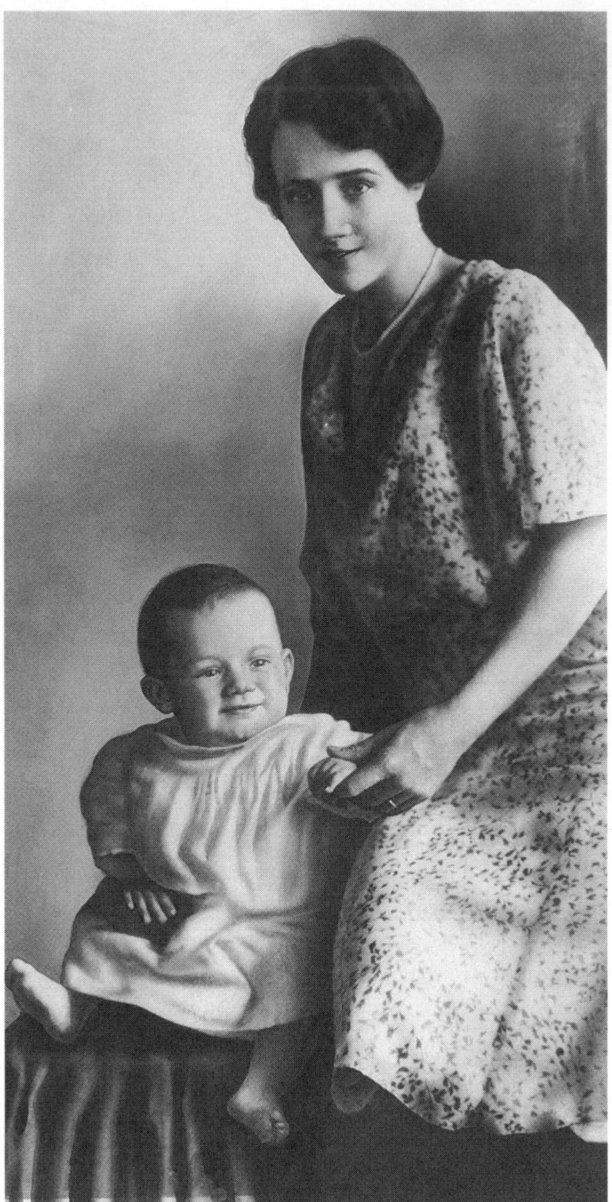

Anne Morrow Lindbergh, wife of famed aviator Charles A. Lindbergh, with toddler Charles Jr., who is kidnapped. The media dub it "The Crime of the Century." **CORBIS-BETTMANN**

Wisconsin enacts first unemployment insurance act.

Tomb of the Unknown Soldier in Arlington National Cemetery (Virginia) is dedicated.

Cost of first-class postage rises to 3 cents an ounce.

Mrs. Hattie W. Caraway of Arkansas becomes first woman elected to U.S. Senate.

Cornerstone is laid for new Supreme Court building.

DEATHS Robert S. Brookings, a founder and benefactor, Brookings Institution; Enoch H. Crowder, World War I Selective Service director; Charles E. Ashburner, first U.S. city manager.

BUSINESS/INDUSTRY/INVENTIONS

Norris-LaGuardia Act prohibits use of injunctions in labor disputes.

David Dubinsky begins 34 years as president of International Ladies Garment Workers Union.

Revlon Inc., cosmetics and fragrance firm, is founded.

William N. Goodwin Jr. patents camera exposure meter.

DEATHS King C. Gillette, safety razor inventor; John J. Carty, engineer who helped develop telephone switchboard; Paul M. Warburg, banker who helped plan Federal Reserve; Julius Rosenwald, Sears executive and philanthropist; Reginald A. Fessenden, inventor of high-frequency alternator; William Wrigley Jr., chewing-gum manufacturer.

TRANSPORTATION

Amelia Earhart becomes first woman to fly solo across Atlantic Ocean (May 20).

Federal gasoline tax of 1 cent per gallon is enacted.

Beech Aircraft Co. is founded; Robert E. Gross purchases Lockheed Aircraft Co. for $40,000.

Auguste Piccard reaches an altitude of more than 55,000 feet in a pressurized balloon.

DEATHS Henry M. Leland, developer of first eight-cylinder engine; Robert Dollar, shipping-line founder.

SCIENCE/MEDICINE

Irving Langmuir is awarded Nobel Prize in chemistry for discoveries in surface chemistry.

Karl G. Jansky determines source of radio waves from outside solar system, begins radio astronomy.

Charles G. King isolates vitamin C.

Yellow-fever vaccine for humans is announced.

Sonic locator, measuring water depth with sound waves, is developed.

DEATH William W. Keen, first U.S. brain surgeon.

EDUCATION

Folger Shakespeare Memorial Library in Washington, D.C., opens.

RELIGION

Norman Vincent Peale becomes pastor of Marble Collegiate Church in New York City.

DEATH Rev. Francis P. (Father) Duffy, chaplain of 165th Infantry in Mexico and Europe.

ART/MUSIC

War Memorial Opera House in San Francisco opens with *Tosca.*

PAINTINGS John Steuart Curry, *Flying Codonàs;* Edward Hopper, *Room in Brooklyn;* Robert Laurent, *Goose Girl;* Thomas Hart Benton, *Cotton Pickers;* Georgia O'Keeffe, *Stables.*

SONGS (POPULAR): "April in Paris," "Brother, Can You Spare a Dime?," "I'm Gettin' Sentimental over You," "Night and Day," "Have You Ever Been Lonely?," "I Surrender, Dear," "I've Got the World on a String," "Lullaby of the Leaves," "One Hour with You," "Try a Little Tenderness," "You're an Old Smoothie."

LITERATURE/JOURNALISM

Teletype Corp. produces its first machine.

Drew Pearson and Robert Allen write "Washington Merry-Go-Round" column.

BOOKS *Tobacco Road* by Erskine Caldwell, *Conquistador* (poetry) by Archibald MacLeish, *Death in the Afternoon* by Ernest Hemingway, *Life Begins at Forty* by Walter B. Pitkin, *Mutiny on the Bounty* by James Hall and Charles B. Nordhoff.

DEATHS Charles W. Chesnutt, first African-American novelist *(Conjure Woman).*

ENTERTAINMENT

PLAYS Leslie Howard stars in *Animal Kingdom,* Ethel Merman in *Take a Chance,* Fred Astaire in Cole Porter's *The Gay Divorce,* Ina Claire in *Biography.*

MOVIES *Grand Hotel* with John Barrymore and Greta Garbo, *A Farewell to Arms* with Helen Hayes and Gary Cooper, *Back Street* with Irene Dunne, *Rebecca of Sunnybrook Farm* with Mary Pickford, *Smilin' Through* with Norma Shearer, *Scarface* with Paul Muni.

New radio shows and personalities include Bing Crosby, Fred Allen, Fred Waring, George Burns and Gracie Allen, Jack Benny, and *One Man's Family.*

Radio City Music Hall in New York City opens; Palace Theater closes as a vaudeville house, becomes movie theater.

DEATHS Minnie Maddern Fiske, actress; Chauncey Olcott, singer, actor, and composer ("My Wild Irish Rose"); Florenz Ziegfeld, theatrical producer; Leonard T. Troland, invented multicolor process for movies.

SPORTS

Winter Olympic Games are held in Lake Placid, New York; U.S. wins 10 gold medals; Summer Games are held in Los Angeles, U.S. wins 16 golds, 9 in swimming.

John McGraw resigns as manager of New York Giants baseball team after 31 years.

Lou Gehrig of New York Yankees becomes first American Leaguer to hit four consecutive home runs.

Hialeah racetrack in Miami, Florida, uses first totalisator (tote board) to record track bets and odds.

WINNERS *Auto racing*—Fred Frame, Indianapolis 500; *Baseball*—New York Yankees, World Series; *Boxing*—Jack Sharkey, heavyweight; Jackie Fields, welterweight; *Football*—Southern California, Rose Bowl; Chicago Bears, NFL; *Golf*—U.S., Walker Cup;

Georgia O'Keeffe, *Cow's Skull with Calico Roses*

Famed for her independent spirit, Georgia O'Keeffe (1887–1986) is one of America's most cherished and enigmatic artists. Her career spanned six decades, and her work as an early American modernist painter is characterized by its clean, fresh colors and profound appreciation of nature. O'Keeffe grew up in Wisconsin and studied art from an early age. Her floral paintings and New York cityscapes gained attention in the 1920s thanks to the efforts of exhibitor and photographer Alfred Stieglitz (whom she later married). In 1929 O'Keeffe began spending summers in New Mexico, and she permanently relocated there in 1946. She became fascinated with the sun-bleached bones littered across the deserts of the Southwest. Her famous *Cow's Skull with Calico Roses*(1932) shows a white skull with roses placed at its right horn and nose. Although this and other desert-inspired canvases have been interpreted as a comment on death and declining creativity, O'Keeffe herself related how "bones are as beautiful as anything I know. To me they are strangely more living than the animals walking around—hair, eyes and all, with their tails switching. The bones seem to cut sharply to the center of something that is keenly alive on the desert even though it is vast and empty and untouchable."

Gene Sarazen, U.S. Open; Olin Dutra, PGA; *Hockey*—Toronto, Stanley Cup; *Horse racing*—Burgoo King, Kentucky Derby and Preakness Stakes; Faireno, Belmont Stakes; *Tennis*—France, Davis Cup; Ellsworth Vines, U.S. Open (men); Helen Jacobs, U.S. Open (women).

DEATH Nat(haniel W.) Niles, pioneer U.S. figure skater.

MISCELLANEOUS

Two-year-old son of Charles and Anne Lindbergh is kidnapped from their New Jersey home; is later found murdered; a carpenter, Bruno Hauptmann, is convicted, executed for crime.

Series of tornadoes in Alabama kill 268.

New York City Mayor Jimmy Walker, charged with corruption, resigns.

1933

INTERNATIONAL

U.S. recognizes U.S.S.R; William C. Bullitt is named ambassador (November 16).

Congress passes law providing independence for Philippine Islands after 12 years (January 13); reserved right to military bases is later modified.

U.S. Marines withdraw from Nicaragua (January 2) after nearly eight years' stay.

American nations sign treaty of nonaggression and conciliation; is ratified by Senate.

Ruth Bryan Owen (Rohde), daughter of William Jennings Bryan, becomes first U.S. woman diplomatic representative (minister to Denmark) (April 12).

NATIONAL

An assassin shoots at President-Elect Franklin D. Roosevelt in Florida, hits Chicago Mayor Anton J. Cermak (February 15); Cermak dies March 6; Joseph Zangara, convicted assassin, is electrocuted (March 20).

President Roosevelt at his inauguration (March 4) states: "The only thing we have to fear is fear itself"; pledges a "good neighbor" policy in world affairs.

For the 100 days between March 9 and June 16, a great many steps are taken by president and Congress to help nation's economy (see also Business and Transportation categories).

President Roosevelt uses the "fireside chat" on radio, tries to keep nation advised of federal actions.

Economy Act (March 20) cuts federal salaries 15%, reduces veterans' pensions, reorganizes government agencies; Volstead Act (Prohibition) is modified (March 22) to permit 3.2% wine and beer; Civilian Conservation Corps (CCC) is created (March 31) to provide 250,000 jobs for unemployed 18–25-year-old men; first camp opens near Luray, Virginia (April 17).

Federal Emergency Relief Administration is created (May 12) to help states with $500 million for relief; Public Works Administration is established (June 16); Federal Surplus Relief Corp. is founded (October 4); Civil Works Administration is created as an unemployment relief program (November 9).

Twenty-first Amendment repealing the Eighteenth (Prohibition) Amendment, goes into effect (December 5).

National debt stands at $22.2 billion.

Francis E. Townsend devises plan for national sales tax with which to pay all retirees $200 per month in scrip, all to be spent within the month.

Francis Perkins, new Secretary of Labor, becomes first woman cabinet member; Eleanor Roosevelt conducts first press conference by a First Lady; Mrs. Nellie Tayloe Ross, first woman governor (Wyoming), becomes first woman to serve as director of U.S. Mint.

Twentieth ("Lame Duck") Amendment is ratified (February 6); called for presidential inauguration January 20 (rather than March); Congress to begin term January 3.

First aircraft carrier *(Ranger)* is launched (February 25).

Admiral William D. Leahy becomes first White House chief of staff, serves until 1949.

DEATH Former President Calvin Coolidge (1923–1929).

BUSINESS/INDUSTRY/INVENTIONS

President Roosevelt proclaims four-day bank holiday (March 6) (most banks already closed by state actions), permits use of scrip, embargoes export of gold, silver, and currency; three-fourths of the banks open March 12.

Farm Credit Administration (March 27) authorizes refinancing farm mortgages at low interest (effective June 16); U.S. officially abandons gold standard (April 19), Congress ratifies action (June 5).

Agricultural Adjustment Act is approved to restore purchasing power of farmers (May 12); Tennessee Valley Authority (TVA) is created to build dams and power plants to improve economy of the area (May 18).

Federal Securities Act (May 27) requires full disclosure of information on new securities.

The defeated Herbert Hoover accompanies Franklin D. Roosevelt to his presidential inauguration. HULTON ARCHIVE/GETTY IMAGES

Federal Savings and Loan Association is authorized (June 13), with first S&L created in Miami (August 8).

Home Owners Loan Corp. is authorized to refinance nonfarm home mortgages (June 13); Federal Deposit Insurance Corp. is created (June 16) to guarantee bank deposits under $5,000.

Congress passes National Industrial Recovery Act, gives federal government control of industry through codes (June 16); the Blue Eagle becomes the NIRA symbol.

National Labor Board is created (August 5); Commodity Credit Corp. is founded (October 16) to help handle agricultural and other commodities; Wages and Hours Act goes into effect, sets minimum wages and maximum weekly hours; seven states pass minimum wage laws.

First "sit-down" strike occurs at Hormel & Co. plant in Austin, Minnesota (November 13).

DEATHS Louis C. Tiffany, developer of Tiffany glass; Edward N. Hurley, founder of pneumatic tool industry.

TRANSPORTATION

Emergency Railroad Transportation Act provides for reorganization of the industry (June 16).

Wiley Post flies solo around the world in 7 days, 18 hours.

Great Lakes-Gulf Waterway between Chicago and New Orleans is completed (June 21).

Construction begins on Golden Gate Bridge; University Bridge in Seattle opens.

SCIENCE/MEDICINE

Thomas H. Morgan is awarded Nobel Prize for physiology/medicine for discoveries on role of chromosomes in heredity.

First large-scale cyclotron ("atom smasher") is developed under direction of its inventor, Ernest O. Lawrence at University of California.

Physicist Carl D. Anderson artificially produces a subatomic particle, the positron, by gamma-ray bombardment.

Dr. Evarts Graham in St. Louis performs first lung removal.

Scientist Albert Einstein arrives from Germany to make his home in Princeton, New Jersey.

EDUCATION

James Bryant Conant begins 20 years as president of Harvard University.

Leonard Bloomfield writes *Language,* an important contribution to linguistics.

Five thousand Chicago schoolteachers, paid in scrip, storm banks for 10 months' back pay.

DEATH John G. Hibben, president of Princeton University (1912–1932).

ART/MUSIC

Diego Rivera and Ben Shahn complete series of murals, *Man at the Crossroads,* in Rockefeller Center; John Flanagan completes the sculpture *Dragon Motif.*

Seattle Art Museum opens.

Aaron Copland composes Short Symphony.

Jazz singer Billie Holiday ("Lady Day") makes first recordings.

Jimmy and Tommy Dorsey form band.

SONGS (POPULAR): "Easter Parade," "It's Only a Paper Moon," "The Last Roundup," "Lazy Bones," "Shuffle Off to Buffalo," "Smoke Gets in Your Eyes," "Sophisticated Lady," "Stormy Weather," "Who's Afraid of the Big Bad Wolf?," "I Like Mountain Music," "Let's Fall in Love," "Maria Elena," "Did You Ever See a Dream Walking?"

LITERATURE/JOURNALISM

Long legal battle ends when Bennett Cerf succeeds in having ban lifted on U.S. publication of James Joyce's *Ulysses.*

American Newspaper Guild organizes with Heywood Broun president.

Newsweek, Esquire, and *U.S. News and World Report* are founded.

Erle Stanley Gardner publishes his first Perry Mason book, *The Case of the Velvet Claws.*

BOOKS *Anthony Adverse* by Hervey Allen, *The Autobiography of Alice B. Toklas* by Gertrude Stein, *Collected Verse* by Robert Hillyer, *God's Little Acre* by Erskine Caldwell, *Miss Lonelyhearts* by Nathanael West, *My Life and Hard Times* by James Thurber.

DEATHS Sara Teasdale, author and poet; Earl Derr Biggers, author (Charlie Chan stories); Richard R. Bowker, founder, American Library Assn. and *Library Journal;* Horace B. Liveright, publisher; Sime Silverman, editor, *Variety* (1905–1933); Ring Lardner, sportswriter and author.

ENTERTAINMENT

Edwin H. Armstrong demonstrates FM (frequency modulation) radio transmission eliminating static.

First drive-in movie theater in U.S. opens in Camden, New Jersey (June 6).

PLAYS Henry Hull stars in *Tobacco Road,* Katharine Cornell in *Alien Corn,* Noel Coward, Alfred Lunt, and Lynn Fontanne in *Design for Living,* Ethel Waters in *As Thousands Cheer* with music by Irving Berlin.

MOVIES *King Kong* with Fay Wray, *State Fair* with Will Rogers, *Flying Down to Rio* with Fred Astaire and Ginger Rogers, *Tugboat Annie* with Marie Dressler, *Dinner at Eight* with Jean Harlow, *Lady for a Day* with May Robson, *Henry the Eighth* with Charles Laughton.

Don McNeill's *Breakfast Club* begins 35-year run on radio; other new shows are *The Lone Ranger, National Barn Dance, Kraft Music Hall, Information Please.*

DEATH Edward H. Sothern, Shakespearian actor.

SPORTS

First major-league baseball All-Star Game is played (July 6); American League wins 4–2, Babe Ruth hits game's first home run.

Boxer Primo Carnera knocks out Ernie Schaaf; Schaaf dies a few days later.

Football goal posts are returned to goal line; forward pass is allowed anywhere behind the line of scrimmage.

WINNERS *Auto racing*—Louis Meyer, Indianapolis 500; *Baseball*—New York Giants, World Series; *Boxing*—Primo Carnera, heavyweight; Jimmy McLarnin, welterweight; Barney Ross, lightweight; *Football*—Southern California, Rose Bowl; Chicago Bears, NFL; *Golf*—Great Britain, Ryder Cup; John Goodman, U.S. Open; Gene Sarazen, PGA; *Hockey*—New York Rangers, Stanley Cup; Boston Olympics, world amateur title; *Horse racing*—Broker's Tip, Kentucky Derby; Head Play, Preakness Stakes; Hurryoff, Belmont Stakes; *Horseshoe pitching*—Ted Allen, national singles; *Tennis*—Fred Perry, U.S. Open (men); Helen Jacobs, U.S. Open (women).

DEATHS William Muldoon, champion wrestler; James J. Corbett, heavyweight boxing champion (1892–1897).

MISCELLANEOUS

Century of Progress Exposition opens in Chicago.

Earthquake at Long Beach, California, claims 115 lives.

Western Union introduces singing telegram.

Clark Gable and Claudette Colbert in the romantic comedy *It Happened One Night.* The film is a hit at the box office and wins all five of the major Academy Awards for 1934. **THE KOBAL COLLECTION**

1934

INTERNATIONAL

All nations who are indebted to the U.S., except Finland, default.

U.S. troops in Haiti are withdrawn.

Trade Agreements Act authorizes President Franklin Roosevelt to negotiate tariffs on a most-favored-nation principle; U.S. and Cuba sign reciprocal trade agreement; duty on sugar is reduced from 2.5 cents to 0.9 cents per pound.

NATIONAL

Congress overrides presidential veto of a bill to restore cuts in federal salaries and pensions.

Federal Communications Commission is created (June 19).

Civil Works Emergency Act provides $950 million for civil works and public relief.

National Archives are founded (June 19).

Naval Parity Act authorizes construction of 100 warships and more than 5,000 planes over a five-year period; National Guard becomes part of U.S. Army during war or emergency.

Anti-New Deal groups emerge: Liberty League and Rev. Charles Coughlin's National Union for Social Justice.

Dust storms occur in Midwest due to overplowing; thousands of tons of topsoil blow away.

Nebraska adopts a unicameral legislature.

Ohio Supreme Court Justice Florence E. Allen is sworn in as the first woman justice of U.S. Circuit Court of Appeals.

Great Smoky Mountains (North Carolina) National Park is established.

DEATH William B. Wilson, first Secretary of Labor (1913–1921).

BUSINESS/INDUSTRY/INVENTIONS

Export-Import Bank organizes to encourage overseas commerce (February 2); Securities & Exchange Commission is created.

Federal Housing Administration is founded (June 28) to insure housing loans; Federal Farm Mortgage Corp. is established (January 31) to refinance farm debts.

Federal Credit Union Act passes (June 26); first credit union is created in Texarkana, Texas (October 1).

U.S. Board of Mediation is organized (July 21); National

A dust storm moves down a road in the 1930s. Thousands of acres of cultivatable midwestern land vanished in such storms **AP/WIDE WORLD PHOTOS**

Labor Relations Board is created (June 19) to replace 1933 National Labor Board.

Federal Trade Commission is reestablished (June 19).

Gold content of dollar is reduced to 13.71 grains.

John C. Garand patents semi-automatic rifle (MI); rifle is adopted by Army in 1936.

Ninety state liquor stores open in Pennsylvania.

Chemist Wallace Carothers of DuPont produces nylon.

National Society of Professional Engineers is founded.

DEATHS Albert B. Dick, founder and head of mimeograph machine company; Ivy L. Lee, developed public relations as a profession; William C. Procter, soap manufacturer (Procter & Gamble); Cass Gilbert, architect (Woolworth Building).

TRANSPORTATION

Railway Labor Act gives workers right to organize and bargain; sets up National Railroad Adjustment Board (June 27).

Streamlined all-steel diesel train, the "Zephyr" of Burlington Railroad, makes first trip (November 11), a round trip from Lincoln, Nebraska, to Kansas City, Missouri.

Jean F. Piccard and wife reach height of 57,500 feet in balloon.

William A. Patterson is named president of United Air Lines; William P. Lear founds Lear Avia Corp.

DEATH Frank J. Sprague, father of electric traction.

SCIENCE/MEDICINE

Harold C. Urey is awarded Nobel Prize in chemistry for discovery of heavy hydrogen; George R. Minot, William P. Murphy, and G. H. Whipple share physiology/medicine prize for work on liver therapy in anemia.

Charles William Beebe descends a then-record 3,028 feet into ocean in a bathysphere that he invented.

Joseph B. Rhine writes book *Extra-Sensory Perception.*

DEATH William H. Welch, pathologist who helped found Johns Hopkins Hospital/Medical School.

EDUCATION

John W. Studebaker becomes U.S. Commissioner of Education.

RELIGION

Merger (June 24) of Reformed Church, founded in 1725, and Evangelical Synod of North America, founded in 1840, creates Evangelical & Reformed church.

Catholic Archbishop of Chicago George W. Mundelein is elevated to cardinal.

ART/MUSIC

Arnold Schoenberg, composer, debuts as conductor with Boston Symphony Orchestra.

Annual Summer Berkshire Symphonic Festival is founded in Tanglewood, Massachusetts.

Metropolitan Opera presents Howard Hanson's opera *Merrymount; Four Saints in Three Acts,* an opera by Virgil Thomson and Gertrude Stein, is produced in Hartford, Connecticut.

Lincoln Kirstein and George Balanchine found School of American Ballet.

Laurens Hammond patents pipeless organ.

Ella Fitzgerald begins singing career with Chick Webb's band; Benny Goodman organizes band.

Walter Piston composes Concerto for Orchestra; William Levi, *Negro Folk* Symphony.

SONGS (POPULAR): "Anything Goes," "I Get a Kick Out of You," "I Only Have Eyes for You," "Moonglow," "Stay as Sweet as You Are," "Wagon Wheels," "Cocktails for Two," "Deep Purple," "June in January," "P.S. I Love You," "Santa Claus Is Coming to Town," "You're the Top," "Solitude," "Be Still, My Heart."

DEATH Otto H. Kahn, banker and one of U.S.'s greatest art patrons.

LITERATURE/JOURNALISM

Milton Caniff draws comic strip "Terry and the Pirates"; Al Capp, the "L'il Abner" strip.

BOOKS *Tender Is the Night* by F. Scott Fitzgerald, *Wine from These Grapes* (poetry) by Edna St. Vincent Millay, *Appointment in Samarra* by John O'Hara, *Heaven's My Destination* by Thornton Wilder, *While Rome Burns* by Alexander Woollcott, *Lust for Life* by Irving Stone, *The Thin Man* by Dashiell Hammett, *Stars Fell on Alabama* by Carl Carmer.

ENTERTAINMENT

Catholic Legion of Decency censors and grades movies.

"March of Time" documentary film series begins.

Decca Records Inc. is established.

PLAYS Walter Huston stars in *Dodsworth,* Ethel Merman in *Anything Goes,* Grace George in *Personal Appearance.*

MOVIES *The Thin Man* with William Powell and Myrna Loy, *It Happened One Night* with Claudette Colbert and Clark Gable, *Of Human Bondage* with Bette Davis and Leslie Howard, *The Gay Divorcee* with Fred Astaire and Ginger Rogers, *The Scarlet Pimpernel* with Leslie Howard.

DEATH Marie Dressler, screen actress.

SPORTS

Ford Frick is named National (baseball) League president.

In baseball All-Star Game, Carl Hubbell strikes out Babe Ruth, Lou Gehrig, Jimmie Foxx, Al Simmons, and Joe Cronin in succession.

Babe Ruth of New York Yankees hits his 700th home run.

First National Hockey League All-Star Game is played.

Golfer Bobby Jones founds annual Masters Tournament.

First ski tow (rope) operates at Woodstock, Vermont.

WINNERS *Auto racing*—Bill Cummings, Indianapolis 500; *Baseball*—St. Louis Cardinals, World Series; *Boxing*—Max Baer, heavyweight; Jimmy McLarnin, welterweight; *Football*—Columbia, Rose Bowl; New York Giants, NFL; *Golf*—U.S., Walker Cup; Olin Dutra, U.S. Open; Paul Runyon, PGA; Horton Smith, first Masters tourney; *Hockey*—Chicago, Stanley Cup; *Horse racing*—Cavalcade, Kentucky Derby; High Quest, Preakness Stakes; Peace Chance, Belmont Stakes; *Tennis*—Great Britain, Davis Cup; Fred Perry, U.S. Open (men); Helen Jacobs, U.S. Open (women); *Wrestling*—Jim Londos, heavyweight; *Yachting*—U.S. boat *Rainbow* retains America's Cup.

DEATH John McGraw, baseball player and manager (New York Giants 1902–1932).

MISCELLANEOUS

Steamer *Morro Castle* burns off Asbury Park, New Jersey; 134 die.

Clyde Barrow and Bonnie Parker, bank robbers, shot to death by Texas Rangers; John Dillinger, Public Enemy No. 1, shot and killed by lawmen outside a Chicago theater.

Florida Keys are hit by hurricane that causes 400 deaths.

Brookfield Zoo in Chicago opens.

American Youth Hostels incorporate.

Clark Gable takes off his shirt in *It Happened One Night,* revealing that he is not wearing an undershirt; undershirt sales immediately plummet.

Shirley Temple, the most popular child star in Hollywood history. CORBIS-BETTMANN

1935

INTERNATIONAL

President Franklin D. Roosevelt approves Philippine Islands constitution (February 8); Senate ratifies (May 14); Manuel Quezon is elected first president (September 17) and Commonwealth of the Philippines is inaugurated (November 15).

After years of consideration, Senate rejects U.S. membership in World Court (January 16).

NATIONAL

Supreme Court in *Schechter* v. *United States* rules that National Industrial Recovery Act of 1933 is unconstitutional (May 27).

Social Security Act is approved (August 24). **SEE PRIMARY DOCUMENT** "The Social Security Act" by Frances Perkins

Senator Huey P. Long of Louisiana is shot and killed in Baton Rouge by Dr. Carl A. Weiss, who is killed by Long's bodyguards.

George H. Gallup founds Institute of Public Opinion, which holds Gallup polls.

First U.S. Savings Bonds ($25 to $100) are issued.

Boulder (later Hoover) Dam is dedicated; produces power (1936) to serve Los Angeles area.

National Youth Administration is formed to aid 16–23 year olds (June 26).

Federal Register is authorized.

Trenton, New Jersey, hosts two-day national conference on crime; 41 states are represented.

Pan American Airways makes first airmail flight across Pacific Ocean.

FBI opens police training school.

Shenandoah (Virginia) National Park is established.

Harry S. Truman begins 10-year service as a senator from Missouri.

DEATHS Oliver Wendell Holmes Jr., Supreme Court justice (1902–1932), known as the Great Dissenter; Jane Addams, social worker (Hull House); Frank H. Hitchcock, Postmaster General (1909–1913) who began parcel post, airmail, and postal savings.

BUSINESS/INDUSTRY/INVENTIONS

United Auto Workers holds first convention; Committee of Industrial Organization, predecessor of CIO, is established.

New National Labor Relations Board is established (July 5).

Congress passes law that provides three-year moratorium on farm foreclosures; Resettlement Administration is created to provide relief to low-income farm families.

Soil Conservation Service is created to stop erosion.

Works Progress Administration (WPA) is created; Harry L. Hopkins administrates.

Public Utility Holding Company Act gives Federal Power Commission more authority over electric transmission and gas, gives Securities & Exchange Commission authority over holding companies practices.

Rural Electrification Administration (REA) is created to provide electricity to rural areas.

Sylvia Porter writes syndicated financial column in *New York Post.*

DEATH David White, developer of carbon ratio theory that leads to development of petroleum industry.

TRANSPORTATION

Supreme Court declares Railroad Retirement Act of 1934 unconstitutional.

Oklahoma City installs first automatic parking meter.

Motor Carrier Act places interstate buses and trucks under Interstate Commerce Commission.

Bell Aircraft Corp. is founded.

Amelia Earhart is first to fly solo across Pacific (Honolulu to Oakland) (January 11).

DEATH John N. Willys, automaker.

SCIENCE/MEDICINE

Arthur Dempster discovers U-235, an isotope of uranium used in nuclear weapons and plants.

DEATHS Franklin H. Martin, founder of American College of Surgeons; Henry Fairfield Osborn, head of American Museum of Natural History (1908–1933).

EDUCATION

Isaiah Bowman begins 14 years as president of Johns Hopkins University.

St. Joseph's College in Philadelphia offers course in combating communism.

RELIGION

Two new Catholic archbishops named: John J. Mitty to San Francisco and Joseph F. Rummel to New Orleans.

Oral Roberts begins evangelistic career.

DEATH Billy Sunday, evangelist and revivalist.

ART/MUSIC

American Ballet, forerunner of New York City Ballet, is founded with George Balanchine director; Littlefield (later Philadelphia) Ballet is formed.

WPA Federal Art Project Gallery opens in New York City; San Francisco Museum of Art opens.

Marian Anderson, one of world's great contraltos, debuts in New York City.

Antonia Brico founds New York Women's Symphony.

Aaron Copland composes *Statements.*

Robert Laurent completes the painting *Spanning the Continent.*

Count Basie forms a band.

SONGS (POPULAR): "I'm in the Mood for Love," "Cheek to Cheek," "Footloose and Fancy Free," "Lullaby of Broadway," "Moon over Miami," "Red Sails in the Sunset," "Summertime," "The Music Goes Round and Round," "Just One of Those Things," "Begin the Beguine."

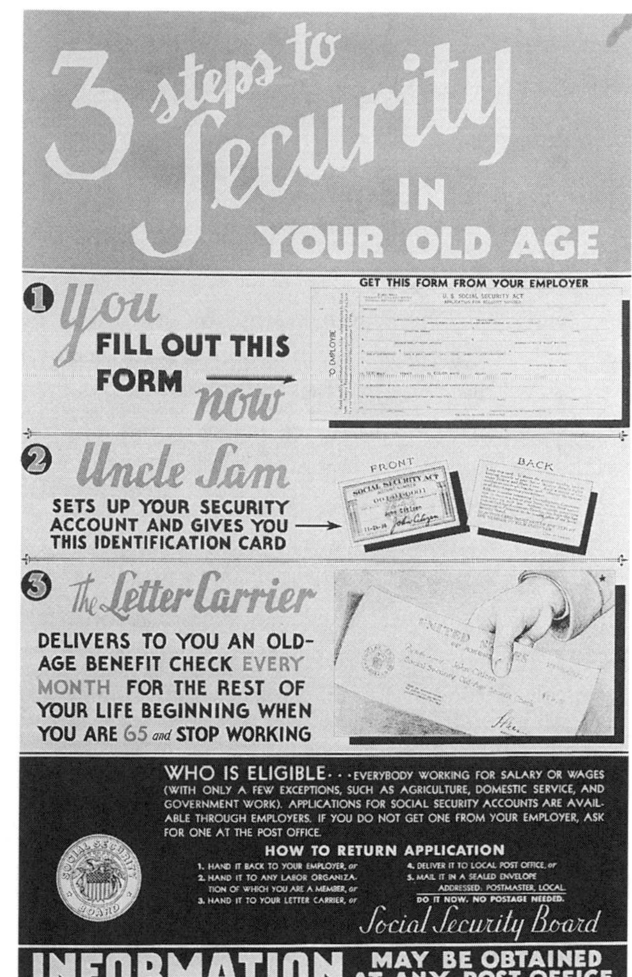

Posters like this instruct the public in how to apply for benefits under the Social Security Act, passed in 1935. CORBIS-BETTMANN

DEATHS Childe Hassam, leading U.S. impressionist painter; Charles Demuth, painter who helped introduce cubist technique to U.S.

LITERATURE/JOURNALISM

Charles S. Addams draws his macabre cartoons for *New Yorker* magazine; Edward R. Murrow joins Columbia Broadcasting System.

Gardner Cowles acquires the *Minneapolis Star.*

BOOKS *Tortilla Flat* by John Steinbeck, *Life with Father* by Clarence S. Day Jr., *It Can't Happen Here* by Sinclair Lewis, *Butterfield 8* by John O'Hara, *Of Time and the River* by Thomas Wolfe, *Vein of Iron* by Ellen Glasgow, *R. E. Lee* by Douglas Southall Freeman.

DEATHS Sidney Smith, cartoonist ("The Gumps"); Adolph S. Ochs, publisher, the *New York Times* (1896–1935); Lucius W. Nieman, endower of jour-

Black Sunday in Kansas

Nicknamed the "dirty thirties," an extended period of drought on the southern Great Plains resulted in unrivaled hardship for western farmers. Dust storms engulfed much of Kansas, ruining agricultural livelihoods with the wholesale destruction of homes, livestock, and wheat crops. The spring of 1935 proved a particularly difficult season. Dust storms darkened most days in March and early April. During a brief respite, many residents of Kansas ventured out on the morning of Sunday, April 14 to take advantage of a rare clear spell of weather. However, in the afternoon, a major dust storm hit unexpectedly. Caught off-guard, residents struggled to find shelter; many were simply lost in the all-consuming dust. The following day the Kansas *Liberal News* described the scene: "The Southwest was plunged into blackness...with only few minutes warning," worsened by the fact that "when the storm struck it was impossible to see one's hand before his face even two inches away." The newspaper went on to claim, "Some people thought the end of the world was at hand when every trace of daylight was obliterated at 4:00 P.M." The severe conditions gave rise to the name Black Sunday. The storm itself moved on to Texas and New Mexico, exacerbating respiratory infections and agricultural hardship across the Southwest. In Perrytown, Texas, citizens referred to the Black Sunday as the worst dust storm in the town's history.

nalism fellowships at Harvard; Edwin Arlington Robinson, poet.

ENTERTAINMENT

Federal Theater Project is founded.

Spyros Skouras founds Twentieth Century-Fox movie company.

PLAYS Leslie Howard and Humphrey Bogart star in *The Petrified Forest,* Burgess Meredith in *Winter-set,* Helen Hayes in *Victoria Regina,* Judith Anderson in *The Old Maid;* George Gershwin's opera *Porgy and Bess* opens on Broadway.

MOVIES *The Informer* with Victor McLaglen, *Mutiny on the Bounty* with Charles Laughton, *Anna Karenina* with Greta Garbo, *Top Hat* and *Roberta* with Fred Astaire and Ginger Rogers, *The Little Colonel* with Shirley Temple, *Magnificent Obsession* with Irene Dunne, *Les Miserables* with Frederic March, *The 39 Steps* with Robert Donat.

New radio shows include *Cavalcade of America, Fibber McGee and Molly, Lights Out, Major Bowes' Original Amateur Hour, Your Hit Parade.*

DEATH DeWolf Hopper, actor.

SPORTS

Roller derby for 50 skaters is held in Chicago.

Sir Malcolm Campbell drives Bluebird Special at 304.33 miles per hour at Bonneville (Utah) Salt Flats.

First night game in major-league baseball is played in Crosley Field, Cincinnati; Reds beat Philadelphia.

Babe Ruth hits his 714th, and last, home run.

Mary Hirsch becomes first woman licensed to train race horses.

New York Downtown Athletic Club presents first Heisman Memorial Trophy; recipient is Jay Berwanger, University of Chicago halfback.

WINNERS *Auto racing*—Kelly Petillo, Indianapolis 500; *Baseball*—Detroit Tigers, World Series; *Boxing*—Jim Braddock, heavyweight; Barney Ross, welterweight; Tony Canzoneri, lightweight; *Football* (bowls)—Alabama, Rose; Bucknell, Orange; Tulane, Sugar; Detroit Lions, NFL; *Golf*—U.S., Ryder Cup; Sam Parks Jr., U.S. Open; Johnny Revolta, PGA; Gene Sarazen, Masters; *Hockey*—Montreal Maroons, Stanley Cup; *Horse racing*—Omaha, third Triple Crown winner (Kentucky Derby, Preakness Stakes, Belmont Stakes); *Skeet shooting*—Lovell S. Pratt, men's national; Esther A. Ingalls, women's; *Tennis*—Great Britain, Davis Cup; Wilmer Allison, U.S. Open (men); Helen Jacobs, U.S. Open (women).

MISCELLANEOUS

Wiley Post and his passenger, Will Rogers, die in an Alaska plane crash.

William G. Wilson and Dr. Robert Smith found Alcoholics Anonymous.

PRIMARY SOURCE DOCUMENT

"The Social Security Act" by Frances Perkins, September 2, 1935

INTRODUCTION Born to middle-class parents in Worcester, Massachusetts, Frances Perkins (1882–1965) first became involved in social reform in the early 1900s by working for the social settlement movement in Illinois, building on the initiatives of Jane Addams at Hull House in 1889. After earning a master's degree in sociology and economics from Columbia University, Perkins worked to improve labor conditions as a staff member of the New York Consumers' League. In 1918, she began a long and distinguished career in public service, eventually earning an appointment as chairperson of New York State's Industrial Commission, a position that brought her into regular contact with the then governor of New York, Franklin D. Roosevelt. Perkins joined Roosevelt's New Deal administration as secretary of labor, becoming the first woman cabinet member in American history.

When Roosevelt became president in 1933, the United States was the only major industrialized nation lacking old-age pensions and unemployment insurance. In June 1934 Perkins headed the Committee on Economic Security to formulate a federal response to the economic crisis of the Great Depression. Perkins and her committee faced pressure to devise social security programs from various fronts. Perkins herself was committed to instituting governmental reforms to ameliorate poverty conditions. However, the Roosevelt administration also faced several powerful social movements calling for old-age pensions, including Upton Sinclair's End Poverty in California movement. The greatest source of pressure for governmental action was a movement inspired by Dr. Frances E. Townsend, an elderly physician from California, whose Old Age Revolving Pension Plan inspired millions of supporters to form Townsend clubs. As a result of Perkins's dedication and skillful manipulation of Congress, the Social Security Act became law in August 1935. The act created various federal aid programs. First, it established an old-age pension program, scheduled to begin in 1942; second, it created means-tested public assistance programs for the blind and handicapped, the elderly poor, and children from single-parent families (Aid to Dependent Children); and third, it legislated unemployment insurance, funded by both employees and employers. The act marked the beginning of a broad commitment on the part of the federal government to the welfare of American citizens affected by poverty, economic distress, and physical disabilities.

Perkins delivered this message on Social Security in a radio broadcast to the American public, a medium of communication that President Franklin D. Roosevelt used effectively during difficult times to reassure Americans that the federal government was working on their behalf during difficult times. Many of the New Deal programs initiated by Roosevelt's administrators addressed the short-term needs of employment. The Social Security Act gave Americans a long-term vision of security, ensuring that such difficult times would never return.

People who work for a living in the United States of America can join with all other good citizens on this forty-eighth anniversary of Labor Day in satisfaction that the Congress has passed the Social Security Act. This act establishes unemployment insurance as a substitute for haphazard methods of assistance in periods when men and women willing and able to work are without jobs. It provides for old-age pensions which I mark great progress over the measures upon which we have hitherto depended in caring for those who have been unable to provide for the years when they no longer can work. It also provides security for dependent and crippled children, mothers, the indigent disabled and the blind.

Old people who are in need, unemployables, children, mothers and the sightless, will find systematic regular provisions for needs. The Act limits the Federal aid to not more than $15 per month for the individual, provided the State in which he resides appropriates a like amount. There is nothing to prevent a State from contributing more than $15 per month in special cases and there is no requirement to allow as much as $15 from either State or Federal funds when a particular case has some personal provision and needs less than the total allowed.

Following essentially the same procedure, the Act as passed provides for Federal assistance to the States in caring for the blind, a contribution by the State of up to $15 a month to be matched in turn by alike contribution by the Federal Government. The Act also contains provision for assistance to the States in providing payments to dependent children under sixteen years of age. There also is provision in the Act for co-operation with medical and health organizations charged with rehabilitation of physically handicapped children. The necessity for adequate service in the fields of public and maternal health and child welfare calls for the extension of these services to meet individual community needs.

Consider for a moment those portions of the Act which, while they will not be effective this present year, yet will exert a profound and far-reaching effect upon millions of citizens. I refer to the provision for a system of old-age benefits supported by the contributions of employer and employees, and to the section which sets up the initial machinery for unemployment insurance.

Old-age benefits in the form of monthly payments are to be paid to individuals who have worked and contributed to the insurance fund in direct proportion to the total wages earned by such individuals in the course of their employment subsequent to 1936. The minimum monthly payment is to be $10, the maximum $85. These payments will begin in the year 1942 and will be to those who have worked and contributed. Because of difficulty of administration not all employments are covered in this plan at this time so that the law is not entirely complete in coverage, but it is sufficiently broad to cover all normally employed industrial workers.…

This vast system of old-age benefits requires contributions both by employer and employee, each to contribute 31% of the much total wage paid to the employee. This tax, collected by the Bureau of Internal Revenue, will be graduated, ranging from the minimum 11% in 1937 to the maximum 3% in 1939 and thereafter. That is, on this man's average income of $100 a month he will pay to passed the usual fund $3 a month and his employer will also pay the same amount over his working years.

In conjunction with the system of old-age benefits, the Act recognizes that unemployment insurance is an integral part of any plan for the economic security of

OVERVIEW

Boom and Bust: The 1920s and the New Deal, 1919–1941

MICHAEL JO, YALE UNIVERSITY

The Return to Normalcy

In 1919 Woodrow Wilson returned from Europe with the Versailles Treaty, but peace continued to elude the American people. That same year, the "Red Scare" resulted in a national crusade against radicals. Labor militancy crested with a general strike in Seattle. Race riots across the country brutally established the power of white supremacy. When the smoke lifted the following year, American politics took a sharp turn away from Progressivism. The Senate rejected the spirit of the Versailles Treaty and Warren G. Harding led the Republicans back into the White House, where they would remain for the next twelve years.

Harding proclaimed that the American people desired a "return to normalcy." In foreign affairs, this meant a return to isolationism. At home, it meant "less government in business and more business in government." Harding's administration was beset by scandals, but when he died in office in 1923, they had not damaged his reputation. Calvin Coolidge, his Vice President, succeeded Harding and then won election in 1924. Echoing his predecessor, he declared that "the business of America is business."

Both Harding and Coolidge steadfastly believed that business leaders were best suited to running the government and the country. Harding appointed Andrew Mellon, an immensely wealthy financier, as secretary of the treasury. He served under three presidential administrations; or, as the joke went, three presidents served under him. Mellon slashed the federal budget and cut taxes on corporate profits and the incomes of the wealthy. His policies, and those of officials like him, sounded the death knell for much Progressive legislation.

The Triumph of Business

The American economy enjoyed unprecedented prosperity in the 1920s. Average per capita income rose from $522 to $716 between 1921 and 1929. Much of this wealth was concentrated in large corporations, which began shifting their attention from heavy industry to consumer products such as fabrics, automobiles, and household appliances. National chain stores gave these companies a nationwide market. Advertising helped stimulate this consumer economy and supported a new mass culture industry of movies, music, magazines, and radio. In many ways, the main features of present-day American economy emerged during the 1920s.

This vaunted prosperity was not enjoyed by everyone, however. In 1929 only the top 0.5 percent of Americans owned 32.4 percent of the nation's wealth. Farmers were particularly hard hit. Low crop prices and corporate buyouts of small farms increased the number of farmers who rented instead of owning their land and created large populations of poor migrant workers.

In these days of business triumph, organized labor was also on the defensive. From 1920 to 1926 the percentage of unionized American workers fell from 12 to 7 percent. This decline reflected employers' untiring offensive against unions, using both the carrot and the stick. Many employers created benefit programs including profit sharing and medical plans. This "welfare capitalism" was intended to make corporations the primary providers of social welfare. When unions did exist, employers fought them with Red Scare smear tactics and a nationwide antiunion campaign. The result was a steady decline in union membership that would last until the 1930s.

---

millions of gainfully under employed workers. It provides for a plan of cooperative Federal-State action by which a State may enact an insurance with system, compatible with Federal requirements and best suited to its individual needs.

The Federal Government attempts to promote and effectuate these State systems, by levying a uniform Federal payroll tax of 31% on employers employing eight or more workers, with the proviso that an employer who contributes to a State unemployment compensation system will receive a credit of 90% of this Federal tax. After 1937, additional credit is also allowable to any employer who, because of favorable employment experience or adequate reserves, is permitted by the State to reduce his payments.

Dreams Deferred

In 1920 the Nineteenth Amendment granted women the right to vote. Soon after, feminists split over a proposed Equal Rights Amendment (ERA) for men and women. Proponents, the equality feminists, argued that women should strive to eliminate sex as a legal category. Opponents, the difference feminists, claimed that the best way to advance women's welfare was to recognize their uniqueness and pass laws protecting them. These divisions would persist for decades.

Growing numbers of women left the household for the work world, and an increasing number of them secured white-collar jobs. Women entered college in greater numbers than ever before, and some high-profile women broke gender barriers in the professional world, sports, and the arts. Young men and women reveled in a more open attitude toward sexuality. However, women still received lower pay than men, were excluded from the highest positions in business, and had minor roles in government.

During World War I many African Americans migrated from the rural South to the industrial cities of the North and Midwest. This "Great Migration" created large urban black communities and in New York fostered the cultural heyday known as the Harlem Renaissance. The "New Negro" of the Harlem Renaissance celebrated African-American culture and took a militant political stand against white supremacy in the South and informal segregation across the nation.

In the 1920s nativism and racism found expression in new organizations and legal measures. The Ku Klux Klan reemerged in 1915 and boasted more than three million members by 1924. This "Second Ku Klux Klan" targeted not only African Americans, but also Catholics, Jews, and radicals, and became a nationwide organization before scandals weakened it by 1929. Conservative Christians formed fundamentalist organizations aimed at combating the church's loss of authority to science and what they saw as the immorality of modern culture. Nativist sentiment culminated in laws that excluded immigrants from southern and eastern Europe, Asia, and Africa.

In 1920 the Eighteenth Amendment prohibited the consumption of alcoholic beverages throughout America. Prohibition was the result of a coalition of Progressives, women reformers, and evangelicals who fought liquor as a form of working-class leisure. Unfortunately, it encouraged rather than outlawed sinful behavior. Organized crime syndicates, such as Al Capone's infamous South side gang, emerged to control the black or bootleg market for liquor. Criticism of Prohibition grew throughout the 1920s, especially from the Democratic Party.

Hoover and the Depression

In 1929 Herbert Hoover, a government "efficiency expert," entered the White House. Like his predecessors he was staunchly pro-business, but he wished to coordinate business activities under governmental supervision instead of giving corporations free rein. Under his vision of an "associative state," government would encourage businesses to work together in associations to pass their own guidelines on prices, production levels, and labor policies.

Hoover had been in office for only a few months when the stock market crashed in October 1929. Inflated stock prices, the inflation of credit through loans, and the unequal distribution of wealth all played a part in this catastrophe. The crisis of confidence in the economy triggered a rash of bank failures, and the Great Depression began. By 1932 thirteen million Americans were unemployed.

Hoover believed that the best way to end the Depression was to assist business. His Reconstruction Finance Corporation provided loans for corporations, but did little for ordinary citizens. Thus, many Americans believed that Hoover was doing nothing to stop their slide into poverty. The shantytowns that were emerging all over the country acquired a new name: "Hoovervilles." In the 1932 presidential election Franklin Delano Roosevelt, governor of New

In addition, the Act provides that after the current fiscal year the Federal Government allocate annually to the States $49,000,000 solely for the administration of their respective insurance systems, thus assuring that all money paid for State unemployment compensation will be reserved for the purpose of compensation to the worker. It has been necessary, at the present time, to eliminate essentially the same groups from participation under the unemployment insurance plan as in the old-age benefit plan, though it is possible that at some future time a more complete coverage will be formulated.

The State of New York, at the present time, has a system of unemployment compensation which might well illustrate the salient factors desired in such a plan; in the event of unemployment, the worker is paid 50% of his

Boom and Bust: The 1920s and the New Deal, 1919–1941 (continued)

York State, soundly defeated Hoover and promised a "New Deal" for the American people.

The First and Second New Deals

In the whirlwind of his "first hundred days," FDR created relief agencies, government work programs to remedy unemployment, price controls and government assistance for agriculture, and the National Recovery Administration (NRA), which would help business regulate itself. Congress also passed the Twenty-First Amendment repealing Prohibition.

Despite its relief measures, this "First New Deal" extended Hoover's philosophy of ending the depression by aiding business. By 1935 this program was in trouble. The Supreme Court, dominated by a conservative majority, ruled many of its initiatives unconstitutional. The economy remained stubbornly in the doldrums, with independent political movements challenging the New Deal.

That year Roosevelt embarked on an ambitious legislative program that became known as the "Second New Deal." The Social Security Act created America's old-age pension system, unemployment insurance, and welfare for the poor. The Wagner Act guaranteed for the first time workers' rights to form unions and bargain collectively with employers for better wages, benefits, and working conditions. The labor movement benefited enormously, reversing its long decline of the 1920s; union members grew to unprecedented numbers. In 1935 a group of unionists also broke away from the American Federation of Labor (AFL) to form the Congress of Industrial Organizations (CIO), a new union devoted to organizing the unskilled industrial workers shunned by the AFL.

In his first term, FDR changed the shape of American government, creating a more active executive branch with a large bureaucracy. Government became involved with people's lives as never before, moving from business regulation and foreign policy toward individual welfare.

wages weekly for a per not exceeding 16 weeks in any 52 weeks. This payment begins within three weeks after the advent of actual unemployment. California, Washington, Utah and New Hampshire have passed unemployment insurance laws in recent months and Wisconsin's law is already in effect. Thirty-five States have old-age pension statutes and mothers' pension acts are in force if but three States.

With the States rests now the responsibility of devising enacting measures which will result in the maximum benefits to the American workman in the field of unemployment compensation. I am confident that impending State action will not fail to take cognizance of this responsibility. The people of the different States favor the program designed to bring them security in the future and their legislatures will speedily appropriate laws so that all may help to promote the general welfare.

Federal legislation was framed in the thought that the attack upon the problems of insecurity should be a cooperative venture participated in by both the Federal and State Governments, preserving the benefits of local administration and national leadership. It was thought unwise to have the Federal Government decide all questions of policy and dictate completely what the States should do. Only very necessary minimum standards are included in the Federal measure wide latitude to the States.

While the different State laws on unemployment in must make all contributions compulsory, the States, in addition to deciding how these contributions shall be levied, have freedom in determining their own waiting periods, rates, maximum benefit periods and the like. Care should be taken that these laws do not contain benefit provisions in excess of collections. While unemployment varies greatly in different States, there is no certainty that States which have had less normal unemployment heretofore will in the future have a more favorable experience than the average for the country.

It is obvious that in the best interests of the worker, industry and society, there must be a certain uniformity of standards. It is obvious, too, that we must prevent the penalizing of competitive industry in any State which plans the early adoption of a sound system of unemployment insurance, and provide effective age guarantees against the possibility of industry in one State having an advantage over that of another. This uniform Federal tax does, as it costs the employer the same whether he pays the levy to the Federal Government or makes a contribution to a State unemployment insurance fund. The amount of the tax itself is a relative assurance that benefits will be standardized in all States, since under the law the entire collection must be the spent on benefits to unemployed.

Reform in Retreat

FDR's landslide victory in the 1936 presidential election demonstrated overwhelming public support for the Second New Deal and its initiatives. African Americans shifted their votes from the Republican Party to the Democrats, whose main constituency was now in the North. Conservative Southern Democrats, alarmed at FDR's liberal policies, began making alliances with Republicans.

However, in 1937 FDR decided to cut federal spending. This move proved ill-advised, for the economy soon began to take somewhat of a nosedive. That year the president also challenged the Supreme Court, which continued to declare a number of his initiatives unconstitutional. FDR proposed to "pack" the Court by expanding it from nine to fifteen justices. The plan outraged some of the president's supporters in Congress, who viewed it as an abuse of executive power. Thus, the "court packing" affair strengthened conservative opposition to FDR. He would pass only one more major piece of social welfare legislation, the Fair Labor Standards Act of 1938, which created America's first national minimum wage and maximum work week laws.

By this time, events abroad were drawing greater national attention. After World War II broke out in Europe in September 1939, FDR proposed to help Great Britain and France by leasing arms to these countries. He also kept a watchful eye on Japanese military expansion in the Pacific. However, the Republicans were determined to maintain America's isolationism. It would take a massive shock to make the nation abandon its long-cherished neutrality.

BIBLIOGRAPHY

For further information on this important period in American history, see Alan Brinkley, *Voices of Protest: Huey Long, Father Coughlin, and the Great Depression* (1982); Lizabeth Cohen, *Making a New Deal: Industrial Workers in Chicago, 1919–1939* (1990); Nancy F. Cott, *The Grounding of Modern Feminism* (1987); William Leach, *Land of Desire: Merchants, Power, and the Rise of a New American Culture* (1993); William E. Leuchtenberg, *Franklin D. Roosevelt and the New Deal, 1932–1940* (1963); David Levering Lewis, *When Harlem Was in Vogue* (1981); Roland Marchand, *Advertising the American Dream: Making Way for Modernity, 1920–1940* (1985).

The social security measure looks primarily to the future and is only a part of the administration's plan to promote sound and stable economic life. We cannot think of it as disassociated from the Government's program to save the homes, the farms, the businesses and banks of the Nation, and especially must we consider it a companion measure to the Works Relief Act which does undertake to provide immediate increase in employment and corresponding stimulation to private industry by purchase of supplies.

While it is not anticipated as a complete remedy for the abnormal conditions confronting us at the present time, it is designed to afford protection for the individual against future major economic vicissitudes. It is a sound and reasonable plan and framed with due regard for the present state of economic recovery. It does not represent a complete solution of the problems of economic security, but it does represent a substantial, necessary beginning. It has been developed after careful and intelligent consideration of all the facts and all of the programs that have been suggested or applied anywhere.

Few legislative proposals have had as careful study, as thorough and conscientious deliberation, as that which went into the preparation of the social security programs. It is embodied in perhaps the most useful and fundamental single piece of Federal legislation in the interest of wage earners in the United States. As President Roosevelt said when he signed the measure: "If the Senate and House of Representatives in their long and arduous session had done nothing more than pass this bill session would be regarded as historic for all time."

This is truly legislation in the interest of the national welfare. We must recognize that if we are to maintain a healthy economy and thriving production, we need to maintain the standard of living of the lower income groups of our population constitute ninety per cent of our purchasing power. The President's Committee on Economic Security, of which I had the honor to be chairman, in drawing up the plan, was convinced that its enactment into law would not only carry us a long way toward the goal of economic security for the individual also a long way toward the promotion and stabilization of purchasing power without which the present economics cannot endure.

That this intimate connection between the maintenance of mass purchasing power through a system of protection individual against major economic hazards is not theoretical is evidenced by the fact that England has been able to withstand the effects of the world-wide depression, even though her prosperity depends so largely upon foreign trade. English economists agree with employers and workers that this ability to weather adverse conditions has been due in no small social insurance benefits and regular payments which served to maintain necessary purchasing power.

Our social security program will be a vital force against the recurrence of severe depressions in the future. We can, as the principle of sustained purchasing power times makes itself felt in every shop, store and mill, grow old without being haunted by the spectre of a poverty-ridden old age or of being a burden on our children.

The costs of unemployment compensation and old-age insurance are not actually additional costs. In some degree they have long been borne by the people, but irregularly, the burden falling much more heavily on some than on others, and none of such provisions offering an orderly or systematic assurance to those in need. The years of depression have brought home to all of us that unemployment entails huge costs to government, industry and the public alike.

Unemployment insurance will within a short time considerably lighten the public burden of caring for those unemployed. It will materially reduce relief costs in future years. In essence, it is a method by which reserves are built up during periods of employment from which compensation is paid to the unemployed in periods when work is lacking.

The passage of this act with so few dissenting votes and with so much intelligent public support is deeply significant of the progress which the American people have made in thought in the social field and awareness of methods of using cooperation through government to overcome social hazards against which the individual alone is inadequate.

During the fifteen years I have been advocating such legislation as this I have learned that the American people want such legislation as the law provides. It will make this great Republic a better and a happier place in which to live—for us, our children, and our children's children.

SOURCE:
Frances Perkins, "The Social Security Act," September 2, 1935, radio address, reprinted in *Vital Speeches of the Day*, I, 1934–1935, 792–794.

1936

INTERNATIONAL

Inter-American Conference is held in Buenos Aires.

NATIONAL

President Franklin D. Roosevelt, Democrat, is reelected, carries every state but Maine and Vermont; receives 27,751,612 popular and 523 electoral votes to Republican Alfred M. Landon's 16,681,913 popular and 8 electoral votes.

Supreme Court in *United States* v. *Butler* declares unconstitutional the Agricultural Adjustment Act (January 24); Congress then passes law to replace the act (February 29), restricts agricultural output through benefit payments to growers practicing soil conservation; Court also deems unconstitutional the Bituminous Coal Conservation Act; upholds the constitutionality of dam building by TVA.

Congress passes bill (January 24) over president's veto to give World War I veterans cash bonuses; distributes more than $1.5 million to about 3 million veterans.

Three dams are completed: Hoover (originally Boulder) Dam on Colorado River, Norris Dam on Clinch River in Tennessee, and Wheeler Dam on Tennessee River in Alabama.

Ford Foundation, philanthropic organization, is established.

DEATHS Former Vice President Charles Curtis (1929–1933); Admiral William S. Sims, commanded World War I naval operations.

BUSINESS/INDUSTRY/INVENTIONS

Drs. Vladimir Zworykin and George Morton describe their invention, the electron tube.

United Auto Workers stage sit-down strikes in several General Motors plants in Flint, Michigan; last 44 days; are copied by other workers.

Philip Murray heads Steel Workers Organizing Committee (later United Steelworkers).

Owens-Illinois Glass Co. completes all-glass windowless packaging laboratory in Toledo, Ohio.

Great American Oil Co. and Hunt Oil Co. are founded.

Government Contracts Act calls for 40-hour week for companies with government contracts, plus time-and-a-half for overtime.

Anti-price discrimination law makes illegal unreasonably low prices by interstate chain stores.

DEATHS William Horlick, originator of malted milk; Edward Weston, inventor of cadmium cell; Hiram P. Maxim, inventor of firearm silencer.

TRANSPORTATION

Triborough Bridge in New York City and San Francisco–Oakland Bridge open.

Socony-Vacuum Oil Co. produces aviation gasoline.

U.S. Maritime Commission replaces Shipping Board, is designed to develop merchant marine.

German dirigible *Hindenburg* arrives at Lakehurst, New Jersey, completing first scheduled transatlantic flight.

Jesse Owens dominates track and field at the 1936 Olympics in Berlin, winning four gold medals. **CORBIS-BETTMANN**

SCIENCE/MEDICINE

Carl D. Anderson shares Nobel Prize in physics with Viktor F. Hess of Austria for discovery of the positron; Otto Loewi shares the prize for physiology/medicine with Sir Henry H. Dale of England for chemical transmission of nerve impulses.

New York State enacts law requiring annual testing of pupils' hearing.

William A. White Foundation founds Washington School of Psychiatry.

EDUCATION

Spring Hill (Alabama) College is chartered; first Catholic college in the deep South.

DEATH Thomas J. Foster, founder of International Correspondence School.

RELIGION

John G. Machen founds Presbyterian Church of America (later becomes Orthodox Presbyterian church).

Evangelical Bishop John S. Stamm becomes president of Board of Bishops.

ART/MUSIC

Sculptor Gutzon Borglum unveils the second 60-foot-high presidential head (Jefferson) at Mt. Rushmore in the Black Hills, South Dakota.

Samuel Barber's Symphony in One Movement is first American work played at Salzburg (Austria) music festival; Walter Piston composes Prelude and Fugue for Orchestra.

William G. Still becomes first African-American to conduct major symphony orchestra (Los Angeles Philharmonic).

Edwin H. Marshfield completes mural *Progress of Civilization* on Library of Congress dome; Paul Burlin completes the painting *The Ghost City;* Louis Guglielmi, *Wedding in South Street;* Charles Sheeler, *City Interior.*

SONGS (POPULAR): "I'm an Old Cowhand," "I've Got You Under My Skin," "Let Yourself Go," "Pennies from Heaven," "Stompin' at the Savoy," "Goody, Goody," "There's a Small Hotel," "These Foolish Things."

DEATHS Ernestine Schumann-Heink, one of greatest contraltos; Lorado Z. Taft, sculptor (Chicago's *Fountain of Time*).

LITERATURE/JOURNALISM

Margaret Bourke-White begins her 33-year career as a *Life* photographer.

BOOKS *How to Win Friends and Influence People* by Dale Carnegie, *Gone with the Wind* by Margaret Mitchell, *A Further Range* (poetry) by Robert Frost, *The People, Yes* (poetry) by Carl Sandburg, *Absalom, Absalom!* by William Faulkner, *Inside Europe* by John Gunther, *Drums Along the Mohawk* by Walter D. Edmonds, *U.S.A.*, a trilogy by John Dos Passos.

DEATHS Arthur Brisbane, newspaper columnist; Lincoln Steffens, reform journalist *(Shame of the Cities).*

SEE PRIMARY DOCUMENT "Dubious Battle in California" by John Steinbeck

ENTERTAINMENT

Eugene O'Neill wins Nobel Prize in literature for his plays.

Washington State Theater in Seattle opens.

PLAYS Katharine Cornell stars in *St. Joan,* Ilka Chase in *The Women,* Alfred Lunt and Lynn Fontanne in *Idiot's Delight,* Ray Bolger in *On Your Toes.*

MOVIES *Mr. Deeds Goes to Town* with Gary Cooper and Jean Arthur, *Modern Times* with Charlie Chaplin, *Camille* with Greta Garbo, *My Man Godfrey* with Carole Lombard, *Poppy* with W. C. Fields, *Follow the Fleet* with Fred Astaire and Ginger Rogers.

RADIO Fanny Brice as "Baby Snooks," *Gangbusters, The Green Hornet,* Edgar Bergen and Charlie McCarthy.

DEATHS Irving Thalberg, movie producer; Samuel L. (Roxy) Rothafel, founder of Radio City Music Hall; John Gilbert, silent-screen actor; H. B. Walthall, pioneer screen actor *(Birth of a Nation).*

SPORTS

U.S. two-man bobsled team wins Winter Olympics gold medal at Garmisch-Partenkirchen, Germany; Jesse Owens wins four golds at Summer Olympics in Berlin, Germany.

Professional football teams draft college players for first time.

Tony Lazzeri of New York Yankees sets American League record by driving in 11 runs in one game with three home runs, two of them grand slams.

Sally Stearns is first woman coxswain of a men's collegiate varsity crew (Rollins College).

WINNERS *Auto racing*—Louis Meyer, Indianapolis 500; *Baseball*—New York Yankees, World Series; *Boxing*—Lou Ambers, lightweight; *Chess*—Samuel Reshevsky, U.S. champion; *Football* (bowls)—Stanford, Rose; Catholic University, Orange; Texas Christian, Sugar; Green Bay, NFL; *Golf*—U.S., Walker Cup; Tony Manero, U.S. Open; Denny Shute, PGA; Horton Smith, Masters; *Hockey*—Detroit, Stanley Cup; *Horse racing*—Bold Venture, Kentucky Derby and Preakness Stakes; Granville, Belmont Stakes; *Table Tennis*—Ruth Aaron, first U.S. woman world champion; *Tennis*—Fred Perry, U.S. Open (men); Alice Marble, U.S. Open (women).

MISCELLANEOUS

Congress charters Veterans of Foreign Wars (VFW).

Tornadoes in Mississippi and Georgia kill 455.

Two expositions are held: Ft. Worth Frontier Centennial and Great Lakes Exposition—Cleveland Centennial.

PRIMARY SOURCE DOCUMENT

"Dubious Battle in California" by John Steinbeck

INTRODUCTION John Steinbeck (1902–1968), born in rural Salinas, California, was the literary voice of the Great Depression, championing the migrant worker, the homeless, and the American worker. In *In Dubious Battle* (1936), *Of Mice and Men* (1937), *The Grapes of Wrath* (1939), and *Cannery Row* (1945), Steinbeck chronicled the Dust Bowl migration of "Okies" and "exodusters" to California and the union struggles and labor conditions of working Americans. Steinbeck won the Pulitzer Prize for *The Grapes of Wrath,* which John Ford made into an Academy-Award winning film, and was awarded a Nobel Prize in Literature in 1962 after publishing *The Winter of Our Discontent* (1961).

The Dust Bowl describes an area encompassing roughly 150,000 square miles of land in the Southern Great Plains that faced a severe drought beginning in 1934. A combination of high winds, loose topsoil, and poor rainfall created swirling dust storms that buried fences, roads and homes, killed livestock, and caused serious health problems. These conditions also decimated the operations of wheat farmers in Colorado, Kansas, Nebraska, Oklahoma, and Texas, precipitating thousands of farm foreclosures. And as formerly independent small farmers fled the Dust Bowl, banks and agricultural corporations bought up land. The Dust Bowl was not a natural disaster, however. The advent of mechanized tractor farming combined with high wheat prices during World War I to turn small-scale farming into large-scale agricultural production, which damaged the Plains' ecosystem.

In this selection from *The Nation,* an important political journal of the New Deal era, Steinbeck focuses on the exploitation that newly arrived farm families faced on California's plantations. Desperate for a fresh start after their worlds collapsed in dust storms and bankruptcies, "exodusters" were forced to accept poor pay and dangerous working conditions as well as harassment from plantation owners, who needed them only on a seasonal basis. Steinbeck helped to build awareness of the general plight of America's millions of farm laborers and of the specific plight of refuges from the southern Plains.

In sixty years a complete revolution has taken place in California agriculture. Once its principal products were hay and cattle. Today fruits and vegetables are its most profitable crops. With the change in the nature of farming there has come a parallel change in the nature and amount of the labor necessary to carry it on....

The drought in the Middle West has very recently made available an enormous amount of cheap labor. Workers have been coming to California in nondescript cars from Oklahoma, Nebraska, Texas, and other states, parts of which have been rendered uninhabitable by drought. Poverty-stricken after the destruction of their farms, their last reserves used up in making the trip, they have arrived so beaten and destitute that they have been willing at first to work under any conditions and for any wages offered. This migration started on a considerable scale about two years ago and is increasing all the time.

For a time it looked as though the present cycle would be identical with the earlier ones, but there are several factors in this influx which differentiate it from the others. In the first place, the migrants are undeniably American and not deportable. In the second place, they were not lured to California by a promise of good wages, but are refugees as surely as though they had fled from destruction by an invader. In the third place, they are not drawn from a peon class, but have either owned small farms or been farms hands in the early American sense, in which the "hand" is a member of the employing family. They have one fixed idea, and that is to acquire land and settle on it. Probably the most important difference is that they are not easily intimidated. They are courageous, intelligent, and resourceful. Having gone through the horrors of the drought and with immense effort having escaped from it, they cannot be herded, attacked, starved, or frightened as all the others were.

Let us see what the emigrants from the dust bowl find when they arrive in California. The ranks of permanent and settled labor are filled. In most cases all resources have been spent in making the trip from the dust bowl. Unlike the Chinese and Filipinos, the men rarely come alone. They bring wives and children, now and then a few chickens and their pitiful household goods, though in most cases these have been sold to buy gasoline for the trip. It is quite usual for a man, his wife, and from three to eight children to arrive in California with no possessions but the rattletrap car they travel in and the ragged clothes on their bodies. They often lack bedding and utensils.

During the spring, summer, and part of the fall the man may find some agricultural work. The top pay for a successful year will not be over $400, and if he has any trouble or is not agile, strong, and quick it may well be only $150. It will be seen that rent is out of the question. Clothes cannot be bought. Every available cent must go for food and a reserve to move the car from harvest to harvest....

The small farmers are not able to maintain camps of any comfort or with any sanitary facilities except one or two holes dug for toilets. The final resource is the squatters' camp, usually located on the bank of some watercourse. The people pack into them. They use the watercourse for drinking, bathing, washing their clothes, and to receive their refuse, with the result that epidemics start easily and are difficult to check....It is often said that no one starves in the United States, yet in Santa Clara County last year five babies were certified by the local coroner to have died of "malnutrition," the modern word for starvation, and the less shocking word, although in its connotation it is perhaps more horrible since it indicates that the suffering has been long drawn out.

In these squatters camps the migrant will find squalor beyond anything he has yet had to experience and intimidation almost unchecked. At one camp it is the custom of deputy sheriffs, who are also employees of the great ranch nearby, to drive by the camp for hours at a time, staring into the tents as though trying to memorize faces. The communities in which these camps exist want migratory workers to come for the month required to pick the harvest, and to move on when it is over. If they do not move on, they are urged to with guns.

These are some of the conditions California offers the refugees from the dust bowl. But the refugees are even less content with the starvation wages and the rural slums than were the Chinese, the Filipinos, and the Mexicans. Having their families with them, they are not so mobile as the earlier immigrants were. If starvation sets in, the whole family starves, instead of just one man. Therefore they have been quick to see that they must organize for their own safety.

Attempts to organize have been met with a savagery from the large growers beyond anything yet attempted....The usual repressive measures have been used against these migrants: shooting by deputy sheriffs in 'self-defense,' jailing without charge, refusal of trial by jury, torture and beating by night riders. But even in the short time that these American migrants have been out here there has been a change. It is understood that they are being attacked not because they want higher wages, not because they are Communists, but simply because they want to organize. And to the men, since this defines the thing not to be allowed, it also defines the thing that is completely necessary to the safety of the workers.

This season has seen the beginning of a new form of intimidation not used before. It is the whispering campaign which proved so successful among business rivals. As in business, it is particularly deadly here because its source cannot be traced and because it is easily spread. One of the items of this campaign is the rumor that in the event of labor troubles the deputy sheriffs inducted to break up picket lines will be armed not with tear gas but with poison gas. The second is aimed at the women and marks a new low in tactics. It is to the effect that in the event of labor troubles the water supply used by strikers will be infected with typhoid germs. The fact that these bits of information are current over a good part of the state indicates that they have been widely planted.

The effect has been far from that desired. There is now in California anger instead of fear. The stupidity of the large grower has changed terror into defensive fury. The granges, working close to the soil and to the men, and knowing the temper of the men of this new race, have tried to put through wages that will allow a living, however small. But the large growers, who have been shown to be the only group making a considerable profit from agriculture, are devoting their money to tear gas and rifle ammunition. The men will organize and the large growers will meet organization with force. It is easy to prophesy this.... There is tension in the valley, and fear for the future.

It is fervently hoped that the great group of migrant workers so necessary to the harvesting of California's crops may be given the right to live decently, that they may not be so badgered, tormented, and hurt that in the end they become avengers of the hundreds of thousands who have been tortured and starved before them.

SOURCE: *The Nation,* New York, September 1936.

1937

INTERNATIONAL

Japanese planes, while bombing China, sink U.S. gunboat *Panay* and three supply ships (December 12); Japan accepts blame, apologizes, pays indemnities.

President Franklin D. Roosevelt urges international quarantine of aggressors as only way to peace.

Congress forbids shipment of arms to either side in Spanish Civil War.

NATIONAL

President Roosevelt submits plan to increase Supreme Court from 9 to 15 if judges decline to retire at 70; calls for increasing number of federal court judges to as many as 50 (February 5); Chief Justice Charles Evans Hughes says court does not need more justices (March 11); Senate by 70–20 vote recommits plan to Judiciary Committee (July 22), where it dies.

Supreme Court upholds series of New Deal measures: Washington minimum-wage law, National Labor Relations Act *(NLRB* v. *Jones & Laughlin Steel),* and Social Security laws.

William H. Hastie is first African-American federal judge.

President Roosevelt, starting his second term, is first to be inaugurated in January rather than March under the Twentieth Amendment.

Bonneville Dam on Columbia River is dedicated.

Lyndon B. Johnson begins 12 years as a representative from Texas.

DEATHS Andrew W. Mellon, Treasury Secretary (1921–1933); Joseph Lee, a leader in playground development; Henry T. Mayo, commander-in-chief, Atlantic Fleet (1916–1919); Frank B. Kellogg, Secretary of State (1925–1929).

BUSINESS/INDUSTRY/INVENTIONS

Congress of Industrial Organizations (CIO) is created with John L. Lewis president (November 14).

U.S. Steel Corp. recognizes Steelworkers union (March 2); Steelworkers demonstrate in front of South Chicago Republic Steel plant, are fired on by police; 4 are killed, 84 are injured.

Rockefeller Center in New York City is completed.

Edwin H. Land founds Polaroid Corp.

General Motors and Chrysler recognize United Auto Workers as bargaining agent for their employees.

DEATHS John R. Pope, architect (National Gallery of Art); Dr. Wallace H. Carothers, research chemist (neoprene, nylon); John D. Rockefeller, Standard Oil founder; Charles E. Hires, root-beer developer; Edward A. Filene, Boston department-store founder; Jacob Schick, razor manufacturer.

TRANSPORTATION

German zeppelin, *Hindenburg,* burns at its mooring in Lakehurst, New Jersey; 36 die.

Golden Gate Bridge opens; first Lincoln Tunnel tube under Hudson River is completed.

Amelia Earhart and pilot Fred Noonan disappear in Pacific Ocean while on round-the-world flight.

SCIENCE/MEDICINE

Clinton J. Davisson shares Nobel Prize in physics with George P. Thomson of England for discovery of the diffraction of electrons by crystals; Albert Szent-Györgyi is awarded prize for physiology/medicine for work on biological combustion processes.

Cook County Hospital, Chicago, establishes first blood bank (March 15).

Physicist I. I. Rabi develops atomic and molecular beam method for observing spectra in radio frequency

This temporary bridge connects the flooded section of Louisville, Kentucky, and the city highlands. The flood, which also hit other cities along the Ohio River, claimed 137 lives in 1937. **CORBIS-BETTMANN**

range; Grote Reber builds first radio telescope; James Hiller develops first practical electron microscope.

National Foundation for Infantile Paralysis and National Cancer Institute are founded.

Dr. Max Theiler develops a vaccine for yellow fever.

DEATH Charles Hayden, a founder of New York City planetarium named for him.

RELIGION

Rev. Norman Vincent Peale and others found American Foundation for Religion and Psychiatry.

Catholic Archbishop Edward F. Mooney of Rochester, New York, becomes first archbishop of Detroit, Michigan.

ART/MUSIC

Andrew Mellon turns over large art collection to federal government and sufficient funds to build and endow National Gallery of Art; Tanglewood in Berkshires is given to Boston Symphony Orchestra as permanent summer-festival home.

Gutzon Borglum unveils the head of President Lincoln, the third head carved on Mt. Rushmore in the Black Hills, South Dakota.

Arturo Toscanini conducts NBC Symphony, especially created for him.

Gian Carlo Menotti composes opera *Amelia Goes to the Ball.*

Glenn Miller forms band.

Museum of Costume Arts incorporates in New York City.

George Biddle completes the painting *William Gropper;* Peter Blume, *The Eternal City;* Lyonel Feininger, *Towers at Halle;* Joseph Hirsch, *Two Men;* Jack Levine, *The Feast of Pure Reason;* John Flanagan completes the sculpture *Triumph of the Egg.*

SONGS (POPULAR): "Bei Mir Bist Du Schön," "Blue Hawaii," "Boo Hoo," "The Lady Is a Tramp," "My Funny Valentine," "Rosalie," "September in the Rain," "Sweet Leilani," "That Old Feeling," "Where or When," "Whistle While You Work."

DEATHS George Gershwin, composer; Bessie Smith, one of the greatest blues singers.

LITERATURE/JOURNALISM

Dr. Seuss (Theodore S. Geisel) completes his first book, *To Think That I Saw It on Mulberry Street.*

Look magazine begins publication.

Babe Didrikson, shown here in 1937, is America's first female superstar. She is an Olympic gold medalist, an accomplished tennis player, and a major force in women's golf, helping to found the Ladies Professional Golfers' Association. CORBIS-BETTMANN

Eleanor M. Patterson leases (later buys) *Washington Herald* and *Washington Times,* combines them.

Edward R. Murrow in London heads CBS European bureau.

BOOKS *Of Mice and Men* by John Steinbeck, *The Late George Apley* by John P. Marquand, *Strictly from Hunger* by S. J. Perelman, *Northwest Passage* by Kenneth Roberts, *The Chute* by Albert Halper, *Patterns of Culture* by Ruth Benedict.

DEATHS Edith Wharton, author; Paul E. More, cofounder of modern humanism.

ENTERTAINMENT

Mobile television units are produced for NBC.

Term *disc jockey* is coined in *Variety.*

PLAYS Luther Adler stars in *Golden Boy,* Gertrude Lawrence in *Susan and God,* Burgess Meredith in *High Tor,* George M. Cohan in *I'd Rather Be Right,* Broderick Crawford in *Of Mice and Men.*

MOVIES *Snow White and the Seven Dwarfs, Lost Horizon* with Ronald Colman, *Heidi* with Shirley Temple, *The Good Earth* with Paul Muni, *Captains Courageous* with Spencer Tracy, *The Awful Truth* with Cary Grant and Irene Dunne, *In Old Chicago* with Alice Faye and Tyrone Power, *A Star Is Born* with Janet Gaynor.

New radio programs include *American Forum of the Air, Big Town, Meet Corliss Archer,* and *Mary Margaret McBride.*

The dance Big Apple sweeps the country.

DEATHS Jean Harlow, screen actress; Mrs. Leslie Carter, actress sometimes called America's Sarah Bernhardt.

SPORTS

WINNERS *Auto racing*—Wilbur Shaw, Indianapolis 500; *Baseball*—New York Yankees, World Series; *Bicycling*—Doris Kopsky, first U.S. women's title; *Boxing*—Joe Louis, heavyweight; Benny Lynch, flyweight; *Football* (bowls)—Pittsburgh, Rose; Duquesne, Orange; Santa Clara, Sugar; Texas Christian, Cotton; Washington, NFL; *Golf*—U.S., Ryder Cup; Ralph Guldahl, U.S. Open; Denny Shute, PGA; Byron Nelson, Masters; *Hockey*—Detroit, Stanley Cup; *Horse racing*—War Admiral wins Kentucky Derby, Preakness Stakes, and Belmont Stakes to become fourth Triple Crown winner; *Tennis*—U.S., Davis Cup; Don Budge, U.S. Open (men); Anita Lizana, U.S. Open (women); *Yachting*—U.S. boat *Ranger* retains America's Cup.

DEATHS Ray C. Ewry, track gold medalist in 1904, 1908 Olympics; Howie Morenz, hockey great.

MISCELLANEOUS

Explosion at New London (Texas) school kills 413 pupils and teachers.

Charles W. Howard conducts one-week "Santa Claus" school in Albion, New York.

First animated cartoon electric sign lights up on Broadway in New York City.

Ohio River floods (especially at Cincinnati and Louisville) result in 137 deaths, $500 million damage.

1938

INTERNATIONAL

Mexico nationalizes British and U.S. oil companies; property valued at $415 million.

President Franklin D. Roosevelt asks Hitler and Mussolini for peaceful solution of growing European problem.

NATIONAL

Congress authorizes $1-billion expansion of two-ocean navy in next 10 years.

House Committee on Un-American Activities is created to investigate subversive activities.

Dr. Francis E. Townsend, old-age pension-plan advocate, is pardoned from 30-day prison term for contempt of Congress.

New York State law requires marriage-license applicants to have medical tests.

Olympic (Washington) National Park is established.

Pickwick Landing Dam on Tennessee River is completed.

DEATHS Helen M. Shepard, endower of American Hall of Fame at New York University; Clarence S. Darrow, defense attorney.

BUSINESS/INDUSTRY/INVENTIONS

Congress reduces taxes on business; the Food, Drug, and Cosmetic Act passes, prohibits misbranding or false advertising of products; Fair Labor Standards Act establishes 40-cents-per-hour minimum wage and 40-hour workweek and sets 16 as minimum age for workers.

Federal Crop Insurance Corp. is authorized; Federal National Mortgage Assn. is created; Agricultural Administration Act is signed.

The Mercury Theater of the Air's dramatization of the science fiction novel *The War of the Worlds*, broadcast on radio October 30, 1938, causes thousands of listeners to panic, fearing an invasion of Martians. Orson Welles provides the voice of the reporter. AP/WIDE WORLD PHOTOS

William McC. Martin becomes first salaried president of New York Stock Exchange.

DuPont Co. announces development of nylon, first usable synthetic fiber.

DEATHS Charles R. Walgreen, founder of drug-store chain; Harvey S. Firestone, rubber company founder.

TRANSPORTATION

Howard Hughes flies around the world in record 3 days, 19 hours, 14 minutes, 28 seconds (July 14); Douglas ("Wrong Way") Corrigan flies from New York to Dublin in 28 hours, 13 minutes, says he thought he was flying to Los Angeles (July 18).

Civil Aeronautics Authority is created to supervise nonmilitary aviation (June 23).

John K. Northrop creates Northrop Aviation Corp.

Honeymoon Bridge at Niagara Falls collapses under pressure of a huge ice jam (January 27); Thousand Islands Bridge over St. Lawrence River opens; bridge connecting Port Huron, Michigan, and Port Edward, Canada, is dedicated.

Airlines carry 1,365,706 revenue passengers.

Massive turbines of the Pickwick Dam are part of the federal government's Tennessee Valley Authority program, which brings affordable electricity to much of the Tennessee Valley during the New Deal. NATIONAL ARCHIVES/CORBIS-BETTMANN

DEATH Joseph B. Strauss, bridge designer (Golden Gate).

SCIENCE/MEDICINE

Enrico Fermi is awarded Nobel Prize in physics for work on nuclear reactions.

National Society for Legalization of Euthanasia is founded.

DEATHS William H. Pickering, astronomer; John J. Abel, who isolated adrenaline and insulin in crystalline form.

EDUCATION

Harvard University observes its tercentenary.

Institute of General Semantics is founded in Chicago.

RELIGION

Mother Francis Xavier Cabrini becomes first American citizen beatified in Catholic church.

Supreme Court upholds right of Jehovah's Witnesses to distribute religious literature without a license.

DEATH Patrick J. Hayes, Catholic archbishop of New York (1919–1938).

ART/MUSIC

Aaron Copland presents ballet *Billy the Kid;* Walter Piston composes First Symphony and *The Incredible Flutist.*

Walter Gropius chairs Harvard Graduate School of Design.

Charles Sheeler completes the painting *Upstairs;* Lyonel Feininger, *Dawn;* Robert Laurent, *Kneeling Woman.*

Benny Goodman's orchestra presents first jazz concert in Carnegie Hall; Lawrence Welk describes his style as "champagne music."

SONGS (POPULAR): "A-Tisket, A-Tasket," "My Heart Belongs to Daddy," "I'll Be Seeing You," "Jeepers Creepers," "Music, Maestro, Please," "One O'Clock Jump," "You Must Have Been a Beautiful Baby," "San Antonio Rose," "Thanks for the Memories."

DEATHS William J. Glackens, artist and illustrator; Alma Gluck, lyric soprano; King (Joseph) Oliver, pioneer jazz cornetist.

LITERATURE/JOURNALISM

Pearl Buck is awarded Nobel Prize in literature for books on China and biographies.

H. V. Kaltenborn, chief CBS news commentator, makes almost nonstop radio broadcasts during Munich crisis; on air 102 times in 18 days.

BOOKS *The Yearling* by Marjorie Kinnan Rawlings, *Benjamin Franklin* by Carl Van Doren, *The Long Valley* by John Steinbeck, *I'm a Stranger Here Myself* (poet-

Behind this billboard advertising comfortable travel conditions are three families of migrants seeking shelter and a new life in California in 1938. John Steinbeck's novel *The Grapes of Wrath,* which will be published in 1939, popularizes the plight of these Dust Bowl refugees during the Great Depression. CORBIS-BETTMANN

ry) by Ogden Nash, *Dynasty of Death* by Taylor Caldwell, *The Unvanquished* by William Faulkner.

DEATHS Thomas Wolfe, author; Elzie C. Segar, cartoonist ("Popeye"); O. O. McIntyre, syndicated newspaper columnist.

ENTERTAINMENT

Radio dramatization of H. G. Wells's *War of the Worlds* by Orson Welles and Mercury Theater is so realistic that it creates a brief nationwide scare.

Marineland, south of St. Augustine, Florida, opens.

Massachusetts Television Institute is established.

Vladimir K. Zworykin develops first practical television camera.

Hedda Hopper syndicates a Hollywood newspaper gossip column.

American Guild of Variety Artists is formed.

PLAYS Raymond Massey stars in *Abe Lincoln in Illinois,* Walter Huston in *Knickerbocker Holiday,* Ethel Waters in *Mamba's Daughters,* Ole Olson and Chic Johnson in *Hellzapoppin;* Thornton Wilder completes *Our Town.*

MOVIES *Room Service* and *A Day at the Circus* with the Marx Brothers, *Boys Town* with Spencer Tracy, *You Can't Take It With You* with Jean Arthur, *Robin Hood* with Errol Flynn, *Algiers* with Charles Boyer, *Jezebel* with Bette Davis.

Bob Hope begins his radio show; Clifton Fadiman moderates *Information Please;* Kay Kyser's *Kollege of Musical Knowledge* debuts.

The British dance, Lambeth Walk, is introduced in U.S.

DEATH Pearl White, silent screen actress *(The Perils of Pauline).*

SPORTS

Johnny Vander Meer of Cincinnati Reds pitches no-hit game against Boston (June 11); repeats no-hitter four days later against Brooklyn Dodgers.

Jockey Eddie Arcaro rides 4,000th winner.

Eastern College Athletic Conference is organized.

WINNERS *Auto racing*—Floyd Roberts, Indianapolis 500; *Baseball*—New York Yankees, World Series; *Baseball*—Temple, first National Invitation Tourney (NIT); *Boxing*—Joe Louis, heavyweight; Henry Armstrong, welterweight and lightweight titles; Joey Archibald, featherweight; *Football* (bowls)—Califor-

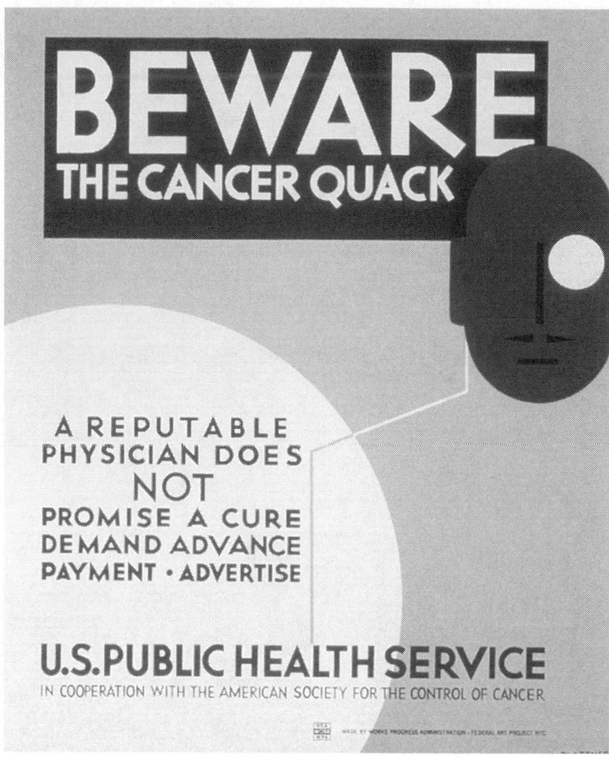

Beware the Cancer Quack, 1938. During the New Deal administration of Franklin Roosevelt, federal agencies become more involved in educating the public about health issues and protecting consumers from quack cures. CORBIS-BETTMANN

nia, Rose; Auburn, Orange; Santa Clara, Sugar; Rice, Cotton; New York Giants, NFL; *Golf*—Great Britain, Walker Cup; Ralph Guldahl, U. S. Open; Paul Runyan, PGA; Henry Picard, Masters; *Hockey*—Chicago, Stanley Cup; *Horse racing*—Laurin, Kentucky Derby; Dauber, Preakness Stakes; Pasteurized, Belmont Stakes; *Tennis*—U.S., Davis Cup; Don Budge, U.S. Open (men); Alice Marble, U.S. Open (women).

DEATH Nathanael G. Herreshoff, designer of America's Cup yachts.

MISCELLANEOUS

Hurricane along Atlantic Coast from Long Island, New York, to Cape Cod, Massachusetts, leaves nearly 700 dead; Southern California floods, landslides kill 144, destroy thousands of homes.

Fairchild Tropical Gardens in Florida is created.

1939

INTERNATIONAL

U.S. declares its neutrality in World War II, which begins in Europe (September 5); Inter-American Conference warns belligerent nations to keep naval actions out of Western Hemisphere.

American arms embargo is repealed, adopts policy of "cash-and-carry" arms exports (November 4).

U.S. agrees to provide financial help to Brazil for economic development.

NATIONAL

President Franklin D. Roosevelt's budget request includes $1.3 billion for national defense (January 5); requests additional $525 million later; president orders purchase of 571 military aircraft, asks for immediate construction of new naval bases.

Federal Security Agency is established to combine activities promoting social and economic security; Federal Works Agency sets up to do the same with public works; Office of Emergency Management is created in Executive Office.

Scientists, including Albert Einstein, notify president of possibilities of an atomic bomb (October 11).

King George VI and Queen Elizabeth arrive in U.S. from Canada for a week's visit, the first by a British monarch.

Social Security amendments are adopted to improve system.

Food-stamp plan that uses agricultural surpluses for those on relief is instituted in Rochester, New York.

Hatch Act passes, prevents federal workers from taking part in political campaigns.

Gunterville Dam on Tennessee River in Alabama is completed.

Transatlantic mail service from New York begins.

Judge Ben Lindsey creates new conciliation court in Los Angeles.

DEATHS Joel Spingarn, a founder and head of NAACP; Robert Fechner, director, Civilian Conservation Corps (1933–1939).

BUSINESS/INDUSTRY/INVENTIONS

Supreme Court upholds right of peaceful assemblage in *Hague* v. *CIO;* Court outlaws sit-down strikes but upholds right to collective bargaining in railroad industry.

Nylon stockings are sold for first time when DuPont puts 4,000 pairs on sale.

DEATH Arthur E. Kennelly, established electrical units and standards, adopted worldwide.

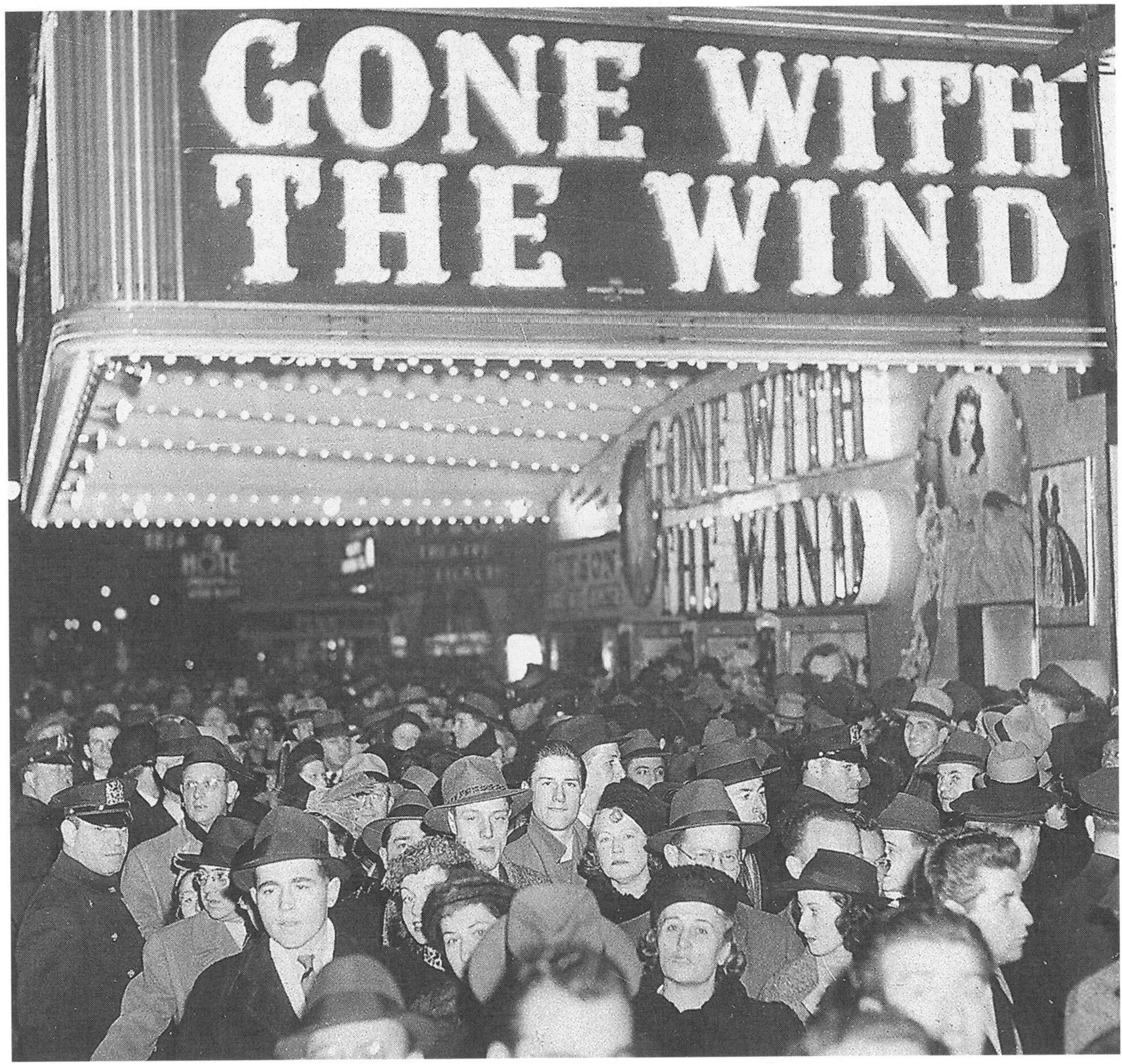

Gone with the Wind premieres in New York. The film will win ten Academy Awards, including best picture. AP/WIDE WORLD PHOTOS

TRANSPORTATION

Pan American Airways begins regular transatlantic passenger air service.

Packard manufactures first air-conditioned automobile.

Igor I. Sikorsky develops first successful helicopter.

McDonnell Aircraft Co. is founded.

Bronx-Whitestone Bridge over East River in New York City and Deer Isle Bridge in Maine open.

SCIENCE/MEDICINE

Ernest O. Lawrence is awarded Nobel Prize in physics for invention of the cyclotron.

Dr. George B. Pegran of Columbia University helps carry out first successful U.S. demonstration of nuclear fission.

DEATHS Dr. Harvey W. Cushing, brain surgeon; Dr. Charles H. Mayo, cofounder of Mayo Clinic.

EDUCATION

Archibald MacLeish begins five years as Librarian of Congress.

Frank Aydelotte is named director of Institute of Advanced Study at Princeton University.

DEATH Henry S. Pritchett, president, Carnegie Foundation for Promotion of Teaching (1906–1930).

Gone with the Wind

In 1939 Metro-Goldwyn-Mayer (MGM) released *Gone with the Wind,* a romantic epic set in the Civil War era. Based on the earlier best-selling novel by Margaret Mitchell, the movie starred Vivien Leigh as Scarlett O'Hara and "King of Hollywood" Clark Gable as Rhett Butler. It cost $4 million to produce over a period of eleven months. *Gone with the Wind* became an instant celluloid classic, thrilling film critics and casual audiences alike with its spectacular cinematography and engaging storyline. The movie contained several memorable scenes, including a frustrated Rhett Butler's response to Scarlett O'Hara's "Oh, where shall I go, what shall I do?,": the indefatigable "Frankly, my dear, I don't give a damn." MGM's movie received ten Academy awards, including best supporting actress honors going to Hattie McDaniel for her role as Mammy. This was the first Oscar presented to an African American actor. Although later criticized for its roseate portrayal of southern Civil War society, *Gone with the Wind* remained a firm favorite with movie fans throughout the latter half of the twentieth century, in spite of its 222-minute running time.

RELIGION

Merger of Methodist Episcopal church, Methodist Church South, and Methodist Protestant church results in 8-million member Methodist church.

Kateri Tekakwitha, "the lily of the Mohawks," is beatified in Rome, first Native American so honored.

Catholic Bishop Francis J. Spellman becomes archbishop of New York; Archbishop Samuel A. Stritch of Milwaukee is transferred to Chicago.

DEATH Catholic Archbishop George W. Mundelein of Chicago (1915–1939).

ART/MUSIC

Mt. Rushmore (South Dakota) presidential sculptures are complete with unveiling of head of Theodore Roosevelt.

Daughters of American Revolution refuse to rent Constitution Hall for a concert by Marian Anderson; First Lady Eleanor Roosevelt resigns from DAR; concert is held Easter Sunday on the Lincoln Memorial steps with 75,000 in attendance.

Museum of Modern Art, New York City, is dedicated.

Arnold Branch completes the painting *Carolina Low Country;* Aaron Bohrod, *Chicago Street;* Ben Shahn, *Seurati's Lunch* and *Handball;* Julian E. Levi, *Fisherman's Family;* Joseph Stella, *The Bridge.*

Frank Sinatra is hired as vocalist with Harry James's orchestra; later moves to Tommy Dorsey's orchestra.

Institute of Design is established in Chicago.

Douglas Moore's opera *The Devil and Daniel Webster* is presented.

SONGS (POPULAR): "God Bless America," "All the Things You Are," "Beer Barrel Polka," "In the Mood," "Little Sir Echo," "Moonlight Serenade," "Over the Rainbow," "Brazil," "I'll Never Smile Again."

DEATH Artur Bodanzky, conductor, Metropolitan Opera Co. (1915–1939).

LITERATURE/JOURNALISM

Pocket Books, inexpensive reprints, are introduced.

Elmer Davis joins CBS News; James B. Reston joins the *New York Times.*

John Crowe Ransom founds *Kenyon Review.*

BOOKS *The Grapes of Wrath* by John Steinbeck, *Wickford Point* by John P. Marquand, *Huntsman, What Quarry?* (poetry) by Edna St. Vincent Millay, *Here Lies* by Dorothy Parker, *The Web and the Rock* by Thomas Wolfe, *The Nazarene* by Sholem Asch, *Children of God* by Vardis Fisher, *Abraham Lincoln* (4 volumes) by Carl Sandburg.

DEATHS Heywood Broun, columnist; Zane Grey, author of Western novels.

ENTERTAINMENT

Grand Ole Opry goes on national television.

PLAYS Tallulah Bankhead stars in *The Little Foxes,* Monty Woolley in *The Man Who Came to Dinner,* Ethel Merman in Cole Porter's *DuBarry Was a Lady,* Bill Robinson in *The Hot Mikado,* Howard Lindsay in *Life with Father,* Gertrude Lawrence in *Skylark.*

MOVIES *Stagecoach* with John Wayne, *Gone with the Wind* with Vivien Leigh and Clark Gable, *The Wizard of Oz* with Judy Garland, *Mr. Smith Goes to Washington* with James Stewart, *Goodbye, Mr. Chips* with Robert Donat, *Wuthering Heights* with Merle Oberon and Laurence Olivier.

Among the new radio shows are *Ellery Queen, The Aldrich Family, Dr. I.Q.*

A new dance, the Samba, arrives from Brazil.

DEATHS Douglas Fairbanks, silent-screen actor; Sidney Howard, playwright; Alice Brady, stage and screen actress.

SPORTS

Baseball Hall of Fame in Cooperstown, New York, is dedicated.

Television comes into sports: first college baseball game (May 17), first major league game (Brooklyn—Cincinnati, August 26), first college football game (Fordham—Waynesburg, September 30), pro football game (Brooklyn—Philadelphia, October 22), first prizefight (June 1).

Lou Gehrig takes himself out of lineup as New York Yankees first baseman (May 2), ends consecutive-game streak at 2,130 (dies less than two years later at 38).

Underwater photography is used for first time to determine finish in swimming races.

WINNERS *Auto racing*—Wilbur Shaw, Indianapolis 500; *Baseball*—New York Yankees, World Series; *Basketball*—Long Island, NIT; Oregon, first NCAA tournament; *Boxing*—Joe Louis, heavyweight; Billy Conn, light heavyweight; Lou Ambers, lightweight; *Football* (bowls)—Southern California, Rose; Tennessee, Orange; Texas Christian, Sugar; St. Mary's, Cotton; Green Bay, NFL; *Golf*—Byron Nelson, U.S. Open; Henry Picard, PGA; Ralph Guldahl, Masters; *Hockey*—Boston, Stanley Cup; *Horse racing*—Johnstown, Kentucky Derby and Belmont Stakes; Challedon, Preakness Stakes; *Tennis*—Australia, Davis Cup; Bobby Riggs, U.S. Open (men); Alice Marble, U.S. Open (women); *Waterskiing*—Bruce Parker, first national title (men); Esther Yates (women).

DEATHS Joe E. Carr, NFL president (1921–1939); Floyd Roberts, winner of 1938 Indianapolis 500 is killed in 1939 race; Jacob Ruppert, brewer and owner, New York Yankees baseball team; James Naismith, developer of basketball.

MISCELLANEOUS

New York World's Fair and Golden Gate Exposition in San Francisco are held.

U.S. submarine *Squalus* sinks at Portsmouth, New Hampshire; 33 of 59 crewmen are saved by using a diving bell.

1940

INTERNATIONAL

World War II (prelude)

President Franklin D. Roosevelt requests $1.8 billion for national defense, $1.2 billion for producing 50,000 planes a year; then asks for $1.3 billion more.

U.S. Air Defense Command is created (February 26); War Department releases outdated stocks (June 3) and transfers 50 overage destroyers to Great Britain in return for bases in Newfoundland and the Caribbean (September 3); U.S. announces embargo on scrap iron and steel to all countries outside the Western Hemisphere except Great Britain (October 16).

Alien Registration Act passes (June 28); 5 million aliens register between August 27 and December 26; Congress approves first peacetime draft for military service of men 21–35 and training of 1.2 million troops and 800,000 reserves in a year (September 16); 16.4 million register by October 16; numbers for the order of service are drawn October 29: first number is 158.

National Defense Research Committee is established, directed by Dr. Vannevar Bush; later becomes Office of Scientific Research and Development.

Pan-American Union approves steps to prevent transfer of European colonies in Western Hemisphere (June 30); all 21 American republics approve Act of Havana (July 30); permits takeover of any colony endangered by aggression.

President Roosevelt and Canadian Prime Minister W. L. McKenzie King agree to set up a Permanent Joint Board on Defense (October 18).

NATIONAL

President Roosevelt is elected to unprecedented third term, receives 27,243,466 popular and 449 electoral votes compared to Republican Wendell L. Willkie's 22,304,755 popular and 82 electoral votes; Republican national convention (June 4) is first to be televised.

Sixteenth census reports national population at 132,164,569.

Chickamauga Dam on Tennessee River and Ft. Peck Dam on Missouri River in Montana are completed.

Benjamin O. Davis becomes first African-American army general.

John F. Kennedy becomes secretary to his father, ambassador to Great Britain.

Franklin D. Roosevelt Library at Hyde Park, New York, is dedicated.

National debt is $43 billion.

DEATH Marcus Garvey, founder of first important African-American organization, Universal Negro Improvement Assn.

In 1940 in Bridgeport, Connecticut, Ivor Sikorsky makes the first successful fully controlled helicopter flight. The device goes straight up for thirty feet, flies two hundred feet around the field, and comes straight down. CORBIS-BETTMANN

BUSINESS/INDUSTRY/INVENTIONS

Chester E. Carlson patents the xerography process.

Charles Eames and Eero Saarinen design revolutionary contour-molded plywood chair that leads to machine-produced furniture.

National unemployment rate reaches 14.6%.

Forty-hour work week goes into effect (October 24).

Philip Murray begins 12 years as president of CIO; George Meany becomes secretary-treasurer of AFL.

Supreme Court upholds the right of peaceful picketing.

DEATHS John T. Thompson, co-inventor of submachine gun; Walter P. Chrysler, founder, Chrysler Corp.; Claude W. Kress, cofounder, dime-store chain; Charles S. Tainter, inventor of Dictaphone.

TRANSPORTATION

National Airport in Washington, D.C., is dedicated.

Lake Washington Floating Bridge in Seattle opens; suspension bridge over the Narrows in Tacoma, Washington, collapses.

Igor I. Sikorsky flies helicopter for 15 minutes at Stamford, Connecticut.

Automobile registrations for year reach 27,465,826.

SCIENCE/MEDICINE

National Institute of Health in Bethesda, Maryland, is dedicated.

Vladimir K. Zworykin demonstrates his electron microscope.

Edwin M. McMillan and Philip H. Abelson discover neptunium (element 93); McMillan and Glenn T. Seaborg discover plutonium (element 94).

DEATHS Raymond Pearl, a founder of biometry; S. Adolphus Knopf, founder of New York City and national tuberculosis associations.

RELIGION

Aurelia H. Reinhardt, president of Mills College, becomes first woman moderator of Unitarian church.

Supreme Court in *Cantwell* v. *Connecticut* upholds right of Jehovah's Witnesses to solicit funds for religious purposes.

Israel Rosenberg becomes president of Union of Orthodox Rabbis.

DEATH Cyrus Adler, a leader of Conservative Judaism.

ART/MUSIC

American Ballet Theater gives its first performance.

Licia Albanese debuts at Metropolitan Opera.

John Steuart Curry completes the painting *Wisconsin Landscape;* Lyonel Feininger, *The River;* Marsden Hartley, *Mount Katahdin, Autumn No. 1;* Joseph Stella, *Full Moon (Barbados);* John Flanagan completes the sculpture *Not Yet.*

A musical quartet written by Benjamin Franklin is found in Paris Conservatory.

Bernard Herrmann composes dramatic cantata *Moby Dick.*

SONGS (POPULAR): "Blueberry Hill," "Fools Rush In," "Frenesi," "How High the Moon," "I'll Never Smile Again," "Pennsylvania 6–5000," "You Are My Sunshine," "All the Things You Are," "Polka Dots and Moonbeams."

DEATHS Hal Kemp, bandleader of 1930s; Jonas Lie, artist *(Brooklyn Bridge).*

LITERATURE/JOURNALISM

Norman Cousins begins 31 years as executive editor of *Saturday Review of Literature.*

BOOKS *For Whom the Bell Tolls* by Ernest Hemingway, *The Heart Is a Lonely Hunter* by Carson McCullers, *Pal Joey* by John O'Hara, *My Name Is Aram* by William Saroyan, *You Can't Go Home Again* by Thomas Wolfe, *Native Son* by Richard Wright, *Homeward to America* (poetry) by John Ciardi, *The Ox-Bow Incident* by Walter V. Clark.

C. C. Beck draws comic strip "Captain Marvel."

DEATHS Edwin Markham, poet ("Man with a Hoe"); F. Scott Fitzgerald, author; Lewis W. Hine, photographer who originated photo story; Robert S. Abbott, publisher, *Chicago Defender* (1905–1940).

ENTERTAINMENT

FM (frequency-modulation) radio introduced (January 5); Peter C. Goldmark develops color television.

American Theater Wing, which operates Stage Door Canteens, originates.

PLAYS Alfred Lunt and Lynn Fontanne star in *There Shall Be No Night,* Ethel Waters in *Cabin in the Sky,* Ethel Merman in *Panama Hattie,* Gene Kelly in *Pal Joey.*

MOVIES *The Great Dictator* with Charlie Chaplin, *The Road to Singapore* with Bing Crosby and Bob Hope, two Disney films *Fantasia* and *Pinocchio, The Grapes of Wrath* with Henry Fonda, *The Philadelphia Story* with Katharine Hepburn, *Rebecca* with Laurence Olivier.

RADIO *The Shadow, Superman, Bell Telephone Hour, Double or Nothing, The Quiz Kids, Truth or Consequences,* and *Abbott and Costello.*

DEATHS Ben Turpin, silent-screen comedian; Tom Mix, silent-screen cowboy.

SPORTS

Cornelius Warmerdam is first to clear 15 feet in pole vault.

Jimmie Foxx of Philadelphia Athletics hits 500th home run.

Belle Martell of Van Nuys, California, becomes first woman licensed as a prizefight referee.

WINNERS *Auto racing*—Wilbur Shaw, Indianapolis 500; *Baseball*—Cincinnati Reds, World Series; *Basketball*—Colorado, NIT; Indiana, NCAA; *Boxing*—Joe Louis, heavyweight; Fritzie Zivic, welterweight; Tony Zale, middleweight; Lew Jenkins, lightweight; *Football* (bowls)—Southern California, Rose; Georgia Tech, Orange; Texas A&M, Sugar; Clemson, Cotton; Chicago Bears, NFL; *Golf*—Lawson Little, U.S. Open; Byron Nelson, PGA; Jimmy Demaret, Masters; *Gymnastics*—Illinois, first intercollegiate title; *Hockey*—New York Rangers, Stanley Cup; *Horse racing*—Gallahadion, Kentucky Derby; Bimelech, Preakness Stakes and Belmont Stakes; *Tennis*—Don McNeill, U.S. Open (men), Alice Marble, U.S. Open (women).

MISCELLANEOUS

Fire in a Natchez, Mississippi, dance hall kills 198.

1941

INTERNATIONAL

World War II

After almost a year of preparing and helping allies under attack, U.S. enters World War II with shocking speed.

Japanese planes in surprise dawn attack December 7 on Pearl Harbor destroy or damage 19 U.S. warships and 150 planes; 2,400 are killed. Japanese also attack Philippines, Guam, Midway, Hong Kong, and the Malay Peninsula.

Congress on December 8 takes 33 minutes to declare war on Japan with Montana Rep. Jeannette Rankin casting the only dissenting vote (she voted the same way

Pearl Harbor

At 7:55 A.M. on December 7, 1941 a total of 360 Japanese fighter planes and bombers from the *Kido Butai* launched an unexpected attack on the U.S. Navy's Pacific Fleet docked at Pearl Harbor, along with other military facilities at Oahu, Hawaii. The bombing lasted for just under two hours. Approximately 2,403 Americans were killed, 183 planes destroyed, and 11 vessels sunk. The *U.S.S. Arizona,* a 26-year-old battleship, was destroyed after a bomb struck one of its gun turrets, resulting in the loss of 1,177 lives. The initial scene was one of confusion and disbelief: The stunning aerial bombardment was totally unexpected, and it represented the first time the U.S. had been attacked on its own soil. The following day President Franklin D. Roosevelt asked Congress for a declaration of war, and the U.S. entered World War II. The memory of Pearl Harbor lingered in American consciousness for many years. Exactly fifty years later, the movie *Pearl Harbor* by Touchstone Pictures (which opened on Memorial Day, 2001) refocused attention on the human tragedy that fateful morning.

in 1917). Germany and Italy declare war on U.S. (December 11); U.S. declares war on them.

Japanese troops land on Luzon in the Philippines (December 10), capture Guam (December 11).

Admiral Chester Nimitz commands Pacific fleet, Admiral Ernest King heads U.S. naval forces.

Before these December events, U.S. had created Lend-Lease Program (March 11), allowing nations deemed vital to U.S. to get arms and equipment by sale, transfer, or lease; $7 billion was appropriated. U.S. promises to help Russia after it is invaded by Germany, granting $1 billion in credit; signs agreement for lend-lease with China.

U.S. pledges defense of Denmark's Greenland after getting right to build installations there (April 9); U.S. lands troops on Denmark's Iceland after agreement on bases (July 7).

U.S. involved in war even before formal entry: merchant ship *Robin Moor* is sunk in the Atlantic by German submarine (May 21); U.S. destroyer *Kearney* is torpedoed (October 17), destroyer *Reuben James* is sunk (October 30). The 1939 Neutrality Act is amended (November 17) to permit arming merchant ships; all German and Italian (and later Japanese) assets in U.S. are frozen.

After a secret meeting at sea, President Franklin D. Roosevelt and British Prime Minister Winston Churchill issue Atlantic Charter (August 14), assures the right of people to choose and retain own governments, renounces territorial ambitions, and calls for disarmament of aggressor nations.

Preparations at home include creation of various agencies: Office of Production Management (January 7), War Shipping Administration (February 7), Office of Price Administration (April 15), Office of Civilian Defense (May 20), Office of Defense Transportation (December 18), Office of Censorship (December 19). United Service Organizations (USO) is formed (April 7).

President proclaims national emergency (May 27), orders closing of German and Italian consulates; a dimout 15 miles wide along the Atlantic Coast is put into effect (April 28) to combat submarine attacks; President orders step-up of production of heavy bombers from 9 a month to 50.

Selective Service is extended for 18 months (August 18), ages change from 21–35 to 20–45; rationing begins with automobile tires (December 27).

U.S. Civil Air patrol is created (December 1) as part of civil-defense operation.

Navy takes over French liner *Normandie* in New York Harbor.

NATIONAL

President enunciates "four freedoms" in a speech to Congress: freedom of speech and religion, freedom from want and fear. **SEE PRIMARY DOCUMENT** "The Four Freedoms" by Franklin D. Roosevelt

Supreme Court Chief Justice Charles Evans Hughes resigns; Associate Justice Harlan F. Stone succeeds him.

Supreme Court in *Edwards* v. *California* rules "Okie" law designed to exclude indigent immigrants unconstitutional; upholds 1938 Fair Labor Standards Act in *United States* v. *Darby.*

Grand Coulee Dam, world's largest hydroelectric facility, generates power in Washington; Los Angeles and other Southern California cities receive water from Colorado River Aqueduct.

Mammoth Cave (Kentucky) National Park is established.

Adam Clayton Powell, pastor of a Harlem Baptist church, becomes first African-American member of New York City Council.

Lanham Act authorizes $150 million for defense housing.

BUSINESS/INDUSTRY/INVENTIONS

National Defense Mediation Board is given power to deal with labor disputes in defense industries; Government takes over North American Aviation plant in Inglewood, California, to end strike impairing defense production.

Fair Employment Practice Committee is set up to curb discrimination in war production and government employment.

Dacron is introduced.

Simmons Co. manufactures electric blankets.

TRANSPORTATION

Ford Motor Co. recognizes United Auto Workers as bargaining agent for its employees.

Rainbow Bridge over Niagara River at Niagara Falls opens.

DEATH Frederic J. Fisher of Fisher Body Co.

SCIENCE/MEDICINE

Glenn T. Seaborg and Emilio Segre produce plutonium, first manufactured fissionable material.

First atomic reactor is built.

EDUCATION

Supreme Court rules that religious training in public schools is unconstitutional.

RELIGION

Rev. Karl M. Block becomes Episcopal bishop of California.

ART/MUSIC

National Gallery of Art opens in Washington, D.C.

Ted Shawn founds Jacob's Pillow Dance Festival in Massachusetts.

Grandma (Anna M.) Moses completes the painting *Black Horses;* Louis Guglielmi, *Terror in Brooklyn;* Joseph Hirsch, *The Senator.*

SONGS (POPULAR): "The Anniversary Waltz," "Bewitched, Bothered, and Bewildered," "Chattanooga Choo Choo," "Deep in the Heart of Texas," "The Last Time I Saw Paris," "I Don't Want to Walk Without You," "Jersey Bounce," "Take the A Train," "There I've Said It Again."

DEATHS Gutzon Borglum, sculptor of Mt. Rushmore president heads; Jelly Roll Morton, jazz musician and composer.

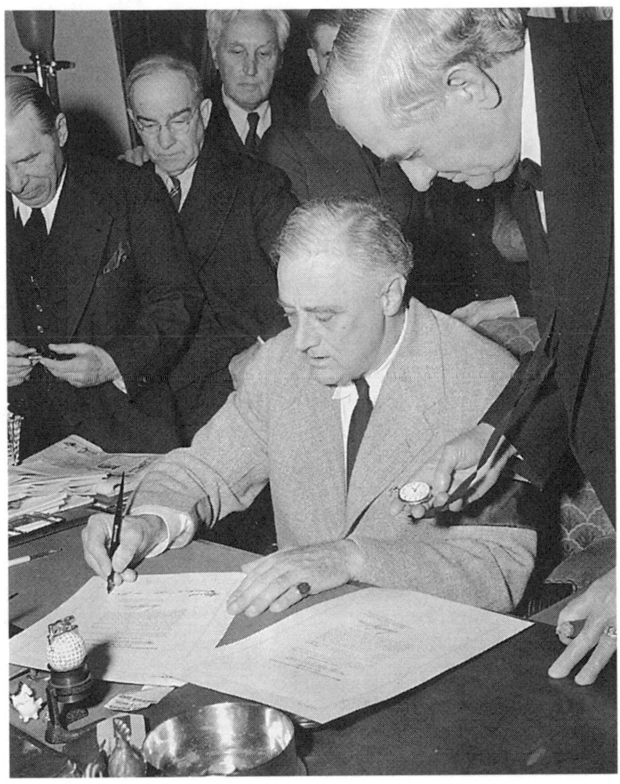

President Franklin D. Roosevelt declares war on Germany at the White House on December 11, 1941. To his right, Sen. Tom Connally notes the exact time of 3:08 P.M. **AP/WIDE WORLD PHOTOS**

LITERATURE/JOURNALISM

Chicago Sun is founded.

BOOKS *The Last Tycoon* by F. Scott Fitzgerald, *Keys of the Kingdom* by A. J. Cronin, *Saratoga Trunk* by Edna Ferber, *H. M. Pulham, Esquire* by John P. Marquand, *Berlin Diary* by William L. Shirer.

DEATH Edward J. H. O'Brien, editor of annual best short-stories collections (1915–1940).

ENTERTAINMENT

WNBT, New York City, shows first audience participation telecast; first commercial television license is issued to NBC (July 1); Nielsen gauges radio ratings.

PLAYS Josephine Hull stars in *Arsenic and Old Lace,* Gertrude Lawrence in *Lady in the Dark,* Mady Christians in *Watch on the Rhine.*

An abandoned house and covered wagon symbolize the wasted landscape of the Dust Bowl of the 1930s and early 1940s. Many residents never return to their land. NATIONAL ARCHIVES AND RECORDS ADMINISTRATION

MOVIES *Citizen Kane* with Orson Welles, *The Maltese Falcon* with Humphrey Bogart, *Sergeant York* with Gary Cooper, *Suspicion* with Cary Grant, *How Green Was My Valley* with Walter Pidgeon, *Sun Valley Serenade* with Sonja Henie.

Milton Berle and Red Skelton begin radio shows; other new programs are *Duffy's Tavern* and *Mr. and Mrs. North.*

DEATH Screen actress Carole Lombard, in plane crash.

SPORTS

American Bowling Congress Hall of Fame is founded.

New York Yankee Joe DiMaggio's consecutive-game hitting streak ends at 56 games.

Lefty Grove of Boston Red Sox wins 300th baseball game.

WINNERS *Auto racing*—Floyd Davis, Mauri Rose, Indianapolis 500; *Baseball*—New York Yankees, World Series; *Basketball*—Long Island, NIT; Wisconsin, NCAA; *Bowling*—John Crimmins, first all-star tournament; *Boxing*—Joe Louis, heavyweight; Gus Lesnevich, light heavyweight; Freddie Cochrane, welterweight; Tony Zale, middlweight; Sammy Angott, lightweight; Chalky Wright, featherweight; *Football* (bowls)—Stanford, Rose; Mississippi State, Orange; Boston College, Sugar; Texas A&M, Cotton; Chicago Bears, NFL; *Golf*—Craig Wood, U.S. Open and Masters; Victor Ghezzi, PGA; *Hockey*—Boston, Stanley Cup; *Horse racing*—Whirlaway wins Kentucky Derby, Preakness Stakes, and Belmont Stakes to become fifth Triple Crown winner; *Tennis*—Bobby Riggs, U.S. Open (men); Sarah Palfrey Cooke, U.S. Open (women).

DEATH Lou Gehrig, baseball player who set consecutive-game record at 2,130 games.

MISCELLANEOUS

Blizzard strikes upper Midwest, claims 70 lives.

PRIMARY SOURCE DOCUMENT

"The Four Freedoms" by Franklin D. Roosevelt, January 6, 1941

INTRODUCTION Franklin Delano Roosevelt, the thirty-second president of the United States, spent most of the 1930s trying to rebuild the crippled American economy and restore Americans' confidence in democracy and capitalism. Grappling with complex economic problems at home and maintaining its traditional policy of isolationism in world affairs, the United States stayed out of the emerging European crisis. In the mid- to late 1930s Congress passed a series of neutrality laws prohibiting the sale of arms and munitions, loans to belligerent nations like Germany and Italy, and travel by American ships in designated war zones. However, the outbreak of war in Europe, starting with Nazi Germany's rapid conquest of Poland, France, and Scandinavia in 1939 and 1940, forced Roosevelt and the country as a whole to look beyond its borders to consider the future. As Adolf Hitler's army marched through Europe, Roosevelt found ways to circumvent the neutrality laws and provide military assistance to Britain on a lend-lease basis (exchanging battleships for the lease of eight British territories). He also established the Selective Service Act of 1940, which created the first American peacetime draft.

Roosevelt was elected to an unprecedented third term in 1940, partly as a result of his promise to not send American boys to war, but he clearly understood that World War II would eventually threaten American security. His 1941 State of the Union address, printed here, stood as a warning to Congress and to the nation that continued isolationism would only prevent the United States from adequately preparing for a possible invasion. In this speech he also announced that a transition from peace to wartime production was already under way. Roosevelt urged Congress to accept the need to supply friendly nations with war material. And that he believed the American people would put "patriotism ahead of pocketbooks" and accept higher taxes to pay for the increased military expenditures required for national defense. On August 14, 1941, the Four Freedoms outlined here were codified in the Atlantic Charter created by Roosevelt and British Prime Minister Winston Churchill to express the joint war aims of the United States and Great Britain.

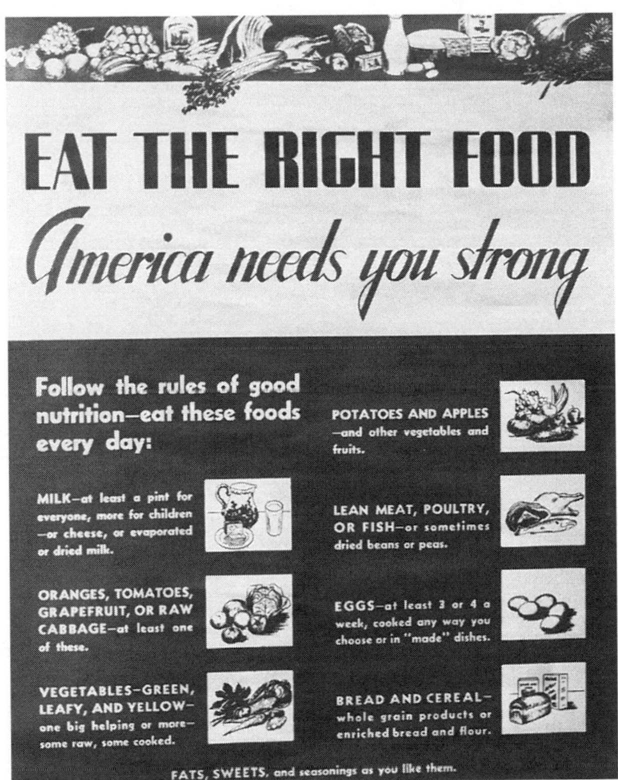

Originating from the office of Defense Health and Welfare Services, this wartime poster reminds every American to "Eat the Right Food." It is the original Food Pyramid that becomes a common tool of the Federal Government to ensure good nutrition and good health. CORBIS-BETTMANN

Mr. Speaker, members of the 77th Congress:

I address you, the members of this new Congress, at a moment unprecedented in the history of the union. I use the word "unprecedented" because at no previous time has American security been as seriously threatened from without as it is today.

Since the permanent formation of our government under the Constitution in 1789, most of the periods of crisis in our history have related to our domestic affairs. And fortunately, only one of these—the four-year war between the States—ever threatened our national unity. Today thank God, 130,000,000 Americans in forty-eight States have forgotten points of the compass in our national unity.

It is true that prior to 1914 the United States often has been disturbed by events in other continents. We have even engaged in two wars with European nations and in a number of undeclared wars in the West Indies, in the Mediterranean and in the Pacific, for the maintenance of American rights and for the Principles of peaceful commerce. But in no case has a serious threat been raised against our national safety or our continued independence. What I seek to convey is the historic truth that the United States as a nation has at all times maintained opposition—clear, definite opposition—to any attempt to lock us in behind an ancient Chinese wall while the procession of civilization went past. Today, thinking of our children and of their children, we oppose enforced isolation for ourselves or for any other part of the Americas....

And in like fashion, from 1815 to 1914—ninety-nine years—no single war in Europe or in Asia constituted a real threat against our future or against the future of any other American nation...Even when the World War broke out in 1941 it seemed to contain only small threat of danger to our own American future. But as time went on, as we remember, the American people began to visualize what the downfall of democratic nations might mean to our own democracy....

I suppose that every realist knows that the democratic way of life is at this moment being directly assailed in every part of the world—assailed either by arms or by secret spreading of poisonous propaganda by those who seek to destroy unity and promote discord in nations that are still at peace.

During sixteen long months this assault has blotted out the whole pattern of democratic life in an appalling number of independent nations, great and small. And the assailants are still on the march, threatening other nations, great and small. Therefore, as your President, performing my constitutional duty to "give to the Congress information of the state of the union," I find it unhappily necessary to report that the future and the safety of our country and of our democ-

Joe Dimaggio's 56-game hitting streak, which begins on May 15, 1941, ends on July 17. **AP/WIDE WORLD PHOTOS**

racy are overwhelmingly involved in events far beyond our borders.

Armed defense of democratic existence is now being gallantly waged in four continents. If that defense fails, all the population and all the resources of Europe and Asia, Africa and Australia will be dominated by conquerors. And let us remember that the total of those populations in those four continents, the total of those populations and their resources greatly exceeds the sum total of the population and the resources of the whole of the Western Hemisphere—yes, many times over.

In times like these it is immature—and, incidentally, untrue—for anybody to brag that an unprepared America, single-handed and with one hand tied behind its back, can hold off the whole world. No realistic American can expect from a dictator's peace international generosity, or return of true independence, or world disarmament, or freedom of expression, or freedom of religion—or even good business. Such a peace would bring no security for us or for our neighbors. Those who would give up essential liberty to purchase a little temporary safety deserve neither liberty nor safety.

As a nation we may take pride in the fact that we are soft-hearted; but we cannot afford to be soft-headed. We must always be wary of those who with sounding brass and a tinkling cymbal preach the ism of appeasement. We must especially beware of that small group of selfish men who would clip the wings of the American eagle in order to feather their own nests. I have recently pointed out how quickly the tempo of modern warfare could bring into our very midst the physical attack which we must eventually expect if the dictator nation win this war.…

The first phase of the invasion of this hemisphere would not be the landing of regular troops. The necessary strategic points would be occupied by secret agents and by their dupes—and great numbers of them are already here and in Latin America. As long as the aggressor nations maintain the offensive they, not we, will choose the time and the place and the method of their attack. And that is why the future of all the American Republics is today in serious danger. That is why this annual message to the Congress is unique in our history. That is why every member of the executive branch of the government and every member of the Congress face great responsibility—great accountability.

The need of the moment is that our actions and our policy should be devoted primarily—almost exclusively—to meeting this foreign peril. For all our domestic problems are now a part of the great emergency. Just as our national policy in internal affairs has been based upon a decent respect for the rights and the dignity of all of our fellow men within our gates, so our national policy in foreign affairs has been based on a decent respect for the rights and the dignity of all nations, large and small. And the justice of morality must and will win in the end.

Our national policy is this: First, by an impressive expression of the public will and without regard to partisanship, we are committed to all-inclusive national defense. Second, by an impressive expression of the public will and without regard to partisanship, we are committed to full support of all those resolute people everywhere who are resisting aggression and are thereby keeping war away from our hemisphere. By this support we express our determination that the democratic cause shall prevail, and we strengthen the defense and the security of our own nation.

Third, by an impressive expression of the public will and without regard to partisanship, we are committed to the proposition that principle of morality and considerations for our own security will never permit us to acquiesce in a peace dictated by aggressors and sponsored by appeasers. We know that enduring peace cannot be bought at the cost of other people's freedom....

Therefore, the immediate need is a swift and driving increase in our armament production. Leaders of industry and labor have responded to our summons. Goals of speed have been set. In some cases these goals are being reached ahead of time. In some cases we are on schedule; in other cases there are slight but not serious delays. And in some cases—and, I am sorry to say, very important cases—we are all concerned by the slowness of the accomplishment of our plans. The Army and Navy, however, have made substantial progress during the past year. Actual experience is improving and speeding up our methods of production with every passing day. And today's best is not good enough for tomorrow....

To change a whole nation from a basis of peacetime production of implements of peace to a basis of wartime production of implements of war is no small task. The greatest difficulty comes at the beginning of the program, when new tools, new plant facilities, new assembly lines, new shipways must first be constructed before the actual material begins to flow steadily and speedily from them....

New circumstances are constantly begetting new needs for our safety. I shall ask this Congress for greatly increased new appropriations and authorizations to carry on what we have begun.

I also ask this Congress for authority and for funds sufficient to manufacture additional munitions and war supplies of many kinds, to be turned over to those nations which are now in actual war with aggressor nations. Our most useful and immediate role is to act as an arsenal for them as well as for ourselves. They do not need manpower, but they do need billions of dollars' worth of the weapons of defense. The time is near when they will not be able to pay for them all in ready cash. We cannot, and we will not, tell them that they must surrender merely because of present inability to pay for the weapons which we know they must have.

I do not recommend that we make them a loan of dollars with which to pay for these weapons—a loan to be repaid in dollars. I recommend that we make it possible for those nations to continue to obtain war materials in the United States, fitting their orders into our own program. And nearly all of their material would, if the time ever came, be useful in our own defense. Taking counsel of expert military and naval authorities, considering what is best for our own security, we are free to decide how much should be kept here and how much should be sent abroad to our friends who, by their determined and heroic resistance, are giving us time in which to make ready our own defense.

For what we send abroad we shall be repaid, repaid within a reasonable time following the close of hostilities, repaid in similar materials, or at our option in other goods of many kinds which they can produce and which we need. Let us say to the democracies: "We Americans are vitally concerned in your defense of freedom. We are putting forth our energies, our resources and our organizing powers to give you the strength to regain and maintain a free world. We shall send you in ever-increasing numbers, ships, planes, tanks, guns. That is our purpose and our pledge".... Yes, and we must prepare, all of us prepare, to make the sacrifices that the emergency—almost as serious as war itself—demands. Whatever stands in the way of speed and efficiency in defense, in defense preparations at any time, must give way to the national need. A free nation has the right to expect full cooperation from all groups. A free nation has the right to look to the leaders of business, of labor and of agriculture to take the lead in stimulating effort, not among other groups but within their own groups....

The nation takes great satisfaction and much strength from the things which have been done to make its people conscious of their individual stake in the preservation of democratic life in America. Those things have toughened the fiber of our people, have renewed their faith and strengthened their devotion to the institutions we make ready to protect. Certainly this is no time for any of us to stop thinking about the social and economic problems which are the root cause of the social revolution which is today a supreme factor in the world. For there is nothing mysterious about the foundations of a healthy and strong democracy.

The basic things expected by our people of their political and economic systems are simple. They are: Equality of opportunity for youth and for others. Jobs

OVERVIEW

World War II, 1939–1945

ROBERT D. JOHNSTON, YALE UNIVERSITY,
WITH THE ASSISTANCE OF SANDY JOHNSTON

The Good War?

World War II remains America's "good war," the war for freedom and democracy, the war against totalitarianism and imperialism. The Allies, primarily the United States, Great Britain, and France, fought against the Axis powers (Germany, Italy, and Japan) in the gravest threat to civilization ever. Adolf Hitler succeeded in killing 6 million Jews in what became known as the Holocaust. He persecuted and murdered many others—homosexuals, gypsies, the disabled, artists, academics, the religious, and political dissidents among them. Japan's rule over its "greater co-prosperity sphere" in Asia was similarly brutal. In total, as many as 60 million people lost their lives during World War II. If this was indeed a good war, that goodness only resulted from its extremely costly defeat of evil.

The Roots of the War

The primary roots of World War II were twofold and lie largely—but not completely—outside U.S. history: in the failed settlement of World War I in Europe and in the scramble for empire in Asia. In many ways, World War II began with the Japanese occupation of much of China, which started in 1931. Across the globe, Hitler, promising to restore his country's greatness after the humiliation of World War I, became head of the German government in 1933 after several key political maneuvers. He and his Nazi Party then dismantled democracy in Germany before taking control of the Rhineland, Austria, and parts of Czechoslovakia between 1936 and March 1939. On September 1, 1939, Hitler made the fateful decision to invade Poland.

Blitzkriegs

After Germany's invasion of Poland, war began to consume the world with dramatic speed. Britain and France asserted their intention to protect Poland from Nazi aggression, and both declared war on Germany within 48 hours of Hitler's lightning war, or blitzkrieg. However, it took the Germans only eighteen days to conquer Poland, and on September 28 they split the territories of the defeated Polish republic in half with their then-ally Russia.

Germany next invaded and occupied Denmark and Norway. The Nazis then rolled across the boundaries of the Netherlands, Belgium, and France in May 1940. They quickly defeated the armies of these countries and drove the British Expeditionary Force (BEF) to the port of Dunkirk, where it was rescued in an operation later described as nothing short of miraculous.

Resistance against the Germans

The Germans next tried to bomb Great Britain into submission, but the Royal Air Force (RAF) defeated these advances but they sustained heavy losses. Hitler then turned his eyes toward the Mediterranean. Fighting also erupted in the Libyan and Egyptian deserts, with the British holding off the Germans there. Meanwhile, Japan was secretly planning a surprise attack on the United States to relieve the pressure on the Japanese economy caused by an American embargo on such key products as oil.

On June 22, 1941, Hitler—against the overwhelming advice of his generals—decided to invade the Soviet Union. German forces advanced to the gates of Moscow before a determined Communist resistance and the fierce Russian winter stopped them. But by this time, events had taken place that would soon capture the attention of the rest of the world.

"A Day That Will Live in Infamy" and the War in the Pacific

Early on the morning of December 7, 1941, a squadron of aircraft commanded by Japanese Adm. Yamamato turned into the wind less than 300 miles

for those who can work. Security for those who need it. The ending of special privilege for the few. The preservation of civil liberties for all. The enjoyment of the fruits of scientific progress in a wider and constantly rising standard of living. These are the simple, the basic things that must never be lost sight of in the turmoil and unbelievable complexity of our modern world. The inner and abiding straight of our economic and political systems is dependent upon the degree to which they fulfill these expectations.

Many subjects connected with our social economy call for immediate improvement. As examples: We should bring more citizens under the coverage of old-age pensions and unemployment insurance. We should widen the opportunities for adequate medical care. We from the huge U.S. naval base at Pearl Harbor, Oahu, Hawaii. These planes took the American fleet entirely by surprise and sank eight battleships and several other vessels. More than 2,200 American sailors died; the Japanese lost twenty-nine planes. Luckily, other vital U.S. carriers had been at sea during the attack, and the first of them, the U.S.S. *Enterprise,* returned the evening of December 7. Standing on the bridge, Adm. William "Bull" Halsey surveyed the wreckage and declared, "Before we're through with them, the Japanese language will be spoken only in hell!"

U.S. President Franklin D. Roosevelt asked Congress to officially declare war on Japan on December 8, 1941, stating that the Japanese attack was "a day that will live in infamy." Hitler declared war on America the next day, and the land of liberty became firmly entrenched in the war on the Allied side. With its Pacific Fleet cut in half, however, the American reaction to Pearl Harbor was initially ineffective. Also, the Japanese launched a series of naval strikes that successfully conquered every Pacific island which was a potential air or navy base, as well as most of southeast Asia. Finally, at the battle of the Coral Sea on May 4–8, 1942, the Japanese were turned back. Subsequently, at the battle of Midway the following month, the United States sank four Japanese aircraft carriers, suffering the loss of only one American ship. U.S. forces then took the offensive, landing on the island of Guadalcanal in the chain of the Soloman Islands in August to begin what would become a long and bloody, but ultimately successful campaign.

At the same time, American industries started the mass production of planes, tanks, guns, bullets, and other necessities of war. This, and the fact that Americans were enlisting in record numbers, encouraged the Allies to make amphibious landings in North Africa, where German Gen. Erwin Rommel and his troops had been dominating the British army for some time. Together, American and British troops finally crushed Hitler's famed Afrika Korps, although the wily German escaped.

The Homefront

On the American homefront, life changed greatly for millions of people not directly involved in the fighting. Most Americans bought war bonds and planted victory gardens in a show of national unity. Still, there were cracks in the country's consensus. African Americans, despite their enthusiastic participation in an anti-racist war, continued to suffer from segregation in the armed forces and from racism in everyday life, particularly in the South. There were also renewed race riots in northern cities such as Detroit.

The most egregious discrimination occurred against those of Japanese ancestry on the West Coast. Whether citizens or resident aliens, nearly 130,000 Japanese Americans were uprooted and sent to internment camps for much of the war. The military and many within government defined all Japanese and Japanese Americans as a security threat, even though later legal action showed that most intelligence had clearly proved they were not. (In the 1980s President Ronald Reagan signed legislation offering an official apology and reparations for the government's actions.)

Although many women suffered the loss of husbands or sons during the war, many also benefited from the gains of steady employment during this period of time: the high pay and social freedom afforded by factory work while the male workforce was away at war. Rosie the Riveter became a powerful symbol of women's efforts in support of the war. Indeed, the number of employed women nearly doubled during the war, rising to nearly twenty million. However, federal daycare facilities remained inadequate. And at the war's end, women were displaced from the most desirable jobs; it was evident that their participation in the factory workforce was viewed by both business and unions as temporary.

One clear-cut victor on the American homefront was the government itself. The federal government intervened in the economy much more than ever before, regulating both production and prices. Citizens took the rationing of meat, sugar, and fuel for granted,

should plan a better system by which persons deserving or needing gainful employment may obtain it. I have called for personal sacrifice, and I am assured of the willingness of almost all Americans to respond to that call. A part of the sacrifice means the payment of more money in taxes. In my budget message I will recommend that a greater portion of this great defense program be paid for from taxation than we are paying for today. No person should try, or be allowed to get rich out of the program, and the principle of tax payments in accordance with ability to pay should be constantly before our eyes to guide our legislation.

If the congress maintains these principles the voters, putting patriotism ahead of pocketbooks, will give you their applause. In the future days which we seek to make

World War II, 1939–1945 (continued)

although with some grumbling. The federal bureaucracy mushroomed, with much of the growth of the government occurring in western states that, ironically, before the war had been the most anti-government. The booming western economy, fueled by military expenditures as well as the increasing exploitation of natural resources such as oil, signified the growth of a previously marginalized region to genuine power.

The Beginning of the End

Despite American success in the Pacific, the campaign against Japan was merely a sideshow to what was unfolding in Europe. On July 10th, 1943, British and American troops captured the Italian island of Sicily. This provided the impetus for the final push of resistance there, and the Italian people soon overthrew Benito Mussolini.

Still, the war in Europe had settled into a stalemate. It took nearly a year more for the allies to make the D-Day landings on the coast of Normandy, France, on June 6, 1944. By the end of 1944 they had liberated Paris, most of France, and the Low Countries. The combined Allied armies had also repulsed a German counterattack at the Battle of the Bulge. At the same time, the Allies used new technology such as sonar devices to drive German submarines, known as U- boats, from the seas, and continuous aerial bombing decimated Germany's cities, their industrial might.

From the east, the Russians were also on the offensive. In 1943, they had stopped the German advance at the battles of Kursk and Stalingrad; next their massive armies invaded Germany itself after liberating Poland, the Ukraine, and part of Czechoslovakia. Finally, Russian troops marched into Berlin. Hitler committed suicide soon thereafter, on April 30, 1945. On May 7, Germany formally surrendered to British Gen. Bernard Montgomery.

From Island Hopping to the Atomic Bomb

The Japanese continued to fight fiercely, but with increasingly ineffective results. By October 1944, Americans had captured the islands of Saipan, Guam, and Tinian, retaken most of New Guinea, and so easily shot down Japanese planes at the battle of the Philippine Sea that the clash was later referred to as "The Great Marianas Turkey Shoot." That same month, American forces began liberating the Philippines. The Japanese navy made one last attempt to crush the combined 5th and 7th fleets of the U.S.

secure, we look forward to a world founded upon four essential human freedoms. The first is freedom of speech and expression—everywhere in the world.

The second is freedom of every person to worship God in his own way—everywhere in the world. The third is freedom from want, which, translated into world terms, means economic understandings which will secure to every nation a healthy peacetime life for its inhabitants—everywhere in the world.

The fourth is freedom from fear, which, translated into world terms, means a world-wide reduction of armaments to such a point and in such a thorough fashion that no nation will be in a position to commit an act of physical aggression against any neighbor—anywhere in the world. That is no vision of a distant millennium. It is a definite basis for a kind of world attainable in our own time and generation. That kind of world is the very antithesis of the so-called "new order" of tyranny which the dictators seek to create with the crash of a bomb.

To that new order we oppose the greater conception—the moral order. A good society is able to face schemes of world domination and foreign revolutions alike without fear. Since the beginning of our American history we have been engaged in change, in a perpetual, peaceful revolution, a revolution which goes on steadily, quietly, adjusting itself to changing conditions without the concentration camp or the quicklime in the ditch. The world order which we seek is the cooperation of free countries, working together in a friendly, civilized society.

This nation has placed its destiny in the hands, heads and hearts of its millions of free men and women, and its faith in freedom under the guidance of God. Freedom means the supremacy of human rights everywhere. Our support goes to those who struggle to gain those rights and keep them. Our strength is our unity of purpose.

To that high concept there can be no end save victory.

SOURCE:

Franklin D. Roosevelt, "Annual Message of the President to the Congress," January 6, 1941, *A Decade of American Foreign Policy: Basic Documents, 1941–49, Prepared at the request of the Senate Committee on Foreign Relations By the Staff of the Committee and the Department of State* (Washington, D.C.: Government Printing Office, 1950).

Navy at the battle of Leyte Gulf, but it was forced to retreat with heavy casualties.

The U.S. war machine next captured, although with staggering losses, the highly strategic islands of Iwo Jima and Okinawa and destroyed much of Japan's industry in regular bombing raids. Submarines prowled the seas surrounding the Home Islands, sinking every craft that flew the flag of Japan. Nevertheless, the Japanese military, perhaps out of the same zealousness that inspired their kamikaze pilots to crash themselves into American ships, was determined to fight to the bitter end. Even so, nothing could prepare them for what would come next.

On the morning of August 6, 1945, *Enola Gay*, the B-29 Superfortress bomber piloted by Col. Paul Tibbets, thundered down the runway at Saipan and launched into the sky. There was only one bomb in its bay, but this single weapon would do as much damage as anything ever known to humanity. When the first atomic bomb was dropped, it nearly obliterated the city of Hiroshima, with between 75,000 and 130,000 people dying instantly. Thousands more would die from the radiation in the weeks and years to come. Three days later, another bomb was dropped on Nagasaki, where between 60,000 to 92,000 were killed. Historians continue to hotly debate the necessity of these nuclear attacks, but they did certainly convince the Japanese to end the war. Japan formally surrendered on September 2, 1945, in Tokyo Bay on the deck of the battleship U.S.S. *Missouri.*

Did this "good war" bring global peace and security? In a formal sense, yes. There has not been a major world war since. But on the other hand, when the bloodshed and arms races of subsequent decades are considered, it is clear that the present world is hardly a peaceful one. Nor unfortunately do hopes for much tranquility in the immediate future seem plausible.

BIBLIOGRAPHY

Martin Gilbert, *The Second World War: A Complete History* (1989) is an exciting narration of the conflict; Richard Natkiel, *Atlas of World War II* (2000) supplies an excellent geographical perspective. For the American homefront, see John Morton Blum, *V is for Victory: Politics and American Culture During World War II* (1977); Americans reminisce in Studs Terkel, ed., *"The Good War": An Oral History of World War II* (1997). On the case of Japanese Americans, see Peter H. Irons, *Justice at War* (1993), for the deadly racial conflicts at the heart of the Pacific conflict, see John Dower, *War Without Mercy: Race and Power in the Pacific War* (1986). Richard Rhodes, *The Making of the Atomic Bomb* (1995) is a powerful account of the origins of the most powerful weapon known to humanity.

1942

INTERNATIONAL

World War II

PACIFIC THEATER Manila and Cavite fall to Japanese (January 2); U.S. and Filipino troops abandon Bataan Peninsula (April 9), 37,000 men are taken prisoner, led on "death march" with about 5,200 dying en route; last stronghold, island fort of Corregidor, falls (May 6).

Pacific fleet attacks Marshall and Gilbert islands (February 1); Allies lose four cruisers, four destroyers in two-day battle of Java Sea and Sunda Strait, a delaying action (February 27); U.S. troops land on New Caledonia (March 12); in Battle of Coral Sea (May 7), Allies halt Japanese drive on Australia; one Japanese carrier is lost, two are damaged; U.S. carrier *Lexington* is lost.

Three-day Battle of Midway (June 3–6) is first defeat of Japanese forces, who lose four aircraft carriers, 275 planes; U.S. loses carrier *Yorktown;* U.S. forces land on Guadalcanal (August 7); Allied naval forces lose four cruisers in Battle of Savo Island; Guadalcanal is gained (November 15).

First battle for Solomon Islands (October 11) costs Japan an aircraft carrier, four destroyers; the second battle, two weeks later, inflicts heavy losses on Japanese fleet; U.S. carrier *Hornet* is sunk.

U.S. B-25s led by Maj. Gen. James H. Doolittle, bomb Tokyo (April 18); Japanese bomb Alaskan bases (June 3), occupy Attu and Kiska in Aleutian Islands.

EUROPEAN THEATER U.S. troops arrive in North Ireland (January 26); U.S. destroyer *Truxton* and cargo ship are sunk off Newfoundland (February 18), 204 perish; agreement is reached with Denmark on military bases in Greenland (April 10); first U.S. air operation in Europe occurs when air force crews take part in British raid on Netherlands (July 4); first U.S. attack by 8th Air Force on railroad yards is at Rouen, France (August 17).

Allied forces land in North Africa (November 8), take Oran, Casablanca, and Algiers; enter Tunisia (November 15).

Major General James Doolittle's squadron of B-25s takes off from the deck of the USS *Hornet* in a bombing raid of Japan. **NATIONAL ARCHIVES AND RECORDS ADMINISTRATION**

Allied nations sign declaration (January 1), affirm Atlantic Charter principles, a joint effort to defeat the Axis powers, and pledge not to make separate peace.

U.S. and Mexico establish joint defense commission (January 12); two-week Rio de Janeiro Conference of 21 American republics ends (January 29) with diplomatic break with Axis, sets up defense for Panama Canal; Act of Chapultepec (March 3) provides that an attack on one American state will be regarded as attack on all, resulting in use of force.

U.S. Great Britain, Russia, and China hold nine-day strategy session; first Moscow Conference meets (August 12), informs Russia that a second European front not possible in 1942.

NATIONAL

American military leadership is created, names Gen. Douglas MacArthur Allied commander in the Pacific (March 17), Gen. Dwight D. Eisenhower commander in Europe (June 11); later Eisenhower becomes Allied commander of North African invasion.

Women's service corps are created: Women Appointed for Voluntary Emergency Service (WAVES), the women's navy branch (July 30), with Wellesley President Mildred McAfee director; Women's Army Auxiliary Corps (WAAC, later WAC) (May 14) with Oveta Culp Hobby director; Women's Auxiliary Ferrying Squadron (WAFS) created by Air Transport Command (September 10); Coast Guard Women's Reserve (SPARS) (November 23), Dorothy C. Stratton, commander.

Various agencies handle war effort: National War Labor Board, which replaces Defense Mediation Board; War Production Board, Office of Civil Defense; Office of Price Administration issues ration books for sugar, coffee, and gasoline; War Shipping Administration, National Housing Agency, War Manpower Commission; Office of War Information, which is headed by Elmer Davis; Office of Strategic Services, which is headed by William Donovan; Office of Economic Stabilization.

Efforts are concentrated on producing war materials: $4-billion program is created to increase synthetic rubber production (January 7); President Franklin D. Roosevelt appeals on radio for scrap rubber; more than 300,000 tons are collected in two weeks.

Manhattan Project is organized (June 18) for production of an atomic bomb; other facilities are at Oak Ridge, Tennessee, and Los Alamos, New Mexico; plutonium production plant is built at Hanford, Washington; Enrico Fermi, Arthur Compton, Leo Szilard, and other scientists at University of Chicago achieve

In *Casablanca* (1942), Humphrey Bogart (right) plays Rick, who defends his true love, played by Ingrid Bergman, and her husband (left), a French Resistance fighter, from the Nazis. **THE KOBAL COLLECTION**

first self-sustaining nuclear chain reaction (December 2), marks beginning of atomic age.

Draft age is lowered from 20 to 18 years.

About 10,000 Japanese Americans on West Coast and in Arizona are relocated to camps in interior area.

V-mail is started.

FBI announces capture of eight Nazi saboteurs who landed by submarine on Long Island and Florida.

First war bond drive opens November 30; nearly $13 billion in bonds are sold by December 23.

Social Justice, publication of Rev. Charles E. Coughlin's radical group, is barred from the mails, ceases publication; his Catholic superiors impose silence on him.

Nationwide daylight saving time goes into effect.

French liner *Normandie,* in conversion to transport duty, capsizes and burns at New York City dock.

BUSINESS/INDUSTRY/INVENTIONS

Kaiser Shipyards, north of Richmond, California, sets record of constructing a ship in 4½ days, builds 1,460 ships during World War II; Henry J. Kaiser, finding it difficult to find enough steel for his shipyards, builds first steel plant on Pacific Coast.

General Electric in Bridgeport produces bazooka rocket gun.

DEATH Ralph Cram, architect, helped design West Point.

TRANSPORTATION

First U.S. jet flight is made in a Bell XP-59A at Edwards Air Force Base, California (October 1).

Pan American Airways completes first round-the-world commercial flight.

Alcan Highway, 1,523 miles from British Columbia to Alaska, is completed (December 1).

Two-place army helicopter makes cross-country helicopter flight from Stratford, Connecticut, to Wright Field, Ohio.

SCIENCE/MEDICINE

Bethesda (Maryland) Naval Medical Center is dedicated.

Permanente (now Kaiser) Foundation, a pioneer nonprofit health maintenance organization, is established.

DEATH Franz Boas, established modern structure of anthropology.

Japanese American citizens, many of whom have been removed from their West Coast homes by the U.S. Army, wait to be placed in the Manzanar internment camp. Many of them lose their homes, their businesses, and their belief in the American dream as a result.
AP/WIDE WORLD PHOTOS

EDUCATION

DEATH Martha M. Berry, founder of schools for underprivileged Georgia children.

RELIGION

Nathan H. Knorr becomes president of Watch Tower Bible and Tract Society.

DEATH Joseph F. Rutherford, head of Jehovah's Witnesses (1916–1942).

ART/MUSIC

William Schuman composes Secular Cantata no. 2; Leonard Bernstein presents first work, Sonata for Clarinet and Piano; Aaron Copland produces *Lincoln Portrait,* for orchestra and speaker, and the ballet *Rodeo;* Gian Carlo Menotti composes opera *The Island God.*

Edward Hopper completes the painting *Nighthawks;* Albert E. Gallatin, *Composition.*

SONGS (POPULAR): "Don't Get Around Much Anymore," "For Me and My Gal," "Manhattan Serenade," "One Dozen Roses," "Praise the Lord and Pass the Ammunition," "Tangerine," "That Old Black Magic," "Don't Sit Under the Apple Tree," "White Christmas."

DEATHS Grant Wood, artist; Tony Sarg, marionette maker; Bunny Berrigan, swing trumpeter.

LITERATURE/JOURNALISM

George Baker draws "Sad Sack" cartoons in *Yank Magazine.*

Negro Digest, a monthly magazine, is founded.

Earl Wilson writes syndicated column "It Happened Last Night."

BOOKS *The Robe* by Lloyd C. Douglas, *Paul Revere* by Esther Forbes, *Admiral of the Ocean Sea* by Samuel Eliot Morison, *A Witness Tree* (poetry) by Robert Frost, *Generation of Vipers* by Philip Wylie, *Dragon Seed* by Pearl Buck, *They Were Expendable* by William L. White, *The Moon Is Down* by John Steinbeck.

DEATH Condé Nast, publisher *(Vanity Fair, Vogue).*

ENTERTAINMENT

PLAYS Fredric March stars in *The Skin of Our Teeth,* Ethel Barrymore in *The Corn Is Green,* Ray Bolger in *By Jupiter,* Arlene Francis in *The Doughgirls.*

MOVIES *Casablanca* with Humphrey Bogart, *Yankee Doodle Dandy* with Jimmy Cagney, *Mrs. Miniver* with Greer Garson, *Holiday Inn* with Bing Crosby,

My Sister Eileen with Rosalind Russell, *For Me and My Gal* with Judy Garland.

CBS signs columnist Ed Sullivan to weekly radio show; other new shows are *Can You Top This?, People Are Funny, Suspense.*

The jitterbug becomes an extremely popular dance.

DEATHS John Barrymore, stage and screen actor; Otis Skinner, actor; George M. Cohan, actor, playwright, and composer; Graham McNamee, radio announcer; Joseph M. Weber of Weber & Fields comedy team.

SPORTS

Paul Waner of Pittsburgh Pirates gets his 3,000th hit.

Cornelius Warmerdam sets outdoor pole vault record of 15 feet, 7¾ inches.

National Boxing Assn. freezes titles of boxers in service.

Torger Tokle breaks own ski jump record, reaches 289 feet.

WINNERS *Baseball*—St. Louis Cardinals, World Series; *Basketball*—West Virginia, NIT; Stanford, NCAA; *Boxing*—Joe Louis, heavyweight; Beau Jack, lightweight; Willy Pep, featherweight; *Football* (bowls)—Oregon State, Rose; Georgia, Orange; Fordham, Sugar; Alabama, Cotton; Washington, NFL; *Golf*—Sam Snead, PGA; Byron Nelson, Masters; *Hockey*—Toronto, Stanley Cup; *Horse racing*—Shut Out, Kentucky Derby and Belmont Stakes; Alsab, Preakness Stakes; *Tennis*—Ted Schroeder, U.S. Open (men); Pauline Betz, U. S. Open (women).

MISCELLANEOUS

Fire in Boston nightclub (Cocoanut Grove) kills 491 people.

James Farmer leads in founding CORE (Congress of Racial Equality).

Eddie Rickenbacker, on government mission with seven others, is forced down in Pacific; survives 23 days with only fish and rainwater to sustain them.

Zoot suits become a popular male garb, featuring a long, one-button jacket with padded shoulders and high-waisted trousers that grip the ankles.

Pvt. Joe Louis says_
"We're going to do our part
...and we'll win because
we're on God's side"

Posters, such as this one depicting Joe Louis as a private during World War II, are effective recruiting devices, particularly in attracting African Americans. Louis's defeat of the German boxer Max Schmelling had made him an American hero.
CORBIS-BETTMANN

1943

INTERNATIONAL

World War II

PACIFIC THEATER In Battle of Bismarck Sea (March 2), Japanese suffer heavy losses (12 troop convoy ships, 10 warships), leads to recapture of much of New Guinea; U.S. begins offensive in South Pacific, retakes most of Solomon Islands (June 30); Allied troops capture Lae, New Guinea (September 16). In Alaska, U.S. forces secure Attu Island after 19 days of fighting (May 30); U.S. and Canadian troops regain Aleutians.

NORTH AFRICA U.S. troops are thrown back at Kasserine Pass (February 14); U.S. troops join British on Mareth Line in Tunisia (March 19), encircle Germans (April 7); British take Tunis; Americans, Bizerte (May 7); section of North African theater collapses when 250,000 Axis troops surrender (May 13).

EUROPEAN THEATER Allied planes hammer Axis positions: Wilhelmshaven (January 27), U.S. planes bomb major oil refineries at Ploesti, Rumania (August 1); ball-bearing plants in Regensburg and Schweinfurt (August 17). U.S. and British forces launch air and sea invasion of Sicily (July 10); Palermo falls (July 14), followed by Catania (August 5) and Messina (August 17), completing island takeover. Allies launch invasion of Italy from Sicily

Winston Churchill (right), Franklin D. Roosevelt (center), and Chiang Kai-shek at the first Cairo conference. **CORBIS-BETTMANN**

(September 3), Italy surrenders (September 8), Germans move into Rome (September 10), Italian fleet surrenders (September 11), Allies take Salerno (September 18); Allied control commission for Italy is established (November 10).

Throughout year, Allied leaders confer: Ten-day Casablanca meeting declares war will go on until "unconditional surrender" is secured (January 24); two-week conference in Washington plans second European front (May 26); President Franklin Roosevelt and British Prime Minister Winston Churchill meet for a week in August; first Cairo Conference finds U.S., British, and Chinese leaders agreeing to fight against Japan until unconditional surrender (November 22); Teheran Conference (November 28) discusses second front in Europe; second Cairo Conference includes Turkish President Ismet Inönü (December 4).

There are also meetings of what became United Nations organizations: Food & Agricultural Organization (May 18), Relief & Rehabilitation Administration (November 9).

DEATH Army Gen. Frank M. Andrews, in plane crash.

NATIONAL

War-related events include: Minimum workweek is lengthened from 40 to 48 hours (with overtime pay for the additional hours) (February 9); War Manpower Commission issues regulations that freeze workers into war jobs; War Production Board halts nonessential housing and highway construction.

Point rationing begins (March 1) for meats, fats and oils, butter, cheese, and processed food; shoes are added later; president orders freeze on prices, wages, and salaries, effective May 12; government takes over Eastern coal mines for a day and later the railroads to prevent a strike.

Office of War Mobilization is created; pay-as-you-go income tax goes into effect (July 1).

Two Depression-era programs end: Civilian Conservation Corps (CCC), which gave young men jobs, and Works Project Administration (WPA), which in eight years employed 8.5 million people on 1.4 million projects that cost $11 billion.

President finds time to dedicate new Merchant Marine Academy, Kings Point, New York, and the Jefferson Memorial in Washington, D.C.

New Defense Department home, the Pentagon, is completed.

White anger over hiring blacks in war plants in Detroit (June 20) sparks race riots, 34 deaths result.

Two Tennessee dams completed: Douglas on French Broad River and Ft. Loudon on Tennessee River.

DEATH Former First Lady Helen H. Taft (1909–1913).

BUSINESS/INDUSTRY/INVENTIONS

World's longest oil pipeline (1,254 miles), between Longview, Texas, and Phoenixville, Pennsylvania, operates.

DEATHS Michael J. Owens, a founder of Libbey-Owens Glass; Nikola Tesla, inventor of many electrical devices and system; J. P. Morgan, banker.

TRANSPORTATION

Chicago's first subway is dedicated (October 16).

DEATH Edsel B. Ford, auto company president (1919–1943).

SCIENCE/MEDICINE

Polio epidemic kills 1,151 persons, cripples thousands.

Otto Stern is awarded Nobel Prize in physics for discovery of magnetic momentum of the proton and contribution to molecular ray method; Edward A. Doisy shares physiology/medicine prize with Henrik C. P. Dam of Denmark for discovery of chemical nature of vitamin A.

Selman A. Waksman, microbiologist, and his coworkers discover antibiotic, streptomycin.

DEATHS Aleš Hrdlička, helped establish U.S. physical anthropology; Clifford W. Beers, public health pioneer; Winford L. Lewis, developer of lewisite (poison gas); George Washington Carver, agronomist, developed hundreds of by-products of peanuts.

EDUCATION

Milton S. Eisenhower becomes president of Kansas State University.

United Negro College Fund is organized.

RELIGION

Supreme Court rules that schoolchildren cannot be compelled to salute the flag if it conflicts with their religion.

ART/MUSIC

WRGB, Schenectady (New York), televises first complete opera *(Hansel and Gretel)* (February 23).

Howard Hanson composes Symphony no. 4, op. 34; Marc Blitzstein, *Freedom Morning;* William H. Schuman, "A Free Song."

PAINTINGS Robert Motherwell, *Pancho Villa, Dead and Alive;* Thomas Hart Benton, *July Hay;* Julio DeDiego, *The Portentous City;* Arshile Gorky, *Waterfall;* Jackson Pollock, *The She-Wolf.*

SONGS (POPULAR): "Besame Mucho," "Holiday for Strings," "I'll Be Home for Christmas," "You'd Be So Nice To Come Home To," "I've Heard That Song Before," "Mairzy Doats," "Pistol Packing Mama."

DEATHS Sergei Rachmaninoff, pianist and composer; Fats Waller, pianist and composer ("Honeysuckle Rose").

LITERATURE/JOURNALISM

Bill Mauldin's cartoons appear in *Stars & Stripes,* the army newspaper.

BOOKS *A Tree Grows in Brooklyn* by Betty Smith, *Western Star* (poetry) by Stephen Vincent Benét, *At Heaven's Gate* by Robert Penn Warren, *The Fountainhead* by Ayn Rand, *The Apostle* by Sholem Asch.

DEATH Albert W. Marquis, founder of *Who's Who.*

ENTERTAINMENT

PLAYS Alfred Drake stars in *Oklahoma!,* Mary Martin in *One Touch of Venus,* Margaret Sullavan in *The Voice of the Turtle,* Moss Hart writes *Winged Victory.*

MOVIES *For Whom the Bell Tolls* with Gary Cooper, *Girl Crazy* with Judy Garland, *Jane Eyre* with Joan Fontaine, *Lassie Come Home* with Roddy McDowall, *Stormy Weather* with Lena Horne, *The Song of Bernadette* with Jennifer Jones.

New radio programs include *Life of Riley, Perry Mason,* and Jimmy Durante.

DEATH Leslie Howard, screen actor.

SPORTS

William D. Cox, part-owner of Philadelphia Phillies baseball team, is banned for life by Commissioner Kenesaw M. Landis for betting on own team.

Women's International Bowling Congress (WIBC) Hall of Fame is founded.

WINNERS *Baseball*—New York Yankees, World Series; *Basketball*—St. Johns, NIT; Wyoming, NCAA; *Bowling*—Ned Day, bowler of year; *Boxing*—Beau Jack, lightweight; *Football* (bowls)—Georgia, Rose; Alabama, Orange; Tennessee, Sugar; Texas, Cotton; Chicago Bears, NFL; *Hockey*—Detroit, Stanley Cup; *Horse racing*—Count Fleet becomes sixth Triple Crown winner taking the Kentucky Derby, Preakness Stakes, and Belmont Stakes; *Tennis*—Joseph Hunt, U.S. Open (men); Pauline Betz, U.S. Open (women).

American women take over as factory workers at home while the men who usually do such work are away fighting the war. GETTY IMAGES

MISCELLANEOUS

Four chaplains aboard the *Dorchester* give up their life jackets to others and go down with the ship.

Two railroad accidents occur: Frankfort Junction in Philadelphia (79 lives are lost), and between Rennert and Buie, North Carolina (72 lives).

1944

INTERNATIONAL

World War II

EUROPEAN THEATER More than 150,000 Allied troops make amphibious landings (June 6) on northern French coast, 4,000 invasion craft and 11,000 planes support; Germans counter with pilotless aircraft (V2s) attacks on London. U.S. troops land on western shore of Cherbourg Peninsula (June 18), take the city (June 27); British capture Caen (July 9), U.S. takes St.-Lô (July 25) and Brest (August 7) and overrun Brittany Peninsula by August 10. Allied troops move rapidly, liberating Paris (August 25), Brussels and Antwerp (September 4), Luxembourg (September 11). U.S. troops enter Germany (September 12), capture Aachen (October 21), Metz (November 22), Strasbourg (November 23).

Germans launch counteroffensive (Battle of the Bulge) (December 16), hoping to split Allied armies; stubborn resistance at Bastogne gives time for Allied reinforcements to arrive (December 26) and end the threat.

Allies are also busy in Italy with amphibious landings at Anzio (January 22), but stiff German resistance stalls drive for months; Rome falls (June 4), U.S. takes Leghorn, the British Florence (July 9). Other Allied forces land in Southern France (August 15), drive up the Rhône Valley.

PACIFIC THEATER U.S. forces advance in southern and central Pacific with invasion of Marshall Islands (January 31); recapture Kwajalein (February 6), Eniwetok (February 22), Admiralty Islands (March 25), Hollandia (April 22); U.S. forces land on Mariana Islands (June 15), take Saipan (July 9), Guam (August 10), Tinian (August 11).

Battle of the Philippine Sea (June 19) costs Japanese 3 aircraft carriers, 200 planes; Gen. Douglas MacArthur returns to Philippines, leads invasion of Leyte (October 20); three-day Battle of Leyte Gulf destroys most remaining Japanese naval strength.

Some activities for postwar living: Forty-four nations attend three-week U.N. Monetary and Financial Conference at Bretton Woods, New Hampshire, create International Monetary Fund and International Bank for Reconstruction and Development. Dumbarton Oaks Conference in Washington follows, lays groundwork for United Nations. An agreement (November 19) is signed at White House to create U.N. Relief and Rehabilitation Administration (UNRRA).

A German plot to assassinate Hitler (July 20) and take over Germany fails.

U.S., Great Britain, and Russia recognize French Provisional Government in Exile; President Franklin Roosevelt and British Prime Minister Winston Churchill meet in Quebec to discuss postwar problems.

NATIONAL

Congress passes GI Bill of Rights, provides benefits to World War II veterans; War Production Board permits limited conversion of industry to civilian production; Office of War Mobilization and Reconversion is created.

President Roosevelt is elected to a fourth term, receives 25,602,505 popular and 432 electoral votes to 22,006,278 popular and 99 electoral votes for Republican Thomas E. Dewey.

Supreme Court upholds wartime exclusion of Japanese Americans from the West Coast.

Soldiers heading toward the beaches of Normandy during the heroic D-Day invasion of Nazi-occupied France on June 6, 1944.
AP/WIDE WORLD PHOTOS

Agreement is reached with Mexico on the shared use of water from Rio Grande, Colorado, and Tijuana rivers.

Big Bend (Texas) National Park is established.

DEATHS Former First Lady Lou Hoover (1929–1933); Wendell Willkie, Republican presidential candidate (1940); Alfred E. Smith, New York governor and 1928 Democratic presidential candidate; Manuel L. Quezon, first Philippines president (1935–1941).

BUSINESS/INDUSTRY/INVENTIONS

Howard H. Aiken of IBM completes Mark I, first large-scale digital computer; it is given to Harvard University.

Marvin Camras patents wire recorder.

DEATHS James H. Rand, devised visible file divider system; Leo H. Baekeland, inventor of Bakelite, a plastic.

TRANSPORTATION

Nation's railroads return to private ownership.

SCIENCE/MEDICINE

Isidor I. Rabi is awarded Nobel Prize in physics for method of recording properties of atomic nuclei; Joseph Erlanger and Herbert S. Gasser share physiology/medicine prize for discoveries of differentiated functions of single nerve fibers.

Dr. Alfred Blalock develops operation to save "blue babies" by increasing oxygen in blood.

New York Hospital establishes first eye bank.

University of California scientists discover three new elements: 95 (americium), 96 (curium), and 97 (berkelium).

DEATHS Thomas Midgley, chemist who discovered antiknock properties of tetraethyl lead in fuel; Joseph M. Flint, surgeon and founder of first mobile hospital for troops.

RELIGION

Methodist Bishop G. Bromley Oxnam becomes president of Federal Council of Churches.

Angus Dun becomes Episcopal bishop of Washington, D.C.

DEATHS Catholic Archbishop Edward J. Hanna of San Francisco; Aimee Semple McPherson, evangelist.

ART/MUSIC

Leopold Stokowski founds, conducts second New York Symphony Orchestra (1944–1945).

Walter Piston composes Second Symphony; Leonard Bernstein composes ballet *Fancy Free* and symphony *Jeremiah;* Aaron Copland composes *Appalachian Spring.*

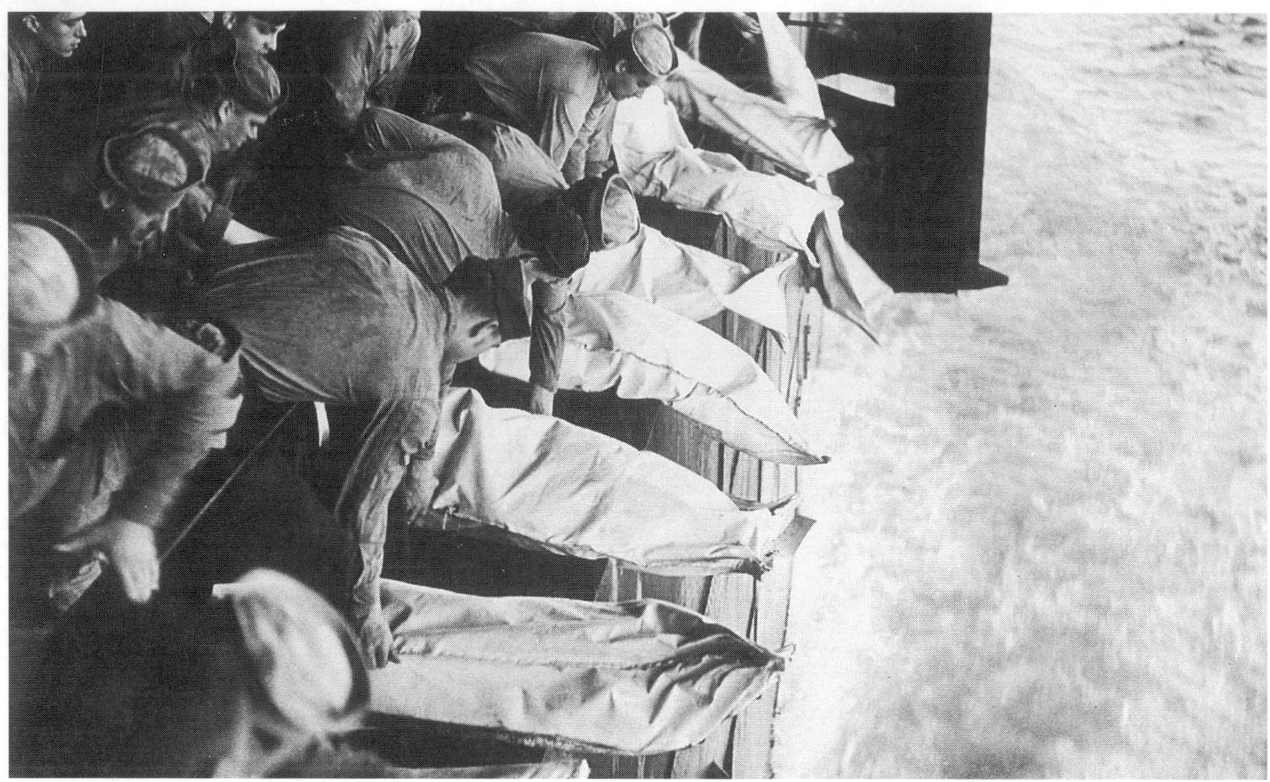

A somber ceremony of burial at sea aboard the USS *Intrepid* after a Japanese attack. Bodies wrapped in bags are held ready to be dropped over the side into the water. HULTON ARCHIVE/GETTY IMAGES

Dizzy Gillespie forms band to play "bop" jazz.

Jackson Pollock completes the painting *Mural.*

SONGS (POPULAR): "Don't Fence Me In," "Spring Will Be a Little Late This Year," "I'll Get By," "Shoo-Shoo Baby," "Swinging on a Star," "I Couldn't Sleep a Wink Last Night."

LITERATURE/JOURNALISM

BOOKS *Brave Men* by Ernie Pyle, *Forever Amber* by Kathleen Winsor, *Strange Fruit* by Lillian Smith, *A Bell for Adano* by John Hersey, *V-Letter and Other Poems* by Karl Shapiro, *The Lost Weekend* by Charles Jackson, *Yankee from Olympus* by Catherine Drinker Bowen.

DEATHS George Ade, humorist *(Fables in Slang);* William Allen White and Harry Chandler, newspaper editors and publishers; two early cartoonists, Billy DeBeck ("Barney Google") and George Herriman ("Krazy Kat"); Ida Tarbell, author of Standard Oil history that led to federal investigation.

ENTERTAINMENT

PLAYS Frank Fay stars in *Harvey,* Eddie Dowling in Tennessee Williams's *The Glass Menagerie,* Celeste Holm in *Bloomer Girl;* Leonard Bernstein writes *On the Town.*

MOVIES *Going My Way* with Bing Crosby, *Meet Me in St. Louis* with Judy Garland, *Up in Arms* with Danny Kaye, *Cover Girl* with Rita Hayworth, *Gaslight* with Charles Boyer, *Pin-Up Girl* with Betty Grable.

Popular new radio shows are *Ozzie and Harriet,* Alan Young, Roy Rogers, and Perry Como.

SPORTS

NCAA adopts two new basketball rules; ban on goaltending, and increased maximum number of personal fouls from 4 to 5.

WINNERS *Baseball*—St. Louis Cardinals, World Series; *Basketball*—St. Johns, NIT; Utah, NCAA; *Chess*—Arnold Danker, U.S. champion; *Football* (bowls)—Southern California, Rose; Louisiana State, Orange; Georgia Tech, Sugar; Randolph Field, Cotton; Green Bay, NFL; *Golf*—Bob Hamilton, PGA; *Hockey*—Montreal, Stanley Cup; *Horse racing*—Pensive, Kentucky Derby and Preakness Stakes; Bounding Home, Belmont Stakes; *Tennis*—Frank Parker, U.S. Open (men); Pauline Betz, U.S. Open (women).

DEATHS Tommy Hitchcock, world-great polo player, in plane crash; Kenesaw M. Landis, baseball commissioner (1921–1944); John L. Griffith, first Big Ten football commissioner.

MISCELLANEOUS

Year is filled with disasters: tornadoes in Ohio, Pennsylvania, West Virginia, and Maryland kill 150; hurricanes along Atlantic Coast from Long Island to Cape Cod kill 400; a fire followed by a stampede at a Hartford (Connecticut) circus kills 168; explosion on Port Chicago, California, pier claims 322 lives, and liquid gas tank explosion followed by widespread fires in Cleveland (Ohio) cause 135 deaths.

1945

INTERNATIONAL

World War II

War on both fronts grinds to a halt, but before it does, the sudden death of President Franklin D. Roosevelt (April 12) shocks world.

PACIFIC THEATER War against Japan ends with dramatic suddenness by use of the first atomic bombs. Two bombs are dropped in early August on Hiroshima and Nagasaki, killing thousands, causing unparalleled devastation; Japanese quickly surrender.

U.S. troops land on Luzon in Philippines (January 9), take Manila (February 23); Marines land on Iwo Jima (February 19), capture island (March 7) at cost of 4,189 killed, 15,308 wounded; Army forces invade Okinawa (March 19), take island (July 21) after more than 11,000 deaths.

First atomic bomb is exploded successfully at Alamogordo (New Mexico) base (July 16); U.S. plane *Enola Gay,* piloted by Col. Paul W. Tibbetts Jr., drops bomb on Hiroshima (August 6), destroys 4 square miles of city, kills or injures 160,000.

A second bomb is dropped on Nagasaki (August 9), kills 40,000. The next day, Japanese offer to surrender, accept terms (August 14). U.S. forces begin occupation (August 27); formal surrender is signed aboard the USS *Missouri* in Tokyo Bay (September 2).

EUROPEAN THEATER U.S. troops drive into Ruhr Valley (February 23), reach the Rhine (March 2), which they cross (March 7) after capturing bridge at Remagen. Cologne and Düsseldorf are taken (March 7), also Mannheim and Frankfurt (March 27), Nuremberg (April 21); U.S. joins Russian troops at Elbe River (April 25).

Mussolini is captured and killed by Italian partisans at Lake Como as he tries to escape to Switzerland (April 28). Provisional German government announces that Hitler committed suicide in Berlin (May 1).

Testing of Atomic Bomb, Alamogordo, New Mexico

At precisely 5:29:45 on the morning of July 16, 1945, Manhattan Project scientists exploded the world's first atomic bomb at Trinity Site, near Alamogordo, New Mexico. The test had been delayed for an hour and a half owing to rain and lightning. As soon as the weather conditions eased, the atomic device was detonated above a 100-foot-high steel tower. A blinding flash stunned scientific and military personnel gathered some distance away. Then a huge mushroom-shaped cloud of dust and debris rose above the southwestern desert. Brig. Gen. Thomas F. Farrell described how "the whole country was lighted by a searing light with the intensity many times that of the midday sun." Physicist Robert Oppenheimer responded with a passage from the *Bhagavad-Gita,* an ancient Hindu text, "I am become death, the shatterer of worlds." The Trinity test was the culmination of the Manhattan Project, a secret government research program inaugurated in June 1942 to develop an atomic weapon before Nazi Germany. The success of the Trinity explosion led to the U.S. Air Force's dropping two atomic bombs, nicknamed Little Boy and Fat Man, on the Japanese cities of Hiroshima and Nagasaki, in early August, effectively bringing about the end of World War II.

Berlin falls to Allies, and German forces in Italy surrender (May 2); German units in the Netherlands, Denmark, and northwest Germany surrender (May 4). Germany agrees to unconditional surrender at "the little red schoolhouse" in Reims, France (May 7); VE Day is proclaimed May 8. Germany is placed under an Allied Control Council (June 5), German occupation zones are established.

United Nations forms as representatives of 50 nations meet in San Francisco (April 25), work out draft charter; President Harry Truman addresses delegates by phone (April 28); Senate approves draft charter (July 28), which is signed by president (August 8); charter goes into effect October 24.

Survivors of the first nuclear bomb, which is dropped on Hiroshima. GETTY IMAGES/ GAMMA LIAISON, INC.

World leaders meet in Yalta February 4–11 to discuss war problems and postwar plans, give Russia important concessions for its declaring war on Japan; meet again (July 7) in Potsdam with emphasis on Japan and war criminals. Allies sign agreement (August 8) to set up International War Crimes Tribunal; trials begin in Nuremberg (November 20), with Supreme Court Justice Robert H. Jackson chief American prosecutor (12 are convicted, 10 hanged in 1946, Hermann Göring commits suicide, Martin Bormann is convicted in absentia).

Lend-Lease program terminates; supplied $50.6 billion in aid to foreign nations.

Point system is announced for the discharge of enlisted men (May 10).

DEATHS Gen. Simon B. Buckner Jr., killed in Okinawa action; Gen. George S. Patton, Third Army commander, in automobile accident in Germany.

NATIONAL

Sudden death of President Roosevelt occurs while he vacations in Warm Springs, Georgia; Vice President Truman is sworn in as president (April 12).

Former Secretary of State Cordell Hull is awarded Nobel Peace Prize for work in founding U.N.

War Production Board (October 4) and Office of Civil Defense (June 30) terminate; gasoline and fuel oil rationing ends; food rationing (except sugar) stops (November 23); daylight saving time ends in September, its use restored to local option.

Eleanor Roosevelt, the president's widow, is named a delegate to United Nations.

Japanese Americans who were evacuated from West Coast in 1943 are free to return home.

New York State Commission Against Discrimination is established; New Jersey adopts new constitution, replacing the 1844 document.

House Un-American Activities Committee is given permanent status; recommends dismissal of 3,800 government employees; Justice Department finds only 36 warranted dismissal.

Atomic Energy Commission is created (August 1).

BUSINESS/INDUSTRY/INVENTIONS

Wage Stabilization Board is created to replace National War Labor Board.

J. Presper Eckhert and John W. Mauchly of the Moore School at the University of Pennsylvania produce ENIAC, the first all-electronic digital computer.

TRANSPORTATION

United Auto Workers stage 113-day strike against General Motors.

Burlington Railroad initiates the "Vista Dome," a car with an observation dome.

Flying Tigers Line is founded.

Second tube of Lincoln Tunnel under Hudson River is completed.

DEATH Vincent Bendix, inventor of automobile starter.

SCIENCE/MEDICINE

Wolfgang Pauli is awarded Nobel Prize in physics for discovery of the exclusion principle.

Grand Rapids, Michigan, becomes first city to fluoridate municipal water.

Weather radar is developed.

DEATH Robert H. Goddard, physicist who pioneered modern rocketry.

EDUCATION

School for Industrial and Labor Relations opens at Cornell University.

Harold Taylor becomes first male president of Sarah Lawrence College, Bronxville, New York.

RELIGION

George A. Smith is elected president of Mormon church.

ART/MUSIC

Leo Sowerby composes *Canticle of the Sun.*

Charles Sheeler completes the painting *Water;* Mark Rothko, *Baptismal Scene;* Isamu Noguchi completes the sculpture *Kouros.*

SONGS (POPULAR): "Have I Told You Lately That I Love You?," "It Might as Well Be Spring," "June Is Bustin' Out All Over," "Laura," "There I've Said It Again," "Rum and Coca-Cola."

DEATHS Jerome Kern, musical-comedy composer; Béla Bartók, composer; Newell C. Wyeth, mural painter and book illustrator.

LITERATURE/JOURNALISM

Ebony magazine begins publication.

BOOKS *The Black Rose* by Thomas B. Costain, *The Egg and I* by Betty McDonald, *The Age of Jackson* by Arthur M. Schlesinger Jr., *Captain from Castile* by Samuel Shellabarger, *Cass Timberlane* by Sinclair Lewis, *Cannery Row* by John Steinbeck, *Stuart Little* by E. B. White.

DEATHS Theodore Dreiser, author; Robert C. Benchley, author and screen actor; Gilbert Patten, author as Burt Standish (Frank and Dick Merriwell series); Ernie Pyle, war correspondent, killed by sniper.

The scene on Wall Street in New York City as Americans celebrate the end of World War II in Europe ("VE Day").
CORBIS-BETTMANN

ENTERTAINMENT

PLAYS John Raitt stars in *Carousel,* Ralph Bellamy in *State of the Union;* Sigmund Romberg writes music for *Up in Central Park.*

MOVIES *National Velvet* with Elizabeth Taylor, *The Bells of St. Mary's* with Bing Crosby, *Spellbound* with Ingrid Bergman, *The Lost Weekend* with Ray Miland, *The Clock* with Judy Garland.

New radio shows include *Break the Bank, Meet the Press, Inner Sanctum, Queen for a Day.*

DEATHS Gus Edwards, entertainer and composer ("School Days"); H. B. Warner, screen actor.

SPORTS

Happy (Albert B.) Chandler is named baseball commissioner.

Servicemen acting as honor guards line the funeral procession route for President Franklin D. Roosevelt on his way to the family burial site in Hyde Park, New York. A similar procession in Washington, D.C., draws huge crowds of mourners. AP/WIDE WORLD PHOTOS

Red (Walter W.) Smith writes syndicated sports column.

WINNERS *Baseball*—Detroit Tigers, World Series; *Basketball*—DePaul, NIT; Oklahoma A&M, NCAA; *Bowling*—Buddy Bomar, bowler of year; *Football* (bowls)—Southern California, Rose; Tulsa, Orange; Duke, Sugar; Oklahoma A&M, Cotton; Cleveland, NFL; *Golf*—Byron Nelson, PGA; *Hockey*—Toronto, Stanley Cup; *Horse racing*—Hoop Jr., Kentucky Derby; Polynesian, Preakness Stakes; Pavot, Belmont Stakes; *Tennis*—Frank Parker, U.S. Open (men); Sarah Palfrey Cooke, U.S. Open (women).

DEATHS Ski champion Torger Tokle killed in action with army; Dwight F. Davis, donor of tennis cup.

MISCELLANEOUS

An army B-25 crashes into Empire State Building in New York City, kills 14 (July 28).

Tornadoes in Oklahoma and Arkansas kill 102.

1946

INTERNATIONAL

Peace conference to end European phase of World War II formally is held in Paris; Japanese war-crimes trial sentences seven to death (hanged in 1948), 14 to life imprisonment.

U.S. gives Philippine Islands independence (July 4).

U.N. General Assembly holds first session in Flushing Meadows on Long Island (October 23); John D. Rockefeller Jr. gives $8.5 million toward purchase of New York City property for permanent U.N. headquarters; Mrs. Eleanor Roosevelt, U.S. delegate to U.N., named head of U.N. Commission on Human Rights.

World Bank organizes with Eugene I. Meyer as president.

British Prime Minister Winston Churchill makes "iron curtain" speech at Westminster College, Fulton, Missouri.

NATIONAL

Atomic explosion tests are held on Bikini Atoll in the Pacific in July.

Emily G. Balch and John R. Mott share Nobel Peace Prize for their work.

Frederick M. Vinson is named Supreme Court Chief Justice.

President Harry S. Truman proposes merging Army and Navy departments into Defense Department.

Hunter College's campus in the Bronx, New York, serves as the interim headquarters for the first meetings of the United Nations Security Council. **CORBIS-BETTMANN/HULTON-DEUTSCH COLLECTION**

President Truman asks for Commerce Secretary Henry A. Wallace's resignation because of his public criticism of U.S. policy on Russia.

Judge William H. Hastie becomes first African-American governor of the Virgin Islands.

New agencies created are the Central Intelligence Agency, Council of Economic Advisors, and Bureau of Land Management in Interior Department.

Republicans gain control of both houses of Congress for first time in 14 years.

DEATHS Gen. Joseph M. ("Vinegar Joe") Stilwell, Burma-China Theater commander; Jimmy Walker, New York City mayor (1926–1932); Gifford Pinchot, first U.S. professional forester; Harry L. Hopkins, federal relief administrator (1933–1938).

BUSINESS/INDUSTRY/INVENTIONS

End of war brings much labor unrest because unions tried to freeze wage increases during the war: 7,700 Western Electric telephone mechanics strike in 44 states, United Electrical Workers in 16 states; United Steelworkers shut down industry briefly, United Mine Workers strike bituminous mines.

Most price and wage controls end.

Hilton Hotels Corp. is organized.

Exchange National Bank, Chicago, provides first bank drive-in service.

Southwestern Bell Telephone Co. initiates mobile telephone service.

DEATHS George W. Hill, American Tobacco Co. president (1925–1946); Sidney Hillman, president, Amalgamated Clothing Workers (1914–1940); Louis K. Liggett, founder and head, United Drug Co.

TRANSPORTATION

Government seizes railroads (May 17) to avert general strike; threat ends a week later.

Four-passenger commercial helicopter (S-51), built by Sikorsky Aircraft, is flown for first time.

SCIENCE/MEDICINE

Percy W. Bridgman is awarded Nobel Prize in physics for discoveries in field of high-pressure physics; James B. Sumner, John H. Northrop, and Wendell M. Stanley share chemistry prize for their work on enzymes and viruses; Hermann J. Muller is awarded physiology/medicine prize for production of mutations by X-ray irradiation.

The first general-purpose electronic calculator, dedicated at the Moore School of Electrical Engineering at the University of Pennsylvania in February 1946. Built to perform ballistic calculations for the U.S. Army, it is called the ENIAC ("Electronic Numerical Integrator and Computer"). **THE LIBRARY OF CONGRESS**

New York Orthopedic Hospital and Hospital for Special Surgery establish bone banks.

Chemist Irving Langmuir develops method to produce rain artificially by seeding clouds with dry ice and silver iodide.

Communicable Disease Center (CDC) is established.

Best-selling book by Dr. Benjamin Spock, *Baby and Child Care,* is published.

EDUCATION

Fulbright Act sets up educational exchange program with foreign countries.

Sarah G. Blanding becomes first woman president of Vassar College.

Oliver C. Carmichael becomes president of Carnegie Foundation for Advancement of Teaching.

Champlain College, primarily for war veterans, opens in Plattsburgh, New York.

RELIGION

United Brethren and Evangelical churches merge to form Evangelical United Brethren church (November 16).

International Council of Religious Education publishes Revised Standard Version of the New Testament.

Mother Cabrini (Francis Xavier Cabrini) becomes first U.S. citizen to be canonized.

Three U.S. Catholic archbishops are elevated to cardinal: John J. Glennon of St. Louis, Missouri, Francis J. Spellman of New York, Samuel A. Stritch of Chicago. Archbishop Joseph E. Ritter of Indianapolis, Indiana, transfers to St. Louis.

Maurice N. Eisendrath becomes president of Union of American Hebrew Congregations.

DEATH Archbishop John J. Glennon of St. Louis (1903–1946).

ART/MUSIC

Grandma Moses completes the painting *From My Window;* Adolph Gottlieb, *The Voyagers' Return;* George Grosz, *The Pit;* Ben Shahn, *Father and Child.*

Gian Carlo Menotti composes the opera *The Medium.*

SONGS (POPULAR): "All I Want for Christmas," "Five Minutes More," "The Girl That I Marry," "Let It Snow," "Shoo Fly Pie," "Zip-a-Dee-Doo-Dah," "On the Atchison, Topeka, and the Santa Fe," "You Always Hurt the One You Love."

DEATHS Alfred Stieglitz, pioneer of modern photography; Arthur G. Dove, first U.S. abstract painter; Carrie Jacobs Bond, composer ("I Love You Truly"); Vincent Youmans, composer ("Tea for Two"); John Steuart Curry, painter; Charles W. Cadman, composer.

LITERATURE/JOURNALISM

Herblock (Herbert Block), editorial cartoonist, joins *Washington Post* staff.

BOOKS *Peace of Mind* by Joshua L. Liebman, *The Foxes of Harrow* by Frank Yerby, *This Side of Innocence* by

Taylor Caldwell, *Lord Weary's Castle* (poetry) by Robert Lowell, *A Member of the Wedding* by Carson McCullers, *Hiroshima* by John Hersey, *Delta Wedding* by Eudora Welty, *All the King's Men* by Robert Penn Warren.

DEATHS Booth Tarkington and Gertrude Stein, authors; Damon Runyon, journalist and author; Joseph M. Patterson, founder and publisher, *New York Daily News.*

ENTERTAINMENT

American Repertory Theatre in New York City opens with Shakespeare's *Henry VIII.*

Arthur Godfrey begins *Talent Scouts* program on radio (later on television).

PLAYS Ethel Merman stars in *Annie Get Your Gun,* Judy Holliday in *Born Yesterday,* Helen Hayes in *Happy Birthday;* Eugene O'Neill writes *The Iceman Cometh.*

DEATHS William S. Hart, silent-screen cowboy; W. C. Fields, actor; "Major" Edward Bowes, amateur-hour originator; George Arliss, actor.

SPORTS

Basketball Association of America, forerunner of National Basketball Assn., is founded.

Bert Bell is named National Football League commissioner; All-American Football Conference begins with eight teams.

Players receive permanent representation on a new baseball governing body; collective-bargaining election is ordered for Pittsburgh Pirates players (vote is 15–3 against American Baseball Guild, most players abstain).

WINNERS *Auto racing*—Gene Robson, Indianapolis 500; *Baseball*—St. Louis Cardinals, World Series; *Basketball*—Kentucky, NIT; Oklahoma A&M, NCAA; *Bowling*—Joseph Wilman, bowler of year; *Boxing*—Joe Louis, heavyweight; Sugar Ray Robinson, welterweight; Tony Zale, middleweight; *Chess*—Samuel Reshevsky, U.S. title; *Football* (bowls)—Alabama, Rose; Miami (Florida), Orange; Oklahoma A&M, Sugar; Texas, Cotton; Chicago Bears, NFL; Cleveland, AAFC; *Golf*—Lloyd Mangrum, U.S. Open; Ben Hogan, PGA; Sam Snead, Masters; Patty Berg, first U.S. Women's Open; *Hockey*—Montreal, Stanley Cup; *Horse racing*—Assault becomes seventh Triple Crown winner; *Tennis*—U.S., Davis Cup; Jack Kramer, U.S. Open (men); Pauline Betz, U.S. Open (women).

DEATHS Former Heavyweight Champion Jack Johnson, in auto accident; Barney Oldfield, first to drive car at more than 60 miles per hour; Walter Johnson, Hall of Fame baseball pitcher.

Life in Kentucky coal country is harsh. The three-room house, owned by the coal company, has no running water or electricity. After 1940 use of coal as an energy source begins to decline. **NATIONAL ARCHIVES AND RECORDS ADMINISTRATION, RECORDS OF THE SOLID FUELS ADMINISTRATION FOR WAR**

MISCELLANEOUS

Forest fire destroys most of Bar Harbor, Maine; damages Acadia National Park; fire in Winecoff Hotel, Atlanta, Georgia, kills 119.

D. S. Harder, Ford vice president, coins word *automation.*

"Ranch-type" houses—low slung, single story—become popular.

1947

INTERNATIONAL

Secretary of State George C. Marshall launches (June 15) European aid plan to promote conditions in which free institutions can exist; 16 nations set up Committee for European Economic Cooperation (July 12); President Harry S. Truman asks approval of $17 billion for Marshall Plan. **SEE PRIMARY DOCUMENT** "The Marshall Plan"

President Truman pledges aid to Greece and Turkey; Congress approves the Truman Doctrine, provides $400 million for aid.

Jackie Robinson (bottom right) breaks baseball's color barrier in 1947, becoming the first African American to play major-league baseball. **CORBIS-BETTMANN**

Peace treaties with Italy, Hungary, Rumania, and Bulgaria are signed (June 14).

North Atlantic Council agrees on integrated European defense under a supreme commander, Dwight D. Eisenhower.

Nineteen American nations sign Treaty of Rio de Janeiro (September 2), a defense pact.

NATIONAL

National Security Act combines Army, Navy, and Air Force departments into Defense Department (July 26), under a Defense Secretary (James E. Forrestal); creates Joint Chiefs of Staff, National Security Council; W. Stuart Symington is sworn in as first Secretary of Air Force (September 18).

Presidential Succession Act revises 1886 law, makes house speaker first in line to succeed president and vice president, followed by president pro tem of Senate, secretary of state, and other cabinet members according to rank.

Selective Service Act for military draft expires.

Sugar rationing ends (June 11).

Former President Hoover leads study of European food and economic conditions, calls for $475 million aid program.

Housing and Home Finance Agency is created, predecessor of Department of Housing and Urban Development.

Puerto Rico is given right to elect own governor; Luis Munoz-Marin, first native appointed governor, is first to be elected.

Supreme Court in *Friedman* v. *Schwellenbach* upholds 1947 loyalty order authorizing dismissal of disloyal federal employees.

Domestic airmail rate drops to 5 cents per ounce.

Everglades (Florida) National Park is established.

Americans for Democratic Action is founded.

Richard M. Nixon begins three years in House from California; John F. Kennedy begins six years in House from Massachusetts; Ronald Reagan begins 13 years as president of Screen Actors Guild.

Freedom Train, a historic exhibit, is dedicated in Philadelphia (September 17) before starting 33,000-mile tour.

DEATHS Former First Lady Frances F. Cleveland (1886–1890, 1894–1898); Carrie Chapman Catt, women's rights leader; Fiorello La Guardia, New York City mayor (1933–1945); Al Capone, gangster.

BUSINESS/INDUSTRY/INVENTIONS

Its inventor, Edwin H. Land, demonstrates Polaroid camera (February 21).

Congress passes Taft-Hartley Act over President Truman's veto; bans closed shop, requires 30 days cooling-off before strike, requires union financial statements, forbids political contributions, and institutes other strict requirements.

DEATH Henry Ford, automaker.

TRANSPORTATION

B. F. Goodrich Co. produces tubeless tires.

Radar for commercial and private planes is demonstrated.

Howard Hughes flies world's largest plane, the 220-ton plywood flying boat, which he designed and built.

Chesapeake & Ohio Railroad absorbs Pere Marquette Railroad.

SCIENCE/MEDICINE

Drs. Carl F. Cori and his wife, Gerty, share Nobel Prize in physiology/medicine for discoveries relating to glycogen.

Mt. Palomar Observatory in California installs a 200-inch telescope lens.

Bell X-1 rocket plane flown by Major Charles E. Yeager breaks sound barrier.

Willard F. Libby develops carbon-14 dating technique.

EDUCATION

Brandeis University in Waltham, Massachusetts, is founded.

Gen Dwight D. Eisenhower is installed as president of Columbia University.

DEATH Nicholas Murray Butler, president, Columbia University (1902–1945).

RELIGION

Conservative Baptist Association of America is founded.

Catholic Bishop Francis P. Keough becomes archbishop of Baltimore, Maryland.

ART/MUSIC

Leopold Stokowski becomes conductor of New York Philharmonic Orchestra.

Walter Piston composes Symphony no. 3; Roger H. Sessions the opera *The Trial of Lucullus;* Gian Carlo Menotti, *The Telephone.*

President Harry S. Truman signing the Foreign Aid Assistance Act, which pledges $400 million in foreign aid to Greece and Turkey to stave off Communist insurgencies, the principles of which become known as the Truman Doctrine. **HULTON ARCHIVE/GETTY IMAGES**

Jackson Pollock completes the painting *Full Fathom Five;* Arshile Gorky, *The Betrothal II.*

SONGS (POPULAR): "Almost Like Being in Love," "How Are Things in Glocca Morra?," "I Believe," "Old Devil Moon," "Sixteen Tons," "Tenderly," "Cool Water," "Open the Door, Richard."

DEATHS Jimmie Lunceford, orchestra leader; Walter Donaldson, composer ("My Blue Heaven").

LITERATURE/JOURNALISM

BOOKS *Gentleman's Agreement* by Laura Z. Hobson, *Tales of the South Pacific* by James A. Michener, *Across the Wide Missouri* by Bernard De Voto, *Rocket Ship Galilee* by Robert A. Heinlein, *The Vixen* by Frank Yerby, *The Big Sky* by A. B. Guthrie.

DEATHS Authors Willa Cather, Hugh Lofting, and Charles B. Nordhoff; Ogden M. Reid, publisher, *New York Tribune, Herald;* Francis W. Crowninshield, editor (*Vanity Fair* 1914–1935); Frederick W. Goudy, type designer.

ENTERTAINMENT

Robert J. Keeshan begins television career as clown

During the "golden age" of jazz, Charlie Parker (right) and his band perform at the Three Deuces in New York City, 1947. Playing with him is Tommy Potter on bass (shown here on left), Miles Davis on trumpet, and Duke Jordan on piano. THE LIBRARY OF CONGRESS

Clarabelle on *Howdy Doody* show; other new shows are *Meet the Press* and *Kraft Television Theater.*

PLAYS Marlon Brando stars in *A Streetcar Named Desire,* Ella Logan in *Finian's Rainbow,* Judith Anderson and John Gielgud in *Medea;* Arthur Miller writes *All My Sons.*

MOVIES *Life with Father* with William Powell, *The Secret Life of Walter Mitty* with Danny Kaye, *Gentleman's Agreement* with Gregory Peck, *Miracle on 34th Street* with Edmund Gwenn, *The Road to Rio* with Bing Crosby and Bob Hope.

DEATHS Grace Moore, opera soprano, in plane crash; Eva Tanguay, entertainer.

SPORTS

Baseball major league annuity plan goes into effect; National Hockey League adopts players' pension fund.

National Hockey League plays first all-star game; World Hockey Assn. organizes with franchises in seven U.S. cities.

National Association for Stock Car Auto Racing (NASCAR) is formed.

Jackie Robinson of Brooklyn Dodgers, first African-American baseball player in majors, plays his first major league game (April 11); Larry Doby becomes first African-American ballplayer in American League (Cleveland) (July 5). **SEE PRIMARY DOCUMENT** "A Negro in the Major Leagues" from *The Sporting News*

Babe Didrikson Zaharias becomes first U.S.-born woman golfer to win British amateur title.

Babe Ruth Day is observed by 58,339 in Yankee Stadium, New York.

WINNERS *Auto racing*—Mauri Rose, Indianapolis 500; *Baseball*—New York Yankees, World Series; *Basketball*—Utah, NIT; Holy Cross, NCAA; Philadelphia, first BAA title; *Bowling*—Buddy Bomar, bowler of year; *Boxing*—Joe Louis, heavyweight; Sugar Ray Robinson, welterweight; Rocky Graziano, middleweight; *Football* (bowls)—Illinois, Rose; Rice, Orange; Georgia, Sugar; Arkansas, Cotton; Chicago Cardinals, NFL; Cleveland, AAFC; *Golf*—U.S., Ryder and Walker cups; Lew Worsham, U.S. Open; Jim Ferrier, PGA; Fred Daly, Masters; *Hockey*—Toronto, Stanley Cup; *Horse racing*—Jet Pilot, Kentucky Derby; Faultless, Preakness Stakes; Phalanx, Belmont Stakes; *Rowing*—Jack Kelly, Henley diamond challenge sculls; *Tennis*—U.S., Davis Cup; Jack Kramer, U.S. Open (men); Louise Brough, U.S. Open (women).

DEATH Charles W. Bidwill, owner of Chicago Cardinals football team.

MISCELLANEOUS

Amvets is chartered by Congress.

Most of Texas City, Texas, is destroyed when a French freighter explodes in harbor (April 16), kills 516.

Big Brothers of America is founded.

Tornadoes in Texas, Oklahoma, and Kansas kill 169; mine disaster in Centralia, Illinois, kills 111; New York City receives heaviest snowfall on record (25.8 inches), paralyzing city, causing 80 deaths.

PRIMARY SOURCE DOCUMENT

"A Negro in the Major Leagues" from *The Sporting News,* April 23, 1947

INTRODUCTION The first African-American baseball player to join the National League that formed in 1876 was Moses Fleetwood Walker, the college-educated son of a minister. As racism began to permeate America after Reconstruction, opportunities for African Americans in organized baseball declined rapidly. After 1898 there was not a single African-American player in an official league until 1946. The color line was fixed, set in stone by the Supreme Court decision *Plessy* v.

Ferguson, that had legitimized the principle of "separate but equal." Although black players formed their own professional teams, it was not until 1920 that an African-American baseball league was established. Rube Foster's Negro National League struggled, but in 1933, with the emergence of stars like Satchel Paige, Josh Gibson, and Cool Papa Bell, it became successful.

In 1945 Brooklyn Dodgers President Branch Rickey began to search the Negro League for the right man to break the color barrier in major league baseball. Although motivated by financial considerations, Rickey was committed to desegregation and he firmly believed that the time had come for such dramatic social change. With the death of baseball commissioner Judge Kenesaw Mountain Landis, a staunch segregationist, came a more progressive commissioner, Happy Chandler, who noted that if an African-American man was allowed to die for his country overseas, then he certainly deserved the chance to play major league baseball. After considering several players, Rickey and his scouts settled on Jackie Robinson as the player with whom to conduct what Rickey referred to as his "noble experiment." Rickey knew Robinson was talented, but more important, he saw him as educated, disciplined, and a man of conviction who would be able to withstand likely racism in pursuit of the important goal of desegregation. Rickey made the right choice.

Jackie Robinson (1919–1972) had joined the Negro League after a stint in the U.S. Army, which was notable for Robinson's resistance to the institutionalized racism then practiced by the armed forces. Robinson had also been a star athlete during his two years at UCLA, the first four-letter athlete in the school's history. Robinson was confident in his own abilities, but he was even more motivated by his commitment to fight discrimination. As a consequence, he felt enormous pressure to succeed on behalf of African Americans everywhere.

Robinson's advancement to the major leagues, here covered in a *Sporting News* editorial published not long after his debut, set off a barrage of media coverage and public scrutiny. With the support of Rickey and his wife Rae, and the friendship of Pee Wee Reese and other teammates, Robinson was able to survive the early years of racial taunts and death threats. He proved that African-American players belonged on the same field as white athletes, and after a ten-year career that included Rookie of the Year and MVP honors, Robinson was elected to the Hall of Fame. In the process, he demonstrated the same nonviolent resistance that would characterize the broader civil rights movement that was soon to sweep the nation.

In the seventy-second year of the National League's history, a Negro has made his appearance on its player rolls for the first time. Jackie Robinson, brought up from the Montreal farm, is listed as a first baseman with the Brooklyn club.

Once Robinson had taken the field with the Dodgers, it was remarked that it was quite odd that a Negro had not been seen in the majors before in the modern history of the game.

To a sport-loving public which had seen Negroes in professional football, Negroes in college gridiron competition, and Negroes winning world boxing championships, Robinson's appearance on a major-league field hardly was a novelty.

To some of the ballplayers, the entry of a Negro into a field of endeavor hitherto closed to that race, albeit open to other non-Caucasians, admittedly was irksome. But that phase of the situation, too, will pass and before long we may expect to see any Negro ballplayer worthy of a place in the major leagues performing in that company.

As Robinson himself admitted when he was purchased by the Brooklyn club, his promotion to the majors involves certain peculiar responsibilities, both for Jackie as an individual, for the Negroes as a race new to the Big Time and for exclusively Negro baseball as a possible feeder of the National and American leagues.

Negro baseball of the past was not too careful about its general conduct. It had no great respect for contracts, for schedules, for a sense of responsibility to Organized Baseball.

Last year, a Negro report on Negro baseball admitted that Negro players had been guilty of certain irregularities which would not be countenanced for one minute by the commissioner of Organized Baseball.

It is up to Negro baseball to recognize the elevation of Robinson to the majors by cleaning house and establishing itself as a clean, well-conducted feeder of the higher company.

To Robinson, no warning is necessary. He is a well-behaved, highly understanding man who recognized his unique position and the fact that on him rests the burden of persuading Organized Baseball to engage more players of his race.

To the Negro fan, let it be said that he must approach the new situation with understanding and patience, two qualities his race long has utilized in its amalgamation into American life, especially in the South.

Pitchers undoubtedly will "test" Robinson's gameness, and there will be other incidents which may make the Negro fan angry.

But Robinson will establish his own position and that of his race in baseball as he established it in the Junior World Series last fall against Louisville.

In games in the Kentucky metropolis, Louisville pitchers sorely tried Jackie's temper. But after every trip into the dirt, he came up smiling. He could take it. And eventually the Colonels forgot Robinson's color and treated him as just another Montreal player.

Jackie Robinson's presence among the Brooklyn personnel marks a vast forward stride for Organized Baseball in the social revolution which has gained a tremendous impetus through the world war.

SOURCE: "Jackie Robinson Editorials: A Negro in the Major Leagues," available at http://www.sportingnews.com/features/jackie.ed4.html. Reproduced by permission.

PRIMARY SOURCE DOCUMENT

"The Marshall Plan," June 1947

INTRODUCTION After World War II, a devastated Great Britain had trouble maintaining its military and economic aid to Greece as a civil war developed between pro-British and pro-communist forces. In response to a British withdrawal from the region, President Harry S. Truman appealed to Congress in March 1947 for foreign aid of $300 million for Greece and $100 million for Turkey to help preserve pro-Western governments. In his speech, which became known as the Truman Doctrine, he justified to the Congress and to the American public his aggressive strategy of fighting communism, which took form in the containment policy. Such a foreign policy was expensive and ran contrary to American isolationist traditions. But the inability of Britain to maintain control in Greece and Turkey, and the general picture of European life after the war, led U.S. officials to fear the rise of communist regimes. Americans traveling through Europe in 1946 and 1947 had seen dark cities, closed or demolished factories, ruined infrastructure, and starving people. The Truman Doctrine, however, would not solve such a problem.

The Marshall Plan, known formally as the European Recovery Program, was named for Gen. George C. Marshall, Truman's Secretary of State. During a June 1947 Harvard University commencement address, Marshall encouraged European nations, as well as the Soviet Union, to approach the United States with plans to rebuild their economies. The Marshall Plan required participating nations to accept American-made goods, which would shield the U.S. economy from a postwar slump, and to account to the American-managed European Recovery Administration for aid expenditures. In effect, the Marshall Plan tied the European market securely to the U.S. economy.

American officials expected Russia to reject the plan as well as to keep its Eastern European allies from participating because it would allow American goods and capital to influence rebuilding plans in Eastern Bloc countries; the Czechs and the Poles did try to participate in the program but were "discouraged" from doing so by the Soviets. The Marshall Plan was a significant step in the evolution of the cold war because it helped to formalize the division of Western Europe and Eastern Europe. It also represented the United States' unilateral assertion of power in Europe beyond the scope of the United Nations.

Their cause helped by a communist coup d'état in Czechoslovakia in early 1948, Truman and Marshall won over the Congress. Over the next four years, roughly $13 billion of American economic aid in the form of capital, machinery, food, and raw materials poured into Western Europe. Although the United States wanted to protect Europe in order to keep its markets open to American investors and goods, the Marshall Plan helped to stabilize European economies and to relieve the suffering of American allies. It combined humanitarian aid, sound foreign policy, and a boost for American capitalism.

I need not tell you gentlemen that the world situation is very serious. That must be apparent to all intelligent people. I think one difficulty is that the problem is one of such enormous complexity that the very mass of facts presented to the public by press and radio make it exceedingly difficult for the man in the street to reach a clear appraisement of the situation. Furthermore, the people of this country are distant from the troubled areas of the earth and it is hard for them to comprehend the plight and consequent reaction of the long-suffering peoples, and the effect of those reactions on their governments in connection with our efforts to promote peace in the world.

In considering the requirements for the rehabilitation of Europe, the physical loss of life, the visible destruction of cities, factories, mines, and railroads was correctly estimated, but it has become obvious during recent months that this visible destruction was probably less serious than the dislocation of the entire fabric of European economy. For the past 10 years conditions have been highly abnormal. The feverish maintenance of the war effort engulfed all aspects of national economics. Machinery has fallen into disrepair or is entirely obsolete. Under the arbitrary and destructive Nazi rule, virtually every possible enterprise was geared into the German war machine. Long-standing commercial ties, private institutions, banks, insurance companies and shipping companies disappeared, through the loss of capital, absorption through nationalization or by simple destruction. In many countries, confidence in the local currency has been severely shaken. The breakdown of the business structure of Europe during the war was complete. Recovery has been seriously retarded by the fact that 2 years after the close of hostilities a peace settlement with Germany and Austria has not been agreed upon. But even given a more prompt solution of these difficult problems, the rehabilitation of the economic structure of Europe quite evidently will require a much longer time and greater effort than had been foreseen.

There is a phase of this matter which is both interesting and serious. The farmer has always produced the foodstuffs to exchange with the city dweller for the other necessities of life. This division of labor is the basis of modern civilization. At the present time it is threatened with breakdown. The town and city industries are not producing adequate goods to exchange with the food-producing farmer. Raw materials and fuel are in short supply. Machinery is lacking or worn out. The farmer or the peasant cannot find the goods for sale which he desires to purchase. So the sale of his farm produce for money which he cannot use seems to him unprofitable transaction. He, therefore, has withdrawn many fields from crop cultivation and is using them for grazing. He feeds more grain to stock and finds for himself and his family an ample supply of food, however short he may be on clothing and the other ordinary gadgets of civilization. Meanwhile people in the cities are short of food and fuel. So the governments are forced to use their foreign money and credits to procure these necessities abroad. This process exhausts funds which are urgently needed for reconstruction. Thus a very serious situation is rapidly developing which bodes no good

OVERVIEW

American High, 1945–1960

PAUL ROSIER, VILLANOVA UNIVERSITY

After World War II America's influence abroad was at an all-time high, while at home many Americans were "riding high" due to postwar economic expansion. America's prosperity was driven by the stability and growth of its industrial sector, undamaged during the war, and its ability to dominate world markets, assisted by government initiatives like the Marshall Plan, which tied lending to the purchase of American-made goods. Government spending on personnel, military hardware, road-building, and other construction projects also fueled economic advances for many Americans, whereas the GI Bill of Rights expanded educational opportunities for veterans. And workers in labor unions found their wages expanding dramatically during the 1950s, helped by the merger of the American Federation of Labor and the Congress of Industrial Organizations (AFL-CIO) in 1955, which enabled organized labor to represent its interests more successfully even as technological advances and automation began to cut into traditional economic sectors. Less successful were African Americans, Native Americans, and other minority groups who found themselves on the margins of an affluent society. However a "liberal consensus" formed that defined America by its anticommunism at home and abroad and its domestic policies of government spending, limited social reform, and free market economics.

The Cold War

By 1946 a "cold war" with the Soviet Union was well underway. As this geopolitical and ideological conflict evolved, the United States asserted its leadership in political, economic, and military realms: The Truman Doctrine suggested the willingness of the United States to oppose left-wing movements; the Marshall Plan provided nearly $13 billion in aid to help rebuild Western Europe; and American forces helped to form and manage the North Atlantic Treaty Organization (NATO).

This leadership role ran counter to the American tradition of isolationism and became very expensive, and thus some politicians found it difficult to accept. One Republican congressman called the Marshall Plan an "international WPA," referring to the Works Progress Administration, a New Deal era work relief program that many conservatives considered socialist in nature. Indeed, the post–World War II period was characterized by an ongoing debate over the role and size of the federal government. Deficit-spending patterns initiated during the New Deal and a continued attempt by Democrats to expand social welfare programs led to a conservative backlash in Congress, which blocked several initiatives of President Harry S. Truman's Fair Deal. This same Congress did, however, adopt some new programs and expand old ones like Social Security.

Anticommunism

When Republicans captured the presidency, the Senate, and the House in 1952, opposition to government expansion was one reason. As important was Truman's perceived failure to halt communist aggression abroad and uncover communist subversion at home. After communists assumed power in China in 1949 by defeating the corrupt Nationalist forces supported by the United States, Truman and his State Department were blamed. At home, Alger Hiss, a U.S. State Department official and former New Dealer, was convicted of perjury in 1950 for lying about past communist activities. The outbreak of war in Korea, which drew U.S. soldiers into battle against North Korean communist forces, also heightened fears of communist aggression. Senator Joseph McCarthy exploited these events to launch what became a witch-hunt for suspected American communists and collaborators. McCarthy, a Republican from Wisconsin, never had proof that the U.S. State Department employed communists, but his

for the world. The modern system of the division of labor upon which the exchange of products is based is in danger of breaking down.

The truth of the matter is that Europe's requirements for the next 3 or 4 years of foreign food and other essential products—principally from America—are so much greater than her present ability to pay that she must have substantial additional help, or face economic, social, and political deterioration of a very grave character.

The remedy lies in breaking the vicious circle and restoring the confidence of the European people in the economic future of their own countries and of Europe as a whole. The manufacturer and the farmer throughout wide areas must be able and willing to exchange their publicized claims served their purpose as anticommunism became a national obsession. Even before McCarthy assumed center stage, the House Committee on Un-American Activities (HUAC) began investigating Communist activity during the New Deal and had actually been again in 1947 with its probe of Hollywood. Truman had also launched a government loyalty program that same year. But McCarthy's shrill anticommunism created a climate of fear that made it difficult for many Americans to speak freely about their beliefs or to champion an agenda that might be considered un-American. A small number of Americans supported the Soviet Union, but many were unfairly labeled "communist" and lost their jobs, families, homes, and, in some cases, their lives as a result. Anticommunism became a functional tool for corporations to attack labor unions, Republicans to scale back New Deal social programs, and Southern democrats (or Dixiecrats) to denounce civil rights activism.

Civil Rights

With Americans' civil liberties under attack, it became increasingly difficult for African Americans to secure civil rights long denied them. Progress was generally restricted to specific institutions. Facing pressure from African-American leaders, President Truman desegregated the armed forces in 1947. A more publicized event was Jackie Robinson's entry into major league baseball in April 1947. The 1954 Supreme Court *Brown* v. *Board of Education* decision outlawed segregation in public schools and ended the "separate but equal" doctrine the Court had established in 1896, giving African Americans additional hope for social and economic change. As lead attorney for the plaintiffs Thurgood Marshall proclaimed after the decision, "The stigma of second class citizenship is on the way out." When Rosa Parks refused to give up her seat on a bus in Montgomery, Alabama, in 1955, she helped inspire thousands of other African Americans to protest their second-class citizenship. Martin Luther King Jr.'s rise to prominence during the Montgomery Bus Boycott of 1955 and 1956 and his help in building organizations like the Southern Christian Leadership Conference (SCLC) set the stage for mass protests in the South. The Court followed its *Brown* decision by outlawing segregation on bus lines, and golf courses, and in other public places, precipitating fierce resistance among southerners everywhere. Dixiecrat congressmen sponsored a "Southern Manifesto" in 1956 to protest government-ordered social change, governors of southern states resisted school integration, and Ku Klux Klan activity flared anew. It would take a decade or more for the federal government to break down such resistance to a new social order.

Women in the 1950s

Gender relations were also in a state of flux immediately following the war. Employment opportunities during World War II had accelerated the movement of women from domestic service and farm labor into more traditionally male jobs like welders, machinists, and railroad workers; women had also found employment in law, medicine, and science, helped by expanded educational opportunities. Although the postwar demand for labor led to employers' continued hiring of married women, women's share of all jobs dropped from 36 to 28 percent soon after the war. Women were laid off at twice the rate of men, especially in the higher-paying industrial sectors. They were exhorted to remember that the returning soldier needed to become "head man again." During the 1950s women's roles were sharply defined along the traditional lines of marriage and motherhood. "Back to the kitchen" was a popular refrain of the 1950s, made by men and women alike. In 1956 a *Life* magazine cover story proudly proclaimed, "Of all the accomplishments of the American woman, the one she brings off with the most spectacular success is having babies."

Baby Boom and Suburban-sprawl

Peaking in 1957, the "baby boom" of the postwar era resulted in roughly doubled fertility rates. As families expanded in size, so too did their communities. New building techniques combined with federal mort-

products for currencies the continuing value of which is not open to question.

Aside from the demoralizing effect on the world at large and the possibilities of disturbances arising as a result of the desperation of the people concerned, the consequences to the economy of the United States should be apparent to all. It is logical that the United States should do whatever it is able to do to assist in the return of normal economic health in the world, without which there can be no political stability and no assured peace. Our policy is directed not against any country or doctrine but against hunger, poverty, desperation, and chaos. Its purpose should be the revival of working economy in the world so as to permit the emergence of political and social conditions in which free institutions can gage-lending programs for veterans to create housing options for many Americans. Thirteen million houses were built in the 1950s, 11 million of which sprouted up in nearly identical suburban communities like Levittown, New York, and Lakewood, California. These new communities were homogenous by design. Levittown homeowners were specifically prohibited from leasing to "members of other than the Caucasian race." By 1960 a quarter of the American population lived in the suburbs. And as these suburbs expanded, so too did the need for consumer items like washing machines, furniture, and cars, helping to fuel economic expansion.

Television and Its Discontents

The suburban life was both expressed through and reinforced by a new medium, television. In 1949 2.3 percent of American homes had a television set. In 1960, 87 percent did, representing a phenomenal increase. Early television programs were sponsored by companies whose products were mentioned or prominently displayed throughout the show. Cold-war concerns also underwrote these early programs. In one drama sponsored by a tobacco company, actors portraying Russian "bad guys" were prohibited from smoking cigarettes lest Americans associate smoking with evil. Television shows of the 1950s reflected advertisers' biggest consumers, white middle-class suburban families. Shows like *Leave it to Beaver, Ozzie and Harriet,* and *Father Knows Best* presented an idealized traditional family life mostly devoid of serious social conflict.

Even as this television culture evolved, other mediums began to challenge such a restricted vision of American life. Films like *Rebel without a Cause* and *The Wild One* depicted an emerging counterculture that rejected suburban conformity. In *The Wild One* a character played by Marlon Brando is asked, "What are you rebelling against?" He replies: "Whaddya got?" The rejection of American society's conventions also found expression in the sexually charged music of Elvis Presley; the Beat movement in literature, exemplified by the work of poet Allen Ginsberg and writer Jack Kerouac; and in the artwork of Jackson Pollock and other American painters of the so-called "New York school." Similar acts of cultural rebellion dominated the 1960s.

Cold-War Fears

Underlying this time of prosperity and confidence were other concerns, driven by an evolving conflict with the Soviet Union. Under President Dwight D. Eisenhower's leadership, U.S. military forces adopted the New Look agenda that emphasized the expansion of American nuclear forces over ground forces, which reflected both a new military strategy and a Republican attempt to cut the huge federal budget. The reliance on nuclear superiority led to an arms race that neither side felt they could lose, giving birth to the principle of mutually assured destruction that guaranteed the devastation of both Soviet and American societies should one side attempt to wage nuclear war. This heightened sense of competition led to other "races." The Soviet Union's launch of the Sputnik satellite in 1957 established the race for space; in response, the United States created the National Aeronautics and Space Administration (NASA) in 1958. The cold war even affected the Olympic Games, as African-American women sprinters came to represent American hopes for victory over Soviet-bloc athletes during the 1956 and 1960 games. In his farewell address to the nation, President Eisenhower warned of the transforming effects of the cold war on American society, in particular the emergence of what he called the military industrial complex, which signaled the rising influence of a military establishment and its industrial partners. America's confidence and comfort in the 1950s would be tested in the 1960s as the conformity created by the cold-war ideology at home and abroad engendered great social conflict that destroyed the idea of consensus.

BIBLIOGRAPHY

For an overview of the period, see William L. O'Neill, *American High: The Years of Confidence, 1945–1960* (1986). On McCarthyism, see Ellen W. Schrecker, *The Age of McCarthyism: A Brief History with Documents* (1994). John Lewis Gaddis reconsiders the cold war in *We Now Know: Rethinking Cold War History* (1997). For a look at the social and cultural history of the 1950s, see Elaine Tyler May, *Homeward Bound: American Families in the Cold War Era* (1988), and Steven Whitfield, *The Culture of the Cold War* (1991).

exist. Such assistance, I am convinced, must not be on a piecemeal basis as various crises develop. Any assistance that this Government may render in the future should provide a cure rather than a mere palliative. Any government that is willing to assist in the task of recovery will find full cooperation, I am sure, on the part of the United States Government. Any government which maneuvers to block the recovery of other countries cannot expect help from us. Furthermore, governments, political parties, or groups which seek to perpetuate human misery in order to profit therefrom politically or otherwise will encounter the opposition of the United States.

It is already evident that, before the United States Government can proceed much further in its efforts to alleviate the situation and help start the European world on its way to recovery, there must be some agreement among the countries of Europe as to the requirements of the situation and the part those countries themselves will take in order to give proper effect to whatever action might be undertaken by this Government. It would be neither fitting nor efficacious for this Government to undertake to draw up unilaterally a program designed to place Europe on its feet economically. This is the business of the Europeans. The initiative, I think, must come from Europe. The role of this country should consist of friendly aid in the drafting of a European program so far as it may be practical for us to do so. The program should be a joint one, agreed to by a number, if not all European nations.

An essential part of any successful action on the part of the United States is an understanding on the part of the people of America of the character of the problem and the remedies to be applied. Political passion and prejudice should have no part. With foresight, and a willingness on the part of our people to face up to the vast responsibilities which history has clearly placed upon our country, the difficulties I have outlined can and will be overcome.

SOURCE: "The Marshall Plan," Harvard University Commencement Address, June 5, 1947.

1948

INTERNATIONAL

Soviet Russia blockades Allied sectors of Berlin (April 1); British and U.S. planes airlift food and coal into city (June 26); when blockade ends in 1949, 276,926 flights had carried 2.3 million tons of supplies.

Economic Cooperation Administration is created to assist foreign countries; $6.1 billion is set aside for program.

Twenty-one Western Hemisphere republics form Organization of American States (OAS) (April 30).

U.N. General Assembly adopts Universal Declaration of Human Rights.

Israel is declared an independent state (May 14); Arabs unsuccessful in military attempt to overthrow action.

NATIONAL

President Harry S. Truman, Democrat, is elected to full term, defeating Republican Thomas E. Dewey with 24,105,802 popular and 303 electoral votes against Dewey's 21,970,065 and 189; Dixiecrat candidate J. Strom Thurmond receives 1,169,063 and 39 votes.

Whittaker Chambers, an admitted communist, accuses Alger Hiss, State Department official, of being a communist; Hiss sues for libel, is indicted for perjury.

New Selective Service Act calls for registration of men 18–25; induction is restricted to 21 months' service in the military for those 19–25.

President Truman issues an executive order outlawing racial segregation in the armed forces.

Three atomic bombs are tested at Eniwetok in the Pacific.

Air Force bombers complete nonstop round-the-world flight, refuel in air four times.

Lyndon B. Johnson begins 12 years of service in Senate from Texas.

DEATHS Former First Ladies Mary S. L. Harrison (1889–1893) and Edith K. C. Roosevelt (1901–1909); Gen. John J. Pershing, head of American World War I forces; Orville Wright, aviation pioneer; Charles Evans Hughes, Supreme Court Chief Justice (1930–1941); John A. Lomax, folklorist.

BUSINESS/INDUSTRY/INVENTIONS

Haloid Corp. and Battelle Institute give first public demonstration of xerography; John Bardeen and Walter H. Brattain demonstrate their invention, the transistor.

Federal Communications Commission authorizes use of telephone recording devices.

More than 350,000 soft-coal miners strike for $100-a-month pensions; agreement is reached a month later.

DEATH John R. Gregg, shorthand-system developer.

TRANSPORTATION

Idlewild (later Kennedy) International Airport opens.

DEATHS William S. Knudsen, General Motors official; Charles W. Nash, pioneer automaker.

SCIENCE/MEDICINE

Blue Cross originates when group of school teachers enter an agreement with Baylor Hospital in Dallas.

Dr. Benjamin M. Duggar discovers aureomycin chlortetracycline, an antibiotic.

Dr. George G. Wright of Army Chemical Laboratory develops anthrax vaccine for humans.

University of Indiana Institute for Sex Research releases report by Dr. Alfred Kinsey on sexual behavior of men.

Dr. Norbert Wiener completes his book, *Cybernetics*.

National Institute of Dental Health is established.

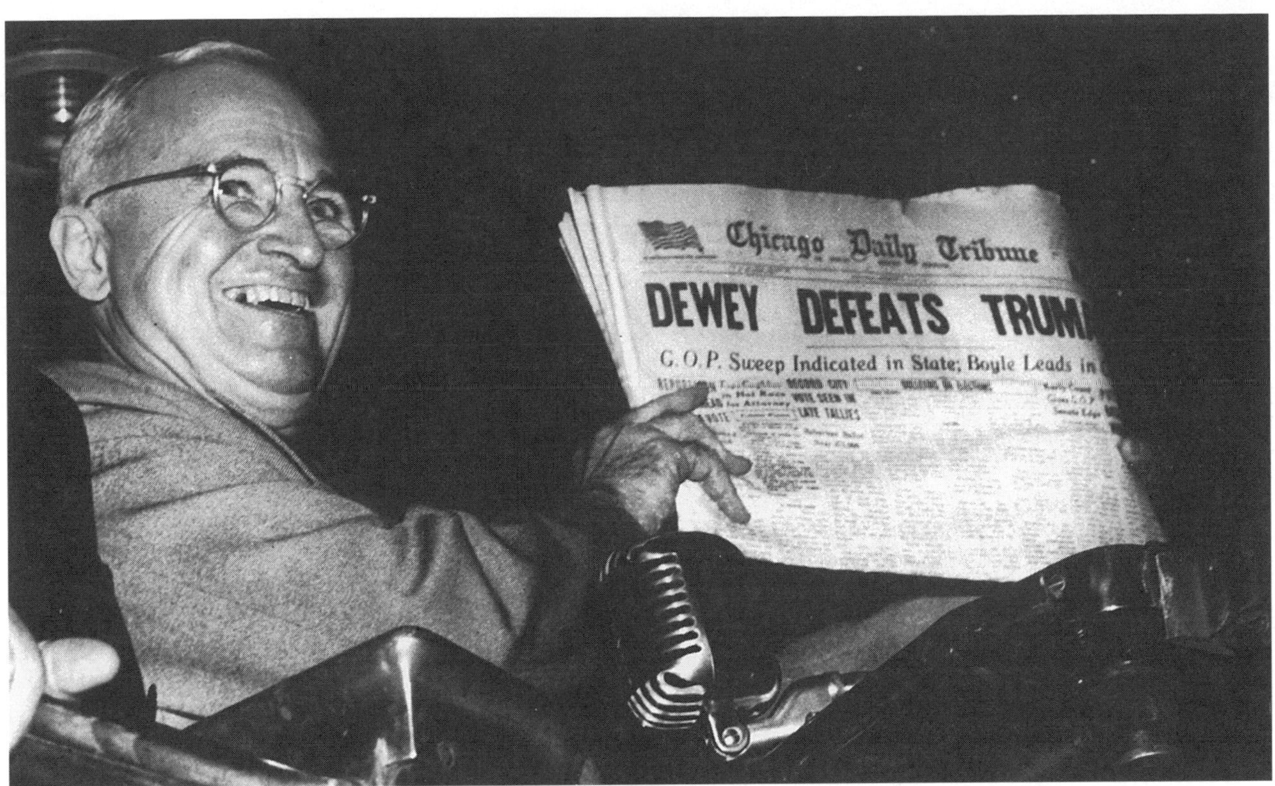

After his victory over Thomas Dewey in the 1948 presidential election, Harry Truman stops in Chicago on his way back to Washington, D.C. He holds up an early edition of the November 4, 1948, *Chicago Tribune*; the erroneous headline was based on early election returns. **AP/WIDE WORLD PHOTOS**

Vitamin B-12 is isolated from liver extract.

DEATHS Abraham A. Brill, pioneer U.S. psychoanalyst; Emily P. Bissell, Christmas Seal founder.

RELIGION

Supreme Court rules religious training in public schools is unconstitutional.

World Council of Churches is founded; Methodist Bishop G. Bromley Oxnam is president.

Helen Kenyon becomes first woman moderator of Congregational-Christian churches.

Christmas Eve midnight mass at St. Patrick's Cathedral in New York City is televised for first time.

Two new Catholic archbishops named: James F. McIntyre of Los Angeles and Patrick A. O'Boyle of Washington, D.C.

ART/MUSIC

New York City Ballet is organized, directed by George Balanchine.

Columbia Records introduces long-playing records, developed by Peter Goldmark; Wire Recording Corp. develops a magnetic tape recorder.

Miles Davis, who started "cool jazz," forms band.

Robert Shaw Chorale is founded.

Mark Rothko completes the painting *No. 2, 1948;* Saul Baizerman completes the sculpture *Slumber.*

Des Moines (Iowa) Art Center is founded.

SONGS (POPULAR): "Hooray for Love," "If I Had a Hammer," "Nature Boy," "On a Slow Boat to China," "Red Roses for a Blue Lady," "Buttons and Bows," "Tennessee Waltz," "Baby, It's Cold Outside."

DEATH Oley Speaks, composer ("On the Road to Mandalay").

LITERATURE/JOURNALISM

Walter C. Kelly draws comic strip "Pogo" for New York papers.

BOOKS *High Towers* by Thomas B. Costain, *The Naked and the Dead* by Norman Mailer, *Guard of Honor* by James G. Cozzens, *Other Voices, Other Rooms* by Truman Capote, *Crusade in Europe* by Dwight D. Eisenhower, *The Seven-Storey Mountain* by Thomas Merton, *The Young Lions* by Irwin Shaw, *The Age of Anxiety* (poetry) by W. H. Auden.

DEATHS Gertrude Atherton, author *(Black Oxen);* James H. McGraw, publisher; Charles A. Beard, historian; Carl T. Anderson, cartoonist ("Henry").

ENTERTAINMENT

Ed Sullivan debuts Sunday night television variety show that lasts 23 years; Milton Berle emcees Texaco Star Theater; Kukla, Fran, and Ollie, part-puppet show, airs; other new shows include *Candid Camera* with Allen Funt, Arthur Godfrey's *Talent Scouts,* and Perry Como.

PLAYS Paul Muni stars in *Key Largo,* Rex Harrison in *Anne of the Thousand Days,* Ray Bolger in *Where's Charley?,* Henry Fonda in *Mr. Roberts,* Alfred Drake in *Kiss Me, Kate.*

MOVIES *The Treasure of Sierra Madre* with Humphrey Bogart, *Fort Apache* with John Wayne, *Johnny Belinda* with Jane Wyman, *Easter Parade* with Fred Astaire and Judy Garland.

Eve Arden stars in radio's *Our Miss Brooks.*

DEATH D. W. Griffith, pioneer filmmaker *(Birth of a Nation).*

SPORTS

Olympic Games are held in London; U.S. wins 33 gold medals, including Bob Mathias's in decathlon.

National Boxing Assn. announces new safety program for professional boxers: more-thorough examinations, 8-ounce gloves, mandatory eight count after a knockdown.

Dick Button becomes first American to win men's world figure-skating championship.

Mel Patton sets record of 9.3 seconds for 100-yard dash.

Satchel Paige, legendary Negro League pitcher, makes first major league start.

WINNERS *Auto racing*—Mauri Rose, Indianapolis 500; *Baseball*—Cleveland Indians, World Series; *Basketball*—St. Louis, NIT; Kentucky, NCAA; Baltimore, BAA; *Bowling*—Andy Varipapa and Val Mikiel, bowlers of year; *Boxing*—Joe Louis, heavyweight; Freddie Mills, light heavyweight; Tony Zale, middleweight; *Chess*—Herman Steiner, U.S. champion; *Football* (bowls)—Michigan, Rose; Georgia Tech, Orange; Texas, Sugar; Southern Methodist, Cotton; Philadelphia, NFL; Cleveland, AAFC; *Golf*—Ben Hogan, U.S. Open and PGA; Henry Cotton, Masters; Babe Didrikson Zaharias, U.S. Women's Open; *Hockey*—Toronto, Stanley Cup; Michigan, NCAA; *Horse racing*—Citation becomes eighth Triple Crown winner taking Kentucky Derby, Preakness Stakes, and Belmont Stakes; *Tennis*—U.S., Davis Cup; Pancho Gonzales, U.S. Open (men); Margaret Osborne du Pont, U.S. Open (women).

DEATHS Babe Ruth, home run king; Jock Sutherland, college football coach.

MISCELLANEOUS

American Association of Registration Executives begins uniform system of birth registration numbering.

Long-playing records ("LPs") begin to replace "78s."

1949

INTERNATIONAL

U.S., Great Britain, Canada, France, Belgium, Italy, Netherlands, Luxembourg, Denmark, Norway, Iceland, Portugal sign North Atlantic Treaty (April 4); create NATO.

President Harry S. Truman calls for Point Four program of assistance to underprivileged areas.

U.S. recognizes Israel after Israel creates a permanent government (January 31).

Berlin airlift ends (September 30) when Russian blockade is lifted; airlift delivered 2.3 million tons of food and coal to Allied portions of Berlin.

U.S., Great Britain, and France agree to establish West German Republic (April 8); President Truman creates office of U.S. High Commissioner for Germany (June 6); John J. McCloy is first commissioner.

Cornerstone is laid for U.N. headquarters in New York City.

Eugenie Anderson becomes first U.S. woman with ambassador rank (to Denmark).

NATIONAL

Supreme Court in *Terminiello* v. *Chicago* upholds free speech even when it causes unrest or disturbances.

Eleven top U.S. Communists are found guilty of conspiring to overthrow the government, are sentenced to five years in prison.

Hoover Commission issues report on government operations; leads to Reorganization Act of 1949.

Salary of president is raised to $100,000 annually; vice president and house speaker to $30,000.

Flag Day, June 14, is established.

General Services Administration (GSA) is established to manage government property.

The Berlin Airlift, 1948–1949. Children in blockaded West Berlin eagerly await American planes bringing supplies. CORBIS-BETTMANN

Gen. Henry H. (Hap) Arnold becomes first general of Air Force; Gen. Omar N. Bradley becomes first permanent chairman of Joint Chiefs of Staff.

William H. Hastie becomes first African-American judge on U.S. Circuit Court of Appeals.

American Museum of Atomic Energy opens at Oak Ridge, Tennessee.

Gerald R. Ford begins 24 years of service in House from Michigan.

National Trust for Historic Preservation is created.

DEATHS James V. Forrestal, first defense secretary; Edward R. Stettinius Jr., first U.S. delegate to the U.N.

BUSINESS/INDUSTRY/INVENTIONS

Supreme Court rules that states have right to ban the closed shop.

Minimum wage is raised from 40 cents an hour to 75 cents, effective 1950.

Federal government seizes North American Aviation plant in Inglewood, California, to end strike.

Goodyear Tire & Rubber Co. manufactures belt conveyor for Weirton mine of National Mines to convey coal 10,000 feet from mine to Monongahela River in West Virginia.

DEATH Atwater Kent, pioneer radio manufacturer.

TRANSPORTATION

More than 5 million (5,119,466) cars are manufactured in year.

SCIENCE/MEDICINE

William F. Giauque is awarded Nobel Prize for chemistry for work on chemical thermodynamics.

Morehead Planetarium at University of North Carolina opens.

EDUCATION

Earl J. McGrath is named U.S. Education Commissioner.

DEATHS Ray Lyman Wilbur, president and chancellor, Stanford University (1916–1949); James R. Angell, Yale University president (1921–1937), a founder of functional psychology.

RELIGION

Billy Graham begins nationwide evangelistic program with eight weeks of meetings in Los Angeles.

Cornerstone is laid for Islamic Center in Washington, D.C.

DEATH Rabbi Stephen S. Wise, co-founder of American Zionist movement.

ART/MUSIC

Roy E. Harris composes *Kentucky Spring.*

Peter Blume completes the painting *The Rock.*

SONGS (POPULAR): "Dear Hearts and Gentle People," "Mule Train," "Rudolph, the Red-Nosed Reindeer," "Some Enchanted Evening," "I'm Gonna Wash That Man Right Out of My Hair."

LITERATURE/JOURNALISM

William Faulkner is awarded Nobel Prize for Literature for contributions to the U.S. novel.

BOOKS *The Big Fisherman* by Lloyd C. Douglas, *Annie Allen* (poetry) by Gwendolyn Brooks, *A Rage to Live* by John O'Hara, *The Man with the Golden Arm* by Nelson Algren, *The Apostle* by Sholem Asch, *The Lottery* by Shirley Jackson, *The Dream Merchants* by Harold Robbins, *The Golden Apples* by Eudora Welty.

The Reporter and *American Heritage* magazines begin publication.

DEATHS Margaret Mitchell and Hervey Allen, authors; Helen Hokinson, cartoonist; John T. McCutcheon, editorial cartoonist (*Chicago Tribune* 1903–1945).

ENTERTAINMENT

PLAYS Mary Martin and Ezio Pinza star in *South Pacific,* Carol Channing in *Gentlemen Prefer Blondes,* Lee J. Cobb in *Death of a Salesman,* Ralph Bellamy in *Detective Story.*

MOVIES *All the King's Men* with Broderick Crawford, *Adam's Rib* with Katharine Hepburn and Spencer Tracy.

New television shows are *Stop the Music* with Bert Parks, *Quiz Kids, One Man's Family, Mama* with Peggy Wood, *Life of Riley* with William Bendix, *Hopalong Cassidy* with William Boyd, *Aldrich Family, Lights Out,* the Fred Waring and Dave Garroway shows.

DEATHS Maxwell Anderson, playwright; Burns Mantle, editor of annual play collection (1919–1947); Wallace Beery, screen actor; Bill ("Bojangles") Robinson, dancer.

SPORTS

Merger of National Basketball League and Basketball Association of America forms National Basketball Assn.; National Football League and All-American Conference merge.

WINNERS *Auto racing*—Bill Holland, Indianapolis 500; Red Byron, NASCAR Winston Cup Champion; *Baseball*—New York Yankees, World Series; *Basketball*—San Francisco, NIT; Kentucky, NCAA; Minneapolis, NBA; *Bowling*—Connie Schwegler and Val Mikiel, bowlers of year; *Boxing*—Ezzard Charles, heavyweight; Jake LaMotta, middleweight; Willie Pep, featherweight; *Football* (bowls)—Northwestern, Rose; Texas, Orange; Oklahoma, Sugar; Southern Methodist, Cotton; Philadelphia, NFL; *Golf*—U.S., Ryder and Walker cups; Cary Middlecoff, U.S. Open; Sam Snead, PGA; Bobby Locke, Masters; Louise Suggs, U.S. Women's Open; *Hockey*—Toronto, Stanley Cup; *Horse racing*—Ponder, Kentucky Derby; Capot, Preakness Stakes and Belmont Stakes; *Tennis*—U.S., Davis Cup; Pancho Gonzales, U.S. Open (men); Margaret Osborne du Pont, U.S. Open (women).

MISCELLANEOUS

Two planes collide over Washington, D.C., kill 55.

Fire in Effingham (Illinois) hospital kills 77 persons.

Bikinis are introduced as swimwear.

1950

INTERNATIONAL

Korean War

One hundred thousand North Koreans invade South Korea (June 25); President Harry Truman orders U.S. air, sea forces to support Korean Republican Army (June 27), adds ground forces (June 30); Gen. Douglas MacArthur is named commander of U.N. troops (July 8). U.S. Marines take Womi Island, Inchon (September 15), U.S. troops recapture Seoul (September 26); 18 Communist China divisions launch surprise attack (September 30), force U.N. retreat to 38th parallel.

North Atlantic Council agrees on integrated European defense force; Gen. Dwight D. Eisenhower becomes NATO commander.

U.S. recalls consular officials from China after U.S. consul general was seized; shipments to Communist China are banned.

U.N. official Ralph Bunche is awarded Nobel Peace Prize for work in Middle East war; U.N. headquarters in New York City is completed.

U.S. sends arms, supplies, and instructors to South Vietnam; military assistance pact is signed with France, Cambodia, Laos, and Vietnam.

U.S. and Canada sign 50-year treaty (February 27), to regulate Niagara Falls power output, preserve falls' beauty.

NATIONAL

Two Puerto Rican nationalists attempt to assassiate President Truman (November 1); one nationalist and a White House guard are killed.

President Truman announces that U.S. will develop hydrogen bomb; Wernher von Braun, German rocket engineer, is named director of missile research facility at Huntsville, Alabama.

U.S. citizenship and limited self-government granted to people of Guam; Puerto Rico Commonwealth Act is signed.

Sixteenth census reports population at 151,325,798.

Annual immigration to U.S. totals 249,187.

Alger Hiss, former State Department official, is found guilty of perjury, is sentenced to five-year prison term.

McCarran Act passes over president's veto, calls for registration of Communists and their internment during national emergencies. **SEE PRIMARY DOCUMENT** Veto of the Internal Security Act

Senate Judiciary Committee televises hearings on organized crime.

Senator Joseph McCarthy of Wisconsin announces in Wheeling, West Virginia, that he has a list of many Communists in the State Department, leading to several years of congressional hearings.

Residential mail deliveries are cut to once a day.

Selective Service for military draft is extended for another year.

National deficit is $3.1 million; public debt climbs to $256.1 billion.

DEATHS Henry L. Stimson, War Secretary (1911–1913, 1940–1945), Secretary of State (1929–1933); Clarence A. Dykstra, Selective Service head (1940–1941); Henry H. (Hap) Arnold, Air Force general.

BUSINESS/INDUSTRY/INVENTIONS

Supreme Court in *American Communications Workers* v. *Douds* upholds Taft-Hartley Act provision that requires non-Communist affidavits from union officers.

Maritime Administration is established.

Grand Coulee Dam in Washington State is dedicated.

Bic Pen Co. is founded; Hazel Bishop forms cosmetics company; J. Paul Getty negotiates oil concessions in Saudi Arabia, Kuwait.

Lucille Ball in *I Love Lucy*, one of the new television shows in 1950. **SPRINGER/CORBIS-BETTMANN**

CIO expels International Longshoremen's and Warehousemen's Union.

Minimum wage becomes 75 cents an hour.

DEATHS Walter H. Beech, founder and head, Beech Aircraft; Charles L. Lawrence, designer of first air-cooled aeronautical engine; Eliel Saarinen, architect.

TRANSPORTATION

President Truman orders seizure of the railroads to prevent general strike (August 27).

New York Port Authority bus terminal opens.

Brooklyn—Battery Tunnel, longest in U.S., opens; Tacoma (Washington) Narrow Bridge is completed.

DEATH Ransom E. Olds, pioneer automaker.

SCIENCE/MEDICINE

Philip S. Hench and Edward C. Kendall share Nobel Prize for physiology/medicine for discoveries about hormones of the adrenal cortex.

President Truman signs act creating National Science Foundation.

Richard H. Lawler performs first kidney transplant from one human to another in Chicago.

Charles Pfizer & Co. announces the antibiotic tetramycin.

Fluoro-record reflector X-ray camera is developed.

Dr. Helen Taussig becomes first woman member of Association of American Physicians.

Element 98 (californium) is discovered at University of California.

DEATHS Charles R. Drew, developer of blood banks; Arthur J. Dempster, builder of first mass spectrometer; George R. Minot, discoverer of liver therapy for anemia.

EDUCATION

Yale University founds Department of Design, headed by Josef Albers; University of North Carolina offers nuclear engineering course.

DEATH Isaiah Bowman, Johns Hopkins University president (1935–1948).

RELIGION

National Council of Churches is formed by 29 major American Protestant, seven Eastern Orthodox churches.

Rose Philippine Duchesne, founder of first American Sacred Heart convent, is beatified.

American Synod of Russian Orthodox church elects New York Archbishop Leonty as Metropolitan for the United States and Canada.

DEATHS William T. Manning, Episcopal bishop of New York (1921–1946); Edwin H. Hughes, senior Methodist bishop (1932–1950).

ART/MUSIC

Age of Anxiety, ballet by Jerome Robbins and Leonard Bernstein, is presented; Gian Carlo Menotti composes opera *The Consul.*

PAINTINGS Jackson Pollock's first "action" work, *Lavender Mist;* Andrew Wyeth's temperas, *Young America* and *Northern Point;* Ben Shahn, *Epoch;* Hans Hofmann, *The Window;* Stuart Davis, *Little Giant Still-Life.*

SONGS (POPULAR): "Mona Lisa," "C'est Si Bon," "A Bushel and a Peck," "From This Moment On," "Good Night, Irene," "May the Good Lord Bless and Keep You."

DEATHS George G. (Buddy) De Sylva, lyricist ("April Showers"); Kurt Weill, composer *(Three-penny Opera);* Walter Damrosch, conductor.

LITERATURE/JOURNALISM

Gwendolyn Brooks, poet, becomes first African-American woman to win Pulitzer Prize (for *Annie Allen*).

Charles M. Schulz creates cartoon "Peanuts."

Walter Cronkite begins CBS television news career.

Tan magazine is founded.

BOOKS *The Wall* by John Hersey, *I, Robert* by Isaac Asimov; *The Disenchanted* by Budd Schulberg, *Kon-Tiki* by Thor Heyerdahl, *The 13 Clocks* by James Thurber, *Complete Poems* by Carl Sandburg, *The Cardinal* by Henry M. Robinson, *The Family Moskat* by Isaac Bashevis Singer, *Giant* by Edna Ferber.

DEATHS Poets Edna St. Vincent Millay and William Rose Benét; authors Edgar Lee Masters, Carl Van Doren, and Edgar Rice Burroughs.

ENTERTAINMENT

CBS television broadcasts in color.

Comedy and musical personalities star on television shows: Jimmy Durante, Steve Allen, Jack Benny, Sid Caesar and Imogene Coca, George Burns and Gracie Allen, and Frank Sinatra; other new shows include *I Love Lucy, Your Hit Parade, What's My Line?, Truth or Consequences, Beat the Clock.*

PLAYS Robert Alda stars in *Guys & Dolls,* Ethel Waters and Julie Harris in *The Member of the Wedding,* Ethel Merman in *Call Me Madam,* Shirley Booth in *Come Back, Little Sheba,* Uta Hagen in *The Country Girl.*

MOVIES *Born Yesterday* with Judy Holliday, *Cyrano de Bergerac* with Jose Ferrer, *The Great Caruso* with Mario Lanza, *Harvey* with James Stewart, *The Asphalt Jungle* with Sterling Hayden, *All About Eve* with Bette Davis.

DEATHS Actresses Julia Marlowe and Jane Cowl; actors Walter Huston and Al Jolson; producers William A. Brady and Brock Pemberton.

SPORTS

Connie Mack retires after managing Philadelphia Athletics baseball team for 50 years.

Florence Chadwick swims English Channel both ways.

Sportswriters and broadcasters name Jack Dempsey greatest prizefighter of 1900–1950 era; George Mikan, best basketball player; Man o' War, greatest racehorse.

U.S. soccer team upsets England in World Cup play; three days later, Chile eliminates U.S.

WINNERS *Auto racing*—Johnny Parsons, Indianapolis 500; Bill Rexford, NASCAR; *Baseball*—New York

Yankees, World Series; *Basketball*—City College of New York, NIT and NCAA; Minneapolis NBA; *Bobsledding*—U.S. four-man team, world title; *Bowling*—Junie McMahon, Marion Ladewig, bowlers of year; *Boxing*—Ezzard Charles, heavyweight; Joey Maxim, light heavyweight; Sugar Ray Robinson, middleweight; Sandy Saddler, featherweight; *Chess*—Arthur B. Bisguier, U.S. Open; *Figure skating*—Dick Button, men's world singles; Peter and Karol Kennedy, first from U.S. to win world pairs; *Football* (bowls)—Ohio State, Rose; Santa Clara, Orange; Oklahoma, Sugar; Rice, Cotton; Cleveland, NFL; *Golf*—Ben Hogan, U.S. Open; Chandler Harper, PGA; Jimmy Demaret, Masters; Babe Didrikson Zaharias, U.S. Women's Open; *Hockey*—Detroit, Stanley Cup; *Horse racing*—Middleground, Kentucky Derby and Belmont Stakes; Hill Prince, Preakness Stakes; *Tennis*—Australia, Davis Cup; Arthur Larsen, U.S. Open (men); Margaret Osborne du Pont, U.S. Open (women).

DEATHS Carl L. Storck, NFL secretary-treasurer (1921–1939)/president (1939–1941); Frank Buck, wild-game hunter.

MISCELLANEOUS

Brinks Express office in Boston is robbed of $2.8 million.

New York City's Aircall, Inc. begins radio paging service.

Standing commuter train in Richmond Hill, New York, is hit by oncoming train, kills 79.

PRIMARY SOURCE DOCUMENT

Veto of the Internal Security Act, September 22, 1950

INTRODUCTION In 1938 the House Un-American Activities Committee began investigating Communist influences in the Roosevelt administration and in the labor movement. This campaign was politically motivated, designed to embarrass President Roosevelt and discredit New Deal programs that Republicans considered un-American. An anti-Communist coalition expanded in the 1940s as ex-Communists began to provide evidence of Communist activity to congressional investigators. These investigations retreated when the Soviet Union became allied with the United States against the Nazi threat, but resumed as the cold war quickly evolved. Harry S. Truman, the thirty-third president of the United States, inherited the presidency when Franklin D. Roosevelt died on April 12, 1945. Truman took a firm stance against the Soviet Union after World War II, resolutely leading the country through the early years of the cold war. Truman also showed a willingness to adopt programs designed to keep members of the American Communist Party or its "sympathizers" out of the government. In March 1947 Truman signed off on a loyalty-security program for government employees and supported the prosecution of individuals with Communist Party ties.

In February 1950 Senator Joseph McCarthy charged that the federal government was riddled with Communist subversives. The campaign was based on false charges, but his publicity stunts, as well as the onset of the Korean War, put additional pressure on the government to detain suspected Communists and either deport or prosecute them. In September 1950, Congress presented Truman with the Internal Security Act, known as the McCarran Act for the bill's sponsor, Nevada's Pat McCarran, who chaired the Senate Judiciary Committee. The legislation would require members of the American Communist Party or its "front groups," organizations affiliated with the Communist Party, to register with the federal government. Truman vetoed the bill, arguing that it was unnecessary, given that existing laws were in place to deter Communist activity, and that it was un-American, in that it would "curb the simple expression of opinion" and thus recreate the very political conditions Americans condemned the Soviet Union for maintaining. Congress overrode Truman's veto, as Truman expected it would, and the McCarran Act became law, giving investigators yet another weapon in their fight against domestic communism. Truman's veto of the Internal Security Act was one of several dramatic protests registered by Democrats as well as by Republicans against the excesses of McCarthyism.

September 22, 1950

To the House of Representatives:

I return herewith, without my approval, H.R. 9490, the proposed "Internal Security Act of 1950."....H.R. 9490 would not hurt the Communists. Instead, it would help them....

...It would actually weaken our existing internal security measures and would seriously hamper the Federal Bureau of Investigation and our other security agencies. It would help the Communists in their efforts to create dissension and confusion within our borders. It would help the Communist propagandists throughout the world who are trying to undermine freedom by discrediting as hypocrisy the efforts of the United States on behalf of freedom...

...Fortunately, we already have on the books strong laws which give us most of the protection we need from the real dangers of treason, espionage, sabotage, and actions looking to the overthrow of our Government by force and violence. Most of the provisions of this bill have no relation to these real dangers....

The idea of requiring Communist organizations to divulge information about themselves is a simple and attractive one. But it is about as practical as requiring thieves to register with the sheriff. Obviously, no such organization as the Communist Party is likely to register voluntarily. Under the provisions of the bill, if an organization which the Attorney General believes should register does not do so, he must request a five-man Subversive Activities Control Board to order the organization to register. The Attorney General would have to produce proof that the organization in question was in fact a Communist-action or a Communist-front organization. To do this he would have to offer evidence relating to every aspect of the organization's activities. The organization could present opposing evidence. Prolonged hearings would be required to allow both sides to present proof and to cross-examine opposing witnesses.

To estimate the duration of such a proceeding involving the Communist Party, we need only recall that on much narrower issues the trial of the eleven Communist leaders under the Smith Act consumed nine months. In a hearing under this bill, the difficulties of proof would be much greater and would take a much longer time....

...Under this bill, the Attorney General would have to attempt the difficult task of producing concrete legal evidence that men have particular ideas or opinions. This would inevitably require the disclosure of many of the FBI's confidential sources of information and thus would damage our national security.

If, eventually, the Attorney General should overcome these difficulties and get a favorable decision from the Board, the Board's decision could be appealed to the courts....

All these proceedings would require great effort and much time. It is almost certain that from two to four years would elapse between the Attorney General's decision to go before the Board with a case, and the final disposition of the matter by the courts.

And when all this time and effort had been spent, it is still most likely that no organization would actually register.

The simple fact is that when the courts at long last found that a particular organization was required to register, all the leaders of the organization would have to do to frustrate the law would be to dissolve the organization and establish a new one with a different name and a new roster of nominal officers...

Unfortunately, these provisions are not merely ineffective and unworkable. They represent a clear and present danger to our institutions. Insofar as the bill would require registration by the Communist Party itself does not endanger our traditional liberties. However, the application of the registration requirements to so-called Communist-front organizations can be the greatest danger to freedom of speech, press, and assembly, since the Alien and Sedition Laws of 1798. This danger arises out of the criteria or standards to be applied in determining whether an organization is a Communist-front organization.

There would be no serious problem if the bill required proof that an organization was controlled and financed by the Communist Party....However, recognizing the difficulty of proving those matters, the bill would permit such a determination to be based solely upon the extent to which the positions taken or advanced by it from time to time on matters of policy do not deviate from those of the Communist movement.

This provision could easily be used to classify as a Communist-front organization any organization which is advocating a single policy or objective which is also being urged by the Communist Party. Thus, an organization which advocates low-cost housing for sincere humanitarian reasons might be classified as a Communist-front organization because the Communists regularly exploit slum conditions as one of their fifth-column techniques.

It is not enough to say that this probably would not be done. The mere fact that it could be done shows clearly how the bill would open a Pandora's box of opportunities for official condemnation of organizations and individuals for perfectly honest opinions which happen to be stated also by Communists.

The basic error of these sections is that they move in the direction of suppressing opinion and belief. This would be a very dangerous course to take, not because we have any sympathy for Communist opinions, but because any governmental stifling of the free expression of opinion is a long step toward totalitarianism.

We can and we will prevent espionage, sabotage, or other actions endangering our national security. But we would betray our finest traditions if we attempted, as this bill would attempt, to curb the simple expression of opinion. This we should never do, no matter how distasteful the opinion may be to the vast majority of our people. The course proposed by this bill would delight the Communists, for it would make a mockery of the Bill of Rights and of our claims to stand for freedom in the world.

And what kind of effect would these provisions have on the normal expression of political views? Obviously, if this law were on the statute books, the part of prudence would be to avoid saying anything that might be construed by someone as not deviating sufficiently from the current Communist propaganda line. And since no one could be sure in advance what views were safe to express, the inevitable tendency would be to express no views on controversial subjects.

The result could only be to reduce the vigor and strength of our political life—an outcome that the Communists would happily welcome, but that free men should abhor....

This is a time when we must marshall all our resources and all the moral strength of our free system in self-defense against the threat of Communist aggression. We will fail in this, and we will destroy all that we seek to preserve, if we sacrifice the liberties of our citizens in a misguided attempt to achieve national security.

SOURCE: From *The Congressional Record*, 81st Cong., 2nd sess., 15629–15632.

1951

INTERNATIONAL

Korean War

Retreating U.N. forces abandon Seoul (January 4) to North Koreans and Chinese; President Harry S. Truman relieves Gen. Douglas MacArthur of his post as U.N. commander and American Far East commander for constant public criticism of U.S. policy (April 11); armistice negotiations in Korea begin (July 10).

Japanese peace treaty is signed in San Francisco by 49 nations (September 8).

U.S., Australia, and New Zealand sign mutual security pact (September 1).

U.S. and Iceland sign agreement calling for U.S. defense of the island in return for right to build major U.S. air base.

NATIONAL

Twenty-second Amendment sets a maximum of two terms for the presidency, is ratified (February 26).

Supreme Court in *Dennis* v. *United States* upholds 1946 Smith Act that makes it a criminal offense to advocate forceful overthrow of the government; also upholds 1949 conviction of 11 American Communist Party leaders.

Gen. Douglas MacArthur, relieved of his Far East posts, addresses a joint session of Congress.

Julius Rosenberg and his wife, Ethel, are convicted of atomic espionage, are sentenced to death.

DEATHS Former Vice President Charles G. Dawes (1925–1929); Lincoln Ellsworth, explorer.

BUSINESS/INDUSTRY/INVENTIONS

Franklin National Bank of New York introduces the credit card.

Electric power is obtained for first time from nuclear energy at Atomic Energy Commission station at Idaho Falls, Idaho.

Pittsburgh Coal Consolidation Co. (Cadiz, Ohio) demonstrates coal pipeline.

Remington Rand builds UNIVAC I, first electronic computer.

Plant in Henderson, Nevada, opens to produce titanium metal from ore.

Dial telephone service coast-to-coast without operators is instituted.

DEATH Will K. Kellogg, cereal company founder.

TRANSPORTATION

First section of New Jersey Turnpike (Bordentown—Deepwater) opens.

Delaware Memorial Bridge at Wilmington opens.

Park-o-Mat Garage (Washington, D.C.), completely automatic push-botton 16-story garage, opens.

Passenger car registrations total 42,700,000.

SCIENCE/MEDICINE

Edwin M. McMillan and Glenn T. Seaborg share Nobel Prize for chemistry for discoveries in chemistry of transuranium elements; Max Theiler is awarded Nobel Prize for physiology/medicine for discoveries concerning yellow fever.

Walter H. Zinn develops first breeder reactor.

EDUCATION

Clarence A. Faust becomes president of Fund for the Advancement of Education.

RELIGION

David O. McKay becomes president of Mormon church on death of George A. Smith.

Catholic Bishop John F. O'Hara becomes archbishop of Philadelphia.

DEATHS Henry A. Ironside, evangelist known as the archbishop of fundamentalists; Catholic Archbishop Dennis J. Dougherty of Philadelphia (1918–1951).

ART/MUSIC

Gian Carlo Menotti writes *Amahl and the Night Visitors,* first opera for television; becomes annual Christmas Eve show.

Gail Kubik composes *Symphony Concertante;* Douglas S. Moore, the opera *Giants in the Earth.*

Dave Brubeck forms his quartet.

Adolph Gottlieb completes the painting *The Frozen Sounds;* David Hare completes the sculpture *Figure Waiting in the Cold.*

SONGS (POPULAR): "Cold, Cold Heart," "I Whistle a Happy Tune," "Kisses Sweeter Than Wine," "Too Young," "In the Cool, Cool, Cool of the Evening," "Getting to Know You."

LITERATURE/JOURNALISM

The Village Voice, New York City newspaper, is founded.

Jet magazine is founded.

South Korean refugees flee from communist invaders. ARCHIVE PHOTOS, INC.

BOOKS *The Sea Around Us* by Rachel Carson, *The Caine Mutiny* by Herman Wouk, *From Here to Eternity* by James Jones, *Collected Poems* by Marianne Moore, *Catcher in the Rye* by J. D. Salinger, *Requiem for a Nun* by William Faulkner, *Piano Player* by Kurt Vonnegut, *A Man Called Peter* by Catharine Marshall.

DEATHS Authors Sinclair Lewis and Lloyd C. Douglas; publishers William Randolph Hearst and Emanuel Haldeman-Julius; Dorothy Dix (Elizabeth M. Gilmer), advice-to-lovelorn columnist.

ENTERTAINMENT

Transcontinental television is inaugurated with President Truman's speech at Japanese peace conference in San Francisco (September 4); Zenith Radio Corp. demonstrates first pay television system.

Philadelphia opens city-owned and -operated playhouse in Fairmount Park.

PLAYS Yul Brynner stars in *The King and I,* Julie Harris in *I Am a Camera,* Barbara Bel Geddes in *The Moon Is Blue,* Shirley Booth in *A Tree Grows in Brooklyn.*

MOVIES *The African Queen* with Katharine Hepburn and Humphrey Bogart, *An American in Paris* with Gene Kelly, *The Lavender Hill Mob* with Alec Guinness, *A Streetcar Named Desire* with Vivien Leigh and Marlon Brando.

New television shows include *Strike It Rich, Mark Saber, Wild Bill Hickok,* and Red Skelton.

SPORTS

Happy Chandler resigns as baseball commissioner, is succeeded by Ford Frick; Warren C. Giles succeeds Frick as National League president.

Bobby Thomson hits three-run home run in the bottom of the ninth against Brooklyn to give New York Giants the playoff and National League pennant.

Norm Van Brocklin of Los Angeles Rams completes 27 passes for record 554 yards, 5 touchdowns.

First Pan-American Games are held.

First NBA all-star basketball game and first Pro Bowl (football) game are played.

Eddie Gaedel, 3-foot, 7-inch baseball player, pinchhits for St. Louis Browns, walks; use of little people in baseball is outlawed by commissioner the next day.

WINNERS *Auto racing*—Lee Wallard, Indianapolis 500; Herb Thomas, NASCAR; *Baseball*—New York Yankees, World Series; *Basketball*—Brigham Young, NIT; Kentucky, NCAA; Rochester, NBA; *Bowling*—Lee Jouglard, Marion Ladewig, bowlers of year; *Boxing*—Jersey Joe Walcott, heavyweight; Sugar Ray Robinson, middleweight; Kid Gavilan, welterweight;

Chess—Larry Evans, U.S. men; Mary Bain, U.S. women; *Figure skating*—Dick Button, world men's title; *Football* (bowls)—Michigan, Rose; Clemson, Orange; Kentucky, Sugar; Tennessee, Cotton; Los Angeles Rams, NFL; *Golf*—U.S., Walker and Ryder cups; Ben Hogan, U.S. Open and Masters; Sam Snead, PGA; Betsy Rawls, U.S. Women's Open; *Hockey*—Toronto, Stanley Cup; *Horse racing*—Count Turf, Kentucky Derby; Bold, Preakness Stakes; Counterpoint, Belmont Stakes; *Tennis*—Australia, Davis Cup; Frank Sedgman, U.S. Open (men); Maureen Connolly, U.S. Open (women).

MISCELLANEOUS

Hart, Schaffner & Marx introduces men's suits made of Dacron.

Mine disaster at West Frankfort, Illinois, kills 119; commuter train plunges through temporary overpass in Woodbridge, New Jersey, kills 85, injures 500; plane plunges into river on takeoff from Elizabeth (New Jersey) Airport taking 56 lives; Kansas and Missouri floods leave 200,000 homeless, 41 dead.

1952

INTERNATIONAL

Korean War continues.

Gen. Matthew B. Ridgway succeeds Gen. Dwight D. Eisenhower as NATO supreme commander.

U.S., Great Britain, France, and West Germany sign peace compact (May 26).

United Nations headquarters in New York City is completed.

NATIONAL

President Harry S. Truman announces that he will not seek reelection; Gen. Eisenhower is picked by Republicans and Adlai E. Stevenson by the Democrats. Eisenhower is elected with 33,900,000 popular and 442 electoral votes to Stevenson's 27,300,000 and 89.

First hydrogen device explodes at Eniwetok in the Pacific (November 1).

Supreme Court clears the Italian film *The Miracle,* declares movies are "a significant medium" for communicating ideas and are fully shielded by First Amendment.

President and Mrs. Truman move back to renovated White House after four-year project.

Puerto Rico becomes first overseas U.S. commonwealth.

Immigration and Naturalization Act removes last racial and ethnic barriers to citizenship.

John F. Kennedy is elected to Senate from Massachusetts.

DEATH Harold L. Ickes, Interior Secretary (1933–1946), headed Public Works Administration.

BUSINESS/INDUSTRY/INVENTIONS

President Truman orders seizure of steel mills to avert strike; Supreme Court rules seizure unconstitutional.

George Meany, AFL secretary-treasurer, succeeds to presidency on death of William Green; Walter P. Reuther, president of United Auto Workers, becomes CIO president after Philip Murray's death.

Lever House in New York City is completed; sets style for office-building design for a decade.

More than 2,500 new television stations are started.

First Holiday Inn (Memphis) opens.

DEATHS Albert D. Lasker, advertising executive; Charles H. Kraft, cofounder of cheese firm.

TRANSPORTATION

Chesapeake Bay Bridge at Annapolis, Maryland, opens.

Two Army helicopters complete transatlantic flight from Westover (Massachusetts) to Germany.

SCIENCE/MEDICINE

Felix Bloch and Edward N. Purcell share Nobel Prize in physics for new methods of nuclear precision measurements; Selman A. Waksman is awarded prize in physiology/medicine for discovery of streptomycin.

More than 21,000 cases of polio are reported in U.S.

University of California scientists identify element 99 (einsteinium).

DEATH Forest R. Moulton, coauthor of spiral nebulae theory.

EDUCATION

Rev. Theodore M. Hesburgh becomes president of Notre Dame University; Henry T. Heald, chancellor of New York University.

DEATH John Dewey, pioneer in progressive education.

RELIGION

Rev. Fulton Sheen appears weekly on television program *Life Is Worth Living.*

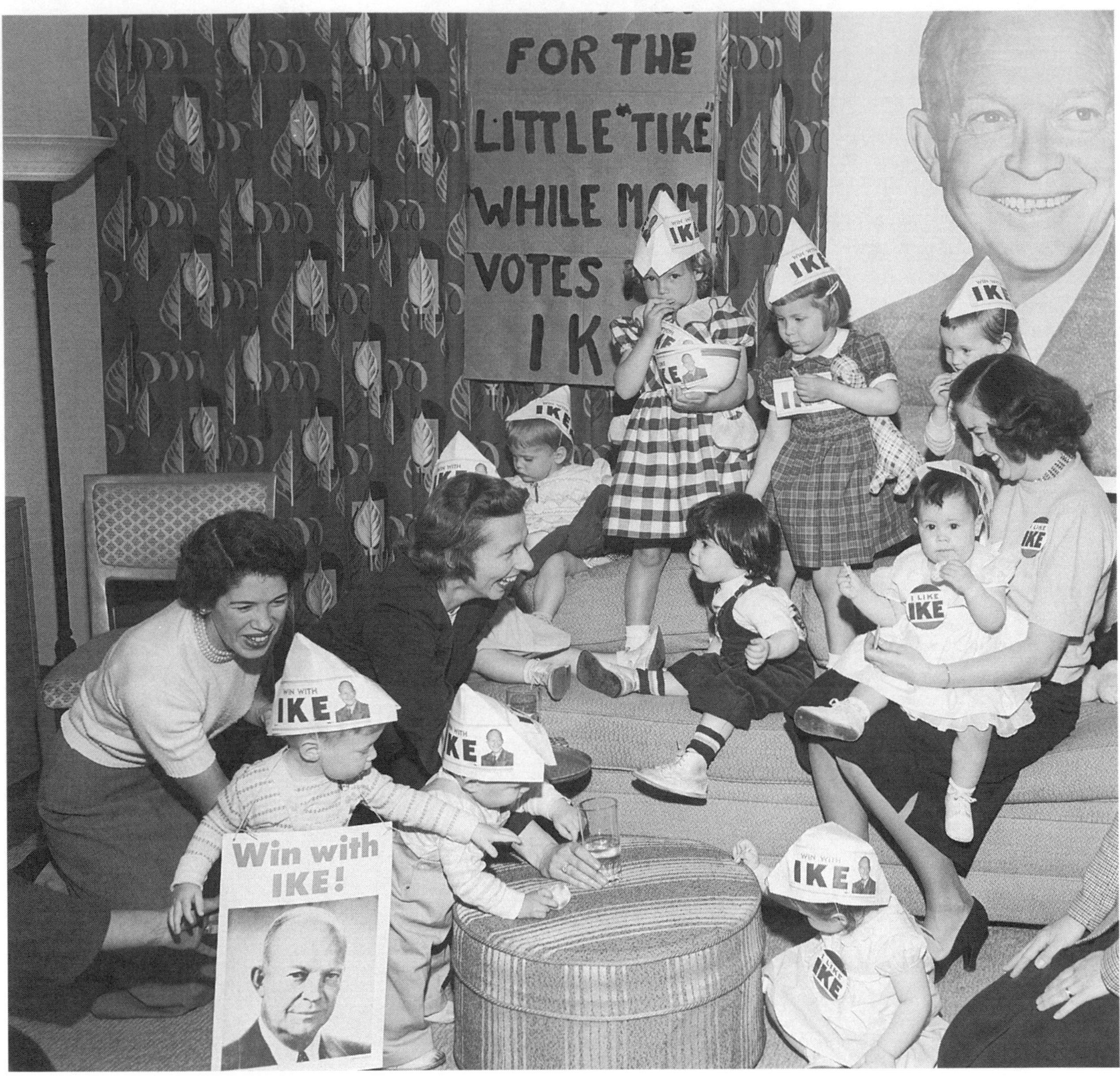

Female supporters of presidential candidate Dwight D. Eisenhower form a baby-sitting service to allow mothers to vote. CORBIS-BETTMANN

ART/MUSIC

Leonard Bernstein composes opera *Trouble in Tahiti;* the Brecht-Weill *Threepenny Opera* is adapted by Marc Blitzstein.

Helen Frankenthaler completes the painting *Mountains and Sea,* Jackson Pollock, *Blue Poles;* Naum Gabo completes the sculpture *Construction Suspended in Space.*

SONGS (POPULAR): "Don't Let the Stars Get in Your Eyes," "I Saw Mommy Kissing Santa Claus," "I'm Yours," "Takes Two to Tango," "You Belong to Me," "High Noon."

LITERATURE/JOURNALISM

BOOKS *The Silver Chalice* by Thomas B. Costain, *East of Eden* by John Steinbeck, *Glory Road* by Bruce Catton, *The Natural* by Bernard Malamud, *Charlotte's Web* by E. B. White, *Invisible Man* by Ralph Ellison, *The Old Man and the Sea* by Ernest Hemingway, *Collected Poems* by Archibald MacLeish, *The Power of Positive Thinking* by Norman Vincent Peale.

DEATH H. T. Webster, cartoonist ("The Timid Soul").

ENTERTAINMENT

Cinerama, a three-film strip process, is demonstrated.

PLAYS Alfred Lunt and Lynn Fontanne star in *Quadrille,* Tom Ewell in *The Seven Year Itch,* Jose Ferrer in *The Shrike.*

MOVIES *Hans Christian Andersen* with Danny Kaye, *Singin' in the Rain* with Gene Kelly, *The Quiet Man* with John Wayne, *Viva Zapata!* with Marlon Brando, *Limelight* with Charlie Chaplin.

New television shows include *This Is Your Life* with Ralph Edwards, *See It Now* with Edward R. Murrow, *I've Got a Secret* with Garry Moore, *Dragnet,* and Ernie Kovacs.

DEATH Gertrude Lawrence, actress.

SPORTS

Winter Olympics are held in Oslo, with U.S. winning four gold medals; Summer Olympics are held in Helsinki, with U.S. winning 40 golds, including Bob Mathias's second decathlon.

Avery Brundage, former head of AAU and U.S. Olympic Assn., begins 20 years as president of International Olympic Committee.

American Bowling Congress approves use of automatic pinspotters.

Professional Golfers Assn. approves participation of African-Americans in golf tournaments.

First U.S. woman bullfighter, Patricia McCormick, debuts in Mexico, kills three bulls.

WINNERS *Auto racing*—Tony Ruttman, Indianapolis 500; Tim Flock, NASCAR; *Baseball*—New York Yankees, World Series; *Basketball*—LaSalle, NIT; Kansas, NCAA; Minneapolis, NBA; *Bowling*—Steve Nagy, Marion Ladewig, bowlers of year; *Boxing*—Rocky Marciano, heavyweight; Archie Moore, light heavyweight; *Figure skating*—Dick Button, U.S. and world men's singles; Tenley Albright, world women's singles; *Football* (bowls)—Illinois, Rose; Georgia Tech, Orange; Maryland, Sugar; Kentucky, Cotton; Detroit, NFL; *Golf*—Julius Boros, U.S. Open; Jim Turnesa, PGA; Sam Snead, Masters; Louise Suggs, U.S. Women's Open; *Hockey*—Detroit, Stanley Cup; *Horse racing*—Hill Gail, Kentucky Derby; Blue Man, Preakness Stakes; One Count, Belmont Stakes; *Tennis*—Australia, Davis Cup; Frank Sedgman, U.S. Open (men); Maureen Connolly, U.S. Open (women).

MISCELLANEOUS

Series of tornadoes in Arkansas, Missouri, and Tennessee claim 208 lives.

DEATH Shipwreck (Alvin) Kelly, flagpole sitter who spent 20,613 hours aloft.

1953

INTERNATIONAL

Armistice in Korea is signed (June 26) after two years of intermittent negotiations; U.S. approves $200 million for Korean relief, rehabilitation (August 3).

President Dwight D. Eisenhower proposes international "atoms for peace" program.

Spain authorizes U.S. to establish military bases there.

U.S. gives $60 million to France to help war in Indochina.

NATIONAL

Former Secretary of State George C. Marshall is awarded Nobel Peace Prize for his plan to assist other nations.

Earl Warren is confirmed as Supreme Court chief justice.

Julius and Ethel Rosenberg are electrocuted in Sing Sing Prison; first civilians executed for wartime espionage, first ever executed for that crime in peacetime.

Former President Hoover is named head of second commission to study reorganization of Executive Department.

Department of Health, Education, and Welfare is created with Oveta Culp Hobby as secretary.

Submerged Land Act gives federal government right to offshore lands of seaboard states.

Refugee Relief Act lifts quota restrictions for 214,000 immigrants wanting to enter U.S.

Two dams completed: Hungry Horse on Flathead River in Montana and McNary on Columbia River in Washington.

DEATHS Robert F. Wagner, New York senator responsible for much social legislation; Jonathan Wainwright, general who defended Bataan, Corregidor; Robert A. Taft, Ohio senator known as Mr. Republican; Supreme Court Chief Justice Frederick M. Vinson (1946–1953).

BUSINESS/INDUSTRY/INVENTIONS

Alcoa Building, 30-story aluminum-faced building in Pittsburgh, is completed.

DEATH William L. Hutcheson, president, Carpenters Union (1915–1952).

TRANSPORTATION

Helicopter service between New York City airports begins.

Julius and Ethel Rosenberg, executed in 1953, are shown here in the U.S. Marshal's van, divided by wire screening, as they leave federal court after their conviction in 1951 on charges of espionage and conspiracy in transmitting atomic secrets to Soviet Russia. **UPI/CORBIS-BETTMANN**

Work begins on Eugene Talmadge Memorial Bridge in Savannah.

DEATH William M. Jeffers, president, Union Pacific Railroad (1937–1946).

SCIENCE/MEDICINE

Fritz A. Lipmann shares Nobel Prize for physiology/medicine with Hans A. Krebs of Great Britain for discovery of coenzyme A.

Dr. Jonas Salk announces successful experimental use of a polio vaccine.

Dr. James D. Watson and Francis C. H. Crick successfully create a three-dimensional molecular model of deoxyribonucleic acid (DNA), a discovery comparable in importance to Newton's laws of motion, Darwin's theory of evolution, and Einstein's relativity theory.

First privately operated atomic reactor put into operation by North Carolina and North Carolina State universities at Raleigh.

University of California scientists identify element 100 (fermium).

Argonne Cancer Research Hospital in Chicago opens.

Companion study to original 1948 study by Institute of Sex Research, *Sexual Behavior in the Human Female,* is published.

DEATH Robert A. Millikan, physicist who was first to isolate the electron.

EDUCATION

Detlev N. Bronk becomes president of Rockefeller Institute; Nathan M. Pusey of Harvard University.

RELIGION

Catholic archbishop James F. McIntyre of Los Angeles is elevated to cardinal; Albert G. Meyer becomes archbishop of Milwaukee, Wisconsin.

ART/MUSIC

New York City Opera presents Aaron Copland's *Tender Land;* Quincy Porter composes Concerto for Two Pianos and Orchestra.

Leonard Bernstein becomes first U.S. composer to conduct at Milan's (Italy) La Scala opera house.

Robert Joffrey founds and directs American Ballet Center.

Andrew D. White Museum of Art at Cornell University opens.

Jackson Pollock completes the painting *Portrait and a Dream;* Helen Frankenthaler, *Open Wall;* Franz Kline, *New York.*

SONGS (POPULAR): "How Much Is That Doggie in the Window?," "From This Moment On," "I Believe," "I Love Paris," "O, Mein Papa," "That's Amore," "Your Cheatin' Heart," "Secret Love."

LITERATURE/JOURNALISM

Hugh Hefner founds *Playboy* magazine.

BOOKS *Poems 1942–53* by Karl Shapiro, *A Stillness at Appomattox* by Bruce Catton, *Go Tell It on the Mountain* by James Baldwin, *The Adventures of Augie March* by Saul Bellow; *The Bridges at Toko-Ri* by James A. Michener, *Fahrenheit 451* by Ray Bradbury.

DEATHS Authors Douglas Southall Freeman and Walter B. Pitkin.

ENTERTAINMENT

The movie *The Robe* introduces Cinemascope.

First U.S. educational television station, KUHT in Houston, broadcasts.

PLAYS Henry Fonda stars in *The Caine Mutiny Court-Martial,* Deborah Kerr in *Tea and Sympathy,* Margaret Sullavan in *Sabrina Fair;* Leonard Bernstein writes music for *Wonderful Town;* Arthur Miller writes *The Crucible;* Paddy Chayefsky, *Marty;* Cole Porter, *Can-Can;* and William Inge, *Picnic.*

MOVIES *From Here to Eternity* with Burt Lancaster and Deborah Kerr, *Shane* with Alan Ladd, *The Desert Song* with Gordon MacRae, *The Bandwagon* with Fred Astaire.

Danny Thomas and Loretta Young premiere television shows, Edward R. Murrow interviews on *Person to Person;* other new shows are *Name That Tune* and *General Electric Theater.*

DEATHS Eugene O'Neill, playwright; Maude Adams, actress who played Peter Pan about 1,500 times.

SPORTS

Supreme Court rules that baseball is a sport, not a business, and therefore not subject to antitrust laws.

National League owners approve transfer of Boston baseball franchise to Milwaukee, Wisconsin; American League, move of St. Louis to Baltimore.

Maureen ("Little Mo") Connolly wins tennis grand slam by winning the Australian, French, British, and U.S. championships in one year.

WINNERS *Auto racing*—Bill Vukovich, Indianapolis 500; Herb Thomas, NASCAR; *Baseball*—New York Yankees, World Series; *Basketball*—Seton Hall, NIT; Indiana, NCAA; Minneapolis, NBA; *Bobsledding*—U.S. four-man team, world title; *Bowling*—Don Carter, Marion Ladewig, bowlers of year; *Boxing*—Rocky Marciano, heavyweight; Carl Olson, middleweight; *Figure skating*—Hayes Jenkins, men's world singles; Tenley Albright, women's world singles; *Football* (bowls)—Southern California, Rose; Alabama, Orange; Georgia Tech, Sugar; Texas, Cotton; Detroit, NFL; *Golf*—U.S., Walker and Ryder cups; Ben Hogan, U.S. Open and Masters; Walter Bukermo, PGA; Betsy Rawls, U.S. Women's Open; *Hockey*—Montreal, Stanley Cup; *Horse racing*—Dark Star, Kentucky Derby; Native Dancer, Preakness Stakes and Belmont Stakes; *Tennis*—Australia, Davis Cup; Tony Trabert, U.S. Open (men); Maureen Connolly, U.S. Open (women); *Wrestling*—Bill Kerslake, first AAU Greco-Roman heavyweight.

DEATHS Jim Thorpe, one of greatest all-around athletes; Bill Tilden, tennis.

MISCELLANEOUS

Tornadoes in Texas kill 114 and in Michigan and Ohio, 142.

U.S. Air Force C-124 crashes and burns near Tokyo, 129 die.

Bermuda shorts become popular among men.

1954

INTERNATIONAL

Senate approves construction of St. Lawrence Seaway; corporation is established to develop, operate, and maintain seaway.

U.S., Australia, Great Britain, France, New Zealand, Pakistan, Philippines, and Thailand create Southeast Asia Treaty Organization (SEATO) (September 8).

U.S., Great Britain, France, Canada, Australia, and South Africa join to explore peacetime uses of atomic energy.

U.S. and Canada agree to create third line of radar stations across northern Canada, the Distant Early Warning (DEW) line.

U.S. signs mutual defense treaties with Japan (March 8) and Nationalist China (December 2).

Libya gives U.S. long-term (to 1970) rights to air base near Tripoli.

NATIONAL

Five members of House of Representatives are slightly wounded by four Puerto Rican nationalists who fire from spectators' gallery (March 1).

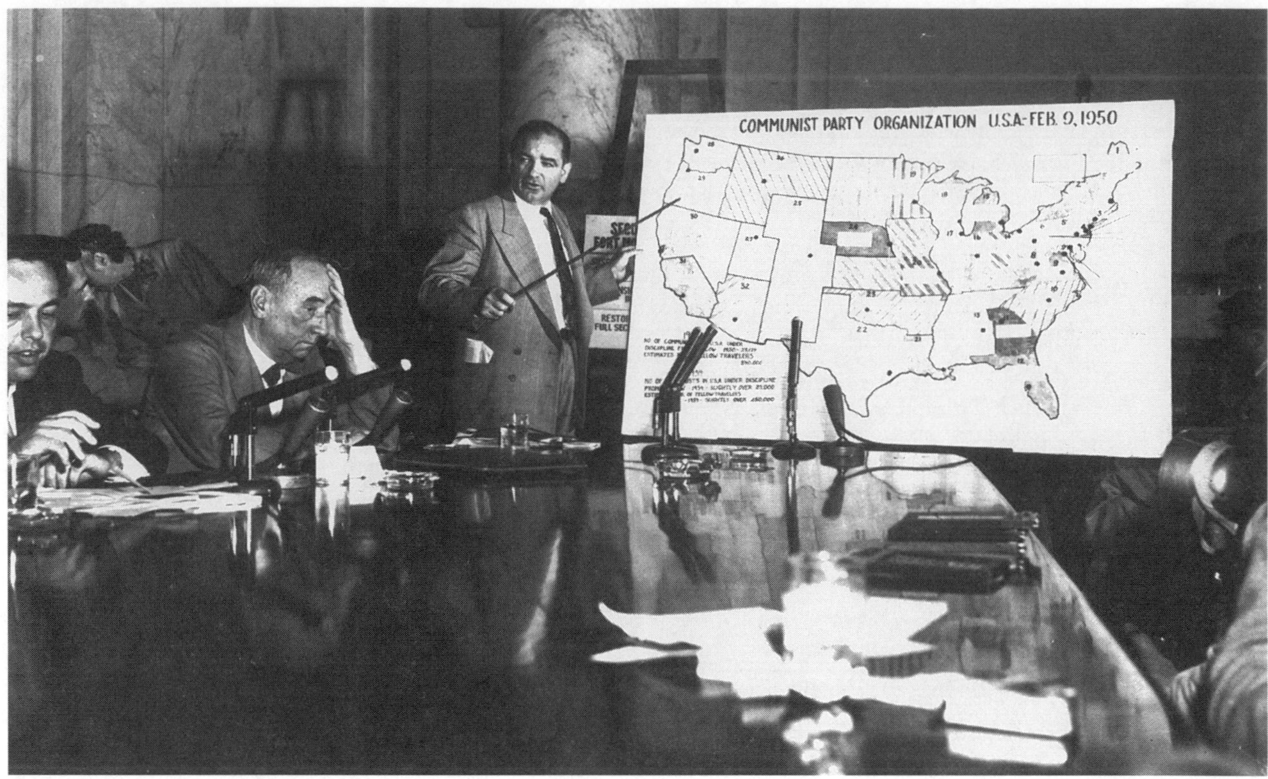

Senator Joseph R. McCarthy shows his view of the growth of communism in the United States at a Senate hearing on June 9, 1954. Army counsel Joseph N. Welch, seated at left, has just denounced McCarthy as a "cruelly reckless character assassin." **UPI/CORBIS-BETTMANN**

Senator Joseph R. McCarthy of Wisconsin attacks alleged Communists in government and Democratic Party; he conducts televised hearings; Senate censures him (December 2) for failing to explain a financial transaction and for abusing fellow senators.

Atomic Energy Commission holds secret hearings on J. Robert Oppenheimer, consultant, for alleged Communist ties; he is cleared as "loyal" but it is recommended that he not be rehired.

Air Force Academy is authorized; opens in temporary quarters at Lowry AFB, then in permanent home at Colorado Springs, Colorado.

Housing Act authorizes construction of 35,000 houses a year for those displaced by federal programs.

Congress outlaws Communist Party.

Benjamin O. Davis Jr. becomes first African-American Air Force general; his father was first African-American Army general.

Nautilus, first atomic-powered submarine, is launched; USS *Forrestal,* largest aircraft carrier, is launched; explosion aboard carrier *Bennington* kills 103.

Second H-bomb experimental explosion occurs at Bikini Atoll in Pacific.

DEATHS Air Force Gen. Hoyt S. Vandenberg; Ruth Bryan (Rohde), first U.S. woman diplomat; Arthur Garfield Hays, director, American Civil Liberties Union (1912–1954).

BUSINESS/INDUSTRY/INVENTIONS

Atomic Energy Act authorizes private power companies to own and use reactors for electric power; ground is broken in Pittsburgh for first atomic power plant.

Buckminster Fuller founds Geodesics Inc. to produce geodesic domes.

Hilton Hotel Corp. acquires controlling interest of Statler Hotels.

TRANSPORTATION

General Motors announces $1 billion expansion program.

First automatic toll-collection station opens at Union Toll Plaza on the Garden State Parkway in New Jersey.

SCIENCE/MEDICINE

Linus Pauling is awarded Nobel Prize for chemistry for research into the nature of chemical bond; John F. Enders, Frederic C. Robbins, and Thomas H. Weller share prize for physiology/medicine for discovery that polio viruses grow in various types of tissue.

First mass inoculation with Salk vaccine begins in Pittsburgh; field trials involving 400,000 children prove vaccine safe and 70% effective in preventing polio.

Rutgers University dedicates Institute of Microbiology.

Plastic contact lenses are introduced.

DEATH Enrico Fermi, nuclear scientist.

EDUCATION

Supreme Court in *Brown* v. *Board of Education* (May 17) holds that racial segregation in public schools violates Fourteenth Amendment guarantee of equal protection of the laws; in a series of decisions (May 24), Court outlaws segregation in tax-supported educational institutions, public housing, and public park, recreational, and entertainment facilities.

University of Alaska at Anchorage is founded.

DEATHS Alain L. Locke, first African-American Rhodes scholar; Liberty H. Bailey, founder of agricultural college at Cornell University.

ART/MUSIC

Annual American jazz festivals begin at Newport, Rhode Island.

Gian Carlo Menotti composes *The Saint of Bleeker Street.*

Elvis Presley makes his first recordings, "That's All Right, Mama" and "Blue Moon of Kentucky."

PAINTINGS *Double Portrait of Birdie* by Larry Rivers, *Light, Earth, and Blue* by Mark Rothko, *Construction with a Piano* by Jasper Johns, *Midi* by Stuart Davis, *The Garden* by John Ferrer.

SONGS (POPULAR): "Fly Me to the Moon," "Hey There," "Home for the Holidays," "Mister Sandman," "Shake, Rattle and Roll," "Sh-Boom," "Smile," "This Ole House."

DEATH Charles Edward Ives, composer of polytonal harmonies, unusual rhythms.

LITERATURE/JOURNALISM

Ernest Hemingway is awarded Nobel Prize in literature.

BOOKS *Poems 1923–54* by e. e. cummings, *A Fable* by William Faulkner, *The Ponder Heart* by Eudora Welty, *Blackboard Jungle* by Evan Hunter, *The Tunnel of Love* by Peter DeVries, *The View from Pompey's Head* by Hamilton Basso, *George Washington* by Douglas Southall Freeman.

DEATHS Maxwell Bodenheim, poet ("Bard of Greenwich Village"); two pioneer cartoonists, George McManus ("Bringing Up Father") and Bud Fisher ("Mutt and Jeff"); Bertie C. Forbes, founder and editor *Forbes Magazine.*

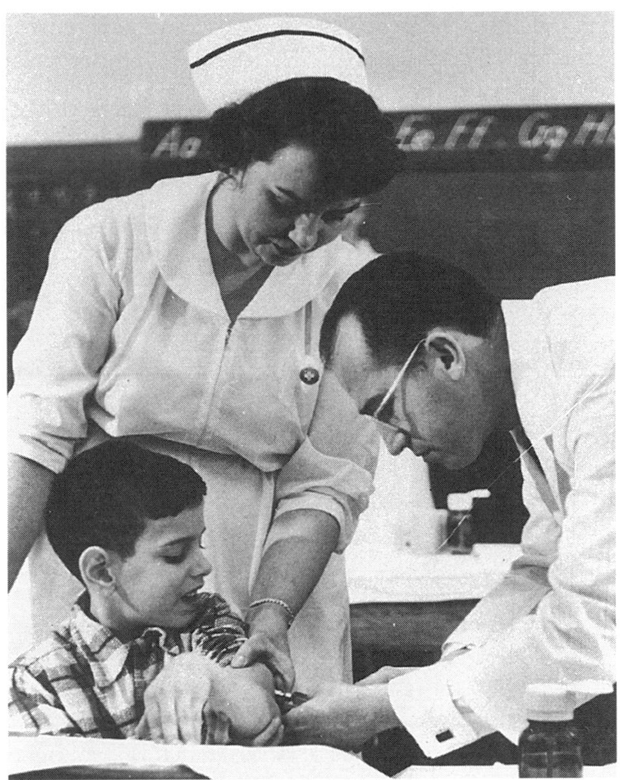

Dr. Jonas E. Salk inoculates a boy with the vaccine Salk has developed that drastically reduces the incidence of paralytic polio in the United States. AP/WIDE WORLD PHOTOS

ENTERTAINMENT

PLAYS Pearl Bailey stars in *House of Flowers,* John Raitt in *The Pajama Game,* Ezio Pinza in *Fanny;* Thornton Wilder writes *The Matchmaker* (which becomes *Hello, Dolly!*).

MOVIES *Rear Window* with James Stewart, *The Country Girl* with Grace Kelly, *A Star Is Born* with Judy Garland, *On the Waterfront* with Marlon Brando, *20,000 Leagues Under the Sea* with James Mason, *The Barefoot Contessa* with Ava Gardner.

New shows on television include *Tonight Show* with Steve Allen, *People Are Funny* with Art Linkletter, *Sid Caesar's Hour, Father Knows Best, The Lineup,* and *Lassie.*

A new dance, the Mambo, becomes popular.

DEATHS Lionel Barrymore, actor; Claude E. Hooper, radio market analyst; Edwin H. Armstrong, developer of FM radio transmission.

SPORTS

NBA adopts rule requiring a shot on basket within 24 seconds after getting the ball.

Parry O'Brien becomes first to throw shot more than 60 feet (60 ft., 5¼ in.).

Maureen Connolly, tennis star, suffers career-ending horseback-riding injury.

American League approves transfer of baseball franchise from Philadelphia to Kansas City, Missouri.

National Ski Hall of Fame is founded.

Sports Illustrated magazine begins publication.

WINNERS *Auto racing*—Bill Vukovich, Indianapolis 500; Lee Petty, NASCAR; *Baseball*—New York Giants, World Series; *Basketball*—Holy Cross, NIT; LaSalle, NCAA; Minneapolis, NBA; *Bowling*—Don Carter, Marion Ladewig, bowlers of year; *Boxing*—Rocky Marciano, heavyweight; Johnny Saxton, welterweight; Jimmy Carter, lightweight; *Chess*—Arthur Bisguier, U.S. title; *Figure skating*—Hayes Jenkins, U.S. and world men's singles; *Football* (bowls)—Michigan State, Rose; Oklahoma, Orange; Georgia Tech, Sugar; Rice, Cotton; Cleveland, NFL; *Golf*—Ed Furgol, U.S. Open; Melvin Harbert, PGA; Sam Snead, Masters; Babe Didrikson Zaharias, U.S. Women's Open; *Hockey*—Detroit, Stanley Cup; *Horse racing*—Determine, Kentucky Derby; Hasty Road, Preakness Stakes; High Gun, Belmont Stakes; *Tennis*—U.S., Davis Cup; Vic Seixas, U.S. Open (men); Doris Hart, U.S. Open (women); Yale, first intercollegiate title.

DEATHS Grantland Rice, sportswriter; Glenn S. (Pop) Warner, college-football coach; Wilbur Shaw, auto racer.

MISCELLANEOUS

Hurricane Hazel rakes Haiti and eastern U.S. for 13 days, kills 347 persons; Hurricane Carol sweeps East Coast, kills 68, causes $500 million damage.

Killing tornadoes hit Waco, Texas (114 die), Flint, Michigan (116), Worcester, Massachusetts (90).

1955

INTERNATIONAL

American occupation of Germany ends (April 21).

U.S. agrees to help train South Vietnamese army.

U.S. and Guatemala sign military assistance pact (June 18); U.S. and Panama sign treaty of cooperation on Panama Canal (January 25).

President Dwight D. Eisenhower and Soviet Premier Nikita Khrushchev discuss disarmament.

NATIONAL

President Eisenhower, on Colorado vacation, suffers heart attack (September 24); resumes limited activities a short time later.

Salaries are raised for vice president by $5,000 to $35,000; members of Congress by $7,500 to $22,500; Supreme Court chief justice by $9,550 to $35,000; associate justices by $10,000 to $30,000.

Rosa Parks refuses to give her seat to a white man on a Montgomery, Alabama, bus (December 1); her arrest leads to major boycott of buses, eventually to Supreme Court decision that outlaws segregation on public transportation.

National Association of Social Workers is established.

DEATHS Cordell Hull, Secretary of State (1933–1944); John R. Mott, YMCA leader; Walter F. White, executive secretary, NAACP (1931–1955); Matthew Henson, who accompanied Peary to North Pole; Maud Park, first president, League of Women Voters.

BUSINESS/INDUSTRY/INVENTIONS

AFL and CIO merge to form 15-million-member union headed by AFL President George Meany.

McDonald's fast-food chain is founded by Ray A. Kroc in Des Plaines, Illinois.

C. G. Glasscock Drilling Co. puts first seagoing oil drill in service.

Tappan Stove Co. introduces electronic range for domestic use.

General Electric researchers form synthetic diamonds.

DEATHS Samuel H. Kress, cofounder of five-and-ten-cent-store chain; Daniel J. Tobin, Teamsters Union president (1907–1952); Glenn L. Martin, aircraft manufacturer.

TRANSPORTATION

President Eisenhower asks Congress for $101 billion over 10 years for interstate highways.

More than 7 million cars (7,920,186) are manufactured in year.

Tappan Zee Bridge over Hudson River at Nyack, New York, opens.

Illinois law requires attachments to which seat belts can be fastened.

SCIENCE/MEDICINE

Polykarp Kusch and Willis E. Lamb share Nobel Prize for physics for precision determination of electron's magnetic moment; Vincent du Vigneaud is awarded chemistry prize for work on sulphur compounds.

Emilio Segre and University of California associates discover new atomic particle, the antiproton; other university scientists discover Element #101 (mendelevium).

National Hurricane Center is established.

DEATHS Albert Einstein, physicist, who originated the Theory of Relativity; George H. Parker, early U.S. experimental zoologist.

EDUCATION

Supreme Court orders "all deliberate speed" in integrating public schools.

White House Conference on Education calls on government to increase financial help for public education.

DEATHS George H. Denny, University of Alabama president (1912–1955); Herbert Putnam, Librarian of Congress (1899–1939).

RELIGION

Betty Robbins of Massapequa, New York, first Jewish woman cantor, sings her first service at Temple Avodah, Oceanside, New York.

DEATH Mary Josephine Rogers, founder of Maryknoll Sisters.

ART/MUSIC

Marian Anderson debuts at Metropolitan Opera, the first African-American to perform at the Met; Arthur Mitchell becomes first African-American to dance with major company (New York City Ballet).

Jackson Pollock completes the painting *Autumn Rhythm;* Willem de Kooning, *Woman: Ochre;* Morris Graves, *Flight of Power;* Herbert Ferber completes the sculpture *Mercury;* David Hare, *Sunrise.*

SONGS (POPULAR): "Ain't That a Shame," "Cry Me a River," "Hearts of Stone," "Love Is a Many-Splendored Thing," "Rock Around the Clock," "Cherry Pink and Apple Blossom White," "Maybellene," "Mack the Knife."

DEATH Charlie Parker, jazz musician and composer who helped develop "bop" or "bebop."

LITERATURE/JOURNALISM

Ann Landers's (Esther P. Friedman Lederer) first advice-to-lovelorn column appears in *Chicago Sun-Times; San Francisco Chronicle* hires her twin sister (Paula E. Friedman Philips) to do similar column ("Dear Abby").

Arrest of Rosa Parks

On December 1, 1955, Rosa Parks was arrested in Montgomery, Alabama, for failing to give up her seat when the "For Whites Only" section of the bus she was riding became full. Parks, a seamstress and a member of the National Association for the Advancement of Colored People (NAACP), defied southern custom by refusing to relinquish her seat when asked. Her defiant act inspired 42,000 people to boycott the city's buses over a period of 381 days, during which time the U.S. Supreme Court declared bus segregation unconstitutional. The Montgomery Bus Boycott marked the beginning of civil rights protests that spread throughout the South during the late 1950s and 1960s. Parks, a diligent and quiet woman, inspired thousands of African Americans to rise up against racism. In 1999 she received the Congressional Gold Medal and a street was named in her honor in Detroit, where she moved in 1957.

William F. Buckley Jr. founds *National Review.*

BOOKS *Marjorie Morningstar* by Herman Wouk, *Andersonville* by MacKinlay Kantor, *Lolita* by Vladimir Nabokov, *10 North Frederick* by John O'Hara, *The Man in the Grey Flannel Suit* by Sloan Wilson, *The Edge of the Sea* by Rachel Carson, *Candy* by Terry Southern.

DEATHS Ham(mond E.) Fisher, cartoonist ("Joe Palooka"); authors Dale Carnegie and James Agee; publishers Joseph A. Pulitzer and Robert R. McCormick.

ENTERTAINMENT

Disneyland in Anaheim, California, opens.

PLAYS Susan Strasberg stars in *The Diary of Anne Frank,* Burl Ives in *Cat on a Hot Tin Roof,* Paul Muni in *Inherit the Wind;* Cole Porter writes *Silk Stockings.*

MOVIES *The Seven Year Itch* with Marilyn Monroe, *Mister Roberts* with Henry Fonda and Jimmy Cagney; *Marty* with Ernest Borgnine, *Rebel Without a Cause* with James Dean, *The Blackboard Jungle* with Glenn Ford, *The Rose Tattoo* with Anna Magnani.

Jackie Gleason stars in *The Honeymooners* with Art Carney and Audrey Meadows; Jim Henson creates first

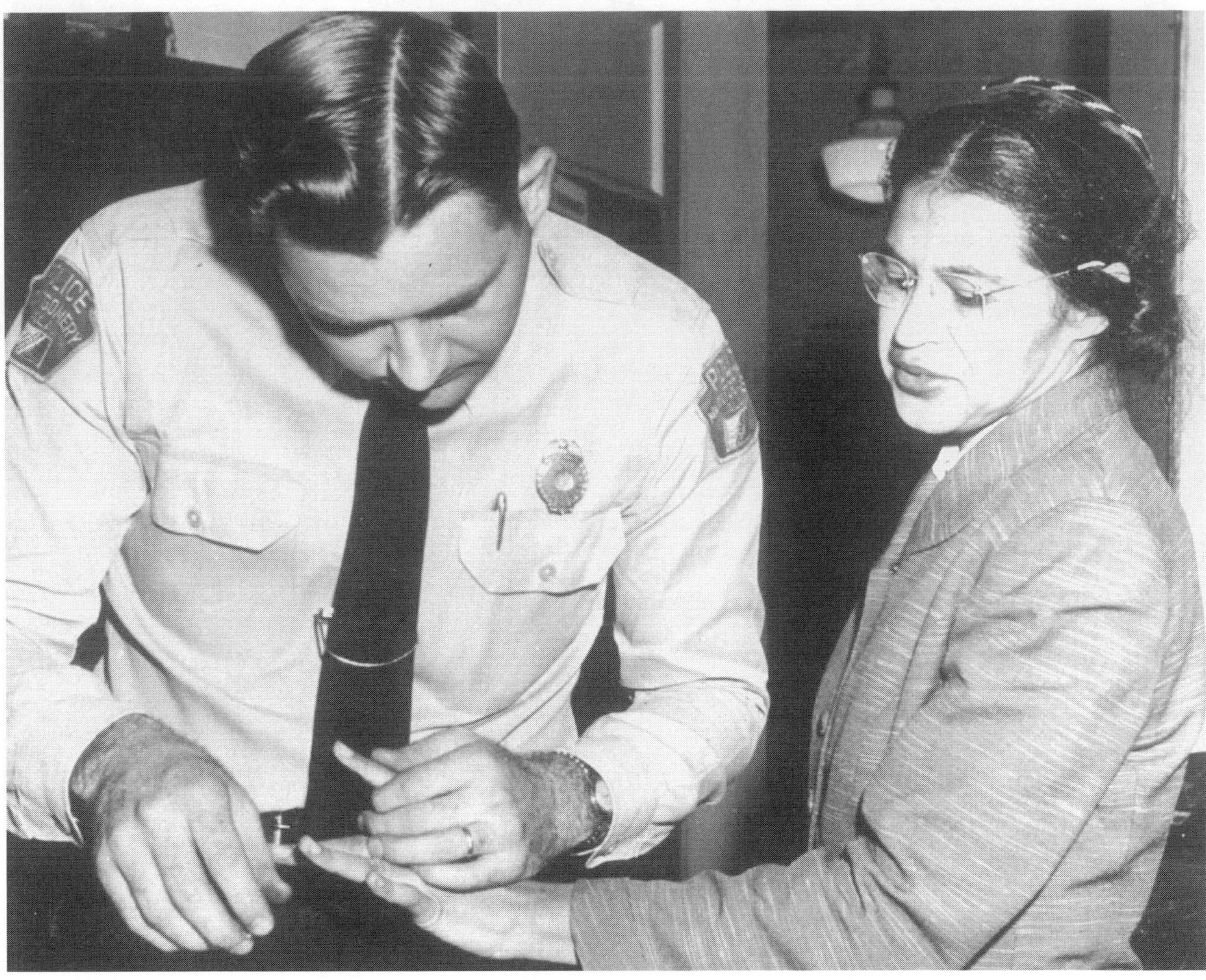

Rosa Parks being fingerprinted by a Montgomery police officer. Mrs. Parks is arrested on December 1, 1955, when she sits in the "white" section of the bus and refuses to give up her seat to a white man. **AP/WIDE WORLD PHOTOS**

of the Muppets, Kermit the Frog; other new television personalities and shows are: Soupy Sales, Phil Silvers, Alfred Hitchcock, *Gunsmoke* with Jim Arness, *The $64,000 Question* with Hal March, *Wyatt Earp* with Hugh O'Brien.

DEATHS James Dean, screen actor; Walter Hampden, actor; Theda Bara, silent-screen "vamp"; Robert E. Sherwood, playwright.

SPORTS

Ted Allen sets horseshoe pitching record of 72 consecutive ringers.

U.S. Auto Club, which sanctions major auto races, is established.

WINNERS *Auto racing*—Bob Sweikert, Indianapolis 500; Tim Flock, NASCAR; *Baseball*—Brooklyn Dodgers, World Series; *Basketball*—Duquesne, NIT; San Francisco, NCAA; Syracuse, NBA; *Bowling*—Steve Nagy, Sylvia Martin, bowlers of year; *Boxing*—Rocky Marciano, heavyweight; Carmen Basilio, welterweight; Sugar Ray Robinson, middleweight; *Figure skating*—Hayes Jenkins, world men's singles; Tenley Albright, U.S. and world women's singles; *Football* (bowls)—Ohio State, Rose; Duke, Orange; Navy, Sugar; Georgia Tech, Cotton; Cleveland, NFL; *Golf*—U.S., Walker and Ryder cups; Jack Fleck, U.S. Open; Doug Ford, PGA; Cary Middlecoff, Masters; Fay Crocker, U.S. Women's Open; Beverly Hanson, LPGA; *Hockey*—Detroit, Stanley Cup; *Horse racing*—Swaps, Kentucky Derby; Nashua, Preakness Stakes and Belmont Stakes; *Tennis*—Australia, Davis Cup; Tony Trabert, U.S. Open (men); Doris Hart, U.S. Open (women).

DEATHS Bill Vukovich, auto racer; Ely Culbertson, bridge expert; baseball greats Honus Wagner and Cy Young.

Elvis Presley has two number-one albums and begins a successful movie career in 1956. CORBIS-BETTMANN

MISCELLANEOUS

Hurricane Diane sweeps Eastern U.S. for two weeks, 400 die; tornadoes in Midwest claim 115 lives; heavy rains in Pacific Northwest cause much damage, claim 74 lives.

1956

INTERNATIONAL

Egypt closes Suez Canal after U.S. and Great Britain stop financing Aswan Dam; Britain and France send troops to retake canal; United Nations intervenes, clears situation; canal reopens 1956.

U.S. and Iceland renew agreement to continue operating U.S. air base.

U.S. signs treaty with Panama to increase canal annuity to $1.93 million.

Eighteen American republics meet in Panama City to discuss economic problems.

NATIONAL

President Dwight D. Eisenhower, Republican, is reelected, receives 35,590,472 popular and 457 electoral votes to 26,022,752 popular and 74 electoral votes for his Democratic challenger, Adlai E. Stevenson; Democrats regain control of Congress.

President Eisenhower suffers an ileitis attack, undergoes successful surgery.

Responding to Supreme Court decision, nonsegregated bus service begins in Montgomery, Alabama; 101 Southern members of Congress call for massive resistance against Court ruling.

The national motto, "In God We Trust," is authorized.

Alaska voters approve territorial constitution.

Virgin Islands National Park is established.

Ft. Randall Dam on Missouri River in South Dakota is completed.

DEATHS Jesse H. Jones, commerce secretary (1940–1945); Former Vice President Alben W. Barkley (1949–1953); Hiram Bingham, explorer who discovered Inca ruins; Admiral Ernest J. King, head of World War II naval operations.

BUSINESS/INDUSTRY/INVENTIONS

Commercial telephone service over transoceanic cable begins; $12 for each three-minute call.

Minimum wage is raised to $1 an hour (March 1).

This street in Levittown, New York, typifies post–World War II suburban growth. Ninety percent of the residents in this development of low-cost, single-story homes are veterans and their families. **CORBIS-BETTMANN**

Smith-Corona Inc. announces portable electric typewriter.

Getty Oil Co. is founded.

Louis Harris & Associates, opinion polling organization, is formed.

DEATHS Clarence Birdseye, inventor of food-freezing process; Harry F. Sinclair, founder and president, Sinclair Oil (1916–1949); Hattie Carnegie, fashion designer.

TRANSPORTATION

Highway Act provides $32.5 billion over 13 years to build 41,000-mile interstate highway system (June 29).

First nonstop transcontinental helicopter flight is completed in 31 hours, 40 minutes.

SCIENCE/MEDICINE

John Bardeen, Walter H. Brattain, and William Shockley share Nobel Prize for physics for discovery of transistor effect; Andre F. Cournand and Dickinson W. Richards Jr. share prize for physiology/medicine for discoveries concerning heart catheterization.

Drs. James W. Watts and Walter Freeman perform first prefrontal lobotomy in Washington, D.C.

DEATH Alfred C. Kinsey, zoologist who headed landmark studies of sexual behavior.

RELIGION

Ninth World Methodist conference meets at Lake Junaluska, North Carolina, representatives from 40 nations are present; Methodist General Conference grants full clergy rights to women in the U.S., orders abolition of racial segregation in Methodist churches.

Congregational Christian and Evangelical and Reformed churches pass vote on proposed merger in 1957.

Margaret Ellen Tanner becomes first woman ordained as Presbyterian minister (October 24).

Universal chapel for eight faiths is dedicated in Universalist Church of the Divine Paternity in New York City.

ART/MUSIC

Robert Joffrey organizes ballet company.

Norman Dello Joio composes *Meditations on Ecclesiastes;* Douglas S. Moore, the opera *The Ballad of Baby Doe.*

Philip Guston completes the painting *Dial;* Grace Hartigan, *City Life;* Georgia O'Keeffe, *Patio with Cloud.*

SONGS (POPULAR): "Blue Suede Shoes," "Don't Be Cruel," "I Could Have Danced All Night," "Memories Are Made of This," "On the Street Where You Live," "Que Será, Será," "I Walk the Line," "Love Me Tender."

DEATHS Jackson Pollock, pop art founder; Albert Von Tilzer, composer ("Take Me Out to the Ball Game"); composer Victor Young ("Love Letters"); bandleader Tommy Dorsey; Art Tatum, jazz pianist.

LITERATURE/JOURNALISM

BOOKS *The Last Hurrah* by Edwin O'Connor, *Peyton Place* by Grace Metalious, *Homage to Mistress Bradstreet* by John Berryman, *Things of This World* (poetry) by Richard Wilbur.

Huntley-Brinkley news report appears on NBC.

DEATHS Clarence E. Mulford, author of Westerns; H. L. Mencken, journalist and author; Alex Raymond, cartoonist ("Flash Gordon").

ENTERTAINMENT

Ampex Corp. demonstrates magnetic tape recorder of sound and picture.

Grace Kelly, screen actress, marries Prince Rainier of Monaco.

Ringling Bros. and Barnum & Bailey Circus closes because of rising costs.

PLAYS Sammy Davis Jr. stars in *Mr. Wonderful,* Rex Harrison and Julie Andrews in *My Fair Lady,* Rosalind Russell in *Auntie Mame;* Leonard Bernstein writes music for *Candide,* Frank Loesser writes *The Most Happy Fella.*

MOVIES *Around the World in 80 Days* with David Niven, *High Society* with Grace Kelly, *Bus Stop* with Marilyn Monroe, *Giant* with Rock Hudson and James Dean, *The King and I* with Yul Brynner, *Picnic* with William Holden.

Ernie Kovacs hosts *The Tonight Show;* new shows include *To Tell the Truth* with Bud Collyer, and Tennessee Ernie Ford.

DEATHS Elsie Janis, entertained troops in World War I; Fred Allen, radio humorist; Bela Lugosi, screen actor.

SPORTS

Don Larsen of New York Yankees pitches first (and only) perfect game in World Series, allows no hits, no walks, no runs against Brooklyn Dodgers (October 8).

Summer Olympic Games are held in Melbourne, Australia; U.S. wins 33 gold medals.

WINNERS *Auto racing*—Pat Flaherty, Indianapolis 500; Buck Baker, NASCAR; *Baseball*—New York Yankees, World Series; *Basketball*—Louisville, NIT; San Francisco, NCAA; Philadelphia, NBA; *Bobsledding*—U.S. four-man team, world title; *Bowling*—Bill Lillard, Anita Canteline, bowlers of year; *Boxing*—Floyd Patterson, heavyweight; Carmen Basilio, welterweight; Joe Brown, lightweight; *Chess*—Arthur B. Bisguier, U.S. title; *Figure Skating*—Hayes Jenkins, men's world singles; Tenley Albright, women's world singles; *Football* (bowls)—Michigan State, Rose; Oklahoma, Orange; Georgia Tech, Sugar; Mississippi, Cotton; New York Giants, NFL; *Golf*—Cary Middlecoff, U.S. Open; Jack Burke, PGA and Masters; Kathy Cornelius, U.S. Women's Open; Marlene Hagge, LPGA; *Hockey*—Montreal, Stanley Cup; *Horse racing*—Needles, Kentucky Derby and Belmont Stakes; Fabius, Preakness Stakes; *Tennis*—Australia, Davis Cup; Ken Rosewall, U.S. Open (men); Shirley Fry, U.S. Open (women).

DEATHS Connie Mack, Philadelphia baseball manager for 50 years; Babe Didrikson Zaharias, one of greatest women athletes.

MISCELLANEOUS

Italian liner *Andrea Doria* and Swedish liner *Stockholm* collide off Nantucket, 51 die.

TWA Super-Constellation and United DC-7 collide over Grand Canyon, 128 die.

1957

INTERNATIONAL

President Dwight D. Eisenhower announces U.S. will use its military and economic power to protect Middle East against Communist aggression (January 5); Congress endorses doctrine.

U.S. ratifies International Atomic Energy Agency treaty, created by 80 nations.

U.S. combat troops withdraw from Japan (August 1).

U.S. renews agreement to maintain air base in Saudi Arabia.

NATIONAL

First civil rights act since 1875 establishes Civil Rights Commission to investigate and seek correction of any violations (September 9).

Supreme Court in *Roth* v. *United States* defines obscenity more permissively than previously accepted; in

Baby Boom

Although the baby boom began in 1946, the peak year of pregnancies occurred in 1957, when 4.3 million babies were born. Yearly totals continued to exceed four million until 1964. As a major demographic event, the baby boom was significant: It bucked the trend toward smaller families that otherwise dominated the twentieth century. However, its cultural effect is perhaps even more important. The post-war baby boom reflected desires among many Americans for a fresh start following wartime experiences, a growing confidence in the national economy, and the widespread appeal of suburban family values. As the baby boom generation entered school, college, and the workplace, they altered the cultural fabric of U.S. society. Many baby boomers protested against the Vietnam War and demonstrated for civil rights in the 1960s. Once considered "forever youthful" (extolling the phrase, "Don't trust anyone over thirty"), the baby boom generation by the 1990s had become part of the establishment. Bill Clinton, elected to the Oval Office in 1991, was the first baby boomer president. He was immediately followed into office by another baby boomer, George W. Bush.

Sweezy v. *New Hampshire,* Court rules that academic freedom is protected by the Constitution's due process clause.

President Eisenhower suffers mild stroke (November 25); recovers quickly, returns to duty in two weeks.

Southern Christian Leadership Conference is founded with Rev. Martin Luther King Jr. as president.

Law providing pensions for former presidents goes into effect.

First underground nuclear explosion occurs at Nevada testing grounds; National Committee for Sane Nuclear Policy is organized.

Queen Elizabeth II and Prince Philip visit Jamestown, Virginia, on 350th anniversary of first English settlement in U.S.

Harry S. Truman Library in Independence, Missouri, is dedicated.

The Dallas Dam on Columbia River and Palisades Dam on Snake River in Idaho are completed.

DEATHS Former First Lady Grace Coolidge (1923–1929); Richard E. Byrd, aviator and polar explorer; Joseph R. McCarthy, Wisconsin senator whose investigative methods gave rise to term *McCarthyism.*

BUSINESS/INDUSTRY/INVENTIONS

Shippingport (Pennsylvania) Atomic Power Station begins operating.

Pittsburgh Consolidation Coal Co. puts 108-mile pipeline to Eastlake (Ohio) power station into operation.

Charles F. Carlson founds Haloid Co., forerunner of Xerox Corp.

Jimmy Hoffa becomes president of Teamsters Union, which was ousted from AFL-CIO on grounds of corruption.

Hamilton Watch Co. introduces electric watch.

First solar-heated building in U.S. is completed in Albuquerque, New Mexico.

DEATHS Sosthenes Behn, founder and head, International Telephone & Telegraph; Ernest T. Weir, founder of Weirton, National Steel companies; Paul Starrett, builder of Empire State Building; Gerard Swope, president, General Electric (1922–1940, 1942–1944).

TRANSPORTATION

Third tube of Lincoln Tunnel under Hudson River is completed.

Mackinac Bridge at Straits of Mackinac, Michigan, and Walt Whitman Bridge in Philadelphia are completed.

Three B-52 Air Force bombers complete round-the-world flight in 45 hours, 19 minutes.

SCIENCE/MEDICINE

Tsung-dao Lee and Chen Ning Yang share Nobel Prize in physics for work on left-right symmetry in physical processes.

World Health Organization begins to use polio vaccine developed by Dr. Albert B. Sabin.

Arthur Kornberg produces artificial DNA, the substance in a cell that carries genetic code.

Argonne National Laboratory announces discovery of Element #102 (nobelicum).

Leon N. Cooper, John Bardeen, and J. R. S. Schrieffer develop theory of superconductivity.

DEATH George W. Merck, pharmaceutical firm head.

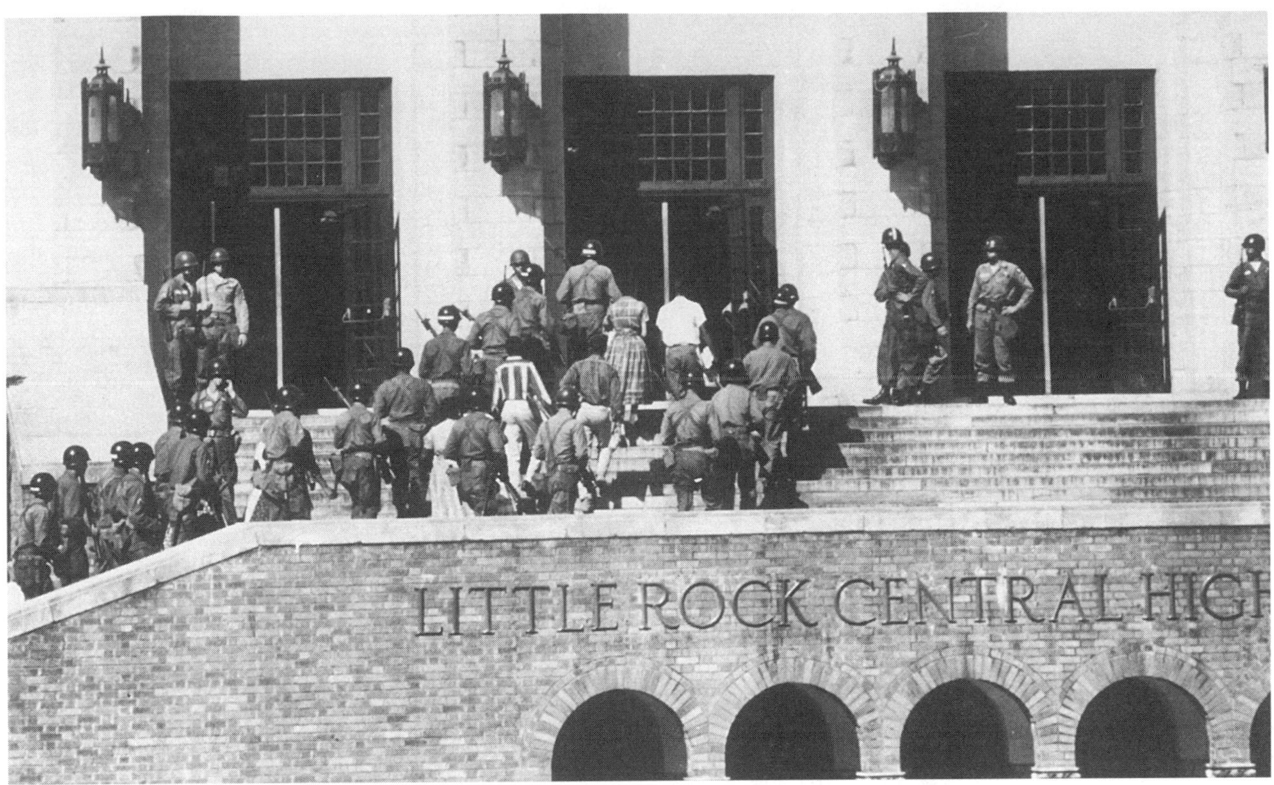

Federal troops enforce desegregation at Central High School in Little Rock, Arkansas, in 1957. CORBIS-BETTMANN

EDUCATION

Arkansas Governor Orval Faubus uses National Guard to keep nine black students from entering all-white high school in Little Rock (September 4); after court order and arrival of federal troops (September 24), students enter.

RELIGION

Evangelical and Reformed Church and Congregational Christian Church merge to form United Church of Christ (June 25).

First worldwide Lutheran meeting in U.S. is held in Minneapolis; Rev. Franklin C. Fry, president of United Lutheran Church in U.S., is named president of world body.

ART/MUSIC

American Ballet Theater is founded; Edward Villela joins New York City Ballet.

Conductor Sarah Caldwell founds Boston Opera Co.

Leontyne Price makes operatic debut with San Francisco Opera.

Leonard Baskin completes the sculpture *Laureate Standing;* Richard Stankiewicz, *Instruction;* Seymour Lipton, *Sorcerer.*

Jasper Johns completes the painting *Book;* Philip Guston, *The Clock.*

Museum for Contemporary Arts in Dallas and Museum for Primitive Art in New York City are founded.

SONGS (POPULAR): "April Love," "Bye Bye Love," "Jailhouse Rock," "Little Darlin'," "Maria," "76 Trombones," "Singin' the Blues," "Tammy," "Wake Up, Little Susie," "Till There Was You."

LITERATURE/JOURNALISM

BOOKS *By Love Possessed* by James G. Cozzens, *Promises* (poetry) by Robert Penn Warren, *A Death in the Family* by James Agee, *How the Grinch Stole Christmas* by Dr. Seuss, *Atlas Shrugged* by Ayn Rand, *The Town* by William Faulkner, *The Wapshot Chronicle* by John Cheever, *On the Road* by Jack Kerouac.

DEATHS Angela Morgan, poet; Edna W. Chase, editor of *Vogue;* Frank E. Gannett, founder of newspaper chain; authors Sholem Asch and Kenneth Roberts.

ENTERTAINMENT

PLAYS Anthony Perkins stars in *Look Homeward, Angel,* Robert Preston in *The Music Man,* Cyril Ritchard in *A Visit to a Small Planet;* Leonard Bernstein writes music for *West Side Story.*

Father and son in a well-stocked fallout shelter near Akron, Michigan. Shelters as well as air raid drills in schools become common during the cold war, especially during the 1950s. NATIONAL ARCHIVES AND RECORDS ADMINISTRATION, RECORDS OF THE DEFENSE OF CIVIL PREPAREDNESS AGENCY

MOVIES *The Bridge on the River Kwai* with Alec Guinness, *St. Joan* with Jean Seberg, *The Three Faces of Eve* with Joanne Woodward, *Twelve Angry Men* with Henry Fonda, *Peyton Place* with Lana Turner.

New television shows include *Wagon Train, The Price Is Right* with Bill Cullen, *Perry Mason* with Raymond Burr, *Maverick* with James Garner, *Leave It to Beaver, Have Gun, Will Travel* with Richard Boone; Jack Paar hosts *The Tonight Show,* Dinah Shore begins program.

DEATHS Oliver Hardy of Laurel and Hardy comedy team; John Van Druten, playwright; Humphrey Bogart, actor; Louis B. Mayer, movie executive.

SPORTS

Two New York teams announce that they will move to Pacific Coast in 1958: New York Giants to move to San Francisco, Brooklyn Dodgers to Los Angeles.

National Hockey League Players Assn. is formed.

Don Bowden becomes first American to run mile in less than 4 minutes (3 min., 58.7 sec.).

Jim Spalding sets nine-game bowling record of 2088 points at ABC tournament.

WINNERS *Auto racing*—Sam Hanks, Indianapolis 500; Buck Baker, NASCAR; *Badminton*—U.S. women's team, world title; *Baseball*—Milwaukee Braves, World Series; *Basketball*—Bradley, NIT; North Carolina, NCAA; Boston, NBA; *Boxing*—Floyd Patterson, heavyweight; Carmen Basilio, middleweight; Alphonse Halimi, featherweight; *Figure skating*—Dave Jenkins, U.S. and world men's singles; Carol Heiss, U.S. and world women's singles; *Football* (bowls) Iowa, Rose; Colorado, Orange; Baylor, Sugar; Texas Christian, Cotton; Detroit, NFL; *Golf*—Great Britain, Walker and Ryder cups; Dick Mayer, U.S. Open; Lionel Hebert, PGA; Doug Ford, Masters; Betsy Rawls, U.S. Women's Open; Louise Suggs, LPGA; *Hockey*—Montreal, Stanley Cup; *Horse racing*—Iron Liege, Kentucky Derby; Bold Ruler, Preakness Stakes; Gallant Man, Belmont Stakes; *Table tennis*—Leah Thall Neuberger, national singles; *Tennis*—Australia, Davis Cup; Malcolm Anderson, U.S. Open (men); Althea Gibson, U.S. Open (women), she also is first African-American to win at Wimbledon.

DEATH Tom Jenkins, wrestling champion.

MISCELLANEOUS

Louisiana and Texas struck by Hurricane Audrey and tidal wave; 531 are dead or missing.

California company introduces the Frisbee.

Sack dresses become popular.

DEATH Elizabeth S. Kingsley, inventor of double-crostic puzzle.

1958

INTERNATIONAL

U.N. announces neutrality in Indonesia civil war.

Marines are sent to Lebanon to restore order after uprising by Arab nationalists.

Vice President Richard M. Nixon makes three-week goodwill tour of eight South American countries; Venezuelans and Peruvians greet him angrily.

NATIONAL

National Aeronautics and Space Administration (NASA) is created.

Atomic-powered submarine *Nautilus* makes first underwater crossing of North Pole; another atomic submarine, *Skate,* crosses Atlantic Ocean both ways submerged in 15 days, 16 hours.

First-class postage increases to 4 cents per ounce.

Robert H. W. Welch Jr. founds John Birch Society.

Nelson A. Rockefeller begins 15 years as New York governor.

DEATH James M. Curley, colorful Boston mayor for 16 years and Massachusetts governor.

BUSINESS/INDUSTRY/INVENTIONS

Arthur Melin and Richard Knerr create hula hoop, a circle of plastic tubing that people twirl on their hips; within year, 25 million such hoops are sold in U.S.

Manufacture of aluminum cans begins.

DEATHS Malcolm Lockheed, airplane manufacturer; James D. Dole, founder of Hawaiian pineapple industry; Arde Bulova, watch manufacturer; Norman Bel Geddes, foremost proponent of streamlining; John Moody, financial analyst; Eugene F. McDonald, founder and head, Zenith Radio Corp.

TRANSPORTATION

First domestic jet airline service begins between New York City and Miami.

Mississippi River Bridge at New Orleans opens.

DEATH Charles F. Kettering, developer of automobile self-starter.

SCIENCE/MEDICINE

George W. Beadle, Edward L. Tatum, and Joshua Lederberg share Nobel Prize in physiology/medicine; Beadle and Tatum for discovery that heredity-transmitting genes do so by chemical reaction; Lederberg for discoveries of genetic recombination and organization of genes in bacteria.

Explorer I is first U.S. satellite placed in orbit (January 31), discovers Van Allen radiation belt; *Score* satellite is launched, transmits first voice messages from space.

Bifocal contact lens is introduced.

More than 11,000 scientists sign petition that is presented to U.N.; demands end to nuclear-weapons testing.

DEATHS Ernest O. Lawrence, developer of cyclotron; Earnest A. Hooton, laid foundation for U.S. physical anthropology.

EDUCATION

Air Force Academy begins operation in permanent home near Colorado Springs, Colorado.

RELIGION

Presbyterian Church (USA) merges with U.S. Presbyterian Church of North America to form United Presbyterian Church (May 28).

Catholic Cardinal Samuel A. Stritch becomes first American named to Roman Curia; Archbishop Albert G. Meyer of Milwaukee is moved to Chicago; Archbishops John F. O'Hara and Richard J. Cushing are elevated to cardinal.

Mimi Jordan, 10, has a snack on her way to breaking the hula-hooping world record. CORBIS-BETTMANN

Bishop Arthur Lichtenberger becomes presiding bishop of American Episcopal Church.

National Council of Churches reports church membership at 109,557,741.

ART/MUSIC

Van (Harvey K.) Cliburn Jr. of Texas wins first prize at International Tchaikovsky Piano Competition in Moscow.

John LaMontaine composes Concerto for Piano and Orchestra; Samuel Barber completes opera *Vanessa;* Walter Piston composes *Seventh Symphony.*

Leonard Bernstein becomes permanent conductor of New York Philharmonic.

Jerome Robbins's *Ballets: USA* tours the country; Alvin Ailey forms ballet company, presents *Blues Suite.*

Stereo long-playing records are introduced.

Isabel Bishop completes the painting *Subway Scene;* Adolph Gottlieb, *Ascent;* Franz Kline, *Siegfried;* Louise Nevelson completes the sculpture *Sky Cathedral;* Alexander Calder, *Spiral.*

Guggenheim Museum in New York City is completed.

SONGS (POPULAR): "The Chipmunk Song," "Gigi," "It's Only Make Believe," "Jingle Bell Rock," "Satin Doll," "Volare," "Summertime," "The Purple People Eater."

DEATHS Artur Rodzinski, conductor; John Held Jr., illustrator of "jazz age"; Doris Humphrey, pioneer of American modern dance; W. C. Handy, blues composer.

LITERATURE/JOURNALISM

United Press and International News Service merge to become UPI.

BOOKS *Anatomy of a Murder* by Robert Traver, *The Travels of Jaimie McPherson* by Robert L. Taylor, *Breakfast at Tiffany's* by Truman Capote, *From the Terrace* by John O'Hara, *Exodus* by Leon Uris, *Only in America* by Harry Golden; *The Dharma Bums* by Jack Kerouac, *Paterson* by William Carlos Williams.

DEATHS George Jean Nathan, editor and drama critic; James Branch Cabell, author.

ENTERTAINMENT

PLAYS Ralph Bellamy stars in *Sunrise at Campobello,* Helen Hayes in *A Touch of the Poet,* Cyril Ritchard in *The Pleasure of His Company;* Archibald MacLeish writes a biblical allegory, *J.B.*, Tennessee Williams, *Suddenly Last Summer.*

MOVIES *The Old Man and the Sea* with Spencer Tracy, *Cat on a Hot Tin Roof* with Elizabeth Taylor, *Gigi* with Leslie Caron, *Damn Yankees* with Gwen Verdon, *Auntie Mame* with Rosalind Russell.

New television shows include 77 *Sunset Strip* with Efrem Zimbalist Jr., *Peter Gunn* with Craig Stevens, *Seahunt* with Lloyd Bridges, and the Garry Moore and Andy Williams shows.

DEATHS Harry M. Warner, Warner Brothers president (1923–1956); Jesse Lasky, movie pioneer; Michael Todd, stage and screen producer; Ronald Colman, screen actor.

SPORTS

Jim Brown, Cleveland running back, rushes for record 1527 yards in season.

Stan Musial, St. Louis Cardinals, gets 3000th base hit.

Glenn Davis sets 100-meter hurdles record of 49.2 seconds.

WINNERS *Auto racing*—Jimmy Bryan, Indianapolis 500; Lee Petty, NASCAR; *Baseball*—New York Yankees, World Series; *Basketball*—Xavier (Ohio), NIT; Kentucky, NCAA; St. Louis, NBA; *Bowling*—Don Carter, Marion Ladewig, bowlers of year; *Boxing*—Don Jordan, welterweight; Sugar Ray Robinson, middleweight; *Figure skating*—David Jenkins, U.S. and world men's singles; Carol Heiss, U.S. and world women's singles; *Football* (bowls)—Ohio State, Rose; Oklahoma, Orange; Mississippi, Sugar; Navy, Cotton; Baltimore, NFL; *Golf*—Tommy Bolt, U.S. Open; Dow Finsterwald, PGA; Arnold Palmer, Masters; Mickey Wright, U.S. Women's Open and LPGA; *Hockey*—Montreal, Stanley Cup; *Horse racing*—Tim Tam, Kentucky Derby and Preakness Stakes; Cavan, Belmont Stakes; *Lawn bowling*—Leonard Schofield, first singles title; *Tennis*—U.S., Davis Cup; Great Britain, Wightman Cup; Ashley Cooper, U.S. Open (men); Althea Gibson, U.S. Open (women); *Yachting*—U.S. sloop *Columbia* retains America's Cup.

DEATHS Mel Ott, New York Giants baseball great; Clarence DeMar, seven-time winner of Boston Marathon.

MISCELLANEOUS

Our Lady of Angels parochial school in Chicago burns; 92 students, 3 teachers die.

1959

INTERNATIONAL

Cuba confiscates U.S.-owned oil refineries and business firms (June 29); U.S. places embargo on Cuban sugar imports, U.S. exports (except food and medicine).

Queen Elizabeth and President Dwight D. Eisenhower dedicate St. Lawrence Seaway (June 26); The Queen and Vice President Richard M. Nixon dedicate St. Lawrence Hydroelectric Power Project at Massena, New York (June 27).

President Eisenhower makes three-week trip to 11 countries in Europe, Asia, and Africa; Soviet Premier Khrushchev makes 12-day visit to U.S.

International Atomic Energy Agency is created to explore peaceful atomic-energy uses.

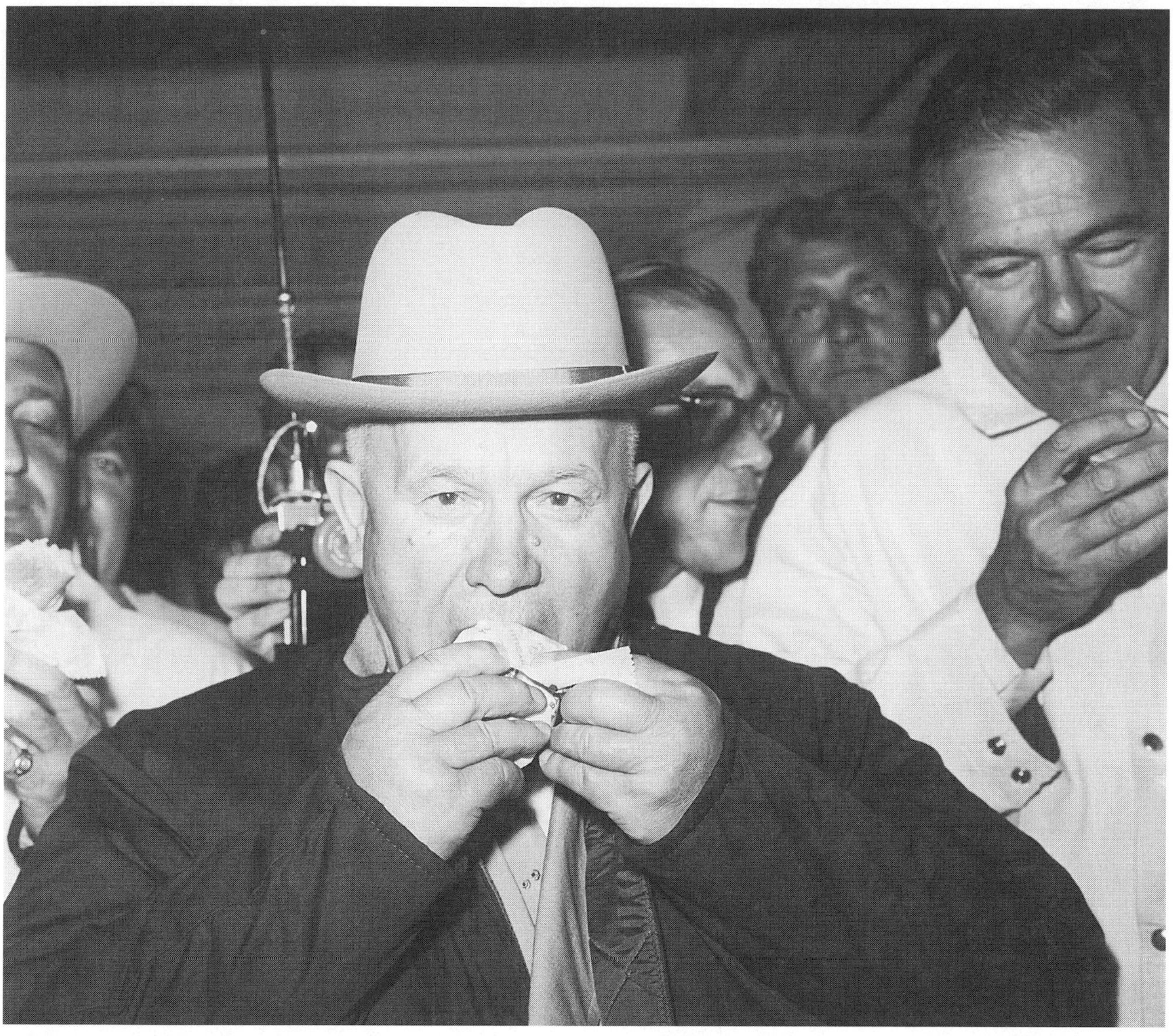

Soviet Premier Nikita Khrushchev in Des Moines, Iowa, enjoying his first hot dog. His visit to the U.S. in 1959 lasts 12 days.
CORBIS-BETTMANN

NATIONAL

Alaska is admitted as 49th state (January 3), Hawaii as 50th (August 21).

Secretary of State John Foster Dulles resigns (April 15) because of an incapacitating illness; dies May 4; Christian A. Herter succeeds him (April 18).

First ballistic missile submarine, *George Washington,* is launched.

DEATHS Admiral William F. Halsey, headed World War II Pacific Fleet; Gen. George C. Marshall, Army chief of staff (1939–1945), Secretary of State (1947–1950).

BUSINESS/INDUSTRY/INVENTIONS

Haloid-Xerox Co. (later Xerox Corp.) introduces first commercial xerographic copier.

Four-month steel strike ends when 80-day federal injunction is issued.

DEATHS Food critic and writer Duncan Hines; Frank Lloyd Wright, architect.

TRANSPORTATION

World's first atomic-powered merchant ship, *Savannah,* is launched in Camden, New Jersey.

SCIENCE/MEDICINE

Albert B. Sabin develops oral polio vaccine.

Owen Chamberlain and Emilio G. Segre share Nobel Prize in physics for discovery of antiproton; Arthur Kornberg and Severo Ochoa share prize in physiology/medicine for contributions to understanding of life process.

Explorer VI satellite is launched to send back pictures of Earth; unmanned spacecraft *Luna 2* lands on moon (September 12); *Luna 3* is first to circle moon (October 4) and send back pictures of far side.

EDUCATION

Federal district court and Virginia Supreme Court both rule that closing public schools to avoid desegregation violates Fourteenth Amendment; desegregation begins in Norfolk and Arlington.

DEATH Abraham Flexner, medical educator, organizer and director (1930–1939), Institute for Advanced Study, Princeton, New Jersey.

RELIGION

Evangelical Lutheran and United Evangelical Lutheran churches merge to form American Lutheran Church.

Unitarian and Universalist churches vote to merge.

Two Catholic archbishops are elevated to cardinal: Aloysius J. Muench of Fargo, North Dakota, and Albert G. Meyer of Chicago.

ART/MUSIC

Elliott Carter composes *Second String Quartet.*

Thomas Hart Benton completes murals in Harry S. Truman Library; Adolph Gottlieb completes the painting *Counterpoise;* Jasper Johns, *Device Circle;* Louise Nevelson completes the sculpture *Dawn's Wedding.*

SONGS (POPULAR): "Climb Every Mountain," "Everything's Coming Up Roses," "Put Your Head on My Shoulder," "My Favorite Things," "There Goes My Baby," "Mister Blue," "Dream Lover," "Lonely Boy."

DEATHS George Antheil, ultramodern composer; Buddy Holly, singer and major influence on rock and roll, in a plane crash; Billie Holiday, jazz singer.

LITERATURE/JOURNALISM

BOOKS *Advise and Consent* by Allen Drury, *Henderson the Rain King* by Saul Bellow, *Hawaii* by James Michener, *The Cave* by Robert Penn Warren, *Two Weeks in Another Town* by Irwin Shaw.

DEATHS Raymond T. Chandler, mystery writer; Edgar A. Guest, columnist and poet.

ENTERTAINMENT

PLAYS Anne Bancroft stars in *The Miracle Worker,* Tom Bosley in *Fiorello!,* Ethel Merman in *Gypsy;* Lorraine Hansberry writes *A Raisin in the Sun,* Lillian Hellman, *The Little Foxes,* Richard Rodgers and Oscar Hammerstein II, *The Sound of Music.*

MOVIES *Ben Hur* with Charlton Heston, *Some Like It Hot* with Jack Lemmon and Tony Curtis, *The Diary of Anne Frank* with Joseph Schildkraut, *Porgy and Bess* with Sidney Poitier, *Rio Bravo* with John Wayne.

Rod Serling writes television series *The Twilight Zone;* a radio soap opera, *One Man's Family,* written by Carlton F. Morse, completes 27-year run of 3,256 episodes; new television shows include *Hawaiian Eye* with Robert Conrad, *Bonanza* with Lorne Greene, *The Untouchables, Bell Telephone Hour.*

DEATHS Lou Costello of Abbott and Costello comedy team; Errol Flynn and Victor McLaglen, screen actors; Cecil B. DeMille, pioneer movie producer and director; Ethel Barrymore, actress; Maxwell Anderson, playwright.

SPORTS

William Harridge, American (baseball) League president since 1931, resigns, is succeeded by Joe Cronin; Continental League forms with Branch Rickey as president.

Supreme Court rules that Louisiana law barring boxing matches between whites and blacks is unconstitutional.

Harvey Haddix, Pittsburgh Pirates, pitches 12 perfect innings but loses in 13th on an error, sacrifice, and hit.

WINNERS *Auto racing*—Roger Ward, Indianapolis 500; Lee Petty, NASCAR; *Baseball*—Los Angeles Dodgers, World Series; *Basketball*—St. Johns, NIT; California, NCAA; Boston, NBA; *Bowling*—Ed Lubanski, Marion Ladewig, bowlers of year; *Boxing*—Ingemar Johansson, heavyweight; Gene Fulmer, middleweight; *Figure skating*—Dave Jenkins, U.S. men's singles; Carol Heiss, U.S. and world women's singles; *Football* (bowls)—Iowa, Rose; Oklahoma, Orange; Louisiana State, Sugar; Texas Christian—Air Force (tie), Cotton; Baltimore, NFL; *Golf*—U.S., Walker and Ryder cups; Billy Casper, U.S. Open; Bob Rosburg, PGA; Art Wall, Masters; Mickey Wright, U.S. Women's Open; Betsy Rawls, LPGA; *Hockey*—Montreal, Stanley Cup; *Horse racing*—Tommy Lee, Kentucky Derby; Royal Orbit, Preakness Stakes; Sword Dancer, Belmont Stakes; *Tennis*—Australia, Davis Cup; Neale Fraser, U.S. Open (men); Maria Bueno, U.S. Open (women).

DEATHS Bert Bell, NFL commissioner; Molla Mallory and Vincent Richards, tennis players; Tim Mara, founder, New York Giants football team; Nap(oleon) Lajoie, baseball; Willie Hoppe, billiards.

1960

INTERNATIONAL

Russia announces it shot down an American U-2 reconnaissance plane (May 1); the pilot, Francis Gary Powers, alive, confesses to spying; President Dwight D. Eisenhower says he had authorized the flight (May 11).

Act of Bogota calls for social and economic reform in Latin America with U.S. help (September 13).

Mob attacks U.S. Embassy in Panama in dispute over flying U.S., Panamanian flags.

NATIONAL

Presidential contenders Republican Vice President Richard M. Nixon and Democratic Senator John F. Kennedy hold four televised debates before election; Sen. Kennedy wins election by a margin of 118,550 popular votes out of 68.8 million cast; Kennedy receives 303 electoral votes, 219 for Nixon.

Four black students stage sit-in at a Greensboro, North Carolina, lunch counter; many such acts follow; Student Non-Violent Coordinating Committee (SNCC) is established.

Connecticut abolishes county governments; state assumes necessary county functions.

Annual immigration to U.S. totals 265,398.

First atomic-powered aircraft carrier, *Enterprise,* is launched.

Eighteenth census reports national population at 179,323,175.

Robert C. Weaver becomes administrator of Housing and Home Finance Agency, predecessor of Department of Housing and Urban Development.

USS *Triton,* nuclear-powered submarine, makes submerged trip around the world, covering 41,500 miles in 84 days.

Garrison Dam on Missouri River in North Dakota is completed.

DEATHS John D. Rockefeller Jr., philanthropist (Colonial Williamsburg, U.N. headquarters); Frank T. Hines, Veterans Administration head (1930–1945).

BUSINESS/INDUSTRY/INVENTIONS

Freeport Sulphur Co. mines sulphur off Louisiana coast.

DEATHS Eugene G. Grace, president, Bethlehem Steel Co. (1913–1946); Sewell Avery, Montgomery Ward president (1931–1955).

TRANSPORTATION

Robert S. McNamara becomes president of Ford Motor Co.

Delaware, Lackawanna & Western, and Erie lines merge to create Erie Lackawanna Railroad.

Auto registrations for the year reach 61,671,390.

Ogdensburg (New York) Bridge over St. Lawrence River opens, connecting the U.S. to Ontario, Canada.

DEATH George N. Borg, helped develop disc auto and truck clutch.

SCIENCE/MEDICINE

Donald A. Glaser is awarded Nobel Prize in physics for inventing bubble chamber to study elementary particles; Willard F. Libby is awarded Chemistry Prize for method of using radioactive carbon to determine age of objects.

Pioneer V satellite is launched (March 11) to investigate space between orbits of Earth and Venus; *Tiros I,* first weather satellite, is launched (April 1); *Echo I,* a giant balloon reflector that relays voice and some TV signals, is launched (August 12); *Courier 1-B,* first successful active communications satellite, is launched (October 10).

Theodore Maiman develops first laser.

Birth-control pills are made available to public.

DEATH Roy Chapman Andrews, naturalist and explorer.

EDUCATION

Kenneth B. Clark, psychologist, becomes first African-American tenured professor (City College of New York).

RELIGION

Inter-Church Center in New York City is completed; becomes headquarters for several church denominations, National Council of Churches.

Catholic Archbishop Joseph E. Ritter of St. Louis is elevated to cardinal.

DEATHS Cardinal John F. O'Hara of Philadelphia; Rev. John W. Keogh, founder of Newman Club.

ART/MUSIC

Aaron Copland composes *Piano Fantasy.*

Leonard Baskin completes the sculpture *Man with Owl;* completed paintings include *Second Story Sunlight* by Edward Hopper, *The Physicist* by Ben Shahn, *The French Line* by Robert Motherwell.

Senator John F. Kennedy (left) and Vice President Richard M. Nixon contend in the second of the "Great Debates," 1960. At center, rear, is moderator Frank McGee of NBC. **CORBIS-BETTMANN**

SONGS (POPULAR): "Cathy's Clown," "If Ever I Should Leave You," "Only the Lonely," "Save the Last Dance for Me," "The Twist," "Why," "I Want to Be Wanted."

DEATHS Lawrence Tibbett, opera baritone; James Montgomery Flagg, illustrator best known for World War I poster ("I Want You"); Dmitri Mitropoulos, conductor.

LITERATURE/JOURNALISM

Many mergers occur in publishing world: Henry Holt & Co. with Rinehart & Winston, Meridian and World, Macmillan and Crowell-Collier, Appleton-Century-Crofts and Meredith, Alfred A. Knopf Inc. and Random House.

Supreme Court clears D. H. Lawrence's novel *Lady Chatterley's Lover* for general distribution.

BOOKS *Times Three* by Phyllis McGinley, *The Rise and Fall of the Third Reich* by William L. Shirer, *Rabbit, Run* by John Updike, *Hard Times* by E. L. Doctorow, *The Child Buyer* by John Hersey, *To Kill a Mockingbird* by Harper Lee.

DEATHS Richard Wright and John P. Marquand, authors; Emily Post, etiquette writer; Franklin P. Adams, columnist and critic; Richard L. Simon, publisher.

ENTERTAINMENT

Broadway theaters close for 10 days because of Actors Equity strike.

PLAYS Richard Burton and Julie Andrews star in *Camelot,* Melvyn Douglas in *The Best Man,* Dick Van Dyke in *Bye, Bye Birdie,* Jason Robards in *Toys in the Attic.*

MOVIES *Butterfield 8* with Elizabeth Taylor, *The Alamo* with John Wayne, *Exodus* with Paul Newman, *Spartacus* with Kirk Douglas, *The Magnificent Seven* with Yul Brynner.

New television shows include *Route 66* with Martin Milner, *My Three Sons* with Fred MacMurray, *The Flintstones,* and *The Andy Griffith Show.*

DEATHS Mack Sennett, pioneer moviemaker; Clark Gable, screen actor; Oscar Hammerstein II, lyricist.

SPORTS

Pete (Alvin) Rozelle becomes National Football League commissioner; American Football League (AFL) debuts eight teams; Chicago Cardinals move to St. Louis.

Candlestick Park in San Francisco opens; demolition begins on Ebbets Field in Brooklyn.

Winter Olympics are held in Squaw Valley, California, U.S. ice hockey team wins gold; Summer Games are held in Rome, U.S. wins 34 gold medals.

Floyd Patterson becomes first to regain heavyweight boxing championship, knocks out Ingemar Johansson.

Continental (baseball) League disbands without playing a game; loses promised four franchises; National League awards franchises to New York and Houston.

John Thomas sets new world high-jump record of 7 feet, 3¾ inches.

Dolph Schayes becomes first NBA player to score 15,000 career points; Elgin Baylor of Los Angeles Lakers sets NBA single-game scoring record of 71 points.

Ted Williams of Boston Red Sox hits 500th home run.

WINNERS *Auto racing*—Jim Rathman, Indianapolis 500; Rex White, NASCAR; *Baseball*—Pittsburgh Pirates, World Series; *Basketball*—Bradley, NIT; Ohio State, NCAA; Boston, NBA; *Bowling*—Don Carter, PBA national title; *Boxing*—Floyd Patterson, heavyweight; *Chess*—Robert Bryce, U.S. Open; *Figure skating*—David Jenkins, U.S. men's singles; Carol Heiss, U.S. and world women's singles; *Football* (bowls)—Washington, Rose; Georgia, Orange; Mississippi, Sugar; Syracuse, Cotton; Philadelphia, NFL; Houston, AFL; *Golf*—Arnold Palmer, U.S. Open and Masters; Jay Herbert, PGA; Betsy Rawls, U.S. Women's Open; Mickey Wright, LPGA; *Hockey*—Montreal, Stanley Cup; *Horse racing*—Venetian Way, Kentucky Derby; Bally Ache, Preakness Stakes; Celtic Ash, Belmont Stakes; *Tennis*—Neale Fraser, U.S. Open (men); Darlene Hard, U.S. Open (women).

MISCELLANEOUS

United DC-8 and TWA Super-Constellation collide in fog over New York City; 134 die.

Fire aboard aircraft carrier *Constellation* under construction in Brooklyn, New York, kills 50, injures 150, does $50 million damage.

Hurricane Donna sweeps across Eastern Seaboard, causes 148 deaths.

1961

INTERNATIONAL

U.S. breaks off diplomatic relations with Cuba (January 3); Bay of Pigs invasion of Cuba by 1,200 anti-Castro exiles is crushed (April 17); President John F. Kennedy says U.S. will not abandon Cuba to Communists (April 20).

President Kennedy offers Alliance for Progress program to raise Latin American living standards (March 13); U.S. and 19 Latin American countries sign the alliance (August 17).

Adlai E. Stevenson is named U.S. ambassador to U.N.

Agency for International Development is created.

U.S. and Canada sign 60-year Columbia River Treaty, agree on waterpower and storage.

NATIONAL

President Kennedy calls for project to land astronaut on the moon and return him safely to Earth by 1970 (May 25); speaking to U.N. General Assembly, he proposes eventual nuclear disarmament.

Twenty-third Amendment is ratified (March 29); allows District of Columbia residents to vote for president.

Peace Corps is created (March 1); Sargent Shriver is named director.

Edward R. Murrow heads U.S. Information Agency; Glenn T. Seaborg becomes first scientist to head Atomic Energy Commission.

Hawaii Volcanoes and Haleakala (Hawaii) national parks are established.

Ice Harbor Dam on Snake River in Washington is completed.

Supreme Court in *Mapp* v. *Ohio* rules that Fourth Amendment guarantee against evidence obtained by unreasonable search and seizure applies to state as well as federal trials.

SEE PRIMARY DOCUMENT John F. Kennedy's Inaugural Address

DEATHS Former First Lady Edith B. Wilson (1915–1921); Sumner Welles, undersecretary of state who laid groundwork for U.S.'s "good neighbor" policy; Sam Rayburn, House Speaker (1937–1961, except for four years); Walter B. Smith, World War II general.

BUSINESS/INDUSTRY/INVENTIONS

Congress votes minimum-wage increase from $1 an hour to $1.25 in two-year period: $1.15 on September 3, $1.25 on September 3, 1963.

President Kennedy dedicates Freeport (Texas) desalinization plant.

DEATHS Alfred C. Gilbert, toymaker; James F. Bell, first president, General Mills (1928–1934); Eero Saarinen, architect; Lee De Forest, various communications inventions.

TRANSPORTATION

Throgs Neck Bridge over Long Island Sound opens.

Ernest Hemingway (center), who takes his own life in 1961. Hemingway won the Nobel Prize for Literature in 1954. **THE GRANGER COLLECTION, NEW YORK**

DEATHS John D. Hertz, founder and head, car rental service; Louis Hupp, pioneer automaker.

SCIENCE/MEDICINE

Robert Hofstadter shares Nobel Prize in physics with Rudolf L. Mossbauer of Germany for discoveries concerning atom nucleus; Melvin Calvin is awarded chemistry prize for discoveries on photosynthesis; George von Bekesy is awarded physiology/medicine prize for discoveries of mechanism of the ear.

Alan B. Shepard becomes first U.S. astronaut to make space flight (May 5).

Lawrence Radiation Laboratory at University of California produces Element #103 (lawrencium).

Experimental reactor near Idaho Falls, Idaho, fails, kills three workers.

DEATH Earle E. Dickson, inventor of adhesive bandage.

EDUCATION

Sterling M. McMurrin is named U.S. Education Commissioner.

RELIGION

National Council of Churches endorses birth control as means of family limitation.

Two Catholic archbishops are named: Lawrence J. Shehan of Baltimore and John J. Krol of Philadelphia.

DEATH Frank N. D. Buchman, founder of Moral Rearmament movement.

ART/MUSIC

Robert Ward composes the opera *The Crucible;* Douglas S. Moore, the opera *Wings of the Dove;* Milton B. Babbitt composes two revolutionary pieces, "Composition for Synthesizer" and "Vision and Prayer."

Jasper Johns completes the painting *Map;* Philip Guston, *The Tale.*

SONGS (POPULAR): "Where Have All the Flowers Gone?," "Big Bad John," "Can't Help Falling in Love," "Hey, Look Me Over," "Moon River," "Travelin' Man," "Hit the Road, Jack," "Please, Mister Postman," "Raindrops."

DEATHS Grandma (Anna M.) Moses, "primitive" painter; Wallingford Riegger, a leader in avant garde twentieth-century music.

LITERATURE/JOURNALISM

President Kennedy holds first live presidential news conference.

BOOKS *Franny and Zooey* by J. D. Salinger; *Nobody Knows My Name* by James Baldwin, *The Agony and the Ecstasy* by Irving Stone, *Mila 18* by Leon Uris, *Catch-22* by Joseph Heller, *The Carpetbaggers* by Harold Robbins.

DEATHS Dashiell Hammett, Ernest Hemingway, and Kenneth Fearing, authors; Hilda Doolittle (HD), poet; James Thurber, author and cartoonist; Dorothy Thompson, columnist.

ENTERTAINMENT

Newton N. Minow, FCC chairman, describes television as "vast wasteland."

PLAYS Robert Morse stars in *How to Succeed in Business without Really Trying,* Kim Stanley in *A Far Country,* Fredric March in *Gideon;* Neil Simon writes *Come Blow Your Horn,* Tennessee Williams writes *The Night of the Iguana.*

MOVIES *The Hustler* with Jackie Gleason, *West Side Story* with Natalie Wood, *The Misfits* with Clark Gable and Marilyn Monroe, *Breakfast at Tiffany's* with Audrey Hepburn.

New television shows include *Sing Along with Mitch, Mr. Ed* with Alan Young, *Hazel* with Shirley Booth, *Dr. Kildare* with Richard Chamberlain, *The Dick Van Dyke Show* with Dick Van Dyke and Mary Tyler Moore, and *The Joey Bishop Show* with Joey Bishop.

DEATHS Playwrights Moss Hart and George S. Kaufman; Gary Cooper, actor.

SPORTS

Roger Maris of New York Yankees hits 61st home run, a new season's record (October 1).

Ralph Boston is first to long jump more than 27 feet (27 ft., ½ in.).

WINNERS *Auto racing*—A. J. Foyt, Indianapolis 500; Ned Jarrett, NASCAR; *Baseball*—New York Yankees, World Series; *Basketball*—Providence, NIT; Cincinnati, NCAA; Boston, NBA; *Bowling*—Dave Soutar, PBA national; *Boxing*—Floyd Patterson, heavyweight; Benny Paret, welterweight; Eder Jofre, bantamweight; *Figure skating*—Bradley Lord, U.S. men's singles; Laurence Owen, U.S. women's singles; *Football* (bowls)—Washington, Rose; Missouri, Orange; Mississippi, Sugar; Duke, Cotton; Green Bay, NFL; Houston, AFL; *Golf*—U.S., Walker and Ryder cups; Gene Littler, U.S. Open; Jerry Barber, PGA; Gary Player, Masters; Mickey Wright, U.S. Women's Open and LPGA; *Hockey*—Chicago, Stanley Cup; *Horse racing* Carry Back, Kentucky Derby and Preakness Stakes; Sherluck, Belmont Stakes; *Tennis*—Roy Emerson, U.S. Open (men); Darlene Hard, U.S. Open (women).

DEATHS Maribel Vinson (Owen), figure-skating; Ty Cobb, baseball.

PRIMARY SOURCE DOCUMENT

John F. Kennedy's Inaugural Address, January 20, 1961

INTRODUCTION John F. Kennedy was born in Brookline, Massachusetts, on May 29, 1917. After graduating from Harvard University in 1940, he joined the Navy, achieving fame in 1943 when he rescued his fellow crewmen on PT 109, a patrol boat sunk by a Japanese destroyer. After the war, Kennedy entered politics, first winning a Democratic seat in the House in 1946 and then the Senate in 1952 and 1958. Nominated for president by the Democratic Party in 1960, Kennedy defeated Vice President Richard M. Nixon by 84 electoral votes, but only by a slim margin in the popular vote: 34,227,000 to 34,109,000. Kennedy's campaign benefited from his strong showing in the nation's first televised presidential debate, watched by an estimated 70 million Americans. Kennedy's youth and good looks contrasted with Nixon's tired demeanor and haggard appearance attracted voters, especially young ones, to his campaign. An excellent turnout by African-American voters also aided Kennedy.

Before the inauguration, Kennedy attended Holy Trinity Catholic Church in Georgetown. When Chief Justice Earl Warren administered the oath of office, Kennedy became the nation's first Roman Catholic president and the youngest Chief Executive ever elected. With the nation's capital blanketed by a heavy snowfall, Robert Frost read one of his poems, appropriately set in nature, as part of the inaugural ceremony. And then came Kennedy's words, which added to a day that sparkled with the promise of a new era.

Like most presidents, Kennedy received input on his speech from a number of advisers and friends, including several clergymen. In the final analysis, though, the speech was of his own making and reflected themes important to him. The most memorable phrase of the speech, "Ask not what your country can do for you—ask what you can do for your country," summarized a key theme of sacrifice expressed in Kennedy's various campaign speeches.

This theme of service inspired countless Americans to join the Peace Corps and other organizations committed to "progress." However, it is worth noting that in his inauguration speech Kennedy made no mention of domestic problems that would explode in America in the 1960s. Kennedy referred to people living in "huts and villages of half the globe," sister republics in Latin America facing grinding poverty, and the new nations of Africa that had won their independence from colonial masters. But he failed to cite certain social conditions in the United States that for many Americans took precedence over those of foreign nations.

The focus of the speech was America's place in the world and its central role in "defending freedom." It was an inspiring speech, combining an idealism not witnessed since the New Deal and a cold war realism that drew on the Truman Doctrine. It is somewhat ironic that the specter of mass destruction and tyranny pervaded the address at a time when cold war tensions were not altogether high. In some ways Kennedy's rhetoric set a standard for vigilance that would compel him to act on all cold war battlefronts.

Vice President Johnson, Mr. Speaker, Mr. Chief Justice, President Eisenhower, Vice President Nixon, President Truman, Reverend Clergy, fellow citizens:

We observe today not a victory of party but a celebration of freedom—symbolizing an end as well as a beginning—signifying renewal as well as change. For I have sworn before you and Almighty God the same solemn oath our forebears prescribed nearly a century and three-quarters ago.

The world is very different now. For man holds in his mortal hands the power to abolish all forms of human poverty and all forms of human life. And yet the same revolutionary beliefs for which our forebears fought are still at issue around the globe—the belief that the rights of man come not from the generosity of the state but from the hand of God.

We dare not forget today that we are the heirs of that first revolution. Let the word go forth from this time and place, to friend and foe alike, that the torch has been passed to a new generation of Americans—born in this century, tempered by war, disciplined by a hard and bitter peace, proud of our ancient heritage—and unwilling to witness or permit the slow undoing of those human rights to which this nation has always been committed, and to which we are committed today at home and around the world.

OVERVIEW

The 1960s

PAUL ROSIER, VILLANOVA UNIVERSITY

From Consensus to Conflict

An estimated 70 million Americans watched the nation's first televised presidential debate in 1960. Democrat John F. Kennedy won the debate and the election, beating Republican Vice President Richard M. Nixon in a tight race to become the nation's first Catholic president and the youngest one ever elected. Kennedy appealed to Americans, "Ask not what your country can do for you—ask what you can do for your country." He inspired countless Americans to join the Peace Corps and other organizations committed to progress. And, he called for the nation to apply its technological energies to reach the moon by the end of the decade. However, by the time Americans landed on the moon in 1969, the age of consensus and conformity had come to an end both abroad and at home. The Cuban Missile Crisis of 1962 raised international tensions and alarmed America's allies, particularly French President Charles De Gaulle, who pulled France out of the NATO alliance in response. The United States' expanding intervention in Vietnam both alienated European allies and divided the nation. By 1974 Americans began to ask the government what *it* could do for a country battered by an unpopular war, inflation, and government scandal.

Liberalism of the 1960s

Kennedy's cold war concerns and a conservative Congress initially prevented him from focusing on domestic issues like poverty and civil rights. Before he was assassinated in November 1963, Kennedy had begun to investigate the face of American racism and poverty, inspired by the expanding civil rights movement and Michael Harrington's 1962 book *The Other America,* which argued that a "culture of poverty" existed in sharp contrast to the picture of an affluent America. Following Kennedy's lead, President Lyndon B. Johnson championed his Great Society agenda, which called for "an end to poverty and racial injustice." Johnson's program encompassed public-housing initiatives, funding for the arts and the humanities, environmental reforms, support for civil rights, and anti-poverty initiatives like Head Start and the Job Corps. The program achieved immediate success as poverty rates dropped from about 20 percent of the population in 1959 to 13 percent in 1968.

The Struggle for Civil Rights

Johnson also supported expanded civil rights for African Americans. In 1960 black activists protested racism through sit-ins, freedom rides, and marches. At the March on Washington for Jobs and Freedom in August 1963, Dr. Martin Luther King Jr.'s stirring "I Have a Dream" speech showed Americans everywhere how powerful the Civil Rights movement had become, both in terms of its broadened constituency and its moral message. The murder of four African-American girls in their Birmingham church two weeks later helped push the government to adopt important federal legislation. The Civil Rights Act of 1964 prohibited discrimination in the workplace and "public accommodations," which included restaurants, motels, and other public meeting places. And, the Voting Rights Act of 1965 eliminated the arbitrary barriers that restricted African-American voting. This legislation did not, however, satisfy all African Americans. As blacks continued to be attacked by white opponents of civil rights, African-American activists began to reconsider the usefulness of Dr. King's nonviolent approach to social change. Malcolm X spoke for some frustrated African Americans in the North by proposing that the bullet might soon replace the ballot if conditions did not improve. Stokely Carmichael called for "Black Power" as a counterweight to poverty, police brutality, and continued attacks on civil rights activists. His ideas helped inspire Huey Newton and Eldridge Cleaver to establish the Black Panther Party, which pledged to protect black citizens and demand better jobs and housing.

Let every nation know, whether it wishes us well or ill, that we shall pay any price, bear any burden, meet any hardship, support any friend, oppose any foe to assure the survival and the success of liberty.

This much we pledge—and more.

To those old allies whose cultural and spiritual origins we share, we pledge the loyalty of faithful friends. United, there is little we cannot do in a host of co-operative ventures. Divided, there is little we can do—for we dare not meet a powerful challenge at odds and split asunder.

To those new states whom we welcome to the ranks of the free, we pledge our word that one form of colonial control shall not have passed away merely to be replaced by a

Racial tensions exploded in a series of riots in the mid-1960s. At one point in 1966 over forty U.S. cities experienced riots. The assassination of Dr. King in 1968 precipitated another round of urban violence that killed scores of Americans.

1968

The year 1968 was a particularly difficult one in America. In addition to Dr. King, presidential candidate Senator Robert F. Kennedy was gunned down while campaigning in California. The so-called Tet offensive by the Viet Cong turned many Americans against the war in Vietnam. And, the clubbing of antiwar protesters by Chicago police outside the Democratic Convention embarrassed the Democratic Party and eased the way for Republican Richard Nixon to capture the White House.

The Vietnam War: What Are We Fighting For?

Before his death, Dr. King had argued that "the promises of the Great Society have been shot down on the battlefield of Vietnam." Vietnam had divided the nation and arrested social progress. The United States' fight against Vietnamese nationalists began after World War II when it supported France's efforts to recolonize Vietnam; it eventually funded nearly 80 percent of the French war effort. The United States helped create South Vietnam by opposing reunification elections sponsored by the 1954 Geneva Accords and then set about defending it. Although President Kennedy sent thousands of advisors to Vietnam during his term, the military buildup did not begin until 1965 when Johnson approved bombing campaigns and the introduction of ground troops. Finally, in 1975 the United States formally withdrew from South Vietnam as North Vietnamese communists took control.

The consequences of the war were tremendous. Nearly 3 million Americans served in the armed forces during the war. An estimated 58,151 American soldiers died; 303,616 were wounded, with 13,167 of them 100 percent disabled. Many Vietnam veterans adjusted to civilian life, but many others suffered from what has become known as posttraumatic stress syndrome, which made the transition to civilian life difficult, if not impossible. The war cost the United States approximately $150 billion, which siphoned money from Johnson's Great Society programs, fueled inflation, and helped to push the country into a recession in 1973. It also prompted significant changes in government. In 1973 Congress passed the War Powers Act, which required the president to notify Congress within 48 hours if military force was to be used, and such military action was limited to 60 days without an official congressional declaration of war.

New Left and Counterculture

Initial opposition to the Vietnam War was voiced by college students before the antiwar movement broadened its base of support to include lawyers, women, clergy, conscientious objectors, and finally Vietnam veterans. In 1960 young Americans emerged on college campuses to challenge the corporate and cold war consensus of the 1950s. Inspired by racism, the fear of nuclear war, and the general stifling of debate about America's future, students formed protest movements to offer a New Left criticism of America. One such organization was Students for a Democratic Society (SDS). In 1962 SDS leaders summarized their views in the Port Huron Statement, which inspired other students to become politically involved in the defining of America. The Free Speech movement at the University of California at Berkeley, begun in 1964, helped radicalize college students, many of whom were driven to political activism when President Johnson expanded the war in Vietnam. Antiwar protests began in 1965 and spread to hundreds of campuses, taking the form of teach-ins, marches, the burning of draft cards, and strikes. A nationwide strike by colleges and high schools in 1968 swelled the ranks of student protesters to nearly a million. The killing of four Kent State students by the Ohio National Guard in 1970 galvanized the movement. In response to Kent State and the murder of two black students at Jackson State College by Mississippi National Guardsmen, 450 colleges shut down in protest.

far more iron tyranny. We shall not always expect to find them supporting our view. But we shall always hope to find them strongly supporting their own freedom—and to remember that, in the past, those who foolishly sought power by riding the back of the tiger ended up inside.

To those people in the huts and villages of half the globe struggling to break the bonds of mass misery, we pledge our best efforts to help them help themselves, for whatever period is required—not because the Communists may be doing it, not because we seek their votes, but because it is right. If a free society cannot help the many who are poor, it cannot save the few who are rich.

To our sister republics south of the border, we offer a special pledge—to convert our good words into good

The 1960s (continued)

The baby-boom generation of mostly white, affluent college students expressed themselves culturally as well as politically, initiating what became known as the counterculture, which was inspired by the Beat generation of poets and writers of the 1950s and the campus activism of the 1960s. Counterculture youth rejected materialism, conservative sexual mores, and corporate life in favor of experimental drug use, rock and roll music, and communal living that stressed the sharing of responsibility as well as sexual partners. The introduction of the birth control pill in 1960 made possible the sexual revolution. The "Age of Aquarius" culminated in the famous Woodstock music festival of 1969, the high point of a broad social movement that combined political protest and cultural rebellion defined by the hippie motto, "Do your own thing."

The Rebirth of American Conservatism

The liberal political agenda and counterculture movement of the 1960s fueled the rebirth of American conservatism as a political force. In his influential book *The Conscience of a Conservative,* published in 1960, Barry Goldwater attacked an expansive federal government and its support of social welfare while proposing to eliminate the income tax, reduce Social Security benefits, and dismantle other New Deal programs like the Tennessee Valley Authority (TVA). The Republican Party nominated him for president in 1964, alarmed by President Johnson's expansion of federal welfare and civil rights programs. Goldwater's views resonated with rightwing Republicans, including intellectuals like William F. Buckley and the college students who formed chapters of Buckley's Young Americans for Freedom. Although Goldwater lost to Johnson by a huge margin, his campaign heralded a new age in Republican Party politics. An East Coast "establishment" elite no longer controlled the party. Ideologues from the American West emerged as its leaders, while southern voters defected from the Democratic Party and its embrace of civil rights. Starting with Nixon's election in 1968, the next nine presidents came from either the South or the West.

Alabama Governor George Wallace also attacked the liberal consensus, running for president in 1964 and 1968. Wallace failed to attract much attention outside of the South, but as an independent candidate in 1968, he won six southern states and 13.5 percent of the popular vote, indicating a shift in southern voting patterns that no longer favored the Democratic Party. In the 1968 election Nixon also appealed to southern voters opposed to court-ordered desegregation and federal welfare policies while campaigning nationwide on a "law and order" agenda that he promised would heal a fragmented and violent America. Nixon's pledge to reestablish law and order would later prove ironic as the Watergate scandal unfolded during his second term, leading to an era of diminished expectations in American life.

BIBLIOGRAPHY

For good overviews of the 1960s, see Alexander Bloom, *Long Time Gone: Sixties America Then and Now* (2001); Todd Gitlin, *The Sixties: Years of Hope, Days of Rage* (1993); and Terry H. Anderson, *The Movement and the Sixties: Protest in America from Greensboro to Wounded Knee* (1995). For perspectives on the Vietnam War, see Loren Baritz, *Backfire: A History of How American Culture Led Us into Vietnam and Made Us Fight the Way We Did* (1985); and George C. Herring, *America's Longest War: The United States and Vietnam, 1950–1975* (1986). For the history of women's rights, see Leila Rupp and Verta Taylor, *Survival in the Doldrums: The American Women's Rights Movement, 1945 to the 1960s* (1987); and Betty Friedan, *The Feminine Mystique* (1963). A good collection on the civil rights movement is Harvard Sitkoff, *The Struggle for Black Equality,* 2nd Ed. (1992). For a concise study of the rebirth of American conservatism in the 1960s, see Mary C. Brennan, *Turning Right in the Sixties* (1995).

deeds—in a new alliance for progress—to assist free men and free governments in casting off the chains of poverty. But this peaceful revolution of hope cannot become the prey of hostile powers. Let all our neighbors know that we shall join with them to oppose aggression or subversion anywhere in the Americas. And let every other power know that this hemisphere intends to remain the master of its own house.

To that world assembly of sovereign states, the United Nations, our last best hope in an age where the instruments of war have far outpaced the instruments of peace, we renew our pledge of support—to prevent it from becoming merely a forum for invective—to strengthen its shield of the new and the weak—and to enlarge the area in which its writ may run.

Finally, to those nations who would make themselves our adversary, we offer not a pledge but a request: that both sides begin anew the quest for peace, before the dark powers of destruction unleashed by science engulf all humanity in planned or accidental self-destruction.

We dare not tempt them with weakness. For only when our arms are sufficient beyond doubt can we be certain beyond doubt that they will never be employed.

But neither can two great and powerful groups of nations take comfort from our present course—both sides overburdened by the cost of modern weapons, both rightly alarmed by the steady spread of the deadly atom, yet both racing to alter that uncertain balance of terror that stays the hand of mankind's final war.

So let us begin anew—remembering on both sides that civility is not a sign of weakness, and sincerity is always subject to proof. Let us never negotiate out of fear. But let us never fear to negotiate.

Let both sides explore what problems unite us instead of belaboring those problems which divide us.

Let both sides, for the first time, formulate serious and precise proposals for the inspection and control of arms—and bring the absolute power to destroy other nations under the absolute control of all nations.

Let both sides seek to invoke the wonders of science instead of its terrors. Together let us explore the stars, conquer the deserts, eradicate disease, tap the ocean depths, and encourage the arts and commerce.

Let both sides unite to heed in all corners of the earth the command of Isaiah—to "undo the heavy burdens…[and] let the oppressed go free."

And if a beachhead of co-operation may push back the jungle of suspicion, let both sides join in creating a new endeavor, not a new balance of power, but a new world of law, where the strong are just and the weak secure and the peace preserved.

All this will not be finished in the first one hundred days. Nor will it be finished in the first one thousand days, nor in the life of this administration, nor even perhaps in our lifetime on this planet. But let us begin.

In your hands, my fellow citizens, more than mine, will rest the final success or failure of our course. Since this country was founded, each generation of Americans has been summoned to give testimony to its national loyalty. The graves of young Americans who answered the call to service surround the globe.

Now the trumpet summons us again—not as a call to bear arms, though arms we need,—not as a call to battle, though embattled we are—but a call to bear the burden of a long twilight struggle, year in and year out, "rejoicing in hope, patient in tribulation"—a struggle against the common enemies of man: tyranny, poverty, disease, and war itself.

Can we forge against these enemies a grand and global alliance, North and South, East and West, that can assure a more fruitful life for all mankind? Will you join in that historic effort?

In the long history of the world, only a few generations have been granted the role of defending freedom in its hour of maximum danger. I do not shrink from this responsibility—I welcome it. I do not believe that any of us would exchange places with any other people or any other generation. The energy, the faith, the devotion which we bring to this endeavor will light our country and all who serve it—and the glow from that fire can truly light the world.

And so, my fellow Americans: ask not what your country can do for you—ask what you can do for your country.

My fellow citizens of the world: ask not what America will do for you, but what together we can do for the freedom of man.

Finally, whether you are citizens of America or citizens of the world, ask of us here the same high standards of strength and sacrifice which we ask of you. With a good conscience our only sure reward, with history the final judge of our deeds, let us go forth to lead the land we love, asking His blessing and His help, but knowing that here on earth God's work must truly be our own.

SOURCE: From *Public Papers of the Presidents of the United States:* John F. Kennedy, 1961, no. 1 (Washington, D.C., 1962), 1–3.

1962

INTERNATIONAL

President John F. Kennedy announces Soviet Russia is building offensive weapons bases in Cuba (October 22); he orders naval and air quarantine of offensive military equipment (October 24); Russia agrees to halt construction, dismantle, and remove Soviet rockets (October 28); dismantling is complete (November 2), U.S. quarantine ends (November 20). **SEE PRIMARY DOCUMENT** Exchange of Letters between John F. Kennedy and Nikita Khrushchev

U.S. military forces are ordered to Laos (May 12); President Kennedy says U.S. advisors in Vietnam will fire if fired on.

NATIONAL

Supreme Court upholds "one-man, one-vote" apportionment of seats in state legislatures; Felix Frankfurter and Charles E. Whittaker resign from the Court; Arthur J. Goldberg and Byron R. White succeed them.

Astronaut John Glenn becomes a national hero after being the first American to orbit the Earth. **NATIONAL AERONAUTICS AND SPACE ADMINISTRATION**

Linus Pauling is awarded Nobel Peace Prize, becomes only person to win two unshared Nobel prizes (awarded 1954 chemistry prize).

U.S. establishes Communications Satellite Corp. (COMSAT).

First U.S. world's fair in more than 20 years, Century 21 Exposition, is held in Seattle, Washington.

Dwight D. Eisenhower Library in Abilene, Kansas, and Herbert Hoover Library in West Branch, Iowa, open.

Trinity Dam on Trinity River in California is completed.

Petrified Forest (Arizona) National Park is established.

DEATHS Former First Lady Eleanor Roosevelt (1933–1945); Vihjalmur Stefansson, Arctic explorer.

BUSINESS/INDUSTRY/INVENTIONS

Cesar Chavez organizes National Farm Workers Assn.; it later merges with United Farm Workers Organizing Committee.

DEATHS Samuel C. Prescott, bacteriologist who found method to keep canned food sanitary; Benjamin Fairless, U.S. Steel president (1938–1952); Arthur V. Davis, Alcoa president (1910–1928), chairman (1928–1957); Abraham Levitt, housing developer; E. F. Hutton, financier.

TRANSPORTATION

William P. Lear founds Lear Corp.

DEATHS Eugene J. Houdry, inventor of catalytic cracking process to make gasoline; Ralph Budd, railroad president (Burlington), introduced streamlined trains.

SCIENCE/MEDICINE

John H. Glenn Jr. becomes first U.S. astronaut to orbit the Earth (February 20).

James D. Watson shares Nobel Prize in physiology/medicine with Frances Crick and Maurice Wilkins of Great Britain for discoveries of molecular structure of deoxyribonucleic acid (DNA), the substance of heredity.

U.S. satellite reaches moon after 229,541-mile flight from Cape Canaveral, Florida (April 26); first U.S. unmanned space flight, *Mariner 2,* passes within 22,000 miles of Venus.

DEATHS William Beebe, naturalist and inventor of bathysphere; Arthur H. Compton, physicist.

EDUCATION

U.S. Circuit Court orders University of Mississippi to admit African-American student James H. Meredith, who had been refused admission (September 24); Meredith is admitted a week later.

Louisiana Archbishop Joseph F. Rummel orders end to segregation in Catholic schools; Atlanta Archbishop Paul J. Hallinan announces Catholic schools will admit students on a nonracial basis.

Supreme Court in *Engel* v. *Vitale* holds sanctioning of religious "utterances," such as reading an official prayer, to be unconstitutional.

Francis Keppel is named U.S. Commissioner of Education.

RELIGION

Merger of United Lutheran Church in America, Augustana Evangelical Lutheran Church, and Finnish Evangelical Church creates Lutheran Church in America.

Rt. Rev. Melville Burgess is consecrated as Suffragan Bishop of Massachusetts, first black Episcopal bishop in a white diocese.

ART/MUSIC

Aaron Copland composes *Connotations for Orchestra;* Samuel Barber, Piano Concerto no. 1.

Leopold Stokowski forms American Symphony Orchestra.

Aerial intelligence photographs like this one of missile erectors in Cuba precipitate the Cuban Missile Crisis of late 1962, which brings the world close to the brink of nuclear conflict. CORBIS-BETTMANN

Lincoln Center in New York City opens.

Robert A. Moog develops first practical electronic synthesizer.

Andy Warhol, pop-art leader, completes the painting *Green Coca-Cola Bottles;* Hans Hofmann, *Sanctum Sanctumorum;* Jasper Johns, *Fool's House.*

SONGS (POPULAR): "Days of Wine and Roses," "I Can't Stop Loving You," "Johnny Angel," "Roses Are Red, My Love," "Stranger on the Shore," "Walk on By," "You Don't Know Me."

LITERATURE/JOURNALISM

John Steinbeck is awarded Nobel Prize in literature.

BOOKS *The Reivers* by William Faulkner, *The Guns of August* by Barbara W. Tuchman, *Herzog* by Saul Bellow, *Silent Spring* by Rachel Carson, *Ship of Fools* by Katherine Anne Porter, *One Flew over the Cuckoo's Nest* by Ken Kesey, *The Wish Tree* by John Ciardi. SEE PRIMARY DOCUMENT Excerpt from *Silent Spring* by Rachel Carson

DEATHS Howard R. Garis, author of children's stories; William Faulkner, author; Robinson Jeffers, poet.

ENTERTAINMENT

Telstar I relays first satellite transmission of television signals between U.S. and Europe.

Johnny Carson emcees *The Tonight Show;* new shows include *The Lucy Show* with Lucille Ball, *McHale's Navy* with Ernest Borgnine, *Beverly Hillbillies* with Buddy Ebsen and Irene Ryan, *Wild Kingdom* with Marlin Perkins.

PLAYS Uta Hagen stars in *Who's Afraid of Virginia Woolf?,* Zero Mostel in *A Funny Thing Happened on the Way to the Forum,* Jason Robards in *A Thousand Clowns.*

MOVIES *Lawrence of Arabia* with Peter O'Toole, *Gigot* with Jackie Gleason, *To Kill a Mockingbird* with Gregory Peck, *The Music Man* with Robert Preston, *The Miracle Worker* with Anne Bancroft.

DEATHS Frank Borzage, screen director and producer; Charles Laughton and Dick Powell, screen actors; Marilyn Monroe, screen actress; Ted Husing, radio announcer of 1920s.

SPORTS

John Uelses is first to clear 16 feet (by a quarter-inch) in pole vault; Jim Beatty becomes first American to break 4-minute mile indoors; Al Oerter first to surpass 200 feet in discus throw (200 ft., 5 in.).

Wilt Chamberlain of Philadelphia scores 100 points in basketball game against New York (36 field goals, 28 free throws).

Dodgers Stadium in Los Angeles opens.

New York Mets receive franchise from National (baseball) League.

WINNERS *Auto racing*—Rodger Ward, Indianapolis 500; Joe Weatherly, NASCAR; *Baseball*—New York Yankees, World Series; *Basketball*—Dayton, NIT; Cincinnati, NCAA; Boston, NBA; *Bowling*—Carmen Salvino, PBA national; *Boxing*—Sonny Liston, heavyweight; Harold Johnson, light heavyweight; Emile Griffith, welterweight; Carlos Ortiz, lightweight; *Chess*—Bobby Fischer, U.S. title; *Figure skating*—Monty Hoyt, U.S. men's singles; Barbara R. Pursley, U.S. women's singles; *Football* (bowls)—Minnesota, Rose; Louisiana State, Orange; Alabama, Sugar; Texas, Cotton; Green Bay, NFL; Dallas, AFL; *Golf*—Jack Nicklaus, U.S. Open; Gary Player, PGA; Arnold Palmer, Masters; Marie Lindstrom, U.S. Women's Open; Judy Kimball, LPGA; *Hockey*—Toronto, Stanley Cup; *Horse racing*—Decidedly, Kentucky Derby; Greek Money, Preakness Stakes; Jaipur, Belmont Stakes; *Tennis*—Rod Laver, U.S. Open (men); Margaret Smith, U.S. Open (women); *Yachting*—U.S. boat *Weatherly* retains America's Cup.

DEATHS Walt Kiesling, football player and coach; Taylor Spink, editor, *Sporting News* (1914–1962).

PRIMARY SOURCE DOCUMENT

Exchange of Letters between John F. Kennedy and Nikita Khrushchev

INTRODUCTION The Cuban Revolution of 1959 created grave tensions between the United States and Cuba's new socialist government led by Fidel Castro. Efforts by the United States to overthrow Castro began shortly after he assumed power. The 1961 Bay of Pigs invasion conducted by CIA-trained Cuban exiles was designed to trigger an anti-Castro uprising, which never materialized. The invasion, conceived during the Eisenhower administration but embraced by President John F. Kennedy, was a disaster for the 1,400 Cuban exiles involved and an embarrassment to the United States. However, the invasion sufficiently alarmed Castro that he was motivated to forge a relationship with the Soviet Union. Castro and Soviet Premier Nikita Khrushchev shared legitimate fears that the United States would again invade Cuba. In the summer of 1962 Castro and Soviet officials reached an agreement to deploy in Cuba, 90 miles from American shores, an extensive arsenal of Soviet weapons, including SS-4 ballistic missiles with a range of 1,020 miles, SS-5 missiles that could reach targets 2,200 miles away, and assorted anti-aircraft defense systems. Khrushchev also saw the arming of Cuba as a necessary response to the United States installing ballistic missiles in Turkey that were capable of reaching the Soviet Union.

On October 14 a U-2 reconnaissance mission over Cuba uncovered evidence of missile sites that the CIA believed could soon be operational (it was later determined that these missile sites contained fully operational tactical nuclear weapons that were backed up by nearly 42,000 Soviet troops, far more than suspected at the time). Although Kennedy and his advisers considered an invasion, a course of action recommended by the Joint Chiefs of Staff, a plan was never fully developed for fear of sustaining high casualties and Soviet retaliation in Europe. Attorney General Robert F. Kennedy, fearing that America would lose its international credibility, opposed air strikes against Soviet positions. Finally, a consensus emerged that the best response was a naval "quarantine" of Cuba, amounting to a U.S. blockade of Soviet ships carrying missiles. President Kennedy announced this decision to a nationwide audience, creating panic among many Americans who feared that nuclear war, the unthinkable, was now a real possibility; Americans in range of Soviet missiles began to study evacuation routes. Although the quarantine succeeded in stopping Soviet ships, tension mounted when Khrushchev denounced Kennedy for bringing the world "to the abyss" of nuclear confrontation.

The letters printed here are part of an important diplomatic exchange between two leaders, the heads of the most powerful countries on earth, as they sought to avert nuclear disaster. Kennedy and Khrushchev eventually reached an agreement calling for the Soviet Union to withdraw its missiles in return for a U.S. pledge not to invade Cuba; the United States also agreed to withdraw its missiles in Turkey within five months, satisfying Khrushchev's basic demand. During October 1962 the world watched with great trepidation as the two superpowers came close to what would have been a catastrophic military confrontation.

Letter from Kennedy to Khrushchev

Washington, October 22, 1962.

Dear Mr. Chairman: A copy of the statement I am making tonight concerning developments in Cuba and the reaction of my Government thereto has been handed to your Ambassador in Washington.(1) In view of the gravity of the developments to which I refer, I want you to know immediately and accurately the position of my Government in this matter.

In our discussions and exchanges on Berlin and other international questions, the one thing that has most concerned me has been the possibility that your Government would not correctly understand the will and determination of the United States in any given situation, since I have not assumed that you or any other sane man would, in this nuclear age, deliberately plunge the world into war which it is crystal clear no country could win and which could only result in catastrophic consequences to the whole world, including the aggressor.

At our meeting in Vienna and subsequently, I expressed our readiness and desire to find, through peaceful negotiation, a solution to any and all problems that divide us. At the same time, I made clear that in view of the objectives of the ideology to which you adhere, the United States could not tolerate any action on your part which in a major way disturbed the existing over-all balance of power in the world. I stated that an attempt to force abandonment of our responsibilities and commitments in Berlin would constitute such an action and that the United States would resist with all the power at its command.

It was in order to avoid any incorrect assessment on the part of your Government with respect to Cuba that I publicly stated that if certain developments in Cuba took place, the United States would do whatever must be done to protect its own security and that of its allies.

Moreover, the Congress adopted a resolution expressing its support of this declared policy.(2)

Despite this, the rapid development of long-range missile bases and other offensive weapons systems in Cuba has proceeded. I must tell you that the United States is determined that this threat to the security of this hemisphere be removed. At the same time, I wish to point out that the action we are taking is the minimum necessary to remove the threat to the security of the nations of this hemisphere. The fact of this minimum response should not be taken as a basis, however, for any misjudgment on your part.

I hope that your Government will refrain from any action which would widen or deepen this already grave crisis and that we can agree to resume the path of peaceful negotiation.

Sincerely,
JFK

SOURCE: Department of State, Presidential Correspondence: Lot 77 D 163. No classification marking. At 7:41 P.M. on October 21 the Department of State had sent Ambassador Kohler the first draft of this message. (Telegram 961 to Moscow; Department of State, Presidential Correspondence: Lot 77 D 163)

Letter from Khrushchev to Kennedy

Moscow, October 24, 1962.

Dear Mr. President: I have received your letter of October 23,(1) have studied it, and am answering you.

Just imagine, Mr. President, that we had presented you with the conditions of an ultimatum which you have presented us by your action. How would you have reacted to this? I think that you would have been indignant at such a step on our part. And this would have been understandable to us.

In presenting us with these conditions, you, Mr. President, have flung a challenge at us. Who asked you to do this? By what right did you do this? Our ties with the Republic of Cuba, like our relations with other states, regardless of what kind of states they may be, concern only the two countries between which these relations exist. And if we now speak of the quarantine to which your letter refers, a quarantine may be established, according to accepted international practice, only by agreement of states between themselves, and not by some third party. Quarantines exist, for example, on agricultural goods and products. But in this case the question is in no way one of quarantine, but rather of far more serious things, and you yourself understand this.

You, Mr. President, are not declaring a quarantine, but rather are setting forth an ultimatum and threatening that if we do not give in to your demands you will use force. Consider what you are saying! And you want to persuade me to agree to this! What would it mean to agree to these demands? It would mean guiding oneself in one's relations with other countries not by reason, but by submitting to arbitrariness. You are no longer appealing to reason, but wish to intimidate us.

No, Mr. President, I cannot agree to this, and I think that in your own heart you recognize that I am correct. I am convinced that in my place you would act the same way.

Reference to the decision of the Organization of American States cannot in any way substantiate the demands now advanced by the United States. This Organization has absolutely no authority or basis for adopting decisions such as the one you speak of in your letter. Therefore, we do not recognize these decisions. International law exists and universally recognized norms of conduct exist. We firmly adhere to the principles of international law and observe strictly the norms which regulate navigation on the high seas, in international waters. We observe these norms and enjoy the rights recognized by all states.

You wish to compel us to renounce the rights that every sovereign state enjoys, you are trying to legislate in questions of international law, and you are violating the universally accepted norms of that law. And you are doing all this not only out of hatred for the Cuban people and its government, but also because of considerations of the election campaign in the United States. What morality, what law can justify such an approach by the American Government to international affairs? No such morality or law can be found, because the actions of the United States with regard to Cuba constitute outright banditry or, if you like, the folly of degenerate imperialism. Unfortunately, such folly can bring grave suffering to the peoples of all countries, and to no lesser degree to the American people themselves, since the United States has completely lost its former isolation with the advent of modern types of armament.

Therefore, Mr. President, if you coolly weigh the situation which has developed, not giving way to passions, you will understand that the Soviet Union cannot fail to reject the arbitrary demands of the United States. When you confront us with such conditions, try to put yourself in our place and consider how the United States would react to these conditions. I do not doubt that if someone attempted to dictate similar conditions to you—the United States—you would reject such an attempt. And we also say—no.

The Soviet Government considers that the violation of the freedom to use international waters and international air space is an act of aggression which pushes mankind toward the abyss of a world nuclear-missile war. Therefore, the Soviet Government cannot instruct the captains of Soviet vessels bound for Cuba to observe the orders of American naval forces blockading that Island. Our instructions to Soviet mariners are to observe strictly the universally accepted norms of navigation in international waters and not to retreat one step from them. And if the American side violates these rules, it must realize what responsibility will rest upon it in that case. Naturally we will not simply be bystanders with regard to piratical acts by American ships on the high seas. We will then be forced on our part to take the measures we consider necessary and adequate in order to protect our rights. We have everything necessary to do so.

Respectfully,
N. Khrushchev(2)

SOURCE: Kennedy Library, President's Office Files, Cuba. A copy of this letter, transmitted in telegram 1070 from Moscow, October 24, arrived in the Department of State at 9:24 P.M. (Department of State, Presidential Correspondence: Lot 66 D 304).

PRIMARY SOURCE DOCUMENT

Excerpt from *Silent Spring* by Rachel Carson

INTRODUCTION Educated as a scientist, Rachel Carson (1907–1964) became a household name in the early 1960s when she became a crusader for environmental awareness with the 1962 publication of *Silent Spring,* one of the most influential books of the twentieth century. Born in Springdale, Pennsylvania, Carson first graduated from the Pennsylvania College for Women before earning her M.S. in Zoology from Johns Hopkins University. Spending her summers at the Marine Biological Laboratory at Woods Hole in Massachusetts, Carson developed a love of the sea, which she later wrote about in *Under the Sea Wind* (1941), *The Sea Around Us* (1951), and *The Edge of the Sea* (1955). *The Sea Around Us* was a best-seller, and was eventually translated into thirty-two languages. She also wrote a series of conservation bulletins while serving as a marine biologist for the U.S. Fish and Wildlife Service.

Carson's love of the natural world, her understanding of its complex biological processes, and her great literary gifts came together most forcefully in *Silent Spring,* which investigated the dangerous effects of DDT and other chemicals on ecological links in nature. Carson feared a world destroyed by the unrestrained use of chemicals, and the title of her book speaks of a future without birds to usher in the arrival of spring. *Silent Spring* also challenged the accepted point of view, one promoted by the powerful chemical industry, that man controlled nature only to good effect. Carson weathered the chemical industry's sustained attack on her character, her scholarship, and her gender. Nevertheless, her scientific research was sound and well documented, and her warnings later proved accurate. She was even defended by President John F. Kennedy, whose Science Advisory Committee endorsed her view that an ecological catastrophe was in the making.

Carson's considerable scientific achievement was matched by uncommon courage. As she wrote *Silent Spring* and while she defended it, Carson underwent treatment for breast cancer. She died from the disease in 1964. Carson's work made the words "environment" and "ecology" part of the national vocabulary, providing an important stimulus for the formation of the modern environmental movement and forcing the U.S. government to consider its responsibilities in protecting citizens from environmental destruction. In effect, Carson demanded an environmental Bill of Rights, arguing that citizens had a right to know when their communities' air, sea, and soil endangered their health and their future.

"The Obligation to Endure"

The most alarming of all man's assaults upon the environment is the contamination of air, earth, rivers, and sea with dangerous and lethal materials. This pollution is for the most part irrecoverable; the chain of evil it initiates not only in the world that must support life but in living tissues is for the most part irreversible. In this now universal contamination of the environment, chemicals are sinister and little—recognized partners of radiation in changing the very nature of the world—the very nature of its life.... [C]hemicals sprayed on croplands or forests or gardens lie long in soil, entering into living organisms, passing from one to another in a chain of poisoning and death. Or they pass through the alchemy of air and sunlight, combine into new forms that kill vegetation, sicken cattle, and work unknown harm on those who drink from once pure wells....

....The figure is staggering and its implications are not easily grasped—500 new chemicals to which the bodies of men and animals are required somehow to adapt each year, chemicals totally outside the limits of biologic experience. Among them are many that are used in man's war against nature. Since the mid-1940's over 200 basic chemicals have been created for use in killing insects, weeds, rodents, and other organisms described in the modern vernacular as 'pests'....Can anyone believe it is possible to lay down such a barrage of poisons on the surface of the earth without making it unfit for all life? They should not be called 'insecticides,' but 'biocides'....

OVERVIEW

The Cold War Between the Soviet Union and the United States, 1945–1989

MARC GALLICHIO, VILLANOVA UNIVERSITY

The cold war did not begin with any single identifiable event comparable to the Confederate shelling of Fort Sumter or the Japanese attack on Pearl Harbor. The two main belligerents, the United States and the Soviet Union, spent billions of dollars arming themselves, but never fought each other. Nevertheless, most Americans in the 1950s and 1960s agreed that if the contest between the United States and the Soviet Union was not like other wars, it was also a far cry from the peace that they had hoped for at the end of World War II.

The cold war was a geopolitical and an ideological struggle. In other words, the United States and Soviet Union competed for the same interests that had long animated the rivalries between independent nations. However, the cold war was about more than gaining territorial and economic advantage over an adversary. It was also a contest to determine which system of social organization would prevail in the world, American democratic capitalism or Soviet communism.

Dissolution

Relations between the United States and the Soviet Union had never been friendly before the two countries and Great Britain became allies against Nazi Germany in December 1941. The Grand Alliance, as this union was called, was a marriage of convenience. Could the relationship forged in war continue after Germany's defeat?

A host of problems awaited cold-war leaders as World War II drew to a close. The Nazis had ravaged Soviet territory and inflicted casualties numbering in the tens of millions. Soviet leader Joseph Stalin pressured his allies for the promise of significant aid in rebuilding Russia. The British, led by Winston Churchill, worried that Soviet control of Eastern Europe, including a portion of Germany, would pose as great a danger to Great Britain's security as Nazi Germany had. The postwar disposition of Germany loomed as the most difficult problem of all. The Soviets' main concern was to ensure that Germany never became strong enough to threaten them again. Germany would have to be militarily and economically enfeebled. The British and Americans also worried that the Soviets would fill the void left by Germany, but they believed that an economically devastated Germany would impede Europe's overall economic recovery, as had been the case after World War I.

The Bomb

Following Germany's defeat, Allied leaders met in Potsdam, a suburb of Berlin, to discuss these problems. The conference ended without resolution of any of the key issues. During the conference, however, President Harry S. Truman learned that the United States had successfully tested an atomic device. Truman could now be sure that Japan would soon surrender without a costly invasion. The president barely mentioned the new weapon to Stalin. On August 6 and 9, 1945, the United States exploded atomic bombs over the Japanese cities of Hiroshima and Nagasaki. The billowing nuclear clouds that formed over the obliterated cities became indelible images of the new atomic age and a potent warning of the horrors that any future war might bring.

The bomb also became one more problem added to the list of postwar issues dividing the Grand

Along with the possibility of the extinction of mankind by nuclear war, the central problem of our age has therefore become the contamination of man's total environment with such substances of incredible potential for harm—substances that accumulate in the tissues of plants and animals and even penetrate the germ cells to shatter or alter the very material of heredity upon which the shape of the future depends....

It is not my contention that chemical insecticides must never be used. I do contend that we have put poisonous and biologically potent chemical indiscriminately into the hands of persons largely or wholly ignorant of their potentials for harm. We have subjected enormous numbers of people to contact with these poisons, without their consent and often without their knowledge. If the Bill of Rights contains no guarantee that a citizen shall be

Alliance. After years of bearing the brunt of war against Germany, the Soviet Union felt vulnerable once again. How could Russians feel secure when another country wielded so much power? Stalin's answer was to acquire atomic weapons of his own. The nuclear arms race, one of the hallmarks of the cold war, had begun.

In the months following the end of World War II, the Allies made little progress in resolving the questions left unsettled at Potsdam. In fact, problems multiplied. As would often be the case in the cold war, the inability to make progress on divisive issues led to a worsening of relations between the United States and the Soviet Union.

Each side saw the turmoil created by the war as benefiting its rival. When civil war erupted in Greece, the Americans concluded that Stalin was aiding the Greek Communist rebels. In March 1947 Truman announced a program of military and economic assistance to Greece and neighboring Turkey. The Truman Doctrine, as the president's speech became known, pledged American support for "free peoples" fighting against armed parties or outside forces trying to seize power by force. In reality, neither Greece nor Turkey had democratically elected governments. Their key qualification for American support was their anticommunism. The next move came in June 1947. Fearful that communism might spread among the desperate and war-ravaged peoples of Europe, America announced its intention to help rebuild Europe through the Marshall Plan, a full-scale economic recovery program named after Secretary of State George C. Marshall. The Marshall Plan and the Truman Doctrine were two important elements of the strategy of containment of Soviet power that would guide American policy throughout the cold war.

Stalin responded to the American moves by solidifying Soviet control over Eastern Europe and obstructing American and British access to their occupation sectors in the jointly controlled city of Berlin, deep within the Soviet zone. The Berlin Blockade, which began in June 1948, brought Europe to edge of war before Stalin backed down and reopened the main access routes. Americans' relief turned to anxiety, however, when the Soviets tested their atomic bomb in 1949. The lines were now drawn in Europe. They would remain largely unchanged until 1989.

Surrogate Wars

Stalemated in Europe, the cold war spread to the third world as the United States and Soviet Union vied to fill the vacuum created by retreating colonial powers. The first of these wars erupted in June 1950, when Soviet-armed North Korean troops invaded South Korea across an internationally recognized boundary that had divided the peninsula since the Japanese surrender. President Truman viewed the North Korean attack as a Soviet attempt to test American resolve. The United States, fighting under the mantle of the United Nations, quickly dispatched troops to a beleaguered South Korea. Chinese Communist troops fresh from their victory over the Nationalists entered the war against the Americans in late 1950. The fighting ended with an armistice in July 1953 that largely restored the prewar boundary of the 38th parallel. The divided peninsula remained a potential flash point for the remainder of the cold war and beyond.

As a consequence of the Korean War, the United States greatly increased military spending and extended aid to other anticommunist governments, many of dubious legitimacy, including the newly formed government of South Vietnam. The United States also engaged in covert operations to overthrow suspected Communist or pro-Soviet regimes throughout the third world, including Iran in 1953, Guatemala in 1954, and Indonesia in 1958.

For its part, the Soviet Union clamped down on any signs of unrest in Eastern Europe and eventually erected the Berlin Wall in 1961 to keep East Germans from escaping to the West. The Russians also sought to gain allies in the third world by aiding revolutionary

secure against lethal poisons distributed either by private individuals or by public officials, it is surely only because our forefathers, despite their considerable wisdom and foresight, could conceive of no such problem.

I contend, furthermore, that we have allowed these chemicals to be used with little or no advance investigation of their effect on soil, water, wildlife, and man himself. Future generations are unlikely to condone our lack of prudent concern for the integrity of the natural world that supports all life.

There is still very limited awareness of the nature of the threat. This is still an era of specialists, each of whom sees his own problem and is unaware of or intolerant of the larger frame into which it fits. It is also an era dominated by movements, such as the one in Vietnam, and providing aid to former colonial countries in Africa and Asia.

Cuban Missile Crisis

The cold war came to a head during the Cuban Missile Crisis, its most dangerous confrontation. In 1961 the United States backed an invasion of Cuba by enemies of Fidel Castro, in the hope that they would overthrow Castro's Marxist government. When the invasion ended in a debacle at the Bay of Pigs, President John F. Kennedy redoubled efforts to harass Castro's regime. Fearing another invasion, Castro asked Soviet leader Nikita Khrushchev to install nuclear missiles in Cuba. Khrushchev obliged. The showdown began in October 1962 when American planes detected the missile installations under construction. Kennedy demanded that Khrushchev remove the missiles. At first the Soviets refused, but finally they relented. In return Kennedy pledged not to invade Cuba and, it was later revealed, to remove American Jupiter missiles from bases in Turkey.

Vietnam

As the two superpowers backed away from the nuclear brink they continued to wage their struggle in the third world. In 1965 American troops entered South Vietnam to aid a failing anticommunist government created by the Americans a decade earlier. After three years of fighting and tens of thousands of casualties, the United States concluded that victory could not be achieved on the battlefield. It took four more years for the United States to extricate itself from Vietnam and leave its ally to stand or fall on its own. South Vietnam fell to Communist forces in 1975.

The End of the Cold War

Humiliated by their defeat in Vietnam and demoralized by a faltering economy, American leaders watched as Soviet influence seemed to grow throughout the third world. During the 1970s President Richard M. Nixon negotiated a Strategic Arms Limitations Treaty (SALT) with the Soviets, arranged for the sale of American grain to Russia, and reopened relations with Communist China, all as part of an elaborate plan to manage the Soviet Union's actions. Critics charged that Nixon's policy of détente only legitimized Soviet rule and encouraged the Russians to expand their influence in the world. Such accusations seemed to have a basis when the Soviet Union invaded neighboring Afghanistan to crush opposition to the Soviet-sponsored government. Soviet forces were soon bogged down in the rugged terrain of Afghanistan.

As Soviet resources dwindled in the fight against Afghan rebels, the cold war entered its final phase. In some ways, this last stage of the cold war resembled the early days of the conflict. Like earlier American presidents, President Ronald Reagan insisted that the United States could not negotiate with the Russians until overwhelming military superiority had been achieved. The president also promulgated the Reagan Doctrine, in which he vowed to aid forces opposing communism throughout the world, such as those fighting in Afghanistan. As was the case with the Truman Doctrine, the United States frequently supported governments that paid only lip service to America's professed values and often inflicted terrible violence on their own citizens in the name of anticommunism.

Nonetheless, conditions during the final phase differed from those of the early days of the cold war in several key respects, perhaps the most important being the emergence of a new and relatively young leadership in Moscow. In 1985 the new Soviet premier, Mikhail Gorbachev, confronted a worsening situation in Afghanistan, rising protest in Eastern Europe, and a decrepit economy at home. Gorbachev enacted policies to restructure the economy and open the Soviet Union to the West and he simultaneously began searching for a way out of the cold war. He withdrew from Afghanistan, loosened Soviet control over Eastern Europe, and started arms reduction talks with Reagan. Events soon outpaced Gorbachev's ability to control them. By 1989 Eastern Europe had broken free of Russian control. The same year East Germans tore down the Berlin Wall. Reunification of Germany quickly followed. In 1991 the Soviet Union

industry, in which the right to make a dollar at whatever costs is seldom challenged. When the public protests, confronted with some obvious evidence of damaging results of pesticide applications, it is fed little tranquilizing pills of half truth. We urgently need an end to these false assurances, to the sugar coating of unpalatable facts. It is the public that is being asked to assume the risks that the insect controllers calculate. The public must decide whether it wishes to continue on the present road, and it can do so only when in full possession of the facts. In the words of Jean Rostand, "The obligation to endure gives us the right to know."

Elixirs of Death

For the first time in the history of the world, every human being is now subjected to contact with dangerous chemicals, from the moment of conception to

The Cold War, 1945–1989 (continued)

virtually collapsed. The cold war had come to a peaceful conclusion.

BIBLIOGRAPHY

Two opinionated and highly readable surveys of the cold war are Warren I. Cohen, *America in the Age of Soviet Power, 1945–1991* (1993) and H. W. Brands, *The Devil We Knew: Americans and the Cold War* (1993). John Lewis Gaddis, *We Now Know: Rethinking Cold War History* (1997) reexamines the development of the cold war in light of the new documentary evidence that became available after the collapse of the Soviet Union. Gary R. Hess's, *Vietnam and the United States* (1990), George C. Herring's *America's Longest War: The United States and Vietnam, 1950–1975* (1986), and Marilyn B. Young's *The Vietnam Wars, 1945–1990* (1991) are excellent introductions to America's involvement in Vietnam.

death.... They have entered and lodged in the bodies of fish, birds, reptiles, and domestic and wild animals so universally that scientists carrying on animal experiments find it almost impossible to locate subjects free from such contamination. They have been found in fish in remote mountain lakes, in earthworms burrowing in soil, in the eggs of birds—and in man himself....

All this has come about because of the sudden rise and prodigious growth of an industry for the production of man-made or synthetic chemicals with insecticidal properties. This industry is the child of the Second World War. In the course of developing agents of chemical warfare, some of the chemicals in the laboratory were found to be lethal to insects. The discovery did not come by chance; insects were widely used to test chemicals as agents of death for man.

The result has been a seemingly endless stream of synthetic insecticides....

What sets the new synthetic insecticides apart is their enormous biological potency. They have immense power not merely to poison but to enter into the most vital processes of the body and change them in sinister and often deadly ways....

The poison may also be passed on from mother to offspring. Insecticide residues have been recovered from human milk in samples tested by Food and Drug Administration scientists. This means that the breast-fed human infant is receiving small but regular additions to the load of toxic chemicals building up in his body. It is by no means his first exposure, however: there is good reason to believe this begins while he is still in the womb....

What of our simultaneous war against the weeds?

The desire for a quick and easy method of killing unwanted plants has given rise to a large and growing array of chemicals that are known as herbicides, or less formally, as weed killers...; the question that here concerns us is whether the weed killers are poisons and whether their use is contributing to the poisoning of the environment.

The legend that the herbicides are toxic only to plants and so pose no threat to animal life has been widely disseminated, but unfortunately it is not true. The plant killers include a large variety of chemicals that act on animal tissue as well as on vegetation. They vary greatly in their action on the organism. Some are general poisons, some are powerful stimulants of metabolism, causing a fatal rise in body temperature, some induce malignant tumors either alone or in partnership with other chemicals, some strike at the genetic material of the race by causing gene mutations. The herbicides, then, like the insecticides, include some very dangerous chemicals, and their careless use in the belief that they are 'safe' can have disastrous results.

Despite the competition of a constant stream of new chemicals issuing from the laboratories, arsenic compounds are still liberally used, both as insecticides...and as weed killers.... The history of their use is not reassuring. As roadside sprays, they have cost many a farmer his cow and killed uncounted numbers of wild creatures. As aquatic weed killers in lakes and reservoirs they have made public waters unsuitable for drinking or even for swimming. As a spray applied to potato fields to destroy the vines they have taken a toll of human and nonhuman life....

Among the herbicides are some that are classified as "mutagens," or agents capable of modifying the genes, the materials of heredity. We are rightly appalled by the genetic effects of radiation; how then, can we be indifferent to the same effect in chemicals that we disseminate widely in our environment?

SOURCE: Rachel Carson, *Silent Spring,* (New York: Houghton Mifflin, 1962).

1963

INTERNATIONAL

U.S., Soviet Russia, and Great Britain agree to Nuclear Test Ban Treaty, ban tests in the atmosphere, outer space, and underwater (August 5); 99 nations agree.

U.S. and Soviet Russia establish a "hot line" for quick communication (August 30).

Former British Prime Minister Winston S. Churchill is granted honorary U.S. citizenship.

By year's end, 15,000 U.S. troops are in Vietnam.

NATIONAL

President John F. Kennedy is assassinated in Dallas (November 22) while traveling in a motorcade through city; Texas Gov. John B. Connally is also shot but not seriously wounded; Lee Harvey Oswald is arrested for the killing; Vice President Lyndon B. Johnson is sworn in as president aboard *Air Force One;* two days later, Oswald is shot to death in city jail by nightclub owner Jack Ruby.

President Johnson pledges to continue policies of late President Kennedy; Warren Commission is created to investigate assassination.

Medgar Evers, NAACP field secretary, is shot to death from ambush in front of his Jackson, Mississippi, home (June 12).

About 200,000 demonstrate peacefully in Washington to support African-Americans' demands for equal rights, hear Dr. Martin Luther King Jr. speech, "I have a dream..." (August 28).

Antisegregation demonstrations begin in Birmingham, Alabama (April 2); race riot follows bombing (September 15) of black church in which four girls are killed, 20 are hurt.

Supreme Court rules congressional districts should have equal populations; in *Gideon* v. *Wainwright,* Court holds that all defendants are entitled to an attorney.

Atomic submarine *Thrasher* sinks in North Atlantic; 29 die.

First-class postage increases to 5 cents.

Jimmy Carter begins four-year term in Georgia state senate.

DEATHS Herbert H. Lehman, New York governor, senator; Elsa Maxwell, noted hostess; Gen. Royal B. Lord, inventor of portable steel cableway.

BUSINESS/INDUSTRY/INVENTIONS

Polaroid introduces color film for its camera.

Minimum wage increases to $1.25 an hour (September 3).

TRANSPORTATION

Chesapeake & Ohio Railroad takes over financially troubled Baltimore & Ohio line.

DEATHS Alfred P. Sloan, General Motors president and chairman (1923–1956); Charles T. Fisher of Fisher Body Corp.

Betty Friedan, *The Feminine Mystique*

Published in February 1963, Betty Friedan's *The Feminine Mystique* revolutionized concepts of womanhood in the U.S., and ushered in a new kind of feminism based on self-realization and career. Its publication is widely accepted as the beginning of the modern women's movement. Friedan, a housewife and freelance writer, attacked the conventional image of the 1950s middle-class suburban female as perfectly content in her role as mother and doting wife most enthralled by what she termed "the feminine mystique." Friedan instead argued that most women were personally repressed and intellectually unfulfilled by a life based on shopping, chauffeuring children to after-school activities, and serving meals to their husbands. In her view, the married woman had become "afraid to ask even of herself the silent question—'Is this all?'" The suburban house was a "comfortable concentration camp" from which women needed to break free. The book became an immediate and sensational best-seller, inspiring great numbers of disenchanted and disillusioned women. Friedan went on to help form the National Organization for Women (NOW), becoming its first president in 1966.

SCIENCE/MEDICINE

Maria Goeppert-Mayer and Eugene P. Wigner share Nobel Prize in physics: Mayer for research on atomic nucleus structure, Wigner for laws of symmetry governing nuclear particle reactions.

DEATHS Dr. Franz Alexander, pioneer in psychosomatic medicine; Otto Struve, astronomer.

EDUCATION

Supreme Court rules in *School District of Abington Township* v. *Schempp* that recitation of Lord's Prayer or Bible verses in public schools is unconstitutional.

Two African-American students enter state university at Birmingham, Alabama, under court order; President Kennedy federalizes Alabama National Guard to speed integration.

Federal government launches $1.2 billion construction program for college buildings.

Antisegregation demonstrations and race riots break out in Birmingham, Alabama. **AP/WIDE WORLD PHOTOS**

One-day boycott is staged in Chicago as 225,000 students stay home to protest segregation.

DEATH Edith Hamilton, popularized classical literature in U.S.

RELIGION

National Council of Churches elects its first woman president, Cynthia C. Wedel.

Lutheran Free Church merges into American Lutheran Church.

Elizabeth Ann Seton, founder of Sisters of Charity, and former Philadelphia Bishop John Neumann are beatified.

Malcolm X becomes "national minister" of the Black Muslims.

Use of English instead of Latin for parts of Catholic mass and sacraments is approved.

DEATH Methodist Bishop G. Bromley Oxnam, a founder of National Council of Churches.

ART/MUSIC

Leonard Bernstein composes the symphony *Kaddish;* Gian Carlo Menotti, the opera *The Last Savage.*

SONGS (POPULAR): "Call Me Irresponsible," "Can't Get Used to Losing You," "Hey Paula," "More," "Our Day Will Come," "Rhythm of the Rain," "Walk Right In," "You Don't Own Me," "Puff the Magic Dragon."

DEATHS Patsy Cline, country-music singer; Dinah Washington, "queen" of blues; Fritz Reiner, conductor.

LITERATURE/JOURNALISM

New York Review of Books begins publication.

BOOKS *The Feminine Mystique* by Betty Friedan, *Raise High the Roof Beams, Carpenter* and *Seymour: An Introduction* by J. D. Salinger, *The Group* by Mary McCarthy, *The Other America* by Michael Harrington.

DEATHS Robert Frost, Theodore Roethke, and William Carlos Williams, poets; Jimmy Hatlo, cartoonist ("Little Iodine"); Alicia Patterson, publisher, *Newsday;* Oliver H. P. La Farge, anthropologist and author *(Laughing Boy).*

ENTERTAINMENT

Robert Redford stars in Neil Simon's play *Barefoot in the Park.*

MOVIES *Cleopatra* with Elizabeth Taylor and Richard Burton, *Hud* with Paul Newman, *Irma la Douce* with Shirley MacLaine and Jack Lemmon, *The Pink Panther* with Peter Sellers.

Following the assassination of President John F. Kennedy in Dallas, Lyndon Baines Johnson takes the Presidential oath of office aboard *Air Force One.* On his right is his wife, Lady Bird, and on his left is Kennedy's widow, Jacqueline. AP/WIDE WORLD PHOTOS

New television shows include *My Favorite Martian* with Ray Walston, *Petticoat Junction* with Bea Benaderet, *Burke's Law* with Gene Barry.

SPORTS

John Pennel clears 17 feet in the pole vault (17 ft., ¾ in.).

Willie Mays of San Francisco Giants hits 400th home run; Early Wynn, Cleveland Indians, pitches his 300th victory.

Pro Football Hall of Fame in Canton, Ohio, opens.

Liberty Bell Racetrack in Philadelphia opens.

WINNERS *Auto racing*—Parnelli Jones, Indianapolis 500; Joe Weatherly, NASCAR; *Baseball*—Los Angeles Dodgers, World Series; *Basketball*—Providence, NIT; Loyola (Illinois), NCAA; Boston, NBA; *Bowling*—Billy Hardwick, PBA National; *Boxing*—Sonny Liston, heavyweight; Willie Pastrano, light heavyweight; Emile Griffith, welterweight; *Figure skating*—Tommy Litz, U.S. men's singles; Lorraine Hanlon, U.S. women's singles; *Football* (bowls)—Southern California, Rose; Alabama, Orange; Mississippi, Sugar; Louisiana State, Cotton; Chicago, NFL; San Diego, AFL; *Golf*—U.S., Walker and Ryder cups; Julius Boros, U.S. Open; Jack Nicklaus, PGA and Masters; Mary Mills, U.S. Women's Open; Mickey Wright, LPGA; *Hockey*—Toronto, Stanley Cup; *Horse racing*—Chateaugay, Kentucky Derby and Belmont Stakes; Candy Spots, Preakness Stakes; *Tennis*—U.S., Davis Cup; Rafael Osuna, U.S. Open (men); Maria Bueno, U.S. Open (women).

DEATHS Two professional football players, Quarterback Bernie Masterson and Eugene "Big Daddy" Lipscomb.

MISCELLANEOUS

Fire in Indiana State Fair Coliseum in Indianapolis kills 73.

1964

INTERNATIONAL

President Lyndon B. Johnson announces U.S. air attacks on North Vietnam in answer to attacks on U.S. warships (August 4); Tonkin Gulf Resolution is passed (August 7), gives president authority to retaliate against North Vietnamese attacks.

Panama suspends relations with U.S. after riots; U.S. offers to renegotiate canal treaty.

The Beatles arrive in America to immediate success. The group wins two Grammy awards in 1964 and becomes a major influence on pop music and culture during the 1960s. **AP/WIDE WORLD PHOTOS**

NATIONAL

President Johnson, Democrat, is elected to full term in biggest landslide of century: 486 electoral votes and 43.1 million popular votes to Republican Sen. Barry M. Goldwater's 52 electoral and 27.1 million popular votes. **SEE PRIMARY DOCUMENT** Barry Goldwater's Acceptance of the Nomination for President at the Twenty-eighth Republic National Convention.

Warren Commission, after investigating President Kennedy's assassination, concludes that Lee Harvey Oswald was lone assassin; Jack Ruby is convicted of killing Oswald and sentenced to death; after appeal, new trial is ordered.

Twenty-fourth Amendment is ratified (January 23), bars the poll tax as a requisite in federal elections.

Civil Rights Act goes into effect (July 2).

Congress approves Office of Economic Opportunity (War on Poverty).

Glen Canyon Dam on Colorado River in Arizona is completed.

Canyonland (Utah) National Park is established.

New Hampshire introduces state lottery to help pay for schools.

Vice President's salary is raised $8,000 to $43,000.

DEATHS Former President Herbert Hoover (1929–1933); Gen. Douglas MacArthur, commander of Pacific forces; Alvin C. York, most decorated U.S. soldier in World War I.

SEE PRIMARY DOCUMENT Nobel Prize Acceptance Speech, Martin Luther King Jr.

TRANSPORTATION

Three major bridges open: Vincent Thomas over Los Angeles Harbor; Verrazano-Narrows over New York Harbor; Chesapeake Bay Bridge Tunnel, 17.6-mile span connecting Eastern Shore of Virginia and Norfolk.

Norfolk and Western Railroad acquires Nickel Plate and Wabash railroads.

SCIENCE/MEDICINE

Charles H. Townes shares Nobel Prize in physics with Nikolai Basov and Aleksander Procherov for work on maser-laser principle of magnifying electromagnetic radiation; Konrad E. Bloch shares prize in physiology/medicine with Feodor Lynen of Germany for work on cholesterol and fatty-acid metabolism.

Surgeon General Luther L. Terry issues warning against cigarette smoking; cigarette manufacturers are required to put hazard notice on cigarette packages.

Mariner 4, unmanned satellite, photographs surface of Mars.

Polio vaccinations cut new cases from 35,600 in 1953 to fewer than 100 in 1964.

DEATHS Dr. Alfred Blalock, developed technique for saving "blue babies"; Norbert Wiener, mathematician, developer of cybernetics.

RELIGION

Presbyterian Church in U.S. votes to permit ordination of women as deacons, elders, and ministers.

First Catholic mass offered completely in English in U.S. is celebrated in St. Louis.

ART/MUSIC

Roger H. Sessions composes opera *Montezuma.*

Vatican exhibit at World's Fair features Michelangelo's *Pieta.*

Thieves steal $410,000 worth of jewels from Museum of Natural History, including world's largest sapphire, 565-carat "Star of India."

Jasper Johns completes the painting *Field Painting.*

SONGS (POPULAR): "Dang Me," "Everybody Loves Somebody," "Hello, Dolly!," "I Want to Hold Your Hand," "My Guy," "Rag Doll," "Walk on By."

DEATHS Jim Reeves, country-music singer; Pierre Monteaux, conductor; Cole Porter, musical comedy composer; Jack Teagarden, trombonist and band leader.

LITERATURE/JOURNALISM

Supreme Court in *The New York Times* v. *Sullivan* upholds freedom of the press, protects the press from libel suits unless malice can be proved.

BOOKS *Flood* by Robert Penn Warren, *The Keepers of the House* by Shirley Ann Grau, *The Wapshot Scandal* by John Cheever, *Reuben, Reuben* by Peter DeVries, *The Honey Badger* by Robert C. Ruark.

DEATHS Percy L. Crosby, cartoonist ("Skippy"); J. Frank Dobie, author of Southwest histories; Rachel Carson, environmental author; Ted Patrick, editor, *Holiday* (1946–1964); Roy W. Howard, Scripps-Howard newspapers executive; Ben Hecht, author and playwright.

ENTERTAINMENT

PLAYS Sammy Davis Jr. stars in *Golden Boy,* Jason Robards in Arthur Miller's *After the Fall,* Barbra Streisand in *Funny Girl,* Carol Channing in *Hello, Dolly!,* Eli Wallach in *Luv.*

MOVIES *Mary Poppins* with Julie Andrews, *My Fair Lady* with Rex Harrison and Audrey Hepburn, *The Night of the Iguana* with Richard Burton, *Dr. Strangelove* with Peter Sellers.

The Beatles arrive for first U.S. tour; their album, *Meet the Beatles,* sells 2 million copies.

Popular rock-and-roll dances are the Watusi and the Frug.

New television shows include *The Man from U.N.C.L.E.* with Robert Vaughn, *Bewitched* with Elizabeth Montgomery, *Daniel Boone* with Fess Parker, *Peyton Place.*

DEATHS Eddie Cantor, entertainer; Joseph Schildkraut, screen actor; Gracie Allen of Burns and Allen comedy team; Alan Ladd, screen actor.

SPORTS

New York Mets open new home park, Shea Stadium.

Billy Mills becomes first American to win Olympic 10,000-meter race; Don Schollander wins four gold medals in swimming.

Astro-Turf, popular covering for baseball and football fields, is first used in Providence, Rhode Island, private school.

WINNERS *Auto racing*—A. J. Foyt, Indianapolis 500; Richard Petty, NASCAR; *Baseball*—St. Louis, World Series; *Basketball*—Bradley, NIT; UCLA, NCAA; Boston, NBA; *Bowling*—Bob Strampee, PBA national; *Boxing*—Muhammad Ali, heavyweight; *Chess*—Pal Benkö, U.S. Open; *Figure skating*—Scott Allen, U.S. men's singles; Peggy Fleming, U.S. women's singles; *Football* (bowls)—Illinois, Rose; Nebraska, Orange; Alabama, Sugar; Texas, Cotton; Cleveland, NFL; Buffalo, AFL; *Golf*—Ken Venturi, U.S. Open; Bob Nichols, PGA; Arnold Palmer, Masters; Mickey Wright, U.S. Women's Open; Mary Mills, LPGA; *Hockey*—Toronto, Stanley Cup; *Horse racing*—Northern Dancer, Kentucky Derby and Preakness Stakes; Quadrangle, Belmont Stakes; *Tennis*—Australia, Davis Cup; Roy Emerson, U.S. Open (men); Maria Bueno, U.S. Open (women).

DEATHS Two Chicago Bears football players: Willie Gallimore and Bo Farrington; Steve Owen, New York Giants football player and coach; Glenn Roberts, auto racer.

MISCELLANEOUS

Earthquake east of Anchorage, Alaska, kills 131, does $500–$700 million damage (March 27).

PRIMARY SOURCE DOCUMENT

Barry Goldwater's Acceptance of the Nomination for President at the Twenty-eighth Republican National Convention

INTRODUCTION Born in Phoenix, Arizona, Barry Goldwater (1909–1998) attended the University of Arizona for one year but did not graduate. After serving in the U.S. Army Air Corps during World War II, he began a successful political career. Elected to the Senate as a Republican in 1952, Goldwater's conservative political ideals ran counter to those of President Dwight D. Eisenhower, whom many conservatives considered to be a Republican moderate supportive of the New Deal, cautious in his anti-communism, and responsible for naming an often liberal-minded Earl Warren as the Chief Justice of the Supreme Court. In contrast, Goldwater defended Joseph McCarthy's actions, publicly attacked labor leader Walter Reuther, and criticized Eisenhower's budget, which, he told Congress, "not only shocks me, but weakens my faith." It was this faith in conservative ideals, particularly a belief in the limited power of the federal government, that helped launch Goldwater's prominent run for presidential office in 1964.

In 1960 Goldwater published a short book entitled *The Conscience of a Conservative,* which quickly sold 500,000 copies. In preparing his manuscript, Goldwater had significant help from former McCarthy speechwriter L. Brent Bozell. One particular passage, which Bozell coauthored, captured the message of Goldwater's book and became a key idea in conservatives' campaign against an expanding federal government: "I have little interest in streamlining government or in making it more efficient, for I mean to reduce its size. I do not undertake to promote welfare, for I propose to extend freedom." Goldwater also proposed to eliminate income tax, reduce Social Security benefits, and dismantle other New Deal programs like the Tennessee Valley Authority.

Despite the success of his book, Goldwater did not capture the Republican Party's presidential nomination in 1960, in part because he did not seek it. His lack of a college education concerned him; he once told the *Chicago Tribune,* "Doggone it, I'm not even sure I've got the brains to be president of the United States." But in 1964, after conservatives watched first John F. Kennedy and then Lyndon B. Johnson expand federal welfare and civil rights programs, the time seemed to have arrived for a Republican like Goldwater to run.

Goldwater's 1964 speech accepting the Republican Party's nomination, printed here, contains the key elements of Goldwater's conservatism, which resonated with right-wing Republicans, including intellectuals like William F. Buckley and the college students who formed chapters of Buckley's Young Americans for Freedom. Goldwater's ideas did not resonate with most Americans, however. His presidential campaign was a disaster. Incumbent Johnson won a landslide victory, receiving 61 percent of the popular vote and 482 electoral votes to Goldwater's 52. Goldwater was a reluctant campaigner prone to gaffes and his Democratic opponents painted a portrait of him as an anticommunist extremist who could not be trusted with nuclear weapons. One Democratic Party campaign button read, "In your guts you know he's nuts."

Despite the embarrassing loss, Goldwater's campaign heralded a new age in Republican Party politics. The GOP was no longer controlled by an East Coast "establishment" elite, but by ideologues from the Sun Belt of the American West. Southerners upset with the desegregation politics of the Democratic Party began to lend their support to the Republican Party. Starting with Richard M. Nixon's election in 1968, six of the next nine presidents came from the West. The Goldwater campaign galvanized a new generation of Republican activists proud of the kind of conservative beliefs Goldwater espoused and determined to make them the guiding principles of the federal government.

...I accept your nomination with a deep sense of humility. I accept, too, the responsibility that goes with it, and I seek your continued help and your continued guidance. My fellow Republicans, our cause is too great for any man to feel worthy of it. Our task would be too great for any man, did he not have with him the heart and the hands of this great Republican Party, and I promise you tonight that every fiber of my being is consecrated to our cause; that nothing shall be lacking from the struggle that can be brought to it by enthusiasm, by devotion, and plain hard work. In this world no person, no party can guarantee anything, but what we can do and what we shall do is to deserve victory, and victory will be ours.

The good Lord raised this mighty Republic to be a home for the brave and to flourish as the land of the free—not to stagnate in the swampland of collectivism, not to cringe before the bully of communism.

Now, my fellow Americans, the tide has been running against freedom. Our people have followed false prophets. We must, and we shall, return to proven ways—not because they are old, but because they are true. We must, and we shall, set the tide running again in the cause of freedom. And this party, with its every action, every word, every breath, and every heartbeat, has but a single resolve, and that is freedom—freedom made orderly for this nation by our constitutional government; freedom under a government limited by laws of nature and of nature's God; freedom—balanced so that liberty lacking order will not become the slavery of the prison cell; balanced so that liberty lacking order will not become the license of the mob and of the jungle.

Now, we Americans understand freedom. We have earned it, we have lived for it, and we have died for it. This Nation and its people are freedom's model in a searching world. We can be freedom's missionaries in a doubting world. But, ladies and gentlemen, first we must renew freedom's mission in our own hearts and in our own homes.

During four futile years, the administration which we shall replace has distorted and lost that faith. It has talked and talked and talked and talked the words of freedom. Now, failures cement the wall of shame in Berlin. Failures blot the sands of shame at the Bay of Pigs. Failures mark the slow death of freedom in Laos. Failures infest the jungles of Vietnam. And failures haunt the houses of our once great alliances and undermine the greatest bulwark ever erected by free nations—the NATO community. Failures proclaim lost leadership, obscure purpose, weakening wills, and the risk of inciting our sworn enemies to new aggressions and to new excesses. Because of this administration we are tonight a world divided—we are a Nation becalmed. We have lost the brisk pace of diversity and the genius of individual creativity. We are plodding at a pace set by centralized planning, red tape, rules without responsibility, and regimentation without recourse.

Rather than useful jobs in our country, people have been offered bureaucratic "make work," rather than moral leadership, they have been given bread and circuses, spectacles, and, yes, they have even been given scandals. Tonight there is violence in our streets, corruption in our highest offices, aimlessness among our youth, anxiety among our elders and there is a virtual despair among the many who look beyond material success for the inner meaning of their lives. Where examples of morality should be set, the opposite is seen. Small men, seeking great wealth or power, have too often and too long turned even the highest levels of public service into mere personal opportunity.

Now, certainly, simple honesty is not too much to demand of men in government. We find it in most. Republicans demand it from everyone. They demand it from everyone no matter how exalted or protected his position might be. The growing menace in our country tonight, to personal safety, to life, to limb and property, in homes, in churches, on the playgrounds, and places of business, particularly in our great cities, is the mounting concern, or should be, of every thoughtful citizen in the United States.

Security from domestic violence, no less than from foreign aggression, is the most elementary and fundamental purpose of any government, and a government that cannot fulfill that purpose is one that cannot long command the loyalty of its citizens. History shows us—demonstrates that nothing—nothing prepares the way for tyranny more than the failure of public officials to keep the streets from bullies and marauders.

Now, we Republicans see all this as more, much more, than the rest: of mere political differences or mere political mistakes. We see this as the result of a fundamentally and absolutely wrong view of man, his nature and his destiny. Those who seek to live your lives for you, to take your liberties in return for relieving you of yours, those who elevate the state and downgrade the citizen must see ultimately a world in which earthly power can be substituted for divine will, and this Nation was founded upon the rejection of that notion and upon the acceptance of God as the author of freedom.

Those who seek absolute power, even though they seek it to do what they regard as good, are simply demanding the right to enforce their own version of heaven on earth. And let me remind you, they are the very ones who always create the most hellish tyrannies. Absolute power does corrupt, and those who seek it must be suspect and must be opposed. Their mistaken course stems from false notions of equality, ladies and gentlemen. Equality, rightly understood, as our founding fathers understood it, leads to liberty and to the emancipation of creative differences. Wrongly understood, as it has been so tragically in our time, it leads first to conformity and then to despotism.

Fellow Republicans, it is the cause of Republicanism to resist concentrations of power, private or public, which enforce such conformity and inflict such despotism. It is the cause of Republicanism to ensure that power remains in the hands of the people. And, so help us God, that is exactly what a Republican president will do with the help of a Republican Congress.

It is further the cause of Republicanism to restore a clear understanding of the tyranny of man over man in the world at large. It is our cause to dispel the foggy thinking which avoids hard decisions in the illusion that a world of conflict will somehow mysteriously resolve itself into a world of harmony, if we just don't rock the boat or irritate the forces of aggression—and this is hogwash.

It is further the cause of Republicanism to remind ourselves, and the world, that only the strong can remain free, that only the strong can keep the peace.

Now, I needn't remind you, or my fellow Americans regardless of party, that Republicans have shouldered this hard responsibility and marched in this cause before. It was Republican leadership under Dwight Eisenhower that kept the peace, and passed along to this administration the mightiest arsenal for defense the world has ever known. And I needn't remind you that it was the strength and the unbelievable will of the Eisenhower years that kept the peace by using our strength, by using it in the Formosa Straits and in Lebanon and by showing it courageously at all times.

It was during those Republican years that the thrust of Communist imperialism was blunted. It was during those years of Republican leadership that this world moved closer, not to war, but closer to peace, than at any other time in the three decades just passed.

And I needn't remind you—but I will—that it's been during Democratic years that our strength to deter war has stood still, and even gone into a planned decline. It has been during Democratic years that we have weakly stumbled into conflict, timidly refusing to draw our own lines against aggression, deceitfully refusing to tell even our people of our full participation, and tragically, letting our finest men die on battlefields (unmarked by purpose, unmarked by pride or the prospect of victory).

Yesterday it was Korea. Tonight it is Vietnam. Make no bones of this. Don't try to sweep this under the rug. We are at war in Vietnam. And yet the President, who is Commander-in-Chief of our forces, refuses to say—refuses to say, mind you, whether or not the objective over there is victory. And his Secretary of Defense continues to mislead and misinform the American people, and enough of it has gone by.

And I needn't remind you, but I will; it has been during Democratic years that a billion persons were cast into Communist captivity and their fate cynically sealed.

Today in our beloved country we have an administration which seems eager to deal with communism in every coin known—from gold to wheat, from consulates to confidence, and even human freedom itself.

The Republican cause demands that we brand communism as a principal disturber of peace in the world today. Indeed, we should brand it as the only significant disturber of the peace, and we must make clear that until its goals of conquest are absolutely renounced and its rejections with all nations tempered, communism and the governments it now controls are enemies of every man on earth who is or wants to be free.

We here in America can keep the peace only if we remain vigilant and only if we remain strong. Only if we keep our eyes open and keep our guard up can we prevent war. And I want to make this abundantly clear—I don't intend to let peace or freedom be torn from our grasp because of lack of strength or lack of will—and that I promise you Americans.

I believe that we must look beyond the defense of freedom today to its extension tomorrow. I believe that the communism which boasts it will bury us will, instead, give way to the forces of freedom. And I can see in the distant and yet recognizable future the outlines of a world worthy our dedication, our every risk, our every effort, our every sacrifice along the way. Yes, a world that will redeem the suffering of those who will be liberated from tyranny. I can see and I suggest that all thoughtful men must contemplate the flowering of an Atlantic civilization, the whole world of Europe unified and free, trading openly across its borders, communicating openly across the world. This is a goal far, far more meaningful than a moon shot.

It's a truly inspiring goal for all free men to set for themselves during the latter half of the twentieth century. I can also see—and all free men must thrill to—the events of this Atlantic civilization joined by its great ocean highway to the United States. What a destiny, what a destiny can be ours to stand as a great central pillar linking Europe, the Americans and the venerable and vital peoples and cultures of the Pacific. I can see a day when all the Americas, North and South, will be linked in a mighty system, a system in which the errors and misunderstandings of the past will be submerged one by one in a rising tide of prosperity and interdependence. We know that the misunderstandings of centuries are not to be wiped away in a day or wiped away in an hour. But we pledge—we pledge that human sympathy—what our neighbors to the South call that attitude of "simpatico"—no less than enlightened self-interest will be our guide.

I can see this Atlantic civilization galvanizing and guiding emergent nations everywhere.

I know this freedom is not the fruit of every soil. I know that our own freedom was achieved through centuries, by unremitting efforts by brave and wise men. I know that the road to freedom is a long and a challenging road. I know also that some men may walk away from it, that some men resist challenge, accepting the false security of governmental paternalism.

And I pledge that the America I envision in the years ahead will extend its hand in health, in teaching and in cultivation, so that all new nations will be at least encouraged to go our way, so that they will not wander down the dark alleys of tyranny or to the dead-end streets of collectivism. My fellow Republicans, we do no man a service by hiding freedom's light under a bushel of mistaken humility.

I seek an America proud of its past, proud of its ways, proud of its dreams, and determined actively to proclaim them. But our example to the world must, like charity, begin at home.

In our vision of a good and decent future, free and peaceful, there must be room for deliberation of the energy and talent of the individual—otherwise our vision is blind at the outset.

We must assure a society here which, while never abandoning the needy or forsaking the helpless, nurtures incentives and opportunity for the creative and the productive. We must know the whole good is the product of many single contributions.

I cherish a day when our children once again will restore as heroes the sort of men and women who—unafraid and undaunted—pursue the truth, strive to cure disease, subdue and make fruitful our natural environment and produce the inventive engines of production, science, and technology.

This Nation, whose creative people have enhanced this entire span of history, should again thrive upon the greatness of all those things which we, as individual citizens, can and should do. During Republican years, this again will be a nation of men and women, of families proud of their role, jealous of their responsibilities, unlimited in their aspirations—a Nation where all who can will be self-reliant.

We Republicans see in our constitutional form of government the great framework which assures the orderly but dynamic fulfillment of the whole man, and we see the whole man as the great reason for instituting orderly government in the first place.

We see, in private property and in economy based upon and fostering private property, the one way to make government a durable ally of the whole man, rather than his determined enemy. We see in the sanctity of private property the only durable foundation for constitutional government in a free society. And beyond that, we see, in cherished diversity of ways, diversity of thoughts, of motives and accomplishments. We do not seek to lead anyone's life for him—we seek only to secure his rights and to guarantee him opportunity to strive, with government performing only those needed and constitutionally sanctioned tasks which cannot otherwise be performed.

We Republicans seek a government that attends to its inherent responsibilities of maintaining a stable monetary and fiscal climate, encouraging a free and a competitive economy and enforcing law and order. Thus do we seek inventiveness, diversity, and creativity within a stable order, for we Republicans define government's role where needed at many, many levels, preferably through the one closest to the people involved.

Our towns and our cities, then our counties, then our states, then our regional contacts—and only then, the national government. That, let me remind you, is the ladder of liberty, built by decentralized power. On it also we must have balance between the branches of government at every level.

Balance, diversity, creativity—these are the elements of Republican equation. Republicans agree, Republicans agree heartily to disagree on many, many of their applications, but we have never disagreed on the basic fundamental issues of why you and I are Republicans.

This is a party, this Republican Party, a Party for free men, not for blind followers, and not for conformists.

Back in 1858 Abraham Lincoln said this of the Republican party—and I quote him, because he probably could have said it during the last week or so: "It was composed of strained, discordant, and even hostile elements" in 1858. Yet all of these elements agreed on one paramount objective: To arrest the progress of slavery, and place it in the course of ultimate extinction.

Today, as then, but more urgently and more broadly than then, the task of preserving and enlarging freedom at home and safeguarding it from the forces of tyranny abroad is great enough to challenge all our resources and to require all our strength. Anyone who joins us in all sincerity, we welcome. Those who do not care for our cause, we don't expect to enter our ranks in any case. And let our Republicanism, so focused and so dedicated, not be made fuzzy and futile by unthinking and stupid labels.

I would remind you that extremism in the defense of liberty is no vice. And let me remind you also that moderation in the pursuit of justice is no virtue.

The beauty of the very system we Republicans are pledged to restore and revitalize, the beauty of this Federal system of ours is in its reconciliation of diversity with unity. We must not see malice in honest differences of opinion, and no matter how great, so long as they are not inconsistent with the pledges we have given to each other in and through our Constitution. Our Republican cause is not to level out the world or make its people conform in computer regimented sameness. Our Republican cause is to free our people and light the way for liberty throughout the world.

Ours is a very human cause for very humane goals.

This Party, its good people, and its unquestionable devotion to freedom, will not fulfill the purposes of this campaign which we launch here now until our cause has won the day, inspired the world, and shown the way to a tomorrow worthy of all our yesteryears.

I repeat, I accept your nomination with humbleness, with pride, and you and I are going to fight for the goodness of our land. Thank you.

SOURCE: The Arizona Historical Foundation.

PRIMARY SOURCE DOCUMENT

Nobel Prize Acceptance Speech, Martin Luther King Jr.

INTRODUCTION After the Civil War, Jim Crow laws and organized violence disenfranchised African Americans in the South and relegated them to the fringes of white society. The modern movement for civil rights began when A. Philip Randolph created a model for organizational action with his threatened "March on Washington" in 1941, forcing President Franklin D. Roosevelt to create the Fair Employment Practice Committee, the first federal response to racial discrimination since the Reconstruction era of 1865 to 1877. The *Brown* v. *Board of Education* decision of 1954 ended legal segregation and compelled American society to address its racial inequalities. Although racism existed throughout America, forcing the South to change would require great effort and even greater sacrifice.

Dr. Martin Luther King Jr. (1929–1968) was one of the driving forces behind the heroic campaign waged for and by African Americans for civil rights long denied them. The civil rights movement largely succeeded because King provided important leadership. Under the call of nonviolence he inspired thousands of African Americans, as well as innumerable white Americans, to risk their lives and jail time by standing up to the rigid caste system of the South. In a series of dramatic protests—punctuated by brutal violence such as the murder of four girls in a Birmingham, Alabama, church bombing and the execution of three young civil rights workers in Mississippi—African Americans boycotted bus lines and businesses; marched peaceably with nearby police brandishing batons, water cannons, and biting dogs; and assembled in Washington, D.C., in August 1963 with a show of force that no presidential administration could ignore. On August 28, 1963, more than 200,000 black and white Americans took part in the March on Washington for Jobs and Freedom, which culminated with King's famous "I Have a Dream" speech from the base of the Lincoln Memorial.

King's dream, and those of millions of African Americans, was partially realized the following year when Congress enacted the Civil Rights Act of 1964, which prohibited discrimination on the basis of race in restaurants and hotels as well as in the workplace. The Voting Rights Act of 1965 outlawed all literacy tests and other measures designed to prevent African Americans from voting. With King's help, voting drives throughout the South swelled the ranks of black voters eager to finally exercise their constitutional rights.

King's approach to social change derived from Gandhi's notion of nonviolent direct confrontation. For adopting and maintaining this strategy of peaceful resistance in the face of police harassment, imprisonment, and verbal abuse, King was awarded the Nobel Peace Prize in 1964. His acceptance speech, delivered in Oslo, Norway in December 1964, is reproduced here. It illustrates King's ideas of nonviolent political action, his views on race in America after a decade-long struggle to secure basic human rights for African Americans and dignity for America herself, and his perspective on race's important role in all international conflict.

The Quest for Peace and Justice

It is impossible to begin this lecture without again expressing my deep appreciation to the Nobel Committee of the Norwegian Parliament for bestowing upon me and the civil rights movement in the United States such a great honor.... I experience this high and joyous moment not for myself alone but for those devotees of nonviolence who have moved so courageously against the ramparts of racial injustice and who in the process have acquired a new estimate of their own human worth. Many of them are young and cultured. Others are middle aged and middle class. The majority are poor and untutored. But they are all united in the quiet conviction that it is better to suffer in dignity than to accept segregation in humiliation. These are the real heroes of the freedom struggle: they are the noble people for whom I accept the Nobel Peace Prize.

This evening I would like to use this lofty and historic platform to discuss what appears to me to be the most pressing problem confronting mankind today. Modern man has brought this whole world to an awe-inspiring threshold of the future. He has reached new and astonishing peaks of scientific success. He has produced machines that think and instruments that peer into the unfathomable ranges of interstellar space....

Yet, in spite of these spectacular strides in science and technology, and still unlimited ones to come, something basic is missing. There is a sort of poverty of the spirit which stands in glaring contrast to our scientific and technological abundance. The richer we have become materially, the poorer we have become morally and spiritually. We have learned to fly the air like birds and swim the sea like fish, but we have not learned the simple art of living together as brothers....

If we are to survive today, our moral and spiritual "lag" must be eliminated. Enlarged material powers spell enlarged peril if there is not proportionate growth of the soul.

....The struggle to eliminate the evil of racial injustice constitutes one of the major struggles of our time. The present upsurge of the Negro people of the United States grows out of a deep and passionate determination to make freedom and equality a reality "here" and "now". In one sense the civil rights movement in the United States is a special American phenomenon which must be understood in the light of American history and dealt with in terms of the American situation. But on another and more important level, what is happening in the United States today is a relatively small part of a world development.

....The deep rumbling of discontent that we hear today is the thunder of disinherited masses, rising from dungeons of oppression to the bright hills of freedom, in one majestic chorus the rising masses singing, in the words of our freedom song, "Ain't gonna let nobody turn us around." All over the world, like a fever, the freedom movement is spreading in the widest liberation in history. The great masses of people are determined to end the exploitation of their races and land. They are awake and moving toward their goal like a tidal wave. You can hear them rumbling in every village street, on the docks, in the houses, among the students, in the churches, and at political meetings....

These developments should not surprise any student of history. Oppressed people cannot remain oppressed forever. The yearning for freedom eventually manifests itself. The Bible tells the thrilling story of how Moses stood in Pharaoh's court centuries ago and cried, "Let my people go." This is a kind of opening chapter in a continuing story. The present struggle in the United States is a later chapter in the same unfolding story. Something within has reminded the Negro of his birthright of freedom, and something without has reminded him that it can be gained. Consciously or unconsciously, he has been caught up by the *Zeitgeist*, and with his black brothers of Africa and his brown and yellow brothers in Asia, South America, and the Caribbean, the United States Negro is moving with a sense of great urgency toward the promised land of racial justice.

Fortunately, some significant strides have been made in the struggle to end the long night of racial injustice. We have seen the magnificent drama of independence unfold in Asia and Africa. Just thirty years ago there were only three independent nations in the whole of Africa. But today thirty-five African nations have risen from colonial bondage. In the United States we have witnessed the gradual demise of the system of racial segregation. The Supreme Court's decision of 1954 outlawing segregation in the public schools gave a legal and constitutional deathblow to the whole doctrine of separate but equal....Then came that glowing day a few months ago when a strong Civil Rights Bill became the law of our land. This bill, which was first recommended and promoted by President Kennedy, was passed because of the overwhelming support and perseverance of millions of Americans, Negro and white. It came as a bright interlude in the long and sometimes turbulent struggle for civil rights: the beginning of a second emancipation proclamation providing a comprehensive legal basis for equality of opportunity....

Another indication that progress is being made was found in the recent presidential election in the United States. The American people revealed great maturity by overwhelmingly rejecting a presidential candidate who had become identified with extremism, racism, and retrogression [reference is to Barry Goldwater]....

Let me not leave you with a false impression. The problem is far from solved. We still have a long, long way to go before the dream of freedom is a reality for the Negro in the United States....But with patient and firm determination we will press on until every valley of despair is exalted to new peaks of hope, until every mountain of pride and irrationality is made low by the leveling process of humility and compassion....

The word that symbolizes the spirit and the outward form of our encounter is *nonviolence*, and it is doubtless that factor which made it seem appropriate to award a peace prize to one identified with struggle. Broadly speaking, nonviolence in the civil rights struggle has meant not relying on arms and weapons of struggle. It has meant noncooperation with customs and laws which are institutional aspects of a regime of discrimination and enslavement. It has meant direct participation of masses in protest, rather than reliance on indirect methods which frequently do not involve masses in action at all....

In a real sense nonviolence seeks to redeem the spiritual and moral lag that I spoke of earlier as the chief dilemma of modern man. It seeks to secure moral ends through moral means. Nonviolence is a powerful and just weapon. Indeed, it is a weapon unique in history, which cuts without wounding and ennobles the man who wields it.

I believe in this method because I think it is the only way to reestablish a broken community. It is the method which seeks to implement the just law by appealing to the conscience of the great decent majority who through blindness, fear, pride, and irrationality have allowed their consciences to sleep....

This approach to the problem of racial injustice is not at all without successful precedent. It was used in a magnificent way by Mohandas K. Gandhi to challenge the might of the British Empire and free his people from the political domination and economic exploitation inflicted upon them for centuries. He struggled only with the weapons of truth, soul force, non-injury, and courage.

In the past ten years unarmed gallant men and women of the United States have given living testimony to the moral power and efficacy of nonviolence. By the thousands, faceless, anonymous, relentless young people, black and white, have temporarily left the ivory towers of learning for the barricades of bias. Their courageous and disciplined activities have come as a refreshing oasis in a desert sweltering with the heat of injustice. They have taken our whole nation back to those great wells of democracy which were dug deep by the founding fathers in the formulation of the Constitution and the Declaration of Independence. One day all of America will be proud of their achievements.

I am only too well aware of the human weaknesses and failures which exist, the doubts about the efficacy of nonviolence, and the open advocacy of violence by some. But I am still convinced that nonviolence is both the most practically sound and morally excellent way to grapple with the age-old problem of racial injustice.

A second evil which plagues the modern world is that of poverty. Like a monstrous octopus, it projects its nagging, prehensile tentacles in lands and villages all over the world. Almost two-thirds of the peoples of the world go to bed hungry at night. They are undernourished, ill-housed, and shabbily clad. Many of them have no houses or beds to sleep in. Their only beds are the sidewalks of the cities and the dusty roads of the villages. Most of these poverty-stricken children of God have never seen a physician or a dentist. This problem of poverty is not only seen in the class division between the highly developed industrial nations and the so-called underdeveloped nations; it is seen in the great economic gaps within the rich nations themselves. Take my own country for example. We have developed the greatest system of production that history has ever known. We have become the richest nation in the world. Our national gross product this year will reach the astounding figure of almost 650 billion dollars. Yet, at least one-fifth of our fellow citizens—some ten million families, comprising about forty million individuals—are bound to a miserable culture of poverty. In a sense the poverty of the poor in America is more frustrating than the poverty of Africa and Asia. The misery of the poor in Africa and Asia is shared misery, a fact of life for the vast majority; they are all poor together as a result of years of exploitation and underdevelopment. In sad contrast, the poor in America know that they live in the richest nation in the world, and that even though they are perishing on a lonely island of poverty they are surrounded by a vast ocean of material prosperity. Glistening towers of glass and steel easily seen from their slum dwellings spring up almost overnight. Jet liners speed over their ghettoes at 600 miles an hour; satellites streak through outer space and reveal details of the moon. President Johnson, in his State of the Union Message, emphasized this contradiction when he heralded the United States' "highest standard of living in the world", and deplored that it was accompanied by "dislocation; loss of jobs, and the specter of poverty in the midst of plenty".

So it is obvious that if man is to redeem his spiritual and moral "lag", he must go all out to bridge the social and economic gulf between the "haves" and the "have nots" of the world. Poverty is one of the most urgent items on the agenda of modern life.

There is nothing new about poverty. What is new, however, is that we have the resources to get rid of it....

A third great evil confronting our world is that of war. Recent events have vividly reminded us that nations are not reducing but rather increasing their arsenals of weapons of mass destruction. The best brains in the highly developed nations of the world are devoted to military technology....

So man's proneness to engage in war is still a fact....A world war—God forbid!—will leave only smoldering ashes as a mute testimony of a human race whose folly led inexorably to ultimate death. So if modern man continues to flirt unhesitatingly with war, he will transform his earthly habitat into an inferno such as even the mind of Dante could not imagine.

Therefore, I venture to suggest to all of you and all who hear and may eventually read these words, that the philosophy and strategy of nonviolence become immediately a subject for study and for serious experimentation in every field of human conflict, by no means excluding the relations between nations. It is, after all, nation-states which make war, which have produced the weapons which threaten the survival of mankind, and which are both genocidal and suicidal in character.

Here also we have ancient habits to deal with, vast structures of power, indescribably complicated problems to solve. But unless we abdicate our humanity altogether and succumb to fear and impotence in the presence of the weapons we have ourselves created, it is as imperative and urgent to put an end to war and violence between nations as it is to put an end to racial injustice. Equality with whites will hardly solve the problems of either whites or Negroes if it means equality in a society under the spell of terror and a world doomed to extinction.

I do not wish to minimize the complexity of the problems that need to be faced in achieving disarmament and peace. But I think it is a fact that we shall not have the will, the courage, and the insight to deal with such matters unless in this field we are prepared to undergo a mental and spiritual reevaluation—a change of focus which will enable us to see that the things which seem most real and powerful are indeed now unreal and have come under the sentence of death....

We will not build a peaceful world by following a negative path. It is not enough to say "We must not wage war." It is necessary to love peace and sacrifice for it....

So we must fix our vision not merely on the negative expulsion of war, but upon the positive affirmation of peace. We must see that peace represents a sweeter music, a cosmic melody that is far superior to the discords of war. Somehow we must transform the dynamics of the world power struggle from the negative nuclear arms race which no one can win to a positive contest to harness man's creative genius for the purpose of making peace and prosperity a reality for all of the nations of the world. In short, we must shift the arms race into a "peace race". If we have the will and determination to mount such a peace offensive, we will unlock hitherto tightly sealed doors of hope and transform our imminent cosmic elegy into a psalm of creative fulfillment.

All that I have said boils down to the point of affirming that mankind's survival is dependent upon man's ability to solve the problems of racial injustice, poverty, and war; the solution of these problems is in turn dependent upon man squaring his moral progress with his scientific progress, and learning the practical art of living in harmony....We have inherited a big house, a great "world house" in which we have to live together—black and white, Easterners and Westerners, Gentiles and Jews, Catholics and Protestants, Moslem and Hindu, a family unduly separated in ideas, culture, and interests who, because we can never again live without each other, must learn, somehow, in this one big world, to live with each other.

This means that more and more our loyalties must become ecumenical rather than sectional. We must now give an overriding loyalty to mankind as a whole in order to preserve the best in our individual societies....

Let us hope that this spirit will become the order of the day. As Arnold Toynbee says: "Love is the ultimate force that makes for the saving choice of life and good against the damning choice of death and evil. Therefore the first hope in our inventory must be the hope that love is going to have the last word."...History is cluttered with the wreckage of nations and individuals that pursued this self-defeating path of hate. Love is the key to the solution of the problems of the world.

Let me close by saying that I have the personal faith that mankind will somehow rise up to the occasion and give new directions to an age drifting rapidly to its doom. In spite of the tensions and uncertainties of this period something profoundly meaningful is taking place. Old systems of exploitation and oppression are passing away, and out of the womb of a frail world new systems of justice and equality are being born. Doors of opportunity are gradually being opened to those at the bottom of society. The shirtless and barefoot people of the land are developing a new sense of "some-bodiness" and carving a tunnel of hope through the dark mountain of despair. "The people who sat in darkness have seen a great light." Here and there an individual or group dares to love, and rises to the majestic heights of moral maturity. So in a real sense this is a great time to be alive. Therefore, I am not yet discouraged about the future. Granted that the easygoing optimism of yesterday is impossible. Granted that those who pioneer in the struggle for peace and freedom will still face uncomfortable jail terms, painful threats of death; they will still be battered by the storms of persecution, leading them to the nagging feeling that they can no longer bear such a heavy burden, and the temptation of wanting to retreat to a more quiet and serene life. Granted that we face a world crisis which leaves us standing so often amid the surging murmur of life's restless sea. But every crisis has both its dangers and its opportunities. It can spell either salvation or doom. In a dark confused world the kingdom of God may yet reign in the hearts of men.

SOURCE: "Nobel Prize Acceptance Speech (1964)" by Martin Luther King Jr.

Dr. Martin Luther King Jr. (right of center) leads a fifty-mile march from Selma to Montgomery, Alabama, to promote civil rights. Others in photo: Coretta Scott King (holding hands with her husband), Dr. Ralph Bunche (next to King), and John Lewis (front row, white jacket) of the Student Non-Violent Coordinating Committee. **AP/WIDE WORLD PHOTOS**

1965

INTERNATIONAL

VIETNAM WAR U.S. air strikes are ordered over North Vietnam (February 8); first combat troops land in South Vietnam, two Marine battalions to defend Danang air base (March 8); additional 50,000 troops are sent, brings total to 125,000; holiday truce begins (December 24).

About 14,000 troops are sent to Dominican Republic during civil war.

NATIONAL

Dr. Martin Luther King Jr. is awarded Nobel Peace Prize.

Police and sheriff's deputies turn back civil rights marchers from Selma, Alabama, as they start for Montgomery (March 7); with an Alabama National Guard escort, the 54-mile march to Montgomery is made two weeks later; Rev. James Reeb, Unitarian clergyman, dies in Selma from beating received while working for civil rights.

Six days of rioting begins (August 11) in Watts section of Los Angeles; results in 34 deaths, 1,000 + injuries, $175 million in fire damage.

Department of Housing and Urban Development is created (September 9); Robert C. Weaver is named Secretary, becomes first African-American cabinet member; Economic Development Administration is established (September 1); Environmental Science Services Administration is created, takes in Coast and Geodetic Survey and Weather Bureau; Equal Employment Opportunity Commission is founded.

Supreme Court rules in *Griswold* v. *Connecticut* that a state cannot prohibit use of contraceptives.

National origins quota system of immigration is abolished (October 3), in effect since 1921.

Arthur J. Goldberg resigns from Supreme Court to become U.N. ambassador; Abe Fortas succeeds him.

A 13½-hour power failure blacks out northeastern U.S. and southeastern Canada (November 9); New York City is hardest hit.

DEATHS Malcolm X, black nationalist, is fatally shot in New York City; Adlai E. Stevenson, Democratic presidential candidate, U.N. ambassador; Bernard M. Baruch, financier; former Vice President Henry A. Wallace.

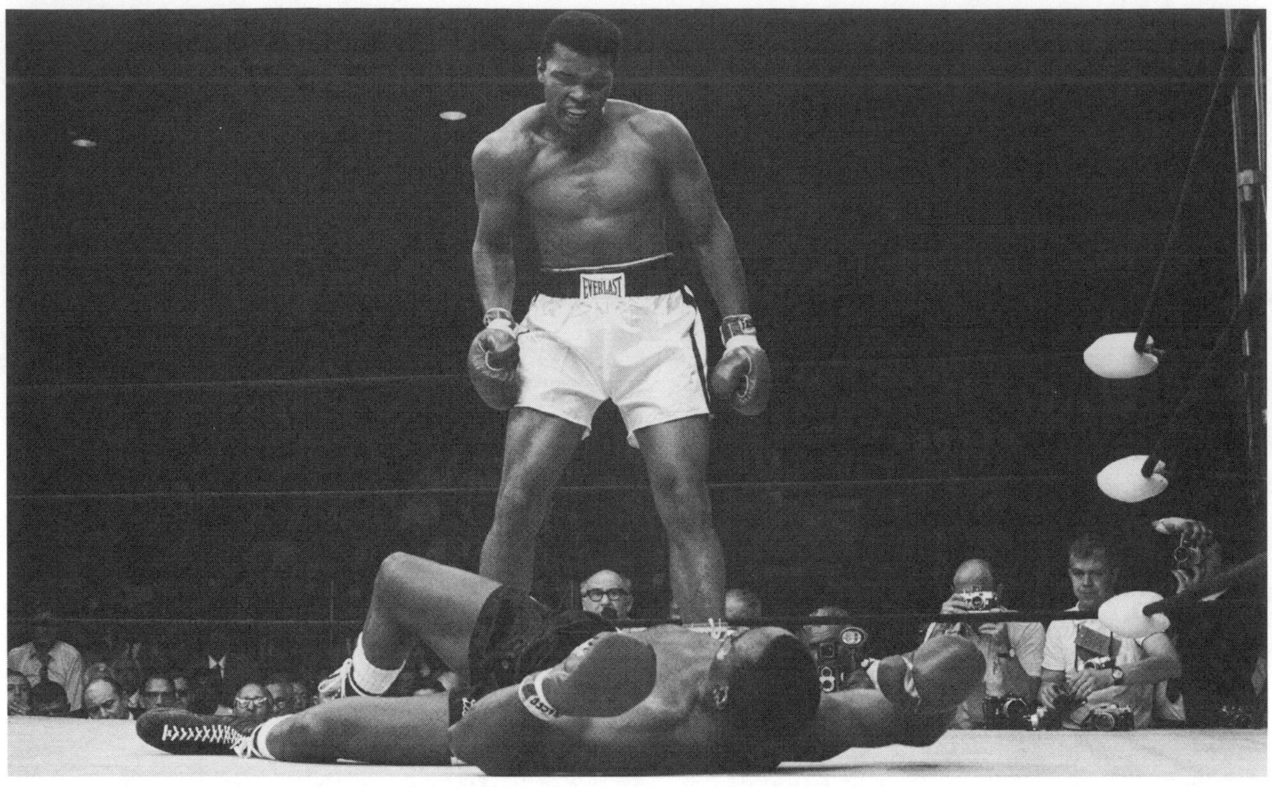

Cassius Clay stands over a fallen Sonny Liston. The newly crowned heavyweight champion of the world soon announces his conversion to Islam and his new name, Muhammad Ali. His draft resistance galvanizes opposition to the Vietnam War and inspires supporters of Black Power during the 1960s. CORBIS-BETTMANN

BUSINESS/INDUSTRY/INVENTIONS

Housing Act providing $7.5 billion for housing and rent subsidies is signed.

DEATHS Colby M. Chester, first president, General Foods (1929–1935); Oscar G. Mayer, meat packer; Allen B. Du Mont, television pioneer; Helena Rubinstein, cosmetics maker; Joshua L. Cowan, inventor of toy electric train.

TRANSPORTATION

Ralph Nader publishes *Unsafe at Any Speed,* a book that shakes automobile industry.

SCIENCE/MEDICINE

Richard P. Feynman and Julius S. Schwinger share Nobel Prize in physics for study of subatomic particles; Robert B. Woodward is awarded chemistry prize for synthesis of complex organic compounds.

James A. McDivitt and Edward H. White II fly 62 orbits in space (June 3), during which White becomes first U.S. astronaut to walk in space.

First commercial satellite, *Early Bird I,* is launched; first space rendezvous is completed (December 15) when astronauts Walter M. Schirra Jr. and Thomas P. Stafford join their spaceship with that of Frank Borman and James A. Lovell Jr.

EDUCATION

Elementary and Secondary Education Act passes, provides large-scale direct federal aid to schools.

RELIGION

Pope Pius VI delivers peace message to U.N. while on visit to U.S.

Catholic Archbishop John P. Cody of New Orleans moves to Chicago; Archbishop Laurence J. Shehan is elevated to cardinal.

DEATH Father Divine (George Baker), founder of Peace Mission.

ART/MUSIC

Leslie Bassett composes *Variations for Orchestra;* Walter Piston composes the Eighth Symphony.

Georgia O'Keeffe completes the painting *Sky above Clouds IV;* James A. Rosenquist, the 51 panels of *F-111;* Robert Motherwell, *Africa;* Alexander Calder, the sculpture *Ticket Window.*

SONGS (POPULAR): "Downtown," "The Game of Love," "I Got You, Babe," "King of the Road," "My Girl," "Over and Over," "The Shadow of Your Smile," "What the World Needs Now," "You've Lost That Lovin' Feelin'," "Back in My Arms Again."

DEATHS Nat "King" Cole, popular singer; Spike Jones, orchestra leader; Paul Manship, sculptor (Prometheus Fountain, Rockefeller Center); Edgard Varèse, conductor and composer.

LITERATURE/JOURNALISM

BOOKS *In Cold Blood* by Truman Capote, *Hotel* by Arthur Hailey, *An American Dream* by Norman Mailer, *A Thousand Days* by Arthur M. Schlesinger Jr.

DEATHS Wilfred J. Funk of Funk & Wagnalls, publishers; Edward R. Murrow, radio and television newsman; Marshall Field IV, editor and publisher; H. V. Kaltenborn, radio news reporter; Shirley Jackson, author; Randall Jarrell, poet.

ENTERTAINMENT

PLAYS Richard Kiley stars in *Man of La Mancha,* Henry Fonda in *Generation,* Lauren Bacall in *Cactus Flower,* Art Carney and Walter Matthau in *The Odd Couple.*

MOVIES *Who's Afraid of Virginia Woolf?* with Richard Burton and Elizabeth Taylor, *The Sound of Music* with Julie Andrews, *Cat Ballou* with Lee Marvin, *Dr. Zhivago* with Omar Sharif, *The Great Race* with Jack Lemmon.

New television shows include *I Spy* with Robert Culp and Bill Cosby, *Green Acres* with Eva Gabor and Eddie Albert, *The FBI* with Efrem Zimbalist Jr., *I Dream of Jeannie* with Barbara Eden and Larry Hagman.

DEATHS Francis X. Bushman, silent-screen actor; David O. Selznick, movie producer; Stan Laurel of Laurel and Hardy comedy team; Clara Bow, 1920s screen actress.

SPORTS

William D. Eckert is named baseball commissioner; Joe Cronin is named president of American League.

Houston Astrodome opens (April 9).

Ernie Banks of Chicago Cubs hits 400th career home run; Willie Mays, San Francisco Giants, his 500th.

Atlanta is awarded National Football League franchise; Miami in American Football League.

Randy Matson is first to throw shot more than 70 feet (70 ft., 7¼ in.).

WINNERS *Auto racing*—Jim Clark, Indianapolis 500; Ned Jarrett, NASCAR; *Baseball*—Los Angeles Dodgers, World Series; *Basketball*—St. Johns, NIT; UCLA, NCAA; Boston, NBA; *Bowling*—Dave Davis, PBA national; *Boxing*—Muhammad Ali, heavyweight; Jose Torres, light heavyweight; Dick Tiger, middleweight; Carlos Ortiz, lightweight; *Figure skating*—Gary Viscount, U.S. men's singles; Peggy Fleming, U.S. women's singles; *Football* (bowls)—Michigan, Rose; Texas, Orange; Louisiana State, Sugar; Arkansas, Cotton; Green Bay, NFL; Buffalo, AFL; *Golf*—U.S., Ryder Cup; Gary Player, U.S. Open; Dave Marr, PGA; Jack Nicklaus, Masters; Carol Mann, U.S. Women's Open; Sandra Haynie, LPGA; *Harness racing*—Egyptian Candor, Hambletonian; *Hockey*—Montreal, Stanley Cup; *Horse racing*—Lucky Debonair, Kentucky Derby; Tom Rolfe, Preakness Stakes; Hail to All, Belmont Stakes; *Tennis*—Manuel Santana, U.S. Open (men); Margaret Smith, U.S. Open (women).

DEATHS Curly (Earl) Lambeau, player, founder, and coach, Green Bay Packers; Jack Mara, New York Giants football team president; Branch Rickey, baseball executive.

MISCELLANEOUS

Hurricane Betsy hits Florida and Louisiana, kills 80 and causes $1.4 billion in damage; 37 tornadoes strike Midwest on Palm Sunday (April 11), kill 271.

Roy Wilkins becomes executive director of NAACP.

Missile silo explodes at Searcy, Arkansas, kills 53.

The miniskirt is introduced into the world of high fashion by Paris designer André Courrèges.

1966

INTERNATIONAL

VIETNAM WAR U.S. resumes bombing of North Vietnam after China rejects peace overtures (January 30); U.S. planes bomb Hanoi area (June 29). Seven-nation Manila Conference pledges to continue efforts in Vietnam until aggression ends (October 25).

President Lyndon Johnson, visiting in Mexico, reaffirms support of the Alliance for Progress.

NATIONAL

Supreme Court in *Miranda* v. *Arizona* rules that suspects in police custody must be informed of their right to remain silent and have right of counsel; also upholds Voting Rights Act of 1965.

The creation of the miniskirt raises eyebrows along with hemlines. American retailers carried miniskirts in 1966. **ARCHIVE PHOTOS/EXPRESS NEWSPAPERS**

Uniform Time Act calls for nationwide daylight saving time; lasts one year, then becomes local option.

Postal Savings Bank System ends after 55 years.

American Revolution Bicentennial Commission is created.

More than 10,000 anti-Vietnam War protestors demonstrate in front of the White House.

Betty Friedan establishes National Organization for Women (NOW).

Andrew F. Brimmer becomes first African-American member of Federal Reserve Board; Edward W. Brooke is elected to U.S. Senate from Massachusetts, the first popularly elected African-American senator.

National Historic Preservation Act goes into effect.

Ronald Reagan is elected governor of California.

Guadalupe Mountains (Texas) National Park is established.

DEATHS Chester W. Nimitz, World War II admiral; Rev. Henry F. Ward, chairman, American Civil Liberties Union (1920–1940); Margaret Sanger, pioneer advocate of birth control.

SEE PRIMARY DOCUMENTS The Black Panther Platform: "What We Want, What We Believe" and National Organization for Women's Statement of Purpose, Adopted at the Organizing Conference in Washington, D.C.

BUSINESS/INDUSTRY/INVENTIONS

Truth in Packaging Law passes, requires clear, accurate statement of ingredients, amounts.

Minimum wage is raised to $1.40 an hour, to be effective February 1, 1967; to $1.60 an hour on February 1, 1968.

RCA uses integrated circuits in television sets.

DEATHS Bernard F. Gimbel, retail merchant; S. S. Kresge, head of five-and-ten-cent-store chain (1907–1966); Elizabeth Arden, founder and owner, cosmetics firm.

TRANSPORTATION

Department of Transportation is established (October 15).

New York City undergoes first subway strike; lasts 12 days.

Interstate Commerce Commission approves merger of Pennsylvania and New York Central railroads.

National Traffic and Motor Vehicle Safety Act passes.

Columbia River Bridge at Astoria, Oregon, opens.

Nation has registered 78 million passenger cars and 16 million trucks and buses.

SCIENCE/MEDICINE

Medicare program to assist elderly goes into effect (July 1).

Robert S. Mulliken is awarded Nobel Prize in chemistry for work on the chemical bond and electronic structure of molecules; Charles B. Huggins and Peyton Rous share physiology/medicine prize, Rous for discovering a cancer virus, Huggins for developing methods of treating cancer.

Surveyor I becomes first U.S. satellite to make soft landing on the moon (June 2).

EDUCATION

Harold Howe II becomes U.S. Education commissioner.

RELIGION

Merger of Methodist and Evangelical United Brethren churches is ratified (November 11), forms largest American Protestant church, the 10,750,000 member United Methodist Church.

National Conference of Catholic Bishops is established, issues rule that Catholics must abstain from eating meat only on Ash Wednesday and Fridays in Lent.

ART/MUSIC

Old Metropolitan Opera House (New York City) gives final performance (April 16); company opens new home in Lincoln Center (September 16) with Samuel Barber's opera *Antony and Cleopatra.*

Barnett Newman completes the painting *Stations of the Cross;* Isamu Noguchi completes the sculpture *Euripides.*

SONGS (POPULAR): "Alfie," "Born Free," "The Impossible Dream," "Lara's Theme," "My Love," "Strangers in the Night," "When a Man Loves a Woman," "Georgy Girl," "If I Were a Carpenter."

DEATHS Hans Hofmann, painter who introduced European styles to U.S.; Malvina Hoffman, sculptor; Deems Taylor, music critic and composer.

LITERATURE/JOURNALISM

BOOKS *The Fixer* by Bernard Malamud, *Giles Goat-Boy* by John S. Barth, *Valley of the Dolls* by Jacqueline Susann, *The Arrangement* by Elia Kazan, *Taipan* by James D. Clavell, *Division Street America* by Studs Terkel.

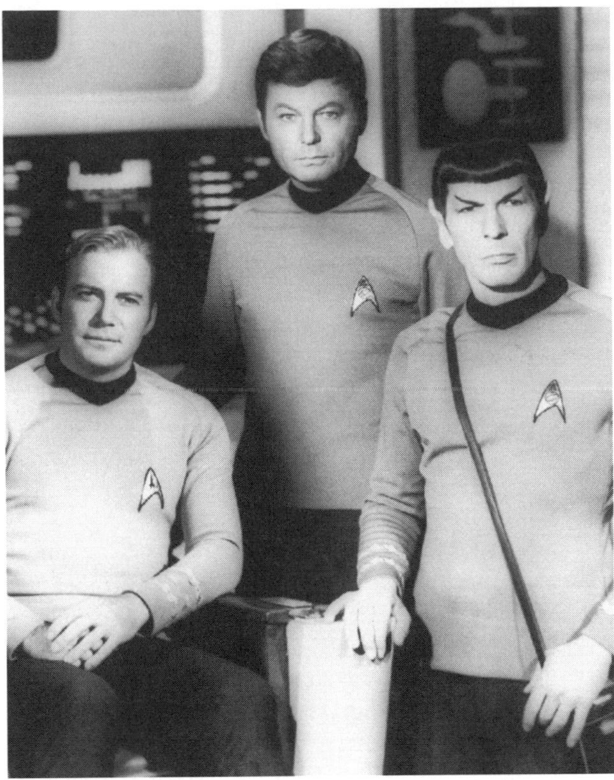

Left to right, William Shatner, DeForest Kelly, and Leonard Nimoy in the television series *Star Trek,* new in 1966. **AP/WIDE WORLD PHOTOS**

ENTERTAINMENT

PLAYS Joel Grey stars in *Cabaret,* Jessica Tandy in *A Delicate Balance,* Gwen Verdon in Neil Simon's *Sweet Charity.*

MOVIES *A Man for All Seasons* with Paul Scofield, *Batman* with Adam West, *The Fortune Cookie* with Walter Matthau, *The Spy Who Came in from the Cold* with Richard Burton.

New television shows include *Mission Impossible, Star Trek* with William Shatner.

DEATHS Russel Crouse, playwright; Sophie Tucker, singer and last of the "red hot mamas"; Hedda Hopper, movie gossip columnist; Billy Rose, producer and composer; Gertrude Berg, radio and television actress; Buster Keaton, silent-screen comedian; Walt Disney, filmmaker and theme-park creator.

SPORTS

American and National Football leagues merge (June 8).

Bill Russell is named player-coach of Boston Celtics, is first African-American coach of a major professional sports team.

Three new stadiums open: Fulton County (Atlanta), California (Anaheim), Busch (St. Louis).

New records are set in track and field: Bob Seagren, indoor pole vault (17 ft., ¼ in.); John Pennel, outdoor pole vault (17 ft., 6¼ in.); Tommie Smith, 220-yard dash (20 sec.); Jim Ryun, mile run (3 min., 51.3 sec.).

WINNERS *Auto racing*—Grahman Hill, Indianapolis 500; David Pearson, NASCAR; *Baseball*—Baltimore Orioles, World Series; *Basketball*—Brigham Young, NIT; Texas Western, NCAA; Boston, NBA; *Bowling*—Wayne Zahn, PBA national; *Boxing*—Muhammad Ali, heavyweight; Emile Griffith, middleweight; Curtis Cokes, welterweight; *Figure skating*—Peggy Fleming, U.S. and world women's title; Scott Allen, U.S. men's; *Football* (bowls)—UCLA, Rose; Alabama, Orange; Missouri, Sugar; Louisiana State, Cotton; *Golf*—Billy Casper, U.S. Open; Al Geiberger, PGA; Jack Nicklaus, Masters; Gloria Ehret, LPGA; Sandra Spuzich, U.S. Women's Open; *Harness racing*—Kerry Way, Hambletonian; *Hockey*—Montreal, Stanley Cup; *Horse racing*—Kaui King, Kentucky Derby and Preakness Stakes; Amberoid, Belmont Stakes; *Tennis*—Fred Stolle, U.S. Open (men); Maria Bueno, U.S. Open (women).

DEATH "Sunny" Jim Fitzsimmons, horse trainer who saddled 2,275 winners.

MISCELLANEOUS

Tornadoes kill 57 in Jackson, Mississippi, 61 others in Alabama and Mississippi.

Huey Newton and Bobby Seale organize Black Panther Party.

Charles Starkweather barricades himself in University of Texas tower, shoots and kills 13, wounds 31 before being killed by law enforcers.

PRIMARY SOURCE DOCUMENT

The Black Panther Platform: "What We Want, What We Believe," October 1966

INTRODUCTION After Congress passed the landmark Civil Rights Act in 1964 and the Voting Rights Act a year later, African Americans had heightened expectations of economic and political progress. However, endemic racism and persistent discrimination in housing and employment as well as police brutality in northern and western cities like Oakland, California, fueled black nationalism. The civil rights movement fractured as a younger generation of activists rejected the integrationist goals and the nonviolent strategy of Dr. Martin Luther King Jr. Stokely Carmichael, an influential exponent of Black Power, left the Student Non-Violent Coordinating Committee in part because the violence civil rights workers faced disturbed him. As he put it in "Black Power," published in *New York Review of Books,* "We cannot be expected any longer to march and have our heads broken in order to say to whites: come on, you're nice guys. For you are not nice guys. We have found you out."

The Black Panther Party for Self-Defense was born in Oakland in October 1966 in response to a matrix of urban problems and fueled by the black nationalism espoused by Carmichael, who later joined the party. In the face of police brutality, founding party officials like Huey P. Newton and Eldridge Cleaver asserted the need to defend their communities with citizens' patrols, forming a paramilitary-style organization that openly carried weapons, which at the time was legal in California. Such public displays captured the attention of the nation and the police, but the Panthers also created a number of community programs that they felt better served the needs of their constituents. Members of the party helped organize food distribution programs and health clinics as well as "liberation schools" that disseminated their particular ideology within the context of the problems with which urban black Americans had to contend.

Considered Marxist-Leninist by many and simply violent thugs by others, including moderate African Americans, the federal government saw the Panthers and their armed assertion of black nationalism as revolutionary and thus dangerous. Crackdowns ensued shortly after the organization began to mobilize and expand in the Midwest and in the East. Newton was imprisoned for killing a policeman, a conviction that was later reversed. Upon his arrest, Newton became a hero for a legion of young African Americans, who donned the Panthers' uniform of a black leather jacket and beret to protest his incarceration. Steady harassment by the FBI and local police forces followed, which included armed assaults and the use of agent provocateurs to incite violence, all of which exacerbated internal divisions and weakened the Panthers' capacity to respond and expand. By 1972 the Black Panthers began to fade from the limelight as a political voice, instead turning their attention to providing social services that emphasized black pride and self-reliance in inner-city communities.

The following document is the platform and program of the Black Panther Party, issued at its founding in October 1966. It reflects the separatist and self-deterministic sentiments of black nationalism.

---

1. We want freedom. We want power to determine the destiny of our Black Community.

We believe that black people will not be free until we are able to determine our destiny.

2. We want full employment for our people.

We believe that the federal government is responsible and obligated to give every man employment or a guaranteed income. We believe that if the white American businessmen will not give full employment, then the means of production should be taken from the businessmen and placed in the community so that the people of the community can organize and employ all of its people and give a high standard of living.

3. We want an end to the robbery by the white man of our Black Community.

We believe that this racist government has robbed us and now we are demanding the overdue debt of forty acres and two mules. Forty acres and two mules was promised 100 years ago as restitution for slave labor and mass murder of black people. We will accept the payment as currency which will be distributed to our many communities. The Germans are now aiding the Jews in Israel for the genocide of the Jewish people. The Germans murdered six million Jews. The American racist has taken part in the slaughter of over twenty million black people; therefore, we feel that this is a modest demand that we make.

4. We want decent housing, fit for shelter of human beings.

We believe that if the white landlords will not give decent housing to our black community, then the housing and the land should be made into cooperatives so that our community, with government aid, can build and make decent housing for its people.

5. We want education for our people that exposes the true nature of this decadent American society. We want education that teaches us our true history and our role in the present-day society.

We believe in an educational system that will give to our people a knowledge of self. If a man does not have knowledge of himself and his position in society and the world, then he has little chance to relate to anything else.

6. We want all black men to be exempt from military service.

We believe that Black people should not be forced to fight in the military service to defend a racist government that does not protect us. We will not fight and kill other people of color in the world who, like black people, are being victimized by the white racist government of America. We will protect ourselves from the force and violence of the racist police and the racist military, by whatever means necessary.

7. We want an immediate end to police brutality and murder of black people.

We believe we can end police brutality in our black community by organizing black self-defense groups that are dedicated to defending our black community from racist police oppression and brutality. The Second Amendment to the Constitution of the United States gives a right to bear arms. We therefore believe that all black people should arm themselves for self defense.

8. We want freedom for all black men held in federal, state, county and city prisons and jails.

We believe that all black people should be released from the many jails and prisons because they have not received a fair and impartial trial.

9. We want all black people when brought to trial to be tried in court by a jury of their peer group or people from their black communities, as defined by the Constitution of the United States.

We believe that the courts should follow the United States Constitution so that black people will receive fair trials. The 14th Amendment of the U.S. Constitution gives a man a right to be tried by his peer group. A peer is a person from a similar economic, social, religious, geographical, environmental, historical and racial background. To do this the court will be forced to select a jury from the black community from which the black defendant came. We have been, and are being tried by all-white juries that have no understanding of the "average reasoning man" of the black community.

10. We want land, bread, housing, education, clothing, justice and peace. And as our major political objective, a United Nations-supervised plebiscite to be held throughout the black colony in which only black colonial subjects will be allowed to participate for the purpose of determining the will of black people as to their national destiny.

When in the course of human events, it becomes necessary for one people to dissolve the political bands which have connected them with another, and to assume, among the powers of the earth, the separate and equal station to which the laws of nature and nature's God entitle them, a decent respect to the opinions of mankind requires that they should declare the causes which impel them to the separation.

We hold these truths to be self evident, that all men are created equal; that they are endowed by their Creator with certain unalienable rights; that among these are life, liberty, and the pursuit of happiness. That, to secure these rights, governments are instituted among men, deriving their just powers from the consent of the governed; that, whenever any form of government becomes destructive of these ends, it is the right of the people to alter or to abolish it, and to institute a new government, laying its foundation on such principles, and organizing its powers in such form, as to them shall seem most likely to effect their safety and happiness. Prudence, indeed, will dictate that governments long established should not be changed for light and transient causes; and accordingly, all experience hath shown, that mankind are more disposed to supper, while evils are sufferable, than to right themselves by abolishing the forms to which they are accustomed. But, when a long train of abuses and usurpations, pursuing invariable the same object, evinces a design to reduce them under absolute despotism, it is their right, it is their duty, to throw off such government, and to provide new guards for their future security.

SOURCE: Black Panther Party 10 Point Program, October 1966. Reproduced by permission.

PRIMARY SOURCE DOCUMENT

National Organization for Women's Statement of Purpose, October 29, 1966

INTRODUCTION The Nineteenth Amendment to the U.S. Constitution, adopted by a slim margin in 1920, gave women the right to vote. Equality was a different matter, however. During the turbulent years of the 1960s, American women again became politicized and organized to secure equal rights and equal opportunity.

During World War II, women worked in traditionally female occupations like office worker and nurse but also in heavy industry as men fought overseas; and for the first time women served, with distinction, in the armed forces in large numbers. But after the war, women's share of all jobs dropped with the return of American soldiers. "Back to the kitchen" became a popular refrain, made by men and women alike. And by 1956, a *Life* magazine cover story was proclaiming, "Of all the accomplishments of the American woman, the one she brings off with the most spectacular success is having babies." This gender culture was influenced by post–World War II suburban prosperity and a conservative and conformist cold war mentality concerned with maintaining the status quo as well as high birth rates.

The birth of the modern feminist movement was driven in part by the 1963 publication of Betty Friedan's *The Feminine Mystique,* which asserted that this postwar gender culture persuaded women that they would find happiness only as mothers and housewives. The book articulated the complaints, insecurities, and hopes of educated women who felt constricted by this false ideal of domestic bliss. Friedan herself was married with three children, a talented writer facing barriers to achieving success outside of the home, which she described as "comfortable concentration camps" in which women were "buried alive," suffering from "a living death" and spiritually "committing a kind of suicide." Friedan's focus was white middle-class educated women, hundreds of whom responded to the book by writing Friedan in support of her conclusions, but her book reached a wide audience and helped inspire women to act politically.

Women were also motivated by the federal government's refusal to enforce Title VII of the 1964 Civil Rights Act, which banned discrimination in the workplace. Millions of women did work in the 1960s and millions of them faced subtle but endemic discrimination as well as sexual harassment. In 1966, Friedan, Kathryn Clarenbach, and other inspired women founded the National Organization of Women (NOW), whose original "Statement of Purpose" is included below. NOW's basic goal was to "bring women into full participation in the mainstream of American society…in truly equal partnership with men." Its original focus was on the workplace, where women did not receive equal pay or equal opportunity. Although a new generation of feminists would focus more on the cultural dimension of sexism than on the political dimension, NOW quickly grew to become the most influential women's organization; its membership rose from 1000 members in 1967 to over 250,000 in 1998.

We, men and women, who hereby constitute ourselves as the National Organization for Women, believe that the time has come for a new movement toward true equality for all women in America, and toward a fully equal partnership of the sexes, as part of the world-wide revolution of human rights now taking place within and beyond our national borders.

The purpose of NOW is to take action to bring women into full participation in the mainstream of American society now, exercising all the privileges and responsibilities thereof in truly equal partnership with men.

We believe the time has come to move beyond the abstract argument, discussion and symposia over the status and special nature of women which has raged in America in recent years; the time has come to confront, with concrete action, the conditions that now prevent women from enjoying the equality of opportunity and freedom of which is their right, as individual Americans, and as human beings.

NOW is dedicated to the proposition that women, first and foremost, are human beings, who, like all other people in our society, must have the chance to develop their fullest human potential. We believe that women can achieve such equality only by accepting to the full the challenges and responsibilities they share with all other people in our society, as part of the decision-making mainstream of American political, economic and social life.

We organize to initiate or support action, nationally, or in any part of this nation, by individuals or organizations, to breakthrough the silken curtain of prejudice and discrimination against women in government, industry, the professions, the churches, the political parties, the judiciary, the labor unions, in education, science, medicine, law, religion and every other field of importance in American society. Enormous changes taking place in our society make it both possible and urgently necessary to advance the unfinished revolution of women toward true equality, now. With a life span lengthened to nearly 75 years it is no longer either necessary or possible for women to devote the greater part of their lives to child-rearing; yet childbearing and rearing which continues to be a most important part of most women's lives—still is used to justify barring women from equal professional and economic participation and advance.

Today's technology has reduced most of the productive chores which women once performed in the home and in mass-production industries based upon routine unskilled labor. This same technology has virtually eliminated the quality of muscular strength as a criterion for filling most jobs, while intensifying American industry's need for creative intelligence. In view of this new industrial revolution created by automation in the mid-twentieth century, women can and must participate in old and new fields of society in full equality—or become permanent outsiders.

Despite all the talk about the status of American women in recent years, the actual position of women in the United States has declined, and is declining, to an alarming degree throughout the 1950's and 60's. Although 46.4% of all American women between the ages of 18 and 65 now work outside the home, the overwhelming majority—75%—are in routine clerical, sales, or factory jobs, or they are household workers, cleaning women, hospital attendants. About two-thirds of Negro women workers are in the lowest paid service occupations. Working women are becoming increasingly…concentrated on the bottom of the job ladder. As a consequence full-time women workers today earn on the average only 60% of what men earn, and that wage gap has been increasing over the past twenty-five years in every major industry group. In 1964, of all women with a yearly income, 89% earned under $5,000 a year; half of all full-time year round women workers earned less than $3,690; only 1.4% of full-time year round women workers had an annual income of $10,000 or more.

Further, with higher education increasingly essential in today's society, too few women are entering and finishing college or going on to graduate or professional school. Today, women earn only one in three of the B.A.'s and M.A.'s granted, and one in ten of the Ph.D.'s.

In all the professions considered of importance to society, and in the executive ranks of industry and government, women are losing ground. Where they are present it is only a token handful. Women comprise less than 1% of federal judges; less than 4% of all lawyers; 7% of doctors. Yet women represent 51% of the U.S. population. And, increasingly men are replacing women in the top positions in secondary and elementary schools, in social work, and in libraries—once thought to be women's fields.

Official pronouncements of the advance in the status of women hide not only the reality of this dangerous decline, but the fact that nothing is being done to stop it. The excellent reports of the President's Commission on the Status of Women and of the State Commissions have not been fully implemented. Such Commissions have power only to advise. They have no power to enforce their recommendations; nor have they the freedom to organize American women and men to press for action on them. The reports of these commissions have, however created a basis upon which it is now possible to build.

Discrimination in employment on the basis of sex is now prohibited by federal law, in Title VII of the Civil Rights Act of 1964. But although nearly one-third of the cases brought before the Equal Employment Opportunity Commission during the first year dealt with sex discrimination and the proportion is increasing dramatically, the Commission has not made clear its intention to enforce the law with the same seriousness on behalf of women as of other victims of discrimination. Many of these cases were Negro women, who are the victims of the double discrimination of race and sex. Until now, too few women's organizations and official spokesmen have been willing to speak out against these dangers facing women. Too many women have been restrained by the fear of being called "feminist."

There is no civil rights movement to speak for women, as there has been for Negroes and other victims of discrimination. The National Organization for Women must therefore begin to speak.

WE BELIEVE that the power of American law, and the protection guaranteed by the U.S. Constitution to the civil rights of all individuals, must be effectively applied and enforced to isolate and remove patterns of sex discrimination, to ensure equality of opportunity in employment and education, and equality of civil and political rights and responsibilities on behalf of women, as well as for Negroes and other deprived groups.

We realize that women's problems are linked to many broader questions of social justice; their solution will require concerted action by many groups. Therefore, convinced that human rights for all are indivisible, we expect to give active support to the common cause of equal rights for all those who suffer discrimination and deprivation, and we call upon other organizations committed to such goals to support our efforts toward equality for women.

WE DO NOT ACCEPT the token appointment of a few women to high-level positions in government and industry as a substitute for a serious continuing effort to recruit and advance women according to their individual abilities. To this end, we urge American government and industry to mobilize the same resources of ingenuity and command with which they have solved problems of far greater difficulty than those now impeding the progress of women.

WE BELIEVE that this nation has a capacity at least as great as other nations, to innovate new social institutions which will enable women to enjoy true equality of opportunity and responsibility in society, without conflict with their responsibilities as mothers and homemakers. In such innovations, America does not lead the Western world, but lags by decades behind many European countries. We do not accept the traditional assumption that a woman has to choose between marriage and motherhood, on the one hand, and serious participation in industry or the professions on the other. We question the present expectation that all normal women will retire from job or profession for 10 or 15 years, to devote their fulltime to raising children, only to reenter the job market at a relatively minor level. This in itself, is a deterrent to the aspirations of women, to their acceptance into management or professional training courses, and to the very possibility of equality of opportunity or real choice, for all but a few women. Above all, we reject the assumption that these problems are the unique responsibility of each individual women, rather

OVERVIEW

Social Movements in Modern America, 1965–2002

ROBERT D. JOHNSTON, YALE UNIVERSITY

Distinctiveness of Social Movements

One of the distinguishing qualities of American history during the last thirty-five years has been the rise of new social movements. During the era of the "New Deal order," from the 1930s to the early 1970s, the relationship between labor and capital and the rise of the welfare state were at the center of American politics and society. Starting in the 1960s, however, a series of insurgencies—peace, feminism, gay and lesbian rights, environmentalism, and multiculturalism—came to the fore and in many ways replaced such economic concerns.

Most of the new social movements can trace their ideological roots to the African-American struggle for freedom. Not only did many feminists and environmentalists participate in the battle for civil rights, they also saw the fight for improved women's status, or against the degradation of the earth, as part of the same general movement for liberation.

The Peace Movement

Arguably, the movement that had the most immediate short-term effect on politics and culture was the peace movement. The roots of the peace movement in American history date back to the nineteenth century. More recently, socialists and Catholic activists who fought against the cold-war political consensus had begun, by the late 1950s, to organize effective protests against the nuclear arms race. By the 1960s these old-time leftists had joined forces with New Left student activists to launch increasingly effective campaigns against the Vietnam War. Historians disagree about whether the peace movement helped shorten the war. There is no doubt, however, that it had a dramatic impact on domestic American society. Even ordinary middle-class Americans who scorned the hippie refrain "make love, not war" recognized the wisdom of the peace movement's objection to the American military commitment to Vietnam. After the war's end, the peace movement regrouped in the 1980s to bring hundreds of thousands of citizens into the streets, on behalf of a freeze of nuclear weapons.

Different Types of Feminism

Women played an increasingly important role in the peace movement, often arguing that they had a "maternal" character inherently opposed to male war-making. Even more significantly, women began to organize on their own behalf as the 1960s drew to a close. Such feminism was frequently viewed with suspicion, indeed with quite a lot of hostility, by other movement activists. African-American men often believed that the struggle for racial equality was paramount and that working toward sexual equality would harm the Civil Rights movement. Likewise, men in the antiwar student movement were often extremely patriarchal in their attempts to limit women's equality.

The result was the flowering of feminism, but not just one kind of feminism. Both "liberal" and "radical" modern feminism were reborn during the late 1960s. Liberals like Betty Friedan and Pauli Murray founded the National Organization for Women (NOW) in 1966, primarily in order to win legal equality for women. NOW had a number of goals, including abortion rights, but their primary objective throughout the 1970s was a constitutional Equal Rights Amendment (ERA).

Radicals, in contrast, challenged liberal feminism's focus on legal equality. Without a full-scale

than a basic social dilemma which society must solve. True equality of opportunity and freedom of choice for women requires such practical, and possible innovations as a nationwide network of child-care center which will make it unnecessary for women to retire completely from society until their children are grown, and national programs to provide retraining for women who have chosen to care for their own children full-time.

WE BELIEVE that it is as essential for every girl to be educated to her full potential of human ability as it is for every boy—with the knowledge that such education is the key to effective participation in today's economy and that, for a girl as for boy, education can only be serious where there is expectation that it be used in society. We believe that American educators are capable of devising means of imparting such expectations to girl students.

assault on patriarchy—the domination of women by men in all realms of life—women would never gain genuine equality. Organizations such as Redstockings therefore centered their attention on the oppressive qualities of the heterosexual family. They argued that "the personal is political," greatly expanding power struggles to decide issues such as who made dinner and who should exercise control in the bedroom.

Gay and Lesbian Rights

Radical feminists paid particular attention to issues of sexual power in a culture that increasingly was undergoing a sexual revolution. A natural extension of their concerns was the rise of a visible movement for gay and lesbian rights. Gay and lesbian subcultures in America dated back to the nineteenth century, but the first organized movements for political equality only developed in the 1950s. In a cautious and small-scale fashion, the Mattachine Society and the Daughters of Bilitis battled police brutality and began to protest the psychiatric stigmatization of same-sex love.

McCarthyism, as well as internal political struggles, put a quick end to these organizations' newfound power. But such "homophile" groups played a crucial role in paving the way for the gay rights movement that evolved after 1969's Stonewall Riot. The Stonewall Inn, a gay bar in New York City's Greenwich Village, was the scene of a riot and revolt after police attempted a standard arrest of its patrons, many of them drag queens. Soon thereafter, lesbians and gays began to "come out of the closet," openly proclaim their sexuality, and argue for full legal and political rights.

During the 1980s the AIDS crisis, which at first primarily affected gay men and intravenous drug users, made organizing gays in America much more difficult. It also exposed some of the political tension between lesbians and gay men. Ultimately, though, AIDS simultaneously radicalized the gay and lesbian movement and helped move the cause into the mainstream. The lack of response on the part of the government and the medical establishment prompted a powerful critique of public health care. At the same time, compelling images of human suffering worldwide led to an awareness of the disease and compassion for its diverse spectrum of victims in some of the most conservative of American communities.

Green Politics

Just as the 1970s witnessed the intensification of sexual politics on all fronts, the decade also saw the full blossoming of an environmental movement. The first Earth Day in 1970 symbolized a renewed consciousness about the fragility of nature. Again, environmentalism had deep roots in American history. During the nineteenth century advocates for wilderness such as John Muir powerfully criticized American economic expansion. The result was the creation of the first national parks. Other activists, known in the early twentieth century as conservationists, fought for the wiser use of natural resources, in particular trees in national forests.

The new environmental movement of the 1970s was in large part the result of postwar affluence. Once the material needs of the masses had been effectively taken care of, many Americans argued that the country should focus on its "quality of life." Tens of thousands of Americans took to national forests to go camping, hiking, boating, and fishing. These ordinary citizens became the rank and file of the environmental movement.

However, this emphasis on mass recreation often conflicted with other kinds of environmentalist politics. Organizations such as Earth First! rejected the very idea of a human-centered nature, even at times advocating the sabotage of logging operations. Nonetheless, environmentalists were able to create an effective American consensus over such issues as recycling and the purity of air and water.

Rainbow Politics

The new social movements had been, since their birth in the late 1960s, primarily the domain of the prosperous white middle class. Increasingly, however,

Moreover, we consider the decline in the proportion of women receiving higher and professional education to be evidence of discrimination. This discrimination may take the form of quotas against the admission of women to colleges, and professional schools; lack of encouragement by parents, counselors and educators; denial of loans or fellowships; or the traditional or arbitrary procedures in graduate and professional training geared in terms of men, which inadvertently discriminate against women. We believe that the same serious attention must be given to high school dropouts who are girls as to boys.

WE REJECT the current assumptions that a man must carry the sole burden of supporting himself, his wife, and family, and that a woman is automatically entitled to lifelong support by a man upon her marriage, or

Social Movements in Modern America, 1965–2002 (continued)

"people of color"—a term itself recently coined—became much more involved. African-American women established their own feminist caucuses, gay Asian Americans mobilized around the devastation of AIDS in their own communities, and Latinos recognized how environmental racism concentrated pollution in poor neighborhoods.

In many ways, struggles over racial identity came to involve the same quest for freedom that had inspired the new social movements. Feminism and gay liberation had led to ever-powerful assertions of "identity politics." Although many on the more traditional union-oriented left viewed identity politics as a form of pseudo-politics, leading to the splintering of the masses, those who embraced it saw identity politics as a powerful form of liberation for previously oppressed groups.

These conflicts came together most intensely in the battles over multiculturalism in the 1990s. Art exhibits, history curricula, Hollywood movies—few parts of American culture were left untouched by arguments over the virtues and defects of multiculturalism.

Conservatism as a New Social Movement

Ironically, the battles over multiculturalism also demonstrated the power of conservatism as a new social movement. Moving at least partially away from its own roots in the defense of wealth and laissez-faire economic liberties, conservatism became a mass movement with powerful moral goals. Christians organized to defend religion in the public arena, and right-wing women mobilized to fight on behalf of traditional domestic roles. Conservatives indeed perfected the use of many of the new forms of mass politics: targeted mailing lists, computers to identify potential constituencies, think tanks, and savvy uses of the media.

The Future

What is the future of social movements? They certainly seem an entrenched part of the political landscape. Environmental legislation does not occur without the input of the Sierra Club, and policy relating to reproductive rights consistently inspires a mass audience organized by feminist groups.

At the same time, some Americans seem to have grown somewhat tired of the culture of "rights" on which so many of the new social movements depend. When women, gays, or Native Americans all demand their rights, such calls seem to some the assertions of special interest groups. On the other hand, those who practice identity politics have increasingly forged alliances with those fighting for economic concerns. During the 1999 "Battle for Seattle," for example, Teamsters and Turtles (unionists and environmentalists) came together in an unexpected antiglobalization alliance. Whether such coalitions remain marginal, or move toward the center of American politics, will be one of the most interesting issues in American life in the new millennium.

BIBLIOGRAPHY

For a study of feminism's roots in the Civil Rights movement, see Sara Evans, *Personal Politics: The Roots of Women's Liberation in the Civil Rights Movement and the New Left* (1976); for background on radical feminism, see Alice Echols, *Daring to Be Bad: Radical Feminism in America, 1967–1975* (1989). The origins of gay politics in the 1950s are imaginatively explored in John D'Emilio, *Sexual Politics: Sexual Communities: The Making of a Homosexual Minority in the United States* (1983). Samuel P. Hays, *Beauty, Health, and Permanence: Environmental Politics in the United States, 1955–1985* (1987), and Kirkpatrick Sale, *The Green Revolution: The American Environmental Movement, 1962–1992* (1993), place the environmental movement in historical context. For a contentious argument about multiculturalism, from one of its principal liberal opponents, see Arthur M. Schlesinger Jr., *The Disuniting of America: Reflections on a Multicultural Society* (1998).

that marriage, home and family are primarily woman's world and responsibility—hers, to dominate—his to support. We believe that a true partnership between the sexes demands a different concept of marriage an equitable sharing of the responsibilities of home and children and of the economic burdens of their support. We believe that proper recognition should be given to the economic and social value of homemaking and child-care. To these ends we will seek to open a reexamination of laws and mores governing marriage and divorce, for we believe that the current state of "half-equality" between the sexes discriminates against both men and women, and is the cause of much unnecessary hostility between the sexes.

WE BELIEVE that women must now exercise their political rights and responsibility as American citizens. They must refuse to be segregated on the basis of sex into separate-and-not-equal ladies auxiliaries in the political parties, and they must demand representation according to their numbers in the regularly constituted part committees—at local, state, and national levels—and in the informal power structure, participating fully in the selection of candidates and political decision-making, and running for office themselves.

IN THE INTERESTS OF THE HUMAN DIGNITY OF WOMEN, we will protest, and endeavor to change, the false image of women now prevalent in the mass media, and in the texts, ceremonies, laws, and practices of our major social institutions. Such images perpetuate contempt for women by society and by women for themselves. We are similarly opposed to all policies and practices—in church, state, college, factory, or office—which, in the guise of protectiveness, not only deny opportunities but also foster in women self-denigration, dependence, and evasion of responsibility, undermine their confidence in their own abilities and foster contempt for women.

NOW WILL HOLD ITSELF INDEPENDENT OF ANY POLITICAL PARTY in order to mobilize the political power of all women and men intent on our goals. We will strive to ensure that no party, candidate, president, senator, governor, congressman, or any public official who betrays or ignores the principle of full equality between the sexes is elected or appointed to office. If it is necessary to mobilize the votes of men and women who believe in our cause, in order to win for women the final right to be fully free and equal human beings, we so commit ourselves.

WE BELIEVE THAT women will do most to create a new image of women by acting now, and by speaking out in behalf of their own equality, freedom, and human dignity—not in pleas for special privilege, nor in enmity toward men, who are also victims of the current, half-equality between the sexes—but in an active, self-respecting partnership with men. By so doing, women will develop confidence in their own ability to determine actively, in partnership with men, the conditions of their life, their choices, their future and their society.

SOURCE: NOW Statement of Purpose, 1966. National Organization for Women. Reproduced by permission.

Super Bowl I

On January 15, 1967, at the Memorial Coliseum in Los Angeles, the Green Bay Packers faced off against the Kansas City Chiefs for the first Super Bowl championship. A crowd of 61,946 gathered inside the California stadium to witness Vince Lombardi's highly regarded Packers, members of the National Football League (NFL), take on the Chiefs, representing the recently formed American Football League (AFL). Kansas City Chiefs owner and AFL founder Lamar Hunt was responsible for the "Super Bowl" name. The game itself was decided when Green Bay quarterback Bart Starr completed a total of 7 throws to receiver Max McGee for a gain of 138 yards and 2 touchdowns. Starr was named the game's most valuable player (MVP). The final score of the first Super Bowl was Packers 35, Chiefs 10. Green Bay retained its title by beating the Oakland Raiders 33–14 the following year.

1967

INTERNATIONAL

U.S., Great Britain, and Russia agree to limit use of outer space for military purposes.

Western Hemisphere nations vote to form Latin American common market.

President Lyndon B. Johnson makes round-the-world trip in a week; meets with Soviet Premier Aleksei Kosygin for three days at Glassboro (New Jersey) State College.

NATIONAL

Twenty-fifth Amendment is ratified, sets up presidential succession (February 10).

Thurgood Marshall becomes first African-American Supreme Court justice (August 30).

Freedom of Information Act goes into effect.

Five days of rioting by African Americans begins in Newark, New Jersey (July 12), 26 persons are killed, 1,500 are injured; week-long rioting begins in Detroit (July 23), results in 43 deaths, 600 injuries, destruction of 5,000 homes.

Tennessee repeals law that forbids teaching of evolution in public schools, which led to 1925 Scopes trial.

U.S. Coast Guard moves from Treasury to new Transportation Department.

First two African-American mayors of major cities are elected: Carl B. Stokes, Cleveland; Richard Hatcher, Gary, Indiana.

National Commission of Product Safety is created.

Nickajack Dam on Tennessee River in Tennessee is completed.

A raid on an after-hours club in 1967 leads to race riots in Detroit that will leave forty-three people dead and hundreds injured.
CORBIS-BETTMANN

Spiro T. Agnew is elected governor of Maryland.

DEATHS Former Vice President John N. Garner (1933–1941); William F. Gibbs, directed production of World War II cargo ships.

BUSINESS/INDUSTRY/INVENTIONS

Teamsters President Jimmy Hoffa begins eight-year prison term for mail fraud and mishandling union funds.

Minimum wage rises to $1.40 an hour (February 1).

DEATHS Henry J. Kaiser, builder of ships, dams, autos; Bruce Barton, advertising executive and author; Roger W. Babson, economist.

TRANSPORTATION

Alan S. Boyd is named first Secretary of Transportation (April 1).

Douglas and McDonnell aircraft companies merge.

Merger of Atlantic Coast Line and Seaboard Air Line railroads forms Seaboard Coast Line.

SCIENCE/MEDICINE

Hans A. Bethe is awarded Nobel Prize in physics for discovery of the energy production of stars; Haldan K. Hartline and George Wald share physiology/medicine prize for discoveries on primary visual processes of the eye.

Fire in spacecraft *Apollo* on ground at Cape Canaveral, Florida, kills three astronauts: Virgil I. Grissom, Edward H. White II, and Roger B. Chaffee (January 27).

DEATHS Elmer V. McCollum, discoverer of vitamin D, codiscoverer of vitamin A; Gregory Pincus, biologist, codeveloper of oral contraceptive pill; J. Robert Oppenheimer, physicist; Bela Schick, pediatrician, developer of diphtheria test; George F. Dick, who with wife, Gladys, isolated scarlet fever germ, developed serum.

EDUCATION

Merger of Case Institute and Western Reserve forms Case-Western Reserve University in Cleveland; merger of Carnegie and Mellon institutes creates Carnegie-Mellon University in Pittsburgh.

RELIGION

Janie McGaughey becomes first Presbyterian woman named moderator of a presbytery (Atlanta).

United Presbyterian Church in the USA adopts new confession, first change since 1647.

A peace offering during a demonstration against the Vietnam War at the Pentagon. The antiwar movement explodes three months later, after the January 1968 Tet Offensive. NATIONAL ARCHIVES AND RECORDS ADMINISTRATION

Two Catholic archbishops are elevated to cardinal: Patrick A. O'Boyle of Washington (D.C.) and John P. Cody of Chicago.

ART/MUSIC

Helen Frankenthaler completes the painting *The Human Edge.*

SONGS (POPULAR): "By the Time I Get to Phoenix," "Can't Take My Eyes off You," "Light My Fire," "A Little Help from My Friends," "Ode to Billy Joe," "Something Stupid," "Up, Up, and Away," "I Heard It Through the Grape Vine."

DEATHS Otis Redding, rhythm-and-blues artist; Geraldine Farrar, dramatic soprano; Paul Whiteman, orchestra leader; Woody Guthrie, folksinger and composer; Muggsy Spanier, Dixieland jazz cornetist; Edward Hopper, painter of contemporary life.

LITERATURE/JOURNALISM

BOOKS *The Confessions of Nat Turner* by William Styron, *The Armies of the Night* by Norman Mailer, *Topaz* by Leon Uris, *Rosemary's Baby* by Ira Levin, *The Chosen* by Chaim Potok.

DEATHS Carl Sandburg, poet and biographer; Carson McCullers, author; Henry R. Luce, publisher; Langston Hughes, "poet laureate" of Harlem.

ENTERTAINMENT

Corporation for Public Broadcasting is established.

PLAYS *Hair* and Clark Gesner's *You're a Good Man, Charlie Brown.*

MOVIES *Guess Who's Coming to Dinner* with Spencer Tracy and Katharine Hepburn; *Bonnie and Clyde* with Warren Beatty and Faye Dunaway, *The Dirty Dozen* with Lee Marvin, *The Graduate* with Dustin Hoffman, *Thoroughly Modern Millie* with Julie Andrews.

New television shows include the Smothers Brothers, Jonathan Winters, Jerry Lewis, Carol Burnett, *The Newlywed Game* with Bob Eubanks, *The Flying Nun* with Sally Field, *Kraft Music Hall.*

DEATHS Bert Lahr, Paul Muni, and Spencer Tracy, actors; Martin Block, disc jockey of 1930–1940s; Nelson Eddy, singer and screen actor.

SPORTS

American League approves transfer of baseball franchise from Kansas City, Missouri, to Oakland, California, authorizes expansion to 12 clubs. National Basketball Assn. grants franchise to San Diego and Seattle; American Basketball Assn. is founded.

Muhammad Ali is sentenced to five years and $10,000 fine for refusing military service; sentence is appealed.

Mickey Mantle, New York Yankees, and Eddie Mathews, Houston Astros, each hit their 500th career home runs.

A. J. Foyt and Dan Gurney become first Americans to win 24 Hours of LeMans sports-car race.

Jim Baaken of St. Louis kicks record seven field goals in a football game.

WINNERS *Auto racing*—A. J. Foyt, Indianapolis 500; Richard Petty, NASCAR; *Baseball*—St. Louis Cardinals, World Series; *Basketball*—Southern Illinois, NIT; UCLA, NCAA; Philadelphia, NBA; *Bowling*—Dave Davis, PBA national; *Boxing*—Muhammad Ali, heavyweight; Emile Griffith, middleweight; *Figure skating*—Peggy Fleming, world and U.S. championship; Gary Visconti, U.S. title (men); *Football* (bowls)—Purdue, Rose; Florida, Orange; Alabama, Sugar; Georgia, Cotton; Green Bay, Super Bowl I; *Golf*—U.S., Walker and Ryder cups; Jack Nicklaus, U.S. Open; Don January, PGA; Gary Brewer Jr., Masters; Catherine Lacoste, U.S. Women's Open; Kathy Whitworth, LPGA; *Harness racing*—Speedy Streak, Hambletonian; *Hockey*—Toronto, Stanley Cup; *Horse racing*—Proud Clarion, Kentucky Derby; Damascus, Preakness Stakes and Belmont Stakes; *Tennis*—John Newcombe, U.S. Open (men); Billie Jean King, U.S. Open (women); *Yachting*—U.S. boat *Intrepid* retains America's Cup.

DEATHS Eleanora Sears, Tennis Hall of Famer; Francis Ouimet, popularized golf in U.S.

MISCELLANEOUS

Silver Bridge over Ohio River that connects Pt. Pleasant, West Virginia, and Kanauga, Ohio, collapses; 46 are killed.

Piedmont Boeing 727 and Cessna 310 collide over Hendersonville, North Carolina; 82 are killed.

Floods damage much of Fairbanks, Alaska.

Aircraft carrier *Forrestal* catches fire off North Vietnam; 134 die.

1968

INTERNATIONAL

VIETNAM WAR Communist forces launch Tet offensive (January 30); U.S. and North Vietnam agree to preliminary talks to end war (May 3); begin a week later.

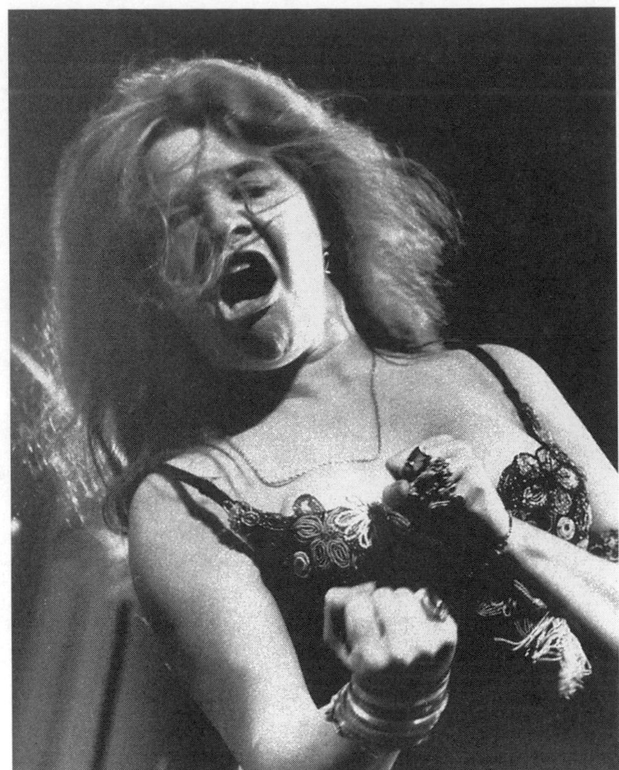

Big Brother and the Holding Company's 1968 album *Cheap Thrills,* featuring the song "Piece of My Heart," sells one million copies in the first month of its release. Singer Janis Joplin is seen here performing live in 1968. AP/WIDE WORLD PHOTOS

North Korea seizes U.S. intelligence ship *Pueblo;* 83 men on board are held as spies.

Island of Iwo Jima is returned to Japan.

NATIONAL

Two assassinations shock nation: Rev. Martin Luther King Jr., civil rights leader, at a Memphis motel (April 4), and Senator Robert F. Kennedy in a Los Angeles hotel (June 5); Kennedy dies the next morning.

President Lyndon B. Johnson announces he will not seek reelection (March 31); Republican Richard M. Nixon is elected president with 31,785,480 popular and 301 electoral votes to Democratic Vice President Hubert H. Humphrey's 31,275,166 popular and 191 electoral votes; Independent George A. Wallace receives 9,906,473 popular and 46 electoral votes.

Supreme Court Chief Justice Earl Warren resigns (June 13).

Nuclear submarine *Scorpion* sinks near the Azores; 99 men are lost.

First-class postage rises to 6 cents.

Walter Cronkite (with microphone) conducts an interview in Vietnam during the Tet Offensive. He returns to the United States to report that America would lose the war. **U.S. MARINE CORPS**

HemisFair 68 opens in San Antonio, Texas, marking city's 200th birthday.

Oroville Dam on Feather River in California is completed.

North Cascades (Washington) and Redwood (California) national parks are established.

Rep. Shirley Chisholm becomes first African-American woman elected to Congress.

DEATHS Helen Keller, blind lecturer on behalf of blind; Norman Thomas, five-time Socialist presidential candidate (1928–1948).

BUSINESS/INDUSTRY/INVENTIONS

Truth in Lending Act is signed.

Minimum wage increases to $1.60 an hour.

DEATHS Sanford L. Cluett, shirt and collar maker, invented Sanforizing process; Chester F. Carlson, inventor of xerography.

TRANSPORTATION

Supreme Court approves merger of Pennsylvania and New York Central railroads, which creates the Penn Central.

Mississippi River Bridge at Baton Rouge, Louisiana, and second span of Delaware Memorial Bridge at Wilmington open.

Lockheed unveils world's largest plane, the C-5A.

Merger of unions representing railway trainmen, locomotive firemen and engineers, switchmen, and conductors forms United Transportation Union.

DEATH Ralph H. Upson, designer of first metalclad airplane.

SCIENCE/MEDICINE

Luis W. Alvarez is awarded Nobel Prize in physics for contributions to physics and detection of elementary particles; Lars Onsager is awarded chemistry prize for work on thermodynamics of irreversible processes; Robert W. Holley, H. Gobind Khorama, and Marshall W. Nirenberg share physiology/medicine prize for interpreting the genetic code and its role in making certain proteins.

Frank Borman, James A. Lovell Jr., and William A. Anders complete six-day first flight to the moon (December 27), send back pictures of moon's surface; earlier, unmanned *Surveyor VII* made soft landing on moon, sending back data and pictures.

Scientists synthesize an enzyme for the first time.

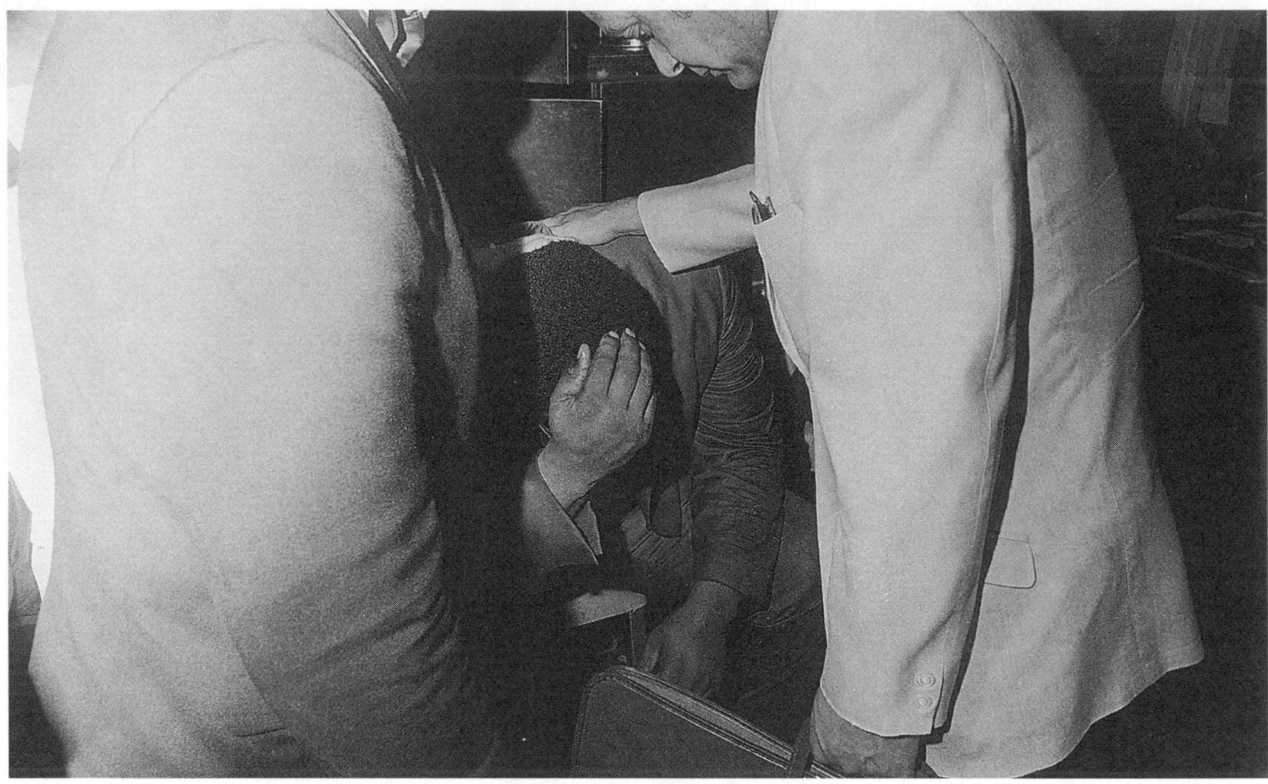

Rosey Grier, a former professional football player and a friend and unofficial bodyguard to Robert F. Kennedy, mourns after Kennedy is assassinated in Los Angeles on June 5, 1968. Kennedy had just won the California primary. **CORBIS-BETTMANN**

Dr. Norman Shumway performs first successful U.S. heart transplant.

EDUCATION

Supreme Court rules that "freedom of choice" desegregation is inadequate if other methods can correct Southern school segregation more rapidly; Court also rules that public-school teachers may not be discharged for good-faith criticism of school officials.

Internal Revenue Service revokes tax-exempt status of private schools that continue to practice racial discrimination in admission policies.

Carnegie Commission on Higher Education urges multibillion-dollar federal aid for colleges and college students.

RELIGION

Terence J. Cooke becomes Catholic archbishop of New York.

DEATH Franklin C. Fry, president, United Lutheran, American Lutheran churches (1944–1968).

ART/MUSIC

New York Philharmonic observes 125th anniversary with Leonard Bernstein conducting Walter Piston's *Ricercare.*

Pop artist Roy Lichtenstein completes painting *Preparedness.*

SONGS (POPULAR): "Do You Know the Way to San Jose?" "The Dock of the Bay," "Hey Jude," "Harper Valley PTA," "Honey," "Mrs. Robinson," "This Guy's in Love with You," "Wichita Lineman," "Piece of My Heart."

DEATH Ruth St. Denis, dancer.

LITERATURE/JOURNALISM

BOOKS *Iberia* by James A. Michener, *Couples* by John Updike, *Myra Breckenridge* by Gore Vidal, *Airport* by Arthur Hailey, *Lonesome Cities* by Rod McKuen.

DEATHS Authors John Steinbeck, Vardis Fisher, Edwin G. O'Connor, Edna Ferber, and Upton B. Sinclair; Harold L. Gray, cartoonist ("Little Orphan Annie").

ENTERTAINMENT

Restored Ford's Theater in Washington, D.C., is dedicated.

Classification of movies begins: "G," "PG," "R," and "X" ratings.

PLAYS Jerry Orbach stars in *Promises, Promises,* James Earl Jones in *The Great White Hope,* Maureen Stapleton and George C. Scott in Neil Simon's *Plaza Suite.*

MOVIES *The Lion in Winter* with Katharine Hepburn, *2001: A Space Odyssey*, *Funny Girl* with Barbra Streisand, *The Green Berets* with John Wayne, *The Detective* with Frank Sinatra.

New television shows include *Laugh-In* with Dan Rowan and Dick Martin, *60 Minutes* with Mike Wallace, *Hawaii 5–0* with Jack Lord.

SPORTS

Club owners fire Baseball Commissioner William D. Eckert with five years left on his contract.

Three new sports facilities open: New York City's Madison Square Center, including a 29-story office building and the Felt Forum; Oakland (California) Coliseum, home of baseball A's; Belmont Park after $30 million renovation.

Naismith Memorial Basketball Hall of Fame opens in Springfield, Massachusetts.

Hank Aaron of Atlanta Braves hits 500th home run.

Olympic Games are held in Mexico City; U.S. wins 45 gold medals.

National Basketball Assn. awards franchises to Milwaukee and Detroit.

National Football League Players Assn. strikes for six days.

Don Drysdale of Los Angeles Dodgers sets record for consecutive scoreless innings pitched (58 2/3).

WINNERS *Auto racing*—Bobby Unser, Indianapolis 500; David Pearson, NASCAR; *Baseball*—Detroit Tigers, World Series; *Basketball*—Dayton, NIT; UCLA, NCAA; Boston, NBA; *Bowling*—Wayne Zahn, PBA national; *Boxing*—Joe Frazier, heavyweight; Bob Foster, light heavyweight; Nino Benevenuti, middleweight; *Figure skating*—Peggy Fleming, U.S. and world titles (women); Tim Wood, U.S. title (men); *Football* (bowls)—Southern California, Rose; Oklahoma, Orange; Louisiana State, Sugar; Texas A&M, Cotton; Green Bay, Super Bowl II; *Golf*—Lee Trevino, U.S. Open; Julius Boros, PGA; Bob Goalby, Masters; Susie M. Browning, U.S. Women's Open; Sandra Post, LPGA; *Harness racing*—Nevele Pride, Hambletonian; *Hockey*—Montreal, Stanley Cup; *Horse racing*—Dancer's Image, Kentucky Derby; Forward Pass, Preakness Stakes; Stage Door Johnny, Belmont Stakes; *Horseshoe pitching*—Elmer Hohe, world title; *Tennis*—U.S., Davis Cup; Arthur Ashe, U.S. Open (men); Virginia Wade, U.S. Open (women).

DEATHS Bill Masterson, Minnesota hockey player, first death in NHL from game injury; Stanislaus Zbyszko, wrestler; Paddy Driscoll, early football great; Earl Sande, one of premier jockeys of 1920s.

Lyndon B. Johnson listens to a tape recording from son-in-law Capt. Chuck Robb, a marine stationed in Vietnam. Despite a successful domestic program, Johnson will be remembered for escalating the Vietnam War during his presidency. **LYNDON BAINES JOHNSON LIBRARY, NATIONAL ARCHIVES AND RECORDS ADMINISTRATION**

MISCELLANEOUS

Explosion and fire in Mannington, West Virginia, coal mine kills 78 miners.

Braniff Electra crashes in storm near Dawson, Texas; 85 die.

1969

INTERNATIONAL

VIETNAM WAR Peace talks to end war in Vietnam begin (January 18); about 250,000 persons take part in anti–Vietnam War demonstration in Washington, D.C. (November 15).

NATIONAL

Warren E. Burger becomes Supreme Court chief justice (June 23); Justice Abe Fortas resigns after criticism of his acceptance of a fee.

The *Apollo 11* lunar landing, July 1969. Astronaut Edwin E. Aldrin Jr. is shown standing beside the U.S. flag. Neil Armstrong takes the photograph with a 70-mm Hasselblad lunar surface camera, while millions of Americans watch the action live on television.

President Richard M. Nixon signs tax reform bill, which was expected to lower taxes by 5%, remove 9 million people from income tax rolls.

Car driven by Sen. Edward M. Kennedy of Massachusetts plunges off bridge on Chappaquiddick Island (Massachusetts); a 28-year-old secretary with him drowns.

Sirhan Sirhan, accused murderer of Sen. Robert Kennedy, is found guilty and sentenced to death; sentence is later commuted to life imprisonment.

World's largest mint opens in Philadelphia.

Destroyer *Evans* collides with an Australian carrier in South China Sea; 74 men are lost.

Vice president's salary is raised from $43,000 to $62,500.

DEATHS Former President Dwight D. Eisenhower (1953–1961); Allen W. Dulles, head of CIA (1953–1961); Assistant Attorney General Thurman Arnold, who filed 230 antitrust suits (1938–1943); World War II Admiral Raymond A. Spruance.

BUSINESS/INDUSTRY/INVENTIONS

DEATHS John L. Lewis, president, United Mine Workers (1920–1960), CIO (1935–1940); Ludwig Mies van der Rohe, architect who developed glass-and-steel skyscraper; Robert E. Wood, merchant (Sears).

TRANSPORTATION

Penn Central completes takeover of bankrupt New York, New Haven & Hartford Railroad.

Metroliner completes first New York City–Washington run in 3 hours, 7 minutes.

Newport Bridge over Narragansett Bay (Rhode Island) is completed.

SCIENCE/MEDICINE

Neil A. Armstrong, Edwin E. Aldrin Jr., and Michael Collins make eight-day flight to the moon; Armstrong becomes first man to set foot on moon (July 20), saying, "That's one small step for a man, one giant leap for mankind."

Murray Gell-Mann is awarded Nobel Prize in physics for discoveries concerning elementary particles; Max Delbruck, Alfred D. Hershey, and Salvador Luria share physiology/medicine prize for discoveries of viruses and viral diseases.

Dr. Denton A. Cooley implants in a human being in Houston world's first totally artificial heart (April 4); patient lives four days.

EDUCATION

Supreme Court rules that schools must end segregation "at once"; school systems must be integrated "now and hereafter"; rules that public school officials cannot interfere with students' nondisruptive public-opinion expressions during school hours; rules that states can spend more on schools in wealthy districts than in disadvantaged areas.

RELIGION

Catholic Church issues revised liturgical calendar, eliminating more than 200 saints (including Christopher, Valentine).

Cynthia C. Wedel becomes first woman president of National Council of Churches.

Norman Vincent Peale becomes president of Reformed Church in America.

Catholic Archbishop Terence J. Cooke of New York is elevated to cardinal.

DEATHS Rev. Francis Brennan, first U.S. dean of Sacred Rota, Catholic Church's highest appeal court; Rev. Harry Emerson Fosdick, leader of modern liberal Christianity.

Popular musicians, including Janis Joplin, Jimi Hendrix, Joan Baez, Joe Cocker, and The Who, draw a crowd at the Woodstock music festival. © **AMALIE ROTHSCHILD/ CORBIS-BETTMANN**

ART/MUSIC

New Juilliard School of Music opens in Lincoln Center, New York City.

Woodstock, music festival attended by about 300,000 young people, is held near Bethel, New York. **SEE PRIMARY DOCUMENT** Woodstock, "A Fleeting, Wonderful Moment of 'Community'"

SONGS (POPULAR): "Aquarius/Let the Sunshine In," "A Boy Named Sue," "Games People Play," "Hair," "Leaving on a Jet Plane," "Something," "Wedding Bell Blues."

DEATHS Ben Shahn, artist of social, political causes; Thomas H. Jones, sculptor of Tomb of the Unknown Soldier in Arlington (Virginia) Cemetery; Frank Loesser, composer.

LITERATURE/JOURNALISM

Jack Anderson takes over "Washington Merry-Go-Round" column on death of Drew Pearson.

BOOKS *Portnoy's Complaint* by Philip Roth, *Slaughterhouse Five* by Kurt Vonnegut, *The Godfather* by Mario Puzo, *The Poseidon Adventure* by Paul Gallico, *The French Connection* by Robin Moore, *The Inheritors* by Harold Robbins.

DEATHS Westbrook Pegler, syndicated columnist; Jack Kerouac, "beat generation" author; Harry Scherman, founder, Book of the Month Club.

ENTERTAINMENT

PLAYS James Coco stars in *Last of the Red Hot Lovers;* Kenneth Tynan contributes to *Oh, Calcutta;* Leonard Gershe writes *Butterflies Are Free;* Woody Allen, *Play It Again, Sam.*

MOVIES *True Grit* with John Wayne, *Butch Cassidy and the Sundance Kid* with Paul Newman and Robert Redford, *Midnight Cowboy* with Jon Voight and Dustin Hoffman, *Easy Rider* with Peter Fonda and Dennis Hopper, *Cactus Flower* with Goldie Hawn.

New on television are *Marcus Welby, M.D.* with Robert Young, *Medical Center* with Chad Everett, *Hee Haw!* with Roy Clark, *The Brady Bunch,* and Merv Griffin, John Davidson, Johnny Cash, Glen Campbell, Dick Cavett, and David Frost.

DEATHS Irene Castle, dancer; Judy Garland, entertainer and screen actress; Boris Karloff, actor.

SPORTS

Bowie Kuhn is named baseball commissioner.

Willie Mays of San Francisco Giants hits his 600th home run.

Jack Murphy (baseball) Stadium in San Diego opens.

WINNERS *Auto racing*—Mario Andretti, Indianapolis 500; David Pearson, NASCAR; *Baseball*—New York Mets, World Series; *Basketball*—Temple, NIT; UCLA, NCAA; Boston, NBA; *Bowling*—Mike McGrath, PBA national; *Boxing*—Joe Frazier, heavyweight; Jose Napoles, welterweight; Mando Ramos, lightweight; *Chess*—Samuel Reshevsky, U.S. title; *Figure skating*—Tim Wood, U.S., world men's titles; Janet Lynn, U.S. women's singles; *Football* (bowls)—Ohio State, Rose; Penn State, Orange; Arkansas, Sugar; Texas, Cotton; New York Jets, Super Bowl III; *Golf*—U.S., Walker Cup; Orville Moody, U.S. Open; Ray Floyd, PGA; George Archer, Masters; Donna Caponi, U.S. Women's Open; Betsy Rawls, LPGA; *Harness racing*—Lindy's Pride, Hambletonian; *Hockey*—Montreal, Stanley Cup; *Horse racing*—Majestic Prince, Kentucky Derby and Preakness Stakes; Arts and Letters, Belmont Stakes; *Tennis*—U.S., Davis Cup; Rod Laver, U.S. Open (men); Margaret Court, U.S. Open (women).

DEATHS Rocky Marciano, heavyweight boxing champion, in plane crash; Arnie Herber, football quarterback; Max Hirsch, dean of U.S. thoroughbred trainers; Walter Hagen, famed golfer.

MISCELLANEOUS

Hurricane Camille strikes Gulf Coast, kills 292, causes $1 billion damage.

Pants suits become acceptable for everyday wear by women.

PRIMARY SOURCE DOCUMENT

Woodstock, "A Fleeting, Wonderful Moment of 'Community'"

INTRODUCTION The Woodstock Festival of Music and Art and Aquarian Exposition of August 1969 was a "wonderful moment of 'community,'" as the following *New Yorker* article described it. It was also "three days of peace and music and love," as the official festival slogan read. And it was "chaos," as Who guitarist Pete Townsend put it. "I thought the whole of America had gone mad," he later said. Given that approximately 500,000 people spent three days living together in a farm pasture, often during downpours, it is not surprising that participants in the Woodstock Festival are unable to describe the experience in one phrase. Originally slated as a weekend music festival expected to draw 100,000, rumors of a massive free concert in upstate New York drew hundreds of thousands of young Americans to Max Yasgur's farm in Bethel, New York (not the town of Woodstock). Local roads and the New York State Thruway were overrun with cars, many of which never reached the concert.

A certain amount of peace existed at the festival. A communal spirit pervaded the scene as strangers found ways to happily coexist amidst the chaos created by limited supplies and facilities. But violence, and even several deaths occurred, as crowded conditions, two days of rain, and drug overdoses created tensions in what became, temporarily, New York State's third largest city. Music was performed by some of the world's greatest bands: Santana, Crosby Stills Nash and Young, Joan Baez, the Who, and Jimi Hendrix were but a few of the prominent names to take center-stage. And free love abounded. One journalist wrote that he had never "seen a society so free of repression."

Woodstock was just one of the great outdoor concerts of the 1960s, although it was certainly the most famous. The Altamont concert in Oakland, California, held four months later witnessed the deaths of four spectators, dashing enthusiasm for such massive musical "be-ins." In many ways Woodstock represented the end of an era rather than the beginning of a new one. It aptly symbolized what the counterculture of the 1960s was all about—the spirit of sharing and community, the pleasures of freedom as experienced through sex, drugs, and rock 'n' roll. But maintaining a society "so free of repression" became difficult, if not impossible, for many of Woodstock's participants, a generation that had rejected a society characterized by the Vietnam conflict, materialism, and constricted sexual mores, to sustain. By the early 1970s many of these "flower children" had traded in bohemian pleasures for bourgeois stability.

Woodstock has endured as a powerful symbol of 1960s unity and an alternative lifestyle. In August 1994 about 200,000 people paid $150 apiece to mark the twenty-fifth anniversary of the original festival in a weekend-long Woodstock "Reunion" held at the Winston Farm in Saugerties, New York. In the audience were many of the same Americans who had traveled to upstate New York in 1969 for "three days of peace and music and love."

We talked with a younger friend of ours—a nineteen-year-old—who had been to the Festival, and he told us he was indignant and discouraged by what the *Times* had had to say about the event. In an editorial headed "Nightmare in the Catskills," the *Times* said, "The dreams of marijuana and rock and roll music that drew 300,000 fans and hippies to the Catskills had little more sanity than the impulses that drive the lemmings to march to their deaths in the sea. They ended in a nightmare of mud and stagnation.... What kind of culture is it that can produce so colossal a mess?" "It wasn't a nightmare," our friend told us. "The mud didn't matter, and it was one of the most remarkable experiences I've ever had. The big point was not that pot was passed around openly but that because there was a minimum of force and restriction—the cops were few, and they were friendly—a huge crowd of people handled itself decently. There were no fights, no hassles, no pushing, no stealing. Everybody shared everything he had, and I've never seen such consideration for others. People volunteered all kinds of jobs—picking up trash, carrying stuff, doing whatever was needed. It was the most extraordinary demonstration of how good people can be—really *want* to be, if they are let alone. It was an ethic shared by a huge mass of people. The *Times* wants to know what kind of culture produces this. In a broad sense, Christian culture produced it."

We asked our young friend, who attends the University of Chicago and has hair neither very short nor very long, to jot down some further notes on his experience....

"I went rather casually," he wrote, "partly because I wanted to hear the music, and partly because I knew, by word of mouth, there would be a tremendous mass of people my age, and I wanted to be part of it. Of course, there was going to be a terrific assemblage of artists—the best this kind of event has to offer—but the main thing was that by listening to the grapevine you could tell the Festival was going to be above and beyond that.... We heard that there wouldn't be any reserved seats, that we'd be free to wander, and that the townspeople weren't calling out the militia in advance. I went, like the others, to meet people, to sit on the grass and play guitars, and to be together. I also knew that people were coming from thousands of miles away, but I had no idea how tremendous the event would be....

"I drove from Rhode Island with a group of friends. When we got on the New York Thruway, we began to see the first signs of how huge it would be—Volkswagens full of kids, motorcycles, hitchhikers carrying signs. Everybody waving at everybody else as people passed. The first traffic jam—about twenty miles from White Lake, on 17B—set the tone. It was a cheerful traffic jam. People talked from car to car. People came up and asked to sit on your hood. Somebody in our car spoke to a girl in a blue Volks next to us and, not having yet caught the tone, remarked that the jam was a drag. 'Oh, no,' she said quickly. 'Everyone here is so beautiful.' She gave us some wine, and we handed over peaches in exchange....

"Finally, we got to a huge parking lot. It cost five dollars and was already full. We were the last car in. We parked and started walking. This was 10 P.M. Thursday. There would be no music until Friday afternoon. We walked along in a stream, exchanging comments with every passerby. There were no houses, no local folks staring us. People became aware of the land around us. Somebody said, 'It's like being part of an encamped army that has won.' We felt as though it were liberated territory. We came to the top of a hill and looked down on a huge meadow—a natural amphitheatre—where the Festival would be. In the center, people were building the stage. People were lying around in sleeping bags or sitting around little fires. The grass was fresh with dew, and the stars were bright. It was wonderful. We went on and found a campground, full of people sitting around sleeping or eating. We unpacked our gear. For fifty cents, we bought 'macroburgers' that some communal people from California had cooked. They were made of soybeans, rice, and vegetable—no meat—between slices of rye bread. The California people also gave slices of huge cucumbers they had grown themselves. It all tasted good. The girl serving the macroburgers gave us water in a plastic cup. She said, 'Save the cup. Somebody else may want it.' The campground was full of the most ingenious shelters. One huge canopy was made of scraps of polyethylene fastened to scraps of wood. Beneath it about forty people were lying down, snuggled against each other, singing and playing music. There was a fence across the campground, and one tough guy—the only tough guy I saw—started to tear down the fence, but people remonstrated with him. They told him it was the farmer's fence and it wasn't necessary to take it down. He was only allowed to take down one panel to make an exit. It was like that through the whole Festival. Where the mass needed an opening, an opening was made. There was no needless destruction. It was a functional thing. There was a woods between us and the amphitheatre. Two paths through the woods had been marked with strings of Christmas lights. One was called the Gentle Path and the other the Groovy Way. Nobody knows who named them. Late that night, we went to sleep in our sleeping bags with the sound of singing and guitars and voices all around us. I slept well.

"In the morning, it was raining lightly, but it didn't last. I went looking for water. I found a tank truck, and there I met a Rhode Island girl I knew who was there brushing her teeth. She hugged me, and the crowd laughed. We breakfasted with some people from the Santa Fe Hog Farm Commune. They were serving out of a great vat of boiled wheat and raisins, scooped onto a paper plate with a dollop of honey on it. It was delicious. It held me all day.

"That day, I just wandered around. I found a group of people who were blowing up a red balloon five feet across, so that their friends could find them, but lots of other people had the same balloons, so these huge red globes dotted the fields. Various groups of people had put up amusement devices for everybody to use free. One was called the Bumblebee Nest. It consisted of forked branches ingeniously fastened together with wooden pegs to support a platform of hay. It was just for the pleasure of sitting on. Somebody had an enclosure of chickens and had brought chicken feed. It was fun to feed the chickens. Somebody else had brought rabbits and made a big pen with benches in it, so you could sit and watch the rabbits and feed them. There was a huge tepeelike construction with a flat stone hung from ropes that you could stand on to swing. All these were free things that people had taken the trouble to provide for others. Most of the day, people wandered around and talked. I read and played cards. In the late afternoon, the music began. The amphitheatre was a mass of people, but there was no pushing. The sound system was excellent. We listened all afternoon and evening. The music was great, and the audience sang and clapped the rhythm. The performers loved it. There was a terrific feeling of unity between the crowd and the stage.

"The next morning, we woke to find it raining hard. Some boys who had got soaked took off their clothes and

OVERVIEW

Women's Rights/ Women's Role, 1848–2002

GRETCHEN BOGER, PRINCETON UNIVERSITY

Women comprise 51 percent of the population. They have always played a key role in the life of the United States. So why is it necessary to study their unique history? Largely because women have not held elected positions of great political power, their history has been ignored until fairly recently. However, women's struggle to participate in society as fully equal citizens has been an important component of the United States' civic and social development.

The Birth of the Women's Rights Movement

In 1848 Lucretia Mott visited her friend Elizabeth Cady Stanton in Seneca Falls, New York, Stanton expressed her frustrations with her isolated life as a young wife and mother in the country. Before marriage, she had traveled to Europe, lived in Boston among friends, and experienced a lively intellectual life. Mott and Stanton had developed a friendship while serving as activists in the antislavery, or abolitionist, movement. Abolitionism provided one of the first opportunities for American women to speak out publicly on questions of government policy, thus giving them experience and exposure in the political sphere.

Many arguments made by abolitionists against slaves' inferior position in American society seemed to apply to women too. Mott, Stanton, and several others decided it was time to host a public meeting on women's issues. They placed an ad in the local paper calling women and men to convene the following week in Seneca Falls. For the event, Stanton drew up a Declaration of Sentiments and Resolutions, including a resolution that women should have the right to vote. In 1848 this was a radical idea, and even Mott suggested that Stanton drop the notion from the meeting's agenda as it was too revolutionary. But among those who supported Stanton was the much-respected abolitionist leader and former slave Frederick Douglass, and Stanton decided to retain the suffrage resolution.

To the organizers' surprise, the Seneca Falls Convention drew more than 200 women and 40 men. All of Stanton's resolutions were passed. Though increasing regional tensions and Civil War would overshadow women's issues in the next two decades, the convention had for the first time articulated a firm position on women's rights: equal participation with men in society and civic affairs. A women's movement had officially been born.

Women's Activism Expands

Although many women considered suffrage a radical idea, increasing numbers began to advocate for other issues in the late nineteenth century. In 1873 women in Ohio spontaneously protested the evils of alcohol. Marching on saloons to demand their closure, these women inspired thousands around the country to do the same, and in 1874 the Woman's Christian Temperance Union—WCTU—was formed. The group viewed alcohol as the great disrupter of home life, which it was their duty to protect. Soon the WCTU expanded to embrace other causes, as president Frances Willard commanded members to "do everything." Women for whom the suffrage movement seemed too revolutionary could comfortably support issues like children's healthcare and a legally required maximum number of workday hours for women.

The WCTU and many similar clubs that formed around women's issues were exclusively white. Denied membership, African-American women organized separate clubs, which joined forces to form the National Association of Colored Women—NACW—in 1896 under the leadership of Mary

walked around naked. It didn't bother anyone. It brought home the idea that this was our land. Nobody was busting them. I was struck by how harmless it was—how the violence of sexuality was missing. The naked boys looked harmless and innocent.

"The concessionaires—hot-dog stands and so on—started out with prohibitive prices, and the kids complained to the management. All day, there were announcements from the stage about where to get free food. Eventually, there was an announcement that the concessionaires had knocked their prices down to cost.

"It rained hard the early part of the day, but the reaction of the crowd was 'Don't fight it.' We sat and listened, soaking wet. The rain really did something to

Church Terrell. One of the key issues to ignite African-American club members in the 1890s was lynching. In 1892 a friend of journalist Ida B. Wells was lynched by a mob for being too successful a businessman. The outraged Wells began an investigation of lynching in the South. In gathering information, she debunked the myth that black men were commonly lynched as punishment for assaults on white women, pointing to underlying racism and sexism as the true causes. Wells continued to lobby for anti-lynching legislation for the rest of her life.

The Suffrage Movement Is Revived

Although women had begun to organize around political issues, they could not yet vote. The need for suffrage grew obvious, and a revived movement culminated in the National American Woman Suffrage Association—NAWSA—founded in 1890 and led for twenty years by Susan B. Anthony. Well-organized campaigns won suffrage in a handful of western states from 1890 to 1912, but the eastern industrial states remained unswayed.

Meanwhile, younger radical suffragists under the leadership of Alice Paul formed a new organization called the National Women's Party—NWP—in 1912. NAWSA disapproved of the blunt, sometimes forceful tactics of the NWP, but the two groups worked toward the same goal. Finally, in 1918, suffragists, sensing enough support in Congress, brought the suffrage amendment to a vote. When it passed the House of Representatives, spectators in the gallery burst into a hymn of praise. Eighteen months later it passed the Senate and—thanks to the tireless campaign of suffragists around the country—was ratified by the states in 1920. Women had at last won legal recognition of their equality as citizens of the United States.

The Cataclysmic Changes of the 1960s

In the decades following 1920, women remained active in various causes and moved into the working world in great numbers during World War II, but they did not again rally around women's rights with such enthusiasm until the 1960s. Then several factors combined to bring women's issues to the fore. The first was the Civil Rights movement. Women's church associations and individual activists like National Association for the Advancement of Colored People—NAACP—southern regional director Ella Baker were instrumental in launching a major civil rights campaign. Younger black women were among the students who formed the Student Nonviolent Coordinating Committee—SNCC—to support boycotts of segregated lunch counters. Black women held leadership roles in the SNCC; they thus gained training in organizing and political work.

Some white middle-class women also developed political skills during the civil rights movement. These students had grown up in a postwar age of prosperity, and many were searching for meaning in their materially comfortable, privileged lives. For many, civil rights seemed a cause worth fighting for. White women who joined SNCC were also impressed with the leadership roles a sizable number of black women had assumed.

White student movements were not as gender-equal. As youth organizations expressing dissatisfaction with American society flourished in the 1960s, a diffuse movement known as the New Left began to challenge the status quo at many levels. However, the new subculture was dominated by male students, who left little room at the top for female leadership. Women students who expressed dissatisfaction with their secondary status were ridiculed. As a result, some began to break away in search of their own movement.

They were not alone: An older generation of women was also expressing dissatisfaction with its unequal status. In 1963 Betty Friedan published the best-selling book *The Feminine Mystique* about housewives' frustrations with their stultifying lives ("the problem that has no name"). In 1966 she and black activist Pauli Murray gathered a group of women to form a new women's organization. The National Organization for Women (NOW) became the leading voice of a revived feminist movement.

reinforce the spirit. There were radios on the campground, and we began to hear news reports that we were in the midst of a mass disaster. At every report, the crowd around the radio laughed. It was such a splendid example of the division between us and the outside world. It dramatized the whole crazy split that the world thought we were having a disaster and we knew we were having no such thing.

"About three o'clock, the sun came out. Everyone took off his clothes to dry. I stripped to my shorts. We lay in the sun and listened to fantastic music. The most popular song was against the Vietnam war. Just as it finished, an Army helicopter flew over. The whole crowd—all those hundreds of thousands of people—looked up and waved their forefingers in the peace sign, and then gave a cheer for themselves. It was an extraordinary thing. Soon

Women's Rights/Women's Role, 1848–2002 (continued)

Nonetheless, many younger women wanted more than the legal victories NOW sought; they demanded fundamental changes in society's attitudes. Declaring "the personal is political," women's liberation activists protested at the 1968 Miss America Pageant, crowning a sheep and inviting women to burn bras, girdles, and other instruments of "female torture." They (and their partners) also launched a sexual revolution, in which sex outside marriage was promoted as acceptable even for "good girls." New openness about sexuality allowed the gay and lesbian communities to become increasingly visible. Although change was slow, lesbian organizations slowly attracted more members over the next decade, allowing lesbian women some room for self-expression.

Momentum and Backlash

A series of significant gains for women in the 1970s and 1980s grew out of the seismic activity of the 1960s. Women moved into new careers in vastly increased numbers, making it more common by 1980 for a woman to work outside the home than not. In elite, high-paying professions, like law and medicine, the increase in the percentage of women working in those fields was dramatic.

In 1972 Title IX of the Educational Amendments Act required that colleges accepting federal funds treat men's and women's programming equally, a major boost for women's athletics. That same year, Congress passed the Equal Rights Amendment—ERA—stating that federal law would not discriminate in any way on the basis of gender—and sent it to the states for ratification. In 1973 the U.S. Supreme Court decided in the case of *Roe* v. *Wade* to make abortion legal throughout the United States.

Such rapid change inevitably produced a countermovement. *Roe* v. *Wade* sparked a highly charged debate between those who supported the Court's decision and those who opposed it, believing abortion was a form of murder. Right-wing activist Phyllis Schlafly headed a campaign to prevent ratification of the ERA, accusing feminists of rejecting their God-given role as mothers and housewives. Working-class and poor women also tended to be less sympathetic with the feminist movement, which they saw as primarily benefiting women at the top of the economic ladder.

A conservative turn in government slowed the pace of change in the 1980s, but by then women's issues were clearly on the agenda. Women's studies programs became common at many universities. Issues like domestic violence and date rape began to receive public attention. The AIDS crisis provided a rallying point for the gay and lesbian community, and, later, activists at large.

At the turn of the twenty-first century, much had been achieved but significant issues remain. The abortion debate continues, the question of child care is critical to most working women, and the need to make the women's movement more accessible to lower-income women is still crucial. It will be the challenge of the next generation of women to take on these causes and pursue change with the same determination and creativity of their foremothers.

BIBLIOGRAPHY

Sara Evans's *Born of Liberty,* 2nd edition (1997) is a clear, highly readable overview of the experience of women throughout American history, from pre-Columbian times to the 1990s. Another extremely readable general text is *No Small Courage: A History of Women in the United States,* edited by Nancy Cott (2000). Cott's *The Grounding of Modern Feminism* (1987) is a classic account of the history of organized women's movements in the United States through the 1920s. Ellen DuBois chronicles the history of woman suffrage in *Woman Suffrage and Women's Rights* (1998). For the history of the modern women's movement, see Ruth Rosen, *The World Split Open: How the Modern Women's Movement Changed America* (2001). DuBois and Vicki Ruiz have edited a groundbreaking volume of essays on previously neglected areas of women's history—various ethnic, religious, and regional minorities—in *Unequal Sisters: A Multi-Cultural Reader in U.S. Women's History,* 3rd edition (2000). Finally, *The Routledge Historical Atlas of Women in America* (2000), edited by Susan Opdycke, offers wonderful visual images of many aspects of women's history.

after that, the farmer who owned the land was introduced, and he got a huge cheer, too.

"Late that afternoon, a 'free stage' began acting as a travellers' aid, where volunteers arranged free rides for people and helped to solve problems. They took up a collection for a ten-year-old boy who had lost his money. They returned a lost child to her mother. They asked for volunteers to pick up garbage, and they made announcements warning those leaving to be careful on the way out—not to take grass with them, because of busts on the highway, and so on.

"There was still another day to go, but I had to leave. We got our stuff together and jammed three hitchhikers into our car and drove it out of the mud. As we went out, people called to us, 'Don't leave! Don't leave!' Nobody wanted to let go of what we'd had there. What we'd had was a fleeting, wonderful moment of what you might call 'community.'"

SOURCE: "A Fleeting, Wonderful Moment of 'Community'," *The New Yorker* Magazine, August 1969. Copyright © 1969, *The New Yorker* Magazine. Reproduced by permission.

1970

INTERNATIONAL

President Richard M. Nixon announces that U.S. troops are being sent into Cambodia (April 30).

Terrorists in Montevideo, Uruguay, kidnap U.S. diplomat Daniel A. Mitrione (July 31); body is found 10 days later.

NATIONAL

Nearly 200,000 postal workers strike (March 18) in New York City; strike spreads through nation (except South), ends six days later.

U.S. Postal Service law is signed (August 12), is effective 1971.

Newly created agencies are Council of Environmental Quality (January 1); Environmental Protection Agency (December 2); National Oceanic and Atmospheric Administration (including Weather Service, Ocean Survey, Marine Fisheries), and Office of Management and Budget (July 1).

Nineteenth census reports national population at 203,302,031.

Two deadly college demonstrations occur: four students at Kent State University are killed by Ohio National Guards during an anti–Vietnam War rally; two students at Jackson (Mississippi) State College are killed when police fire on demonstrators.

Norman E. Borlaug is awarded Nobel Peace Prize for contributions to spurring food production in developing nations.

First draft lottery since World War II is held.

Guam and Virgin Islands elect their first governors.

National debt is reported at $370.1 billion.

First Earth Day is observed (April 22).

DEATHS Benjamin O. Davis, first African-American Army general; Gen. Leslie R. Groves, headed Manhattan Project that developed atomic bomb.

BUSINESS/INDUSTRY/INVENTIONS

IBM has sold 18,000 mainframe computer systems in U.S. since early 1950s; Intel introduces its first memory chip, which holds one kilobyte of information.

Paul A. Samuelson is awarded Nobel Prize in economics for raising level of scientific analysis in economic theory.

Occupational Safety and Health Act is signed, authorizes setting of federal standards.

DEATHS Walter P. Reuther, United Auto Workers president (1946–1970); Richard J. Neutra, architect, introduced international style to U.S.; Harry A. Noyes, developer of food-freezing process.

TRANSPORTATION

General Motors redesigns cars to operate on lower octane gas.

President Nixon signs clean-air bill that sets six-year deadline for auto industry to develop pollution-free engine.

Merger of Chicago, Burlington, and Northern and Northern Pacific roads creates Burlington Northern Railroad.

Lee Iacocca becomes president of Ford Motor Co.

DEATHS William T. Piper, designer of Piper Cub planes; Arthur W. S. Herrington, developer of World War II jeep.

SCIENCE/MEDICINE

Julius Axelrod shares Nobel Prize in physiology/medicine with Sir Bernard Katz of Great Britain and Ulf Von Euler of Sweden for independent basic research on chemistry of nerve transmission.

Apollo 13 mission develops serious problems about 200,000 miles from Earth when oxygen tanks and service module explode; completes mission around moon, returns to Earth successfully (April 17).

EDUCATION

Supreme Court rules that election of school board members must adhere to one-man, one-vote principle.

University of Hawaii is established.

RELIGION

Joseph Fielding Smith becomes tenth head of Mormon Church, on death of David O. McKay.

Catholic Bishop Humberto S. Medeiros is named archbishop of Boston following death of Archbishop Richard J. Cushing (1947–1970).

ART/MUSIC

Mario Davidovsky composes *Synchronisms #6.*

One of the four students killed by the Ohio National Guard during an antiwar demonstration at Kent State University.
UPI/CORBIS-BETTMANN

SONGS (POPULAR): "Bridge over Troubled Water," "Everything Is Beautiful," "I Never Promised You a Rose Garden," "Let It Be," "No Sugar Tonight," "Raindrops Keep Fallin' on My Head," "We've Only Just Begun."

DEATHS Mark Rothko, artist of abstract expressionism who during year completed *Black on Grey;* George Szell, conductor; Janis Joplin, rock star.

LITERATURE/JOURNALISM

BOOKS *Jonathan Livingston Seagull* by Richard D. Bach, *Hard Times* by Studs Terkel, *The Rising Sun* by John Toland, *The Trumpet of the Swan* by E. B. White, *Love Story* by Erich Segal, *Rich Man, Poor Man* by Irwin Shaw.

DEATHS Richard Hofstadter, historian; Rube Goldberg, cartoonist; Erle Stanley Gardner and John O'Hara, authors; Joseph Wood Krutch, editor, *The Nation* (1924–1952).

ENTERTAINMENT

PLAYS Dean Jones stars in *Company,* Lauren Bacall in *Applause;* Paul Zindel writes *The Effect of Gamma Rays on Man-in-the-Moon Marigolds.*

MOVIES *Airport* with Burt Lancaster and Helen Hayes, *Patton* with George C. Scott, *Catch-22* with Alan Arkin, *Love Story* with Ali McGraw, *The Reivers* with Steve McQueen.

New television shows include *The Odd Couple* with Tony Randall and Jack Klugman, *The Partridge Family* with Shirley Jones, *The Mary Tyler Moore Show,* and *The Flip Wilson Show.*

DEATHS Gypsy Rose Lee, entertainer; Billie Burke, screen actress.

SPORTS

Two college football teams and staff are killed in air crashes: Wichita State University in Colorado, 29 die; Marshall University in West Virginia, 43 die.

Bill Shoemaker rides 6,033rd winning horse to set new record.

Three baseball parks open: Texas Rangers in Arlington, Riverfront Stadium in Cincinnati, and Three Rivers Stadium in Pittsburgh.

International Lawn Tennis Assn. approves ninepoint tie-breaking scoring.

National Basketball Assn. expands to 18 teams, awards franchises to Buffalo, Cleveland, Houston, and Portland, Oregon.

Charles S. Feeney becomes National (baseball) League president.

In 1970 William Ruckelshaus is named director of the newly created Environmental Protection Agency. The same year the first Earth Day reinforces the idea that Americans demanded federal action to clean up and to protect the environment. CORBIS-BETTMANN

Hank Aaron of Atlanta Braves and Willie Mays of San Francisco Giants each gets his 3,000th hit.

Tom Dempsey kicks longest field goal (63 yards) in NFL history.

Gary Gabelich sets land speed record of 622.407 miles per hour.

Seattle baseball franchise moves to Milwaukee.

WINNERS *Auto racing*—Al Unser, Indianapolis 500; Bobby Isaac, NASCAR; *Baseball*—Baltimore Orioles, World Series; *Basketball*—Marquette, NIT; UCLA, NCAA; New York, NBA; *Bowling*—Mike McGrath, PBA national; *Boxing*—Joe Frazier, heavyweight; Billy Backus, welterweight; Carlos Monzon, middleweight; Ismael Laguna, lightweight; *Figure skating*—Tim Wood, U.S. and world men's titles; Janet Lynn, U.S. women's; *Football* (bowls)—Southern California, Rose; Penn State, Orange; Mississippi, Sugar; Texas, Cotton; Kansas City, Super Bowl IV; *Golf*—Tony Jacklin, U.S. Open; Dave Stockton, PGA; Billy Casper, Masters; Donna Caponi, U.S. Women's Open; Shirley Engelhorn, LPGA; *Harness racing*—Timothy T., Hambletonian; *Hockey*—Boston, Stanley Cup; *Horse racing*—Dust Commander, Kentucky Derby; Personality, Preakness Stakes; High Echelon, Belmont Stakes; *Marathon*—Gary Muhrcke, first New York City race; Sara Berman, first woman's championship; *Tennis*—U.S., Davis Cup; Ken Rosewall, U.S. Open (men); Margaret Court U.S. Open (women); *Yachting*—U.S. boat *Intrepid* retains America's Cup.

DEATHS Vincent Lombardi, football coach; Harold S. Vanderbilt, winner of America's Cup three times, developer of contract bridge.

MISCELLANEOUS

North tower of World Trade Center in New York City tops out, world's tallest (1,350 feet).

Tornado strikes Lubbock, Texas, kills 26, causes $135 million in damage.

1971

INTERNATIONAL

VIETNAM WAR U.S. bombs Vietnam for five days, beginning December 26, for alleged violations of 1968 bombing halt.

Treaty is signed, returns Okinawa to Japan; Ryukyu and Daito islands are also returned.

Silicon Valley, California

In 1971 Don C. Hoefler, a journalist for *Electronic News,* first described the technological community of Santa Clara County and its surrounding regions (including parts of San Mateo, Alameda and Santa Cruz) as "Silicon Valley." Silicon is the primary ingredient in the manufacture of semiconductors, and the region had links with the electronics and computer industry dating back to 1937, when two Stanford University graduates established the Hewlett-Packard Company in a Palo Alto garage. The early 1970s marked a remarkable period of change and growth for Silicon Valley, as the military and aerospace markets took a back seat to the computer industry. Electronics firms expanded to meet a growing demand for semiconductors, with sales rising by approximately twenty-five percent each year. In the mid-1980s competition from Japanese manufacturers resulted in a period of recession in Silicon Valley. However, valley entrepreneurs rebounded by pioneering better computer systems and forging successful new companies, including Sun Microsystems and Silicon Graphics. In the late 1990s Silicon Valley rode the wave of the first Internet communications boom, until the sudden collapse of dot.com businesses in 2001.

Trade embargo on Communist China is lifted after 21 years.

Japanese Government allows Chrysler Motors to acquire 35% interest in Mitsubishi Motors over three-year period.

NATIONAL

National voting age is lowered to 18 with ratification of Twenty-sixth Amendment (July 1).

President Richard M. Nixon announces 90-day wage-price freeze (August 15); Cost of Living Council is established.

U.S. Postal Service comes into existence, replaces Post Office Department.

Radical Weather Underground bombs a room in Capitol; no one is injured, $300,000 damage.

Kennedy Center for the Performing Arts in Washington, D.C., opens.

First-class postage rises to 8 cents an ounce (May 16).

Three-day holiday weekends (Washington's Birthday, Memorial Day, Columbus Day, Veterans Day) go into effect (January 1).

More than 1,000 New York State troopers and police storm Attica prison to end four-day uprising; 9 hostages, 28 convicts are killed.

Lyndon B. Johnson Library at University of Texas is dedicated.

ACTION is created as an independent agency to administer volunteer programs (Peace Corps, VISTA, Foster Grandparents, and others.).

Jimmy Carter is elected Georgia governor.

Cowans Ford Dam on Catawba River in North Carolina is completed.

DEATHS Thomas E. Dewey, New York governor, twice Republican presidential candidate; Arthur B. Spingarn, NAACP president (1940–1965); Dean G. Acheson, secretary of state (1949–1953); Rosey (Emmett) O'Donnell, Air Force general; Ralph Bunche, U.N. undersecretary.

BUSINESS/INDUSTRY/INVENTIONS

Simon Kuznets is awarded Nobel Prize in economics for developing economic interpretation of national growth.

Cigarette advertising is banned from television.

Interior Department recommends trans-Alaska oil pipeline to help meet critical oil need.

Texaco completes world's deepest producing oil well at Stockton, Texas.

DEATHS James C. Penney, department-store-chain founder; Gar Wood, boat racer and builder (Navy PT boat); Philo T. Farnsworth, television pioneer.

TRANSPORTATION

Amtrak announces rates and schedules, begins operations (May 1); Alan S. Boyd is named chief executive officer.

Dent Bridge in Clearwater County, Idaho, opens.

SCIENCE/MEDICINE

Earl W. Sutherland Jr. is awarded Nobel Prize in physiology/medicine for discoveries concerning hormone action.

EDUCATION

Supreme Court upholds constitutionality of busing to eliminate segregation; also overturns Mobile, Alabama, desegregation plan.

Sidney P. Marland Jr. is named U.S. Education Commissioner.

Ford Foundation announces six-year, $100-million program to assist African American private colleges and minority students.

RELIGION

Supreme Court rules unconstitutional the reimbursement of religious schools for secular instruction.

DEATH Reinhold Niebuhr, theologian.

ART/MUSIC

Jacob Druckman composes the work *Windows;* Leonard Bernstein composes *Mass* for opening of Kennedy Center.

SONGS (POPULAR): "Joy to the World," "Knock Three Times," "Me and Bobby McGee," "Mister Bojangles," "Put Your Hand in the Hand," "She's a Lady," "Take Me Home, Country Road," "You've Got a Friend," "Day by Day."

DEATHS Rockwell Kent, artist and author; Louis (Satchmo) Armstrong, jazz musician, singer, and orchestra leader; Ted Fio Rito, early orchestra leader and composer.

LITERATURE/JOURNALISM

The *New York Times* publishes classified Pentagon Papers, followed soon after by the *Washington Post*; Supreme Court upholds right to their publication.

Look magazine ceases publication.

BOOKS *Rabbit Redux* by John Updike, *The Winds of War* by Herman Wouk, *The Betsy* by Harold Robbins, *Wheels* by Arthur Hailey, *Yazoo* by Willie Morris, *Wonderland* by Joyce Carol Oates, *Our Gang* by Philip Roth.

DEATHS Bennett Cerf, publisher; Margaret Bourke-White, *Life* photographer; Ogden Nash, poet; James F. Stevens, author of Paul Bunyan stories.

ENTERTAINMENT

PLAYS Peter Falk stars in *The Prisoner of Second Avenue;* John M. Tebelak and Stephen Schwartz write *Godspell;* Tim Rice and Andrew Lloyd Webber, *Jesus Christ Superstar.*

MOVIES *A Clockwork Orange* with Malcolm McDowell, *The French Connection* with Gene Hackman, *Dirty Harry* with Clint Eastwood, *Klute* with Jane Fonda, *The Last Picture Show* with Timothy Bottoms and Jeff Bridges.

New television shows include *All in the Family* with Carroll O'Connor, *Sonny and Cher, Hollywood Squares, Columbo* with Peter Falk.

SPORTS

Supreme Court overturns conviction of Muhammad Ali as a draft evader; rules that he qualified as a conscientious objector.

New York (football) Giants announce move to Flushing Meadows in New Jersey in 1975; Washington Senators baseball club announces move to Texas in 1972.

Iron Eyes Cody

In 1971 a Cree-Cherokee actor named Iron Eyes Cody was featured in a television commercial against littering paid for by the "Keep America Beautiful" campaign. Cody, dressed in traditional Native-American costume, paddled his canoe across a polluted river before standing on the edge of a freeway, with litter thrown at his feet from passing vehicles. A single tear fell from Cody's face. A monotone voiceover uttered, "People start pollution. People can stop it." The "Crying Indian" commercial, as it came to be known, proved hugely successful in the 1970s. Aired just one year after the first Earth Day, the advertisement tapped a growing interest in environmentalism and green living. Cody, born in Fort Gibson, Oklahoma, was a veteran of the entertainment industry, first touring with his father in a Wild West show before moving on to movies. He played an Indian chief in *Paleface,* the 1948 film starring Bob Hope, and a medicine man in the 1970 motion picture *A Man Called Horse,* with Richard Harris. His television credits included guest roles in *Rawhide, Bonanza,* and *Gunsmoke.* Despite a career spanning seven decades, Cody became synonymous with the "Crying Indian" of the "Keep America Beautiful" series. It is estimated that Americans witnessed his plea for environmental stewardship a total of fifteen billion times. Cody died in Los Angeles on January 4, 1999 at the age of 94.

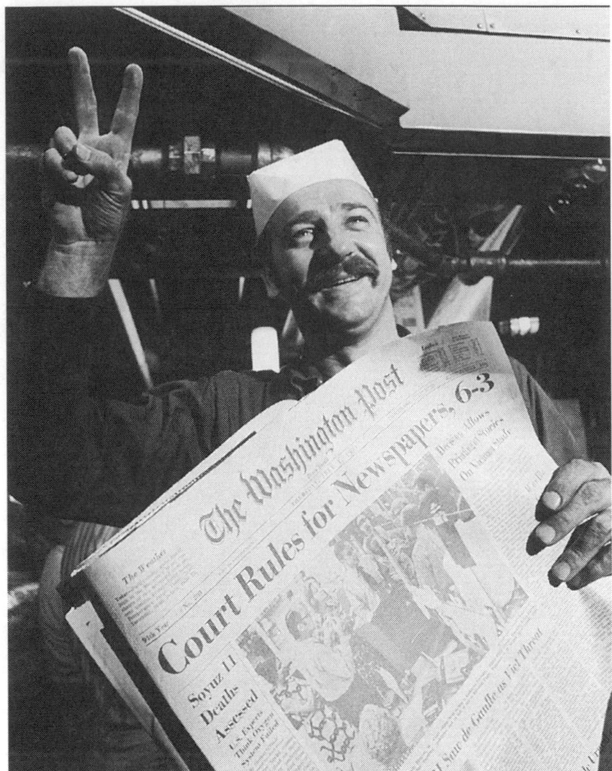

William Frazee, chief of the presses for the *Washington Post*, celebrates the 1971 Supreme Court decision allowing newspapers to resume publication of top secret Pentagon Papers on the Vietnam War. CORBIS-BETTMANN

World Hockey Assn. is founded; to begin play in 1972.

New York City begins first legal off-track horserace betting in U.S.

Hank Aaron of Atlanta Braves hits 600th home run.

WINNERS *Auto racing*—Al Unser, Indianapolis 500; Richard Petty, NASCAR; *Baseball*—Pittsburgh Pirates, World Series; *Basketball*—North Carolina, NIT; UCLA, NCAA; Milwaukee, NBA; *Bowling*—Mike Lemongello, PBA national; *Boxing*—Joe Frazier, heavyweight; Jose Napoles, welterweight, Ruben Olivares, bantamweight; *Figure skating*—John M. Petkevich, U.S. men's title; Janet Lynn, U.S. women's; *Football* (bowls)—Stanford, Rose; Nebraska, Orange; Tennessee, Sugar; Notre Dame, Cotton; Baltimore, Super Bowl V; *Golf*—Great Britain, Walker Cup; U.S., Ryder Cup; Lee Trevino, U.S. Open; Jack Nicklaus, PGA; Charlie Coody, Masters; JoAnne Carner, U.S. Women's Open; Kathy Whitworth, LPGA; *Harness racing*—Speedy Crown, Hambletonian; *Hockey*—Montreal, Stanley Cup; *Horse racing*—Canonero II, Kentucky Derby and Preakness Stakes; Pass Catcher, Belmont Stakes; *Tennis*—U.S. Davis Cup; Stan Smith, U.S. Open (men); Billie Jean King, U.S. Open (women).

DEATHS Bobby Jones, golfer; Will Harridge, American (baseball) League president (1931–1958).

MISCELLANEOUS

Hurricane Agnes kills 130, does $2 billion damage along Atlantic Coast; tornado in Mississippi Delta kills 110.

Earthquake rocks San Fernando Valley in California; 64 are killed, damage is set at $1 billion.

Alaska Airlines Boeing 727 crashes into mountain near Juneau, 111 die.

1972

INTERNATIONAL

VIETNAM WAR North Vietnam forces launch attack across demilitarized zone (March 30); U.S. resumes bombing Hanoi and Haiphong (April 15); peace talks resume April 27; bombing resumes December 18 after peace talks stall.

U.S. and Russian representatives sign Strategic Arms Limitation Treaty I (SALT I) in Moscow (May 26); in effect until 1977.

President Nixon makes week-long visit to China; first president to visit a nation not recognized by U.S.; restriction on China travel by U.S. ships and planes is lifted.

President Nixon visits Russia in May.

NATIONAL

President Nixon, Republican, is elected to second term, receives 47,165,234 popular and 520 electoral votes to 29,170,774 popular and 17 electoral for Democratic Sen. George S. McGovern.

Alabama Gov. George A. Wallace is shot at a Laurel (Maryland) political rally, is paralyzed from waist down; this ends his effort to attain Democratic presidential nomination; Arthur Bremer is sentenced to 63 years for the crime.

Five men are arrested for breaking into Democratic national headquarters in Watergate building in Washington (June 17).

Supreme Court rules the death penalty to be unconstitutional in *Furman* v. *Georgia*.

Consumer Product Safety Commission is created.

American Museum of Immigration opens at base of Statue of Liberty.

President Richard Nixon and his entourage walk the Great Wall of China during the president's historic visit in 1972. **NATIONAL ARCHIVES AND RECORDS ADMINISTRATION**

Eisenhower Center, including library, in Abilene, Kansas, and Herbert Hoover Library in West Branch, Iowa, are dedicated.

DEATHS Former President Harry S. Truman (1945–1953); J. Edgar Hoover, FBI director (1924–1972); James F. Byrnes, Supreme Court justice, secretary of state (1945).

BUSINESS/INDUSTRY/INVENTIONS

Kenneth J. Arrow shares Nobel Prize in economics with John R. Hicks of Great Britain for contributing to general economic equilibrium theory and welfare theory.

Dow-Jones industrial average closes above 1,000 for the first time.

Near-total ban on use of DDT goes into effect.

Congress overrides president's veto of a 20% increase in railroad retirement benefits.

Major cigarette companies agree to include health warning in advertising.

DEATHS Howard H. Aiken, inventor of Mark I, forerunner of digital computer; Howard Johnson, restaurant and hotelchain founder; Igor Sikorsky, engineer, developer of several planes, helicopter.

TRANSPORTATION

Senate passes antihijacking bill; U.S. airlines tighten security to prevent acts of sabotage; government orders search of all carry-on luggage, boarding passengers.

First portion of San Francisco's BART transit system opens.

Merger of Gulf, Mobile and Ohio Railroad and Illinois Central Railroad forms Illinois Central Gulf Railroad.

SCIENCE/MEDICINE

John Bardeen, Leon N. Cooper, and John R. Schrieffer share Nobel Prize for physics for theory of superconductivity; Christian B. Anfinsen, Stanford Moore, and William H. Stine share chemistry prize for major contributions to enzyme chemistry; Gerald M. Edelman shares prize in physiology/medicine with Rodney R. Porter of Great Britain for research on chemical structure of antibodies.

President Nixon approves plan to develop space shuttle.

Pioneer 10 is launched, is designed to explore asteroid belt and fly by Jupiter.

Acupuncture is used for first time in U.S.

EDUCATION

Congress provides $2 billion to help public schools

Marlon Brando (foreground) and Robert Duvall in a scene from *The Godfather.* The film wins an Academy Award for best picture for 1972. **CORBIS-BETTMANN**

desegregate, establishes federal aid program for college and university students.

National Institute of Education is established to conduct, coordinate basic and applied educational research.

RELIGION

Supreme Court rules that state laws requiring school attendance violate constitutional freedom of religion, rules that Amish children cannot be required to attend beyond eighth grade.

Historic separation of white and black Methodist conferences in South Carolina ends.

Sally J. Priesand becomes first U.S. woman rabbi; Judith Herd becomes first woman Lutheran pastor.

Four Episcopal bishops defy church law, ordain 11 women priests; Rev. Harold S. Jones is consecrated Episcopal bishop of South Dakota, the first Sioux Indian bishop; Rt. Rev. Paul Moore Jr. becomes Episcopal bishop of New York.

Harold B. Lee heads the Mormon Church on the death of Joseph Fielding Smith.

ART/MUSIC

Elliott Carter composes String Quartet no. 3.

SONGS (POPULAR): "Alone Again," "Baby, Don't Get Hooked on Me," "The Candy Man," "I Can See Clearly Now," "Lean on Me," "Song Sung Blue," "Without You."

DEATHS Ferde Grofé and Rudolf Friml, composers; Howard Barlow, conductor; Mahalia Jackson, gospel singer.

LITERATURE/JOURNALISM

Supreme Court rules that journalists have no right to withhold confidential information from grand juries.

Gloria Steinem founds *Ms.* magazine.

BOOKS *The Optimist's Daughter* by Eudora Welty, *Chimera* by John Barth, *Up Country* by Maxine Kumin, *The Ward* by Irving Wallace, *The Blue Knight* by Joseph Wambaugh.

DEATHS Four Poets: John Berryman, Ezra Pound, Marianne Moore, and Mark Van Doren; reporters: Walter Winchell, Louella Parsons, and Gabriel Heatter; Edmund Wilson, *New Yorker* critic and author; Walter van Tilburg Clark, author.

ENTERTAINMENT

PLAYS Ben Vereen stars in *Pippin,* Jack Albertson and Sam Levene in *The Sunshine Boys;* Jason Miller writes *That Championship Season*, Jim Jacobs and Warren Casey write *Grease.*

MOVIES *The Godfather* with Marlon Brando, *Cabaret* with Liza Minelli, *Lady Sings the Blues* with Diana Ross, *The Poseidon Adventure* with Gene Hackman, *The Candidate* with Robert Redford.

New television shows include *Maude* with Bea Arthur, *M*A*S*H* with Alan Alda, *Sanford and Son* with Redd Foxx, *The Waltons,* and *Bob Newhart.*

SPORTS

Winter Olympics are held in Sapporo, Japan; U.S. wins 3 gold medals; Summer Games are held in Munich, Germany, with U.S. winning 33 golds, including 7 by swimmer Mark Spitz.

New York State Athletic Commission approves letting women journalists into dressing rooms at boxing, wrestling matches when men are "properly attired."

Cincinnati pro basketball team moves to Kansas City, Missouri.

John Wooten is first to be enshrined in Basketball Hall of Fame as a player (Purdue 1960) and coach (UCLA).

Roberto Clemente of Pittsburgh Pirates gets his 3,000th hit.

WINNERS *Auto racing*—Mark Donohue, Indianapolis 500; Richard Petty, NASCAR; *Baseball*—Oakland Athletics, World Series; *Basketball*—Maryland, NIT; UCLA, NCAA (for sixth consecutive year); Immaculata, first AIAW title; *Bowling*—Johnny Guenther, PBA title; *Boxing*—Joe Frazier, heavyweight; Roberto Duran, lightweight; Enrique Pinder, bantamweight; *Chess*—Bobby Fischer, first American to win world title; *Figure skating*—Janet Lynn, U.S. women's title; Ken Shelley, U.S. men's; *Football* (bowls)—Stanford, Rose; Nebraska, Orange; Oklahoma, Sugar; Penn State, Cotton; Miami, Super Bowl VI; *Golf*—U.S., Ryder Cup; Jack Nicklaus, U.S. Open and Masters; Gary Player, PGA; Susie M. Berning, U.S. Women's Open; Kathy Ahem, LPGA; *Harness racing*—Super Bowl, Hambletonian; *Hockey*—Boston, Stanley Cup; *Horse racing*—Riva Ridge, Kentucky Derby and Belmont Stakes; Bee Bee Bee, Preakness Stakes; *Soccer*—New York Cosmos, North American League; *Tennis*—U.S., Davis Cup; Ilie Nastase, U.S. Open; Billie Jean King, U.S. Open (women).

DEATHS Gil Hodges, baseball player and manager; Roberto Clemente, baseball player; Jackie Robinson, first African-American major league baseball player; Nat Fleischer, founder and editor, *Ring Magazine* (1922–1972).

MISCELLANEOUS

Eastern Airlines plane crashes on approach to Miami Airport; 101 die.

Tropical Storm Agnes hits U.S. from Florida to New York in nine-day period, kills 177, causes $3 billion damage.

Flash flood in Rapid City, South Dakota, causes 237 deaths, $160 million damage; dam at Buffalo Creek, West Virginia, collapses; 118 die.

1973

INTERNATIONAL

VIETNAM WAR U.S., South and North Vietnam sign cease-fire (January 27), end Vietnam War.

Arab oil producers reduce exports to U.S. and other pro-Israel nations by 5% (October 17); Saudi Arabia reduces exports 10% (October 18); Mideast nations ban all exports (October 19); Iraq nationalizes Exxon and Mobil oil properties.

U.S. and Cuba sign treaty, calls for extradition or punishment of air pirates.

Ambassador Cleo A. Noel Jr. and Chargé d'Affaires George C. Moore are killed by Palestinian guerrillas in Khartoum, Sudan.

U.S. and China agree to set up in each country permanent liaison offices.

NATIONAL

WATERGATE Senate establishes Select Committee headed by Sen. Sam Ervin (February 7); Archibald Cox is named special prosecutor (April 17); three top presidential aides—H. R. Haldeman, John Ehrlichmann, and John W. Dean—and Attorney General Richard Kleindienst resign (April 30); Senate committee holds nationally televised hearings (May 17); Court of Appeals orders President Richard M. Nixon to turn over Watergate tapes to Judge John Sirica (October 14); President orders Special Prosecutor Cox fired (October 20); Attorney General Elliot Richardson resigns rather than fire Cox; Deputy William Ruckelshaus is fired for refusing to fire Cox; Leon Jaworski is named special prosecutor (November 1).

Vice President Spiro T. Agnew resigns in wake of a tax scandal (October 10), is succeeded by Rep. Gerald R. Ford of Michigan.

Secretary of State Henry Kissinger shares Nobel Peace Prize with Le Duc Tho of North Vietnam.

American Withdrawal from Vietnam

On March 29, 1973 the last U.S. combat troops left Vietnam to return home. Under a cease-fire agreement signed in Paris, France, on January 27, 1973 by all warring factions, the U.S. government agreed to withdraw its forces. A total of 539 U.S. prisoners of war were freed from a Hanoi prison, nicknamed the "Hanoi Hilton," and several other North Vietnamese prisons. Air Force Capt. Ronald Bliss, captured in 1966, saw his wife for the first time in seven years. The peace settlement had taken three years of official and informal negotiations. Beginning in August 1969, President Richard Nixon systematically reduced the number of GIs in Vietnam from 540,000 to less than 100,000, while promoting a "Vietnamization" of the war effort by focusing on the training of South Vietnamese military personnel. To improve their bargaining positions, before the negotiations, both North Vietnam and the U.S. engaged in new offensives. During 1972 the communists captured the city of Quangtri while American planes bombed Hanoi and Haiphong. In the U.S., the end of the war was greeted with relief, coupled with an overwhelming desire to put behind the entire Vietnam experience. Without American support, the South Vietnamese government buckled in April 1975 when communist troops entered the capital of Saigon.

Military draft ends.

Price control on gas, oil, and refinery products is reimposed; government lifts price controls on automobile industry.

Supreme Court in *Roe* v. *Wade* rules that a state may not prevent a woman from having an abortion in the first six months of pregnancy.

Confrontation between American Indian Movement (AIM) protesters and white authorities over a murder case leads to AIM takeover of village of Wounded Knee, South Dakota; two activists are killed during 71-day standoff, ends when activist leaders sign a "peace pact" with the government.

Atlanta becomes first major Southern city to elect an African-American mayor, Maynard Jackson.

DEATHS Former President Lyndon B. Johnson (1963–1969); Jeannette Rankin of Montana, first woman member of Congress, voted against U.S. entry in both World Wars.

BUSINESS/INDUSTRY/INVENTIONS

Congress and the president approve construction of trans-Alaska pipeline.

Federal Trade Commission charges eight major companies with conspiring for 23 years to monopolize petroleum refining.

Wassily Leontief is awarded Nobel Prize in economics for development of input-output method.

DEATHS William Benton, advertising executive, founder, Voice of America; Alfred C. Fuller, of brush fame; Eddie Rickenbacker, World War I flying ace, Eastern Airlines president (1938–1963).

TRANSPORTATION

Volvo announces it will build $100 million assembly plant in Chesapeake, Virginia.

Grand Central Station in New York City closes from 1:30 to 5:30 A.M.; new passenger terminal at remodeled Newark (New Jersey) Airport opens.

Dallas–Ft. Worth Airport opens.

Largest American merchant ship is christened at Brooklyn (New York) Navy Yard; first Soviet passenger ship in 25 years arrives in New York.

SCIENCE/MEDICINE

Ivar Giaever shares Nobel Prize in physics with Lee Esaki of Japan and Brian Josephson of Great Britain for work on semiconductors and superconductors.

EDUCATION

Supreme Court upholds lower court ruling that Richmond, Virginia, desegregation plan is unconstitutional; rules Denver's school districting unconstitutional because it represents state-imposed segregation; strikes down as unconstitutional New York State financial assistance to private and parochial schools.

Student Loan Marketing Assn. (Sallie Mae) is created to support $4.5 billion federal student-loan program.

DEATH Ada Louise Comstock, president, Radcliffe College (1923–1943).

RELIGION

Rev. Lawrence W. Bottoms is named moderator of Pres-

Members of the American Indian Movement stand guard outside the Sacred Heart Catholic Church in Wounded Knee, South Dakota, during negotiations with federal officials on March 3, 1973. **CORBIS-BETTMANN**

byterian Church of the U.S., first African-American leader in Southern denomination in 113 years.

Judge M. A. Haywood of Washington, D.C., is named moderator of United Church of Christ general synod, first African-American woman named to leadership position in U.S. biracial denomination.

Spencer W. Kimball is named president of Mormon Church.

Conservatives in Presbyterian Church of the U.S. form National Presbyterian Church.

Catholic Archbishop Humberto S. Medeiros of Boston is elevated to cardinal.

DEATH Maurice N. Eisendrath, president, Union of American Hebrew Congregations (1946–1973).

ART/MUSIC

Donald Martino composes *Notturno.*

SONGS (POPULAR): "Send in the Clowns," "Bad Bad Leroy Brown," "Delta Dawn," "Killing Me Softly with His Song," "Midnight Train to Georgia," "My Love," "Tie a Yellow Ribbon Round the Old Oak Tree," "Keep on Truckin'."

DEATHS Jim Croce, rock star; Gene Krupa, drummer and band leader; Lauritz Melchior, opera tenor; Edward Steichen, pioneer photographer; Vaughn Monroe, singer and orchestra leader.

LITERATURE/JOURNALISM

BOOKS *Burr* by Gore Vidal, *Fear of Flying* by Erica Jong, *Gravity's Rainbow* by Thomas Pynchon, *The Dolphin* by Robert Lowell, *The Last of the Southern Girls* by Willie Morris.

DEATHS Poets W. H. Auden and Conrad Aiken; Cartoonists Chic Young ("Blondie") and Walter C. Kelly ("Pogo"); Pearl S. Buck, author.

ENTERTAINMENT

PLAYS Stephen Sondheim writes *A Little Night Music;* Lanford Wilson, *Hot-L Baltimore.*

MOVIES *The Way We Were* with Barbra Streisand, *The Exorcist* with Ellen Burstyn, *The Sting* with Paul Newman and Robert Redford, *Serpico* with Al Pacino.

New television shows are *Kojak* with Telly Savalas, *Barnaby Jones* with Buddy Ebsen.

DEATH John Ford, screen director.

SPORTS

American League approves trial of designated hitter; Ron

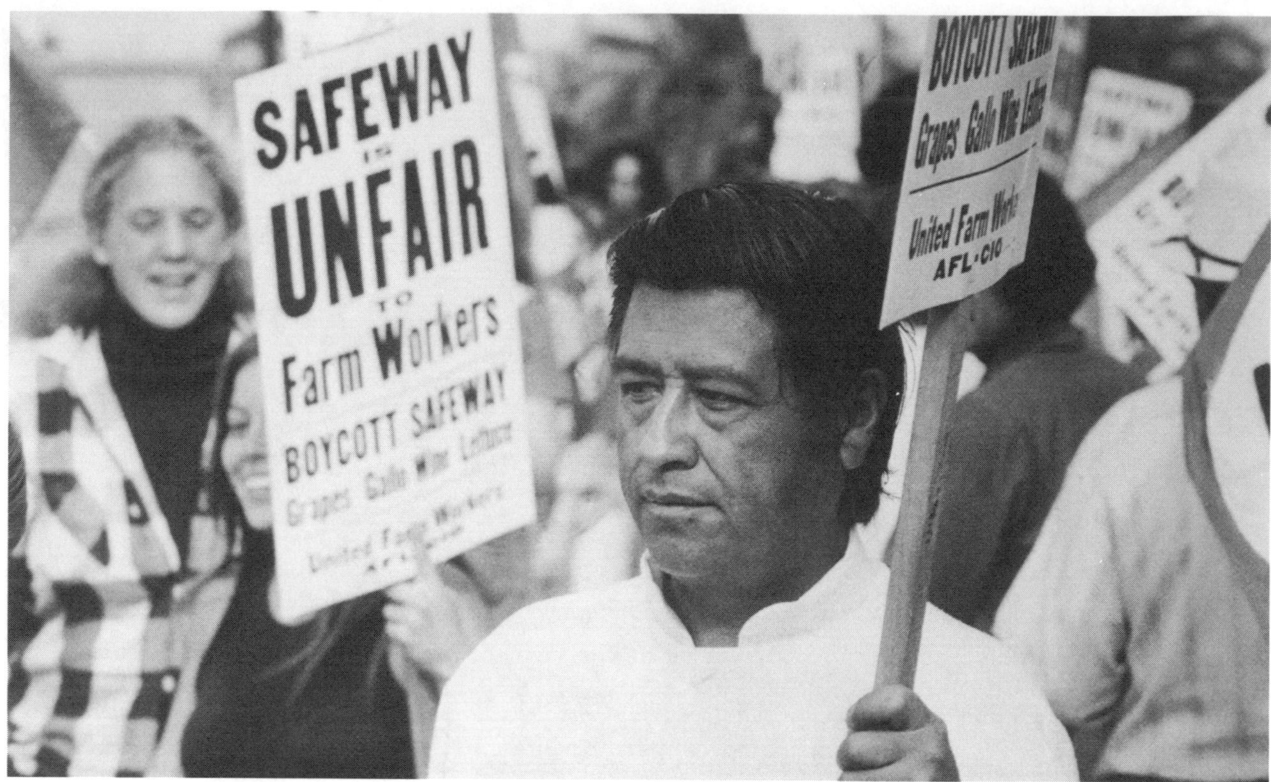

Cesar Chavez, executive director of the United Farm Workers, which will bring civil rights techniques to the world of migrant farm workers, especially those of the grape industry. Here he protests the arrests of fellow activists in 1973. **CORBIS-BETTMANN**

Blumberg of New York Yankees is first designated hitter; he walks with bases loaded.

Baseball players and owners sign three-year contract, end spring training boycott; NBA and players sign first comprehensive contract, which provides $20,000 minimum annual salary, pensions.

National Hockey League Hall of Fame opens in Eveleth, Minnesota.

O. J. Simpson of Buffalo sets football season rushing record of 2,003 yards.

WINNERS *Auto racing*—Gordon Johncock, Indianapolis 500; Benny Parsons, NASCAR; *Baseball*—Oakland Athletics, World Series; *Basketball*—Virginia Tech, NIT; UCLA, NCAA; Immaculata, AIAW; New York, NBA; *Bowling*—Earl Anthony, PBA; *Boxing*—George Foreman, heavyweight; *Figure skating*—Janet Lynn, U.S. women; Gordon McKellen Jr., U.S. men; *Football* (bowls)—Southern California, Rose; Nebraska, Orange; Oklahoma, Sugar; Texas, Cotton; Miami, Super Bowl VII; *Golf*—Johnny Miller, U.S. Open; Jack Nicklaus, PGA; Tommy Aaron, Masters; Susie M. Berning, U.S. Women's Open; Mary Mills, LPGA; *Harness racing*—Firth, Hambletonian; *Hockey*—Montreal, Stanley Cup; *Horse racing*—Secretariat, ninth Triple Crown winner, takes the Kentucky Derby, Preakness Stakes, and Belmont Stakes; *Tennis*—Australia, Davis Cup; John Newcombe, U.S. Open (men); Margaret Court, U.S. Open (women).

MISCELLANEOUS

Delta jetliner crashes in fog at Boston's Logan Airport; 89 die.

Mississippi River floods cause $322 million damage, leave 35,000 homeless.

1974

INTERNATIONAL

President Gerald R. Ford becomes first incumbent president to visit Japan, confers with leaders; goes to Vladivostok where he and Russian leader Leonid Brezhnev set framework for more-comprehensive agreement on offensive nuclear arms (November 24); earlier, President Richard M. Nixon signed treaty with Russia that limited underground testing of nuclear weapons.

Ambassador to Cyprus, Rodger P. Davies, is killed by a sniper in Nicosia.

American composer and band leader Duke Ellington (left) dies in 1974. Here he collaborates with Louis Armstrong during the heyday of big band music in the 1940s. **AP/WIDE WORLD PHOTOS**

NATIONAL

WATERGATE Watergate scandal ends with resignation of President Nixon (August 9); he is succeeded by Vice President Ford; vice presidency is filled by Nelson A. Rockefeller (December 19). Before these events, former Attorney General John N. Mitchell and presidential aides John Erlichmann and H. R. Haldeman were found guilty of coverup charges (January 1); House of Representatives authorized an impeachment investigation (February 6), voted three articles of impeachment (July 27–30) and without debate approved impeachment articles (412–3) (August 20); Supreme Court ruled (July 24) that President Nixon must turn over 64 tapes to Watergate prosecutor. **SEE PRIMARY DOCUMENT** President Richard M. Nixon's Resignation Speech

President Ford grants an unconditional pardon to former President Nixon (September 8) for offenses he "committed or may have committed" while in office.

Most Arab oil-producing countries lift ban on shipments to U.S. (March 18) after five-month embargo; wage and price controls end.

Supreme Court rules that women must receive equal pay for equal work.

Violent protests in Boston as white students opposed to busing for school desegregation attack African-American students (September–November).

Cost of first-class postage increases to 10 cents; soon thereafter, to 13 cents.

Life expectancy in U.S. rises to 71.3 years; 10.3% of population (21.8 million) is older than 65.

Expo '74 held in Spokane, Washington.

DEATHS Charles A. Lindbergh, first to fly solo nonstop across Atlantic (1927); Earl Warren, Supreme Court chief justice (1953–1969); Gen. Carl Spaatz, first Air Force chief of staff; Gen. Creighton Abrams, commanding general in Vietnam War (1968–1972).

BUSINESS/INDUSTRY/INVENTIONS

Work begins on trans-Alaska oil pipeline.

Justice Department files civil antitrust suit against ATT.

Franklin National Bank of New York City fails, largest U.S. bank failure.

Two-stage coal gasification process is patented; can also be used for producing synthetic oil and gasoline.

Minimum wage rises to $2 an hour (May 1).

Sears Tower in Chicago, 110 stories, is completed; world's tallest building.

Departing Washington after his resignation, Richard Nixon raises his arms in a victory stance at the door of the presidential helicopter. **AP/WIDE WORLD PHOTOS**

DEATHS H(aroldson) H. Hunt, oil magnate; Vannevar Bush, builder of first analog computer; Edwin G. Nourse, first chairman, Council of Economic Advisers; Alexander P. De Seversky, aeronautical engineer and inventor.

TRANSPORTATION

President Nixon signs law, sets highway speed limit at 55 miles per hour.

Union Pacific and Rock Island railroads merger is approved.

Supreme Court rules that cities can levy high taxes on downtown parking to try to reduce congestion.

Commodore Barry Bridge at Chester, Pennsylvania, opens.

SCIENCE/MEDICINE

Paul J. Flory is awarded Nobel Prize in chemistry for developing analytic methods to study properties, architecture of long chain molecules; Albert Claude and George E. Palade share prize in physiology/medicine for contributions to understanding inner workings of living cells.

Spacecraft *Pioneer II* passes planet Jupiter on way to Saturn.

DEATH Selman A. Waksman, codiscoverer of streptomycin.

EDUCATION

Supreme Court rules that female teachers cannot be forced to take maternity leave before last weeks of pregnancy; also rules that states may provide funds for nonsectarian purposes to church-affiliated schools.

Federal district court rules that Boston's schools are racially segregated; orders dismantling of dual system.

RELIGION

Christian Science Church Center opens in Boston.

Bishop John M. Alin is installed as presiding bishop of Episcopal Church; Harold L. Wright becomes first African-American Episcopal bishop in New York diocese.

ART/MUSIC

Hirshhorn Museum in Washington, D.C., opens.

Dominick Argento composes *From the Diary of Virginia Woolf.*

SONGS (POPULAR): "Annie's Song," "Don't Let the Sun Go Down on Me," "Having My Baby," "My Melody of Love," "Seasons in the Sun," "The Streak," "Time in a Bottle."

DEATHS Harry Ruby, composer ("Three Little Words"); Duke Ellington, jazz pianist and composer; Johnny Mercer, composer.

LITERATURE/JOURNALISM

BOOKS *The Power Broker* by Robert A. Caro; *Jaws* by Peter Benchley, *Centennial* by James A. Michener, *The Fan Club* by Irving Wallace, *The Rhinemann Exchange* by Robert Ludlum.

DEATHS Francis M. Flynn, publisher, *New York Daily News* (1947–1973); Abel Green, editor, *Variety;* Chet Huntley of Huntley-Brinkley television news team; Otto Soglow, cartoonist ("The Little King"); Walter Lippmann, author and columnist.

ENTERTAINMENT

PLAYS Edward Albee writes *Seascape;* Bob Randall, *The Magic Show.*

MOVIES *The Towering Inferno* with Paul Newman, *Blazing Saddles* with Gene Wilder, *The Godfather, Part II* with Al Pacino, *The Great Gatsby* with Robert Redford, *Harry and Tonto* with Art Carney.

New television shows include *The Tony Orlando and Dawn Show, The Rockford Files* with James Garner, *Little House on the Prairie* with Michael Landon, *Happy Days* with Henry Winkler.

DEATHS Three comedians die: Jack Benny, Bud Abbott of Abbott and Costello, and Charlie Weaver; Samuel Goldwyn, movie producer; Charles Boyer, screen actor; Ed Sullivan, variety-show master of ceremonies; Tex Ritter, singer and Western screen actor; Katharine Cornell, actress.

SPORTS

Henry Aaron of Atlanta Braves hits 715th home run (April 8), breaks 39-year-old record of 714 set by Babe Ruth.

Frank Robinson becomes first African-American major league baseball manager (Cleveland Indians).

President Ford dedicates Golf Hall of Fame in Pinehurst, North Carolina.

Baseball Commissioner Bowie Kuhn suspends George Steinbrenner of New York Yankees for two years because of his federal conviction for illegal political contributions.

Consecutive winning streak of UCLA basketball team ends at 88 by Notre Dame.

New Jersey Superior Court rules that girls must be permitted to play in Little League baseball games.

Al Kaline of Detroit Tigers gets his 3,000th base hit; Lou Brock of St. Louis Cardinals steals 700th base, ends season with record 118.

Tom Waldrop sets world indoor-mile record of 3 minutes, 55 seconds.

WINNERS *Auto racing*—Johnny Rutherford, Indianapolis 500; Richard Petty, NASCAR; *Baseball*—Oakland Athletics, World Series; *Basketball*—Purdue, NIT; North Carolina State, NCAA; Immaculata, AIAW; Boston, NBA; *Bowling*—Earl Anthony, PBA; *Boxing*—Muhammad Ali, heavyweight; *Figure skating*—Gordon McKeller, U.S. men's; Dorothy Hamill, U.S. women's; *Football* (bowls)—Ohio State, Rose; Penn State, Orange; Notre Dame, Sugar; Nebraska, Cotton; Miami, Super Bowl VIII; *Golf*—Hale Irwin, U.S. Open; Lee Trevino, PGA; Gary Player, Masters; Sandra Haynie, U.S. Women's Open and LPGA; *Harness racing*—Christopher T., Hambletonian; *Hockey*—Philadelphia, Stanley Cup; *Horse racing*—Cannonade, Kentucky Derby; Little Current, Preakness Stakes and Belmont Stakes; *Tennis*—Jimmy Connors, U.S. Open (men); Billie Jean King, U.S. Open (women); *Yachting*—U.S. yacht *Courageous* retains America's Cup.

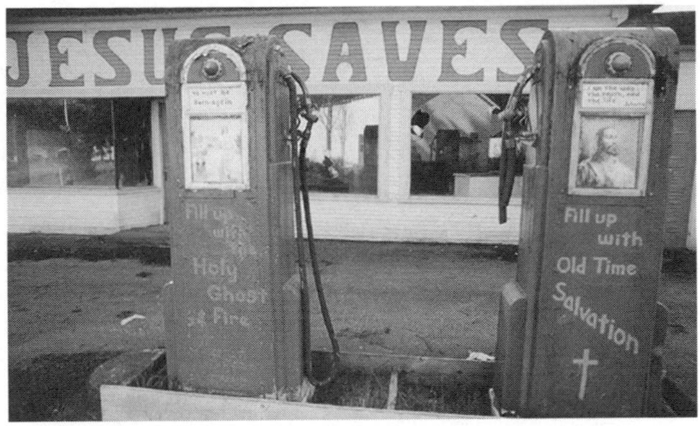

During the five-month fuel crisis that lasts until March 1974, abandoned gas stations are often used for other purposes. This Potlatch, Washington, station has been turned into a religious meeting place. NATIONAL ARCHIVES AND RECORDS ADMINISTRATION, RECORDS OF THE ENVIRONMENTAL PROTECTION AGENCY

MISCELLANEOUS

Thirteen states are hit by 148 tornadoes in 24 hours (April 3–4); the storms kill 315, injure 600, destroy or damage 27,000 homes.

David Kunst is first to circle the Earth on foot, returns to Waseca, Minnesota, after 14,500 miles in 4 years, 3 months, 16 days.

"Streaking," a fad involving running naked in public, sweeps the nation.

PRIMARY SOURCE DOCUMENT

President Richard M. Nixon's Resignation Speech, August 8, 1974

INTRODUCTION The Watergate scandal began with a bungled burglary and ended with a presidential pardon. On June 17, 1972, seven employees of the Republican Party's Committee to Reelect the President were caught burgling the headquarters of the Democratic National Committee (DNC), located in the Watergate building complex of commercial offices and private residences. These employees, including a former CIA employee and Cuban exiles associated with various anti-Castro campaigns, were attempting to place wiretaps on DNC phones as part of Operation Gemstone, a long-running campaign of "dirty tricks" designed to discredit Democratic challengers to Richard M. Nixon's presidency. Nixon was reelected in November 1972, but *Washington Post* reporters Carl Bernstein and Robert Woodward uncovered important links between the burglars and top Nixon aides John Ehrlichman and H. R. Haldeman; they were assisted by an unnamed government official nicknamed "Deep Throat." The *Post* articles led to a wider investigation that included fifty-three days of televised Senate hearings on a White House ordered cover-up of the burglary. Contributing to the constitutional crisis, Vice President Spiro I. Agnew was forced to resign while the hearings were in progress because he had failed to pay sufficient taxes on his previous income as Maryland governor.

In response to Nixon's attempts to derail the investigation, the House Judiciary Committee adopted three articles of impeachment in July 1974 on the grounds that Nixon obstructed justice by refusing to turn over tape recordings of Oval Office meetings that could provide evidence of his participation in the cover-up. The U.S. Supreme Court ordered Nixon to produce the tapes in *United States* v. *Nixon,* rejecting his claim of executive privilege. The tapes produced "smoking gun" evidence showing that he knew of the cover-up and had, in fact, obstructed justice. Facing an impeachment trial as well as the increasing hostility of the nation, Nixon elected to resign the presidency. In his final speech to the nation, printed here, he does not explain "the Watergate matter," as he calls it, but focuses instead on a summary of the highlights of his presidency. After Nixon left office, his successor, Gerald R. Ford, pardoned him for his crimes and misdemeanors. His co-conspirators were not so lucky, as many of them, including Ehrlichman and Haldeman, served time in prison.

Good evening.

This is the 37th time I have spoken to you from this office, where so many decisions have been made that shaped the history of this Nation. Each time I have done so to discuss with you some matter that I believe affected the national interest.

In all the decisions I have made in my public life, I have always tried to do what was best for the Nation. Throughout the long and difficult period of Watergate, I have felt it was my duty to persevere, to make every possible effort to complete the term of office to which you elected me.

In the past few days, however, it has become evident to me that I no longer have a strong enough political base in the Congress to justify continuing that effort. As long as there was such a base, I felt strongly that it was necessary to see the constitutional process through to its conclusion, that to do otherwise would be unfaithful to the spirit of that deliberately difficult process and a dangerously destabilizing precedent for the future.

But with the disappearance of that base, I now believe that the constitutional purpose has been served, and there is no longer a need for the process to be prolonged.

I would have preferred to carry through to the finish whatever the personal agony it would have involved, and my family unanimously urged me to do so. But the interest of the Nation must always come before any personal considerations.

From the discussions I have had with Congressional and other leaders, I have concluded that because of the Watergate matter I might not have the support of the Congress that I would consider necessary to back the very difficult decisions and carry out the duties of this office in the way the interests of the Nation would require.

I have never been a quitter. To leave office before my term is completed is abhorrent to every instinct in my body. But as President, I must put the interest of America first. America needs a full-time President and a full-time Congress, particularly at this time with problems we face at home and abroad.

To continue to fight through the months ahead for my personal vindication would almost totally absorb the time and attention of both the President and the Congress in a period when our entire focus should be on the great issues of peace abroad and prosperity without inflation at home.

Therefore, I shall resign the Presidency effective at noon tomorrow. Vice President Ford will be sworn in as President at that hour in this office.

As I recall the high hopes for America with which we began this second term, I feel a great sadness that I will not be here in this office working on your behalf to achieve those hopes in the next 2½ years. But in turning over direction of the Government to Vice President Ford, I know, as I told the Nation when I nominated him for that office 10 months ago, that the leadership of America will be in good hands.

In passing this office to the Vice President, I also do so with the profound sense of the weight of responsibility that will fall on his shoulders tomorrow and, therefore, of the understanding, the patience, the cooperation he will need from all Americans.

As he assumes that responsibility, he will deserve the help and the support of all of us. As we look to the future, the first essential is to begin healing the wounds of this Nation, to put the bitterness and divisions of the recent past behind us, and to rediscover those shared ideals that lie at the heart of our strength and unity as a great and as a free people.

By taking this action, I hope that I will have hastened the start of that process of healing which is so desperately needed in America.

I regret deeply any injuries that may have been done in the course of the events that led to this decision. I would say only that if some of my judgments were wrong, and some were wrong, they were made in what I believed at the time to be the best interest of the Nation.

To those who have stood with me during these past difficult months, to my family, my friends, to many others who joined in supporting my cause because they believed it was right, I will be eternally grateful for your support.

And to those who have not felt able to give me your support, let me say I leave with no bitterness toward those who have opposed me, because all of us, in the final analysis, have been concerned with the good of the country, however our judgments might differ.

So, let us all now join together in affirming that common commitment and in helping our new President succeed for the benefit of all Americans.

I shall leave this office with regret at not completing my term, but with gratitude for the privilege of serving as your President for the past 5½ years. These years have been a momentous time in the history of our Nation and the world. They have been a time of achievement in which we can all be proud, achievements that represent the shared efforts of the Administration, the Congress, and the people.

But the challenges ahead are equally great, and they, too, will require the support and the efforts of the Congress and the people working in cooperation with the new Administration.

We have ended America's longest war, but in the work of securing a lasting peace in the world, the goals ahead are even more far-reaching and more difficult. We must complete a structure of peace so that it will be said of this generation, our generation of Americans, by the people of all nations, not only that we ended one war but that we prevented future wars.

We have unlocked the doors that for a quarter of a century stood between the United States and the People's Republic of China.

We must now ensure that the one quarter of the world's people who live in the People's Republic of China will be and remain not our enemies but our friends.

In the Middle East, 100 million people in the Arab countries, many of whom have considered us their enemy for nearly 20 years, now look on us as their friends. We must continue to build on that friendship so that peace can settle at last over the Middle East and so that the cradle of civilization will not become its grave.

Together with the Soviet Union we have made the crucial breakthroughs that have begun the process of limiting nuclear arms. But we must set as our goal not just limiting but reducing and finally destroying these terrible weapons so that they cannot destroy civilization and so that the threat of nuclear war will no longer hang over the world and the people.

We have opened the new relation with the Soviet Union. We must continue to develop and expand that new relationship so that the two strongest nations of the world will live together in cooperation rather than confrontation.

Around the world, in Asia, in Africa, in Latin America, in the Middle East, there are millions of people who live in terrible poverty, even starvation. We must keep as our goal turning away from production for war and expanding production for peace so that people everywhere on this earth can at last look forward in their children's time, if not in our own time, to having the necessities for a decent life.

Here in America, we are fortunate that most of our people have not only the blessings of liberty but also the means to live full and good and, by the world's standards, even abundant lives. We must press on, however, toward a goal of not only more and better jobs but of full opportunity for every American and of what we are striving so hard right now to achieve, prosperity without inflation.

For more than a quarter of a century in public life I have shared in the turbulent history of this era. I have fought for what I believed in. I have tried to the best of my ability to discharge those duties and meet those responsibilities that were entrusted to me.

Sometimes I have succeeded and sometimes I have failed, but always I have taken heart from what Theodore Roosevelt once said about the man in the arena, "whose face is marred by dust and sweat and blood, who strives valiantly, who errs and comes short again and again because there is not effort without error and shortcoming, but who does actually strive to do the deed, who knows the great enthusiasms, the great devotions, who spends himself in a worthy cause, who at the best knows in the end the triumphs of high achievements and who at the worst, if he fails, at least fails while daring greatly."

I pledge to you tonight that as long as I have a breath of life in my body, I shall continue in that spirit. I shall continue to work for the great causes to which I have been dedicated throughout my years as a Congressman, a Senator, a Vice President, and President, the cause of peace not just for America but among all nations, prosperity, justice, and opportunity for all of our people.

There is one cause above all to which I have been devoted and to which I shall always be devoted for as long as I live.

When I first took the oath of office as President 5½ years ago, I made this sacred commitment, to "consecrate my office, my energies, and all the wisdom I can summon to the cause of peace among nations."

I have done my very best in all the days since to be true to that pledge. As a result of these efforts, I am confident that the world is a safer place today, not only for the people of America but for the people of all nations, and that all of our children have a better chance than before of living in peace rather than dying in war.

This, more than anything, is what I hoped to achieve when I sought the Presidency. This, more than anything, is what I hope will be my legacy to you, to our country, as I leave the Presidency.

To have served in this office is to have felt a very personal sense of kinship with each and every American. In leaving it, I do so with this prayer: May God's grace be with you in all the days ahead.

1975

INTERNATIONAL

VIETNAM WAR Saigon is shelled; remaining U.S. military evacuated (April 27); South Vietnam announces its unconditional surrender to Vietcong (April 30). **SEE PRIMARY DOCUMENT** "Looking at U.S. Role in Vietnam" by R. W. Apple Jr.

All-out attack results in recovery of U.S. ship *Mayaguez*, which Cambodian forces captured (May 14).

U.S. vetoes admission of North and South Vietnam to U.N.

NATIONAL

President Gerald R. Ford is unharmed in two apparent assassination attempts; Secret Service agent grabs pistol aimed at the president in Sacramento (September 5), and a political activist fires at him and misses in San Francisco (September 22).

Ohio Gov. John Rhodes and 27 of the National Guard are exonerated in 1970 Kent State shooting in which four students were killed.

Supreme Court rules that federal government has exclusive rights to oil and gas resources beyond 3-mile limit in Atlantic Ocean.

Nuclear Regulatory Agency is established, takes over functions of Atomic Energy Commission.

First-class postage rises to 13 cents an ounce (December 31).

U.S. military academies open to women.

DEATH Gen. Anthony J. McAuliffe, commander at Bastogne, remembered for answer ("Nuts!") to German surrender demand.

BUSINESS/INDUSTRY/INVENTIONS

Automobile companies give rebates to stimulate sales.

Minimum wage is raised to $2.10 an hour for nonfarmworkers, $1.80 for farmworkers (January 1).

Tjalling Koopmans shares Nobel Prize in economics with Leonid Kantrovich of U.S.S.R. for contributions to theory of "optimum allocation of resources."

Jimmy Hoffa, former Teamsters Union president, mysteriously disappears.

Altair, a microcomputer kit that takes hobbyists 40 or more hours to assemble, appears on the cover of *Popular Electronics.*

TRANSPORTATION

Plan to revitalize six bankrupt northeastern and midwestern railroads is announced.

Staten Island ferry fare, which had been 5 cents since 1898, is raised to 25 cents.

SCIENCE/MEDICINE

L. James Rainwater shares Nobel Prize in physics with Ben Mottelson and Aage Bohr of Denmark for discovery of connection between collective and particle motion in atomic nucleus; David Baltimore, Renato Dulbeco, and Howard Temin share prize in physiology/medicine for discoveries of interaction between tumor viruses and genetic cell material.

U.S. and Russian spacecraft link up 140 miles above Earth, exchange visits.

DEATHS Detlev W. Bronk, founder of biophysics; John R. Dunning, first to demonstrate fission of uranium 235.

EDUCATION

Supreme Court rules that school pupils cannot be suspended without notice of charges against them and a chance to be heard; rules that school officials who discipline pupils unfairly cannot claim ignorance of pupils' rights if sued; rules that states may permit teachers to spank misbehaving students.

Federal district court orders Detroit to begin school integration.

Louisville and Jefferson County, Kentucky, becomes first metropolitan area to achieve racial balance in public schools by cross-district busing.

DEATH Robert G. Sproul, president of University of California (1930–1958).

RELIGION

Elizabeth Ann Seton is canonized, first U.S.-born Catholic saint (September 24).

Internal Revenue Service announces that tax exemption will be denied to church-affiliated schools that refuse to accept children of all racial and ethnic groups.

A helicopter is cast overboard from the USS *Blue Ridge* to make way for more evacuees from Saigon, South Vietnam. **AP/WIDE WORLD PHOTOS**

ART/MUSIC

Beverly Sills debuts with Metropolitan Opera.

Ned Rorem composes "Air Music."

SONGS (POPULAR): "Have You Never Been Mellow," "I'm Sorry," "Love Will Keep Us Together," "Mandy," "Rhinestone Cowboy," "Thank God, I'm a Country Boy," "Another Somebody Done Somebody Wrong Song."

DEATHS Thomas Hart Benton, artist of realistic portraits; Richard Tucker, opera tenor; "Cannonball" Adderly, jazz saxophonist; Vincent Lopez, pianist and orchestra leader.

LITERATURE/JOURNALISM

BOOKS *Humboldt's Gift* by Saul Bellow, *Shogun* by James D. Clavell, *Ragtime* by E. L. Doctorow, *Looking for Mr. Goodbar* by Judith L. Rossner, *In the Beginning* by Chaim Potok.

DEATHS Authors Thornton Wilder, P. G. Wodehouse, and Rex Stout; George Baker, cartoonist.

ENTERTAINMENT

A Chorus Line is written by Michael Bennett, Marvin Hamlisch, and others; F. Murray Abraham stars in *The Ritz;* Ellen Burstyn in *Same Time, Next Year.*

MOVIES *One Flew over the Cuckoo's Nest* with Jack Nicholson, *Shampoo* with Warren Beatty, *The Sunshine Boys* with George Burns and Walter Matthau, *Jaws* with Roy Scheider and Richard Dreyfuss.

New television shows include *Welcome Back, Kotter* with John Travolta, *Wheel of Fortune, One Day at a Time* with Bonnie Franklin, *The Jeffersons* with Sherman Hemsley, *Barney Miller* with Hal Linden.

DEATHS Fredric March, screen actor; Rod Serling, television playwright *(Twilight Zone).*

SPORTS

Bowie Kuhn is reelected baseball commissioner; former postmaster Lawrence R. O'Brien is named NBA commissioner.

Bobby Fischer forfeits world chess championship after rule changes that he requests for a match are refused.

Three sports facilities are completed: New Orleans Superdome; Pontiac (Michigan) Metropolitan Stadium, home of Detroit Lions; Meadowlands Harness Track in the sports complex near Hackensack, New Jersey.

World Football League disbands after two years.

WINNERS *Auto racing*—Bobby Unser, Indianapolis 500; Richard Petty, NASCAR; *Baseball*—Cincinnati Reds,

World Series; *Basketball*—Princeton, NIT; UCLA, NCAA; Golden State, NBA; *Bowling*—Earl Anthony, PBA; *Boxing*—Muhammad Ali, heavyweight; Victor Galindez, light heavyweight; Carlos Monzon, middleweight; *Figure skating*—Gordon McKellen Jr., U.S. men; Dorothy Hamill, U.S. women; *Football* (bowls)—Southern California, Rose; Notre Dame, Orange; Nebraska, Sugar; Penn State, Cotton; Pittsburgh, Super Bowl IX; *Golf*—Lou Graham, U.S. Open; Jack Nicklaus, PGA and Masters; Sandra Palmer, U.S. Women's Open; Kathy Whitworth, LPGA; *Harness racing*—Bonefish, Hambletonian; *Hockey*—Philadelphia, Stanley Cup; *Horse racing*—Foolish Pleasure, Kentucky Derby; Master Derby, Preakness Stakes; Avatar, Belmont Stakes; *Tennis*—Manuel Orantes, U.S. Open (men); Chris Evert, U.S. Open (women).

DEATHS Jockey Alvaro Pineda in accident at starting gate; Steve Prefontaine, runner; Jim Londos, wrestler; Casey Stengel, baseball player and manager; Avery Brundage, leader in national, international amateur athletics.

MISCELLANEOUS

Air Force plane carrying Vietnamese children crashes near Saigon, 172 are killed; Eastern Boeing 727 crashes in storm at Kennedy Airport, 113 die.

PRIMARY SOURCE DOCUMENT

"Looking at U.S. Role in Vietnam" by R. W. Apple Jr., April 29, 1975

INTRODUCTION The Vietnam War lasted through six presidential administrations, from Harry S. Truman to Gerald R. Ford. It cost over 58,000 American soldiers and support personnel their lives and caused another 300,000 casualties, many of whom suffered alienation and isolation upon returning to a country deeply divided over the war. Nearly 1.5 million Vietnamese lost their lives; 10 million more became refugees, including over 30,000 children born to U.S. soldiers and Vietnamese women.

The rising death toll in the late 1960s, and the failure of American politicians to adequately justify it, triggered a traumatic cultural conflict in American society that divided families, communities, and the nation itself. Protest against the war escalated after the Tet offensive of 1968, with television bringing horrific images of a brutal war into Americans' living rooms on a nightly basis. After National Guardsmen shot and killed four Kent State University protesters in 1970, students at four hundred colleges and universities went on strike, the first general student strike in the history of the United States. A highly diverse protest movement comprising men and women, poor and rich, white and black, young and old, as well as Vietnam veterans, emerged and took to the streets. Even high school students got into the act, starting about 500 newspapers to protest the war.

Additional pressure to end the war came in 1971 when the *New York Times* published the Pentagon Papers, a massive collection of documents which provided clear evidence that as early as 1965 American intelligence officers thought the war was "unwinnable" and that the objective of continued military activity was to avoid "a humiliating defeat" in the context of the cold war.

Even before the Vietnam War ended in 1975 it created changes in how the government waged war. In 1973 Congress passed the War Powers Act, which required the President to notify Congress within 48 hours if military force was to be used. It also limited such military action to 60 days without a congressional declaration of war. The Vietnam War cost $167 billion, which siphoned money from much-needed social programs during the 1960s and 1970s, fueled inflation that devastated the middle class, and increased the federal deficit. The war additionally spawned general distrust of the government, which was compounded by the Watergate crisis that became front-page headlines in 1973.

In January 1973 the United States signed the Paris Peace Accords, which established terms for American withdrawal from South Vietnam; the South Vietnamese, with American advisors' help, took over the war's effort. On May 1, 1975, that effort finally collapsed when North Vietnamese communist forces seized control of Saigon and all of Vietnam.

The following document is a *New York Times* article published the day before the last remaining American advisors and soldiers frantically evacuated Saigon. Reporter R.W. Apple Jr. captures the diverse and divided sentiments of key participants in and observers of the Vietnam War as it came to a bitter end.

The following dispatch was written before the Saigon Government surrendered to Communist forces.

WASHINGTON, April 29—For many Americans it may have been a day of simple emotions—relief, perhaps, that the long war in Vietnam was near an end, or bitterness that the United States and its ally had in the end lost.

But for many Americans who played prominent parts in the long Indochinese struggle—senior officials in Washington, leaders of the antiwar movement, reporters who covered the war, officials who served in the American Embassy in Saigon—reactions were more complex.

Some talked of fear for their friends' well-being; some dwelt on mistakes they felt they and their country had made; some expressed hope that the future would be better.

Here are what some of them had to say on the day the last American officials left Vietnam, ending an involvement of two decades at a cost of vast blood and treasure:

ROBERT W. KOMER, former chief of the pacification program in Vietnam and adviser to President Lyndon B. Johnson:

"I feel terrible frustration and depression about all the things that we should have done and could have done and didn't do. In hindsight, it was a disaster, but that's easy.

"I haven't thought about much in the last month except the people who are still there—waking up in the middle of the night, worrying about people like Colonel Be [a Vietnamese pacification expert]. We'll recover, but will they?"

WILLIAM J. PORTER, former Deputy Ambassador in Saigon and chief negotiator at the Paris peace talks, now Ambassador to Canada:

"All of my worries of all these years about how it was going to end have materialized. We didn't understand the place, we didn't know how to fight there. It was a sad epoch.

"There are lessons to be drawn from it, very clear lessons. We should never have tried to get by with half-measures, because you can't do that and control the outcome. The national moral is that you apply power if you have it."

BARRY ZORTHIAM, former chief information officer for the United States Embassy in Saigon, now an executive of Time Inc.:

"I feel a real sense of horror about the awful way in which we had to get out combined with a sense of relief that it's finally over. But then there are the beginnings of analysis, second thoughts, recriminations, distillations.

"Where did things go wrong? Could there have been a different result? I'm not sure, but I sometimes think we would have been better to have let them solve it their way 10 years ago. To what degree was it our desires, our ambitions, our pressures that kept putting them through this?"

ANTHONY LAKE, former Foreign Service officer in Vietnam and aide to Secretary of State Kissinger, who resigned to protest the American invasion of Cambodia:

"I'm glad the fighting is coming to an end, but I feel shame that it took so long and that we played the role we did in extending it for so long. It has been inevitable that they would win the war for so many years.

"Now here's a chance to figure out what kind of foreign policy we should have instead of having Vietnam rip us apart. That hasn't been possible before, not when anyone who objected to military aid for Saigon automatically was being called neo-isolationist."

MORTON H. HALPERIN, former Defense Department official and aide to Secretary Kissinger, whose telephone was tapped:

"I'm relieved that it's over and that we didn't go back again. My fear was that Vietnam was a film that would keep running backwards and forward and would never end.

"Then dismay that people talk of losing Vietnam or the fall of Vietnam. That country has not fallen and we didn't have it to lose. Vietnam will now be independent."

RICHARD HOLBROOKE, former Foreign Service officer in Vietnam who now edits Foreign Policy, *a quarterly:*

"I'm just sort of weary. We never belonged there even though so many people tried to do so many good things.

"And I'm angry at the gullibility of Nixon and Ford and Kissinger for believing that the South Vietnamese could survive this offensive without the vertebra of American fire power, when they couldn't survive any of the earlier ones without us. By this colossal foreign policy failure we provided for our own humiliation, we made the worst of a bad situation.

"Why did we never go to Thieu, after Paris and the Congressional arms cutoff, and tell him that this was a new world and he had better negotiate unless he wanted defeat?"

W. AVERELL HARRIMAN, long-time participant in American foreign policy, who turned against the war in the late nineteen-sixties:

"It is tragic that President Roosevelt's determination not to let the French back into Indochina after World War II was not carried out. It would have saved France, the United States and the Vietnamese people this desperate experience."

DEAN RUSK, Secretary of State under President Johnson and President John F. Kennedy:

"Obviously, I'm very saddened by recent developments, but also concerned where the story ends. We haven't seen the final bill yet. The American people around 1968 decided that if we couldn't tell them when the war would end, we might as well chuck it. Part of this decision was to take the consequences, and that's what we are going to have to do now.

"I can't avoid my responsibility for what happened in Southeast Asia, but I don't think others, including the peace movement, should either for what will happen now."

CORA WEISS, antiwar activist who helped establish contact with Hanoi concerning American prisoners of war:

"It's a very exciting and tragic moment at the same time. Exciting because no more lives will be wasted, because the people of Vietnam will be able to determine their lives without foreign interference. Tragic because one can't forget the needless death and destruction.

"For 25 years the United States has tried to control 25 million people on a tiny strip of land and we couldn't do it and we should never try to do it again anywhere else."

SAM BROWN, one of the organizers of the Vietnam moratorium demonstrations, now Treasurer of the State of Colorado:

"There were some people here today suggesting a celebration. That's so far from what I feel. We started that era with great hopes and expectations, and Vietnam crushed them and our sense of the future. Now I feel no sense of rebirth; something has ended but nothing has started.

"Unfortunately, we still think we should play with the destinies of other countries; we only think our tactics were bad in Vietnam. We're in for a period not of real soul-searching, which we need, but of blame-assessing."

PROF. RICHARD FALK of Princeton University, a key antiwar theoretician:

"It goes back to the Paris cease-fire accords. We were caught in a trap.

"We couldn't get our prisoners back without Thieu's agreement, and we could only get Thieu's agreement if we promised to support his opposition to bringing about peace. The result was an unnecessary added interlude of suffering."

WARD S. JUST, a former Washington Post correspondent in Vietnam, now a novelist:

"I was asked the other day to write something about all this and it just wouldn't go, it just wouldn't write. I had nothing helpful or enlightening or ameliorative to say.

"You can only look on it with a kind of horrified fascination. I don't believe the cultures mix. It was a kind of failure of our national temperament; we felt that if we kept plugging away even if we were on the wrong course, by the triumph of American innocence everything would come out all right. It didn't."

MORLEY SAFER, a CBS news correspondent in Vietnam:

"I feel a deep unhappiness, a sense that surely there must have been a better way, sorrow for the Vietnamese who saw the momentary advantage of going along with us.

"It's vital to refight this war for a long time to come so that we understand just what we did over there, not only to ourselves but to them, and why we did it. We don't understand it yet, and we have to make the effort."

Some of those who supported the American effort to the end, including both journalists and military officers, said they were either too bitter or too sensitively situated professionally to comment on the day's events.

SOURCE:
R. W. Apple Jr., "Looking at U.S. Role in Vietnam" *New York Times*, April 29, 1975. Copyright© 1975 by the New York Times Company. Reproduced by permission.

1976

INTERNATIONAL

Ambassador to Lebanon Francis E. Maloy Jr. and an aide are killed by an unidentified man.

Cuban Premier Fidel Castro cancels antihijacking pact with U.S., charges U.S. complicity in crash of a Cuban airliner.

NATIONAL

Democrat Jimmy Carter is elected president, defeats President Gerald R. Ford; Carter receives 40,828,929 popular and 297 electoral votes against 39,149,940 popular and 240 electoral for Ford.

Nation celebrates 200th anniversary with a "tall ships" parade in New York Harbor, presidential visit to Independence Hall in Philadelphia, and other events throughout the country.

Supreme Court in *Gregg* v. *Georgia* holds that death penalty in first-degree murder cases is not in and of itself cruel and unusual punishment.

Pesticides containing mercury are banned.

Supreme Court rules that the president has right to impose fees on imported oil.

Homestead Act of 1862 is repealed for all states except Alaska because there no longer is cultivable public land available.

DEATHS James A. Farley, former postmaster general (1933–1940); Richard J. Daley, Chicago mayor (1955–1976); Perle Mesta, Washington hostess (model for play *Call Me Madam*); Howard R. Hughes, reclusive millionaire.

BUSINESS/INDUSTRY/INVENTIONS

Milton Friedman is awarded Nobel Prize in economics for work in consumption analysis and monetary history and theory.

Minimum wage rises to $2.30 an hour (January 1).

Stephen G. Wozniak and Steven P. Jobs introduce Apple I desktop computer.

DEATHS William Zeckendorf, real-estate developer; J. Paul Getty, oil industry leader.

TRANSPORTATION

Transportation Department postpones mandatory air bags in all cars for two years.

Approval is given for $2.4 million aid to improve commuter rail service between Washington (D.C.), New York, and Boston.

Washington, D.C., subway service begins.

Concorde SST service from Paris and London to Washington begins.

Astronaut Frank Borman is named chairman of Eastern Air Lines.

SCIENCE/MEDICINE

Burton Richter and Samuel C. C. Ting share Nobel Prize in physics for discoveries of new type of elementary particle (PSI or J); William N. Lipscomb is awarded prize in chemistry for studies on structure of boranes; Baruch S. Blumberg and Daniel C. Gajdusek share prize in physiology/medicine for discoveries of new mechanisms for origin and dissemination of infectious diseases.

Flu-shot program is launched (March 24), halts after 58 persons suffered paralysis from shots.

Unmanned spacecraft successfully lands on Mars (July 20).

A mysterious "Legionnaire's disease" kills 29 persons who attended convention in Philadelphia.

DEATH Morris Fishbein, editor, *AMA Journal* (1924–1949).

EDUCATION

Supreme Court rules that courts cannot require school authorities to readjust attendance zones each year to keep up with population shifts; also rules that private nonsectarian schools cannot exclude African-American children because of race.

U.S. Appeals Court upholds court-ordered integration of Boston schools.

RELIGION

International Eucharistic Congress is held in Philadelphia.

Episcopal Church bishops and deputies' vote to permit ordination of women as priests and bishops is approved by general convention.

Thelma D. Adair is elected moderator of United Presbyterian Church, first African-American woman to hold that post.

Catholic Archbishop William W. Baum of Washington, D.C., is elevated to cardinal.

ART/MUSIC

Richard Wernick composes *Visions of Terror and Wonder.*

Fireworks over the Statue of Liberty in New York harbor during the nation's bicentennial celebration, July 4, 1976. © JAN LUCAS/ PHOTO RESEARCHERS, INC.

Christo, the artist, designs *Running Fence,* a 24-mile curtain of fabric along Pacific Coast.

SONGS (POPULAR): "I Write the Songs," "Tonight's the Night," "Disco Lady," "Fifty Ways to Leave Your Lover," "If You Leave Me Now."

DEATHS Lily Pons, opera soprano; Alexander Calder, sculptor; Eddie Condon, Dixieland band leader; painters Man Ray, surrealist, and Mark Tobey.

LITERATURE/JOURNALISM

Saul Bellow is awarded Nobel Prize in literature.

BOOKS *Beautiful Swimmers* by William W. Warner, *The Deep* by Peter Benchley, *Roots* by Alex Haley, *The Boys from Brazil* by Ira Levin, *Trinity* by Leon Uris, *The Zodiac* by James Dickey, *Collected Poems* by W. H. Auden, *Slapstick* by Kurt Vonnegut.

DEATHS Samuel Eliot Morison, historian; Munro Leaf, author and illustrator *(Ferdinand, Wee Gillis);* Arnold Gingrich, founder and publisher, *Esquire* magazine; Mary Margaret McBride, radio commentator.

ENTERTAINMENT

PLAYS Jules Feiffer writes *Knock, Knock;* David Rabe, *Streamers.*

MOVIES *Network* with Peter Finch, *Rocky* with Sylvester Stallone, *All the President's Men* with Dustin Hoffman and Robert Redford, *Marathon Man* also with Hoffman, *Taxi Driver* with Robert DeNiro.

TELEVISION *Wonder Woman* with Lynda Carter, *Laverne and Shirley* with Penny Marshall and Cindy Williams, *Charlie's Angels, The Muppets,* and Donny and Marie Osmond.

DEATHS Jo Mielziner, stage designer for 360 Broadway plays; Rosalind Russell, stage and screen actress; Busby Berkeley, stage and screen choreographer; Paul Robeson, singer and actor.

SPORTS

Winter Olympics are held in Innsbruck, Austria; Bill Koch becomes first from U.S. to win medal (silver) in Nordic events; Summer Games are held in Montreal, U.S. wins 34 golds.

NBA's 18 teams merge with four of remaining six teams of American Basketball Assn.

Baseball owners and players agree to change in reserve clause, give players free agency after five years.

New York's Yankee Stadium opens after $70 million renovation.

Dan Ripley sets pole-vault record of 18 feet, 1¼ inches.

U.S. Croquet Assn. is founded.

WINNERS *Auto racing*—Johnny Rutherford, Indianapolis 500; Cale Yarborough, NASCAR; *Baseball*—Cincinnati Reds, World Series; *Basketball*—Kentucky, NIT; Indiana, NCAA; Boston, NBA; *Bowling*—Paul Colwell, PBA; *Boxing*—Muhammad Ali, heavyweight; *Figure skating*—Dorothy Hamill, U.S. and world women's title; Terry Kubicka, U.S. men's; *Football* (bowls)—UCLA, Rose; Oklahoma, Orange; Alabama, Sugar; Arkansas, Cotton; Pittsburgh, Super Bowl X; *Golf*—Jerry Pate, U.S. Open; Dave Stockton, PGA; Ray Floyd, Masters; Jo Anne Carner, U.S. Women's Open; Betty Burfeindt, LPGA; *Harness racing*—Steve Lobell, Hambletonian; *Hockey*—Montreal, Stanley Cup; *Horse racing*—Bold Forbes, Kentucky Derby and Belmont Stakes; Elocutionist, Preakness Stakes; *Tennis*—Jimmy Connors, U.S. Open (men); Chris Evert, U.S. Open (women).

MISCELLANEOUS

Ferry and tanker collide in Mississippi River near Luling, Louisiana; 77 die; *Argo Merchant* runs aground off Nantucket Island, causes 7.7-million-gallon oil spill.

Museum of American Jewish History opens in Philadelphia.

1977

INTERNATIONAL

President Jimmy Carter and Panamanian Gen. Omar Herrera sign treaties to transfer control of Panama Canal to Panama by year 2000.

U.S. and Soviet Russia agree to continue abiding by SALT I treaty to limit strategic arms despite its 1977 expiration date.

U.S. and Canada agree on joint construction of 2,700-mile natural-gas pipeline from Alaska to continental U.S.

U.S. and Great Britain reach new civil aviation agreement.

NATIONAL

President Carter pardons most Vietnam War draft resisters.

Department of Energy is created (August 9) with James R. Schlesinger as first secretary; functions of Federal Power Commission transfer to new department.

President Carter restores gasoline price controls.

DEATHS Alice Paul, women's rights leader; Gen. Lewis B. Hershey, head, Selective Service System (1941–1970).

BUSINESS/INDUSTRY/INVENTIONS

Oil flows in 800-mile trans-Alaska pipeline, arrives in southern terminus, Valdez.

Five oil companies agree to build and operate Louisiana offshore oil port.

Sales of Apple computers reach $2.5 million; Paul Allen and William Henry Gates III form Microsoft, which will by early 1990s be world's largest manufacturer of personal-computer software, operating systems, and programming languages.

TRANSPORTATION

Supreme Court rules that Concorde SST may land at Kennedy Airport; issues rules limiting Concorde operation in U.S.

Pipe and cigar smoking is banned on all commercial airlines.

Federal court orders imposition of tolls on 13 East River and Harlem River bridges to reduce New York City mass-transit fares.

Francis Scott Key Bridge in Baltimore opens.

First overnight-cruise paddle-wheel steamboat is built in 50 years in U.S.; the 500-passenger *Mississippi Queen* is commissioned.

A space shuttle being transported on the back of a 747. Though the first orbital flight will not occur until 1981, extensive tests are carried out starting in 1977. NATIONAL AERONAUTICS AND SPACE ADMINISTRATION

SCIENCE/MEDICINE

John H. Van Vleck and Philip W. Anderson share Nobel Prize in physics for work basic to development of computer memories; Rosalyn S. Yalow, Roger C. Guillemin, and Andrew V. Schally share prize in physiology/medicine, Yalow for development of radio immunoassay, Schally and Guillemin for research in production of peptide hormones in the brain.

DEATHS Wernher von Braun, rocket scientist; Eli Lilly, pharmaceutical firm head.

EDUCATION

Supreme Court upholds right of federal courts to order citywide school desegregation plans; upholds plan for Detroit.

Health, Education, and Welfare Department issues regulations to prevent discrimination against disabled schoolchildren.

Ernest L. Boyer is named U.S. Education Commissioner.

DEATH Robert M. Hutchins, educator.

RELIGION

John N. Neumann, Catholic bishop of Philadelphia (1852–1860), becomes first U.S. man to be canonized.

Rev. Jacqueline Means becomes first woman ordained an Episcopal priest; some Episcopalians opposed to feminine ordination form Anglican Church of North America.

Supreme Court rules that states may finance counseling for parochial school children on off-school "neutral" sites.

ART/MUSIC

Michael Colgrass composes *Déjà Vu* for percussion and orchestra.

SONGS (POPULAR): "Evergreen," "How Deep Is Your Love," "Slip, Slidin' Away," "Southern Nights," "You Light Up My Life," "Baby, Come Back."

DEATHS Elvis Presley, singer; Leopold Stokowski, conductor; Bing Crosby, singer and actor; Guy Lombardo, orchestra leader; Ethel Waters, singer and actress; Maria Callas, opera soprano.

LITERATURE/JOURNALISM

BOOKS *The Dragons of Eden* by Carl Sagan, *The Thorn Birds* by Colleen McCullough, *Dreams Die First* by Harold Robbins, *Condominium* by John D. MacDonald, *Falconer* by John Cheever, *Collected Poems* by Howard Nemerov.

DEATHS MacKinlay Kantor, author; Bruce Bliven, editor, *New Republic* (1923–1955).

ENTERTAINMENT

PLAYS Andrea McArdle stars in *Annie,* Judd Hirsch in *Chapter Two,* Jessica Tandy and Hume Cronyn in *The Gin Game;* Michael Cristofer writes *The Shadow Box.*

MOVIES *Annie Hall* with Diane Keaton; *Close Encounters of the Third Kind* with Richard Dreyfuss; *New York, New York* with Liza Minnelli; *Oh, God!* with George Burns; *Smokey and the Bandit* with Burt Reynolds; *Star Wars* with Mark Hamill, Harrison Ford, and Carrie Fisher; *Saturday Night Fever* with John Travolta.

New television shows include the miniseries *Roots, The Love Boat* with Gavin McLeod, *Eight Is Enough* with Dick Van Patten, *Chips* with Erik Estrada.

DEATHS Zero (Sam) Mostel, actor; Joan Crawford and Charlie Chaplin, screen actors; Alfred Lunt, actor; Groucho Marx, entertainer and actor.

SPORTS

Reggie Jackson of New York Yankees hits three consecutive home runs on three consecutive pitches against Los Angeles Dodgers in World Series game.

Lou Brock of St. Louis Cardinals breaks Ty Cobb's base-stealing record of 892.

Two baseball stadiums open: King Dome in Seattle and Olympic Stadium in Montreal.

National Hockey League rejects merger with World Hockey League.

Fifteen members of Evansville (Indiana) University basketball squad die in plane crash.

Jockey Steve Cauthen sets record for purses in a year: $6,151,750.

Janet Guthrie becomes first woman to drive in Indianapolis 500 auto race; mechanical problems force her out after 27 laps.

WINNERS *Auto racing*—A. J. Foyt, Indianapolis 500; Cale Yarborough, NASCAR; *Baseball*—New York Yankees, World Series; *Basketball*—St. Bonaventure, NIT; Marquette, NCAA; Portland, NBA; *Bowling*—Tommy Hudson, PBA; *Boxing*—Muhammad Ali, heavyweight; *Figure skating*—Linda Fratianne, U.S. and world women's titles; Charles Tickner, U.S. men's; *Football* (bowls)—Southern California, Rose; Ohio State, Orange; Pittsburgh, Sugar; Houston, Cotton; Oakland, Super Bowl XI; *Golf*—Hubert Green, U.S. Open; Lanny Wadkins, PGA; Tom Watson, Masters; Hollis Stacy, U.S. Women's Open; Chako Higuchi, LPGA; *Harness racing*—Green Speed, Hambletonian; *Hockey*—Montreal, Stanley Cup; *Horse racing*—Seattle Slew becomes 10th Triple Crown winner, wins Kentucky Derby, Preakness Stakes, and Belmont Stakes; *Tennis*—Australia, Davis Cup; Guillermo Vilas, U.S. Open (men); Chris Evert, U.S. Open (women); *Yachting*—U.S. yacht *Courageous* retains America's Cup.

MISCELLANEOUS

Fire in a Southgate, Kentucky, nightclub kills 164.

A Boeing 747 completes round-the-world flight over both poles in 54 hours, 7 minutes, 12 seconds.

1978

INTERNATIONAL

Senate approves two treaties to turn Panama Canal over to Panama by year 2000 (March 16, April 18); President Jimmy Carter and General Herrera of Panama sign the treaties.

Talks begin at Camp David, Maryland, between President Carter, Egyptian President Anwar Sadat, and Israeli Prime Minister Menachem Begin to seek Mideast peace.

Solomon Islands become independent; U.S. protectorate since World War II.

NATIONAL

Members of the People's Temple in South America shoot Rep. Leo J. Ryan of California and four other U.S. citizens to death; soon thereafter, 900 members of the Temple are murdered or commit suicide.

Supreme Court refuses to allow firm quota system in affirmative action plans; also rules that New York City can prohibit construction of 53-story office building atop landmark Grand Central Terminal.

President Carter places more than 56 million acres of Alaska federal lands into National Park system.

Cost of first-class postage increases to 15 cents.

DEATH Former Vice President Hubert H. Humphrey (1965–1969).

BUSINESS/INDUSTRY/INVENTIONS

Herbert A. Simon is awarded Nobel Prize in economics for research in decision-making process in economic organizations.

Minimum wage increases to $2.65 an hour (January 1).

Longest U.S. coal strike, nearly four months, ends (March 25).

DEATHS John D. MacArthur, Bankers Life Insurance Co. president; Edward Durrell Stone, architect (Kennedy Center); Charles Eames, furniture designer; William P. Lear, aircraft manufacturer.

TRANSPORTATION

First Volkswagen comes off New Stanton, Pennsylvania, assembly line; first U.S. mass production of foreign cars.

Ben Abruzzo, Max Anderson, and Larry Newman make first successful balloon crossing of Atlantic.

Airline industry is freed from federal regulation.

Seaboard Coast Line Industries and Chessie Systems announce merger to form largest U.S. railroad.

SCIENCE/MEDICINE

Arno Penzies and Robert Wilson share Nobel Prize in physics for discovery of cosmic microwave background radiation; Daniel Nathans and Hamilton O. Smith share prize in physiology/medicine for discovery of restriction enzymes.

DEATH Margaret Mead, anthropologist.

EDUCATION

Federal appeals court bars mandatory retirement at 65.

Supreme Court rules that a student dismissed from medical school for low grades and poor performance has little right to challenge the action; also upholds constitutionality of college admissions programs that give special advantage to minorities.

Hannah H. Gray becomes president of University of Chicago, first woman president of a major U.S. university.

Congress passes legislation, makes more than 1 million students from middle-income families eligible for college tuition help.

DEATH James Bryant Conant, Harvard University president (1933–1953).

RELIGION

Reformed Protestant Dutch Church of New York City celebrates its 350th anniversary.

Rev. M. William Howard Jr., at 32, becomes youngest president of National Council of Churches.

ART/MUSIC

Joseph Schwantner composes *Aftertones of Infinity;* Leonard Bernstein, *An American Song Book.*

Norman Rockwell, who died in 1978, captured the lives of working-class Americans in his engaging magazine illustrations. ARCHIVE PHOTOS, INC.

SONGS (POPULAR): "Three Times a Lady," "With a Little Luck," "You Don't Bring Me Flowers," "You Needed Me," "If I Can't Have You," "Shadow Dancing."

DEATH Norman Rockwell, painter and illustrator.

LITERATURE/JOURNALISM

Isaac Bashevis Singer is awarded Nobel Prize in literature.

Life magazine reappears as a monthly.

BOOKS *Now and Then Poems* by Robert Penn Warren, *The World According to Garp* by John Irving, *Chesapeake* by James A. Michener, *War and Remembrance* by Herman Wouk, *The Coup* by John Updike, *A Distant Mirror* by Barbara Tuchman.

DEATHS Phyllis McGinley, poet; Faith Baldwin, novelist; Bruce Catton, Civil War historian.

ENTERTAINMENT

PLAYS Jack Lemmon stars in *Tribute,* Fats (Thomas) Waller in *Ain't Misbehavin',* Bob Fosse produces *Dancin',* Ira Levin writes *Deathtrap.*

MOVIES *The Boys from Brazil* with Gregory Peck, *The Deer Hunter* with Robert DeNiro, *Grease* with John Travolta, *Superman* with Christopher Reeve.

President Jimmy Carter, Israel's Prime Minister Menachem Begin, and Egyptian President Anwar Sadat join hands after signing the historic Camp David Accords on September 17, 1978, which establishes a framework for creating peace in the troubled Middle East.
© ROBERT DAUGHERTY/ AP/WIDE WORLD PHOTOS

New television shows include *Dallas* with Larry Hagman, *Mork and Mindy* with Robin Williams, *20/20.*

DEATHS Edgar Bergen, ventriloquist; Jack Warner, movie executive.

SPORTS

Pete Rose gets his 3,000 hit; ties National League consecutive game-hitting streak (44).

College Football Hall of Fame is dedicated at King's Island, Ohio.

WINNERS *Auto racing*—Al Unser, Indianapolis 500; Cale Yarborough, NASCAR; *Baseball*—New York Yankees, World Series; *Basketball*—Texas, NIT; Kentucky, NCAA; Washington, NBA; *Bowling*—Warren Nelson, PBA; *Boxing*—Muhammad Ali, heavyweight; *Figure skating*—Charles Tickner, U.S., world men's titles; Linda Fratianne, U.S. women's title; *Football* (bowls)—Washington, Rose; Arkansas, Orange; Alabama, Sugar; Notre Dame, Cotton; Dallas, Super Bowl XII; *Golf*—Andy North, U.S. Open; John Mahaffey, PGA; Gary Player, Masters; Hollis Stacy, U.S. Women's Open; Nancy Lopez, LPGA; *Harness racing*—Speedy Somoli, Hambletonian; *Hockey*—Montreal, Stanley Cup; *Horse racing*—Affirmed becomes 11th Triple Crown winner, wins Kentucky Derby, Preakness Stakes, and Belmont Stakes; *Tennis*—U.S., Davis Cup; Jimmy Connors, U.S. Open (men); Chris Evert, U.S. Open (women).

DEATHS Theresa W. Blanchard, figure skater; Ford Frick, baseball commissioner (1961–1965).

MISCELLANEOUS

Boeing 727 and Cessna 172 collide over San Diego, 150 die.

1979

INTERNATIONAL

Iranian militants seize U.S. Embassy in Teheran (November 4), hold 63 U.S. hostages; release African Americans and women hostages (November 19); President Jimmy Carter orders immediate suspension of oil imports from Iran (November 12).

Mob attacks U.S. Embassy in Islamabad, Pakistan, four are killed (November 21).

Muslim extremists in Kabul kill Ambassador Adolph Dubs in Afghanistan.

U.S. and Soviet Union sign SALT II treaty in Vienna to continue limitations on strategic weapons; treaty not ratified because President Carter withdraws it from Senate consideration after Soviets invade Afghanistan.

Panama assumes control of Panama Canal Zone.

China and U.S. resume full diplomatic relations; U.S. severs relations with Taiwan.

NATIONAL

President Carter announces deferral in production of neutron bomb; approves development of MX missile.

Congress approves bill to divide Department of Health, Education, and Welfare into the Department of Health and Human Services and the Department of Education; Patricia R. Harris becomes Secretary of HHS; Shirley Hufstedler, of Education.

Congress approves windfall profits tax that is expected to raise $23.2 billion.

Supreme Court rules that police cannot stop motorists at random unless there is some reason to believe motorist is violating the law; upholds voluntary affirmative action programs.

John F. Kennedy Memorial Library is dedicated in Boston.

DEATHS Omar N. Bradley, World War II general; former Vice President Nelson A. Rockefeller (1974–1977); former First Lady Mamie Eisenhower (1953–1961); Jacob L. Devers, World War II general who led southern France invasion; Rexford G. Tugwell, New Deal "brain truster."

BUSINESS/INDUSTRY/INVENTIONS

Worst U.S. nuclear accident occurs at Three Mile Island reactor at Middletown, Pennsylvania; coolant loss and partial core meltdown are symptoms; no deaths or injuries (March 28).

Theodore W. Schultz shares Nobel Prize in economics with Sir Arthur Lewis of Great Britain for work on economic problems of developing nations.

President Carter decontrols price of heavy crude oil.

Minimum wage increases to $2.90 an hour (January).

DEATHS A. Philip Randolph, labor and civil-rights leader; Conrad Hilton, hotel-chain founder; Cyrus S. Eaton, financier, industrialist.

Checking radiation in the Susquehanna River after the accident at the Three Mile Island nuclear power plant, visible in the background. UPI/CORBIS-BETTMANN

TRANSPORTATION

Lee Iacocca becomes chief executive officer of Chrysler Motors; Congress approves $1.5 billion federal loan to save Chrysler.

Southern Railway Co. is fined $1.9 billion for providing shippers free use of three company-owned resorts.

SCIENCE/MEDICINE

Steven Weinberg and Sheldon L. Glashow share Nobel Prize in physics for theory of unity of electromagnetic and weak atomic forces; Herbert C. Brown shares prize in chemistry with George Wittig of Germany for development of temporary chemical links for complex molecules; Alan M. Cormack shares prize in physiology/medicine with Godfrey N. Hounsfield of Great Britain for developing the CAT scan.

EDUCATION

House defeats a bill to ban busing as a means of desegregating schools.

RELIGION

Reformed Church of America votes to allow ordination of women as ministers.

Supreme Court rules unconstitutional Tennessee law that bans priests and ministers from running for public office; last such state law.

Pope John Paul II becomes first pope to be received in the White House.

DEATHS Catholic Archbishop James F. McIntyre of Los Angeles; Catholic Bishop Fulton Sheen, popular radio and television personality.

ART/MUSIC

David Del Tredici composes *In Memory of a Summer Day.*

Opera star Beverly Sills becomes music director of New York City Opera Co.

The Icebergs, a painting by Frederick E. Church, is auctioned for $2.5 million, highest price for an American painting.

SONGS (POPULAR): "Sad Eyes," "Please Don't Go," "Rise," "Le Freak," "Reunited," "Too Much Heaven," "No More Tears," "I Will Survive."

DEATHS Stan Kenton, band leader; Dimitri Tiomkin, composer of film scores; Richard Rodgers, composer of musicals; Leonide Massine, ballet dancer and choreographer; Arthur Fiedler, founder and conductor, Boston Pops (1930–1979).

LITERATURE/JOURNALISM

BOOKS *The Executioner's Song* by Norman Mailer, *The Island* by Peter Benchley, *Sophie's Choice* by William Styron, *Broca's Brain* by Carl Sagan, *The Strength of Fields* by James Dickey, *Great Days* by Donald Barthelme.

DEATHS Malcolm Muir, founder of *Business Week* and editor-in-chief, *Newsweek* (1937–1961); Al Capp, cartoonist ("Lil Abner"); Allen Tate, poet and critic.

ENTERTAINMENT

PLAYS Neil Simon writes *They're Playing Our Song;* Patti LuPone stars in *Evita,* Angela Lansbury in *Sweeney Todd* with music by Stephen Sondheim; Michael Weller writes *Loose Ends.*

MOVIES *Kramer versus Kramer* with Dustin Hoffman and Meryl Streep, *Apocalypse Now* with Martin Sheen, *The China Syndrome* with Jane Fonda, *Rocky II* with Sylvester Stallone, *Star Trek* with William Shatner.

New television shows include *Knots Landing, Hart to Hart* with Robert Wagner, *The Dukes of Hazzard.*

DEATHS Merle Oberon, screen actress; Mary Pickford, early screen star called America's Sweetheart; John Wayne, screen actor; Darryl F. Zanuck, screen producer.

SPORTS

First all-sports cable network, ESPN (Entertainment, Sports Network), debuts on the air (September 9).

Four World Hockey League franchises (New England, Quebec, Winnipeg, Edmonton) merge into National Hockey League.

Stan Barrett sets land-speed record of 739.66 miles per hour in a rocket-powered car at Edwards Air Force Base, California, is first to break sound barrier on the ground.

Carl Yastrzemski of Boston at 40 and Lou Brock of St. Louis each gets his 3,000th base hit.

Pro Rodeo Hall of Champions and Museum of the American Cowboy opens in Colorado Springs, Colorado.

WINNERS *Auto racing*—Rick Mears, Indianapolis 500; Richard Petty, NASCAR; *Baseball*—Pittsburgh Pirates, World Series; *Basketball*—Indiana, NIT; Michigan State, NCAA; Seattle, NBA; *Bowling*—Mike Aulby, PBA; *Boxing*—Larry Holmes, heavyweight; Matthew Franklin, light heavyweight; Vito Antuofermo, middleweight; *Figure skating*—Linda Fratianne, U.S. and world women's titles; Charles Tickner, U.S. men's title; Tai Babilonia and Randy Gardner, world pairs title; *Football* (bowls)—Southern California, Rose; Oklahoma, Orange; Alabama, Sugar; Notre Dame, Cotton; Pittsburgh, Super Bowl XIII; *Golf*—Hale Irwin, U.S. Open; David Graham, PGA; Fuzzy Zoeller, Masters; Jerilyn Britz, U.S. Women's Open; Donna Caponi, LPGA; *Harness racing*—Legend Hanover, Hambletonian; *Hockey*—Montreal, Stanley Cup; *Horse racing*—Spectacular Bid, Kentucky Derby and Preakness Stakes; Coastal, Belmont Stakes; *Tennis*—U.S., Davis Cup; John McEnroe, U.S. Open (men); Tracy Austin, U.S. Open (women).

DEATHS Thurman Munson, New York Yankees catcher; Warren Giles, National (baseball) League president.

MISCELLANEOUS

Hurricane David rakes Caribbean and eastern U.S. for a week; 1,100 die.

American Airlines jet crashes on takeoff at Chicago's O'Hare Airport killing all 272 aboard.

1980

INTERNATIONAL

U.S. severs diplomatic relations with Iran as a result of 1979 takeover of U.S. Embassy; military mission to rescue U.S. hostages in Teheran aborts after plane and helicopter collide; Secretary of State Cyrus Vance resigns over the mission.

U.S. and Great Britain announce increase in reciprocal air service; U.S. and China sign first airline service pact since 1949.

NATIONAL

Ronald Reagan, Republican, is elected president, receives 43,889,248 popular and 489 electoral votes to President Jimmy Carter's 35,481,435 popular and 49 electoral votes.

Twentieth census reports national population at 226,542,203.

President Carter orders evacuation of 710 families from Love Canal area in Niagara Falls, a former toxic-waste dump.

Nineteen- and twenty-year-old men are required to register for the military draft.

Three Alaska national parks are created: Katmai, Kenai Fjords, and Lake Clark; Mt. McKinley National Park is renamed Denali National Park.

DEATH William O. Douglas, Supreme Court justice (1939–1976).

BUSINESS/INDUSTRY/INVENTIONS

Lawrence R. Klein is awarded Nobel Prize in economics for development, analysis of empirical models of business fluctuations.

Standard Oil Co. (Indiana) agrees to settle price-violations charges by reimbursing $300 million and spending $400 million on new refining and production facilities, and exploration.

Minimum wage increases to $3.10 an hour (January 1).

DEATHS George Meany, AFL-CIO president (1955–1979); John W. Mauchly, co-inventor of electronic computer.

TRANSPORTATION

Honda Motor Co. announces that it will build assembly plant in Ohio; Nissan Motor Co. to build plant near Smyrna, Tennessee.

Interstate trucking industry is deregulated.

Two railroad mergers complete: Seaboard Coast Line and Chessie form CSX Inc. and Southern and Norfolk Western.

Interstate Commerce Commission denies railroads the power to set freight rates collectively; Civil Aeronautics Board agrees to give airlines more freedom to change domestic rates without government approval.

American hockey players celebrate their upset 4-3 victory over the Soviet Union in a semi-final game of the 1980 Winter Olympics hockey tournament. The Americans go on to beat Finland for the gold medal. CORBIS-BETTMANN

Maxie Anderson and son, Kim, complete first nonstop transcontinental balloon flight.

DEATH Jacqueline Cochran, aviator.

SCIENCE/MEDICINE

James W. Cronin and Val L. Fitch share Nobel Prize in physics for research on subatomic particles that reveal that natural laws of symmetry can be violated; Paul Berg and Walter Gilbert share prize in chemistry for development of methods for detailed mapping of DNA structure and function; Barruj Benacerraf and George Snell share prize in physiology/medicine for research in immunology.

Unmanned spacecraft *Voyager I* passes within 77,000 miles of Saturn, sends back data.

Supreme Court rules that biological organisms can be patented.

EDUCATION

Supreme Court rules that unionizing faculty members of private universities are not protected by federal law because they are "managerial" employees.

Steam and ash rise some 60,000 feet in the air as Mt. St. Helens erupts, July 22, 1980. Mt. Hood is visible in the background.
UPI/CORBIS-BETTMANN NEWSPHOTOS

Federal court rules unconstitutional a Texas law that bars children of illegal aliens from attending public schools.

St. Louis public schools integrate after eight-year program of desegregation.

RELIGION

Rev. Marjorie S. Mathews of Traverse City, Michigan, is elected Methodist bishop, is first woman named to ruling hierarchy of a U.S. church.

Mormons travel from around the world to Salt Lake City to observe church's 150th anniversary; convention rejects ordination of women.

Jesuit order forbids Rev. Robert Drinan, only priest in Congress, from running for reelection.

U.S. Appeals Court bars students from holding prayer meetings in public schools.

National Council of Churches calls for major effort to introduce "nonsexist" language in worship.

DEATHS Henry K. Sherrill, Episcopal presiding bishop; Dorothy Day, publisher, *Catholic Worker.*

ART/MUSIC

Former Beatle John Lennon is murdered outside his New York City apartment.

Eugene Ormandy ends 44 years as musical director of Philadelphia Symphony; Mikhail Baryshnikov becomes director of American Ballet Theater.

John Williams, composer and conductor, conducts Boston Pops Orchestra.

SONGS (POPULAR): "Call Me," "Funkytown," "Magic," "Starting Over," "Upside Down," "All the Gold in California," "Coward of the County," "On the Road Again," "Stand by Me."

DEATH André Kostelanetz, conductor.

LITERATURE/JOURNALISM

BOOKS *Loon Lake* by E. L. Doctorow, *The Transit of Venus* by Shirley Hazzard, *Floater* by Calvin Trillin, *The Ring* by Danielle Steel, *China Men* by Maxine H. Kingston.

DEATH Rube Goldberg, cartoonist.

ENTERTAINMENT

PLAYS Mark Meddoff writes *Children of a Lesser God; 42nd Street* is produced.

MOVIES *Coal Miner's Daughter* with Sissy Spacek; *The Empire Strikes Back* with Harrison Ford, Carrie Fisher, and Mark Hamill; *Raging Bull* with Robert DeNiro; *The Hunter* with Steve McQueen; *Nine to*

The Mariel boatlift brings thousands of Cubans to the shores of the United States in search of prosperity and political freedom in 1980. These Cuban refugees wait for U.S. Immigration officials off Key West on April 23. **CORBIS-BETTMANN**

Five with Dolly Parton; *Urban Cowboy* with John Travolta.

New on television are Barbara Mandrell, Tim Conway, and *Magnum P.I.* with Tom Selleck.

DEATHS Jimmy Durante, entertainer; Steve McQueen, screen actor; Gower Champion, dancer and director; Alfred Hitchcock, director; Mae West, screen and stage actress; Marc Connelly, playwright.

SPORTS

President Carter announces U.S. will not participate in Summer Olympics in Moscow because of Soviet invasion of Afghanistan; Winter Games held in Lake Placid, New York; U.S. wins six gold medals, five of them by speed skater Eric Heiden. **SEE PRIMARY DOCUMENT** "The Golden Goal" by E. M. Swift

Baseball owners and players sign four-year contract.

Plane crash at Warsaw Airport takes the lives of 22 U.S. amateur-boxing team members.

WINNERS *Auto racing*—Johnny Rutherford, Indianapolis 500; Dale Earnhardt, NASCAR; *Baseball*—Philadelphia Phillies, World Series; *Basketball*—Virginia, NIT; Louisville, NCAA; Los Angeles, NBA; *Bowling*—Johnny Petraglia, PBA; *Boxing*—Larry Holmes, heavyweight; Marvin Hagler, middleweight; Sugar Ray Leonard, welterweight; *Football* (bowls)—Southern California, Rose; Oklahoma, Orange; Alabama, Sugar; Houston, Cotton; Pittsburgh, Super Bowl XIV; *Golf*—Jack Nicklaus, U.S. Open and PGA; Severiano Ballesteros, Masters; Amy Alcott, U.S. Women's Open; Sally Little, LPGA; *Harness racing*—Burgomeister, Hambletonian; *Hockey*—New York Islanders, Stanley Cup; *Horse racing*—Genuine Risk, Kentucky Derby; Codex, Preakness Stakes; Temperance Hill, Belmont Stakes; *Tennis*—John McEnroe, U.S. Open (men); Chris Evert, U.S. Open (women); *Yachting*—U.S. boat *Freedom* retains America's Cup.

DEATH Stella Walsh, Olympic runner.

MISCELLANEOUS

Mt. St. Helens, Washington volcano, erupts for first time in 123 years, kills 26; 46 missing.

Week-long Hurricane Allen hits Caribbean and Texas, 272 die.

Freighter rams Sunshine Skyway Bridge over Tampa (Florida) Bay, collapses one span; 35 die.

Fire in MGM Grand Hotel in Las Vegas kills 84; fire in Stouffer Inn, Harrison, New York, kills 26.

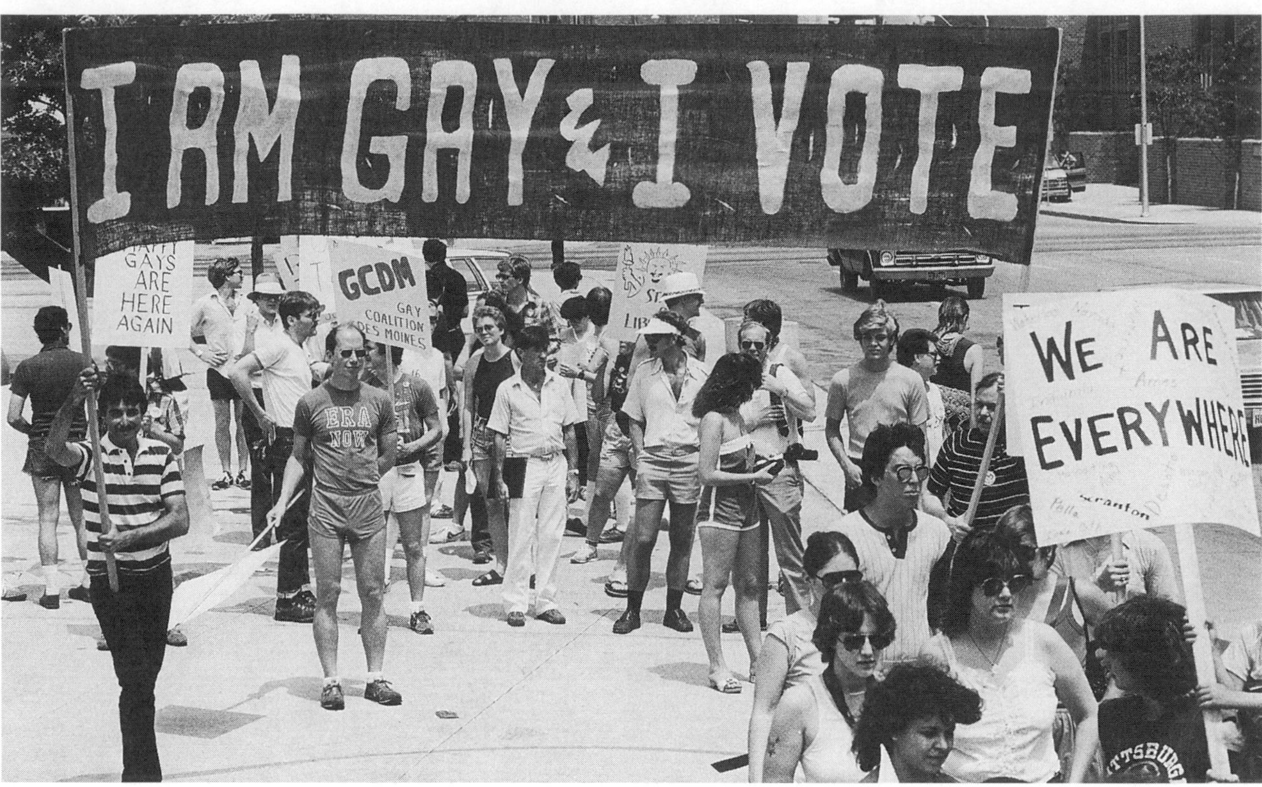

Gay and Lesbian Pride parades become common sights and sources of political protest in the 1970s and 1980s as activists become a vocal constituency demanding an end to discrimination. **CORBIS-BETTMANN**

Two days of rioting in New Mexico State Prison result in 33 deaths.

Searchers find wreckage of *Titanic* 12,000 feet deep in Atlantic Ocean, 400 miles southeast of Newfoundland; liner sank on its maiden voyage (April 14, 1912).

PRIMARY SOURCE DOCUMENT

"The Golden Goal" by E. M. Swift

INTRODUCTION Two weeks before their February 22, 1980, semifinal match in the Winter Olympics, the U.S. Olympic Hockey team had been soundly beaten by the Soviet team by seven goals. The Soviet Union had previously won twenty-one straight Olympic hockey contests, dominating international hockey for decades. It appeared that the Americans had no chance against such a formidable foe. But, then came the "goal heard around the world," a 20-foot wrist shot by Mike Eruzione, the captain of the American team. It is fitting that Eruzione scored the goal, as his name means "eruption" in Italian. And an eruption is indeed what happened after the United States won the game 4–3. The team erupted, the crowd attending the game in Lake Placid, New York, erupted, and the nation erupted with joy after a stunning upset often referred to as the "miracle on ice." Sports commentator Al Michaels described the event as follows: "You didn't have to be a sports fan to appreciate this—it transcended sports." What was all the excitement about?

Beyond the excitement of seeing their team defeat the heavily favored Soviets and earn the chance to win gold, many Americans saw the game as a moral victory in a larger struggle with the Soviet Union, as the cold war raged beyond the walls of the Olympic Village. The Soviet Union had invaded Afghanistan the year before and President Jimmy Carter was considering a boycott of the Olympic Summer Games in Moscow in retaliation. Just as important, fifty-three Americans had been held hostage by Iranian militants since November 1979, a disheartening situation that marked the end of a difficult decade which saw Watergate and defeat in Vietnam eat away at the nation's collective confidence. America needed a victory and it got one on Olympic ice.

The U.S. team, composed mostly of college students, continued their winning streak by defeating the exceptional Finnish team, twice rallying from one-goal deficits and scoring three goals in the final period to win the first U.S. gold medal in hockey since 1960. Even if the American team had lost in the final round of competition, it would still be remembered for its victory over the Soviet Union, the ensuing excitement driven in part by the nation's hunger for good news.

"This is the team of destiny; you can't explain what's happened here," said defenseman Bill Baker after winning gold. "It just happened." After it happened, American boys and girls everywhere were inspired to play hockey and to emulate a new group of American heroes.

An account of this exciting week in sports history is captured in a *Sports Illustrated* piece published shortly after the U.S. hockey team won the Olympic gold medal.

For millions of people, their single lasting image of the Lake Placid Games will be the infectious joy displayed by the U.S. hockey team following its 4-3 win over the Soviet Union last Friday night. It was an Olympian moment, the kind the creators of the Games must have had in mind, one that said: Here is something that is bigger than any of you. It was bizarre, it was beautiful. Upflung sticks slowly cartwheeled into the rafters. The American players—in pairs rather than in one great glop—hugged and danced and rolled on one another.

The Soviet players, slightly in awe, it seemed, of the spectacle of their defeat, stood in a huddle near their blue line, arms propped on their sticks, and waited for the ceremonial postgame handshakes with no apparent impatience. There was no head-hanging. This was bigger, even, than the Russians.

"The first Russian I shook hands with had a smile on his face," said Mark Johnson, who had scored two of the U.S. goals. "I can't believe it. I still can't believe it. We beat the Russians."

In the streets of Lake Placid and across the country, it was more of the same. A spontaneous rally choked the streets outside the Olympic Ice Center, snarling bus traffic for the umpteenth time since the start of the Games. A sister of one of the U.S. hockey players—in between cries of "The Russians! I can't believe we beat the Russians!"—said that she hadn't seen so many flags since the '60s. "And we were burning them then," she added. So move over, Dallas Cowboys. The fresh-faced U.S. hockey team had captured the imagination of a country. *This* was America's Team. When the score of the U.S.-Soviet game was announced at a high school basketball game in Athens, Ohio, the fans—many of whom had probably never seen a hockey game—stood and roared and produced dozens of miniature American flags. In a Miami hospital, a TV set was rolled into the surgical intensive care unit and doctors and nurses cheered on the U.S. between treating gunshot wounds and reading X-rays. In Atlanta, Leo Mulder, the manager of the Off Peachtree restaurant, concocted a special drink called the Craig Cocktail, after U.S. goalie Jim Craig, whose NHL rights belong to the Atlanta Flames. What's in a Craig Cocktail? "Everything but vodka," Mulder said. Impromptu choruses of *The Star-Spangled Banner* were heard in restaurants around Lake Placid, while down in the U.S. locker room—you still doubt this is America's Team?—the players leather-lunged their way through *God Bless America*!

"Someone started it as a joke, I think," said Dave Silk, the right wing who had set up the tying goal. "But all of a sudden we were all singing. We got to the part after 'land that I love ...' and nobody knew the words. So we kind of hummed our way to ' ...from the mountains, to the prairies...' and we finished it. It was great."

Great as it was, there was a still a little matter of the gold medal to take care of. Going into Sunday's game against Finland, it was possible for any of the four medal-round teams—the U.S., Finland, Sweden, the U.S.S.R.—to win the gold. Despite its astonishing string of upsets and its 5-0-1 record, the U.S. wasn't even assured of a bronze. But America's Team had come too far to lose.

"To be one game away from the gold medal is the dream of a lifetime," said forward John Harrington. "There was no way we were going to blow it."

They didn't, but it wasn't easy. Finnish goalie Jorma Valtonen made 14 stops in the first period as Finland took a 1-0 lead—the sixth time in seven games the Americans had surrendered the first goal. Steve Christoff tied the game in the second period, but the Finns scored a power-play goal two minutes later.

So, after two periods, this U.S. squad found itself in almost the same position that another American Olympic hockey team had been in 1960 at Squaw Valley. After having beaten the Soviets the day before, the '60 team was trailing Czechoslovakia 4-3 with one period to play. The U.S. players then came out and scored six unanswered goals. One of the leaders of that comeback was Billy Christian, and 20 years later it was his son, David, who sparked the decisive rally.

With just under $2\frac{1}{2}$ minutes gone in the third period, Christian broke up-ice and slid a pass to Phil Verchota, who broke around the defense and beat Valtonen to tie the game at 2-2. Then, at 6:05, Christian backhanded a shot from the point that the ubiquitous Johnson picked up behind the net and passed out front to Rob McClanahan. After waiting calmly for Valtonen to make the fatal first move, McClanahan slipped the puck between the goaltender's legs for a 3-2 U.S. lead.

The drama built as the Americans were called for three penalties between 6:48 and 15:45 and the Finns pressed the attack. Finally, with $3\frac{1}{2}$ minutes to play, the U.S. scored perhaps its most spectacular goal of the entire tournament—a shorthanded one at that. Christoff slammed a startled Finn against the boards and centered a pass to Johnson.

"I was going to shoot it right away but the puck was bouncing, so I pulled it around, went in and took a backhand," Johnson said. Valtonen sprawled and blocked Johnson's shot, but with two defenders on him, the 5-foot, 9-inch, 155-pound Johnson rapped the rebound into the net. It was his team-high 11th point of the tournament. "We knew we'd never be in this situation again," Johnson would say. "I just sit here in awe."

It was the only time all week that any of the U.S. players had been in awe of anything. Coach Herb Brooks had told them so many times over the past few months that Soviet captain Boris Mikhailov looks like Stan Lau-

OVERVIEW

The Age of Diminished Expectations: From Watergate to the Rise of Conservatism, 1974–1992

MICHAEL MULLINS, YALE UNIVERSITY

Blows to America

With the resignation of President Richard M. Nixon and the end of the Vietnam era, the United States seemed to lurch at once backward and forward in time. Although the presidency remained in the hands of the Republican Party with Gerald R. Ford succeeding Nixon, Watergate symbolically called into question the foundation of leadership that claimed to have guided the nation out of the tumultuous 1960s and into a new era of "law and order." The Vietnam War also dealt American self-confidence a crippling blow both on the world stage and at home. The country's proven vulnerabilities, whether through a humiliating military defeat or the economic disruption of a 1973 oil embargo imposed by the Organization of Petroleum Exporting Countries (OPEC), resulted in new forms of uncertainty.

Economic Problems

The onset of a severe economic recession at the close of 1974 made this sense of threat more immediate and shaped the nation's economic prospects for the remainder of the decade and beyond. Many heavy industries and manufacturing firms either closed down or moved their operations abroad, accelerating a pattern of deindustrialization that cost hundreds of thousands of American jobs. This process established the importance of the "service sector"—jobs linked to human services, such as health care, education, and business sales and services—in place of traditional industrial production.

Decline of Labor

The nation's labor movement, anchored in many of those industries on the decline, was generally unable to keep pace with this transformation. Over the next two decades, the percentage of unionized American workers declined to a record low, a number not witnessed since the beginning of the century. Meanwhile, those business interests that were able to weather the economic changes tended to be large, multinational corporations prepared to embrace the globalization of trade. They also had, like the computer giant IBM, a stake in the media and were in touch with the technological advances of the increasingly important Information Age. Simultaneously, the dollar's continued inflation caused significant price hikes for American consumers and helped to trigger an overall trade deficit in 1976. This began a pattern of more American imports than exports that would endure almost every year for the remainder of the century.

Survival of Social Movements

The anxieties surrounding the economy did not derail many bold cultural initiatives in American society, a number of them direct extensions of the political movements of the previous two decades. Perhaps the most visible struggle involved the Equal Rights Amendment (ERA), the centerpiece of the women's rights movement for most of the 1970s. Although it ultimately fell short of the necessary number of ratifying states, the campaign for the ERA coincided with the cultural assimilation of women into many formerly male-dominated institutions and professions, most notably, all of the nation's preeminent universities. With African Americans and other racial minorities, women also began to benefit from affirmative action

rel that, well, it was impossible for them to treat Mikhailov, or any of his teammates, with reverence. "Every time we watched a film of the Russians," said Harrington, "he'd keep saying, 'Stan Laurel, Stan Laurel, look at Stan Laurel.'"

Harrington, Silk and captain Mike Eruzione have compiled a 16-page booklet entitled *Brooksisms*—and "Stan Laurel" is an entry. An old-fashioned motivator, Brooks repeats favored aphorisms with enough regularity that they make an impression. Among them:

—You're playing worse every day, and right now you're playing like the middle of the next month.

—Gentlemen, you don't have enough talent to win on talent alone.

laws, despite the partial Supreme Court rejection of these laws in 1977. Amid such changes in opportunities and civil rights, the United States was also rapidly becoming a different kind of population. An increase in the overall number of immigrants reflected the importance of the landmark Immigration Act of 1965, but equally significant was the general shift in immigration patterns, away from Europe and solidly rooted in Asia, Latin America, and Africa.

Reagan Era

A host of circumstances combined, at the very beginning of the 1980s, to signal a sharp new turn in the national climate. It was marked most obviously by the election of President Ronald Reagan. In truth, Reagan's victory was merely the result of a deeper, longer-term change in American political alignment. The 1980 census indicated for the first time that the population in the American South and West outnumbered that in the North and Midwest. These regions were rapidly becoming the center of an emerging *conservative coalition*: evangelical Christians, fiscal conservatives, and proponents of law-and-order policies and aggressive opposition to communist governments. President Jimmy Carter's outgoing administration, saddled with the blame for so-called "stagflation" and a perception of American weakness abroad, became a popular target for Reagan. Reagan unveiled an ambitious plan to revive the American economy through a program of regressive tax cuts and business-friendly policies. On the other hand, he pledged to revive American optimism at home and rebuild the nation's military might throughout the world.

Downsizing the government was a central concern of Reaganomics, but the administration's approach also emphasized the free rein of capitalism in every sense, at home and abroad. Another benchmark of Reagan's tenure was his 1982 stand-off with the air traffic controllers union (PATCO) that threatened to strike for higher wages and a reduction in stressful workload. Invoking the national interest, Reagan dissolved the union and set an aggressive precedent against union militancy in other industries. Ultimately, however, the priorities of the Reagan administration involved a far more selective rollback of the federal government than his rhetoric suggested. One major beneficiary of new federal investment was the armed forces, whose neglect, according to Reagan, had come to endanger the entire free world against the menace of the "evil empire," Reagan's famous description of the former Soviet Union. Much new military investment centered on the modernization of the armed forces, with numerous contracts further bolstering the influence of the aerospace and defense industries. Capitalizing on a revived popular interest in space exploration after the commissioning of the Space Shuttle in the early 1980s, federal officials also announced plans for the Strategic Defense Initiative, a nuclear missile shield popularly called "Star Wars."

Conservative Coalition

In many ways, Reagan's attack on the "evils" of the Soviet Union recalled the domestic agenda of the conservative coalition that he led, especially those initiatives linked to the so-called *religious right.* By the early 1980s, increasing numbers of evangelical and conservative Christians wielded political power on both the local and national levels. Largely through their efforts, the decade witnessed the emergence of solid grassroots organizations determined to restrict or outlaw abortion, allow prayer in public schools, permit parents some choice in the schools their children attended, and legislate other kinds of "values." It also witnessed rising concern over youth violence and the threats of illegal drug use, fueling a series of highly punitive criminal laws. The prosecution of this war on drugs initiated with the "Just Say No" campaign helped to double the American prison population, with a disproportionate number of African-American and Latino young men, in the course of merely a decade.

The Opposition

Despite conservatives' growing influence during the Reagan era, their comparative dominance did not go unchecked. In 1987 the Iran-Contra hearings captured national attention and cast serious doubts on

—Boys, in front of the net it's bloody-nose alley.

—Don't dump the puck in. That went out with short pants.

—Throw the puck back and weave, weave, weave. But don't just weave for the sake of weaving.

—Let's be idealistic, but let's also be practical.

—You can't be common because the common man goes nowhere. You have to be uncommon.

The U.S. hockey team was anything but common. Before the previous week's upset win over Czechoslovakia, Christian sat in a locker room and secretly fashioned something out of a cardboard Budweiser packet. When he put on his helmet, there were a set of wings and a tail the post-Vietnam legacy of U.S. interventions abroad, such as those in Nicaragua and El Salvador. The stock market fell alarmingly during that same year, prompting some measure of caution in a culture that had increasingly come to celebrate Wall Street and speculative investment. And a variety of social movements, from environmental groups to organizations formed in response to the AIDS crisis, succeeded in winning partial but decisive victories on issues largely ignored or opposed by conservatives in power.

The Bush Presidency

None of the problems that plagued the Reagan administration, however, prevented Vice President George Herbert Walker Bush from carrying forward Reagan's agenda for another four years. Bush's campaign defeat of Democrat Gov. Michael Dukakis—specifically his condemnation of the Democrats for "tax-and-spend" policies and for weak resolve on crime and other moral issues—helped to solidify the growing stigma attached to "liberalism" as a force in American politics and culture. This pointed national defeat for the Democratic Party, merely two decades after the glory of the Kennedy-Johnson years, set the stage for the party's move to the right-center in the decade to come. So too did the growing consensus, among Republicans and Democrats alike, surrounding such formerly divisive issues as the need for lower taxes and an all-out war on crime.

The four years of the Bush presidency reflected a stark divide between dramatic displays of U.S. power abroad and significant turmoil in the domestic sphere. Domestic anxieties seemed to largely deepen during these years—from high-crime inner cities to beleaguered family farms. Bush drew perhaps the sharpest criticism for failing his own party's litmus test when he signed a tax increase in 1991. Simultaneously, in rapid succession, America watched as the nations of the former Soviet republic gave way to reform movements and new constitutions. In a process that climaxed with the demolition of the Berlin Wall and the reunification of Germany, the power of the U.S.S.R. crumbled. The cold war had officially ended. Equally significant, the United States wasted little time in seeking to fill political voids in the former Soviet nations. In conjunction with the World Bank and the International Monetary Fund (IMF), the United States led a coalition of Western nations in favoring a restructuring process based on foreign investment, corporate capitalism, and the institutions of liberal democracy. Simultaneously, the country's armed forces focused rapidly on a different part of the world, repelling Iraq's invasion of Kuwait during the Gulf War of 1991. The war foreshadowed the increasing importance of the Islamic world for United States foreign policy in the 1990s. Thus, even as the year 1992 prompted heated debate over commemorations of Christopher Columbus and the five-hundred-year colonial settlement of the Americas, modern-day Americans—in dramatically different degrees of wealth and poverty—faced the future as the world's lone superpower.

BIBLIOGRAPHY

For a broad chronological account of changes in American politics after Nixon, see Thomas and Mary Edsall's *Chain Reaction: the Impact of Race, Rights and Taxes on American Politics* (1992). Alan Crawford's *Thunder on the Right* (1980) offers a more detailed portrait of the "New Right," and opposition to the "liberal establishment," based on accounts of individual leaders and various political organizations. In *The Great U-Turn: Corporate Restructuring and the Polarizing of America* (1988), Bennett Harrison and Barry Bluestone analyze the same period in terms of rapidly shifting economic power, income inequality, and prospects for the labor movement. Bruce J. Schulman, in *The Seventies: The Great Shift in American Culture, Society, and Politics* (2001), analyzes the cultural and political legacies of the often-neglected decade. Randy Shilts's *And the Band Played On: Politics, People, and the AIDS Epidemic* (2000) is an excellent account of the political and social deliberations, and broader federal health policy changes, that followed the discovery of AIDS. *The End of the Cold War: Its Meaning and Implications* (1992), edited by Michael Hogan, offers diverse academic history and contemporary commentary on the shift in world power. Finally, for a sweeping and very readable political biography of Reagan, analyzing many foundations of the Reagan revolution, see Garry Wills's *Reagan's America* (1987).

sticking out of the airholes. "Boy, am I going to be flying tonight," Christian announced.

In the next game, against Norway, the U.S. fell behind 1-0 after the opening period and appeared frustrated. In the locker room between the first and second periods, Silk said something impassioned about how everyone had to support everyone else and suggested that they all tell each other nothing but nice things. There was a brief silence. Then:

"Eric, your hair looks marvelous."

"Phil, that's a wonderful job of taping your shin pads."

"Jimmy, your eyes are a lovely shade of blue."

As Eruzione noted later, "We may be young, but we're immature."

The U.S. players performed fearlessly and the public ate it up. Even before the Americans beat the Soviets, Lake Placid restaurant managers sent over complimentary bottles of wine, and New York State Troopers asked for autographs. At one point, Silk's mother, Abigail, who was housed with 40 other hockey parents and relatives in an abode they called the Hostage House, was riding a bus when she heard a young man tell the girl he was embracing that he was on the hockey team.

"Really? And who are you?" Mrs. Silk asked, cruelly.

"I'm Dave Silk," he said, undaunted.

"I'm Dave Silk's mom," she replied.

The girl fled.

So it was that people actually sensed the impending upset of the Soviets, as if wishing could make it so. It was such an unreasonable hope—virtually unthinkable for anyone who had seen the U.S.S.R's 10-3 rout of the U.S. at Madison Square Garden three days before the Olympics opened. Tickets for the rematch were scalped for as much as $340 a seat, and Johnson heard of one lady who had offered $600. "Are you telling me it wasn't worth it?" he said two hours after the upset, while watching a replay of the game with teammates in the Holiday Inn. "I'd have paid a thousand to have been in that atmosphere."

It was electric. Craig, superlative throughout the Olympics, gave up two first-period goals but made 16 saves, most of them tough ones. Indeed, he kept the U.S. alive. Then, with three seconds remaining in the period, the U.S. made the key play of the game. Christian took a 100-foot slap shot from beyond center ice that goaltender Vladislav Tretiak let rebound off his pads. Johnson, busting toward the net, weaved through the two Soviet defenseman and picked up the puck. He feinted, dropping his shoulder as if to shoot, and Tretiak went to his knees. Johnson pulled the puck back, moved to his left a bit and slid the puck behind Tretiak and into the net just before time expired. That was all for Tretiak, who was promptly yanked from the game in favor of Vladimir Myshkin. And when Aleksandr Maltsev made it 3-2 at 2:18 of the second period, that was all the scoring for the Soviets.

All told, the U.S. outscored its opponents 27-6 in the second and third periods, testimony to the team's depth and conditioning. Charged up by the chants of "U.S.A! U.S.A!" the Americans tied the score at 8:39 of the third period. Silk sent a pass through two defensemen to Johnson, who picked the puck off a Soviet skate and fired it under Myshkin. The game winner came 1:21 later, Eruzione beating Myshkin through a screen. Eruzione means "explosion" in Italian, and his goal sent repercussions rinkwide, nationwide, indeed worldwide.

After it was all over on Sunday and the U.S. players were wearing their gold medals, it was left to Harrington to find a fitting Brooksism for the whole improbable series of upsets. He didn't have to think about it long. "Boys, we went to the well again, and the water was colder and the water was deeper."

It was sweeter, too.

SOURCE: *Sports Illustrated,* March 3, 1980, for "The Golden Goal," by E. M. Swift.

1981

INTERNATIONAL

Iran releases 52 U.S. hostages whom they held more than a year in Teheran.

President Ronald Reagan imposes sanctions on Polish military government for its role in cracking down on Polish independent labor unions.

U.S. and Japan reach agreement to reduce Japanese car exports to U.S. for three years.

NATIONAL

President Reagan is shot and seriously wounded in downtown Washington by John W. Hinckley; Press Secretary James Brady, Secret Service Agent Timothy J. McCarthy, and Thomas Delahanty, a Washington police officer, are also wounded (March 30).

Sandra Day O'Connor becomes first woman Supreme Court justice (September 25).

Cost of first-class postage increases to 18 cents (March 22), then to 20 cents (November 1).

Federal Trade Commission drops eight-year-old antitrust suit against eight major oil firms.

Price controls on domestic oil and gasoline are lifted.

Henry G. Cisneros is first Mexican American elected mayor of a U.S. city (San Antonio, Texas).

Gerald R. Ford Library in Ann Arbor, Michigan, is dedicated.

DEATHS Roy Wilkins, NAACP leader; Robert Moses, New York state and city park commissioner, headed 1964–1965 World's Fair.

BUSINESS/INDUSTRY/INVENTIONS

James Tobin is awarded Nobel Prize in economics for analysis of financial markets and their effect on how people spend and save money.

Louisiana Offshore Oil Port opens, costs $100 million.

Crowds in Washington, D.C., swarm buses bringing U.S. hostages home. Iran releases the Americans shortly after President Ronald Reagan is inaugurated. **CORBIS-BETTMANN**

United Auto Workers rejoins AFL-CIO after 13-year separation.

Minimum wage increases to $3.35 an hour (January 1).

Two mergers of the year are Du Pont with Conoco Oil and Marathon Oil Co. with U.S. Steel.

IBM introduces a personal computer.

DEATH Wallace K. Harrison, architect (U.N. building, Rockefeller Center).

TRANSPORTATION

Ben Abruzzo, Larry Newman, Rocky Aoki, and Ron Clark complete first nonstop balloon crossing of Pacific Ocean (November 12).

Professional Air Traffic Controllers Assn. strikes nationwide (August 3); most of the 12,000 controllers are fired and replaced.

Ford Motor Co. turns down proposal to merge with Chrysler Motors.

Pan American Airways begins New York to Peiping (now Beijing) air service.

SCIENCE/MEDICINE

First manned space shuttle, *Columbia,* orbits earth 36 times (April 12–14); crew is John W. Young and Robert L. Crippen.

Nicolass Bloembergen and Arthur Schaalow share Nobel Prize in physics for work in developing technologies with lasers and other devices to study matter; Roald Hoffmann shares prize in chemistry with Kenichi Fukui of Japan for work in applying theories of quantum mechanics to predict course of chemical reactions; Roger W. Sperry, David H. Hubel, and Tosten N. Wiesel share prize in physiology/medicine for studies of the brain.

DEATH Harold C. Urey, chemist who discovered heavy hydrogen.

EDUCATION

Terrell H. Bell becomes Secretary of Education.

Former Indiana congressman, John Brademas, is named president of New York University.

RELIGION

Supreme Court upholds constitutionality of religious services by college student organizations in campus buildings.

Representatives from 56 nations attend Christian Science Church convention in Boston.

Christ Episcopal Church in Stevensville, Maryland, observes its 350th anniversary.

The anti-nuclear movement expands rapidly in the early 1980s in response to heightened cold-war tensions and the 1979 crisis at the Three Mile Island nuclear power plant. Here, activists protest the operation of the Diablo Canyon nuclear power plant. © ROGER RESSMEYER/CORBIS-BETTMANN

ART/MUSIC

Roger Sessions composes Concerto for Orchestra.

SONGS (POPULAR): "Endless Love," "I Love a Rainy Night," "Jessie's Girl," "Rapture," "Elvira," "Games People Play," "Nine to Five."

LITERATURE/JOURNALISM

BOOKS *Rabbit Is Rich* by John Updike, *Zuckerman Unbound* by Philip Roth, *Gorky Park* by Martin C. Smith, *Remembrance* by Danielle Steel.

DEATHS Three publishers die: DeWitt Wallace, cofounder, *Reader's Digest;* John S. Knight, founder of newspaper chain; and Robert F. DeGraff, founder, Pocket Books; authors Anita Loos, William Saroyan, and Will Durant, coauthor of 11-volume *Story of Civilization;* Lowell Thomas, radio news reporter and author.

ENTERTAINMENT

PLAYS Charles Fuller writes *A Soldier's Play;* Beth Henley, *Crimes of the Heart;* Charles Egan and Henry Krieger, *Dreamgirls;* Lanford Wilson, *The Fifth of July.*

MOVIES *Chariots of Fire* with Ben Cross, *On Golden Pond* with Katharine Hepburn and Henry Fonda, *Raiders of the Lost Ark* with Harrison Ford, *Mommie Dearest* with Faye Dunaway.

New television shows include *Dynasty* with John Forsythe and Linda Evans, *Harper Valley PTA* with Barbara Eden, *Hill St. Blues.*

DEATHS Playwrights Mary C. Chase *(Harvey)* and Paul E. Green *(Lost Colony, In Abraham's Bosom);* Melvyn Douglas, stage and screen actor.

SPORTS

Baseball players strike for seven weeks over free-agent compensation.

Jockey Willie Shoemaker rides his 8,000th winner.

Coach Paul (Bear) Bryant of Alabama sets record (315) for college football wins.

Phil Mahre becomes first American to win World Cup Alpine skiing title.

WINNERS *Auto racing*—Bobby Unser, Indianapolis 500; Darrell Waltrip, NASCAR; *Baseball*—Los Angeles Dodgers, World Series; *Basketball*—Tulsa, NIT; Indiana, NCAA; Boston, NBA; *Bowling*—Earl Anthony, PBA; *Boxing*—Larry Holmes, heavy-weight; Sugar Ray Leonard, middleweight; *Figure*

skating—Scott Hamilton, U.S. and world men's titles; Elaine Zayak, U.S. women's; *Football* (bowls)—Michigan, Rose; Oklahoma, Orange; Georgia, Sugar; Alabama, Cotton; Oakland, Super Bowl XV; *Golf*—David Graham, U.S. Open; Larry Nelson, PGA; Tom Watson, Masters; Pat Bradley, U.S. Women's Open; Donna Caponi, LPGA; *Harness racing*—Shiaway St. Pat, Hambletonian; *Horse racing*—Pleasant Colony, Kentucky Derby and Preakness Stakes; Summing, Belmont Stakes; *Tennis*—U.S., Davis Cup; John McEnroe, U.S. Open (men); Tracy Austin, U.S. Open (women).

DEATHS Joe Louis, heavyweight boxing champion (1937–1949); Jim Morgan, bobsled driver, killed in world-title race.

MISCELLANEOUS

Two "skywalks" in Hyatt Regency Hotel in Kansas City, Missouri, collapse; 113 are killed.

1982

INTERNATIONAL

U.S. imposes an embargo on Libyan oil imports, curtails export of high technology to Libya because of its support of terrorism.

U.S. and Soviet Union hold arms-control talks in Geneva.

SEE PRIMARY DOCUMENT President Ronald Reagan's Speech to the House of Commons

NATIONAL

Equal Rights Amendment to Constitution fails when three state legislatures do not approve it before the midnight deadline on June 30.

Cyanide-laced Tylenol capsules cause seven deaths in Chicago area; killer is not found; federal regulations are issued (November 4), require tamper-proof packaging for nearly all nonprescription drugs.

Supreme Court rules that individuals may sue state and local officials and agencies directly in federal court; also rules that federal and state officials are entitled to "qualified immunity" from civil damage suits for their official acts and that the president cannot be sued for damages for any official act.

Federal jury finds John W. Hinckley Jr. not guilty in shooting of President Reagan and three others by virtue of insanity.

Secretary of State Alexander M. Haig resigns; George P. Shultz succeeds him.

Supreme Court rules that members of Old Order Amish Church who operate businesses must pay Social Security and unemployment taxes despite their religious belief that paying taxes is a sin.

World's Fair is held in Knoxville, Tennessee.

Death penalty is reinstated in New Jersey.

DEATHS Former First Lady Bess Truman (1945–1953); Leon Jaworski, Watergate special prosecutor.

BUSINESS/INDUSTRY/INVENTIONS

George J. Sigler is awarded Nobel Prize in economics for research on industry and role of government regulation in economics.

Justice Department drops antitrust suit against ATT.

Supreme Court rules that seniority systems that outlaw race or sex discrimination are legal.

Cities Service and Occidental Petroleum merge.

Johns Manville Co. files for bankruptcy.

Sales of Apple computers reach $1 billion.

DEATH David Dubinsky, president, International Ladies Garment Workers Union (1932–1966).

TRANSPORTATION

U.S. Appeals Court rules that new cars sold after September 1983 must be equipped with air bags or automatic seat belts; House of Representatives rejects Federal Trade Commission rules that require used-car dealers to disclose major defects in cars to buyers.

Ford Motor Co. workers accept contract that trades wages and benefits for increased job security.

U.S. Appeals Court upholds government decision to decertify striking Professional Air Traffic Controllers Organization.

Intercity bus industry is freed from many government regulations.

Braniff Airways suspends all operations (May 12), files for bankruptcy; is first airline to do so.

Congress approves 5-cents-per-gallon tax increase and higher taxes for heavy trucks.

Missouri Pacific, Western Pacific, and Union Pacific railroads merge.

SCIENCE/MEDICINE

Kenneth G. Wilson is awarded Nobel Prize in physics for his method of analyzing basic changes in matter under influence of pressure and temperature.

First "permanent" artificial heart is implanted in a human being, 61-year-old Barney Clark, at Univer-

A scene from Steven Spielberg's film, *E.T. The Extra-Terrestrial*, 1982. **THE KOBAL COLLECTION**

sity of Utah Medical Center; he lives about three months.

Center for Disease Control terms AIDS, disease that has spread to 24 states, an epidemic; initially disease spreads predominantly among young homosexual men.

Space shuttle completes nine-day mission, makes numerous scientific studies; June flight includes first U.S. woman astronaut, Sally K. Ride.

Supreme Court upholds order that permits doctors to advertise nontraditional arrangements for medical practice.

EDUCATION

Supreme Court rules that law that bars sex discrimination in federally aided education programs applies to employees as well as students; upholds lower-court ruling that children of illegal aliens must have access to free public education; rules that handicapped children are entitled to public education from which they derive "some educational benefit."

New Jersey Senate passes bill over governor's veto that requires public schools to start each day with a minute of "silent contemplation and introspection."

Arkansas federal judge strikes down Arkansas law that requires teaching of creation based on the Bible in schools where theory of evolution is taught, rules that this violates separation of church and state.

Supreme Court rules that First Amendment limits discretion of public school officials to remove books they deem offensive from school libraries.

RELIGION

Agreement is announced to merge American Lutheran Church, Association of Evangelical Lutheran Churches, and Lutheran Church in America.

Presbyterian Church in the U.S. and the United Presbyterian Church in the U.S. vote to merge, end 122-year-old schism caused by slavery question.

Seven largest African-American denominations with 65,000 churches and 20 million members create Congress of National Black Churches.

National Cathedral in Washington, D.C., celebrates its 75th anniversary by unveiling new west front; two more towers remain to be built.

Dr. Norman Vincent Peale celebrates 50th anniversary with Marble Collegiate Church in New York City.

Catholic Archbishop Joseph L. Bernardin of Cincinnati is moved to Chicago.

President Reagan proposes constitutional amendment to permit organized prayer in schools.

ART/MUSIC

Ellen T. Zwilich composes *Three Movements for Orchestra;* William Bolcom, *Songs of Innocence* and *Songs of Experience;* John Corigliano, *Three Hallucinations for Orchestra* and *Pied Piper Fantasy.*

Edward Kienholz completes the painting *Bout, Round Eleven.*

SONGS (POPULAR): "Ebony and Ivory," "Eye of the Tiger," "I Love Rock and Roll," "Up Where We Belong," "Chariots of Fire," "Heartbreak Express," "Mountain Music," "What's Forever For."

DEATHS Arthur Rubinstein, pianist; Calvin Simmons, first African-American conductor of a major orchestra (Oakland Symphony); Earl ("Fatha") Hines, jazz pianist and orchestra leader.

LITERATURE/JOURNALISM

BOOKS *The Color Purple* by Alice Walker, *The Dean's December* by Saul Bellow, *Crossings* by Danielle Steel, *Prizzi's Honor* by Richard Condon.

DEATHS Erwin D. Canham, editor, *Christian Science Monitor* (1941–1974); Archibald MacLeish, poet; John Cheever, author; cartoonists Hal Foster ("Prince Valiant") and Ernie Bushmiller ("Nancy").

ENTERTAINMENT

PLAYS Andrew Lloyd Webber writes *Cats,* which becomes U.S.'s longest-running play; Arthur Kopit and Maury Yeston, *Nine;* Lanford Wilson, *Angels Fall.*

MOVIES *Gandhi* with Ben Kingsley, *Tootsie* with Dustin Hoffman, *Blade Runner* with Harrison Ford, *Cannery Row* with Nick Nolte, *Pennies from Heaven* with Steve Martin, *Sophie's Choice* with Meryl Streep, *Victor/Victoria* with Julie Andrews, *E.T., The Extra-Terrestrial* directed by Steven Spielberg.

DEATHS Henry Fonda, actor; Ingrid Bergman, actress.

SPORTS

National Football League players strike for nine weeks; U.S. Football League is founded, set to play in Spring 1983; federal jury finds NFL guilty of antitrust action in trying to block Oakland Raiders' move to Los Angeles; NFL owners accept five-year $2 billion television contract.

Club owners refuse to renew Bowie Kuhn's contract as baseball commissioner.

Wayne Gretzky of Edmonton, Canada, becomes first National Hockey League player to surpass 200 points in a season, first to be selected unanimously as NHL most-valuable player.

International Olympic Committee restores amateur status and approves posthumously the two gold medals won by Jim Thorpe in 1912 Olympics; they were taken from him for amateur-rule violation.

WINNERS *Auto racing* Gordon Johncock, Indianapolis 500; Darrell Waltrip, NASCAR; *Baseball*—St. Louis Cardinals, World Series; *Basketball*—Bradley, NIT; North Carolina, NCAA; Louisiana Tech, first NCAA (women); Los Angeles, NBA; *Bowling*—Earl Anthony, PBA; *Boxing*—Larry Holmes, heavyweight; Sugar Ray Leonard, welterweight; *Figure skating*—Scott Hamilton, U.S. and world men's titles; Elaine Zayak, world women's; Rosalynn Sumners, U.S. women's; *Football* (bowls)—Washington, Rose; Clemson, Orange; Pittsburgh, Sugar; Texas, Cotton; San Francisco, Super Bowl XVI; *Golf*—Tom Watson, U.S. Open; Ray Floyd, PGA; Craig Stadler, Masters; Janet Alex, U.S. Women's Open; Jan Stephenson, LPGA; *Harness racing*—Speed Bowl, Hambletonian; *Hockey*—New York Islanders, Stanley Cup; *Horse racing*—Gato del Sol, Kentucky Derby; Aloma's Ruler, Preakness Stakes; Conquistador, Belmont Stakes; *Swimming*—Florida, first NCAA women's title; *Tennis*—U.S., Davis Cup; Jimmy Connors, U.S. Open (men); Chris Evert, U.S. Open (women).

DEATHS Gordon Smiley, auto racer; Salvador Sanchez, featherweight boxing champion; Red (Walter W.) Smith, syndicated sports columnist.

MISCELLANEOUS

Air Florida 737 crashes into Potomac River after takeoff at Washington's (D.C.) National Airport, 78 die; Pan Am 727 crashes after takeoff in Kenner, Louisiana, 153 die.

Women become full-fledged firefighters in New York City with graduation of 11 from Fire Academy.

PRIMARY SOURCE DOCUMENT

President Ronald Reagan's Speech to the House of Commons, June 8, 1982

INTRODUCTION Ronald Reagan, the nation's fortieth president, was instrumental in ending the cold war between the United States and the Soviet Union. Soon after defeating Jimmy Carter for the presidency, Reagan focused his diplomatic efforts on attacking Soviet communism and its practice of denying democratic elections. In June 1982 he addressed the British House of Commons (the British equivalent of the U.S. House of Representatives) to outline his "crusade for freedom." This speech, reproduced below, set a new tone for the cold war in the

1980s. By going on the offensive against communism, Reagan brought an end to the U.S. policy of détente, a relaxation of cold war tensions with the Soviet Union that he believed had caused a "deadening accommodation with totalitarian evil."

Under Reagan, the United States accelerated the arms race and exacerbated international tensions, initiated a massive build-up of American military forces that turned the United States into the world's largest debtor nation, and funded and armed anti-Communist guerilla groups in Latin America, which triggered the Iran-Contra scandal of the mid-1980s. Nonetheless, Reagan's aggressive policies helped to convince Soviet Premier Mikhail Gorbachev that his country could not sustain the cost of this new phase of the cold war. Gorbachev steered the Soviet Union toward some of the principles espoused in Reagan's speech to the House of Commons, adopting the policy of *glasnost,* or openness, in domestic life. Reagan supported Gorbachev in his efforts to enact change, proving to be as flexible with Gorbachev as he was fervent in attacking the policies of his predecessors.

[Editor's Note: Although Reagan does not use the term "evil empire" in this address, it is commonly referred to as the "evil empire" speech. In an address at the National Association of Evangelicals Convention a year later, Reagan built on themes established in the speech to the House of Commons and attacked "the aggressive impulses of an evil empire."]

We're approaching the end of a bloody century plagued by a terrible political invention—totalitarianism. Optimism comes less easily today, not because democracy is less vigorous, but because democracy's enemies have refined their instruments of repression. Yet optimism is in order because day by day democracy is proving itself to be a not at all fragile flower. From Stettin on the Baltic to Varna on the Black Sea, the regimes planted by totalitarianism have had more than thirty years to establish their legitimacy. But none—not one regime—has yet been able to risk free elections. Regimes planted by bayonets do not take root.

The strength of the Solidarity movement in Poland demonstrates the truth told in an underground joke in the Soviet Union. It is that the Soviet Union would remain a one-party nation even if an opposition party were permitted because everyone would join the opposition party....

Historians looking back at our time will note the consistent restraint and peaceful intentions of the West. They will note that it was the democracies who refused to use the threat of their nuclear monopoly in the forties and early fifties for territorial or imperial gain. Had that nuclear monopoly been in the hands of the Communist world, the map of Europe—indeed, the world—would look very different today. And certainly they will note it was not the democracies that invaded Afghanistan or suppressed Polish Solidarity or used chemical and toxin warfare in Afghanistan and Southeast Asia.

If history teaches anything, it teaches self-delusion in the face of unpleasant facts is folly. We see around us today the marks of our terrible dilemma—predictions of doomsday, antinuclear demonstrations, an arms race in which the West must, for its own protection, be an unwilling participant. At the same time we see totalitarian forces in the world who seek subversion and conflict around the globe to further their barbarous assault on the human spirit. What, then, is our course? Must civilization perish in a hail of fiery atoms? Must freedom wither in a quiet, deadening accommodation with totalitarian evil?

Sir Winston Churchill refused to accept the inevitability of war or even that it was imminent. He said, "I do not believe that Soviet Russia desires war. What they desire is the fruits of war and the indefinite expansion of their power and doctrines. But what we have to consider here today while time remains is the permanent prevention of war and the establishment of conditions of freedom and democracy as rapidly as possible in all countries."

Well, this is precisely our mission today: to preserve freedom as well as peace. It may not be easy to see; but I believe we live now at a turning point.

In an ironic sense Karl Marx was right. We are witnessing today a great revolutionary crisis, a crisis where the demands of the economic order are conflicting directly with those of the political order. But the crisis is happening not in the free, non-Marxist West but in the home of Marxism- Leninism, the Soviet Union. It is the Soviet Union that runs against the tide of history by denying human freedom and human dignity to its citizens. It also is in deep economic difficulty. The rate of growth in the national product has been steadily declining since the fifties and is less than half of what it was then.

The dimensions of this failure are astounding: a country which employs one-fifth of its population in agriculture is unable to feed its own people. Were it not for the private sector, the tiny private sector tolerated in Soviet agriculture, the country might be on the brink of famine. These private plots occupy a bare 3 percent of the arable land but account for nearly one-quarter of Soviet farm output and nearly one-third of meat products and vegetables. Overcentralized, with little or no incentives, year after year the Soviet system pours its best resources into the making of instruments of destruction. The constant shrinkage of economic growth combined with the growth of military production is putting a heavy strain on the Soviet people. What we see here is a political structure that no longer corresponds to its economic base, a society where productive forced are hampered by political ones.

The decay of the Soviet experiment should come as no surprise to us. Wherever the comparisons have been made between free and closed societies—West Germany and East Germany, Austria and Czechoslovakia, Malaysia and Vietnam—it is the democratic countries that are prosperous and responsive to the needs of their people. And one of the simple but overwhelming facts of our time is this: of all the millions of refugees we've seen in the modern world, their flight is always away from, not toward the Communist world. Today on the NATO line, our military forces face east to prevent a possible invasion. On the other side of the line, the Soviet forces also face east to prevent their people from leaving.

The hard evidence of totalitarian rule has caused in mankind an uprising of the intellect and will. Whether it is the growth of the new schools of economics in America or England or the appearance of the so-called new philosophers in France, there is one unifying thread running through the intellectual work of these groups—rejection of the arbitrary power of the state, the refusal to subordinate the rights of the individual to the superstate, the realization that collectivism stifles all the best human impulses....

Chairman Brezhnev repeatedly has stressed that the competition of ideas and systems must continue and that this is entirely consistent with relaxation of tensions and peace.

Well, we ask only that these systems begin by living up to their own constitutions, abiding by their own laws, and complying with the international obligations they have undertaken. We ask only for a process, a direction, a basic code of decency, not for an instant transformation.

We cannot ignore the fact that even without our encouragement there has been and will continue to be repeated explosion against repression and dictatorships. The Soviet Union itself is not immune to this reality. Any system is inherently unstable that has no peaceful means to legitimize its leaders. In such cases, the very repressiveness of the state ultimately drives people to resist it, if necessary, by force.

While we must be cautious about forcing the pace of change, we must not hesitate to declare our ultimate objectives and to take concrete actions to move toward them. We must be staunch in our conviction that freedom is not the sole prerogative of a lucky few but the inalienable and universal right of all human beings. So states the United Nations Universal Declaration of Human Rights, which, among other things, guarantees free elections.

The objective I propose is quite simple to state: to foster the infrastructure of democracy, the system of a free press, unions, political parties, universities, which allows a people to choose their own way to develop their own culture, to reconcile their own differences through peaceful means.

This is not cultural imperialism; it is providing the means for genuine self-determination and protection for diversity. Democracy already flourishes in countries with very different cultures and historical experiences. It would be cultural condescension, or worse, to say that any people prefer dictatorship to democracy. Who would voluntarily choose not to have the right to vote, decide to purchase government propaganda handouts instead of independent newspapers, prefer government to worker-controlled unions, opt for land to be owned by the state instead of those who till it, want government repression of religious liberty, a single political party instead of a free choice, a rigid cultural orthodoxy instead of democratic tolerance and diversity.

Since 1917 the Soviet Union has given covert political training and assistance to Marxist-Leninists in many countries. Of course, it also has promoted the use of violence and subversion by these same forces. Over the past several decades, West European and other social democrats, Christian democrats, and leaders have offered open assistance to fraternal, political, and social institutions to bring about peaceful and democratic progress. Appropriately, for a vigorous new democracy, the Federal Republic of Germany's political foundations have become a major force in this effort.

We in America now intend to take additional steps, as many of our allies have already done, toward realizing this same goal. The chairmen and other leaders of the national Republican and Democratic party organizations are initiating a study with the bipartisan American Political Foundation to determine how the United States can best contribute as a nation to the global campaign for democracy now gathering force. They will have the cooperation of congressional leaders of both parties, along with representatives of business, labor, and other major institutions in our society. I look forward to receiving their recommendations and to working with these institutions and the Congress in the common task of strengthening democracy throughout the world.

It is time that we committed ourselves as a nation—in both the public and private sectors—to assisting democratic development....

What I am describing now is a plan and a hope for the long term—the march of freedom and democracy which will leave Marxism-Leninism on the ash heap of history as it has left other tyrannies which stifle the freedom and muzzle the self-expression of the people. And that's why we must continue our efforts to strengthen NATO even as we move forward with our zero-option initiative in the negotiations on intermediate-range forces and our proposal for a one-third reduction in strategic ballistic missile warheads.

Our military strength is a prerequisite to peace, but let it be clear we maintain this strength in the hope it will never be used, for the ultimate determinant in the struggle that's now going on in the world will not be bombs and rockets but a test of wills and ideas, a trial of spiritual resolve, the values we hold, the beliefs we cherish, the ideals to which we are dedicated.

The British people know that, given strong leadership, time, and a little bit of hope, the forces of good ultimately rally and triumph over evil. Here among you is the cradle of self-government, the Mother of Parliaments. Here is the enduring greatness of the British contribution to mankind, the great civilized ideas: individual liberty, representative government, and the rule of law under God.

I've often wondered about the shyness of some of us in the West about standing for these ideals that have done so much to ease the plight of man and the hardships of our imperfect world. This reluctance to use those vast resources at our command reminds me of the elderly lady whose home was bombed in the blitz. As the rescuers moved about, they found a bottle of brandy she'd stored behind the staircase, which was all that was left standing. And since she was barely conscious, one of the workers pulled the cork to give her a taste of it. She came around immediately and said, "Here now—there now, put it back. That's for emergencies."

Well, the emergency is upon us. Let us be shy no longer. Let us go to our strength. Let us offer hope. Let us tell the world that a new age is not only possible but probable.

During the dark days of the Second World War, when this island was incandescent with courage, Winston Churchill exclaimed about Britain's adversaries, "What kind of people do they think we are?" Well, Britain's adversaries found out what extraordinary people the British are. But all the democracies paid a terrible price for allowing the dictators to underestimate us. We dare not make that mistake again. So, let us ask ourselves, "What kind of people do we think we are?" And let us answer, "Free people, worthy of freedom and determined not only to remain so but to help others gain their freedom as well."

Sir Winston led his people to great victory in war and then lost an election just as the fruits of victory were about to be enjoyed. But he left office honorably and, as it turned out, temporarily, knowing that the liberty of his people was more important than the fate of any single leader. History recalls his greatness in ways no dictator will ever know. And he left us a message of hope for the future, as timely now as when he first uttered it, as opposition leader in the Commons nearly twenty-seven years ago, when he said, "When we look back on all the perils through which we have passed and at the mighty foes that we have laid low and all the dark and deadly designs that we have frustrated, why should we fear for our future? We have," he said, "come safely through the worst."

Well, the task I've set forth will long outlive our own generation. But together, we too have come through the worst. Let us now begin a major effort to secure the best—a crusade for freedom that will engage the faith and fortitude of the next generation. For the sake of peace and justice, let us move toward a world in which all people are at last free to determine their own destiny.

SOURCE: Ronald Reagan: "Speech to the House of Commons," June 8, 1982. *Public Papers of the Presidents of the United States: Ronald Reagan,* 1982 (Washington, D.C., 1983), vol. 1, 742–748.

1983

INTERNATIONAL

U.S. Embassy in Beirut is bombed (April 18), 17 U.S. citizens die; a bomb-filled truck smashes through barriers at U.S. Marine compound in Beirut, kills 241 Americans (October 23).

U.S. troops land on Grenada in West Indies to halt Cuban buildup and protect U.S. students (October 25); island is secured within few days.

Russians shoot down Korean Airlines plane that had drifted over Soviet territory (September 1); all 269 aboard, including 52 Americans, die.

NATIONAL

Social Security is amended to include federal employees after April 1, 1984; raises age of eligibility from 65 to 66 by year 2009, to 67 by 2027.

Third Monday in January becomes national holiday in honor of Dr. Martin Luther King Jr.

Chicago elects its first African-American mayor, Harold Washington.

Supreme Court upholds constitutionality of windfall profits tax on decontrolled crude oil.

BUSINESS/INDUSTRY/INVENTIONS

Apple introduces "mouse," hand-held computer pointing device, and screens with pictures ("icons") to represent programs.

Supreme Court approves an agreement that settles antitrust suit against ATT (August 5); ATT gives up its 22 Bell System companies; in return it is permitted to enter previously prohibited areas (data processing, equipment sales, and others).

General Motors agrees to pay $42.5 million to settle charges of employment discrimination against blacks, Hispanics, and women.

A marine stands in front of the ruins of the operation center in Beirut, Lebanon, where a suicide bomber slammed a truck loaded with TNT into the U.S. Marine base in October 1983, killing 241 Americans. **AP/WIDE WORLD PHOTOS**

Gerard Debreu is awarded Nobel Prize in economics for work on the way prices operate to balance supply and demand.

Job Training Partnership Act establishes job training and employment services for underprivileged persons.

Compact discs ("CDs") begin to appear in record stores, replacing LP records.

DEATHS R. Buckminster Fuller, developer of geodesic dome; Earl S. Tupper, developer of Tupperware.

TRANSPORTATION

Federal Trade Commission approves plan by General Motors and Toyota for joint production of a subcompact car.

Federal gasoline tax increases 5 cents per gallon to pay for highway, bridges, and mass-transit improvements.

Connecticut Turnpike bridge over Mianus River at Greenwich collapses; three are killed.

American Airlines simplifies fare structure to four basic fees tied to miles traveled.

Houston voters reject $2.35-billion bond issue for urban rail system.

Mississippi River Bridge at Luling, Louisiana, opens.

SCIENCE/MEDICINE

Subrahmanyan Chandrasekhar and William A. Fowler share Nobel Prize in physics for work on what happens when stars age; Barbara McClintock is awarded prize in physiology/medicine for discovery that genes can move on chromosomes of plants and effect of the moves on future plants.

Eighth successful shuttle flight is completed; first flight for an African-American astronaut, Guion S. Buford III.

EDUCATION

Federal District Court rules that New Jersey law that mandates a minute of silence or meditation for public school students is unconstitutional (see 1982).

National Commission on Excellence in Education reports that U.S. elementary and secondary education is "mediocre."

Supreme Court rules that IRS can deny tax exemptions to private schools that practice racial discrimination.

RELIGION

National Conference of Catholic Bishops condemns nuclear arms race, calls for end of nuclear arms production and deployment.

National Council of Churches completes translation of Bible readings to eliminate references to God as solely male.

Presbyterian Church (USA) comes into being as the United Presbyterian Church and the Presbyterian Church in the U.S. formally merge; Rev. John R. Taylor of Charlotte, North Carolina, is named first moderator of merged church.

Catholic Archbishop Joseph L. Bernardin of Chicago is elevated to cardinal.

ART/MUSIC

Bernard Rands composes *Canti del Sole.*

SONGS (POPULAR): "All Night Long," "Beat It," "Down Under," "Every Breath You Take," "Islands in the Stream," "Say Say Say," "Total Eclipse of the Heart," "Somebody's Baby," "Sweet Dreams."

DEATHS George Balanchine, choreographer; Eubie Blake, pianist and composer; Harry James, trumpeter and bandleader; Marty Robbins, country-music singer and composer; Ira Gershwin, lyricist for brother, George.

LITERATURE/JOURNALISM

BOOKS *Ironweed* by William Kennedy, *American Primitive* by Mary Oliver, *Winter's Tale* by Mark Helprin, *Voice of the Heart* by Barbara T. Bradford, *Thurston House* by Danielle Steel.

ENTERTAINMENT

PLAYS David Mamet writes *Glengarry Glen Ross;* Neil Simon, *Brighton Beach Memoirs;* Marsha Norman, *'Night, Mother;* Stockard Channing stars in *The Lady and the Clarinet.*

MOVIES *Terms of Endearment* with Shirley MacLaine; *Return of the Jedi* with Harrison Ford, Carrie Fisher, and Mark Hamill; *The Big Chill* with Glenn Close; *Breathless* with Richard Gere; *Sudden Impact* with Clint Eastwood; *Silkwood* with Meryl Streep.

DEATHS Tennessee Williams, playwright; screen personalities Norma Shearer, Gloria Swanson, Raymond Massey, and Pat O'Brien; television hosts Dave Garroway and Arthur Godfrey; Lynn Fontanne, actress.

SPORTS

Peter F. Ueberroth becomes baseball commissioner.

American Medical Assn. urges ban on boxing because of brain damage resulting from bouts.

ABC and NBC agree to pay $1.1 billion for six years of regular-season baseball broadcasts.

U.S. District Court awards $11.5 million in antitrust damages to Los Angeles Raiders, $4.86 million to Los Angeles Coliseum in suit against NFL.

Nolan Ryan records 3,509th strikeout, breaking Walter Johnson's long-standing record; Brian Downing, California Angels outfielder, sets record of 244 consecutive errorless games; Steve Garvey of San Diego Padres sets National League playing record, 1,207 consecutive games.

WINNERS *Auto racing*—Tom Sneva, Indianapolis 500; Bobby Allison, NASCAR; *Baseball*—Baltimore Orioles, World Series; *Basketball*—Fresno State, NIT; North Carolina State, NCAA; Southern California, NCAA (women); Philadelphia, NBA; *Bowling*—Earl Anthony, PBA; *Boxing*—Larry Holmes, heavyweight; Sugar Ray Leonard, welterweight; Vito Antuofermo, middleweight; *Figure skating*—Scott Hamilton, U.S. and world men's title; Rosalynn Sumners, U.S. and world women's title; *Football* (bowls)—UCLA, Rose; Nebraska, Orange; Penn State, Sugar; Southern Methodist, Cotton; Washington, Super Bowl XVII; Michigan, first USFL title; *Golf*—Larry Nelson, U.S. Open; Hal Sutton, PGA; Severiano Ballesteros, Masters; Jan Stephenson, U.S. Women's Open; Patty Sheehan, LPGA; *Harness racing*—Duenna, Hambletonian; *Hockey*—New York Islanders, Stanley Cup; *Horse racing*—Sunny's Halo, Kentucky Derby; Deputed Testamony, Preakness Stakes; Caveat, Belmont Stakes; *Skiing*—Phil Mahre, world Alpine Cup; Tamara McKinney, first American to win world women's title; *Tennis*—Jimmy Connors, U.S. Open (men); Martina Navratilova, U.S. Open (women); *Yachting*—Australian boat *Australia II* wins America's Cup, first U.S. loss since race began in 1851.

DEATHS Jack Dempsey, heavyweight boxing champion (1919–1926); George Halas, pro-football pioneer; Paul (Bear) Bryant, Alabama football coach.

MISCELLANEOUS

Worst snowstorm in 36 years blankets 600-mile stretch of the East Coast.

1984

INTERNATIONAL

Explosives-filled truck strikes U.S. Embassy annex in Beirut; 23 are killed.

U.S. Marines are withdrawn from Beirut (February 26); three Americans are kidnapped in that city: TV

Geraldine Ferraro, a New York congresswoman, is the first woman vice presidential candidate of a major party. On October 11, 1984, she debates Vice President George Bush on national television. CORBIS-BETTMANN

reporter Jeremy Levin, who escapes later; CIA Station Chief William Buckley, who is killed (March 7); and Presbyterian Minister Benjamin Weir (May 8).

U.S. and Vatican resume full diplomatic relations after 117 years (January 10); William A. Wilson is named ambassador to the Vatican.

U.S. withdraws from UNESCO (U.N. Educational, Scientific, and Cultural Organization) because of agency's mismanagement and politicization.

Kuwaiti plane en route to Pakistan is hijacked; 161 in plane are held hostage at Teheran; Iranian security men capture plane; two Americans are killed before rescue.

President Ronald Reagan makes six-day visit to China.

NATIONAL

President Reagan, Republican, is reelected, receives 54,281,858 popular and 525 electoral votes to 37,457,215 popular and 13 electoral votes for former vice president Walter Mondale; Rep. Geraldine Ferraro is Mondale's vice presidential candidate, the first woman nominated by a major party.

Supreme Court rules that the Federal Aviation Administration (and by inference, other agencies) cannot be sued for damages for mistakes that contribute to disasters.

Vietnam Memorial in Washington, D.C., is dedicated.

DEATHS Mark W. Clark, World War II and Korea general; William A. Egan, first Alaska governor; George H. Gallup, pollster.

BUSINESS/INDUSTRY/INVENTIONS

ATT divests itself of 22 wholly owned local Bell telephone companies (January 1) as a result of 1982 consent decree with Justice Department.

E. F. Hutton brokerage firm pleads guilty to 2,000 federal charges of checking-account manipulations.

Stock market sets record when 236 million shares change hands in one day; 696 million shares are traded in week.

Environmental Protection Agency proposes 90% reduction of lead in gasoline by 1986, complete elimination by 1995.

Major U.S. oil companies agree to allow service-station operators to sell any gasoline they choose.

Mergers during the year include Gulf Oil and Chevron, Texaco and Getty Oil, Superior Oil and Mobil, Carnation and Nestle, Electronic Data Systems and General Motors.

TRANSPORTATION

Joe Kittinger completes first successful transatlantic balloon flight (September 17).

New York becomes first state to require driver and front-seat passenger seat belts.

SCIENCE/MEDICINE

Bruce Merrifield is awarded Nobel Prize in chemistry for research that revolutionized study of proteins.

Astronaut Bruce McCandless becomes first person to walk in space with no ties to the mother ship; Astronaut Kathryn D. Sullivan becomes first American woman to walk in space.

Astronauts successfully repair in space damaged satellite that had been inoperative for four years.

DEATH Dr. John Rock, codeveloper of oral contraceptive pill.

EDUCATION

Supreme Court rules that prohibition of sex discrimination by federally aided schools and colleges applies only to department or program that receives the aid, not entire school; also upholds law that makes college men who fail to register for the draft ineligible for federal scholarships.

New York State Board of Regents issues strict new high school graduation requirements.

RELIGION

Supreme Court reaffirms its ruling that organized prayer in public schools is unconstitutional; also rules that public financing of a Nativity scene does not of itself violate doctrine of separation of church and state.

Senate rejects proposed constitutional amendment to permit silent or spoken prayers in public schools.

Congress approves measure that permits public high school students to hold religious meetings in the schools during off-hours.

Basis is reached for merging nine Protestant denominations by Consultation on Church Union after 22 years of effort.

Two Catholic archbishops are named: John J. O'Connor of New York and Bernard F. Law of Boston.

ART/MUSIC

Stephen Albert composes *Symphony RiverRun.*

John Baldessori completes the painting *Kiss/Panic.*

SONGS (POPULAR): "Against All Odds," "Footloose," "Ghostbusters," "I Just Called to Say I Love You," "Jump," "What's Love Got to Do with It?," "When Doves Cry," "Another Woman in Love."

DEATHS Ansel Adams, photographer; Mabel Mercer, jazz singer; Meredith Willson, composer *(The Music Man);* Jan Peerce, opera tenor; two orchestra leaders, Fred Waring and Count Basie.

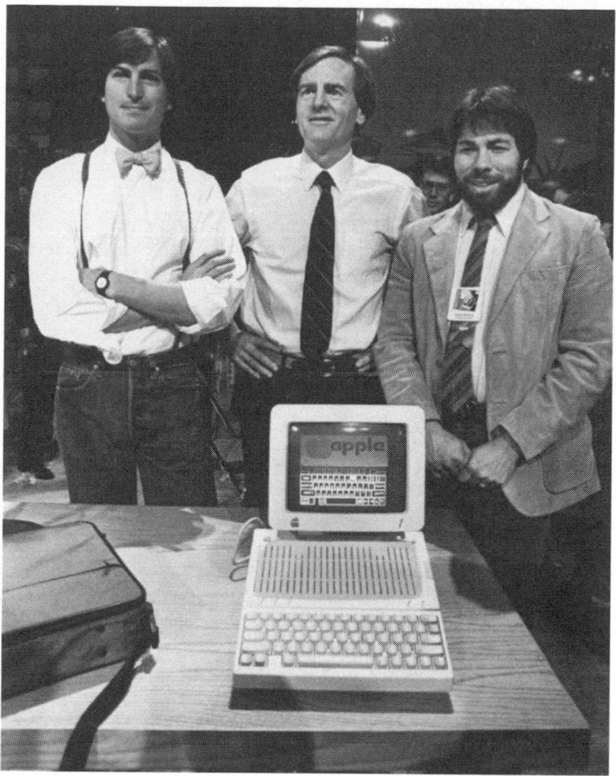

Apple Computer co-founders Steve Jobs (left) and Steve Wozniak (right), pictured here with new company president John Sculley, introduce the new Apple IIc computer in 1984. In the same year, they also develop the Macintosh. UPI/CORBIS-BETTMANN

LITERATURE/JOURNALISM

BOOKS *The American Blues* by Ward Just, *Duplicate Keys* by Jane Smiley, *Full Circle* by Danielle Steel, *The Good War* by Studs Terkel, *Yin* by Caroline Kizer.

DEATHS Authors Irwin Shaw and Truman Capote.

ENTERTAINMENT

PLAYS Stephen Sondheim and James Lapine write *Sunday in the Park with George;* Jerry Herman, *La Cage aux Folles.*

MOVIES *Indiana Jones and the Temple of Doom* with Harrison Ford, *Beverly Hills Cop* with Eddie Murphy, *Falling in Love* with Robert DeNiro, *The Terminator* with Arnold Schwarzenegger, *Harry and Son* with Paul Newman, *The Natural* with Robert Redford, *Romancing the Stone* with Michael Douglas.

Olympic gold medalist Mary Lou Retton performs on the balance beam. © NEAL PRESTON/ CORBIS-BETTMANN

DEATHS Lillian Hellman, playwright; William Powell, screen actor; Brooks Atkinson, *New York Times* drama critic.

SPORTS

Supreme Court rules that NCAA's exclusive control of college-football television coverage violates antitrust laws; five universities form National Independent Football Network.

Supreme Court rules that NFL cannot prevent teams from moving to other cities.

U.S. Football League abandons spring playing schedule, to play in fall.

Winter Olympics are held in Yugoslavia; Bill Johnson first from U.S. to win gold medal in skiing; Debbi Armstrong, a gold in women's giant slalom; Russia announces that it will not participate in Summer Games in Los Angeles; Karen Stives becomes first U.S. woman to win an equestrian event; Mary Lou Retton, first to win all-around women's gymnastics; Joan Benoit, the first women's marathon.

Reggie Jackson hits 500th home run; Elvin Hayes of Houston ends basketball career with record 1,303 games; Kareem Abdul Jabbar becomes pro basketball's leading scorer with 31,421 points; Walter Payton of Chicago Bears breaks career rushing record with 12,400 yards; Eric Dickerson of Los Angeles Rams sets single-season rushing record with 2,105 yards.

WINNERS *Auto racing*—Rick Mears, Indianapolis 500; Tery Labonte, NASCAR; *Baseball*—Detroit Tigers, World Series; *Basketball*—Michigan, NIT; Georgetown, NCAA; Southern California, NCAA (women); Boston, NBA; *Bowling*—Bob Chamberlain, PBA; *Boxing*—Thomas Hearns, superwelterweight; Marvin Hagler, middleweight; Livingston Bramble, lightweight; *Figure skating*—Scott Hamilton, U.S. and world men's titles; Rosalynn Summers, U.S. women's title; *Football* (bowls)—UCLA, Rose; Miama (Florida), Orange; Auburn, Sugar; Georgia, Cotton; Los Angeles Raiders, Super Bowl XVIII; *Golf*—Fuzzy Zoeller, U.S. Open; Lee Trevino, PGA; Ben Crenshaw, Masters; Hollis Stacy, U.S. Women's Open; Pat Sheehan, LPGA; *Harness racing*—Historic Freight, Hambletonian; *Hockey*—Edmonton, Stanley Cup; *Horse racing*—Swale, Kentucky Derby and Belmont Stakes; Gate Dancer, Preakness Stakes; *Tennis*—Sweden, Davis Cup; John McEnroe, U.S. Open (men); Martina Navratilova, U.S. Open (women).

DEATHS Johnny Weissmuller, swimmer and screen actor (Tarzan); Walter Alston, baseball manager (Dodgers 1954–1976); Anne Townsend, leading U.S. field-hockey player.

1985

INTERNATIONAL

Cruise ship *Achille Lauro* is hijacked in Mediterranean; one U.S. citizen is killed before rescue.

Barber B. Conable, former New York congressman, is named president of World Bank.

Four U.S. citizens are kidnapped in Beirut: Catholic priest Lawrence Jenco; Terry Anderson, Associated Press correspondent; Thomas Sutherland, American University dean; and David Jacobsen, director, American University hospital; Rev. Benjamin Weir, kidnapped in 1984, is released.

U.S. and Soviet Union disarmament talks begin in Geneva.

President Ronald Reagan and Canadian Prime Minister Brian Mulroney sign several agreements, create joint committee to study acid rain.

NATIONAL

President Reagan undergoes successful abdominal surgery (July 13).

First-class postage rises to 22 cents an ounce (February 17).

Philadelphia police bomb house to evict MOVE, a radical group; results in fire that causes 11 deaths, destruction of 61 houses (May 13).

Labor Secretary Raymond Donovan resigns after being indicted for business practices before becoming secretary.

U.S. District Court finds Yonkers, New York, guilty of "illegally and intentionally" segregating public schools and housing.

DEATHS Henry Cabot Lodge, legislator, ambassador to South Vietnam; Sam Ervin, North Carolina senator who headed Watergate committee.

BUSINESS/INDUSTRY/INVENTIONS

General Electric buys RCA for $6.28 billion; other corporate combinations of year are General Motors and Hughes Aircraft, Nabisco and R. J. Reynolds.

Largest U.S. civil judgment ($10.53 billion) assessed against Texaco Inc. in favor of Penzoil Co.

President Reagan vetoes bill that would limit imports of textiles.

Bank failures nearly double in year to 120.

Franco Modigoliani is awarded Nobel Prize in economics for analyzing behavior of household savers and functioning of financial markets.

DEATH Robert W. Woodruff, Coca-Cola president and chairman (1923–1955).

TRANSPORTATION

Chrysler Corp. and Mitsubishi Motors Corp. announce joint venture to build subcompact cars in U.S.

Groundbreaking is held in Michigan for new Mazda auto plant; Honda Motors says it will build engines for a subcompact at an Ohio plant.

Lock of Welland Canal that connects Lakes Erie and Ontario collapses, halts shipping (October 15).

Norfolk Southern Corp. is chosen to take over government-controlled Conrail system.

Court of Appeals finds Exxon Corp. guilty of overcharging customers; fines it $1.9 billion.

Texas Air Corp. announces it will acquire TWA (Trans World Airlines).

New security measures against airline and airport terrorism are issued.

Ford Motor Co. announces it will cut its white-collar force by 20% over next five years.

"We Are the World," written by Michael Jackson and Lionel Richie and produced by Quincy Jones, wins a Grammy for song of the year. The project brings together twenty-one solo vocalists with proceeds going to famine victims in Ethiopia. **AP/WIDE WORLD PHOTOS**

SCIENCE/MEDICINE

Herbert A. Hauptman and Jerome Karle share Nobel prize in chemistry for developing techniques used to determine structures of molecules vital to life; Michael S. Brown and Joseph L. Goldstein share prize in physiology/medicine for research on cholesterol.

DEATHS John F. Enders, developer of tissue culture of polio virus that led to Salk vaccine; Charles F. Richter, developer of scale for measuring earthquakes.

EDUCATION

Supreme Court rules that public school systems may not send teachers into parochial schools for remedial or enriched instruction; also rules that public school teachers and officials may search students if there are "reasonable grounds" to believe search will give evidence of law or school-rule violation.

William J. Bennett becomes Secretary of Education.

RELIGION

Supreme Court strikes down Alabama law that permits one minute of prayer or meditation in public schools.

Ezra Taft Benson is named president of Mormon Church.

Amy Eilberg is ordained as first woman Conservative rabbi.

Episcopal Bishop Edmund L. Browning of Hawaii is elected presiding bishop.

Two Catholic archbishops are elevated to cardinal: John J. O'Connor of New York and Bernard F. Law of Boston.

DEATHS Eugene Carson Blake, general secretary, World Council of Churches (1966–1972); Catholic Cardinal Terence J. Cooke of New York.

ART/MUSIC

George Perle composes *Wind Quintet IV;* John Corigliano composes *Fantasia on an Obstinato.*

SONGS (POPULAR): "Can't Fight This Feeling," "Careless Whisper," "Everybody Wants to Rule the World," "I Want to Know What Love Is," "Money for Nothing," "The Power of Love," "Say You, Say Me," "We Are the World."

DEATHS Rick Nelson, rock 'n' roll star; Wayne King, orchestra leader; Johnny Marks, composer ("Rudolph, the Red-Nosed Reindeer"); Eugene Ormandy, concert violinist and conductor; Roger Sessions, opera composer.

LITERATURE/JOURNALISM

BOOKS *Lonesome Dove* by Larry McMurtry, *Caracole* by Edmund White, *Family Album* by Danielle Steel, *The Mammoth Hunters* by Jean M. Auel, *Galapagos* by Kurt Vonnegut Jr.

DEATHS E. B. White and Taylor Caldwell, authors; Chester Gould, cartoonist ("Dick Tracy").

ENTERTAINMENT

Capital Cities Communications Inc. purchases ABC (American Broadcasting Co.).

MOVIES *Back to the Future* with Michael Fox, *Out of Africa* with Meryl Streep, *Rambo, First Blood* with Sylvester Stallone, *The Color Purple* with Whoopi Goldberg, *Pale Rider* with Clint Eastwood, *Into the Night* with Michelle Pfeiffer.

DEATHS Phil Silvers, entertainer; Yul Brynner, actor; Burr Tillstrom, puppeteer *(Kukla, Fran, and Ollie);* Rock Hudson, screen actor, of AIDS, encouraging open national discussion of the disease.

SPORTS

Basketball Hall of Fame in Springfield, Massachusetts, is dedicated.

Eddie Robinson, Grambling University football coach, becomes winningest coach with 324th win; later rises to 371.

U.S. Olympic Committee to test U.S. athletes for drugs up to 1988 games; major league baseball personnel, except unionized players, to submit to drug tests.

Nolan Ryan of Houston Astros becomes first pitcher to achieve 4,000 career strikeouts; Tom Seaver, Chicago White Sox, and Phil Niekro, New York Yankees, each wins his 300th game; Pete Rose of Cincinnati Reds breaks Ty Cobb's 1928 record with 4,192 career base hits; Rod Carew of California Angels scores his 3,000th base hit.

WINNERS *Auto racing*—Danny Sullivan, Indianapolis 500; Darrell Waltrip, NASCAR; *Baseball*—Kansas City Royals, World Series; *Basketball*—UCLA, NIT; Villanova, NCAA; Old Dominion, NCAA (women); Los Angeles Lakers, NBA; *Bowling*—Mike Aulby, PBA; *Boxing*—Michael Spinks, heavyweight; Marvin Hagler, middleweight; Donald Curry, welterweight; *Figure skating*—Brian Boitano, U.S. men's title; Tiffany Chin, U.S. women's title; *Football* (bowls)—Southern California, Rose; Washington, Orange; Nebraska, Sugar; Boston College, Cotton; San Francisco, Super Bowl XIX; *Golf*—Andy North, U.S. Open; Hubert Green, PGA; Bernhard Langer, Masters; Kathy Baker, U.S. Women's Open; Nancy Lopez, LPGA; *Harness racing*—Prakas, Hambletonian; *Hockey*—Edmonton, Stanley Cup; *Horse racing*—Spend a Buck, Kentucky Derby; Tank's Prospect, Preakness Stakes; Creme Fraiche, Belmont Stakes; *Rowing*—Princeton, Men's Intercollegiate; Washington, Women's; *Tennis*—Ivan Lendl, U.S. Open (men); Hana Mandlikova, U.S. Open (women).

DEATHS Peter Desjardins, Olympic diving champion; Pelle Lindbergh, Philadelphia goaltender, in car crash; Roger Maris, current holder of season home-run record (61).

MISCELLANEOUS

Charter DC-8 bringing troops home for Christmas crashes at Gander, Newfoundland; 256 are killed.

1986

INTERNATIONAL

President Ronald Reagan signs secret order, authorizes arms shipments to Iran (January 17); National Security Advisor John M. Poindexter resigns (November 25); his aide, Lt. Col. Oliver North is dismissed after it is learned that some Iran arms sales proceeds went to finance military aid for Nicaraguan Contras.

U.S. planes bomb "terrorist" targets in Libya (April 15).

Two U.S. hostages in Beirut are released, three others kidnapped; released are Rev. Lawrence Jenco and David Jacobsen; kidnapped are Frank Reed, educator; Edward Tracy, writer; and Joseph Cicippio.

Congress overrides presidential veto to impose economic sanctions against South Africa.

Canada and U.S. agree on plan to reduce acid rain.

NATIONAL

President Reagan announces that Supreme Court Chief Justice Warren Burger will retire, nominates Associate Justice William Rehnquist for post; he is confirmed September 17.

Congress virtually eliminates mandatory retirement at 70.

Congress passes major tax-reform law.

More than 5 million Americans join hands trying to form a human chain across the nation in Hands Across America, designed to raise money for the hungry.

Titan 34-D rocket carrying secret military payload explodes shortly after liftoff.

Supreme Court denies Yonkers, New York, a stay in effecting court-ordered desegregation plan for schools and housing; also rules that police cannot question defendant at arraignment if his requested lawyer is not present; also rules that military personnel cannot sue superiors for damages even if their constitutional rights are violated.

Senate ratifies U.N. treaty outlawing genocide.

Elie Wiesel is awarded Nobel Peace Prize.

President Carter Memorial Library in Atlanta is dedicated.

DEATH Admiral Hyman Rickover, father of atomic-powered Navy.

BUSINESS/INDUSTRY/INVENTIONS

James M. Buchanan is awarded Nobel Prize in economics for pioneering new methods of analyzing economic and political decision-making.

Dow Jones industrial average drops 86.61 points when a record 237.6 million shares change hands (September 11); drops another 34.17 points the following day.

Year's bank failures climb to 145.

LTV Corp. becomes largest U.S. corporation to file for bankruptcy.

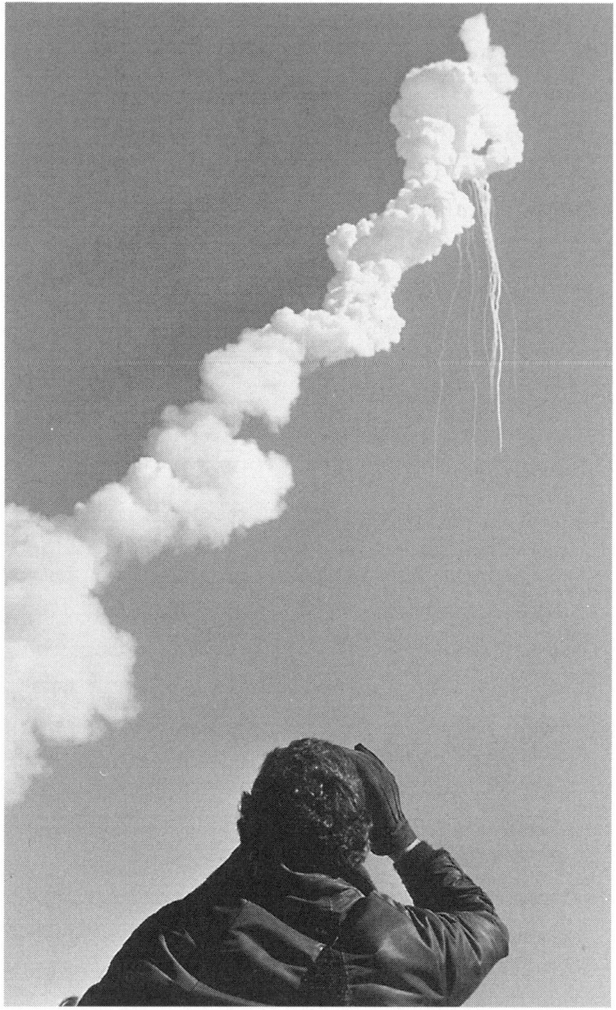

As viewed from the Kennedy Space Center in Cape Canaveral, Florida, the space shuttle *Challenger* explodes during take-off, January 28, 1986. UPI/CORBIS-BETTMANN

Among the year's mergers are Beatrice Foods and KKR (Kohlberg Kravis Roberts), General Foods and Philip Morris, Sperry and Burroughs, Allied Stores and Campeau.

DEATHS Abram N. Pritzger, founder of Hyatt Hotels; J. Willard Marriott, founder of hotel/restaurant chain; Minoru Yamasaki, architect (New York's World Trade Center).

TRANSPORTATION

Supreme Court upholds ruling that Exxon Corp. pay $2.1 billion in refunds for overcharges.

Some airline mergers and purchases occur: Northwest buys Republic, United acquires Frontier, Texas Air buys People's Express, Delta and Western plan merger, Texas Air purchases Eastern.

General Motors announces that it will close 11 plants as

part of modernization program; Excel, small car built by Hyundai Corp. of South Korea, goes on sale in U.S.

Interstate Commerce Commission rejects proposed merger of Southern Pacific and Santa Fe railroads.

Pan Am begins shuttle service from La Guardia Airport in New York to Washington (D.C.) and Boston.

Last stretch of Interstate 80, a five-mile segment in Salt Lake City, is completed.

SCIENCE/MEDICINE

Space shuttle *Challenger,* with a crew of seven, explodes moments after liftoff, kills entire crew (January 28).

Voyager, an experimental plane piloted by Dick Rutan and Jeana Yeager, completes round-the-world nonstop flight without refueling, landing at Edwards AFB, a flight of nearly 26,000 miles in 9 days, 3 minutes, 44 seconds (December 23).

Dudley Herschbach and Yuan T. Lee share Nobel Prize in chemistry for helping create first detailed understanding of chemical reactions; Rita Levi-Montalcini and Stanley Cohen share Prize in physiology/medicine for major contributions to understanding substances that influence cell growth.

Surgeon General C. Everett Koop calls for widespread education, condom distribution, and antibody testing to prevent the spread of AIDS.

EDUCATION

Norfolk, Virginia, school board votes to end 15 years of busing for racial balance, returns to neighborhood elementary schools.

Barbara A. Black becomes dean of Columbia Law School, first woman to head major private law school.

Carnegie Foundation for the Advancement of Teaching urges overhaul of undergraduate education, including dropping of standardized admission tests.

Carnegie Corporation to establish nation's first system of certifying elementary and high school teachers.

RELIGION

United Methodist Council of Bishops calls for "clear and unconditional" opposition to use of nuclear weapons.

ART/MUSIC

John Harbison composes *The Flight into Egypt.*

Jeff Koons completes the sculpture *Statuary.*

SONGS (POPULAR): "Addicted to Love," "How Will I Know?" "Kiss," "On My Own," "Rock Me Amadeus," "That's What Friends Are For," "West End Girls."

LITERATURE/JOURNALISM

Robert Penn Warren is named first official U.S. poet laureate.

Supreme Court overturns several statutes that put burden of proof on news organizations in libel cases.

BOOKS *Bearing the Cross* by David J. Garrow, *Thomas and Beulah* by Rita Dove, *The Counterlife* by Philip Roth, *Wanderlust* by Danielle Steel, *A Summons to Memphis* by Peter Taylor.

DEATH Theodore H. White, author of "making of the president" books.

ENTERTAINMENT

PLAY August Wilson writes *Fences.*

MOVIES *Top Gun* with Tom Cruise, *Crocodile Dundee* with Paul Hogan, *Platoon* with Charlie Sheen, *Hoosiers* with Gene Hackman, *Heartburn* with Meryl Streep, *Delta Force* with Chuck Norris.

L.A. Law appears on television.

DEATHS Screen actors Ray Milland and Jimmy Cagney; Desi Arnaz of *I Love Lucy* show; Marlin Perkins, zoo director and television personality; Otto Preminger, movie director.

SPORTS

Supreme Court upholds move of Oakland Raiders to Los Angeles.

NCAA adopts three-point field goal in men's basketball.

Federal jury awards $1 in damages to U.S. Football League in its $1.7 million suit against NFL; USFL cancels its fall season, hopes to start larger, stronger league in 1987.

NFL increases drug testing of players; repeat users to be suspended for life.

A. Bartlett Giamatti, Yale University president, is elected president of National (baseball) League.

Jackie Joyner sets women's heptathlon record with 7,158 points.

WINNERS *Auto racing*—Bobby Rahal, Indianapolis 500; Dale Earnhardt, NASCAR; *Baseball*—New York Mets, World Series; *Basketball*—Ohio State, NIT; Louisville, NCAA; Texas, NCAA (women); Boston, NBA; *Bowling*—Tom Crites, PBA; *Boxing*—Michael Spinks, heavyweight; Lloyd Moneghan, welterweight; *Figure skating*—Brian Boitano, U.S. and world men's titles; Debi Thomas, U.S. and world women's titles; *Football* (bowls)—UCLA, Rose; Oklahoma, Orange; Tennessee, Sugar; Texas A&M, Cotton; Chicago, Super Bowl XX; *Golf*—Ray Floyd, U.S. Open; Bob Tway, PGA; Jack Nicklaus, Masters; Jane Geddes, U.S. Women's Open; Pat Bradley, LPGA; *Harness racing*—Nuclear Kosmos, Hambletonian; *Hockey*—Montreal, Stanley Cup; *Horse racing*—Ferdinand, Kentucky Derby; Snow Chief, Preakness Stakes; Danzig Connection, Belmont Stakes; *Tennis*—Ivan Lendl, U.S. Open (men); Martina Navratilova, U.S. Open (women).

DEATH Billy Haughton, harness-race driver.

MISCELLANEOUS

Fire in DuPont Plaza Hotel in Puerto Rico kills 96.

1987

INTERNATIONAL

U.S. and Soviet Union resolve differences in treaty to ban medium- and shorter-range missiles; Soviet President Mikhail Gorbachev comes to Washington to sign treaty (December 9).

U.S. and Canada agree on free trade that will eliminate all tariffs by 1999; must be approved by national legislatures (October 3).

Four U.S. citizens are kidnapped in Beirut: Charles Glass, television reporter who is released two months later, Robert Polhill, Jonathan Turner, and Alan Steen.

An Iraqi missile strikes the USS *Stark* in the Persian Gulf; kills 37 sailors.

NATIONAL

President Ronald Reagan signs bill ratifying international genocide treaty, drafted 40 years ago; victory for Wisconsin Sen. William Proxmire who made 3,300 daily speeches over 19 years urging ratification.

President Reagan nominates Robert H. Bork for the Supreme Court; Bork is not confirmed.

President Reagan submits the first trillion-dollar budget.

Iran-Contra hearings by Congress continue for three months to try to get facts about diversion of Iran arms-sales profits to Nicaraguan Contras.

Former Labor Secretary Raymond J. Donovan is acquitted of grand larceny and fraud charges in actions prior to his government service.

March on Washington for Gay and Lesbian Rights

In October 1987, 600,000 protesters marched on Washington, D.C. in support of gay and lesbian rights. It was the second march on the Capitol—the first in 1979 had drawn 100,000 people, while a third march in 1993 attracted 1 million. The 1980s represented a difficult period for gay activists. In the 1986 legal decision *Bowers* v. *Hardwick,* the Supreme Court ruled 5-4 in favor of upholding existing sodomy laws. With enormous media attention surrounding the spread of Acquired Immuno-Deficiency Syndrome (AIDS), gay Americans found themselves unfairly stigmatized because of their lifestyle. The 1987 march, along with civil disobedience protests by the AIDS Coalition to Unleash Power (ACT UP), demonstrated the increasing visibility of gay Americans in U.S. society and aided their continuing quest for equal rights and social recognition.

Supreme Court rules that states may force Rotary clubs to admit women to membership; Kiwanis International ends 77-year-old men-only policy.

Former Sen. Gary Hart drops out of race for Democratic presidential nomination after publicity about his affair with a model.

First Lady Nancy Reagan undergoes successful mastectomy.

Great Basin (Nevada) National Park is dedicated.

DEATHS Commerce Secretary Malcolm Baldrige; two World War II generals, Maxwell D. Taylor and L. Lawton Collins; Bayard Rustin, civil rights leader.

BUSINESS/INDUSTRY/INVENTIONS

Stock market shows great activity: Dow-Jones industrial average closes above 2,000 for first time (January 23) and daily trading volume exceeds 300 million shares for first time; then in steady climb passes 2,300 and 2,400 early in spring, 2,500 and 2,700 in the summer; turnaround comes when average drops 91.55 points (October 6); 10 days later 338.4 million shares change hands and average falls 108.36 points (October 16), falls 508 points two weeks later.

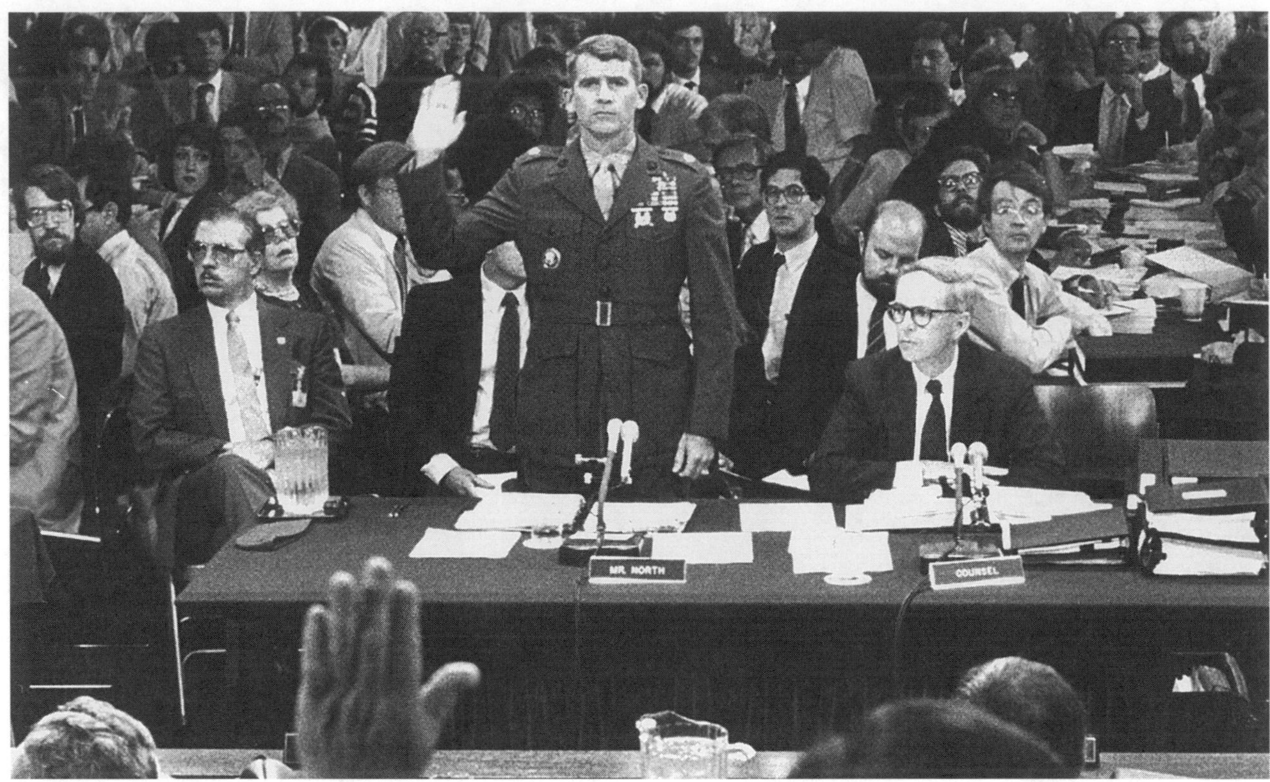

Oliver North's first appearance before the Senate Iran-Contra Committee in the summer of 1987. UPI/CORBIS-BETTMANN

Robert M. Solow is awarded Nobel Prize in economics for seminal contributions to theory of economic growth.

Mergers and new combinations in year include Standard Oil and British Petroleum, Dome Petroleum and Amoco, Chesebrough-Ponds and Unilever NV, Celanese and American Hoechst.

Bank failures for year reach 184.

TRANSPORTATION

Chrysler Corp. buys American Motors Co. from France's Renault for $1.5 billion.

Conrail is sold to private investors for $1.65 billion after decade of federal operation.

Texaco files for bankruptcy; Texaco and Penzoil sign settlement of $10.3 billion suit.

Continental Airlines absorbs People's Express, USAir takes over Piedmont Aviation.

Senate gives states right to raise speed limit to 65 miles per hour.

Volkswagen announces that it will close its New Stanton, Pennsylvania, plant in 1988.

Interstate highway bridge on New York Thruway near Amsterdam collapses; 10 are killed.

DEATH Henry Ford II, chief executive officer, Ford Motor Co. (1945–1980).

SCIENCE/MEDICINE

Donald J. Cram and Charles J. Pedersen share Nobel Prize in chemistry for wide-ranging research, including creation of artificial molecules.

IBM announces production of ceramic material capable of handling much greater amounts of electric current.

As the Third International AIDS Conference meets in Washington, D.C., 36,000 cases have been diagnosed, with 21,000 deaths.

EDUCATION

Three lower-court rulings are reversed: Alabama law banning 31 textbooks for promoting "religion of secular humanitarianism," Louisiana law requiring equal time for teaching of evolution theory and divine creation as a science; Hawkins County, Tennessee, law excusing children from classes using textbooks that are offensive to parents' religious beliefs.

Los Angeles puts its 618 schools and 592,000 pupils on a year-round schedule.

The AIDS quilt, brainchild of gay activist Cleve Jones, displays the names of thousands of people who have died of the disease. It is displayed in the Washington Mall in 1987. © LEE SNIDER/ CORBIS-BETTMANN

RELIGION

Rev. Pat Robertson resigns leadership of his religious broadcasting empire to run for Republican presidential nomination.

ART/MUSIC

William Bolcom composes *12 New Études for Piano;* John Conigliaro composes the opera *A Figaro for Antonia.*

DEATHS Jascha Heifetz, concert violinist; Sammy Kaye, orchestra leader; Andy Warhol, pop-art painter.

LITERATURE/JOURNALISM

Joseph Brodsky, exiled Soviet-born poet, is awarded Nobel Prize in literature.

Richard Wilbur is second U.S. poet laureate.

BOOKS *Beloved* by Toni Morrison, *Look Homeward* by David H. Donald, *Breathing the Water* by Denise Levertov, *Fine Things* and *Kaleidoscope* by Danielle Steel.

ENTERTAINMENT

PLAYS Alfred Uhry writes *Driving Miss Daisy;* Terrence McNally, *Frankie and Johnny in the Clair de Lune;* Tina Howe, *Coastal Disturbances.*

MOVIES *The Predator* with Arnold Schwarzenegger; *Wall Street* with Michael Douglas; *Moonstruck* with Cher; *Tin Men* with Richard Dreyfuss; *Good Morning, Vietnam* with Robin Williams; *The Last Emperor,* directed by Bernardo Bertolucci.

DEATHS Dancers Ray Bolger and Fred Astaire; Liberace, pianist; actors Danny Kaye and Robert Preston; actresses Mary Astor and Rita Hayworth; Clare Boothe Luce, playwright; Jackie Gleason, actor and entertainer; director and choreographer Bob Fosse; screen directors John Huston and Mervyn Leroy; David Susskind, producer and talk-show host; Bill Baird, puppeteer.

SPORTS

NBA awards four new franchises: Miami and Orlando, Florida; Charlotte, North Carolina, Minneapolis.

NFL players strike for three weeks.

WINNERS *Auto racing*—Al Unser, Indianapolis 500; Dale Earnhardt, NASCAR; *Baseball*—Minnesota Twins, World Series; *Basketball*—Southern Mississippi, NIT; Indiana, NCAA; Tennessee, NCAA (women); Los Angeles Lakers, NBA; *Bowling*—Randy Pedersen, PBA; American women, world title; *Boxing*—Mike Tyson, heavyweight; Sugar Ray Leonard, middleweight; *Figure skating*—Brian Boitano, U.S. men; Jill Trenary, U.S. women; *Football* (bowls)—Arizona State, Rose; Oklahoma, Orange; Nebraska, Sugar; Ohio State, Cotton; New York Giants, Super Bowl XXI; *Golf*—Scott Simpson, U.S. Open; Larry Nelson, PGA; Larry Mize, Masters; Laura Davies, U.S. Women's Open; Jane Geddes, LPGA; *Harness racing*—Mack Lobell, Hambletonian; *Hockey*—Edmonton, Stanley Cup; *Horse racing*—Alysheba, Kentucky Derby and Preakness Stakes; Bet Twice, Belmont Stakes; *Tennis*—Ivan Lendl, U.S. Open (men); Martina Navratilova, U.S. Open (women); *Yachting*—U.S. boat *Stars and Stripes* regains America's Cup.

MISCELLANEOUS

Tornado wipes out Saragosa, Texas, a town of 350; 30 are killed, 121 are injured.

Northwest airliner crashes after takeoff in Romulus, Michigan; 156 die.

1988

INTERNATIONAL

U.S. naval gunners mistakenly shoot down an Iranian passenger plane over the Persian Gulf thinking it was a warplane; all 290 aboard die (July 3).

Senate approves free-trade agreement with Canada.

President Ronald Reagan authorizes "a substantive dialogue" with Palestine Liberation Organization.

Senate ratifies Intermediate Range Nuclear Forces Treaty between U.S. and Soviet Union.

Car bomb kills U.S. military attaché in Athens, Navy Capt. William E. Nordeen.

NATIONAL

Vice President George Bush, Republican, is elected president, receives 48,881,221 popular and 426 electoral votes against 41,805,422 popular and 111 electoral votes for his Democratic challenger Michael S. Dukakis.

President Reagan vetoes civil rights bill; it passes over his veto (March 22).

Reparations bill is signed, gives $20,000 to each of about 60,000 surviving Japanese Americans interned during World War II.

New York State declares Love Canal area in Niagara Falls safe to live in; declared disaster area (1978) because of chemical contamination.

Veterans Administration becomes 14th cabinet department; effective 1989.

President Reagan signs $3.9 billion drought-relief bill.

Supreme Court rules that children in sexual abuse cases must confront their alleged abusers.

First-class postage increases by 3 cents to 25 cents.

DEATH Stuart Symington, senator, first secretary of Air Force.

BUSINESS/INDUSTRY/INVENTIONS

Securities and Exchange Commission accuses Drexel Burnham Lambert Group and junk-bond leader Michael Milken of extensive fraud.

Most of nation suffers severe drought, with half of the agricultural counties designated disaster areas; fire destroys about 4 million acres of forest.

Reported bank failures are at a record high, 221 in year.

Important mergers and takeovers during year: Kohlberg Kravis Roberts acquires RJR Nabisco for $24.9 billion; Philip Morris acquires Kraft for $11.5 billion; Campeau acquires Federated Department Stores for $7.4 billion; Pillsbury becomes part of Grand Metropolitan; Bridgestone acquires 75% of Firestone Tire for $1 billion.

TRANSPORTATION

Smoking is banned on Long Island and Metro-North Commuter railroads (New York) and all Northwest Airlines flights in North America.

Chrysler Corp. closes its 5,500-worker Kenosha, Wisconsin, plant.

Texaco agrees to pay $1.25 billion to settle overcharge complaints.

Transportation Department orders drug testing for 4 million transportation workers.

Donald Trump buys Eastern Airlines Northeast shuttle; Interstate Commerce Commission approves purchase of Southern Pacific Railroad for $1.2 billion by Rio Grande Industries.

SCIENCE/MEDICINE

Leon M. Lederman, Melvin Schwartz, and Jack Steinberger share Nobel Prize in physics for research that improved understanding of elementary particles and forces; Gertrude B. Elion and George H. Hitchings share prize in physiology/medicine for discovering principles for drug treatment.

Senate by 87–4 vote approves a $1 billion program for prevention and treatment of AIDS.

The Lockerbie crash in 1988 kills all passengers and crew, most of them American. Airline security is tightened after the crash, and after a massive manhunt the killers are brought to justice. © BRYN COLTON/ ASSIGNMENTS PHOTOGRAPHERS/CORBIS-BETTMANN

Space shuttle *Discovery* is first U.S. space shot since the *Challenger* disaster (1986).

DEATHS Walter H. Brattain, co-inventor of transistor; Luis W. Alvarez, codeveloper of ground-controlled radar.

EDUCATION

Education Secretary William Bennett resigns; Lauro F. Cavazos, first Hispanic cabinet member, succeeds him.

Supreme Court rules that public school officials have right to censor school newspapers and plays.

Dade County, Florida, turns over management of 32 schools to teams including teachers and parents; Illinois legislature restructures Chicago public schools, shifting power to run schools mostly to parents.

NAACP drops 15-year desegregation suit against Los Angeles schools because of changes in school population composition.

RELIGION

Barbara Harris is elected suffragan bishop of Boston by Massachusetts Episcopal Diocese, first woman named by the Anglican Church in 450 years (September 24).

Mother Katharine Drexel, a Philadelphia nun, is beatified; born to wealth, she took vow of poverty, founded Sisters of the Blessed Sacrament; Rev. Junipero Serra, founder of California missions, is beatified.

Televangelist Jimmy Swaggart confesses sins to 8,000 of his Baton Rouge (Louisiana) congregation, takes indefinite leave; Assemblies of God Church defrocks him when he refuses to stop preaching for a year; televangelist Jim Bakker is indicted on 24 federal charges of fraud and conspiracy.

Catholic Bishop Eugene A. Marino of Atlanta becomes first African-American archbishop; two archbishops are elevated to cardinal: James A. Hickey of Washington, D.C., and Edmund C. Szoka of Detroit, Michigan.

Merger of American Lutheran Church, Lutheran Church in America, and Association of Evangelical Lutheran Churches creates Evangelical Lutheran Church.

ART/MUSIC

Roger Reynolds composes *Whispers out of Time.*

Gala in Carnegie Hall celebrates Irving Berlin's 100th birthday; Smithsonian Institution stages exhibition on his life and works.

National Gallery (Washington, D.C.) constructs 23 new

Toni Morrison stands with her 1987 novel *Beloved,* which earned her the Pulitzer Prize for fiction in 1988. © DAVID BOOKSTAVER/AP/WIDE WORLD PHOTOS

galleries in East Building to display twentieth-century art.

DEATH Frederick Loewe, musical comedy composer.

LITERATURE/JOURNALISM

Maxwell Communications acquires Macmillan Publishing Co.

BOOKS *New and Collected Poems* by Richard Wilbur, *A Bright Shining Lie* by Neil Sheehan, *The Bonfire of the Vanities* by Tom Wolfe, *Anything for Billy* by Larry McMurtry, *Greenlanders* by Jane Smiley.

DEATHS Milton Caniff, cartoonist; Robert A. Heinlein, science-fiction writer.

ENTERTAINMENT

PLAYS Michael Crawford stars in *The Phantom of the Opera;* Wendy Wasserstein writes *The Heidi Chronicles.*

MOVIES *Rain Man* with Tom Cruise and Dustin Hoffman, *Who Framed Roger Rabbit?* with Bob Hoskins, *Coming to America* with Eddie Murphy, *Twins* with Arnold Schwarzenegger.

Congress passes bill, limits number of commercials in children's television programs, is vetoed by President Reagan.

DEATH John Houseman, actor, director, and producer.

SPORTS

A. Bartlett Giamatti, National League president, becomes baseball commissioner; effective 1989.

First game is played under lights in Chicago's Wrigley Field (August 9).

St. Louis Cardinals football team moves to Phoenix.

Roosevelt Raceway in Westbury, New York, announces it will close.

WINNERS *Auto racing*—Rick Mears, Indianapolis 500; Bill Elliott, NASCAR; *Baseball*—Los Angeles Dodgers, World Series; *Basketball*—Connecticut, NIT; Kansas, NCAA; Louisiana Tech, NCAA (women); Los Angeles Lakers, NBA; *Bowling*—Brian Voss, PBA; *Boxing*—Mike Tyson, heavyweight; *Figure skating*—Brian Boitano, U.S., Olympic, and world titles; Debi Thomas, U.S. women's; *Football* (bowls)—Michigan State, Rose; Miami (Florida), Orange; Syracuse—Auburn (tie), Sugar; Texas A&M, Cotton; Washington, Super Bowl XXII; *Golf*—Curtis Strange, U.S. Open; Jeff Shuman, PGA; Sandy Lyle, Masters; Liselotte Neumann, U.S. Women's Open; Sherri Turner, LPGA; *Harness racing*—Ambro Goal, Hambletonian; *Hockey*—Edmonton, Stanley Cup; *Horse racing*—Winning Colors, Kentucky Derby; Risen Star, Preakness Stakes and Belmont Stakes; *Tennis*—Mats Wilander, U.S. Open (men); Steffi Graf, U.S. Open (women); *Yachting*—U.S. boat *Stars and Stripes* retains America's Cup.

DEATHS Pete Maravich, basketball star; Jockey Mike Venezia in Belmont Park race; Hap (Leighton) Emms and Babe (Walter) Pratt, hockey greats; Carl Hubbell, Hall of Fame pitcher.

MISCELLANEOUS

Pan Am airliner en route to U.S. explodes over Lockerbie, Scotland, killing all 259 aboard, 11 on the ground; cause is determined to be bomb in a suitcase.

Diesel-fuel storage tank collapses, pours about 1 million gallons into Monongahela River at West Elizabeth, Pennsylvania.

1989

INTERNATIONAL

U.S. troops (20,000) invade Panama, overthrow regime of Gen. Manuel A. Noriega (December 20); Noriega surrenders (January 3, 1990), flies to Miami to stand trial on drug charges; four days of fighting result in 23 U.S. and about 250 Panamanian deaths; Canal traffic closes for one day.

Two U.S. fighter planes shoot down two Libyan jets over Mediterranean, north of Tobruk (January 4).

U.S. warships are permitted to protect neutral shipping in Persian Gulf.

U.S. to return Iranian assets ($567 million) frozen since 1979 as result of hostage-taking.

Free-trade agreement between U.S. and Canada goes into effect (January 1); over a 10-year period, will create a largely free market of 270 million people.

Islamic militants announce that they killed U.S. hostage Lt. Col. William R. Higgins.

President George Bush becomes first U.S. president to address Hungarian parliament.

NATIONAL

Supreme Court leaves intact constitutional right to abortion but encourages states to set limits; upholds mandatory urine testing of railroad employees involved in accidents, Customs Service employees who seek drug enforcement jobs; rules alcoholism to be "willful misconduct," allows Veterans Administration to deny benefits to alcoholic veterans.

House Ethics Committee unanimously charges Speaker James C. Wright with 69 violations of House rules; Wright resigns (June 6); Thomas S. Foley succeeds him.

Largest oil spill in North American history occurs when Exxon tanker, *Exxon Valdez,* runs aground on reef near Valdez, Alaska; damages miles of beaches, destroys wildlife.

Explosion in gun turret of USS *Iowa* kills 47 crewmen.

Department of Veterans Affairs begins operations (March 15); Edward J. Derwinski is secretary.

Richard B. Cheney is named defense secretary after former Senator John Tower's nomination is rejected; Gen. Colin L. Powell becomes first African-American chairman of Joint Chiefs of Staff.

Pennsylvania is first state to restrict abortions (November 18) since *Roe* v. *Wade* Supreme Court decision.

New Jersey Supreme Court finds surrogate mother agreements illegal in "Baby M" case.

U.S. Appeals Court Judge Robert Vance is killed by mail bomb at his home near Birmingham, Alabama; two days later, a civil rights lawyer, Robert Robinson, is killed by a mail bomb in Savannah, Georgia.

David N. Dinkins is first African-American mayor elected by New York City.

DEATH Gen. Albert C. Wedemeyer, World War II commander in China.

BUSINESS/INDUSTRY/INVENTIONS

Rescue package of $159 billion is set up for ailing savings and loan industry; Resolution Trust Corp. is created.

Minimum wage is raised to $4.25 an hour, effective 1991.

Mergers and takeovers include Warner Communications and *Time* magazine, Squibb and Bristol-Myers, Sony and Columbia Pictures.

Dow-Jones industrial average reaches record high of 2,734.64 (August 24).

Bank failures total 209 in year.

TRANSPORTATION

Eastern Airlines files for bankruptcy protection.

American Airlines and Delta Air Lines form partnership to operate global computer reservations system.

SCIENCE/MEDICINE

Space shuttle *Atlantis* launches *Magellan* space probe to map Venus (May 4); five months later *Atlantis* launches spacecraft *Galileo* to begin six-year journey to Jupiter; *Voyager II,* in space 12 years, passes planet Neptune (August 24).

Norman F. Ramsey and Hans G. Dehmelt share Nobel Prize in physics for developing methods of isolating atoms and subatomic particles; Thomas R. Cech and Sidney Altman share prize in chemistry for independent discoveries about active role of RNA in chemical cell reactions; J. Michael Bishop and Harold E. Varmus share prize in physiology/medicine for discovery of normal genes that can cause cancer when they go awry.

Government extends 20-month-old ban on federal financing of research using transplanted fetal tissue.

Congress repeals Medicare Catastrophic Coverage Act, including surtax to finance program.

Senate votes $1 billion anti-AIDS program.

DEATH William B. Shockley, co-inventor of transistor.

EDUCATION

Annual federal assessment finds student performance "merely average" and "stagnant" with no improvement despite increased spending.

Players watch fans leave Candlestick Park in San Francisco as the October 17, 1989 earthquake disrupts the World Series. **AP/WIDE WORLD PHOTOS**

RELIGION

American Episcopal bishops approve election of Barbara Harris, first women bishop in church, consecrate her as suffragan bishop of Boston (February 11); Episcopal Synod of America is formed by Episcopalians upset by the consecration (June 2).

Televangelist Jim Bakker is sentenced to 45 years and $500,000 fine for fraud and conspiracy.

Catholic Archdiocese of Detroit closes 43 of 112 churches because of dwindling membership and high operating costs.

Moral Majority, religious right-wing political lobby, disbands.

ART/MUSIC

Senate votes to bar National Endowment for the Arts from supporting "obscene or indecent" works; House refuses to concur.

Mel Powell composes *Duplicates.*

SONGS (POPULAR): "Wind Beneath My Wings," "Look Away."

DEATHS Irving Berlin, composer of 800+ songs ("White Christmas," "God Bless America"); Alvin Ailey, ballet dancer and choreographer; Vladimir Horowitz, pianist.

LITERATURE/JOURNALISM

BOOKS *In Our Image* by Stanley Karnow, *All I Really Need to Know I Learned in Kindergarten* by Robert Fulghum, *Star* by Danielle Steel, *Swan Lake* by Mark Helprin.

Waldenbooks and other chains remove Salman Rushdie's *The Satanic Verses* from shelves after threats by Iran; Waldenbooks later changes its mind.

DEATHS Robert Penn Warren, first U.S. poet laureate; authors Irving Stone, Barbara W. Tuchman, and Mary McCarthy.

ENTERTAINMENT

PLAYS August Wilson writes *The Piano Lesson;* Jerome Robbins produces *Jerome Robbins' Broadway.*

Kirk Kerkorian sells MGM/UA Communications Co., including United Artists studio and 4,000-film library, to Quintex Group of Australia for $1 billion.

MOVIES *Driving Miss Daisy* with Jessica Tandy, *Dead Poets' Society* with Robin Williams, *Steel Magnolias* with Julia Roberts, *Born on the Fourth of July* with Tom Cruise, *Mississippi Burning* with Gene Hackman.

DEATHS Laurence Olivier, actor; Bette Davis and Lucille Ball, actresses.

SPORTS

A. Bartlett Giamatti becomes seventh baseball commissioner (April 1); dies suddenly (September 1); Fay Vincent, deputy commissioner, is elevated to commissioner; William D. White becomes National League president.

Pete Rozelle resigns as NFL commissioner after 30 years (March 22), is succeeded by Paul Tagliabue (October 26).

Sky Dome, home of Toronto baseball team, opens; San Francisco voters reject $115 million bond issue for downtown baseball stadium.

New York Supreme Court rules that U.S. boat *Stars and Stripes* violated spirit of race in winning 1988 America's Cup; decision is appealed.

Art Shell is named coach of Los Angeles Raiders; first African-American coach in NFL.

Four golfers shoot holes-in-one on same hole in less than two hours during U.S. Open tournament; there had only been 21 aces in previous 94 Opens.

Pete Rose is banished from baseball for gambling activities.

Michael Chang becomes first U.S. tennis player to win French Open in 34 years.

Steve Largent catches 100th touchdown pass to set career record; Wayne Gretzky sets hockey-career scoring record with 1,851 points.

Greg LeMond wins Tour de France bicycle race by 8 seconds for second win.

Driver Hervé Filion becomes first harness-race driver to win 800 races in a year.

National Hockey League votes to expand league from 21 to 28 teams by year 2000; first teams will join 1992–1993.

Nolan Ryan of Houston Astros records 5,000th strikeout.

Randy Barnes sets world indoor record for shotput with toss of 74 feet, 4¼ inches.

WINNERS *Auto racing*—Emerson Fittipaldi, Indianapolis 500; Rusty Wallace, NASCAR; *Baseball*—Oakland Athletics, World Series; *Basketball*—St. Johns, NIT; Michigan, NCAA; Tennessee, NCAA (women); Detroit, NBA; *Bowling*—Peter Weber, PBA; *Boxing*—Mike Tyson, heavyweight; Sugar Ray Leonard, middleweight; *Figure skating*—Christopher Bowman, U.S. men; Jill Trenary, U.S. women; *Football* (bowls)—Michigan State, Rose; Miami (Florida), Orange; Florida State, Sugar; UCLA, Cotton; San Francisco, Super Bowl XXIII; *Golf*—Curtis Strange, U.S. Open; Payne Stewart, PGA; Nick Faldo, Masters; Betsy King, U.S. Women's Open; Nancy Lopez, LPGA; *Harness racing*—Park Avenue Joe, Hambletonian; *Hockey*—Calgary, Stanley Cup; *Horse racing*—Sunday Silence, Kentucky Derby and Preakness Stakes; Easy Goer, Belmont Stakes; *Tennis*—Boris Becker, U.S. Open (men); Steffi Graf, U.S. Open (women).

DEATHS Larry Fleisher, organizer, NBA Players Assn.; Lee Calhoun, Olympic hurdler; Claude Harmon, golfer; Billy Martin, baseball player and manager; Doug Harvey, hockey great; Sugar Ray Robinson, boxing champion.

MISCELLANEOUS

Severe earthquake hits northern California (October 17); more than 60 are killed, several thousand are injured, 100,000 homes are damaged; hardest hit are San Francisco, Oakland; quake occurs at 5:04 P.M. during rush hour and minutes before start of World Series game in Candlestick Park; park is not damaged, no spectators are hurt.

Hurricane Hugo hits Caribbean and southeastern U.S.; 504 die.

Truck hits school bus in Alton, Texas, killing 16 students, injuring 64; hurricane-force winds blow down cafeteria wall at Newburgh, New York, school during lunch hour, killing 7.

United DC-10 crashes during emergency landing at Sioux City, Iowa; 111 are killed.

1990

INTERNATIONAL

U.N. approves resolutions condemning Iraq's occupation of Kuwait; U.N. forces begin air attacks on Iraq to force withdrawal.

Soviet President Gorbachev and President George Bush hold summit meeting in Washington, agree to reduce long-range nuclear weapons by about a third over seven years.

Two U.S. hostages kidnapped in Lebanon are freed: Robert Polhill after more than three years, Robert Reed after nearly five years.

Congress increases annual immigration limit from 500,000 to 700,000 in 1992–1994 period.

NATIONAL

President Bush signs Americans with Disabilities Act to prevent discrimination against the handicapped.

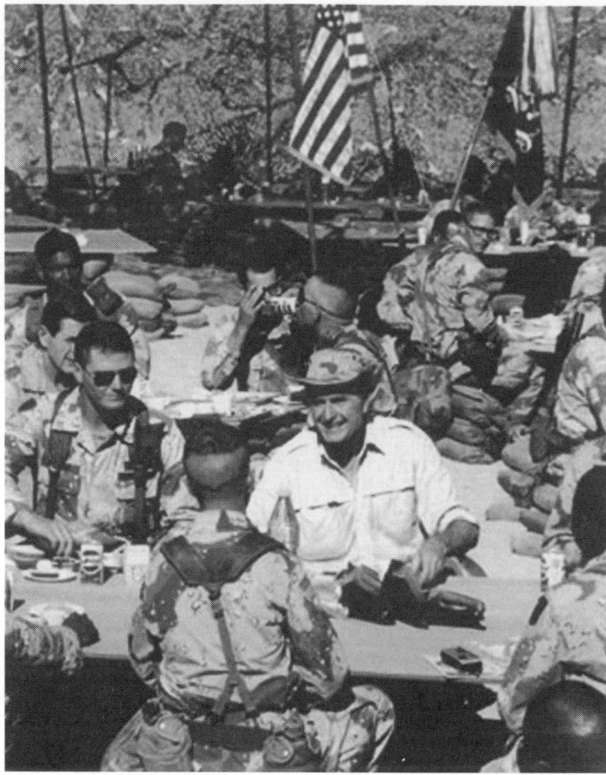

George Bush visits American troops in the Persian Gulf for a Thanksgiving dinner during Operation Desert Storm, a U.S.-led campaign to restore the sovereignty of Kuwait after Iraq's 1990 invasion. **GEORGE BUSH LIBRARY, NATIONAL ARCHIVES AND RECORDS ADMINISTRATION**

Proposed constitutional amendment to permit prosecution of flag burners of desecrators fails to pass either house of Congress.

Former National Security Advisor John Poindexter is found guilty of five felony counts in Iran-Contra case, is sentenced to six months; Appeals Court suspends three felony convictions of Oliver North.

Senate Ethics Committee studies five senators' involvement with Charles Keating, head of a failed California savings and loan; find "credible evidence" of misconduct by Sen. Alan Cranston of California.

Supreme Court Justice William Brennan Jr. retires after nearly 34 years; Appeals Court Judge David Souter succeeds him.

Twenty-first census reports national population of 249,632,692.

Washington Mayor Marion Barry is found guilty on one charge of drug possession, is sentenced to six months.

Congress passes clean air and deficit reduction legislation, President Bush signs it but vetoes a civil rights bill, arguing that it would require quotas for hiring and promotion.

Mrs. Imelda Marcos, widow of former Philippines president, is found not guilty on charges of racketeering, fraud, and obstruction of justice.

DEATH Ralph B. Abernathy, civil rights leader.

BUSINESS/INDUSTRY/INVENTIONS

Drexel Burnham Lambert Group, a securities firm, files for bankruptcy; Michael Milken, former "junk bond" king, pleads guilty to securities fraud, agrees to pay $600 million in fines, restitution, is sentenced to 10 years in prison.

Harry M. Markowitz, William F. Sharpe, and Merton H. Miller share Nobel Prize in economics for work in providing new tools to weigh risks and rewards of different investments and valuing stocks and bonds.

Joseph Hazelwood, captain of the *Exxon Valdez,* which spilled millions of gallons of oil in Alaskan waters, is found guilty of negligence.

Contel and GTE, communications firms, merge.

Allied/Federal Stores and Ames Department Stores file for bankruptcy; year's bank failures total 169.

Dow-Jones industrial average reaches an all-time high of 2,999.75 (July 16–17).

DEATHS Joseph Schumpeter, economist; Lewis Mumford, architectural and urban design critic; Harry Bridges, West Coast longshoremen's union president; Gordon Bunshaft, architect; Halston, designer.

TRANSPORTATION

Three Chrysler Corp. engineers develop first fully electronic force-fed automatic transmission.

Space shuttle *Discovery* deploys the $1.5-billion Hubble telescope; soon after launch, it is learned that serious design flaws will mar many of its experiments; *Magellan* space probe sends back image strips taken in its 1½ orbits of the planet Venus.

Joseph E. Murray and E. Donnell Thomas share Nobel Prize in physiology/medicine for pioneering work in organ transplantations; Jerome I. Friedman and Henry W. Kendall share prize in physics for experiments confirming existence of quarks, fundamental to all matter; Elias J. Corey is awarded prize in chemistry for new ways to synthesize complex molecules.

Supreme Court rules that a person whose wishes are clearly known has right to refuse life-sustaining medical treatment.

Four-year-old girl becomes first human recipient of gene therapy when she is infused with white blood cells containing copies of the gene she lacked.

DEATH Karl Menninger, psychiatrist.

EDUCATION

DEATH Bruno Bettelheim, psychoanalyst specializing in autistic children.

ART/MUSIC

Twelve artworks valued at about $100 million are stolen from Gardner Museum in Boston.

Record price for a painting is set when Vincent Van Gogh's *Portrait of Dr. Gachet* sells for $82.5 million.

William S. Paley bequeaths major collection of art to Museum of Modern Art.

Kurt Masur is named musical director of New York Philharmonic Orchestra, succeeding Zubin Mehta.

SONGS (POPULAR): "Blaze of Glory," "Knockin' Boots," "Hold On," "Step by Step," "All Around the World."

DEATHS Jimmy Van Heusen and David Rose, popular songwriters; Kurt Weill, composer; Buddy DeSylva, lyricist; Sarah Vaughan and Pearl Bailey, singers; Leonard Bernstein and Aaron Copland, composers and conductors.

LITERATURE/JOURNALISM

St. Louis Sun folds after only seven months of publication.

Mark Strand is fourth U.S. poet laureate.

Supreme Court rules that First Amendment does not automatically shield opinions in newspaper columns from being found libelous.

BOOKS *Hocus Pocus* by Kurt Vonnegut Jr., *The Witching House* by Anne Rice, *Deception* and *Patrimony* by Philip Roth, *Clear and Present Danger* by Tom Clancy.

DEATHS Malcolm Forbes, magazine publisher; Marquis Childs, columnist; Laurence J. Peter, developer of the Peter Principle.

ENTERTAINMENT

A Chorus Line closes (March 31) after 6,104 performances.

PLAYS Maggie Smith stars in *Lettice and Lovage; Six Degrees of Separation* by John Guare.

MOVIES *Pretty Woman* with Julia Roberts, *Home Alone* with Macauley Culkin, *Dances with Wolves* with Kevin Costner.

DEATHS Five noted screen actresses, Paulette Goddard, Barbara Stanwyck, Ava Gardner, Irene Dunne, and Greta Garbo; Rex Harrison, actor; Mary Martin, actress; Sammy Davis Jr., entertainer and actor; William S. Paley, CBS head; three radio/television celebrities: Jim Henson, creator of the Muppets; Bill Cullen, game-show host; and Ray Goulding, of Bob and Ray comedy team.

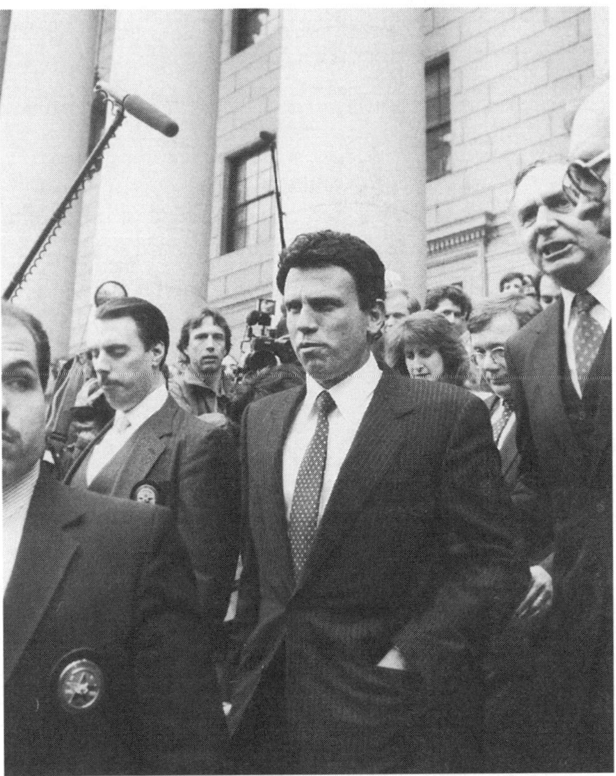

Financial executive Michael Milken pleads guilty to securities fraud. CORBIS-BETTMANN

SPORTS

Baseball Commissioner Fay Vincent forces George Steinbrenner to resign as New York Yankees managing general partner for associating with a "known gambler."

Oakland, California, and Al Davis agree on $602-million, 15-year deal to bring the football Raiders back to Oakland; popular referendum rejects the deal.

Baseball owners and players agree on settlement of claims for free-agent violations: $280 million in damages.

New York Court of Appeals upholds awarding 1988 America's Cup to *Stars and Stripes* (see 1989).

Pete Rose, barred from baseball, pleads guilty to filing false income tax returns, is sentenced to five-month prison term, is fined $50,000.

Greg LeMond wins Tour de France bicycle race for third time in five years.

Willy Shoemaker, 58, rides final race (February 3); won 8,833 races in 40,350 starts.

CBS fires sportscaster Brent Musburger after 15 years (April 10); he signs with ABC (May 2).

Cleveland voters approve higher taxes for downtown stadium/arena.

Rickey Henderson of Oakland Athetics sets new American League career stolen-base record (893); Nolan Ryan of Houston Astros pitches record sixth no-hit game, wins 300th game.

Comiskey Park in Chicago closes after 80 seasons; new baseball stadium to open in Spring 1991.

Wayne Gretzky of Los Angeles becomes first NHL player to score 2,000 points.

WINNERS *Auto racing*—Ariel Luyendyk, Indianapolis 500; Dale Earnhardt, NASCAR; *Baseball*—Cincinnati Reds, World Series; *Basketball*—Vanderbilt, NIT; UNLV, NCAA; Stanford, NCAA (women); Detroit, NBA; *Bowling*—Jim Pencak, PBA; *Boxing*—Evander Holyfield, heavyweight; Pernell Whittaker, lightweight; *Figure skating*—Jill Trenary, U.S. and world women's titles; Todd Eldredge, U.S. men's; *Football* (bowls)—Southern California, Rose; Notre Dame, Orange; Miami, Sugar; Tennessee, Cotton; San Francisco, Super Bowl XXIV; *Golf*—Hale Irwin, U.S. Open; Wayne Grady, PGA; Nick Faldo, Masters; Betsy King, U.S. Women's Open; Beth Daniel, LPGA; *Harness racing*—Harmonious, Hambletonian; *Hockey*—Edmonton, Stanley Cup; *Horse racing*—Unbridled, Kentucky Derby; Summer Squall, Preakness Stakes; Go and Go, Belmont Stakes; *Tennis*—Pete Sampras, U.S. Open (men); Gabriele Sabatini, U.S. Open (women).

DEATHS Hap Day, hockey great; Fortune Gordien, Olympic discus thrower; Bronko Nagurski, football star (University of Minnesota, Chicago Bears); Lawrence O'Brien, former NBA commissioner.

MISCELLANEOUS

Colombian jet liner crashes on Long Island, New York, kills 73.

Social club fire in New York City claims 87 lives.

Mt. Kilauea in Hawaii and Mt. Redoubt in Alaska erupt.

NASA reports that the average global temperature in year is 59.81 degrees, the warmest since 1880.

1991

INTERNATIONAL

GULF WAR Operation Desert Storm (the war in Iraq) begins (January 17) with U.S.-led air units striking Iraqi targets; ground-war fighting begins (February 24), virtually ends in five days.

Oklahoma law professor Anita Hill testifies before the Senate judiciary committee considering the nomination of Clarence Thomas to the U.S. Supreme Court. Her claim of sexual harassment stimulates discussion across the nation about the meaning of the term. AP/WIDE WORLD PHOTOS

Queen Elizabeth of Great Britain makes two-week visit to U.S., addresses Congress (May 16); first by a British monarch.

President George Bush lifts economic sanctions against South Africa.

President Bush and Soviet President Mikhail Gorbachev sign treaty to reduce nuclear-weapons stockpile.

American Edward Tracy, a hostage since 1986, released in Lebanon.

Philippines Senate rejects renewal of lease for Subic Bay Naval Station; U.S. to withdraw within three years; eruption of Mt. Pinatubo forces the evacuation and eventual abandonment of Clark Air Force Base, 10 miles from volcano.

NATIONAL

Commission recommends that 34 U.S. military bases be closed, 48 be realigned; Congress approves (July 30).

Senate votes 52 to 48 to confirm Clarence Thomas as Supreme Court associate justice (October 15), succeeding retiring Thurgood Marshall; action comes after controversial hearings.

Special prosecutor drops charges against Oliver North in Iran-Contra investigation.

Trial of Gen. Manuel Noriega, former Panama leader, on drug trafficking and money laundering charges begins in Miami.

First-class postage rises to 29 cents an ounce (February 3).

Bank that served House of Representatives to close at year's end after revelations that members had written 8,331 bad checks in one year.

Supreme Court lets stand New York City's prohibition of begging in subways; rules police can search trunk of a car and its contents without a warrant; rejects challenge to punitive damage awards, leaving juries with historic broad discretion.

Remains of President Zachary Taylor are exhumed at request of a historical novelist who thought he may have died of arsenic poisoning rather than acute gastrointestinal illness; study shows no trace of arsenic.

DEATHS Senator John Heinz of Pennsylvania and former Senator John Tower of Texas in separate plane crashes.

BUSINESS/INDUSTRY/INVENTIONS

Ronald H. Coase is awarded Nobel Prize in economics for work on role of institutions in the economy.

Supreme Court rules that employers cannot bar women from jobs where they might be exposed to materials hazardous to developing fetuses.

Three major bank mergers occur: Chemical Banking Corp. and Manufacturers Hanover, NCNB Corp. and C. & S. Sovran to form Nations Bank, and Bank America Corp. and Security Pacific Corp.; ATT and NCR complete their merger.

Federal regulators take over Bank of New England Corp. after huge fourth-quarter loss and run on bank.

Minimum wage increases to $4.25 an hour (January 1).

Five-millionth patent is given by Patent Office, to researchers at University of Florida for a genetically engineered microbe; other patents issued include one for a machine to measure fats, oils, and moisture in baked goods as they come off assembly line, and a magnetic hammer to make it easier to drive nails without hitting one's fingers.

TRANSPORTATION

Pan American World Airways files for bankruptcy, sells most of its remaining assets to Delta; Eastern Airlines stops flying, sells most of its assets; bankrupt Midway Airlines ceases operating.

Nissan Motors plans to build second U.S. plant at Decherd, Tennessee.

General Motors announces it will close 21 of 125 assembly and parts plants in North America over the next few years, eliminating more than 70,000 jobs.

General Motors begins building first commercially available electric car in modern times in Lansing, Michigan.

SCIENCE/MEDICINE

National Association of Health Commissioners selects nine private health-insurance policies as supplements to Medicare, replacing the large number now available.

Federal government announces new nationwide fee schedule under which family doctors and general practitioners will receive more (but less than expected), specialists will receive less.

Operation Desert Storm

Operation Desert Storm began at 23:30 GMT on January 16, 1991. It signaled the beginning of the Gulf War, the first significant post-Cold War conflict, and the start of an air offensive against Iraqi military facilities. An international coalition led by the U.S. challenged Iraq for its invasion of neighboring Kuwait on August 2, 1990. Before Desert Storm commenced, President George Bush sent a letter to Congress explaining the need for military action given Iraqi leader Saddam Hussein's unresponsiveness to economic sanctions and diplomatic initiatives. The technological superiority of U.S. armed forces, including the deployment of the F-117 Stealth bomber and the Tomahawk sea-launched cruise missile, proved decisive in securing victory. Allied planes flew over 100,000 combat sorties in the space of six weeks. On February 24, U.S.-led ground forces entered enemy territory in Operation Desert Sabre. Under the command of Gen. Norman Schwarzkopf, the U.S. military (aided by thirty-four other nations including Great Britain, France, and Saudi Arabia) liberated Kuwait on February 27, 1991. The success of the Gulf War helped ease the memory of the American retreat in Vietnam.

Kuwaiti oil fields and an Iraqi tank burn during Operation Desert Storm. **AP/WIDE WORLD PHOTOS**

NASA reports that a satellite above Antarctica found ozone level in the atmosphere to be lowest on record.

AIDS spreads rapidly among the poor, African Americans and Hispanic Americans, and women and children. A variety of drugs are available to patients, who often live ten or more years with the disease.

EDUCATION

Supreme Court rules that school desegregation busing could end if school districts have done everything "practicable" to eliminate "vestiges" of past discrimination.

President Bush calls for national education tests and for redirecting federal money to help disadvantaged students who choose to go to private schools or parochial schools.

RELIGION

Survey shows that 90% of Americans identify with some church.

Southern Baptists who are unhappy with conservative leadership create 6,000-member Cooperative Baptist Fellowship.

Catholic archbishops Roger M. Mahoney and Anthony J. Bevilacqua are elevated to cardinal; Bishop Daniel A. Cronin is named archbishop of Hartford, Connecticut.

ART/MUSIC

Supreme Court rules 5–4 that, while nude dancing is entitled to protection under the First Amendment's freedom of expression, states may ban it in the "interest of protecting order and morality."

Carnegie Hall celebrates 100th birthday with two gala concerts (May 5).

Walter H. Annenberg bequeaths about $1 billion worth of impressionist and postimpressionist art to Metropolitan Museum of Art; also donates $10 million to Los Angeles County Museum of Art.

Willie Nelson releases special recording designed to raise $15 million owed in back taxes to Internal Revenue Service.

DEATHS Robert Motherwell, abstract expressionist painter; Miles Davis, jazz trumpeter.

LITERATURE/JOURNALISM

Joseph Brodsky becomes fifth U.S. poet laureate.

Rupert Murdoch, faced with huge debt burden, sells nine magazines (including *Racing Form, New Woman,*

Seventeen, New York) for more than $600 million to K-III Holdings.

Robert Maxwell, British publisher, agrees to buy *New York Daily News* after reaching agreement with 13 labor unions.

Supreme Court reverses New York State law that prohibits criminals from profiting from stories sold to publishers.

Dallas Times Herald folds.

BOOKS *A Soldier of the Great War* by Mark Helprin, *Sliver* by Ira Levin, *Pinocchio in Venice* by Robert Coover, *Harlot's Ghost* by Norman Mailer, *Scarlett* by Alexandra Ripley.

DEATHS Isaac Bashevis Singer and Dr. Seuss (Theodore Seuss Geisel), authors.

ENTERTAINMENT

FCC votes to relax but not eliminate rule that prohibits television networks from owning and selling reruns of shows they broadcast.

New television shows include *America's Most Wanted, Beverly Hills 90210, Thirtysomething.*

MOVIES *Cape Fear* with Nick Nolte, *Field of Dreams* with Kevin Costner, *Bugsy* with Warren Beatty, *Thelma and Louise* with Susan Sarandon and Geena Davis, Disney's *Beauty and the Beast.*

DEATHS Frank Capra, movie director; Eva Le Gallienne and Colleen Dewhurst, actresses; Joseph Papp, theatrical producer; Redd Foxx, television entertainer.

SPORTS

Dennis Martinez of Montreal Expos pitches perfect game (13th to do so); Rickey Henderson of Oakland Athetics sets new career stolen-base record (939).

Mike Powell breaks 23-year-old long-jump record with leap of 29 feet, 4½ inches; Carl Lewis sets world 100-meter record of 9.86 seconds.

The National, first sports daily, folds after 18 months.

Don Shula, coach of Miami Dolphins, coaches his 300th career football-game victory.

WINNERS *Auto racing*—Rick Mears, Indianapolis 500; Dale Earnhardt, NASCAR; *Baseball*—Minnesota Twins, World Series; *Basketball*—Duke, NCAA; Stanford, NIT; Tennessee, NCAA (women); Chicago, NBA; *Bowling*—Mike Miller, PBA; *Boxing*—Evander Holyfield, heavyweight; *Figure skating*—Kristi Yamaguchi, world women's title; Todd Eldredge, U.S. men's; Tonya Harding, U.S. women's; *Football* (bowls)—Washington, Rose; Colorado, Orange; Tennessee, Sugar; Miami (Florida), Cotton; New York Giants, Super Bowl XXV; *Golf*—U.S., Walker and Ryder cups; Payne Stewart, U.S. Open; Ian Woosnam, Masters; John Daly, PGA; Meg Mallon, U.S. Open (women); *Harness racing*—Giant Victory, Hambletonian; *Hockey*—Pittsburgh, Stanley Cup; *Horse racing*—Strike the Gold, Kentucky Derby; Hansel, Preakness Stakes and Belmont Stakes; *Tennis*—Stefan Edberg, U.S. Open (men); Monica Seles, U.S. Open (women).

DEATH Lyle Alzado, football player.

1992

INTERNATIONAL

President George Bush and Russian President Boris Yeltsin announce (December 30) agreement on a nuclear arms reduction treaty that would reduce their countries' strategic arms by two-thirds, eliminate land-based multiple-warhead missiles by 2003; the agreement, to be signed January 3, 1993, in Moscow, must be ratified by the Senate and the legislatures of Russia and three other Soviet republics.

U.S. forces land in Somalia (December 3) to protect food shipments for the starving populace; for many months, shipments were looted by native gangs; U.N. forces join U.S. in securing airports and towns, protecting relief centers.

U.S. planes shoot down an Iraqi jet when it violates U.N.-created no-fly zone in southern Iraq (December 27).

U.S., one of 178 nations attending the U.N. Environment and Development Conference in Rio de Janeiro, does not sign the international treaty designed to preserve the world's plants, animals, and natural resources; argues that treaty is "seriously flawed" by not protecting U.S. patents on biological inventions; U.S. does sign a treaty to try to halt global warming.

Representatives from Canada, Mexico, and the U.S. approve (August 12) draft agreement (NAFTA) that establishes free trade among the three in 15 years; treaty is signed by the nations' leaders (December 17), must be ratified by legislatures of the nations.

President Bush visits Australia, Singapore, South Korea, and Japan to improve U.S. international trade, collapses during a state dinner in Japan, recovers quickly, diagnosed as having had intestinal flu.

Bush Administration lifts sanctions against China's transfer of high technology after China pledges to abide by restrictions on missile sales to Mideast.

Firefighters contend with the effects of the riots in Los Angeles following the verdict in the Rodney King case, April 1992.
REUTERS/CORBIS-BETTMANN

Supreme Court lifts injunction that bars U.S. from returning Haitian refugees held at base at Guantanamo Bay, Cuba.

NATIONAL

Democratic Gov. Bill (William J.) Clinton of Arkansas is elected president, defeats President Bush and independent candidate H. Ross Perot; Clinton receives 370 electoral and 43,682,624 popular votes; Bush, 168 and 38,117,331; Perot, no electoral votes and 19,217,213 popular votes; Tennessee Senator Albert Gore is elected vice president. Carol M. Braun becomes first African-American woman senator, wins in Illinois; California fills both Senate seats with women, San Francisco Mayor Diane Feinstein and Rep. Barbara Boxer.

Supreme Court upholds part of Pennsylvania law that imposes strict limits on a woman's right to abortion (June 29), but its 5–4 vote also upholds "essence" of constitutional right to abortion. Bush Administration rules that doctors in federally funded family-planning clinics may give limited advice on abortion but nurses and counselors may not.

Rioting sweeps through south central Los Angeles (April 29) after a jury acquits four white police officers on all but one count in the beating of Rodney King, a black man; 52 are killed in riots that go on for several days.

House Ethics Committee reports (March 5) that 329 present and former House members wrote almost 20,000 overdrafts on their accounts in the House bank in nearly three years; the private bank serves only House members.

Twenty-seventh Amendment to Constitution, approved by Congress in 1789, is finally ratified (May 7) when Michigan legislature acts favorably; amendment, proposed by James Madison, provides that congressional pay raises cannot take effect until a new Congress takes office.

President Bush pardons former Defense Secretary Caspar Weinberger and five other former Reagan administration executives accused of lying to Congress about Iran-Contra acts.

Congress approves bill to extend benefit payments for 13 weeks to long-term unemployed persons during a recession; president signs it.

Former Panama military ruler Manuel Noriega is convicted for racketeering, drug trafficking, and money laundering.

Sweeping law that requires businesses to give equal access to disabled Americans goes into effect (January 27).

California Insurance Commissioner, in first case since voter-approved rollback of auto insurance, orders 20th Century Insurance Co. to refund more than $100 million to 650,000 policyholders; California, where legislature and governor cannot agree on a budget, runs short of cash, begins to pay bills with IOUs.

More than a million votes are cast to select a portrait of the late Elvis Presley to be used on a postage stamp.

DEATHS Philip Habib, Mideast negotiator; Wilbur Mills, head of House Ways and Means Committee 17 years; George Murphy, screen actor, California senator; John J. Sirica, judge who presided at Watergate trials.

BUSINESS/INDUSTRY/INVENTIONS

Gary S. Becker is awarded Nobel Prize in economics for extending economic theory to human behavior dealt with by other social sciences.

R. H. Macy & Co., owner of 251 retail stores; Wang Laboratories, computer maker; and Zale department stores file for bankruptcy.

Economic depression in defense industry leads to layoffs and consolidations: General Dynamics sells its jet-fighter division to Lockheed, its missile division to Hughes Aircraft; Martin Marietta buys General Electric's aerospace division; LTV Corp. sells aircraft and missile divisions.

President Bush directs U.S. manufacturers to stop producing virtually all ozone-destroying chemicals by end of 1995.

First food irradiation plant in U.S. (Mulberry, Florida) ready for service, begins to irradiate strawberries for shipment, other produce follows.

Charlotte Beers becomes first woman chairman of a major advertising group (Ogilvy & Mather).

Dow-Jones industrial average hits record high of 3,280.64 (February 20).

Federal Communications Commission proposes opening many radio frequencies for "emerging technologies."

DEATHS William McGowan, former MCI head whose antitrust suit against ATT led to competition in telecommunications; Sam Walton, founder of Wal-Mart stores; George J. Stigler, Nobel Prize economist.

TRANSPORTATION

"Big Three" automakers report huge losses for year: Chrysler, $895 million; Ford, $2.26 billion; General Motors, $4.5 billion. Ford announces investment of $3 billion in new machinery and plant, some to be used for new minivan in late 1993; GM announces first stage of three-year plan to close 21 plants in U.S. and Canada.

Trans World Airlines (TWA) files for bankruptcy.

Chrysler Corp. selects Robert G. Eaton, a GM executive, to succeed Lee A. Iacocca as chief executive January 1993; GM replaces its chairman, Robert C. Stempel, with John G. Smale as head of executive committee.

Federal officials estimate (December 29) that 1992 traffic deaths will drop below 40,000 for first time in 30 years.

President Bush signs bill to end strike that shut down nation's freight lines; calls for 20-day cooling-off period, then (if needed) binding arbitration.

British Airways and USAir plan to form world's largest airline partnership with British Airways buying 44% of USAir; deal falls through when Britain refuses to open more air space to U.S. carriers; Northwest Airlines and KLM Royal Dutch Airlines combine operations; Air Canada buys Continental Airlines.

Senate passes energy bill to encourage development of alternative-fuel vehicles.

SCIENCE/MEDICINE

Edmond H. Fischer and Edwin G. Krebs share Nobel Prize in physiology/medicine for discovering a regulatory mechanism affecting most cells; Rudolph A. Marcus is awarded prize in chemistry for finding way to predict certain interactions between molecules in solution.

NASA reports that danger of ozone depletion over northeastern U.S. and eastern Canada has increased as chemicals harmful to ozone reach record levels.

Three space-shuttle crew members, working more than eight hours outside the spacecraft, succeed in capturing a communications satellite that went off course; after repairs, the satellite returns to proper orbit; Richard H. Truly resigns as head of NASA after long battle with White House over direction of space program; Daniel S. Goldin succeeds him.

Food and Drug Administration orders moratorium on sale and implantation of silica gel breast implants while safety of implant operations is studied.

Scientists discover what could be oldest, largest living organism on Earth: a giant fungus, possibly 10,000 years old, that covers more than 30 acres near Crystal Falls, Michigan; Washington scientists dispute claim, saying that a fungus near Mt. Adams, New Hampshire, is 40 times as large.

DEATHS Barbara McClintock, Nobel Prize scientist; Robert M. Page, physicist who helped develop radar.

EDUCATION

Supreme Court rules that nonsectarian prayers at a public high school graduation in Providence, Rhode Island, were unconstitutional.

Supreme Court rules that Mississippi failed to prove that it erased segregation in its state university system; also rules that students can sue schools and colleges for sexual harassment and other forms of sex discrimination.

Yale University President Benno C. Schmidt Jr. resigns (effective January 1, 1993) to head a project to create a national private school system; Whittle Communications funds project with $60 million; Michael I. Sovran to step down June 1993 as president of Columbia University; other 1992 resignations are Hannah H. Gray of University of Chicago, H. Keith Brodie of Duke University, and Donald Kennedy of Stanford University.

RELIGION

Harvey W. Wood, longtime chairman of Christian Science Church, resigns amid bitter dispute over church's direction and finances.

Center for Christian-Jewish Understanding is created at Sacred Heart University in Fairfield, Connecticut.

DEATH Frederick W. Franz, president, Jehovah's Witnesses (1977–1992).

ART/MUSIC

President Bush dismisses John E. Frohnman as chairman of National Endowment for the Arts after criticism of some grants made by agency.

J. Carter Brown retires after 27 years as director of National Gallery of Art.

Philip Glass's opera *The Voyage* is produced to commemorate Christopher Columbus's trip; Lyric Opera of Chicago presents William Bolcom's opera *McTeague.*

SONGS (POPULAR): "Here Comes the Hammer," "Justify My Love," "I Do It for You," "Ropin' the Wind," "Unforgettable," "End of the Road," "Baby Got Back."

Many New Yorkers switch to country music as alternative to hip-hop and rap; WYNY-FM claims largest country-music audience in world.

DEATHS John Cage, experimental music composer; William Schuman, composer, founding director of Juilliard School; Lawrence Welk, orchestra leader.

LITERATURE/JOURNALISM

Mona Van Duyn becomes sixth U.S. poet laureate; first woman so honored.

BOOKS *Memories of the Ford Administration* by John Updike, *Women of Sand and Myrrh* by Hanan el-Shaykh, *The First Dissident* by William Safire, *The Way Things Ought to Be* by Rush Limbaugh.

Two new magazines begin publication: *Worth* by Fidelity Investments and *Smart Money* by Hearst Corp. and Dow Jones; former *Vanity Fair* editor Tina Brown edits *The New Yorker.*

Arthur Ochs Sulzberger, publisher of the *New York Times* for 29 years, steps down, is succeeded by son, Arthur O. Jr.

DEATHS William Shawn, editor, *The New Yorker* (1957–1992); author Isaac Asimov (468 books), Alex Haley *(Roots),* and Frank Yerby, novelist; CBS newsman Eric Sevareid.

ENTERTAINMENT

Johnny Carson retires after 29 years as emcee of *The Tonight Show,* succeeded by Jay Leno.

Federal Communications Commission allows television networks to buy local cable systems.

MOVIES *A Few Good Men* with Tom Cruise, *Hoffa* with Jack Nicholson, *Home Alone 2* with Macauley Culkin, *Batman Returns* with Michael Keaton, *Sister Act* with Whoopi Goldberg, Disney's *Aladdin, Malcolm X* with Denzel Washington.

PLAYS Alan Alda stars in *Jake's Women* by Neil Simon, Judd Hirsch in *Conversations with My Father,* Gregory Hines in *Jelly's Last Jam,* Brid Brennan in *Dancing at Lughnasa;* Wendy Wasserstein writes *The Sisters Rosensweig.*

DEATHS Stage/screen/TV actors Shirley Booth, Judith Anderson, Ralph Bellamy, Sandy Dennis, Marlene Dietrich, Jose Ferrer, Allan Jones, Fred MacMurray, Gene Tierney, Molly Picon; Hal Roach, pioneer screen comedy writer and producer; Mark Goodson, TV game-show producer *(The Price Is Right, What's My Line?);* country-music greats Roy Acuff, Tennessee Ernie Ford, Roger Miller.

SPORTS

Fay Vincent resigns as baseball commissioner after majority of owners ask him to step down; John Ziegler quits as National Hockey League president after 15 years.

Earvin "Magic" Johnson, basketball star who contracted AIDS virus, resigns for second time; Hall of Fame

Jockey Angel Cordero Jr. retires after racing accident; Larry Bird, Boston Celtics star, retires.

Winter Olympics are held in Albertville, France; U.S. wins 5 golds, with Bonnie Blair winning 2 in speed skating; Summer Games held in Barcelona, Spain; U.S. wins 37 golds.

Former heavyweight boxing champion Mike Tyson is convicted of rape in Indianapolis, is sentenced to six-year prison term.

National Hockey League players begin first strike (April 2) after rejecting contract proposal; return 10 days later with new contract.

Baseball club owners approve sale of Seattle Mariners to group of investors including Nintendo Co. of Japan as a minority stockholder.

WINNERS *Auto racing*—Al Unser, Indianapolis 500; Alan Kulwicki, NASCAR; *Baseball*—Toronto Blue Jays, World Series; *Basketball*—Virginia, NIT; Duke, NCAA; Stanford, NCAA (women); Chicago, NBA; *Boxing*—Evander Holyfield, heavyweight; Virgil Hill, light heavyweight; Reggie Johnson, middleweight; *Figure skating*—Kristi Yamaguchi, Olympics, world, U.S. singles, women; Christopher Bowman, U.S. singles, men; *Football* (bowls)—Washington, Rose; Miami (Florida), Orange; Notre Dame, Sugar; Florida State, Cotton; Washington, Super Bowl XXVI; *Golf*—Tom Kite, U.S. Open; Nick Price, PGA; Fred Couples, Masters; Patty Sheehan, U.S. Women's Open; Betsy King, LPGA; *Harness racing*—Alf Palema, Hambletonian; *Hockey*—Pittsburgh, Stanley Cup; *Horse racing*—Lil E. Tee, Kentucky Derby; Pine Bluff, Preakness Stakes; A. P. Indy, Belmont Stakes; *Tennis*—Stefan Edberg, U.S. Open (men); Monica Seles, U.S. Open (women); *Yachting*—U.S. retains America's Cup.

DEATHS Carl Stotz, founder of Little League baseball; baseball players Billy Herman, Ken Keltner, Eddie Lopat; football players Buck Buchanan, Mel Hein; Red (Walter H.) Barber, baseball announcer; Samuel Reshevsky, U.S. chess champion.

MISCELLANEOUS

Hurricane Andrew devastates part of southern Florida and Louisiana (August 24); 30 are killed, 85,000 homes are destroyed or damaged, leaving 250,000 homeless; estimated loss of $7.3 billion; Hurricane Iniki strikes Hawaii (September 11), kills 3, causes about $1 billion in damage.

Most powerful earthquake in California in 40 years strikes 125 miles east of Los Angeles, near Landers, followed by another three hours later; one death, numerous injuries, much property damage.

About 250 million gallons of water from Chicago River flood into downtown tunnels, basements in Chicago; forces evacuation of 200,000 people for several days.

1993

INTERNATIONAL

United States and 116 other countries agree to GATT (General Agreement on Tariffs and Trades), remove export barriers, tariffs on thousands of manufactured products, include agriculture and service industries in world trade rules; to be signed April 1994 in Morocco; must be approved by nations' legislatures; effective 1995.

Congress approves NAFTA (North American Free Trade Agreement), the House by 234–200, the Senate by 61–38, to phase out tariffs between U.S., Canada, and Mexico in 15 years.

U.S. is one of more than 120 countries that sign agreement not to manufacture, stockpile, or use chemical weapons.

U.S. hands control of relief efforts in Somalia to U.N. after six-month effort to remove weapons in the streets, safeguard food distribution. Twenty U.S. soldiers killed in Mogadishu, Somalia, in fierce clash with Somali warlord forces. Incident leads to increasing U.S. military presence and the decision to bring U.S. troops home by March 31, 1994.

U.S., French, and British planes bomb missile sites in southern Iraq when Iraq defies terms ending Persian Gulf war; another strike at Baghdad suburb when Iraq refuses to guarantee safety of U.N. inspectors.

President Bush and Russian President Boris Yeltsin sign second Strategic Arms Reduction Treaty; later in year, President Bill Clinton meets with Yeltsin to arrange aid to Russia.

U.S. naval forces patrol waters around Haiti to enforce U.N. sanctions imposed when Haitian military leaders refuse to let elected president return.

President Clinton attends economic summit of major industrial nations in Tokyo; reaches accord with Japan to resolve trade disputes; later, U.S. is host to APEC (Asia Pacific Economic Cooperation) forum designed to reduce or eliminate trade disputes.

President Clinton announces U.S. will sign international treaty protecting rare and endangered species, follow timetable to reduce threat of global warming; both items were rejected by President Bush.

Michael Jordan, star of the Chicago Bulls, retires from basketball—temporarily, as it turns out—in 1993.

NATIONAL

President Clinton proposes plan to assure health insurance for all Americans and to lower healthcare costs.

House (218–216) and Senate (51–50) approve bill to reduce federal budget deficit by $496 billion over five years.

Congress passes Family Leave Act to permit employees of government and companies of 50 or more workers to take up to 12 weeks of unpaid annual leave to deal with family problems.

Janet Reno is confirmed as first woman U.S. Attorney General; Ruth Bader Ginsburg becomes second woman Supreme Court justice, succeeds retiring Byron White.

Women become eligible to pilot combat aircraft and serve on fighter and bomber crews in all services.

Defense Base Closure and Realignment Commission recommends closure of 33 major military bases, 100 smaller facilities, realignment of 45 others; President Clinton and Congress approve.

President Clinton dismisses FBI Director William Sessions after probe of alleged use of FBI funds for personal purposes; Louis J. Freeh succeeds him. Gen. Colin Powell resigns as joint chiefs of staff chairman; Gen. John Shalishkashvili succeeds him; Defense Secretary Les Aspin resigns; Retired Admiral Bobby Ray Inman is nominated as successor.

Administration announces program to streamline federal government, designed to save $108 billion over five years, lower federal employment by 252,000 jobs.

Supreme Court rules 6–3 that federal judges may not bar protestors from blockading abortion clinics; President Clinton signs order repealing ban on abortion counseling at U.S.-funded clinics.

Majority of Puerto Rican residents vote to remain a U.S. commonwealth, turning down proposal to become a state.

U.S. Holocaust Museum in Washington, D.C., is dedicated by President Clinton.

DEATHS Thurgood Marshall, Supreme Court justice; Gen. Matthew B. Ridgway, led American troops in Normandy, U.N. forces in Korea; John B. Connally, Texas governor wounded when President Kennedy was assassinated; former First Lady Pat Nixon (1969–1974).

BUSINESS/INDUSTRY/INVENTIONS

Robert W. Fogel and Douglass C. North share Nobel Prize in economics for leadership in field of "new economic history."

IBM announces $4.97 billion loss in 1992, largest one-year loss by an American firm; also announces first employee layoffs.

Sears to stop publishing annual catalogs, a marketing tool since 1896; will close 113 of 859 stores, eliminate 50,000 jobs. Other announced layoffs include McDonnell Douglas 8,700, Boeing 20,000, Pratt & Whitney 6,700, Procter & Gamble 13,000 jobs and closure of 30 factories.

Bell Atlantic Corp. and Tele-Communications Inc. announce plans to merge, will create company able to develop, deliver many types of new programming. Primamerica proposes acquisition of Travelers' Insurance; Amax Inc. and Cyprus Minerals Co. to merge into one of largest mining companies.

Supreme Court upholds law allowing banks to sell insurance nationwide.

DEATHS Thomas J. Watson, former IBM head; Cesar Chavez, farmworkers labor leader; Julio Gallo, winemaker.

TRANSPORTATION

Los Angeles opens 4.4-mile portion of its first subway.

Following a gunfight between federal officers and David Koresh and his followers, the Branch Davidian compound in Waco, Texas, burns on April 19, 1993. **AP/WIDE WORLD PHOTOS**

General Motors to build 20,000 cars annually in U.S. for sale in Japan under Toyota name.

GM, Ford, and Chrysler consider joint building of electric car to meet requirements of clean-air acts in California and elsewhere.

Greyhound Lines Inc. and drivers union settle three-year-old strike.

DEATH Olive A. Beech, cofounder and chairwoman, Beech Aircraft Co.

SCIENCE/MEDICINE

Princeton University researchers produce strongest controlled-nuclear-fusion reaction on record: 3 million watts of energy, later 5.6 million; may eventually lead to inexhaustible supply of energy.

Kary B. Mullis shares Nobel Prize in chemistry for work on amplifying (or copying) DNA; Joseph H. Taylor and Russell A. Halse share physics prize for discovering first known binary pulsar; Philip S. Sharp and Richard J. Roberts share prize in physiology/medicine for independent discovery of split genes.

Mars Observer spacecraft, $980-million craft launched in September 1992, ceases communication as it approaches Mars; NASA space crew repairs Hubble space telescope launched in 1991; repairs are expected to give telescope ability to provide new space views.

Four men and four women emerge from glass-enclosed "Biosphere 2" in desert near Tucson, Arizona, after two-year experiment in enclosed ecosystem.

DEATHS Robert W. Holley, Nobel biologist; Vincent J. Schaefer, chemist who developed cloud "seeding"; Polykarp Kusch, Nobel physicist.

EDUCATION

George E. Rupp is named president of Columbia University; Richard C. Levin as Yale University president.

President Clinton's plan to give students help for tuition, living allowances for college and vocational training in return for two years of community service is enacted by Congress.

DEATH Dr. Jean Mayer, Tufts University chancellor.

RELIGION

Pope John Paul II visits U.S. to participate in youth festival in Colorado.

Supreme Court rules unanimously that schools must allow church groups the same after-hours access to facilities as secular community groups.

The Vietnam Veterans Memorial Wall becomes a literal touchstone for many Americans. This young woman visits the wall during a dedication ceremony for the Vietnam Women's Memorial Sculpture. November 11, 1993. © WALLY MCNAMEE/ CORBIS-BETTMANN

Supreme Court rules that ban by Hialeah, Florida, of a ritual animal sacrifice violates religious freedom of Santeria religion followers. Later, Court passes law overturning 1990 decision that made it easier for government to pass laws that infringe on religious beliefs.

DEATH Norman Vincent Peale, minister, noted author.

ART/MUSIC

Cezanne painting *Still Life with Apples* sells for $28.6 million at Sotheby's auction.

New York Philharmonic celebrates 150th anniversary with year-long observances.

DEATHS Richard Diebenkorn, abstractionist painter; Rudolf Nureyev, ballet dancer; Sammy Cahn, popular songwriter; Bob Crosby, bandleader; Billy Eckstine, popular singer; Dizzy Gillespie, jazz trumpeter; Marian Anderson, world-renowned contralto; Agnes de Mille, choreographer; Conway Twitty, country-music star.

LITERATURE/JOURNALISM

Rita Dove becomes seventh U.S. poet laureate, first African American so honored.

Toni Morrison becomes first African-American writer *(Songs of Solomon, Beloved, Jazz)* to win Nobel Prize in literature.

BOOKS *Feather Crowns* by Bobbie Ann Mason, *Remembering Babylon* by David Malouf, *Lenin's Tomb* by David Remnick, *See, I Told You So* by Rush Limbaugh, *Without Remorse* by Tom Clancy.

The *New York Times* acquires *Boston Globe* over five years in $1.1-billion merger; Mortimer B. Zuckerman purchases *New York Daily News.*

Federal Appeals Court upholds 1991 ruling that regional Bell telephone companies may own information services.

DEATHS Authors Kay Boyle, John Hersey *(Hiroshima),* and William Golding *(Lord of the Flies);* newspaper publishers William R. Hearst Jr. and Joseph Pulitzer Jr.; Vincent T. Hamlin, creator of "Alley Oop" comic strip; Harrison E. Salisbury and William Shirer, foreign correspondents and authors.

ENTERTAINMENT

Federal Communications Commission orders cuts in cable TV rates that could total $1.2 billion annually nationwide; six months later, state and federal investigations begin study into the rates that increased rather than decreased.

David Letterman moves late-night show from NBC to CBS; Chevy Chase begins and quickly ends late-night TV show.

MOVIES *Jurassic Park* sets record of $18.2 million for opening-day gross ticket sales; *Sleepless in Seattle* with Tom Hanks and Meg Ryan, *Falling Down* with Michael Douglas, *The Firm* with Tom Cruise, *Schindler's List* with Ralph Fiennes, *The Remains of the Day* with Anthony Hopkins, *Philadelphia* with Tom Hanks, *The Fugitive* with Harrison Ford.

THEATER *Putting It Together* with Julie Andrews, *Kiss of the Spider Woman* with Chita Rivera, *The Who's Tommy, Angels in America* with Ron Liebman.

DEATHS Actresses Lillian Gish (last of the silent-film stars), Helen Hayes ("first lady" of American theater), Audrey Hepburn, Eugenie Leontovich, Ruby Keeler; Joseph Mankiewicz, film director and producer; Raymond Burr, actor; Carlton E. Morse, radio writer *(One Man's Family).*

SPORT

Marge Schott, baseball-team owner (Cincinnati Reds), is suspended for year for racist remarks.

Michael Jordan (Chicago Bulls) retires from basketball.

National Football League and players agree on seven-year contract that allows players freedom to move to other teams.

Monica Seles, top-ranked tennis star, is stabbed by a spectator at a German match; muscle tear side-lines her for a time.

Madison Square Garden presents final boxing match (July 8), ending almost 70 years of boxing.

WINNERS *Auto racing*—Emerson Fitipaldi, Indianapolis 500; Dale Earnhardt, NASCAR; *Baseball*—Toronto Blue Jays, World Series; *Basketball*—Chicago Bulls, NBA; North Carolina, NCAA; Texas Tech, NCAA (women); Minnesota, NIT; *Bowling*—Norm Duke, ABC Masters; George Branham 3rd, Tournament of Champions; *Boxing*—Riddick Bowe, Evander Holyfield, heavyweight; Gerald McClellan, light heavyweight; Pernell Whittaker, welterweight; Julio Chavez, lightweight; *Figure skating*—Scott Davis, U.S. men's title; Nancy Kerrigan, U.S. women's; *Football* (bowls)—Alabama, Sugar; Michigan, Rose; Notre Dame, Cotton; Florida State, Orange; Dallas, Super Bowl XXVII; *Golf*—Bernhard Langer, Masters; Lee Janzen, U.S. Open; Lauri Merten, U.S. Women's Open; Paul Azinger, PGA; Patty Sheehan, LPGA; *Harness racing*—American Winner, Hambletonian; *Hockey*—Montreal, Stanley Cup; Maine, NCAA; *Horse racing*—Sea Hero, Kentucky Derby; Prairie Bayou, Preakness Stakes; Colonial Affair, Belmont Stakes; *Tennis*—Pete Sampras, U.S. Open (men); Steffi Graf, U.S. Open (women).

DEATHS Arthur Ashe, former tennis champion; Baseball Hall of Famers Charley Gehringer, Bill Dickey, Johnny Mize, Roy Campanella, Don Drysdale; Hank Iba, basketball coach; auto racer Alan Kulwicki and Davey Allison; Willie Mosconi, billiards champion.

MISCELLANEOUS

Explosion in underground parking garage at World Trade Center in New York City kills six, forces temporary closing of complex; seven men are arrested. FBI uncovers second bomb plot, arrests nine men; Sheikh Omar Abdel Rahman, whose followers were arrested in both plots, is detained.

Four agents of Bureau of Alcohol, Tobacco and Firearms are killed in shootout with members of Branch Davidian religious cult, outside Waco, Texas, when Bureau tries to arrest leader David Koresh; group holds out until government use of force ends standoff two months later (April 19), killing 55 adults and 17 children.

March blizzard in eastern U.S. causes 200 deaths; summer flooding in nine midwestern states results in about 50 deaths, more than 700,000 homeless, $12 billion in property damage.

In Amtrak's deadliest wreck, 47 die as train plunges into Alabama bayou when bridge collapses after being struck by a barge.

Bagels become country's latest food craze.

1994

INTERNATIONAL

U.S. and North Korea agree in principle (January 5) on inspection of nuclear facilities; talks break down. Former President Carter convinces North Korea to resume discussions (June 22); two nations sign agreement (August 6) that allows U.N. inspections of nuclear plants. Late in year, a U.S. helicopter accidentally flies into North Korean territory and is shot down; one airman is killed, the other is held prisoner briefly.

President Clinton lifts 19-year-old trade embargo against Vietnam (February 3).

President and Mrs. Clinton participate in 50th-anniversary commemoration of D-Day (June 6) in France. President attends meeting of industrial nations in Naples; then becomes first U.S. president to visit Baltic nations.

Former President Carter, Georgia Sen. Sam Nunn, and Retired Gen. Colin Powell negotiate peaceful end

(September 18) to Haiti's military rule, return of deposed president, Jean-Bertrand Aristide. U.S. troops arrive to keep peace until restored government is in place.

Special session of Congress in December ratifies GATT (General Agreement on Tariffs and Trade), which is designed to lower tariffs on manufactured and agricultural products among 117 nations.

NATIONAL

Final report on Iran-Contra scandal is issued (January 18) by Lawrence Walsh, independent counsel who headed 6½-year investigation.

Supreme Court Justice Harry A. Blackmun resigns after 24 years of service; Circuit Court Judge Stephen Breyer succeeds him.

President Clinton's proposed health plan is not voted on by Congress and is withdrawn.

Congress approves (August 28) $30.2 billion crime bill, providing funds for hiring 100,000 police, helping to establish new prisons, and banning some automatic weapons.

Social Security Administration, part of Health and Human Services Department, is scheduled to become an independent agency March 31, 1995.

Republicans win control of Congress (November 8) for first time since 1952.

Small plane crashes (September 12) on White House lawn, skids against building; pilot is killed; presidential family not at home. Gunman sprays White House with bullets from an assault rifle (October 29); no one is injured; the gunman is captured.

Several Administration officials resign: Agriculture Secretary Michael Espy (succeeded by former Kansas congressman Dan Glickman); Treasury Secretary Lloyd Bentsen (succeeded by Robert Rubin); Surgeon General Dr. Joycelyn Elders; and CIA Director R. James Woolsey.

Letter from former President Reagan (November 5) discloses that he suffers from Alzheimer's disease.

DEATHS Former President Richard M. Nixon; former First Lady Jacqueline Kennedy Onassis.

BUSINESS/INDUSTRY/INVENTIONS

Dow-Jones industrial average passes 3,800 mark for first time (January 6); two weeks later (January 21), it closes at more than 3,900.

Viacom Inc. gains control of Paramount Communications for about $10 billion, after it agrees to buy Blockbuster Entertainment Corp. for $8.4 billion.

Lockheed and Martin Marietta agree to merge, creating Lockheed Marietta, the largest U.S. defense contractor.

John C. Harsanyi and John F. Nash share Nobel Prize in economics for pioneering work in the field of game theory.

Orange County, California, declares bankruptcy when its $7.8 billion investment fund covering 180 cities and agencies suffers a more than $2 billion loss.

Federal legislation permits banks to operate branches across the nation.

DEATHS William Levitt, developer ("Levittowns"); Dave Beck, Teamsters Union president.

TRANSPORTATION

Federal court in Anchorage, Alaska, orders Exxon to pay $5 billion to more than 34,000 persons for damages resulting from the oil spill from the *Exxon Valdez* tanker in 1989.

Three plane crashes occur during year: a commuter plane near Gary, Indiana, killing all 68 aboard; a USAir jet on approach to Pittsburgh, killing 132; and a USAir jet near Charlotte, North Carolina, killing 37 of 67 aboard.

SCIENCE/MEDICINE

First Russian astronaut flies as crew member on U.S. shuttle *Discovery* (February 3–11).

Space shuttle *Endeavor* carries first space radar laboratory, maps Earth's surface in three dimensions.

A doctor who performed abortions and his escort are shot to death outside a Pensacola, Florida, abortion clinic; two workers are shot to death in two Brookline, Massachusetts, clinics.

George A. Olah wins Nobel Prize in chemistry for his contributions to hydrocarbon research; Clifford G. Shull shares prize in physics with Bertram N. Brockhouse of Canada for techniques to use neutron probes into atomic structure of matter; Alfred G. Gilman and Martin Rodbell share prize in physiology/medicine for research in natural substances that help cells control fundamental life processes.

DEATH Linus Pauling, winner of Nobel Prizes in chemistry and peace.

EDUCATION

A court orders The Citadel, state-financed military college in Charleston, South Carolina, to admit female students, holding school in violation of constitutional equal protection provisions; school appeals ruling.

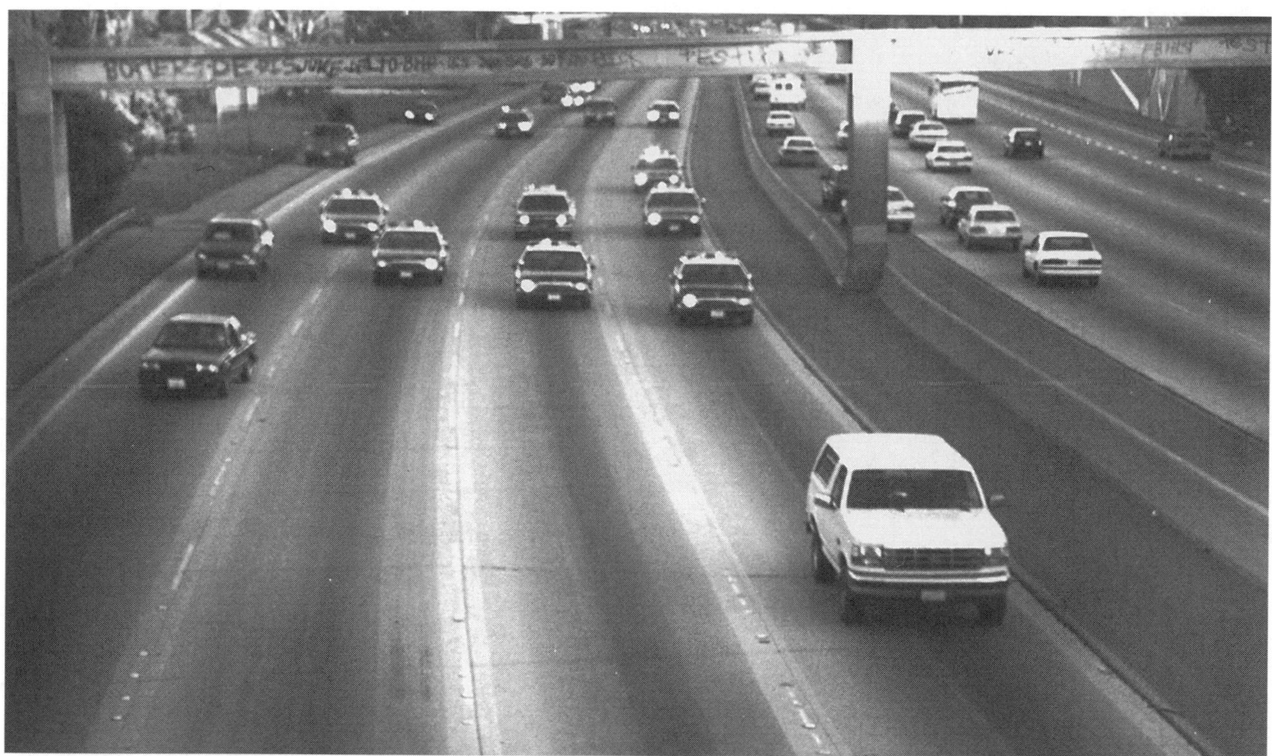

Police cars chase the white Ford Bronco carrying former football star O. J. Simpson on a California freeway on June 17, 1994. Simpson fled police after being named a suspect in the murder of his estranged wife, Nicole Simpson, and her acquaintance Ronald Goldman. **AP/WIDE WORLD PHOTOS**

RELIGION

DEATHS Ezra Taft Benson, head of Mormon Church (1985–1994); Menachem M. Schneerson, leader of a Jewish Hassidic sect.

ART/MUSIC

Concerts (August 12–14) at Saugerties, New York, mark 25th anniversary of the Woodstock concert in Bethel, New York, which was attended by about 500,000; about 350,000 attend Saugerties concerts.

POPULAR MUSIC Albums: *Waymore's Blues, Part II* with Waylon Jennings; *Turbulent Indigo* with Joni Mitchell; *Natural Ingredients* with Luscious Jackson; *Let the Picture Paint Itself* with Rodney Crowell. Songs: "Lost in America," Alice Cooper; "Dignity," Bob Dylan; "The Farmer's Daughter," Vince Gill; "California Dreamin'," American Music Club.

DEATHS Cab Calloway, orchestra leader and singer; singers Dinah Shore, Dorothy Collins, and Carmen McRae; composers Henry Mancini ("Moon River," "Days of Wine and Roses") and Jule Styne.

LITERATURE/JOURNALISM

BOOKS *The Shipping News* by E. Annie Proulx, *The Hot Zone* by Richard Preston, *No Ordinary Time* by Doris K. Goodwin, *A Map of the World* by Jane Hamilton, *The Celestine Prophecy* by James Redfield, *Gal* by Ruthie Bolton.

DEATHS Ralph Ellison, author *(Invisible Man);* Lawrence Spivak, originator and first moderator, *Meet the Press.*

ENTERTAINMENT

MOVIES *The Lion King* with the voice of Jeremy Irons, *Forrest Gump* with Tom Hanks, *Nobody's Fool* with Paul Newman, *Pulp Fiction* with John Travolta, *Speed* with Keanu Reeves, *The Santa Clause* with Tim Allen.

PLAYS *Passion* by Stephen Sondheim with Donna Murphy, *Angels in America: Perestroika* with Stephen Spinella, *Any Given Day* by Frank D. Gilroy with Sada Thompson, *Laughter on the 23d Floor* by Neil Simon.

DEATHS Actors Cesar Romero, Telly Savalas, Joseph Cotten, Vincent Price, Martha Raye, Burt Lancaster, Don Ameche, Myrna Loy, Jessica Tandy; Henry Morgan, television comedian; Harriet Nelson of *Ozzie and Harriet* show; Garry Moore, television host.

SPORTS

Winter Olympics are held in Lillehammer, Norway; U.S. wins 13 medals, the most it has won in a single winter games.

U.S. plays host for first time to World Soccer tournament; Brazil wins title.

New York Rangers win hockey's Stanley Cup for first time in 54 years; defeat Vancouver 4 games to 3.

Labor disputes affect two major sports: baseball players strike (August 12), force cancellation of remainder of season and World Series; hockey players and owners fail to reach agreement, force delay of season (October 1). Neither dispute is resolved at year's end.

George Foreman becomes oldest heavyweight boxing champion at 45, knocks out Michael Moorer (November 5) to regain title he lost to Muhammad Ali 20 years earlier.

WINNERS *Auto racing*—Al Unser Jr., Indianapolis 500; Dale Earnhardt, NASCAR; *Basketball*—Houston Rockets, NBA; Arkansas, NCAA; North Carolina, NCAA (women); Villanova, NIT; *Bowling*—Steve Fehr, ABC Masters; Norm Duke, Tournament of Champions; *Boxing*—George Foreman, heavyweight (WBA, IBF); Oliver McCall, heavyweight (WBC); *Figure skating*—Scott Davis, U.S. men; *Football* (bowls)—Wisconsin, Rose; Florida State, Orange; Florida, Sugar; Notre Dame, Cotton; Dallas, Super Bowl XXVIII; *Golf*—Ernie Els, U.S. Men's Open; Nick Price, PGA; Jose Maria Olazabal, Masters; Patty Sheehan, U.S. Women's Open; Laura Davies, LPGA; *Harness racing*—Victory Dream, Hambletonian; *Hockey*—New York Rangers, Stanley Cup; *Horse racing*—Go for Gin, Kentucky Derby; Tabasco Cat, Preakness Stakes and Belmont Stakes; *Tennis*—Andre Agassi, U.S. Open (men); Arantxa Sanchez Vicario, U.S. Open (women).

DEATHS Charles Feeney, president, National (baseball) League; Wilma Rudolph, track star; Jersey Joe Walcott and Jack Sharkey, boxing champions; Vitas Gerulaitis, tennis star; Allie Reynolds, baseball pitcher; Julius Boros, golfer.

MISCELLANEOUS

Predawn earthquake in Los Angeles area kills 61, injures more than 9,300, damages or destroys 45,000 residences; damage is estimated at $13–$20 billion.

Series of tornadoes in Alabama, Tennessee, and North and South Carolina kills 52; flooding in Georgia and Alabama results in 32 deaths.

Four men are convicted of bombing the World Trade Center in New York City in 1993; each is sentenced to prison for 240 years.

1995

INTERNATIONAL

U.S. leads United Nations effort to end 3½ years of fighting in Bosnia; agreement is reached (November 21) by Balkan leaders in Dayton, Ohio, calling for a U.N. force, including 20,000 U.S. troops, to maintain peace; U.S. troops arrive in December.

U.S. also is principal backer of Israeli-Palestinian peace talks; agreement is signed in Washington, D.C., in October.

Nobel Peace Prize is awarded to British physicist Joseph Rotblat, who was a member of the Manhattan Project that developed the U.S. atomic bomb, but resigned when it was clear Germany was not working on a nuclear weapon.

U.S. announces plan to place 100% tariff on Japanese-made luxury cars because Japanese markets are closed to U.S. cars. Japanese automakers agree to buy more U.S. parts; tariff plan is dropped.

U.S. eases trade embargo against North Korea in effect since Korean War. Vietnam and U.S. exchange low-level diplomats in July.

U.S. peace-keeping forces in Haiti are replaced (March 31) by a U.N. mission.

NATIONAL

First Republican-controlled Congress since 1953 convenes (January 4); adopts "Contract with America" to be accomplished in year. Session is marked by Clinton-Congress fights over budget and deficit, which lead to two government shutdowns—one very brief, the second in 17th day at year's end.

Oklahoma City federal building is bombed (April 19); 160 people killed. Two men with ties to right-wing U.S. militia group are charged.

An unidentified terrorist, the Unabomber, believed responsible for 17 deaths, demands publication of 35,000-word manifesto calling for revolt against industrial-technological society. He threatens to bomb an airliner if it is not published; The *New York Times* and *Washington Post* print it in September.

United Nations observes 50th anniversary in October, with nearly 140 heads of state attending ceremonies in New York City.

National 55-mile speed limit is repealed, effective December 8; some states set maximum at 75, Montana sets no daytime limit.

Supreme Court in 5–4 decision invalidates a Georgia congressional district whose boundary lines were drawn with race as a "predominant factor."

NAACP, faced with a $4-million debt, names Rep. Keisi Mfume of Maryland as its new head. Nation of Islam leader Louis Farrakhan organizes "Million Man March" (October 16) in Washington, D.C., to create unity among African-American men.

Gen. Colin Powell, a potential Republican 1996 presidential candidate, announces he will not run.

Cost of first-class postage rises to 32 cents per ounce (January 1).

A number of congressmen announce they will not seek reelection in 1996, including Senators Bill Bradley (New Jersey), Sam Nunn (Georgia), Mark Hatfield (Oregon), Alan Simpson (Wyoming), and Nancy Kassebaum (Kansas).

Senator Robert Packwood (Oregon) retires (September 7) after Ethics Committee recommends his expulsion because of sexual misconduct and influence peddling.

Defense Base Closure Commission's recommendations to close 79 bases and consolidate 26 others are approved.

DEATHS Warren E. Burger, former Supreme Court chief justice; Dean Rusk, former Secretary of State; Oveta Culp Hobby, first director of WAC, first HEW secretary; Margaret Chase Smith, first woman elected to both houses of Congress; Orval Faubus, Arkansas governor.

The Oklahoma Bombing

At 9:02 A.M., April 19, 1995 a bomb exploded outside the Alfred P. Murrah Building in Oklahoma City, resulting in the loss of 169 lives. The nine-story federal facility was partially destroyed by the blast, with seven other nearby buildings significantly damaged. The Oklahoma Bombing, as the tragic event soon became known, represented the most serious terrorist attack on the U.S. up until that time. Timothy J. McVeigh, from Pendleton, New York, and Terry Lynn Nichols, originally from Michigan, were tried and convicted of the bombing. Angry over what he felt was the federal government's growing encroachment on personal freedom, McVeigh, a decorated veteran of the Gulf War, considered his act a justified declaration of war. The date of the bombing tellingly marked the two-year anniversary of a showdown between federal agents and an armed religious community led by David Koresh near Waco, Texas. Eighty-one of Koresh's devotees died in the resulting fire. McVeigh was executed by lethal injection on June 11, 2001.

BUSINESS/INDUSTRY/INVENTIONS

Acquisitions and mergers mark the year, including combinations of Time Warner and Turner Broadcasting, Disney Co. and Capital Cities/ABC, Westinghouse Electric and CBS; Seagram acquires MCA, Kimberly Clark acquires Scott Paper; Martin Marietta and Lockheed merge; Rite Aid and Revco join, forming a 4,500-drugstore chain; Chase Manhattan and Chemical Bank merge under Chase name to form $297-billion-assets bank.

Dow-Jones industrial average, which began July 3, 1884, when Charles Dow published first averages, passes the 4,000 mark (February 23) and 5,000 (November 21).

Three large industrial unions, auto workers, steelworkers, and machinists, vote to merge by year 2000. AFL-CIO President Lane Kirkland retires in August after 16 years.

Nobel Prize in economics is awarded to Robert E. Lucas, the fifth Nobel prize–winning economist at University of Chicago in six years; selected for his mathematical critiques of activist governmental policies.

Congress for first time overrides a President Clinton veto (December 22), thereby approving legislation that limits stockholders' ability to sue for fraud; opponents argue that small investors will suffer.

DEATHS John V. Atanasoff, electronic computer inventor; Edward Bernays, public relations pioneer; J. Peter Grace, corporation head; Orville Redenbacher, agricultural scientist, popcorn manufacturer; George Romney, president, American Motors.

TRANSPORTATION

DEATH Douglas (Wrong Way) Corrigan, transatlantic flier, who said he thought he was flying to California when he landed in Ireland (July 1938).

SCIENCE/MEDICINE

Galileo spacecraft, launched October 1989, reaches within 130,000 miles of Jupiter; launches probe into Jupiter's orbit (December 7), diving into planet's atmosphere, collecting atmospheric data. Spacecraft

The north side of the Alfred Murrah Federal Building in Oklahoma City shows the devastation caused by the truck bomb that detonates early on April 19, 1995. © ERIC DRAPER/ AP/WIDE WORLD PHOTOS

begins first of 11 orbits around Jupiter that will last until November 1997.

Swiss scientists report discovery of new planet in constellation Pegasus; American astronomers Geoffrey March and Paul Butler confirm the findings.

F. Sherwood Rowland shares Nobel Prize in chemistry with Paul Chutzen of Netherlands and Mario Molina of Mexico for warning of ozone depletion; Martin Perl and Frederick Raines share physics prize for discovery of subatomic particles; Edward B. Lewis and Eric F. Wieschaus share medicine/physiology prize for research into fruit flies.

U.S. shuttle *Atlantis* and Russian space station *Mir* join in space (June 29) for six days.

American Museum of Natural History in New York City opens largest, most scientifically ambitious dinosaur exhibit in the world.

DEATHS Jonas Salk, developer of first polio vaccine; Nobel prize–winning physicists Eugene Wigner and Subrahmanyan Chandrasekhar; Apollo 14 astronaut Stuart A. Roosa.

EDUCATION

Shannon Faulkner, after long legal battle, is admitted as a cadet at The Citadel (August 11); she resigns after four days of training. Legal efforts to change all-male admission policy at the state-supported Virginia Military Institute begin, reach Supreme Court where a decision is expected by mid-1996.

DEATH Former Arkansas Senator J. William Fulbright, whose fellowship legislation aided higher education.

RELIGION

Pope John Paul II issues his 11th encyclical, opposes abortion, birth control, and euthanasia; makes his fourth visit to U.S. in October.

Supreme Court rules 5–4 that a student-run religious publication must be funded by University of Virginia just as any other student publication.

Billy Graham, 77-year-old evangelist, reduces his activities after he suffers a fall; designates his son, Franklin, as his eventual successor.

DEATH Howard W. Hunter, Mormon Church leader.

ART/MUSIC

Private funds enable opening of long-awaited Vermeer art exhibit at National Gallery of Art, closed because of a federal government shutdown.

Barnes Foundation, renowned private art collection in Merion, Pennsylvania, reopens after 30-month renovation.

The Grateful Dead, a rock-and-roll group, folds after its founder, Jerry Garcia, dies. Selena, the queen of Tejano music, is murdered; event creates quick popularity rise in her music and Latin pop music.

MUSIC Albums include *The Ghost of Tom Joad* by Bruce Springsteen, *To Bring You My Love* by P. J. Harvey, *The Hits* by Garth Brooks, *Any Man of Mine* by Shania Twain, *Thinkin' About You* by Trisha Yearwood.

DEATHS Band leaders Phil Harris, Lee Elgart, and Jerry Garcia; jazz trumpeter Don Cherry; singers Burl Ives, Charlie Rich, and Maxene Andrews; Eazy-E, cofounder of "gangsta" rap group.

LITERATURE/JOURNALISM

Mergers and acquisitions continue in television field as Cable News Network launches a 12-hour daily financial news service (CNNfn); Microsoft and NBC team up to develop 24-hour cable news and Internet service, expects to begin operations in mid-1996.

Robert Haas is named the eighth U.S. poet laureate.

Robert MacNeil, co-anchor of *MacNeil-Lehrer News Hour* for 20 years, retires.

BOOKS *Stories* by Vladimir Nabokov, *Familiar Heat* by Mary Hood, *Collected Short Fiction* by Bruce Jay Friedman, *The Road Ahead* by Bill Gates.

DEATHS Ian Ballantine, publisher; Alfred Eisenstadt, *Life* photographer; John Cameron Swayze, early TV newsman; James (Scotty) Reston, *New York Times* reporter.

ENTERTAINMENT

Carol Channing, who first starred in *Hello, Dolly!* in 1964 through nearly 4,500 performances, starts a revival in October.

MOVIES *Apollo 13* with Tom Hanks, *Bridges of Madison County* with Meryl Streep and Clint Eastwood, *Star Trek* with William Shatner, *Toy Story,* first entirely computer-animated full-length feature.

Television programs include *ER* (a medical drama), *Friends, Murder One,* and *The Single Guy.*

DEATHS George Abbott, playwright and director; actors Eva Gabor, Ida Lupino, Ginger Rogers, Lana Turner, and Dean Martin; Jerry Lester, early television host.

SPORTS

Cal Ripken Jr., Baltimore Orioles shortstop, breaks (September 6) Lou Gehrig's consecutive-game streak of 2,130 games, set in 1939.

Michael Jordan returns to the Chicago Bulls basketball team.

Baseball strike ends after NLRB and federal court action; sides agree to 144-game season, instead of usual 162. National Hockey League and players agree on new contract and 48-game season, instead of usual 84.

Cleveland Browns football team announces move to Baltimore in 1996; Houston Oilers to move to Nashville soon. Local opposition arises and Browns face lawsuits before moving.

Sergei Grinkov, who with his wife, Ekaterina Gordeyeva, won Olympic gold medals (1988, 1994) for pairs skating, dies of a heart attack while practicing in Lake Placid, New York.

Mike Tyson completes three-year prison term, wins his first fight with an 89-second TKO of Peter McNeely.

WINNERS *Auto racing*—Jacques Villaneuve, Indianapolis 500; Jeff Gordon, NASCAR; *Baseball*—Atlanta Braves, World Series; *Basketball*—Houston Rockets, NBA; UCLA, NCAA; University of Connecticut, NCAA (women); Virginia Tech, NIT; *Bowling*—Mike Aulby, ABC Masters and Tournament of Champions; *Football* (bowls)—Penn State, Rose; Nebraska, Orange; Florida State, Sugar; Southern California, Cotton; San Francisco, Super Bowl XXIX; *Golf*—Corey Pavin, U.S. Men's Open; Steve Elkington, PGA; Ben Crenshaw, Masters; Anika Sorenstam, U.S. Women's Open; Kelly Robbins, LPGA; *Harness racing*—Tagliabue, Hambletonian; *Hockey*—New Jersey, Stanley Cup; *Horse racing*—Thunder Gulch, Kentucky Derby and Belmont Stakes; Timber Country, Preakness Stakes; *Tennis*—Pete Sampras, Wimbledon and U.S. Open (men); Steffi Graf, Wimbledon and U.S. Open (women).

DEATHS Sportscasters Howard Cosell and Lindsey Nelson; baseball players Leon Day and Mickey Mantle; auto racer Juan Manuel Fangio; tennis stars Pancho Gonzales, Bobby Riggs, and Fred Perry; basketball player and coach Nat Holman.

MISCELLANEOUS

Heavy March rains in California cause 15 deaths and $2 billion damage; 1,001 tornadoes in Midwest create second-most-active season, and 8 tropical storms and 11 hurricanes make for worst season since 1933.

July heat wave causes more than 800 deaths in Midwest and Northeast.

O. J. Simpson, football star, after a 16-month trial, is found not guilty of murdering his former wife and her friend.

1996

INTERNATIONAL

A bomb explodes at military complex near Dhahran, Saudi Arabia, 19 U.S. servicemen die, several hundred are wounded.

Troops from U.S. and other countries monitor peace accord among the three warring factions in Bosnia-Herzegovina.

Senate approves (January 26) the Second Strategic Arms Reduction Treaty, which was signed three years earlier by presidents Bush and Yeltsin.

President Clinton announces that he will authorize renewal of most-favored-nation trade status for China, which would provide lower export tariffs on trade to U.S.; many oppose action because of Chinese human-rights violations.

President Clinton visits Japan and South Korea, signs agreements on joint security.

Cuban jets shoot down two unarmed planes carrying four Cuban exiles based in Miami (February 24); U.S. says planes were shot down over international waters. Economic embargo against Cuba is strengthened by President Clinton (March 12).

NATIONAL

President Clinton is re-elected, the first Democratic president re-elected since Franklin D. Roosevelt. The president receives 47,401,185 popular votes and 379 electoral votes while Sen. Robert Dole, the Republican candidate, receives 39,197,469 popular and 159 electoral votes and the Reform Party candidate Ross Perot draws 8,085,294 popular votes but no electoral votes.

President nominates Madeleine Albright, U.S. representative to United Nations, to become Secretary of State, the first woman in that post.

Legislative battle of 1995 ends (January 26) when President Clinton signs stopgap bill to keep government operating into March. Later (September 30), another bill takes care of rest of fiscal year and funds for fiscal year 1997.

Federal agents in Montana seize Theodore Kaczynski, former mathematics professor, for possession of bomb-making materials. He is believed to be the Unabomber, the object of a search since 1978 for sending mail bombs that killed 3, injured 23.

Montana is also the scene of FBI confrontation with the Freemen, an antigovernment group (March 25). Group surrenders without incident (June 13), is charged with defrauding businesses of $1.8 billion, conducting seminars on how to defraud. A plot to bomb seven government buildings is thwarted when a 12-man paramilitary group is arrested in Phoenix, Arizona, area.

President Clinton signs legislation that changes welfare program to state programs using federal funds. Other enacted legislation includes line-item veto by president of parts of spending and tax bills, $1 billion to fight terrorism over four-year period, and gradual elimination of farm subsidy program.

A commission recommends changes in how to determine Consumer Price Index, which could result in reducing inflation rate and cost-of-living raises tied to CPI.

Supreme Court holds a Colorado law unconstitutional for excluding homosexuals from civil rights protection; upholds right of law-enforcement officials to seek criminal penalties against a defendant and seize the defendant's property.

DEATHS Spiro T. Agnew, former Vice President (1969–1973) and Maryland governor; Ronald Brown, Commerce Secretary (April 3); Edmund S. Muskie, Secretary of State (1980) and Maine governor, senator; Quentin Burdick, North Dakota senator for 32 years; Edmund G. (Pat) Brown, California governor; William E. Colby, CIA director (1973–1976); McGeorge Bundy, former national security advisor; Carl B. Stokes, first African-American mayor of major city (Cleveland, 1967–1971); Barbara Jordan, Texas legislator; Alger Hiss, former official accused of spying.

BUSINESS/INDUSTRY/INVENTIONS

Dow-Jones industrial average passes 6,000 mark for first time (October 14); ends year at 6,448.27, a 26% gain over 1995.

President Clinton signs (February 8) Telecommunications Reform Act deregulating in large measure telephone, mobile phone, and cable television service.

President Clinton approves regulations to curb sale of tobacco products to young persons. A major tobacco company, Liggett Group Inc., breaks with industry, agrees to a settlement in a class-action suit.

Boeing Co. buys McDonnell Douglas for $13.3 billion and Rockwell aerospace and defense operations; several mergers are made, including Pacific Telesis Group and SBC Communications, Continental Cablevision and U.S. West Media Group, and Nation's Bank and Boatmen's Bancshares.

Minimum wage increases from $4.25 an hour to $4.75 (October 1) and set to rise to $5.15 on September 1, 1997. President Clinton signs bill that allows workers changing jobs to maintain their health insurance.

Two corporations settle actions against them: Archer Daniels Midland agrees to pay $100 million fine for conspiring to fix prices on two products; Texaco agrees to pay $520 million to settle employees' racial-bias suit.

DEATHS Canadian-born American William Vickery, shares 1996 Nobel Prize in economics, dies suddenly three days later (October 11); James W. Rouse, developer of malls, "cities"; Max Factor, cosmetics manufacturer; David Packard, electronics industry pioneer.

TRANSPORTATION

Valujet DC-9 crashes (May 11) into Florida Everglades, kills all 110 aboard; accident caused by fire in cargo hold. TWA Flight 800 traveling from New York to Paris explodes, crashes shortly after takeoff, kills all 230 people aboard (July 17).

Mid-Atlantic state businesses like this Washington, D.C., restaurant face unfamiliar complications from a January 1996 blizzard that causes more than a billion dollars in damages up and down the coast. © RON EDMONDS/ AP/WIDE WORLD PHOTOS

SCIENCE/MEDICINE

NASA Administrator Daniel Goldin says that evidence found in a small meteorite points to possible existence of life beyond Earth. Meteorite reportedly originated on Mars $4\frac{1}{2}$ billion years ago.

Mars Environmental Survey *Pathfinder* space shuttle, first of 13 Mars flights, is successfully launched.

David M. Lee, Robert C. Richardson, and Douglas C. Osheroff share Nobel Prize in physics; Robert F. Curl Jr. and Richard Smalley share chemistry prize.

President Clinton vetoes bill that would ban late-term abortions, which, he says, are few but often important to save life; efforts to override fail.

Dr. Jack Kevorkian, retired pathologist who was present at 27 suicides, is acquitted of violating Michigan law against assisted suicide.

DEATHS Carl Sagan, astronomer who popularized space study; Mary Leakey, anthropologist; Roger Tory Peterson, author and illustrator of bird books; Paul Erdos, founder of discrete mathematics.

EDUCATION

Supreme Court rules (June 26) that Virginia Military Institute, state-supported school, may not bar women from admission. The Citadel, a South Carolina state-supported school, which began admitting women in previous year, admits four women (August 24).

DEATH Arthur S. Flemming, University of Oregon president, HEW secretary.

RELIGION

DEATHS Two Catholic cardinals and archbishops: Joseph Bernardin of Chicago (1982–1996) and John J. Krol of Philadelphia (1961–1988); a Catholic priest, Lawrence M. Jenco, who had been a hostage in Lebanon for 18 months.

ART/MUSIC

SONGS "Unchained" by Johnny Cash, "Because You Loved Me" by Diane Warren, "Mystery Box" by Mickey Hart, "Blue" by LeAnn Rimes, "Give Me One Reason" by Tracy Chapman; *25th Anniversary Metropolitan Opera Gala* by James Levine.

DEATHS Henry Lewis, first African-American conductor of major U.S. orchestra (New Jersey Symphony); Morton Gould, composer and conductor; Lincoln Kirstein, cofounder New York City Ballet; Juliet

Ted Kaczynski, dubbed the Unabomber, is arrested in 1996 and accused of waging a terrorist campaign that killed three people and injured twenty-three. He later is sentenced to life imprisonment. **AP/WIDE WORLD PHOTOS**

Prowse, dancer; Gerry Mulligan, saxophonist and band leader; Ella Fitzgerald, singer; Bill Monroe, founder of bluegrass music; Tiny Tim, falsetto singer; Tupac Shakur, rap superstar.

LITERATURE/JOURNALISM

BOOKS *The First Man* by Albert Camus, *All the Days and Nights* by William Maxwell, *The Body Is Water* by Julie Schumacher, *The Tailor of Panama* by John le Carré, *Lily White* by Susan Isaacs, *Executive Orders* by Tom Clancy, *The Christmas Box* by Richard P. Evans.

DEATHS John Chancellor, television newsman; Erma Bombeck, author and humorist; Joseph Brodsky, exiled Soviet poet who became U.S. poet laureate and Nobel prize-winner in literature.

ENTERTAINMENT

Television executives agree to implement use of v-chip (*v* for violence) that can be installed in sets to block out programs. At year's end, industry adopts six-tier rating system for sex and violence of its shows, similar to system used by movies.

MOVIES *Grumpier Old Men* with Jack Lemmon and Walter Matthau, *Fargo* with Frances McDormand, *The Crucible* with Daniel Day-Lewis and Winona Ryder, *Shine* with Geoffrey Rush, *Secrets and Lies* with Brenda Blethyn.

PLAYS *State Fair* with John Davidson and Kathryn Crosby; *Big* with Daniel Jenkins and Crista Moore; *Rent* with Adam Pascal, Anthony Rapp, and Daphne Rubin-Vega.

DEATHS Movie actors Dorothy Lamour, Claudette Colbert, Greer Garson, Martin Balsam, Lew Ayres; television actors Audrey Meadows of *The Honeymooners;* Vince Edwards, who played Dr. Ben Casey on television; Morey Amsterdam; singer and dancer Gene Kelly; veteran comic George Burns, almost 100; country-music star Minnie Pearl.

SPORTS

Summer Olympic Games open in Atlanta (July 19); eight days later a pipe-bomb explodes in Centennial Park in downtown Atlanta, kills one person; does not affect the games.

Evander Holyfield, former heavyweight champion, upsets Mike Tyson to regain WBA boxing title that Tyson retook earlier in year.

Baseball club owners approve five-year agreement with players, calling for revenue sharing by clubs and interleague play; owners turn down pact (November 6), then reverse themselves (December 9).

National Football League owners approve moves of Cleveland Browns to Baltimore for 1996–1997 season and Houston Oilers to Nashville in 1998.

Twenty-year-old Eldrick "Tiger" Woods wins U.S. amateur golf title for record third year, turns pro.

Eddie Murray of Baltimore Orioles hits 500th home run, the 15th player to hit that many.

New York Jets Nick Lowery kicks field goal (October 13) to become all-time career field goal kicker with 346.

Major League Soccer (MLS) debuts with 31,683 watching San Jose Clash beat DC United 1–0.

WINNERS *Auto racing*—Buddy Lazier, Indianapolis 500; Terry Labonte, NASCAR; *Baseball*—New York Yankees, World Series; *Basketball*—Chicago, NBA; Kentucky, NCAA; Tennessee, NCAA (women); Nebraska, NIT; *Bowling*—Ernie Schliegel, ABC Masters; Dave D'Entremont, Tournament of Champions; *Figure skating* (world)—Todd Eldredge, men; Michelle Kwan, women; *Football* (bowls)—Southern California, Rose; Florida State, Orange; Virginia Tech, Sugar; Colorado, Cotton; Dallas, Super Bowl XXX; *Golf*—Nick Faldo, Masters; Steve Jones, U.S. Men's Open; Mark Brooks, PGA; Annika Sorenstam,

U.S. Women's Open; Laura Davies, LPGA; *Harness racing*—Continentalvictory, Hambletonian; *Hockey*—Colorado, Stanley Cup; *Horse racing*—Grindstone, Kentucky Derby; Louis Quatorze, Preakness Stakes; Editor's Note, Belmont Stakes; *Tennis*—Richard Krajcek, Wimbledon (men), Pete Sampras, U.S. Open (men); Steffi Graf, U.S. Open and Wimbledon (women).

DEATHS Pete Rozelle, NFL commissioner (1960–1989); Charles O. Finley, baseball club owner (Kansas City, Oakland); Mel Allen, baseball sportscaster; Roger Crozier, hockey goalie; Minnesota Fats (Rudolf Wanderone), legendary pool hustler; Jimmy ("The Greek") Snyder, oddsmaker and sportscaster.

MISCELLANEOUS

Blizzard deposits up to three feet of snow on mid-Atlantic and New England states (January 7–8), causing more than $1 billion in damage; tornadoes (March 28–29) cause 52 deaths in Alabama, Tennessee, Georgia, and the Carolinas.

Hurricane Bertha arrives (July 5) near Jacksonville, North Carolina, causes $270 million in damage; Hurricane Fran comes ashore (September 6) at Cape Fear, North Carolina, causes 34 deaths, $3.2 billion in damage.

A seven-year-old girl, trying to become the youngest to pilot a plane across the U.S., is killed along with her father and flight instructor in a crash in Wyoming.

Four-day auction of about 5,900 items owned by the late Jacqueline Kennedy Onassis brings in more than $34 million.

99% of approximately 97 million homes in U.S. have a color television; 82% have a videocassette recorder (VCR).

Civil trial against O. J. Simpson, former football star, begins; Simpson was acquitted (1995) of murdering his wife and her friend, now is being sued for damages.

1997

INTERNATIONAL

Iraqi President Saddam Hussein refuses in October to allow United Nations arms inspections to continue unless American members are removed; U.N. Security Council orders inspections to continue; Iraq orders U.S. inspectors to leave; entire U.N. team leaves (October 29). U.S. begins military buildup; Russia leads move to end impasse; inspectors return after three-week absence, but haggling over inspection sites continues.

Global warming conference in Tokyo reaches tentative agreement (December 11) to reduce fossil fuels in the future, marking first historic steps to binding reductions in industrial gases.

Iranian President Muhammad Khatami (December 14) calls for talks with U.S., changing his nation's nearly 20-year-old anti-American attitude.

Seventy countries in World Trade Organization agree to open banking, insurance, and securities markets to outside firms; open policy is already in effect in U.S.

Although U.S. opposes immediate ban of land mines, the international banning group and its coordinator, Jody Williams of Poultney, Vermont, convince many nations to sign ban. The group and Williams are awarded Nobel Peace Prize.

U.S. and Russia are among 146 nations to sign Comprehensive Test Ban Treaty; only eight countries have ratified pact (U.S. and Russia have not). Senate ratifies Chemical Weapons Treaty in April, making U.S. 75th nation to approve elimination of such weapons by 2007.

President Jiang Zemin of China visits U.S. in November; signs nuclear proliferation treaty, agrees to end nuclear assistance to Iran.

U.S. and Mexico agree on broader efforts to fight drug trafficking.

President Clinton visits U.S. troops in Bosnia at Christmastime, tells them of decision to extend their stay.

NATIONAL

Senate (March 4) defeats for third time in three years a proposed constitutional amendment requiring a balanced federal budget. White House and Congress agree in May to balance federal budget by 2002.

Line Item Veto bill, which would allow president to veto individual expenditures in large spending bills, is held to be unconstitutional (April 19) by a district judge; Supreme Court (June 26) dismisses challenge. President Clinton uses new veto power (August 11) on three specific items.

Timothy McVeigh is found guilty of 1995 bombing of Oklahoma City federal building that killed 168 people; death penalty is imposed. Terry Nichols, his alleged accomplice, is found guilty in December of conspiracy and involuntary manslaughter.

Jury is selected in December to try Theodore Kaczynski, the alleged Unabomber, in January 1998.

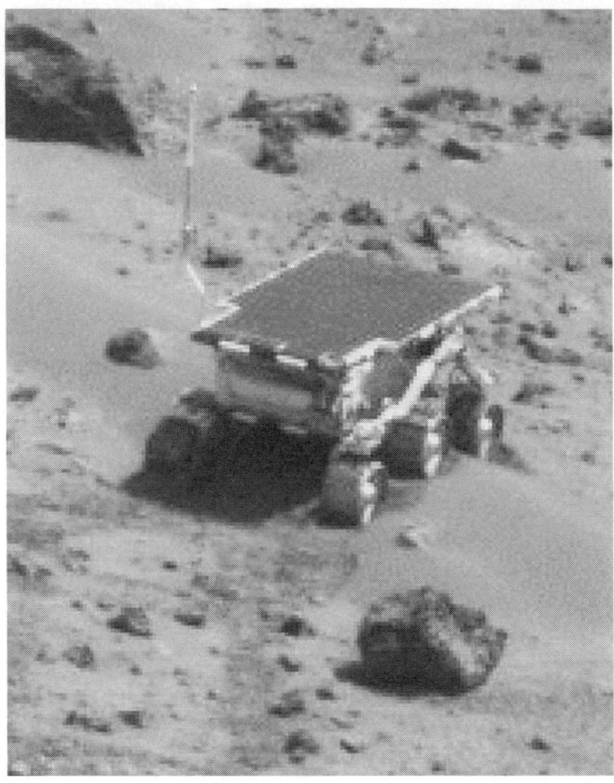

Dark tracks on the Martian Mermaid Dune show the path of the surface rover "Sojourner," during the 1997 Pathfinder mission. **AP/WIDE WORLD PHOTOS**

Four major tobacco companies and several state attorneys general agree on a settlement costing the companies $368.5 billion; approval is needed from president, Congress, and health community. Florida becomes second state, after Mississippi, to settle claims with tobacco industry in August.

California law bars state from race- or gender-based preferences in school admission, public hiring, or contracting (August 28).

President Clinton suffers serious knee injury (March 14) in Palm Beach, Florida.

Arizona Gov. Fife Symington resigns (September 5) after federal jury finds him guilty of fraud in actions prior to his election.

DEATHS William J. Brennan Jr., former Supreme Court justice; Pamela Harriman, ambassador to France; Robert C. Weaver, first African-American cabinet member, first HUD secretary.

BUSINESS/INDUSTRY/INVENTIONS

United Parcel Service (UPS) and Teamsters Union settle 15-day strike (August 19) that costs UPS an estimated $600 million in revenues. Federal official orders new election of Teamsters president (August 22) after investigation finds that Ron Carey received illegal contributions to his campaign.

In August, Dow-Jones average reaches all-time high of 8,259.31; economic problems in southeast Asia cause drop of 554 points (October 27), biggest single-day drop. Year closes at 7,908, the third consecutive year with more than a 20% increase.

Justice Department files complaint against Microsoft Corp. for allegedly forcing computer companies to use its browser program; court (December 11) orders Microsoft to stop practice.

Federal minimum wage rises to $5.15 an hour (September 1) from $4.75; unemployment rate for year is 4.6%, a 24-year low.

Morgan Stanley Group Inc. reports that it will merge with Dean Witter, Discover & Co., creating largest U.S. securities group. Three other mergers are announced: NYNEX and Bell Atlantic, Northrup Grumman and Lockheed, Hughes Aircraft and Raytheon.

U.S. trade deficit for 1996 is reported at $114.23 billion, up 8.7% from 1995.

DEATHS Robert Goizueta, Coca-Cola president; Robert W. Sarnoff of RCA; James A. Ryder, pioneer in truck leasing.

TRANSPORTATION

A British racing team breaks sound barrier on land (October 15) when a jet-powered Thrust SSC reaches 763.035 miles per hour on Black Rock Desert in Nevada.

FBI completes its investigation of TWA Flight 800 crash, states there is no evidence of any criminal action.

SCIENCE/MEDICINE

American spacecraft, the Mars *Pathfinder,* lands (July 4) on planet Mars; sends back pictures.

President Clinton (March 4) bans use of federal funds for human embryo research in wake of successful cloning of adult sheep in Scotland.

Immense Hale-Bopp comet with a 25-mile wide icy core reaches its point closest to Earth, about 122 million miles; first appearance near Earth in 4,200 years.

Paul D. Boyers shares Noble Prize in chemistry with John E. Walker of Great Britain and Jens C. Skou; Steven Chu and William D. Phillips share prize in physics, and Stanley B. Prusiner is awarded prize in physiology/medicine.

In June, Supreme Court upholds Washington and New York state laws that make it a crime for doctors to help patients end their lives.

DEATHS Biochemists Melvin Calvin, John C. Kendrew, and George Wald; physicists Robert Dicke and Edward Purcell; surgeons Alfred D. Hershey and Charles B. Huggins; astronomer Clyde V. Tombaugh.

EDUCATION

George Bush Memorial Library opens in College Station, Texas.

RELIGION

Promise Keepers, an evangelical group, organizes a rally (October 4) in Washington, D.C., for Christian men to reaffirm their faith and to help restore and preserve the nation and families.

DEATH Ruffin Bridgeforth, first African-American Mormon high priest.

ART/MUSIC

Performing arts center opens in downtown Newark, New Jersey; Los Angeles opens a new Getty art museum.

SONGS "Candle in the Wind," Elton John's eulogy for Princess Diana, "Crash into Me" by the Dave Matthews Band.

DEATHS Rudolph Bing, Metropolitan Opera manager (1950–1972); Helen Jepson, opera singer; John Denver, singer and composer; songwriter Irving Caesar; orchestra conductor Georg Solti; artists Willem de Kooning and Roy Lichtenstein.

LITERATURE/JOURNALISM

Supreme Court rules 7–2 in June to extend right of free speech to the Internet.

Robert Pinsky is named the ninth U.S. poet laureate.

Some books of the year are *Cold Mountain* by Charles Frazier, *The God of Small Things* by Arundhati Roy, *Midnight in the Garden of Good and Evil* by John Berendt, *Angela's Ashes* by Frank McCourt, *Into Thin Air* by Jon Krakauer.

DEATHS Poets James Dickey and Allen Ginsberg; columnists Mike Royko, Murray Kempton, and Herb Caen; TV performer and author Charles Kuralt of *On the Road* fame; authors James Michener, Harold Robbins, Leon Edel, Vance Packard, Leo Rosten.

ENTERTAINMENT

Major television networks, except NBC, agree (July 9) to revised, expanded TV rating system; revision expands contents ratings of January.

Tiger Woods celebrates on the eighteenth green of the Augusta National Golf Club after winning the 1997 Masters Tournament on April 13, 1997. He sets a new course record of 270 strokes and becomes both the youngest and the first African American to win this major tournament. © JOHN KUNTZ/ ARCHIVE PHOTOS, INC.

The musical *Cats* becomes longest-running show in Broadway history (June 19) with its 6,138th performance, passes *A Chorus Line.*

MOVIES *LA Confidential, Titanic, Amistad, As Good as It Gets, The Ice Storm, Men in Black.*

PLAYS *The Lion King, Ragtime* with Brian Stokes Mitchell, and *A Doll's House* with Janet McTeer.

DEATHS Screen actors Burgess Meredith, Robert Mitchum, Jimmy Stewart; TV and film comic Red Skelton; pioneer TV announcer and game-show host Dennis James; Brandon Tartikoff, NBC executive; screen director Fred Zinneman.

SPORTS

Tiger Woods sets new record (270 strokes) in winning Masters golf tournament (April 13); also youngest (21) event winner and first African American to win major tourney.

Tara Lipinski becomes youngest (14) U.S. figure-skating champion (February 16).

Evander Holyfield retains WBA heavyweight boxing title (June 28) when Mike Tyson is disqualified after biting Holyfield's ear several times.

Retirees in sports world include Dean Smith, University of North Carolina basketball coach for 36 years with a record 879 wins, and Eddie Robinson, Grambling College football coach for 56 years with 408 wins.

Baseball salaries hit new high when Boston Red Sox sign pitcher Pedro Martinez (December 10) to six-year $75 million contract. Baseball also enters new era (June 12) with start of regular season interleague play.

Detroit hockey coach Scotty Bowman becomes (February 8) first NHL coach to achieve 1,000 wins; later (June 7) his Red Wings win Stanley Cup for first time in 43 years.

WINNERS *Auto racing*—Ariel Luyendyk, Indianapolis 500; Jeff Gordon, NASCAR; *Baseball*—Florida Marlins, World Series; *Basketball*—Chicago, NBA; Houston, WNBA (women), Columbus, ABL (women); Kentucky, NCAA; Tennessee, NCAA (women); Michigan, NIT; *Bowling*—John Gant, Tournament of Champions; Jason Queen, Masters; *Figure skating*—Tara Lipinski, U.S., world women's title, Todd Eldredge, U.S. men's title; *Football* (bowls)—Ohio State, Rose; Nebraska, Orange; Florida, Sugar; Brigham Young, Cotton; Green Bay, Super Bowl XXXI; *Golf*—Ernie Els, U.S. Men's Open; Davis Love III, PGA; Tiger Woods, Masters; Allison Nicholas, U.S. Women's Open; Chris Johnson, LPGA; *Harness racing*—Malabar Man, Hambletonian; *Horse racing*—Silver Charm, Kentucky Derby, Preakness Stakes; Touch Gold, Belmont Stakes; *Tennis*—Patrick Rafter, U.S. Open (men); Pete Sampras, Wimbledon (men); Martina Hingis, U.S. Open, Wimbledon (women).

DEATHS Pro football club owners Jack Kent Cooke and Robert Irsay; golfer Ben Hogan; baseball players Johnny Vander Meer, Buck Leonard, and Curt Flood; football star Don Hutson; Eddie Arcaro, only jockey to ride two Triple Crown winners; tennis star Helen Jacobs; boxer Tony Zale.

MISCELLANEOUS

Bobbi McCaughey of Carlisle, Iowa, gives birth to first set of living septuplets (October 26) in nearby Des Moines; all seven doing well at year's end.

Flood-swollen rivers force about 100,000 persons in upper Midwest from their homes in April; a month earlier, floods in Ohio River Valley claim 35 lives.

Tornadoes in central Arkansas (March 1) kill 26; six tornadoes rip through central Texas; one kills 27 persons in Jarrell.

Ted Turner, media and sports leader, announces donation of $1 billion over 10 years to United Nations agencies.

Approximately 41% of U.S. homes have a personal computer.

1998

INTERNATIONAL

Asia is beset with one economic calamity after another in a growing list of countries, including South Korea, Thailand, Indonesia, Malaysia, the Philippines and Japan. Problems include plunging currencies, troubled banking systems, shrinking gross domestic products, and tumbling stock market values.

Russia effectively devalues the ruble and imposes a 90-day moratorium on repayment of many foreign debts.

John Hume and David Trimble share the Nobel Peace Prize for their work in resolving the conflict in Northern Ireland.

Violence erupts in Kosovo, where the 90% ethnic Albanian population struggles for self-determination. For the first time, U.S. troops are deployed for the purpose of ending ethnic cleansing.

DEATH Pol Pot, notorious Cambodian dictator.

NATIONAL

President Bill Clinton comes under fire once again when the U.S. House of Representatives approves two articles of impeachment for perjury and obstruction of justice. The House accuses Clinton of lying about his relationship with White House intern Monica Lewinsky when interviewed in a sexual harassment case against him, brought by Paula Jones in 1998.

Newt Gingrich, the darling of the 1994 Republican revolution, steps down as Speaker of the House. His replacement, Rep. Bob Livingston of Louisiana, also resigns after revelations that he had an extramarital affair. Rep. Dennis Hastert of Illinois, a former high school wrestling coach, assumes the post.

Former mental patient Russell E. Weston Jr. takes a gun through a metal detector at the Capitol and shoots officer Jacob Chestnut. He is apprehended while running toward the offices of Minority Whip Tom DeLay.

Theodore Kaczynski sentenced to four consecutive life terms after his trial in the Unabomber case. His entire cabin was transported to Sacramento for the proceedings.

Aaron James McKinney (right), co-defendant in the Matthew Shepard murder. Russell Henderson (not pictured) has already been convicted of felony murder. Shepard is brutally beaten on October 7, 1998, apparently because he is gay. © ED ANDRIESKI/ ARCHIVE PHOTOS, INC.

Wildfires rage in Florida, causing 100,000 people to be evacuated from their homes and 120 miles of Interstate 95 to be closed. Damage is estimated at $300 million and the cost of fighting the fire exceeds $100 million.

Matthew Shepard, a gay student at the University of Wyoming, is killed by Russell Henderson and Aaron McKinney in Laramie. The murder is classified as a hate crime.

James Byrd Jr., an African-American resident of Jasper, Texas, is tied to the back of a pick-up truck and dragged to his death by three racists. The men are charged with murder.

Forty-six states and five U.S. territories sign a $200 billion deal with four tobacco companies, Phillip Morris, Lorillard, R.J. Reynolds, and Brown & Williamson. The settlement also forbids the use of cartoons in cigarette advertising.

Senate Majority Leader Trent Lott blocks a vote which would allow James Hormel, who is admittedly gay, to become U.S. Ambassador to Luxembourg.

Jesse "The Body" Ventura, a former professional wrestler and political independent, defeats Hubert Humphrey Jr. and Norm Coleman to become governor of Minnesota.

DEATHS Bella Abzug, feminist and former U.S. representative; Barry Goldwater, former U.S. senator and presidential candidate; Tom Bradley, first African-American mayor of Los Angeles; George Wallace, former Alabama governor; Eldridge Cleaver, former Black Panther; James Earl Ray, convicted assassin of Dr. Martin Luther King Jr.

BUSINESS/INDUSTRY/INVENTIONS

The Justice Department, twenty states, and the District of Columbia file suit against Microsoft for violating anti-trust laws. Judge Thomas Penfield Jackson hears the case.

Chrysler and Mercedes merge, creating one of the world's largest car companies.

Preparations are made to correct potential problems arising from computer programs misreading the year 2000 as 1900. The media cover the phenomenon, referred to as the Y2K bug, extensively.

Consumer optimism remains at incredibly high levels in the U.S. and the stock market surges to new heights.

DEATH Walter Diemer, accidental inventor of bubble gum.

TRANSPORTATION

World-renowned AIDS researcher Dr. Jonathan Mann and 228 others are killed when SwissAir Flight 111 crashes off Peggy's Cove, Nova Scotia.

In December 1998 members of the House Judiciary Committee listen to testimony about allegations that President Bill Clinton lied under oath. President Clinton later becomes the second U.S. president to be impeached. © WALLY MCNAMEE/ CORBIS-BETTMANN

SCIENCE/MEDICINE

Seventy-seven-year-old Senator John Glenn returns to space on the shuttle *Discovery* 36 years after orbiting the earth in the *Friendship 7* capsule.

Pfizer releases Viagra, the first non-surgical erection enhancer that is successful for seven out of ten men. Over 3 million prescriptions are written in the first five months, although some possible health risks exist.

The FDA approves PREVEN, a morning-after contraceptive kit that researchers say could cut unintended pregnancies and the abortion rate in half.

Advances in gene therapy raise ethical questions about concepts like cloning and stem cell research.

DEATHS Marjorie Stoneman Douglas, Everglades crusader; Alan Shepard, first American in space; Dr. Jonathan Mann, AIDS expert; Ted Fujita, scientist.

EDUCATION

Yale Professor Antonio Lasaga is arrested for creating and possessing child pornography.

DEATH Dr. Benjamin Spock, pediatrician and parenting educator.

RELIGION

As many as 1 million Cubans cheer Pope John Paul II when he visits Havana's Revolution Square. The pope calls on Castro's government to give more freedom to the people and criticizes the U.S. trade embargo.

A United Methodist court falls one vote short of convicting the Rev. Jimmy Creech, an Omaha pastor, of violating church doctrine by performing a same-sex marriage ceremony.

Karla Faye Tucker, a pick-ax killer turned born-again Christian, is executed in Texas, despite appeals from such figures as Pat Robertson and Pope John Paul II.

ART/MUSIC

SONGS "Du Hast" by Rammstein, "Slide" by the Goo Goo Dolls, and "Celebrity Skin" by Hole.

DEATHS Jerome Robbins, choreographer; Shari Lewis, puppeteer of Lamb Chop; Gene Autry, singing cowboy; Jeffrey Moss, *Sesame Street* writer.

LITERATURE/JOURNALISM

BOOKS *The Poisonwood Bible* by Barbara Kingsolver, *A Man in Full* by Tom Wolfe, *The Essence of the Thing* by Madeline St. John, *Lindbergh* by A. Scott Berg, *Jack Maggs* by Peter Carey.

DEATHS Martha Gellhorn, writer and ex-wife of Ernest

The site of the U.S. embassy in Nairobi, Kenya, following the Al Qaeda–sponsored bombing. Bombers also strike the embassy in Dar Es Saalam, Tanzania. The August 1998 bombings leave more than a hundred people dead and thousands wounded. © DAVID BUTOW/CORBIS SABA

Hemingway; Ted Hughes, poet; Octavio Paz, Nobel Prize winner; writers Allen Drury, Dorothy West.

ENTERTAINMENT

PLAYS *The Lion King, Ragtime, Beauty Queen, Corpus Christi.*

MOVIES *Still Crazy, Waking Ned Devine, Pleasantville* with William H. Macy and Joan Allen, *Saving Private Ryan* with Tom Hanks and Matt Damon, *Life Is Beautiful* with Roberto Benigni, *Shakespeare in Love* with Gwyneth Paltrow, *The Truman Show* with Jim Carrey.

DEATHS Singers Frank Sinatra, Carl Perkins, Roy Rogers, Sonny Bono, Rob Pilatus; actors Hugh Reilly, Maureen O'Sullivan, Buffalo Bob Smith, Jack Lord; Akira Kurosawa, film director; Phil Hartman, comedian.

SPORTS

John Elway leads the Denver Broncos to a stunning upset of the defending champion Green Bay Packers, earning his first Super Bowl victory.

France defeats Brazil 3-0 after Zinedane Zidane scores two goals, to win its first World Cup on home turf. The celebrations last well into the next month.

Mark McGwire and Sammy Sosa attempt to break Roger Maris's record of 61 home runs. McGwire eventually hits 70 and Sosa 66. Sosa also wins his first MVP award.

Ricky Williams of Texas sets the college football record for most yards rushing on his way to winning the Heisman Trophy.

Former champion Mike Tyson's boxing license is revoked following his 1997 fight in which he bit off part of Evander Holyfield's ear.

WINNERS *Auto Racing*—Eddie Cheever Jr., Indianapolis 500; Dale Earnhardt, Daytona 500; *Baseball*—New York Yankees, World Series; *Basketball*—Chicago, NBA; Kentucky, NCAA; Tennessee, NCAA (women) *Bowling*—Mike Aulby, ABC Masters; Dennis Horan Jr., Tournament of Champions; *Figure Skating*—Ilia Kulik, Olympics (men); Tara Lipinski, Olympics (women); *Football*—Nebraska, Orange Bowl; Michigan, Rose Bowl; Florida State, Sugar Bowl; Kansas State, Fiesta Bowl; Denver, Super Bowl XXXII; *Golf*—Mark O'Meara, Masters and British Open; Lee Janzen, U.S. Open; Vijay Singh, PGA Championship; *Harness racing*—Muscles Yankee, Hambletonian; *Hockey*—Detroit; Stanley Cup; *Horse racing*—Real Quiet, Kentucky Derby and Preakness Stakes; Victory Gallop, Belmont Stakes; *Tennis*—Patrick Rafter,

After a nine-day mission on the Space Shuttle *Discovery*, Senator John Glenn discusses his return to space with the media. The image in the background is a 1962 photograph of Glenn from his former days as an astronaut. **AP/WIDE WORLD PHOTOS**

U.S. Open (men); Pete Sampras, Wimbledon (men); Lindsay Davenport, U.S. Open (women); Jana Novotna, Wimbledon (women).

DEATHS Florence Griffith Joyner, record-setting sprinter; Harry Caray, Chicago Cubs announcer; Archie Moore, boxer; Sid Luckman, football player; Doak Walker, famed running back; Dan Quisenberry, relief pitcher.

1999

INTERNATIONAL

Devastating earthquakes hit Turkey and Japan, killing thousands. Over 32,000 people are killed worldwide in natural disasters.

European monetary union becomes a reality, with 11 member states of the European Union adopting a single currency, for accounting purposes.

East Timor votes to separate from Indonesia, which had occupied the area since 1975. Indonesia sends in troops to loot and pillage, but UN forces intervene and the nation becomes independent.

Doctors Without Borders, a worldwide medical organization, wins the Nobel Peace Prize for its international public health efforts.

On the heels of Desert Storm, U.S. and British forces continue to bomb targets in Iraq in hopes of destroying weapons depots.

DEATH King Hussein, ruler of Jordan.

NATIONAL

Hurricane Floyd, a category 4 hurricane, touches down on the U.S.'s East Coast, causing severe flooding in North Carolina and Virginia and resulting in $1 billion in losses and 40 deaths.

Dylan Klebold, 18, and Eric Harris, 17, open fire at Columbine High School in Littleton, Colorado, killing 12 students and a teacher before committing suicide. Investigators reveal the pair had plotted to kill 500 students and blow up the school. Other school shootings occur in Richmond, Va; Conyers, Ga; Deming, N.Mex; and Fort Gibson, Oklahoma.

A plane piloted by John F. Kennedy Jr. crashes into the Atlantic off the Massachusetts coast. Kennedy, his wife Carolyn Bessette Kennedy, and her sister Lauren Bessette are killed instantly.

President Bill Clinton becomes the second president to be impeached. Congress refuses to convict him of perjury and obstruction of justice charges and he remains in office. However, the American public learns about his sexual indiscretions in incredible detail from the Kenneth Starr report. **SEE PRIMARY DOCUMENT** Proceedings of the Impeachment of President Bill Clinton

The Melissa virus, a macrovirus that forwards files to other e-mail addresses, hits the U.S. Worries over privacy issues grip lawyers and doctors. A 30-year-old New Jersey man is arrested for creating the bug.

Forty-one people are killed as 12 tornadoes roar across the plains in Oklahoma and Kansas.

DEATHS John Chaffee, former Rhode Island senator; Daisy Bates, civil rights leader; Elliot Richardson, former attorney general; John F. Kennedy Jr., publisher.

BUSINESS/INDUSTRY/INVENTIONS

MP3 digital music players are declared legal and MP3.com has a highly successful IPO.

Judge Thomas Penfield Jackson rules that Microsoft is a monopoly.

Carleton "Carly" Fiorina becomes CEO of Hewlett Packard (HP). The former Lucent executive replaces Lewis Platt as HP's chief executive after a search. She is the highest-ranking woman in a Fortune 500 company.

Each day, 1.5 million web surfers place bids on eBay, an online auction site.

The Sega Dreamcast, which flopped in Japan, sells over 1 million systems in the U.S. The system, which costs $199, also allows users to surf the net.

DEATHS Jay Pritzker, founder of Hyatt Hotels; Forrest Mars Sr., creator of M&Ms; Akio Morita, Sony CEO; Jules Lederer, founder of Budget Rent-a-Car.

TRANSPORTATION

Egypt Air Flight 990 crashes off of Nantucket, killing 217. Rumors circulate that the pilot had ties to terrorist groups.

A Gates Learjet carrying champion golfer Payne Stewart crashes in Aberdeen, South Dakota. Five others die with Stewart in the crash.

SCIENCE/MEDICINE

Scientists announce a near complete sequence for chromosome 22, a significant development in mapping the human genome.

Scientists create a new type of gas called Fermium condensate that could be the basis for new types of clocks and lasers.

Jesse Gelsinger becomes the first patient to die as a result of gene therapy. The University of Pennsylvania where Gelsinger's therapy was performed puts a moratorium on all gene therapy research.

DEATHS Apollo 12 astronaut Pete Conrad; Glenn Seaborg, named Nobel Prize winner for discovery of plutonium.

EDUCATION

President Clinton in his state-of-the-union address unveils a five-point plan for improving America's public schools, for the first time holding states and school districts accountable for progress and rewarding them for results.

DEATH Paul Mellon, philanthropist.

RELIGION

Congressman Bob Barr and others demand that Wicca and other minority religions be outlawed in the U.S. military, despite constitutional protection of freedom of religion.

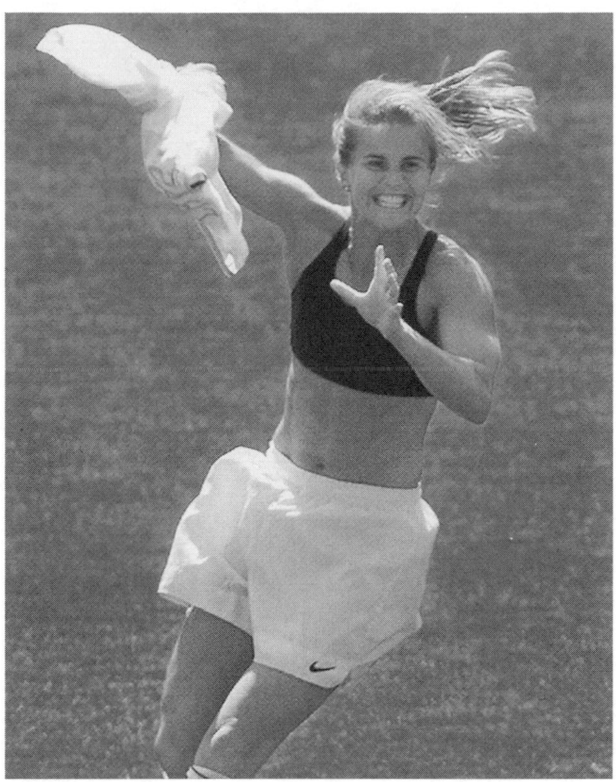

Brandi Chastain removes her shirt after her winning penalty kick clinched the American women's July 1999 World Cup victory over China, which kick-starts enormous interest in women's soccer. © ERIC RISBERG/AP/WIDE WORLD PHOTOS

More than 10,000 followers of Falun Gong gather in Beijing to protest the practices of the Communist regime. Afterward, the Chinese government bans the controversial faith and arrests hundreds of its followers.

The Kansas State school board publishes an evolution-free set of teaching guidelines, bringing the Scopes Trial–era creation and evolution debate back into the spotlight.

ART/MUSIC

Woodstock '99, an overly commercial tribute to the famous 1969 concert, is held in Rome, New York. Moby, Kid Rock, Creed, Dave Matthews Band, Jewel, Wyclef Jean, Offspring, and Buckcherry perform.

SONGS "The Next Movement" by The Roots, "Guerrilla Radio" by Rage Against the Machine, "Smooth" by Rob Thomas and Santana, and "We're in This Together" by Nine Inch Nails.

DEATHS Robert Shaw, chorale director; Yehudi Menuhin, violinist; Saul Steinberg, *New Yorker* cartoonist; Grover Washington Jr., jazz musician; Shel Silverstein, popular artist and poet.

Willie Nelson performs for the crowd on the closing day of Woodstock '99, a three-day music festival celebrating the thirty-year anniversary of the music festival that attracted more than 300,000 people in 1969. AP/WIDE WORLD PHOTOS

LITERATURE/JOURNALISM

BOOKS *Harry Potter and the Prisoner of Azkaban* by J. K. Rowling, *Personal Injuries* by Scott Turow, *Waiting* by Ha Jin, *The Big Test* by Nicholas Lemman, *Dangerous Friend* by Ward Just.

DEATHS Iris Murdoch, author; Mario Puzo, author of *The Godfather*; Marion Zimmer Bradley, author of *The Mists of Avalon*; Martha Rountree, co-creator of *Meet the Press.*

ENTERTAINMENT

Who Wants to Be a Millionaire?, a quiz show imported from Britain and hosted by Regis Philbin, jumps to the top of the television ratings chart.

MOVIES *All About My Mother, The Matrix, American Beauty, Election, South Park: Bigger, Longer, and Uncut, The Talented Mr. Ripley, The End of the Affair.*

PLAYS *The Iceman Cometh* with Kevin Spacey, *Contact* with Deborah Yates, *Death of a Salesman* with Brian Dennehy, *The Lonesome West* with Brian O'Byrne.

DEATHS Gene Siskel, film reviewer; singers Mel Torme, Dusty Springfield; actors George C. Scott, Madeline Kahn, Desmond Llewelyn, Dana Plato, Gary Morton, David Strickland.

SPORTS

The U.S. women's soccer team wins its second World Cup by defeating China 5-4 before a sellout crowd at the Rose Bowl. Brandi Chastain scores the winning kick and waves her shirt in celebration, becoming an American icon.

Cyclist Lance Armstrong wins the Tour de France two years after being given less than a 50% chance to survive testicular cancer.

Hockey great Wayne Gretzky retires.

The NBA season does not begin until after the All-Star break due to a lockout. San Antonio wins the NBA title in the shortened season.

The U.S. golf team makes the largest comeback in Ryder Cup history, winning 9 of 12 matches on the final day to defeat the European squad.

WINNERS *Auto Racing*—Kenny Brack, Indianapolis 500; Dale Jarrett, NASCAR; *Baseball*—New York Yankees, World Series; *Basketball*—San Antonio, NBA; Connecticut, NCAA (men); Purdue NCAA (women) *Bowling*—Brian Boghosian, ABC Masters; Gryan Goebel, Tournament of Champions; *Football*—Florida, Orange Bowl; Wisconsin, Rose Bowl; Ohio State, Sugar Bowl; Tennessee, Fiesta Bowl; Denver, Super Bowl XXXIII; *Golf*—Jose Maria Olazabal, Masters; Paul Lawrie, British Open; Payne Stewart, U.S. Open; Tiger Woods, PGA Championship; *Harness racing*—Self Possessed, Hambletonian; *Hockey*—Dallas, Stanley Cup; *Horse racing*—Charismatic, Kentucky Derby and Preakness Stakes; Lemon Drop Kid, Belmont Stakes; *Tennis*—Andre Agassi, U.S. Open (men); Pete Sampras, Wimbeldon (men); Serena Williams, U.S. Open (women); Lindsay Davenport, Wimbeldon (women).

DEATHS Joe DiMaggio, legendary baseball player; Wilt Chamberlain, celebrated NBA center; Payne Stewart, golfer; Walter Payton, NFL rushing leader.

PRIMARY SOURCE DOCUMENT

Proceedings of the Impeachment of President Bill Clinton, February 12, 1999

INTRODUCTION On February 12, 1999, after a five-week trial followed closely by most Americans, the U.S. Senate acquitted President Bill Clinton on charges of perjury and obstruction of justice. It was only the second impeachment trial in the nation's history, coming 131 years after Andrew Johnson's, which also ended in an acquittal. President Richard M. Nixon resigned in

1974 rather than face an impeachment trial in the Senate. The scandal, and the general crisis in American politics that it triggered, began as the outgrowth of an investigation into President Clinton's real estate dealings of the 1980s. The "Whitewater" investigation failed to uncover any impropriety on Clinton's part, but the congressional committee and its special prosecutor Kenneth Starr expanded its inquiry by looking into Clinton's rumored sexual relationship with a former White House intern, Monica Lewinsky. After initially denying the relationship, Clinton eventually admitted to the infidelity to the nation in a dramatic nationally televised address. Because he had also denied the relationship in a deposition in a civil suit brought against him in Arkansas, the U.S. House of Representatives found grounds for impeachment, charging him with perjury and obstruction of justice.

Some analysts considered the impeachment of Clinton largely promoted and then supported by Republicans as revenge for Nixon's forced resignation, whereas others saw it as an effort to restore morality and civility to American politics. Although opinion polls showed that the public overwhelmingly did not support impeachment, the scandal damaged Clinton's reputation and embarrassed the nation; even Democrats who voted against conviction felt betrayed. However, the scandal had larger implications as it also raised questions about the character of public officials in general. Several Republican congressmen who had aggressively pushed for Clinton's impeachment, including Henry Hyde, Newt Gingrich, and Robert Livingston (Gingrich's successor as Speaker of the House of Representatives), admitted to adulterous affairs as the Clinton impeachment case played out.

The document below is an excerpt of the written record for the February 12 Senate session in which senators voted on the two articles of impeachment brought by the House of Representatives; Article I alleged Clinton had committed perjury, and Article II charged Clinton with obstruction of justice. The Senate failed to reach the two-thirds vote required for conviction on either charge. Five moderate Republicans joined Democratic senators in voting for acquittal. In addition, an attempt by Republican senators to officially censure Clinton for "shameful, reckless and indefensible" conduct fell short of the necessary two-thirds majority.

Feb. 12: Final Votes
From the *Congressional Record*
Friday, February 12, 1999

....The CHIEF JUSTICE [William H. Rehnquist, Chief Justice of the United States Supreme Court]. The Sergeant at Arms will make the proclamation.

The Sergeant at Arms, James W. Ziglar, made proclamation as follows:

Hear ye! Hear ye! Hear ye! All persons are commanded to keep silent, on pain of imprisonment, while the Senate of the United States is sitting for the trial of the articles of impeachment exhibited by the House of Representatives against William Jefferson Clinton, President of the United States....

Closed Session

(At 9:44 A.M., the doors of the Chamber were closed. The proceedings of the Senate were held in closed session until 12:04 P.M., at which time the following occurred.)

Jesse Ventura, a former professional wrestler and Navy Seal, takes the oath as governor of Minnesota in 1999 after his stunning victory in the November 1998 election as the Reform Party candidate. AP/WIDE WORLD PHOTOS

Open Session

Mr. LOTT. Will Senators return to their desks? Managers, thank you for joining us. Would Senators stand, and the gallery, as the Chief Justice enters the Chamber, please.

The CHIEF JUSTICE. The Senate will be in order.

Mr. LOTT. Mr. Chief Justice, Members of the Senate, the Senate has met almost exclusively as a Court of Impeachment since January 7, 1999, to consider the articles of impeachment against the President of the United States. The Senate meets today to conclude this trial by voting on the articles of impeachment, thereby, fulfilling its obligation under the Constitution. I believe we are ready to proceed to the votes on the articles. And I yield the floor.

The CHIEF JUSTICE. The Chair would inform those in attendance in the Senate galleries, that under rule XIX of the Standing Rules of the Senate, demonstrations of approval or disapproval are prohibited, and it is the duty of the Chair to enforce order on its own initiative.

Article I. The CHIEF JUSTICE. The clerk will now read the first Article of impeachment.

The legislative clerk read as follows:

A tribute to a young John F. Kennedy Jr. sits among flowers left near his New York City residence days after Kennedy, his wife Carolyn, and her sister Lauren die in a plane crash on July 16, 1999. **AP/WIDE WORLD PHOTOS**

Article I

In his conduct while President of the United States, William Jefferson Clinton, in violation of his constitutional oath faithfully to execute the office of President of the United States and, to the best of his ability, preserve, protect, and defend the Constitution of the United States, and in violation of his constitutional duty to take care that the laws be faithfully executed, has willfully corrupted and manipulated the judicial process of the United States for his personal gain and exoneration, impeding the administration of justice, in that: On August 17, 1998, William Jefferson Clinton swore to tell the truth, the whole truth, and nothing but the truth before a Federal grand jury of the United States. Contrary to that oath, William Jefferson Clinton willfully provided perjurious, false and misleading testimony to the grand jury concerning one or more of the following: (1) the nature and details of his relationship with a subordinate Government employee; (2) prior perjurious, false and misleading testimony he gave in a Federal civil rights action brought against him; (3) prior false and misleading statements he allowed his attorney to make to a Federal judge in that civil rights action [refers to the sexual harassment case brought by Paula Jones]; and (4) his corrupt efforts to influence testimony of witnesses and to impede the discovery of evidence in that civil rights action. In doing this, William Jefferson Clinton has undermined the integrity of his office, has brought disrepute on the Presidency, has betrayed his trust as President, and has acted in a manner subversive of the rule of law and justice, to the manifest injury of the people of the United States. Wherefore, William Jefferson Clinton, by such conduct, warrants impeachment and trial, and removal from office and disqualification to hold and enjoy any office of honor, trust, or profit under the United States.

The CHIEF JUSTICE. The Chair reminds the Senate that each Senator, when his or her name is called, will stand in his or her place and vote 'guilty' or 'not guilty' as required by rule XXIII of the Senate rules on impeachment.

The Chair also refers to article I, section 3, clause 6, of the Constitution regarding the vote required for conviction on impeachment. Quote: '[N]o Person shall be convicted without the Concurrence of two-thirds of the Members present.'

Vote on Article I. The CHIEF JUSTICE. The question is on the first article of impeachment. Senators, how say you? Is the respondent, William Jefferson Clinton, guilty or not guilty? A rollcall vote is required.

The clerk will call the roll.

The legislative clerk called the roll.

Rollcall Vote No. 17

The flight data recorder from Egypt Air Flight 990 (seen here on November 10, 1999), which crashes off Nantucket Island on October 31, 1999, killing all 217 persons aboard. AP/WIDE WORLD PHOTOS

[Rollcall Vote No. 17]

Subject: Article I—Articles of Impeachment Against President William Jefferson Clinton

[SUBJECT: ARTICLE I—ARTICLES OF IMPEACHMENT AGAINST PRESIDENT WILLIAM JEFFERSON CLINTON]

GUILTY—45 [Note: List of Senators voting guilty follows]

NOT GUILTY—55 [Note: List of Senators voting not guilty follows]

The CHIEF JUSTICE. On this article of impeachment, 45 Senators having pronounced William Jefferson Clinton, President of the United States, guilty as charged, 55 Senators having pronounced him not guilty, two-thirds of the Senators present not having pronounced him guilty, the Senate adjudges that the respondent, William Jefferson Clinton, President of the United States, is not guilty as charged in the first article of impeachment.

Article II. The CHIEF JUSTICE. The clerk will read the second article of impeachment.

The legislative clerk read as follows:

Article II

In his conduct while President of the United States, William Jefferson Clinton, in violation of his constitutional oath faithfully to execute the office of President of the United States and, to the best of his ability, preserve, protect, and defend the Constitution of the United States, and in violation of his constitutional duty to take care that the laws be faithfully executed, has prevented, obstructed, and impeded the administration of justice, and has to that end engaged personally, and through his subordinates and agents, in a course of conduct or scheme designed to delay, impede, cover up, and conceal the existence of evidence and testimony related to a Federal civil rights action brought against him in a duly instituted judicial proceeding [refers to the sexual harassment case brought by Paula Jones]. The means used to implement this course of conduct or scheme included one or more of the following acts:

(1) On or about December 17, 1997, William Jefferson Clinton corruptly encouraged a witness in a Federal civil rights action brought against him to execute a sworn affidavit in that proceeding that he knew to be perjurious, false and misleading.

(2) On or about December 17, 1997, William Jefferson Clinton corruptly encouraged a witness in a Federal civil rights action brought against him to give perjurious,

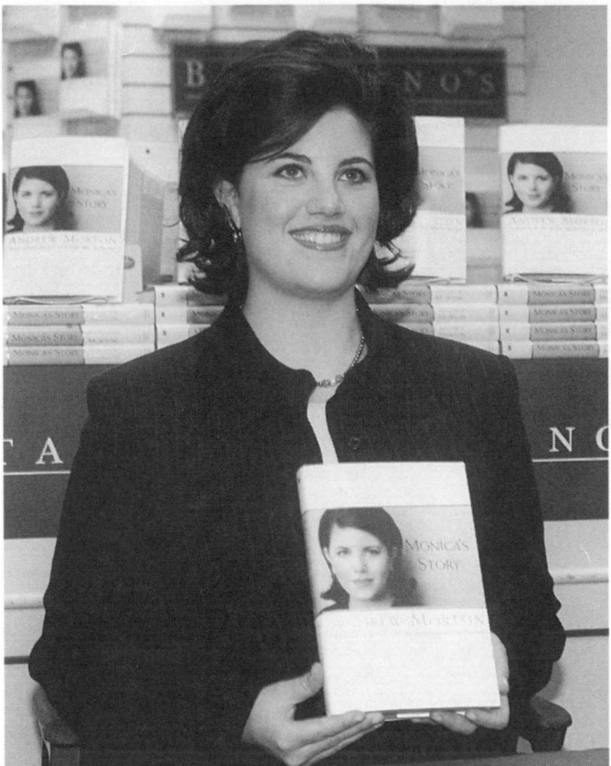

At a Los Angeles bookstore former White House intern Monica Lewinsky poses with a copy of her book, *Monica's Story,* her account of the scandal that tainted Bill Clinton's presidency. **AP/WIDE WORLD PHOTOS**

false and misleading testimony if and when called to testify personally in that proceeding.

(3) On or about December 28, 1997, William Jefferson Clinton corruptly engaged in, encouraged, or supported a scheme to conceal evidence that had been subpoenaed in a Federal civil rights action brought against him.

(4) Beginning on or about December 7, 1997, and continuing through and including January 14, 1998, William Jefferson Clinton intensified and succeeded in an effort to secure job assistance to a witness in a Federal civil rights action brought against him in order to corruptly prevent the truthful testimony of that witness in that proceeding at a time when the truthful testimony of that witness would have been harmful to him.

(5) On January 17, 1998, at his deposition in a Federal civil rights action brought against him, William Jefferson Clinton corruptly allowed his attorney to make false and misleading statements to a Federal judge characterizing an affidavit, in order to prevent questioning deemed relevant by the judge. Such false and misleading statements were subsequently acknowledged by his attorney in a communication to that judge.

(6) On or about January 18 and January 20–21, 1998, William Jefferson Clinton related a false and misleading account of events relevant to a Federal civil rights action brought against him to a potential witness in that proceeding, in order to corruptly influence the testimony of that witness.

(7) On or about January 21, 23, and 26, 1998, William Jefferson Clinton made false and misleading statements to potential witnesses in a Federal grand jury proceeding in order to corruptly influence the testimony of those witnesses. The false and misleading statements made by William Jefferson Clinton were repeated by the witnesses to the grand jury, causing the grand jury to receive false and misleading information. In all of this, William Jefferson Clinton has undermined the integrity of his office, has brought disrepute on the Presidency, has betrayed his trust as President, and has acted in a manner subversive of the rule of law and justice, to the manifest injury of the people of the United States. Wherefore, William Jefferson Clinton, by such conduct, warrants impeachment and trial, and removal from office and disqualification to hold and enjoy any office of honor, trust, or profit under the United States.

Vote on Article II. The CHIEF JUSTICE. The question is on the second article of impeachment. Senators, how say you? Is the respondent, William Jefferson Clinton, guilty or not guilty?

The clerk will call the roll.

The bill clerk called the roll.

The result was announced—guilty 50, not guilty 50, as follows:

Rollcall Vote No. 18

[Rollcall Vote No. 18]

Subject: Article II—Articles of Impeachment against President William Jefferson Clinton

[SUBJECT: ARTICLE II—ARTICLES OF IMPEACHMENT AGAINST PRESIDENT WILLIAM JEFFERSON CLINTON]

GUILTY—50 [Note: List of Senators voting guilty follows]

NOT GUILTY—50 [Note: List of Senators voting not guilty follows]

The CHIEF JUSTICE. The galleries will be in order.

On this article of impeachment, 50 Senators having pronounced William Jefferson Clinton, President of the United States, guilty as charged, 50 Senators having pronounced him not guilty, two-thirds of the Senators present not having pronounced him guilty, the Senate adjudges that the respondent, William Jefferson Clinton, President of the United States, is not guilty as charged in the second article of impeachment.

Colorado teenagers Dylan Klebold and Eric Harris walk through the cafeteria of Columbine High School on April 20, 1999, the day they kill a teacher and twelve fellow students and horrify the nation. AP/WIDE WORLD PHOTOS

The Chair directs judgment to be entered in accordance with the judgment of the Senate as follows:

The Senate, having tried William Jefferson Clinton, President of the United States, upon two articles of impeachment exhibited against him by the House of Representatives, and two-thirds of the Senators present not having found him guilty of the charges contained therein: it is, therefore, ordered and adjudged that the said William Jefferson Clinton be, and he is hereby, acquitted of the charges in this said article.

The Chair recognizes the majority leader.

Communication to the Secretary of State and to the House of Representatives. Mr. LOTT. Mr. Chief Justice, there is an order at the desk.

The CHIEF JUSTICE. The clerk will read the order.

The legislative clerk read as follows:

Ordered, that the Secretary be directed to communicate to the Secretary of State, as provided by Rule XXIII of the Rules of Procedure and Practice in the Senate when sitting on impeachment trials, and also to the House of Representatives, the judgment of the Senate in the case of William Jefferson Clinton, and transmit a certified copy of the judgment to each.

The CHIEF JUSTICE. Without objection, the order will be entered.

Statement by the Chief Justice of the United States on the Senate Trial. The CHIEF JUSTICE. The Chair wishes to make a brief statement, without objection on such. (Laughter.)

More than a month ago, I first came here to preside over the Senate sitting as the Court of Impeachment. I was a stranger to the great majority of you. I underwent the sort of culture shock that naturally occurs when one moves from the very structured environment of the Supreme Court to what I shall call, for want of a better phrase, the more free-form environment of the Senate. (Laughter.)

I leave you now a wiser but not a sadder man. I have been impressed by the manner in which the majority leader and the minority leader have agreed on procedural rules in spite of the differences that separate their two parties on matters of substance.

I have been impressed by the quality of the debate in closed session on the entire question of impeachment as provided for under the Constitution. Agreed-upon procedures for erring on substantive divisions must be the hallmark of any great deliberative body.

Our work as a Court of Impeachment is now done. I

OVERVIEW

America at Century's End: The Age of Bill Clinton and George W. Bush, 1993–2002

ROBERT D. JOHNSTON, YALE UNIVERSITY

History of the Present

Writing the history of recent times is always a risky endeavor. How can a historian, who is supposed to at least try to be fair and impartial, remove him or herself from the swirl of current events and objectively evaluate what has happened in one's own lifetime?

Ultimately, complete detachment is impossible. However, most historians would agree on the events and trends that are likely to be considered "historic" a century from now. These include, in the political realm alone, the troubled dominance of Bill Clinton as a political leader in the 1990s, the challenges to Clinton from conservatives such as Newt Gingrich, the impeachment crisis, and the event that dramatically marked the century's end: the stalemated 2000 presidential election. Outside the political arena, in the realm of everyday life, few people used e-mail at the beginning of the 1990s; by the decade's end, fewer still were not touched by the rise of the Internet. Cell phones abound. Nonetheless, all these events and new technologies seemed to pale in comparison to the stunning attack on the United States by Islamic terrorists on September 11, 2001.

The Era of Bill Clinton

The era of conservatism, best symbolized by Presidents Ronald Reagan and George Herbert Walker Bush, came to an abrupt end with the election of a youthful Bill Clinton in 1992. In defeating Bush, Clinton fought off concerns about his avoiding the Vietnam draft and possible drug use. Clinton articulated a political program that would defend the interests of "the forgotten middle class," but even more important, he, like Jack Kennedy in 1960, radiated youthful vigor and a sense of hope.

Stalemate of Liberalism and the Contract with America

Most Americans believed Clinton to be a liberal, even if a moderate one. But his attempts to implement liberal policies did not succeed. He quickly retreated from an attempt to promote equality for gays in the military, and he abandoned his nominee for the top civil rights position in the Justice Department, Lani Guinier, after opponents claimed that she was a "quota queen" who believed in the worst forms of affirmative action. African Americans, however, remained Clinton's most devoted followers, with novelist Toni Morrison even declaring Clinton the first effectively black president. Clinton's worst political debacle, however, occurred when he unveiled a national health insurance plan—devised largely by his wife, lawyer Hillary Rodham Clinton, and by policy advisor Ira Magaziner—that involved sweeping reforms. The ensuing legislative push completely failed. Two years into his presidency, Clinton suffered another stinging rebuke at the hands of the electorate when the Republicans swept both houses of Congress. Newt Gingrich, the ultra-conservative Georgian who became Speaker of the House, spoke of a new conservative revolution. He and his allies composed a Contract with America that promised to cut taxes; restore American military might; and fight for one of the decade's new innovations in American politics, term limits for elected officials.

From these defeats, Clinton rebounded with amazing skill. He handily defeated Senator Bob Dole, a much-decorated World War II veteran, in the 1996 presidential election. Two years later, he seemed to have also vanquished the conservative revolution

leave you with the hope that our several paths may cross again under happier circumstances.

The majority leader.

Mr. LOTT. Mr. Chief Justice, we thank you for your comments.

Expression of Gratitude to the Chief Justice of the United States. Adjournment Sine Die of the Court of Impeachement:

Mr. LOTT. Now, Mr. Chief Justice, I move that the Senate, sitting as a Court of Impeachment on the articles exhibited against William Jefferson Clinton, adjourn sine die.

The motion was agreed to, and at 12:43 P.M., the Senate, sitting as a Court of Impeachment, adjourned sine die.

when the Republicans did much worse than expected in the 1998 congressional elections. Gingrich suddenly resigned from Congress; yet his conservatism continues to have a palpable effect on lawmakers. After his first year in office, Clinton became much more of a centrist politician. He joined with Republicans and conservative Democrats to balance the federal budget and terminate the sixty-year-old federal program of aid to families with dependent children. Many heralded this reform as the end of welfare. More, in 1996 Clinton himself announced that "the era of big government is over."

The Impeachment Crisis

Even after his reelection by a wide margin, conservative Republicans continued to attack Clinton. An investigation led by Special Prosecutor Kenneth Starr scrutinized his financial, political, and personal dealings, as well as those of his wife Hillary Rodham Clinton. Republicans in the House of Representatives succeeded in impeaching him in December 1998 on charges of perjury and obstruction of justice. Clinton was only the second president ever impeached and the first in the twentieth century. He had lied about his sexual affair with White House intern Monica Lewinsky in court testimony concerning his alleged earlier sexual harassment of Arkansas government employee Paula Jones. The question ultimately boiled down to whether or not the offenses with which Clinton was charged were serious enough to justify ending his presidency. In the end, the Senate could not muster the two-thirds majority necessary to remove him from office.

Economic Prosperity and Globalization

Against this backdrop of scandal, President Clinton had presided over the longest period of economic prosperity in decades. The skyrocketing fortunes of high-tech companies such as Bill Gates's Microsoft buoyed an increasingly information-driven economy. Nonetheless, the social landscape of America was in many ways not terribly hopeful during the 1990s. Despite the boom in the economy, many worried about the decline of the middle class as the gulf between the rich and poor deepened. The expansion of economic ties between different countries, known as globalization, inspired large political protests based on anxieties about job loss and environmental degradation.

Racial Conflicts Intensify

During this period of prosperity, racial conflicts also became much more serious. The worst race riot in decades occurred in Los Angeles in 1992. Los Angeles policemen were videotaped beating an African-American motorist, Rodney King. The city erupted when a jury declared four white officers not guilty on all but one count of police brutality. Three days of rioting resulted in the deaths of fifty-three people and the destruction of five hundred buildings. Los Angeles was also the site of another racially charged spectacle: the trial of former football star O. J. Simpson for the alleged murder of his ex-wife Nicole Brown and her friend Ronald Goldman. Millions of televisions were turned to this "trial of the century," with blacks and whites often holding diametrically opposed viewpoints on the case.

Although O. J. Simpson's trial was compatible with a long tradition of American racial conflict and division, the bombing of the Oklahoma City federal building on April 19, 1995, was a new and horrifying development. The bombers, Timothy McVeigh and Terry Nichols, were former U.S. servicemen who had become seriously disenchanted with the bureaucracy of big government and its "oppression" of the average citizen. Their actions were influenced by racist and neo-Nazi propaganda, as well as motivated by revenge for the FBI's botched operation at Ruby Ridge. In total, 168 deaths resulted, a great many of them children trapped in a day-care center. The Oklahoma City bombing, along with a spate of deadly shootings by disaffected students at schools such as Columbine High School in Colorado, created a new fear of violence.

Multiculturalism and Its Discontents

Despite the advance of the worst forms of racism, the 1990s also was a decade when American racial diver-

Escorting of the Chief Justice...Censure Resolution. Mr. ASHCROFT. Mr. President, the debate we will be having in the Senate is on whether to suspend the rules of the Senate to consider a resolution censuring the President's conduct.

A motion will be made to indefinitely postpone the motion to suspend the rules. These votes will occur before Senators have the opportunity to amend the resolution censuring the President's conduct.

I take the floor of the Senate to make clear that I am opposed to a censure resolution of President Clinton.

The Impeachment Trial of President William Jefferson Clinton is over. The Senate has faithfully discharged its constitutional obligation by serving as impartial

America at Century's End: The Age of Bill Clinton and George W. Bush, 1993–2002 (continued)

sity flourished. Americans began to think of race as much less an issue of black and white, and much more a matter of a mosaic that additionally included Native Americans, Latinos, and Asian Americans. This diversity was often called multiculturalism, and it greatly influenced school curricula as well as television programs. However, not all agreed that multiculturalism, in its "politically correct" attempt to acknowledge the contributions of different groups to American politics and culture, was a good thing. Critics such as prominent historian Arthur M. Schlesinger, Jr., feared that emphasizing distinct cultures might lead to a "disuniting of America."

American Foreign Policy

At the end of the twentieth century, American foreign policy also entered a new era. How should the United States exercise its power in a post–cold war era? Conservatives such as Pat Buchanan argued that America should go it alone. This isolationist sentiment was widespread enough that President Clinton was extremely cautious about sending troops into foreign conflicts, even if they evolved into genocide as happened in Rwanda and the former Yugoslavia.

Election of 2000

Despite Bill Clinton's many problems, his vice president, Al Gore, entered the 2000 campaign season the clear presidential favorite. However, Republican nominee Gov. George W. Bush (the son of the 41st president) gradually narrowed Gore's lead in the polls. With populist Green Party candidate Ralph Nader also in the running, the race seemed to be a dead heat as voters went to their polling places. What followed was a remarkable 36-day drama to determine who the next president would be.

Gore won the popular vote, but in the election's immediate aftermath the winner of the majority of votes in the electoral college remained unclear. All eyes turned to the incredibly close race in Florida, where many voting irregularities had occurred and both candidates claimed victory, with the Democrats demanding a recount. Whoever won Florida would gain the votes necessary to put him over the top in the

jurors of the Articles of Impeachment approved by a bipartisan majority of the U.S. House of Representatives.

The Senate has rendered its verdict, and has found the President not guilty as charged. The consequence of this action by the Senate is to keep the President in office where he is to fully and faithfully discharge the constitutional duties of his office.

The trial is over. It is time for the Senate to focus on the national legislative agenda.

On this last point, I chose my words carefully. I did not say it is time for the Senate to turn to the people's business.

Some have said we should not have had the trial or should have adjourned the trial much earlier so that we could turn to the people's business.

I reject that notion. I firmly believe that conducting the trial was doing the people's business.

But the truth is the trial is over. I do not see any place for the pending resolution censuring the President. It is not the business of the Senate to punish President Clinton.

As Senator Byrd has concluded censure, unlike impeachment, is 'extra-constitutional.' The Constitution empowers the Senate to try a President impeached by the House and remove him if 67 Senators agree.

The Constitution does not empower the Senate to punish a President, in the absence of 67 votes to remove. The impeachment trial is over.

The Senate should move on and leave President Clinton alone.

The Constitution recognizes that if a President cannot be removed through impeachment, he should not be weakened by censure. Although the Senate passes sense of the Senate resolutions on many subjects, censure is different because the Constitution requires a 2/3 vote before the Senate can discipline the President and requires removal upon conviction for impeachable offenses. Censure is an effort to end-run these constitutional requirements.

One final problem is that any censure resolution will have to be weak. Even proponents of censure concede that a censure resolution that actually punished the President would be an unconstitutional bill of attainder. Any censure that is consistent with the Bill of Attainder Clause is too weak to be worth doing.

The highest form of censure the Constitution allows is impeachment by the House. The failure to convict the electoral college. For the first time in American history, the Supreme Court stepped in to decide the election after a number of legal maneuvers by both sides. By a 5-4 vote, the justices effectively declared Bush the winner in Florida and thus the next president.

A New Millenium of Terror

The 2000 election captivated Americans for weeks, inspiring contentious, and often creative, arguments about the nature of American democracy. A year later, though, few people spoke of the divisions caused by the election. Instead, Americans were united in their grief over the catastrophic events of September 11, 2001. That morning, Islamic terrorists associated with long-time American adversary Osama bin Laden hijacked four passenger planes full of explosive jet fuel. They flew the jets into the Pentagon and the twin towers of the World Trade Center. Passengers aboard the fourth plane apparently struggled with the hijackers, causing that plane to crash before it could reach its intended target—perhaps the White House in Washington, D.C. Thousands were killed in the deadliest terror attack ever on American soil, and a nation went into mourning.

In response, President Bush declared that he would eliminate the sources of terror. The United States, along with other staunch allies like Great Britain, invaded Afghanistan in order to topple the radical Islamic Taliban government that shielded and supported bin Laden and his Al Qaeda network. Expressions of fierce patriotism—flags, t-shirts, bumper stickers—returned to the United States in a way not seen in perhaps half a century. Whether such unity will continue now that American has entered the Age of Terror is, however, impossible to say.

BIBLIOGRAPHY

For insights into the politician who dominated the decade, see David Maraniss, *The First in His Class: The Biography of Bill Clinton* (1996); for information on his administration, see Bob Woodward, *The Agenda: Inside the Clinton White House* (1995). For contrasting perspectives on the historical deadlock in the presidential election, see Alan Dershowitz, *Supreme Injustice: How the High Court Hijacked Election 2000,* and Richard Posner, *Breaking the Deadlock: The 2000 Election, the Constitution, and the Courts* (2001). For a critical view of worldwide trends, see Benjamin R. Barber, *Jihad vs. McWorld: How Globalism and Tribalism are Re-Shaping the World* (1996).

President will not erase that action by the House. It is time for the Senate to move on.

SOURCE:
"Proceedings of the Impeachment Trial of President Bill Clinton," *Congressional Record,* February 12, 1999.

2000

INTERNATIONAL

Concorde flight AF4590 crashes in Gonesse, France, shortly after take-off from Charles DeGaulle Airport. All Concorde flights are subsequently grounded.

Six-year-old Elian Gonzalez arrives on the Florida coast after escaping from Cuba on a raft with his mother who died en route. This touches off a diplomatic controversy. Eventually the Justice Department orders the boy's return to his father in Cuba.

The Russian submarine *Kursk* sinks in the Arctic Ocean near Murmansk. Despite an international rescue effort, over 100 men die aboard the craft.

South Korean leader Kim Dae-Jung wins the Nobel Peace prize for his efforts at reconciliation with North Korea.

DEATHS Pierre Trudeau, Canadian Prime Minister; Ginetta Sagan, founder of Amnesty International.

NATIONAL

Election watchers worldwide are stunned when the U.S presidential election is called incorrectly by all major television stations. Only thirty-eight days after the election is the contest resolved and Democrat Al Gore is defeated by Republican George W. Bush. Ballot irregularities in Florida are at the heart of the controversy over which candidate won that state's electoral college votes. **SEE PRIMARY DOCUMENT** Remarks from the Candidates on the Presidential Election of 2000

The South Carolina state government comes under fire for flying the confederate flag on top of its state capitol. Many social justice groups encourage a boycott of South Carolina businesses.

The Bridgestone/Firestone Company and Ford recall 14.4 million tires because of safety concerns, many of which were on Ford Explorer SUVs.

Hispanic Population Rises in the 2000 Census

The 22nd Census, the largest survey of U.S. population trends ever conducted, continued to invite interpretation and discussion throughout 2000 and 2001. Of significance was the fact that the population of the U.S. had risen by a figure greater than that of the 1950s baby boom. Between 1990 and 2000 the total population of the U.S. jumped from 248.7 to 281.4 million, representing a 32.7 million increase. During the 1950s the population had grown by 28 million. A rising Hispanic population contributed to the demographic boom. Between 1990 and 2000 the total number of Spanish-speaking Americans (including those of Mexican, Puerto Rican, Cuban, and South and Central American descent) rose from 22.4 to 35.3 million, a gain of 57.9 percent. Geographically, more than three-quarters of the Hispanic population was found to live in the West and the South, with California and Texas topping the chart. The leap was partly explained by immigration and partly attributed to poor counting and unsuccessful outreach compromising prior surveys. Census Bureau forecasts meanwhile anticipated the population of the U.S. doubling by 2100 thanks to further immigration and improved life expectancy. Experts predicted that by the end of the century 571 million people would inhabit the country, with minority groups comprising 60 percent of that total. The Hispanic population was expected to number upwards of 190 million, while 5 million Americans would be over 100 years in age. The 2000 Census figures and projections attested to the growing ethnic and racial diversity of the U.S. at the beginning of the new millennium.

Almost 14,000 operators and technicians at Verizon go on strike, causing 25 million customers to experience delays in repairs, installation and operator service.

The American ship U.S.S. *Cole* is bombed by Islamic terrorists during a refueling stop in Aden, Yemen. Seventeen sailors are killed and thirty-nine more injured in the blast.

Missouri Governor and Senatorial candidate Mel Carnahan dies when his Cessna 335 crashes in Hillsboro, Missouri. His wife Jean runs for Senate in his place and wins.

DEATHS Carl Albert, Speaker of the House (1971–1977); Frank Willis, security guard who uncovered the Watergate break-in.

BUSINESS/INDUSTRY/INVENTIONS

The Y2K bug proves to be harmless. Almost no computers in the world experience trouble.

Intel buys many companies, especially in the telecom markets. Ziatech, for example, is purchased for $240 million in cash.

DEATH Mark Reynolds Hughes, founder of Herbalife.

SCIENCE/MEDICINE

A pair of 1.7-million-year-old fossil skulls are found in Asia offering a glimpse into the first species of human ancestors to exit Africa.

Sleep scientists find evidence suggesting that sleep contributes to certain types of memory formation.

Two rival groups, one public and one private, announce that each has read most of the 3 billion or so DNA subunits that spell out the human genome.

DEATHS Rene Favaloro, inventor of bypass surgery; David Brauer, executive director of the Sierra Club.

EDUCATION

The Supreme Court abolishes school-sanctioned, student-led prayers at high school football games in *Santa Fe Independent School District* v. *Doe.*

DEATHS Victor Serebriakoff, IQ test designer; Florynce Kennedy, lawyer and lecturer.

RELIGION

Pope John Paul II issues a historic apology for the sins of Roman Catholics throughout history, especially wrongs committed toward non-Catholics during the Inquisition.

The survivors and relatives of the Branch Davidians who died in the 1993 FBI assault on their Waco, Texas, compound sue the U.S. government for wrongful death and seek $675 million in damages.

ART/MUSIC

SONGS "Kryptonite" by Three Doors Down, "Natural Blues" by Moby, "Last Resort" by Papa Roach, and "It's My Life" by Bon Jovi.

New York City Mayor Rudolph Giuliani reveals to the media that he has prostate cancer at an April 27, 2000, press conference.
AP/WIDE WORLD PHOTOS

DEATHS Charles M. Schulz, *Peanuts* cartoonist; Edward Gorey, *Amphigorey* cartoonist; Tito Puente, mambo king; Frank Patterson, Irish tenor; Victor Borge, comedian/pianist; Jeff MacNelly, *Shoe* cartoonist.

LITERATURE/JOURNALISM

BOOKS *A Heartbreaking Work of Staggering Genius* by Dave Eggers, *In the Heart of the Sea* by Nathaniel Philbrick, *New Jack: Guarding Sing Sing* by Ted Conover, *Driving Mr. Albert* by Michael Paterniti, *Ghost Light* by Frank Rich.

DEATHS Judd Rose, CNN/ABC journalist; Gwendolyn Brooks, first African-American woman to win a Pulitzer Prize; Ring Lardner Jr., columnist; Barbara Cartland, romance novelist; Carl Rowan, columnist.

ENTERTAINMENT

The success of CBS series *Survivor* touches off a reality-TV craze. *Survivor,* won by Richard Hatch, becomes a national obsession.

MOVIES *Gladiator, Dancer in the Dark, Crouching Tiger, Hidden Dragon, Nurse Betty, Chicken Run, Wonder Boys.*

PLAYS *The Producers, The Invention of Love, The Play about the Baby, Proof, Urinetown.*

DEATHS Singers Kirsty MacColl, Screamin' Jay Hawkins, Johnnie Taylor, Vicky Sue Robinson; actors Douglas Fairbanks Jr., Walter Matthau, Sir Alec Guinness, Jason Robards, Jim Ernest Varney.

SPORTS

Tiger Woods wins three out of four major golf championships and earns nearly $10 million in prize money.

Football players Rae Carruth and Ray Lewis are tried for murder in separate cases: Carruth is convicted for his role in killing his pregnant girlfriend, and Lewis is acquitted of a Super Bowl weekend stabbing.

Indiana University fires legendary coach Bobby Knight.

Shortshop Alex Rodriguez signs a 10-year, $252 million contract with the Texas Rangers, the most lucrative deal in the history of professional sports.

The Summer Olympics are held in Sydney, Australia. Australian swimmer Ian Thorpe is the most popular athlete.

Future Hall of Fame football quarterbacks, Dan Marino of the Miami Dolphins and Steve Young of the San Francisco 49ers, retire.

WINNERS *Auto Racing*—Juan Montoya, Indianapolis 500; Dale Jarrett, Daytona 500; *Baseball*—New York

The controversial Confederate flag flies over the South Carolina State House before its removal in July, after an intense campaign waged by the NAACP; however, another version of the flag appears on the State Capitol's lawn. AP/WIDE WORLD PHOTOS

Yankees, World Series; *Basketball*—L.A. Lakers, NBA; Michigan State, NCAA (men); Connecticut, NCAA (women) *Bowling*—Mika Koivuniemi, ABC Masters; Jason Couch, Tournament of Champions; *Football*—Michigan, Orange Bowl; Wisconsin, Rose Bowl; Florida State, Sugar Bowl; Nebraska, Fiesta Bowl; St. Louis, Super Bowl XXXIV; *Golf*—Vijay Singh, Masters; Tiger Woods, British Open, U.S. Open, and PGA Championship; *Harness racing*—Yankee Paco, Hambletonian; *Hockey*—New Jersey, Stanley Cup; *Horse racing*—Fusaichi Pegasus, Kentucky Derby; Red Bullet, Preakness Stakes; Commendable, Belmont Stakes; *Tennis*—Marat Safin, U.S. Open (men); Pete Sampras, Wimbledon (men); Venus Williams, U.S. Open and Wimbledon (women).

DEATHS Derrick Thomas, football player; Malik Sealy and Bobby Phills, basketball players; Robert Trent Jones, Augusta National Golf Course designer.

PRIMARY SOURCE DOCUMENT

Remarks from the Candidates on the Presidential Election of 2000

INTRODUCTION On November 7, 2000, the American people went to the polls to vote for a new president: either Vice President Al Gore, the Democratic Party candidate, Gov. George W. Bush of Texas, the Republican Party candidate, or consumer activist Ralph Nader, the Green Party candidate. Over a month later, the victor was named after a contentious and controversial legal battle that was ultimately decided by the U.S. Supreme Court.

The drama began election night when an extraordinarily close race got even closer. Gore had won the important states of Illinois, Michigan, and Pennsylvania, whereas Bush claimed victory in Missouri, Ohio, and Gore's home state of Tennessee. Election results in Wisconsin, Iowa, New Mexico, and Oregon remained too close to call. In the end, however, it all came down to Florida. Whichever candidate won Florida's critical electoral votes would become the forty-third president of the United States.

Early reports showed Gore winning the state, but about 8:00 P.M. (EST) television analysts determined that the outcome was in doubt. Shortly after 2:00 A.M. the following morning, the networks declared Bush the winner. As a result, Gore conceded the election in a phone call to Bush. Incredibly, an hour later Gore retracted his concession in a second phone call to Bush after learning that Bush's lead in Florida had shrunk considerably. And by 4:15 A.M. the networks had retracted their prediction of a Bush victory. Florida state election law called for an automatic recount in the event of a close vote, and it was this recount that would delay the outcome of the election and keep the nation on edge for over a month.

The presidential election, normally the domain of the American people, became a legal matter, a contest between two well-financed and highly partisan legal dream teams. The controversy in Florida rested on the mechanics of Florida voting procedures. Confusion over the punch cards commonly used throughout Florida led a number of voters, especially in traditionally democratic Palm Beach County, to complain that their votes intended for Gore went to another candidate by mistake. Complicating matters, African Americans in some parts of Florida charged that they were denied rightful access to the polls.

As several Florida counties conducted manual recounts of the paper ballots, Bush lawyers filed suit to stop these recounts, an action ordered by Florida's secretary of state, Katharine Harris. Democrats charged that Harris's actions were politically motivated since she was an appointee of Gov. Jeb Bush, George W. Bush's brother. On November 21, the Florida Supreme Court, over Harris's objections, ordered the hand counts to proceed. On December 8, after several lawsuits and countersuits, the court again ordered manual recounts in several Florida counties to resume.

The status of these recounts ultimately reached the U.S. Supreme Court after Bush's legal team sought an injunction against further vote counts. On December 9, the Supreme Court ruled, in a 5-4 decision, that the manual recounts should cease until a hearing could be held to consider arguments by both Gore's and Bush's lawyers. On December 11, Bush's lawyers contended that the Florida Supreme Court had no constitutional authority to order a manual recount, whereas Gore's lawyers argued that the U.S. Supreme Court had no jurisdictional authority to intervene in a state election. Siding with the Bush campaign, the U.S. Supreme Court declared the Florida Supreme Court's action unconstitutional. Bush's victory in Florida was sealed. The nation then waited for Gore's next action. Would he challenge the Supreme Court ruling? Would he find some other way to continue his determined fight for the presidency? Or would he concede the election to Bush and help to unite a divided nation? The documents below contain Gore's and Bush's responses to the momentous Supreme Court decision.

Jean Carnahan, the widow of U.S. Senator Mel Carnahan, who died in an October 2000 plane crash, greets the media in Missouri on November 9, 2000, after filling his Senate seat. AP/WIDE WORLD PHOTOS

Remarks of Al Gore

Good evening.

Just moments ago, I spoke with George W. Bush and congratulated him on becoming the 43rd president of the United States.

And I promised him that I wouldn't call him back this time.

I offered to meet with him as soon as possible so that we can start to heal the divisions of the campaign and the contest through which we just passed.

Almost a century and a half ago, Senator Stephen Douglas told Abraham Lincoln, who had just defeated him for the presidency, "Partisan feeling must yield to patriotism. I'm with you, Mr. President, and God bless you."

In that same spirit, I say to President-elect Bush that what remains of partisan rancor must now be put aside, and may God bless his stewardship of this country.

Neither he nor I anticipated this long and difficult road. Certainly neither of us wanted it to happen. Yet it came, and now it has ended, resolved, as it must be resolved, through the honored institutions of our democracy.

Over the library of one of our great law schools is inscribed the motto, "Not under man but under God and law." That's the ruling principle of American freedom, the source of our democratic liberties. I've tried to make it my guide throughout this contest as it has guided America's deliberations of all the complex issues of the past five weeks.

Now the U.S. Supreme Court has spoken. Let there be no doubt, while I strongly disagree with the court's decision, I accept it. I accept the finality of this outcome which will be ratified next Monday in the Electoral College. And tonight, for the sake of our unity of the people and the strength of our democracy, I offer my concession.

I also accept my responsibility, which I will discharge unconditionally, to honor the new president elect and do everything possible to help him bring Americans together in fulfillment of the great vision that our Declaration of Independence defines and that our Constitution affirms and defends.

Let me say how grateful I am to all those who supported me and supported the cause for which we have fought.

Tipper and I feel a deep gratitude to Joe and Hadassah Lieberman [Joseph Lieberman, U.S. Senator from Connecticut, was Gore's running mate] who brought passion and high purpose to our partnership and opened new doors, not just for our campaign but for our country.

Sarah Gauna, right, mourns with her family at the graveside service for her son Timothy in Ennis, Texas, on October 25, 2000. Gauna was one of seventeen U.S. sailors killed on the USS *Cole* after it is attacked in Yemen on October 12. **AP/WIDE WORLD PHOTOS**

This has been an extraordinary election. But in one of God's unforeseen paths, this belatedly broken impasse can point us all to a new common ground, for its very closeness can serve to remind us that we are one people with a shared history and a shared destiny.

Indeed, that history gives us many examples of contests as hotly debated, as fiercely fought, with their own challenges to the popular will.

Other disputes have dragged on for weeks before reaching resolution. And each time, both the victor and the vanquished have accepted the result peacefully and in the spirit of reconciliation.

So let it be with us.

I know that many of my supporters are disappointed. I am too. But our disappointment must be overcome by our love of country.

And I say to our fellow members of the world community, let no one see this contest as a sign of American weakness. The strength of American democracy is shown most clearly through the difficulties it can overcome.

Some have expressed concern that the unusual nature of this election might hamper the next president in the conduct of his office. I do not believe it need be so.

President-elect Bush inherits a nation whose citizens will be ready to assist him in the conduct of his large responsibilities. I personally will be at his disposal.

And I call on all Americans—I particularly urge all who stood with us to unite behind our next president.

This is America. Just as we fight hard when the stakes are high, we close ranks and come together when the contest is done.

And while there will be time enough to debate our continuing differences, now is the time to recognize that that which unites us is greater than that which divides us.

While we yet hold and do not yield our opposing beliefs, there is a higher duty than the one we owe to political party.

This is America and we put country before party. We will stand together behind our new president.

As for what I'll do next, I don't know the answer to that one yet. Like many of you, I'm looking forward to spending the holidays with family and old friends.

I know I'll spend time in Tennessee and mend some fences, literally and figuratively.

Some have asked whether I have any regrets and I do have one regret: that I didn't get the chance to stay and fight for the American people over the next four years, especially for those who need burdens lifted and barriers removed, especially for those who feel their voices have not been heard.

I heard you—and I will not forget.

I've seen America in this campaign and I like what I see. It's worth fighting for and that's a fight I'll never stop.

As for the battle that ends tonight, I do believe as my father once said, that no matter how hard the loss, defeat might serve as well as victory to shape the soul and let the glory out.

So for me this campaign ends as it began: with the love of Tipper and our family; with faith in God and in the country I have been so proud to serve, from Vietnam to the vice presidency; and with gratitude to our truly tireless campaign staff and volunteers, including all those who worked so hard in Florida for the last 36 days.

Now the political struggle is over and we turn again to the unending struggle for the common good of all Americans and for those multitudes around the world who look to us for leadership in the cause of freedom.

In the words of our great hymn, "America, America": "Let us crown thy good with brotherhood, from sea to shining sea."

And now, my friends, in a phrase I once addressed to others, it's time for me to go.

Thank you and good night, and God bless America.

SOURCE: Text from website of former White House administration, available at http://clinton4.nara.gov/textonly/WH/EOP/OVP/speeches/election.html.

Remarks of George W. Bush

...Thank you very much. Good evening, my fellow Americans. I appreciate so very much the opportunity to speak with you tonight.

Mr. Speaker, Lieutenant Governor, friends, distinguished guests, our country has been through a long and trying period, with the outcome of the presidential election not finalized for longer than any of us could ever imagine.

Vice President Gore and I put our hearts and hopes into our campaigns. We both gave it our all. We shared similar emotions, so I understand how difficult this moment must be for Vice President Gore and his family.

He has a distinguished record of service to our country as a congressman, a senator and a vice president.

This evening I received a gracious call from the vice president. We agreed to meet early next week in Washington and we agreed to do our best to heal our country after this hard-fought contest.

Six-year-old Elian Gonzalez plays outside his Miami relatives' home. Department of Justice officials later return him home to Cuba to live with his father, creating an uproar in Miami's Cuban-American community. **AP/WIDE WORLD PHOTOS**

Tonight I want to thank all the thousands of volunteers and campaign workers who worked so hard on my behalf.

I also salute the vice president and his supports for waging a spirited campaign. And I thank him for a call that I know was difficult to make. Laura and I wish the vice president and Senator Lieberman and their families the very best.

I have a lot to be thankful for tonight. I'm thankful for America and thankful that we were able to resolve our electoral differences in a peaceful way.

I'm thankful to the American people for the great privilege of being able to serve as your next president.

I want to thank my wife and our daughters for their love. Laura's active involvement as first lady has made Texas a better place, and she will be a wonderful first lady of America.

(APPLAUSE)

I am proud to have Dick Cheney by my side, and America will be proud to have him as our next vice president.

(APPLAUSE)

President-elect George W. Bush meets with Vice President Al Gore at Gore's official residence in Washington, December 19, 2000, after a bitter election battle that is decided by the Supreme Court. AP/WIDE WORLD PHOTOS

Tonight I chose to speak from the chamber of the Texas House of Representatives because it has been a home to bipartisan cooperation. Here in a place where Democrats have the majority, Republicans and Democrats have worked together to do what is right for the people we represent.

We've had spirited disagreements. And in the end, we found constructive consensus. It is an experience I will always carry with me, an example I will always follow.

I want to thank my friend, House Speaker Pete Laney, a Democrat, who introduced me today. I want to thank the legislators from both political parties with whom I've worked.

Across the hall in our Texas capitol is the state Senate. And I cannot help but think of our mutual friend, the former Democrat lieutenant governor, Bob Bullock. His love for Texas and his ability to work in a bipartisan way continue to be a model for all of us.

(APPLAUSE)

The spirit of cooperation I have seen in this hall is what is needed in Washington, D.C. It is the challenge of our moment. After a difficult election, we must put politics behind us and work together to make the promise of America available for every one of our citizens.

I am optimistic that we can change the tone in Washington, D.C.

I believe things happen for a reason, and I hope the long wait of the last five weeks will heighten a desire to move beyond the bitterness and partisanship of the recent past.

Our nation must rise above a house divided. Americans share hopes and goals and values far more important than any political disagreements.

Republicans want the best for our nation, and so do Democrats. Our votes may differ, but not our hopes.

I know America wants reconciliation and unity. I know Americans want progress. And we must seize this moment and deliver.

Together, guided by a spirit of common sense, common courtesy and common goals, we can unite and inspire the American citizens.

Together we will work to make all our public schools excellent, teaching every student of every background and every accent, so that no child is left behind.

Together we will save Social Security and renew its promise of a secure retirement for generations to come.

Together we will strengthen Medicare and offer prescription drug coverage to all of our seniors.

Together we will give Americans the broad, fair and fiscally responsible tax relief they deserve.

Together we'll have a bipartisan foreign policy true to our values and true to our friends, and we will have a military equal to every challenge and superior to every adversary.

Together we will address some of society's deepest problems one person at a time, by encouraging and empowering the good hearts and good works of the American people.

This is the essence of compassionate conservatism and it will be a foundation of my administration.

These priorities are not merely Republican concerns or Democratic concerns; they are American responsibilities.

During the fall campaign, we differed about the details of these proposals, but there was remarkable consensus about the important issues before us: excellent schools, retirement and health security, tax relief, a strong military, a more civil society.

We have discussed our differences. Now it is time to find common ground and build consensus to make America a beacon of opportunity in the 21st century.

I'm optimistic this can happen. Our future demands it and our history proves it. Two hundred years ago, in the election of 1800, America faced another close presidential election. A tie in the Electoral College put the outcome into the hands of Congress.

After six days of voting and 36 ballots, the House of Representatives elected Thomas Jefferson the third president of the United States. That election brought the first transfer of power from one party to another in our new democracy.

Shortly after the election, Jefferson, in a letter titled "Reconciliation and Reform," wrote this: "The steady character of our countrymen is a rock to which we may safely moor; unequivocal in principle, reasonable in manner. We should be able to hope to do a great deal of good to the cause of freedom and harmony."

Two hundred years have only strengthened the steady character of America. And so as we begin the work of healing our nation, tonight I call upon that character: respect for each other, respect for our differences, generosity of spirit, and a willingness to work hard and work together to solve any problem.

I have something else to ask you, to ask every American. I ask for you to pray for this great nation. I ask for your prayers for leaders from both parties. I thank you for your prayers for me and my family, and I ask you to pray for Vice President Gore and his family.

Jesse Jackson attends church with his wife Jackie in January 2000, his first public appearance following the disclosure an affair that resulted in a child born out of wedlock. © AFP/ CORBIS-BETTMANN

I have faith that with God's help we as a nation will move forward together as one nation, indivisible. And together we will create an America that is open, so every citizen has access to the American dream; an America that is educated, so every child has the keys to realize that dream; and an America that is united in our diversity and our shared American values that are larger than race or party.

I was not elected to serve one party, but to serve one nation.

The president of the United States is the president of every single American, of every race and every background.

Whether you voted for me or not, I will do my best to serve your interests and I will work to earn your respect.

I will be guided by President Jefferson's sense of purpose, to stand for principle, to be reasonable in manner, and above all, to do great good for the cause of freedom and harmony.

The presidency is more than an honor. It is more than an office. It is a charge to keep, and I will give it my all.

Thank you very much and God bless America.

(APPLAUSE)

Chinese official Chen Ci discusses the negotiations over twenty-four soon-to-be released U.S. crewmen, who have made an emergency landing on Chinese soil after a mid-air collision that kills a Chinese fighter pilot in Haikou, China. AP/WIDE WORLD PHOTOS

2001

INTERNATIONAL

Crown Prince Dipendra of Nepal, massacres the country's entire royal family. Those killed include his mother, Queen Aiswarya; his father, King Birendra; his sister, Princess Shruti; and brother, Prince Nirajan, leaving the tiny Himalayan nation in shock.

The Nationalist Party is defeated for the first time in a Taiwanese national election.

New Labour's Tony Blair easily wins reelection as British Prime Minister over William Hague.

A U.S. jet collides with a Chinese fighter near Hainan Island off the Chinese coast. In one of his first actions as Secretary of State, Colin Powell eases the U.S. out of a tenuous diplomatic situation.

London-born Richard Reid attempts to light explosives in his shoes on a transatlantic flight. Reid is later found to have ties to the Al-Qaeda terrorist organization.

DEATHS Leopold Senghor, first president of Senegal; Nguyen Van Thieu, president of South Vietnam (1967–1975); King Birendra, Nepalese monarch.

NATIONAL

America comes under terrorist attack when two hijacked planes fly into the towers of the World Trade Center in New York, one hits the Pentagon, and another crashes in Shanksville, Pennsylvania. Over 3,300 Americans die and life in New York City comes to a standstill as its residents, led by Mayor Rudolph Giuliani, cope with the aftermath of the attack. Firemen and policemen in New York and Washington perform heroic deeds in saving thousands of lives. Sixty countries join the U.S. and Britain in a coalition against worldwide terrorism, including the Al Qaeda network. **SEE PRIMARY DOCUMENTS** Eyewitness Accounts of the Attacks on the World Trade Center and Transcript of Osama Bin Laden Videotape

The coalition led by the U.S. starts bombing Afghanistan, but after 100 days Osama bin Laden, leader of Al Qaeda, is still nowhere to be found.

In the wake of September 11, tighter airport security measures are passed, resulting in delays at many airports.

Anthrax turns up in the U.S. mail system, killing postal workers in New York, a journalist in Florida, and an elderly Connecticut woman. Letters sent to congressmen contain the disease.

George W. Bush, the son of the 41st President George H.W. Bush, assumes office in January despite losing the popular vote.

After several stays, Timothy McVeigh, the convicted bomber of the Alfred P. Murrah Federal Building in Oklahoma City, is executed in Terra Haute, Indiana, by lethal injection.

President Bush authorizes a rebate of $300 dollars ($600 for families) for every American taxpayer.

The economy is officially in recession and Alan Greenspan and the Federal Reserve drop interest rates at a record pace.

BUSINESS/INDUSTRY/INVENTIONS

The AbioCor artificial heart, a softball-sized, self-contained mechanical heart is implanted in 59-year-old Robert Tools in Louisville, Kentucky. Tools lives for eleven days with the new heart before dying.

Following September 11, the White House approves $5 billion in federal aid for major airline carriers. The industry is estimated to have lost $10 billion in the weeks following the attack.

The Millenium Bridge, which is able to pivot to one side to avoid approaching ships, is built by Wilkinson Eyre Architects to connect Gateshead and Newcastle, England.

An energy crisis puts Pacific Gas & Electric into bankruptcy and results in rolling blackouts in California. Utilities report billions in losses.

DEATH Isao Okawa, CEO of Sega Corporation.

TRANSPORTATION

Security at airports in the U.S. and the world increases dramatically in the wake of the September 11 attacks.

Congress considers legislation that would restrict the visas for international students and crack down on foreign nationals in America.

SCIENCE/MEDICINE

Advanced Cellular Technologies succeed in cloning an early human embryo from an adult cumulus cell nucleus, leading to a variety of legal and moral debates.

The debate over the usage of stem cells for scientific purposes rages in Congress. President Bush eventually creates a compromise solution where only existing cell lines could be used.

A Chinese farmer in Liaoning finds a strange dragon-like fossil called caudipteryx that scientists say helps link dinosaurs with birds.

Researchers uncover the fossil remains of an early hominid called *Ardipithecus,* which at 4.4 million years old is the oldest human ancestor found to date.

DEATHS Sir Fred Hoyle, astrophysicist who coined the term "Big Bang"; Dr. Robert Kerr, athletic trainer who encouraged steroid use; Christiaan Barnard, pioneering heart surgeon.

EDUCATION

President Bush signs the *No Child Left Behind Act of 2001* enacting sweeping reforms to help minority and disadvantaged students close the achievement gap.

RELIGION

The Reverend Jesse Jackson admits to having fathered an illegitimate child with a Rainbow Coalition staffer. Jackson apologizes and says he will step out of the public eye to spend time with his family.

The Prayer of Jabez, a book about a little-known biblical prayer by Atlanta Rev. Bruce Wilkinson, becomes a surprise best-seller.

ART/MUSIC

SONGS "Short Skirt/Long Jacket" by Cake, "Everyday" by Dave Matthews Band, "Island in the Sun" by Weezer, and "Peaceful World" by John Mellencamp.

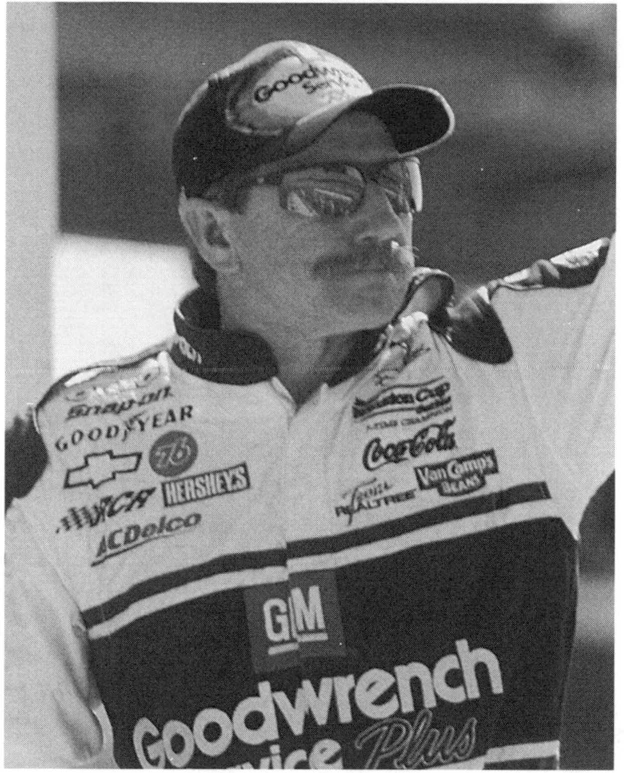

The immensely popular Dale Earnhardt waves to fans before the start of the Daytona 500 on February 18, 2001. He dies in a crash during the race, saddening the world of NASCAR racing.
AP/WIDE WORLD PHOTOS

DEATHS George Harrison, Beatle; Imogene Coca, comedienne; Jack Haley Jr., producer; Balthus, French painter; Louis Faurer, photographer.

LITERATURE/JOURNALISM

A federal judge commutes the death sentence of former Black Panther and journalist Mumia Abu-Jamal, who had become a cause célèbre of the anti-death penalty movement while in prison in Pennsylvania.

Billy Collins is named poet laureate of the United States. Collins is known for his humorous, contemplative works.

BOOKS *John Adams* by David McCullough, *Harry Potter and the Goblet of Fire* by J.K. Rowling, *A Painted House* by John Grisham, *The Bonesetter's Daughter* by Amy Tan.

DEATHS Mordecai Richler, Canadian author; James Parton, publisher; Anne Morrow Lindbergh, author and wife of aviator Charles Lindbergh; Douglas Adams, author of *Hitchhiker's Guide to the Galaxy;* R.K. Narayan, Indian author.

ENTERTAINMENT

MOVIES *Moulin Rouge, Gosford Park, Amélie, Lord of the*

Michael Jordan returns to the court to play for the Washington Wizards. His competitive fire and mature leadership help the Wizards improve, but not enough to return them to the playoffs. AP/WIDE WORLD PHOTOS

Rings: Fellowship of the Ring, In the Bedroom, and *A Beautiful Mind.*

PLAYS *The Producers, Metamorphoses, The Glory of Living,* and *Topdog/Underdog.*

DEATHS Gunther Gebel-Williams, lion tamer; actors Jack Lemmon, Anthony Quinn, and Carroll O'Connor; Aaliyah Haughton, singer and actor.

SPORTS

The Arizona Diamondbacks defeat the defending champions the New York Yankees. Arizona wins a title faster than any other expansion team, doing it in just four years.

Veteran outfielder Barry Bonds hits seventy-three home runs for the San Francisco Giants, breaking Mark McGwire's record of seventy.

With his win at the Masters, Tiger Woods holds all four major titles at once, the first golfer in over fifty years to do so.

Dale Earnhardt, one of NASCAR's most successful and charismatic drivers, dies in a fiery crash at the Daytona 500.

College and professional football teams come under fire for their practice methods after Minnesota Vikings lineman Korey Stringer and Northwestern defensive back Rashidi Wheeler die from heat stroke.

Beijing is named as the site for the 2008 summer Olympic Games, marking the first time that the Olympics will be held in China.

WINNERS *Auto Racing*—Helio Castroneves, Indianapolis 500; Michael Waltrip, Daytona 500; *Baseball*— Arizona, World Series; *Basketball*—L.A. Lakers, NBA; Duke, NCAA (men); Notre Dame, NCAA (women) *Bowling*—Parker Bohn III, ABC Masters; Walter Ray Williams Jr., PBA National; *Football*—Oklahoma, Orange Bowl; Washington, Rose Bowl; Miami, Sugar Bowl; Oregon State, Fiesta Bowl; Baltimore, Super Bowl XXXV; *Golf*—Tiger Woods, Masters; David Duval, British Open; Retief Goosen, U.S. Open; David Toms, PGA Championship; *Harness racing*— Scarlet Knight, Hambletonian; *Hockey*—Colorado, Stanley Cup; *Horse racing*—Monarchos, Kentucky Derby; Point Given, Preakness Stakes and Belmont Stakes; *Tennis*—Lleyton Hewitt, U.S. Open (men); Goran Ivanisevic, Wimbeldon (men); Venus Williams, U.S. Open and Wimbeldon (women).

DEATHS Earl Anthony, champion bowler; Affirmed, Triple Crown Winner; Dale Earnhardt, NASCAR driver; Charley Pell, football coach; Tommie Agee, baseball player; Eddie Matthews, baseball player; Al McGuire, basketball coach.

PRIMARY SOURCE DOCUMENT

Eyewitness Accounts of the Attacks on the World Trade Center, September 11, 2001

INTRODUCTION There are a thousand stories to be told about September 11, 2001, that brilliantly sunny morning that will truly live in infamy. In three hijacked passenger airplanes, terrorists attacked symbols of American pride and power: the World Trade Center in New York City and the Pentagon in Washington, D.C. September 11 began like any other day. Countless men and women were en route to their offices; others were already at their desks hard at work. But the world changed forever at 8:46 A.M. when American Airlines Flight 11 from Boston crashed into the north tower of the World Trade Center. Early reports suggested that the crash might be an accident. At 9:06 A.M. United Airlines Flight 175, which had originated in Boston, flew into the south tower of the World Trade Center. These events were not an accident but a carefully planned attack, mounted by radical Muslim terrorists connected to the Al-Qaeda network and associated with Osama bin Laden, a wealthy Saudi Arabian exile. The scope of the attack widened shortly after the World Trade Center towers were hit. At 9:40 A.M. American Airlines Flight 77, hijacked from nearby Dulles Airport, slammed into the Pentagon, the nerve center of America's military. If not for the heroism of the men and women on United Airlines Flight 93, which soon crashed in rural Pennsylvania before it could reach its intended unknown target, the impact of the attack might have been even more horrific.

The towers of the World Trade Center in New York City are struck by hijacked planes on September 11. Several thousand people of many different nationalities die in the attack. ©GULNARA SAMOILOVA/ AP/WIDE WORLD PHOTOS

The magnitude of the event, its death toll, and the ensuing human tragedy widened considerably when both towers of the World Trade Center collapsed: the south tower at 10:00 A.M., the north tower at 10:29 A.M. After the hijacked planes crashed into the towers, emergency crews throughout New York City and its surrounding areas sprung into action, streaming into the burning buildings to rescue the injured or trapped. Hundreds of firefighters, police, and medical personnel were killed along with several thousand World Trade Center workers. As the towers fell, alternating shock and confusion, horror and grief consumed the Manhattan streets below. It is this spectrum of emotions that reporters from *U.S. News and World Report* capture in dramatic fashion.

"A Smoky Sprint to Safety and 'Flesh in the Street'" by Lisa Stein

As usual, I was running late. I'd missed the 8:30 a.m. shuttle to Washington and was rushing to catch the 9:30. At about 8:45, I heard a thunderous explosion. I looked out the window of my 27th-floor hotel room and saw enormous shards of concrete, streaming, screaming to the ground from the World Trade Center. Flames and smoke spewed from the building. I instantly thought it was a terrorist attack.

I heard another explosion. Then I began to run for my life. I sprinted down 27 flights of stairs, in an eerily quiet stairwell, my heart pounding. The lobby teemed with people, some injured, some seeking shelter, others, like me, preparing to flee. Hotel workers dutifully passed out orange juice and bottles of water. Dana Wanamaker, 45, was in the lobby, her blouse blood-splattered, a bandage above her eye. "I saw somebody's hand and foot," she said. "There was flesh in the street."

My hotel was just three blocks from the World Trade Center, and the view of the orange-red flames shooting from the building was vivid and haunting. As I left the hotel, police ordered everyone to head south toward Battery Park so that rescue squads could reach the scene. Fire trucks, police cars, and ambulances filled the streets, their sirens piercing the air. Strangers comforted each other.

"I will not leave."

Some stopped to watch the Trade Center burn. It was sickening. I knew that the people in there could never get out, and I couldn't see any way firefighters could reach the blaze. Police pleaded with one woman in her parked Jeep to leave the area. "There are people in there I know," she said. "There are people in there I love. I will not leave. My heart is in that building."

Others who had escaped mutely watched the rescue efforts. James Cutler, 31, said he was in a ground-level restaurant in the towers. "It was like three consecutive booms-boom, boom, boom." He thought it was a kitchen fire. Then the restaurant doors blew open. Soon the room was engulfed in smoke and ash. "And the ceiling fell in." Suddenly, the damage became apparent, and the human tragedy. "I'm a Gulf War veteran, and I've never seen anything like this," Cutler said. "It was total mayhem."

As we talked at the intersection of West Street and Battery Place, one of the towers collapsed. All hell broke loose. The air filled with thick smoke and ash. Emergency crews screamed at us to leave. There was a new sense of danger and panic. People rushed to get to the tip of Manhattan. Some people screamed for people to run. Others appealed for calm.

I decided to remain calm and run. But the smoke was moving so fast I could barely breathe or see. I thought we were going to choke to death. Everyone was drenched in soot and smoke. People covered their faces with their shirts or anything they could find to keep from inhaling ash and smoke.

I knew we could run only so far until we would have nowhere to go but the Hudson River. I was enveloped in a cloud of smoke and ash. We reached a restaurant, American Park at the Battery. People were banging on the glass doors, but they were locked. We were trapped. And the smoke kept coming. It was a typically eclectic New York crowd. There were people with babies and pets, stockbrokers in suits. All covered in soot. The straps of my sandals broke as I ran, so I ditched them and went barefoot.

Desperation

People screamed to be let in the restaurant. One man told everyone to step back and he smashed the glass with a hammer. I helped push the glass out, and people poured into the restaurant. Eventually, the manager opened the doors and let people in. He was contrite, and like all of us, didn't really know what to do. It must have been the only restaurant for blocks without a TV, so we didn't really know what was going on.

Minutes later, another part of the Trade Center collapsed, and more people ran toward Battery Park. About an hour later, a New York Waterway ferry began shuttling those of us in the restaurant across the Hudson to Jersey City. Police said we had to leave. There was no way to go back into the city.

It was sad chugging across the Hudson, watching the plumes of black smoke where the magnificent twin towers used to be. The Statue of Liberty was framed in a blue sky. It was the bluest sky I've ever seen.

SOURCE: Lisa Stein, "Eyewitness to Terror: A Smoky Sprint to Safety and 'Flesh in the Street'," *U.S. News and World Report* Special Report, September 14, 2001.

"A Ghastly Sight"

From the passenger seat of a taxi I heard the cabbie curse. Alarmed, I looked out the window—just in time to see the plane hit the north tower. We were heading south on the West Side Highway, back to my hotel at the World Trade Center plaza. Minutes later, ambulances and squad cars were screaming down the highway past us. My reporter's instincts took over, and I told the driver to follow them.

Below the towers, thousands watched as debris tumbled from the building. Paper cascaded from windows; some onlookers speculated that it was office workers trying to alert rescuers. Trapped workers were falling from the building, a ghastly sight as the bodies cartwheeled to earth like rag dolls. Some of the spectators said they saw pieces of flesh flying through the air. One man leapt from a horrible height to certain death. The man beside me said, "That's the ninth I've seen." Watching the flames licking the tower's facade, I couldn't imagine the choice: Jump or burn to death.

Anywhere Else

The crowd's thoughts turned to terrorism. President Bush will react soon, someone said in the crowd. Another: "He'd better." Floor traders from the New York Mercantile Exchange tried to fetch their belongings. Office workers tried to get a water shuttle home to New Jersey.

And then, the second explosion. It transformed what had been a scene of disaster into mass panic. Parents with strollers, hotel maids in uniforms, Wall Street workers in dress shoes and heels—all began to flee, going somewhere, anywhere.

The cops were shouting: Leave now! Hugging the shore of the Hudson River, I lingered. Then a second boom, and a third. I gave up on the idea of getting close to the action and joined the throngs streaming north. I had gone only about 200 yards when someone said the unthinkable: "One of the towers is gone." A man told me to stay near walls. Looking up at the north tower, the one still standing, I imagined a nightmarish scenario: A collapsing building could kill me and the others in an instant.

A bit farther north, near the Chelsea Piers entertainment complex, volunteers were handing out cups of water. Cellphones were of no use; pay phones were jammed. New Yorkers turned friendly, offering advice and directions. Then, suddenly, the second tower started to fall. I watched, horrified. The tower collapsed in on itself, leaving just the exterior shell. Seconds later, that, too, fell in.

People reacted in weirdly different ways. At 33rd Street and 10th Avenue, a man held up an American flag, inviting hornblowing. Four blocks away, a young man sat on a fire hydrant and stopped to read Scripture. Then I realized my family and friends were also viewing the carnage—on TV. They knew I was staying at a hotel next to the towers. I had left one panicked voice-mail message for my wife just after the crash. Otherwise they had no idea where I was, or whether I was alive. When I made contact, the tears flowed. My wife, beside herself, demanded I return home. My mother's voice quaked. My boss told me she thought I was dead. Their reactions gave me just a small dose of the sorrow felt by the families of those who perished. Grateful to be alive, I spent the rest of the day in a haze, breathing deeply.

SOURCE: Noam Neusner, "Eyewitness to Terror: 'A Ghastly Sight,'" *U.S. News and World Report* Special Report, September 14, 2001.

PRIMARY SOURCE DOCUMENT

Transcript of Osama Bin Laden Videotape

INTRODUCTION After terrorist attacks on New York City and Washington, D.C., on September 11, 2001, the United States, in conjunction with several of its staunchest allies and the Northern Alliance (Afghani forces opposed to the ruling Taliban government), began searching for Osama bin Laden and other leaders of the Al Qaeda terrorist network believed to be responsible for planning and conducting the attacks. U.S. armed forces operating in Afghanistan acquired huge quantities of weapons, computer data, and intelligence gleaned from captured terrorists. Although they did not find bin Laden, they did confiscate a videotape that provided evidence of his role in the attacks. In a December 13, 2001, Defense Department news release, Secretary of Defense Donald H. Rumsfeld said, "There was no doubt of bin Laden's responsibility for the September 11 attacks before the tape was discovered." But the videotape, reportedly taken from a private home in Jalalabad, Afghanistan, in late November was released, according to the Defense Department, because of "the value of having the world fully appreciate what we are up against in the war against terrorism."

The video was likely shot in mid-November weeks after the terrorist attacks. It features Osama bin Laden visiting with a Saudi Arabian sheik ("Shaykh" in the transcript); at least two other men are also present. Bin Laden inquires about reaction to the attacks elsewhere in the Arab world and celebrates the extent of the damage. In several passages bin Laden openly speaks of his knowledge of the operation and his role in planning it. He noted that "due to my experience in this field, I was thinking that the fire from the gas in the plane would melt the iron structure of the building and collapse the area where the plane hit and all the floors above it only. This is all that we had hoped for." Speaking of the "martyrs" who carried out the attacks, he said, "But they were trained and we did not reveal the operation to them until they are there and just before they boarded the planes."

The following transcript of the videotape was issued by the U.S. Department of Defense. The document includes introductory remarks included in the Defense Department report. [Note: Although most Americans are familiar with the name Osama bin Laden, the Defense Department spells it Usama bin Laden, abbreviated as UBL in the transcript.]

December 13, 2001

(Transcript and annotations independently prepared by George Michael, translator, Diplomatic Language Services; and Dr. Kassem M. Wahba, Arabic language program coordinator, School of Advanced International Studies, Johns Hopkins University. They collaborated on their translation and compared it with translations done by the U.S. government for consistency. There were no inconsistencies in the translations.)

In mid-November, Usama Bin Laden spoke to a room of supporters, possibly in Qandahar, Afghanistan. These comments were video taped with the knowledge of Bin Laden and all present.

Note: The tape is approximately one hour long and contains three different segments: an original taping of a visit by some people to the site of the downed U.S. helicopter in Ghazni province (approximately 12 minutes long); and two segments documenting a courtesy visit by Bin Laden and his lieutenants to an unidentified Shaykh, who appears crippled from the waist down. The visit apparently takes place at a guesthouse in Qandahar. The sequence of the events is reversed on the tape—the end of his visit is in the beginning of the tape with the helicopter site visit in the middle and the start of the Usama bin Laden visit beginning approximately 39 minutes into the tape. The tape is transcribed below according to the proper sequence of events.

Due to the quality of the original tape, it is *not* a verbatim transcript of every word spoken during the meeting, but does convey the messages and information flow.

EDITOR'S NOTE: 39 minutes into tape, first segment of the bin Laden meeting, begins after footage of helicopter site visit.

Shaykh: (...inaudible...) You have given us weapons, you have given us hope and we thank Allah for you. We don't want to take much of your time, but this is the arrangement of the brothers. People now are supporting

People line up in the Russell Senate Office Building to be tested for exposure to anthrax on October 17, 2001, after several dozen people test positive for exposure to it in Sen. Tom Daschle's office. AP/WIDE WORLD PHOTOS

us more, even those ones who did not support us in the past, support us more now. I did not want to take that much of your time. We praise Allah, we praise Allah. We came from Kabul. We were very pleased to visit. May Allah bless you both at home and the camp. We asked the driver to take us, it was a night with a full moon, thanks be to Allah. Believe me it is not in the country side. The elderly...everybody praises what you did, the great action you did, which was first and foremost by the grace of Allah. This is the guidance of Allah and the blessed fruit of jihad.

UBL: Thanks to Allah. What is the stand of the Mosques there (in Saudi Arabia)?

Shaykh: Honestly, they are very positive. Shaykh Al-Bahrani (phonetic) gave a good sermon in his class after the sunset prayers. It was videotaped and I was supposed to carry it with me, but unfortunately, I had to leave immediately.

UBL: The day of the events?

Shaykh: At the exact time of the attack on America, precisely at the time. He (Bahrani) gave a very impressive sermon. Thanks be to Allah for his blessings. He (Bahrani) was the first one to write at war time. I visited him twice in Al-Qasim.

UBL: Thanks be to Allah.

Shaykh: This is what I asked from Allah. He (Bahrani) told the youth: "You are asking for martyrdom and wonder where you should go (for martyrdom)?" Allah was inciting them to go. I asked Allah to grant me to witness the truth in front of the unjust ruler. We ask Allah to protect him and give him the martyrdom, after he issued the first fatwa. He was detained for interrogation, as you know. When he was called in and asked to sign, he told them, "don't waste my time, I have another fatwa. If you want me, I can sign both at the same time."

UBL: Thanks be to Allah.

Shaykh: His position is really very encouraging. When I paid him the first visit about a year and half ago, he asked me, "How is Shaykh Bin-Ladin?" He sends you his special regards. As far as Shaykh Sulayman 'Ulwan is concerned, he gave a beautiful fatwa, may Allah bless him. Miraculously, I heard it on the Quran radio station. It was strange because he ('Ulwan) sacrificed his position, which is equivalent to a director. It was transcribed word-by-word. The brothers listened to it in detail. I briefly heard it before the noon prayers. He ('Ulwan) said this was jihad and those people were not innocent people (World Trade Center and Pentagon victims). He swore to Allah. This was transmitted to Shaykh Sulayman Al ['Umar] Allah bless him.

UBL: What about Shaykh Al-[Rayan]?

Shaykh: Honestly, I did not meet with him. My movements were truly limited.

UBL: Allah bless you. You are welcome.

Shaykh: (Describing the trip to the meeting) They smuggled us and then I thought that we would be in different caves inside the mountains so I was surprised at the guest house and that it is very clean and comfortable. Thanks be to Allah, we also learned that this location is safe, by Allah's blessings. The place is clean and we are very comfortable.

UBL: (...Inaudible...) when people see a strong horse and a weak horse, by nature, they will like the strong horse. This is only one goal; those who want people to worship the lord of the people, without following that doctrine, will be following the doctrine of Muhammad, peace be upon him.

(UBL quotes several short and incomplete Hadith verses, as follows):

"I was ordered to fight the people until they say there is no god but Allah, and his prophet Muhammad."

"Some people may ask: why do you want to fight us?"

"There is an association between those who say: I believe in one god and Muhammad is his prophet, and those who don't (...inaudible...)

"Those who do not follow the true fiqh. The fiqh of Muhammad, the real fiqh. They are just accepting what is being said at face value."

UBL: Those youth who conducted the operations did not accept any fiqh in the popular terms, but they accepted the fiqh that the prophet Muhammad brought. Those young men (...inaudible...) said in deeds, in New York and Washington, speeches that overshadowed all other speeches made everywhere else in the world. The speeches are understood by both Arabs and non-Arabs—even by Chinese. It is above all the media said. Some of them said that in Holland, at one of the centers, the number of people who accepted Islam during the days that followed the operations were more than the people who accepted Islam in the last eleven years. I heard someone on Islamic radio who owns a school in America say: "We don't have time to keep up with the demands of those who are asking about Islamic books to learn about Islam." This event made people think (about true Islam) which benefited Islam greatly.

Shaykh: Hundreds of people used to doubt you and few only would follow you until this huge event happened. Now hundreds of people are coming out to join you. I remember a vision by Shaykh Salih Al-[Shuaybi]. He said: "There will be a great hit and people will go out by hundreds to Afghanistan." I asked him (Salih): "To Afghanistan?" He replied, "Yes." According to him, the only ones who stay behind will be the mentally impotent and the liars (hypocrites). I remembered his saying that hundreds of people will go out to Afghanistan. He had this vision a year ago. This event discriminated between the different types of followers.

UBL: (...Inaudible...) we calculated in advance the number of casualties from the enemy, who would be killed based on the position of the tower. We calculated that the floors that would be hit would be three or four floors. I was the most optimistic of them all. (...Inaudible...) due to my experience in this field, I was thinking that the fire from the gas in the plane would melt the iron structure of the building and collapse the area where the plane hit and all the floors above it only. This is all that we had hoped for.

Shaykh: Allah be praised.

UBL: We were at (...inaudible...) when the event took place. We had notification since the previous Thursday that the event would take place that day. We had finished our work that day and had the radio on. It was 5:30 p.m. our time. I was sitting with Dr. Ahmad Abu-al-[Khair]. Immediately, we heard the news that a plane had hit the World Trade Center. We turned the radio station to the news from Washington. The news continued and no mention of the attack until the end. At the end of the newscast, they reported that a plane just hit the World Trade Center.

Shaykh: Allah be praised.

UBL: After a little while, they announced that another plane had hit the World Trade Center. The brothers who heard the news were overjoyed by it.

Shaykh: I listened to the news and I was sitting. We didn't...we were not thinking about anything, and all of a sudden, Allah willing, we were talking about how come we didn't have anything, and all of a sudden the news came and everyone was overjoyed and everyone until the next day, in the morning, was talking about what was happening and we stayed until four o'clock, listening to the news every time a little bit different, everyone was very joyous and saying "Allah is great," "Allah is great," "We are thankful to Allah," "Praise Allah." And I was happy for the happiness of my brothers. That day the congratulations were coming on the phone non-stop. The mother was receiving phone calls continuously. Thank Allah. Allah is great, praise be to Allah.

(Quoting the verse from the Quran)

Shaykh: "Fight them, Allah will torture them, with your hands, he will torture them. He will deceive them and he will give you victory. Allah will forgive the believers, he is knowledgeable about everything."

Shaykh: No doubt it is a clear victory. Allah has bestowed on us…honor on us…and he will give us blessing and more victory during this holy month of Ramadan. And this is what everyone is hoping for. Thank Allah America came out of its caves. We hit her the first hit and the next one will hit her with the hands of the believers, the good believers, the strong believers. By Allah it is a great work. Allah prepares for you a great reward for this work. I'm sorry to speak in your presence, but it is just thoughts, just thoughts. By Allah, who there is no god but him. I live in happiness, happiness…I have not experienced, or felt, in a long time. I remember, the words of Al-Rabbani, he said they made a coalition against us in the winter with the infidels like the Turks, and others, and some other Arabs. And they surrounded us like the days…in the days of the prophet Muhammad. Exactly like what's happening right now. But he comforted his followers and said, "This is going to turn and hit them back." And it is a mercy for us. And a blessing to us. And it will bring people back. Look how wise he was. And Allah will give him blessing. And the day will come when the symbols of Islam will rise up and it will be similar to the early days of Al-Mujahedeen and Al-Ansar (similar to the early years of Islam). And victory to those who follow Allah. Finally said, if it is the same, like the old days, such as Abu Bakr and Othman and Ali and others. In these days, in our times, that it will be the greatest jihad in the history of Islam and the resistance of the wicked people.

Shaykh: By Allah my Shaykh. We congratulate you for the great work. Thank Allah.

Tape ends here

Second segment of Bin Laden's visit, shows up at the front of the tape

UBL: Abdallah Azzam, Allah bless his soul, told me not to record anything (…inaudible…) so I thought that was a good omen, and Allah will bless us (…inaudible…). Abu-Al-Hasan Al-[Masri], who appeared on Al-Jazeera TV a couple of days ago and addressed the Americans saying: "If you are true men, come down here and face us." (…inaudible…) He told me a year ago: "I saw in a dream, we were playing a soccer game against the Americans. When our team showed up in the field, they were all pilots!" He said: "So I wondered if that was a soccer game or a pilot game? Our players were pilots." He (Abu-Al-Hasan) didn't know anything about the operation until he heard it on the radio. He said the game went on and we defeated them. That was a good omen for us.

Shaykh: May Allah be blessed.

Unidentified Man Off Camera: Abd Al Rahman Al-(Ghamri) said he saw a vision, before the operation, a plane crashed into a tall building. He knew nothing about it.

Shaykh: May Allah be blessed!

Sulayman [Abu Guaith]: I was sitting with the Shaykh in a room, then I left to go to another room where there was a TV set. The TV broadcasted the big event. The scene was showing an Egyptian family sitting in their living room, they exploded with joy. Do you know when there is a soccer game and your team wins, it was the same expression of joy. There was a subtitle that read: "In revenge for the children of Al Aqsa', Usama Bin Ladin executes an operation against America." So I went back to the Shaykh (meaning UBL) who was sitting in a room with 50 to 60 people. I tried to tell him about what I saw, but he made gesture with his hands, meaning: "I know, I know…"

UBL: He did not know about the operation. Not everybody knew (…inaudible…). Muhammad [Atta] from the Egyptian family (meaning the Al Qa'ida Egyptian group), was in charge of the group.

Shaykh: A plane crashing into a tall building was out of anyone's imagination. This was a great job. He was one of the pious men in the organization. He became a martyr. Allah bless his soul.

Shaykh (referring to dreams and visions): The plane that he saw crashing into the building was seen before by more than one person. One of the good religious people has left everything and come here. He told me, "I saw a vision, I was in a huge plane, long and wide. I was carrying it on my shoulders and I walked from the road to the desert for half a kilometer. I was dragging the plane." I listened to him and I prayed to Allah to help him. Another person told me that last year he saw, but I didn't understand and I told him I don't understand. He said, "I saw people who left for jihad…and they found themselves in New York…in Washington and New York." I said, "What is this?" He told me the plane hit the building. That was last year. We haven't thought much about it. But, when the incidents happened he came to me and said, "Did you see…this is strange." I have another man…my god…he said and swore by Allah that his wife had seen the incident a week earlier. She saw the plane crashing into a building…that was unbelievable, my god.

UBL: The brothers, who conducted the operation, all they knew was that they have a martyrdom operation and we asked each of them to go to America but they didn't know anything about the operation, not even one letter. But they were trained and we did not reveal the operation to them until they are there and just before they boarded the planes.

UBL: (…inaudible…) then he said: Those who were trained to fly didn't know the others. One group of people did not know the other group. (…inaudible…)

(Someone in the crowd asks UBL to tell the Shaykh about the dream of [Abu-Da'ud]).

UBL: We were at a camp of one of the brother's guards in Qandahar. This brother belonged to the majority of the group. He came close and told me that he saw, in a dream, a tall building in America, and in the same dream he saw Mukhtar teaching them how to play karate. At that point, I was worried that maybe the secret would be revealed if everyone starts seeing it in their dream. So I closed the subject. I told him if he sees another dream, not to tell anybody, because people will be upset with him.

(Another person's voice can be heard recounting his dream about two planes hitting a big building).

UBL: They were overjoyed when the first plane hit the building, so I said to them: be patient.

UBL: The difference between the first and the second plane hitting the towers was twenty minutes. And the difference between the first plane and the plane that hit the Pentagon was one hour.

Shaykh: They (the Americans) were terrified thinking there was a coup.

[Note: Ayman Al-Zawahri says first he commended UBL's awareness of what the media is saying. Then he says it was the first time for them (Americans) to feel danger coming at them.]

UBL (reciting a poem): I witness that against the sharp blade They always faced difficulties and stood together...When the darkness comes upon us and we are bit by a Sharp tooth, I say..."Our homes are flooded with blood and the tyrant Is freely wandering in our homes"...And from the battlefield vanished The brightness of swords and the horses...And over weeping sounds now We hear the beats of drums and rhythm... They are storming his forts And shouting: "We will not stop our raids Until you free our lands"...

Bin Laden visit footage complete. Footage of the visit to the helicopter site follows the poem.

SOURCE: Department of Defense.

2002

INTERNATIONAL

On January 1, the Euro, the new currency of the European Union, goes into circulation.

American *Wall Street Journal* reporter Daniel Pearl is captured and killed by a Pakistani extremist group.

Violence again riddles the Middle East as Palestinian suicide bombers kill Israeli civilians.

Israeli troops besiege Yasir Arafat at his compound in Ramallah. On May 1, weeks after the offensive started, Arafat is permitted to leave his headquarters on the West Bank.

Robert Steinhaeuser, a student expelled from the Gutenberg School in Erfurt, Germany, attacks his former classmates, killing eighteen.

A coup briefly ousts Venezuelan president Hugo Chavez, but after two days he returns to power, promising a better government.

Jean-Marie Le Pen, an anti-immigration candidate, places second in the race for French Prime Minister, outpolling current President Lionel Jospin. Prime Minister Jacques Chirac defeats Le Pen in a run-off election.

In Argentina, the government of Fernando de la Rua falls as the nation's economy enters a crisis. Edward Duhalde of the Peronista Party becomes head of state.

DEATHS Queen Elizabeth, "the queen mum"; Princess Margaret of England.

NATIONAL

Enron Corporation, at one time the seventh largest U.S. company, sees its share price collapse when news emerges that the company had been concealing losses by setting up shell companies. Enron eventually goes bankrupt. Chief Executive Kenneth Lay pleads the fifth during Senate testimony. Another Enron executive, Clifford Baxter, commits suicide. President Bush and his administration come under fire for their association with Lay.

Alexander Garvin, a New York-based city planner and Yale professor is named to oversee the redesign of the former World Trade Center site.

Andrea Yates, the Texas mother who drowned her five children, is convicted of first-degree murder by a Houston jury. Her husband, Russell Yates, sues the psychiatrists who treated his wife.

On March 20th, the Senate votes 60–40 to pass a long-awaited campaign finance reform bill championed by Senators John McCain and Russ Feingold.

Marjorie Knoller is convicted of second-degree murder and her husband Robert Noel of involuntary manslaughter in the death of lacrosse coach Diane Whipple. The couple's Presa Canario killed Whipple last year.

The Benevolence International Foundation, a Muslim charity, and its longtime executive director, Enaam

Andrea Yates, center, looking back at her mother (outside of photo), after being found guilty of capital murder on March 12, 2002, in Houston, Texas. Yates, 37, had killed all five of her children; she is sentenced to life in prison. **AP/WIDE WORLD PHOTOS**

Arnaout, are accused of funneling money to Osama bin Laden's terrorist network.

White House counselor Karen Hughes, considered by many to be "the most influential person" in President Bush's administration, resigns in order to move back to Texas.

Billionaire businessman Michael Bloomberg is inaugurated as the 108th mayor of New York City on Jan. 1, 2002.

SEE PRIMARY DOCUMENT President George W. Bush's State of the Union Address

BUSINESS/INDUSTRY/INVENTIONS

Fixed-rate mortgages drop for five consecutive weeks as inflation remains at bay in the U.S. economy.

DEATHS Ruth Handler, inventor of Barbie dolls; Dave Thomas, founder of Wendy's; Pat Weaver, creator of *The Today Show;* Gordon Matthews, inventor of voicemail.

SCIENCE/MEDICINE

A U.S. National Research Council report finds that the greatest threat to a manned mission to Mars is hexavalent chromium, the chemical that affected citizens in the movie *Erin Brockovich.*

South African Internet entrepreneur Mark Shuttleworth pays for a ride into space aboard a Russian rocket, becoming the second "space tourist."

EDUCATION

The National Center for Public Policy and Higher Education finds that college costs are outpacing inflation and family income.

Congressional investigators urge lawmakers to create a single agency to oversee food safety after discovering that tainted school food is sickening more U.S. children every year.

RELIGION

The American Catholic Church is rocked by sex abuse scandals. Cardinals Bernard Law of Boston and Edward Eagan of New York come under fire for not bringing abuse cases to the attention of local law-enforcement officials and reassigning known offenders to other parishes. In remarks from the Vatican, the Pope encourages Catholics to maintain close ties with their priests.

ART/MUSIC

The Museum of Modern Art, "MoMA," a long-time Manhattan fixture, moves to Long Island City, Queens while its current site undergoes renovations.

SONGS "What's Luv?" by Fat Joe; "Ain't It Funny" by Jennifer Lopez, "How You Remind Me" by Nickelback, and "Video" by India.Arie.

DEATHS Lisa "Left Eye" Lopes, Waylon Jennings, singers; Chuck Jones, Daffy Duck animator.

LITERATURE/JOURNALISM

BOOKS *Austerlitz* by W.G. Sebald, *Bel Canto* by Ann Patchett, *Daddy's Little Girl* by Mary Higgins Clark, *Dust to Dust* by Tami Hoag Bantam, *John Henry Days* by Colson Whitehead.

DEATH Astrid Lindgren, author of Pippi Longstocking.

ENTERTAINMENT

Actor Robert Blake is charged with the 2001 murder of his wife Bonny Lee Bakley.

MOVIES *The Scorpion King, Kissing Jessica Stein, Collateral Damage, Blade 2, Spiderman,* and *Death to Smoochy.*

PLAYS *The Full Monty, The Producers, Some Like It Hot, Hairspray.*

DEATHS Linda Lovelace, former porn star turned anti-porn crusader; Milton Berle, comedian; actors Dudley Moore, John Agar; Billy Wilder, director.

SPORTS

Salt Lake City, Utah, hosts the Winter Olympics despite evidence that local leaders bribed IOC officials. The Games are racked by claims of unfair judging, as reflected in the IOC's decision to award two gold medals in the Figure Skating pair event.

Led by quarterback Tom Brady, the New England Patriots upset the heavily favored St. Louis Rams 20–17 on a last-second field goal by Adam Vinatieri.

Yao Ming, a 7-foot, 5-inch, Chinese center, arrives in America to train to play on professional basketball teams. Yao is expected to be one of the top picks in the upcoming NBA draft.

Jason Kidd becomes the first New Jersey Nets player to be named to the All-NBA first team.

The World Cup is held in May and June in South Korea and Japan.

WINNERS *Basketball*— Maryland, Men's NCAA; University of Connecticut, Women's NCAA; *Figure skating*— Sarah Hughes, Olympics (women); Alexei Yagudin, Olympics (men); *Football*— New England, Super Bowl XXXVI; *Golf*— Masters, Tiger Woods.

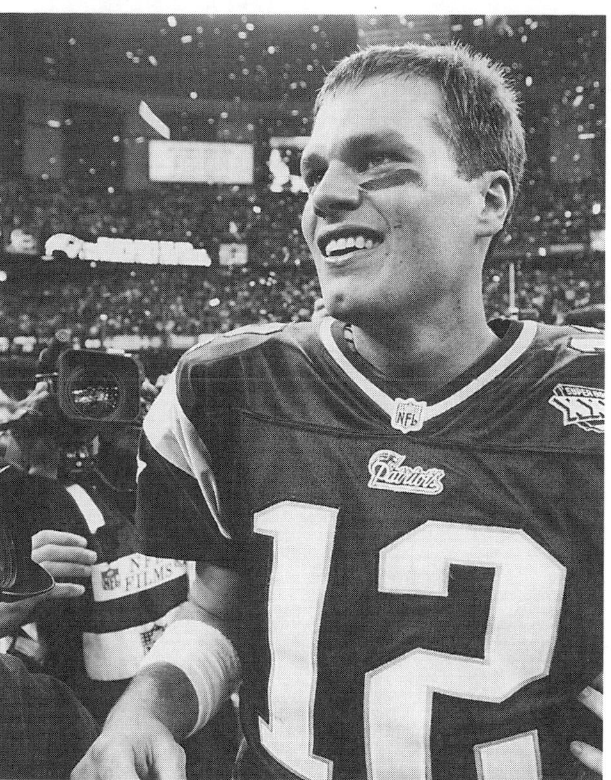

MVP quarterback Tom Brady celebrates after the New England Patriots beat the St. Louis Rams 20-17 in Super Bowl XXXVI at the Louisiana Superdome, Sunday, February 3, 2002. **AP/WIDE WORLD PHOTOS**

PRIMARY SOURCE DOCUMENT

President George W. Bush's State of the Union Address

INTRODUCTION Millions of Americans tuned in to President George W. Bush's first State of the Union address on January 29, 2002, with great anticipation. The nation had spent the previous four months recovering from the September 11 attacks on New York City and Washington, D.C. Families and friends of the victims were grieving over the loss of their loved ones. A well-financed terrorist network still posed a threat to the nation's security even as American soldiers battled overseas to shut it down. More and more Americans found themselves out of work as the economy slumped further. The ignominious collapse of Enron, a giant energy trader from Bush's home state, had weakened Americans' confidence in the stock market. The nation wanted to know how President Bush would respond to these disturbing developments.

Sitting near First Lady Laura Bush were Interim Afghan Prime Minister Hamid Karzai, the widow of slain CIA officer Johnny Michael Spann, and two soldiers wounded in action in Afghanistan. Speaking as the nation's capital was enveloped by incredibly tight security, Bush outlined what lay ahead for America: a long-term struggle against loosely organized terrorists and what he called an "axis of evil." Identifying Iran, Iraq, and North Korea as a threat to international peace and stability, Bush vowed to fight this "axis of evil" by enlarging American military forces abroad and doubling the budget for "homeland security."

Bush discussed other matters of national importance, in particular, his plan to end the recession and to create safeguards for Americans' 401(k) and pension plans. Though he did not mention Enron by name, he said that corporate America "must be made more accountable to employees and shareholders and held to the highest standards of conduct." His focus, however, was on how America would regain its confidence and its sense of security. Bush expressed his pride at how America had responded to a series of tragedies; he had been "humbled" in seeing "the true character of this country in a time of testing." In the end, he sent a message to nations everywhere that the United States was resolute in its fight against terrorism. If other countries "do not act," he said, "America will."

THE PRESIDENT: Thank you very much. Mr. Speaker, Vice President Cheney, members of Congress, distinguished guests, fellow citizens: As we gather tonight, our nation is at war, our economy is in recession, and the civilized world faces unprecedented dangers. Yet the state of our Union has never been stronger.

We last met in an hour of shock and suffering. In four short months, our nation has comforted the victims, begun to rebuild New York and the Pentagon, rallied a great coalition, captured, arrested, and rid the world of thousands of terrorists, destroyed Afghanistan's terrorist training camps, saved a people from starvation, and freed a country from brutal oppression.

Photograph sent by kidnappers of Daniel Pearl, a *Wall Street Journal* reporter investigating terrorist networks in Pakistan. He is brutally killed by Islamic terrorists after a massive manhunt fails to locate him. CNN/GETTY IMAGES

The American flag flies again over our embassy in Kabul. Terrorists who once occupied Afghanistan now occupy cells at Guantanamo Bay. And terrorist leaders who urged followers to sacrifice their lives are running for their own.

America and Afghanistan are now allies against terror. We'll be partners in rebuilding that country. And this evening we welcome the distinguished interim leader of a liberated Afghanistan, Chairman Hamid Karzai.

The last time we met in this chamber, the mothers and daughters of Afghanistan were captives in their own homes, forbidden from working or going to school. Today women are free, and are part of Afghanistan's new government. And we welcome the new Minister of Women's Affairs, Doctor Sima Samar.

Our progress is a tribute to the spirit of the Afghan people, to the resolve of our coalition, and to the might of the United States military. When I called our troops into action, I did so with complete confidence in their courage and skill. And tonight, thanks to them, we are winning the war on terror. The men and women of our Armed Forces have delivered a message now clear to every enemy of the United States: Even 7,000 miles away, across oceans and continents, on mountaintops and in caves—you will not escape the justice of this nation.

For many Americans, these four months have brought sorrow, and pain that will never completely go away. Every day a retired firefighter returns to Ground Zero, to feel closer to his two sons who died there. At a memorial in New York, a little boy left his football with a note for his lost father: "Dear Daddy, please take this to heaven. I don't want to play football until I can play with you again some day."

Last month, at the grave of her husband, Michael, a CIA officer and Marine who died in Mazur-e-Sharif, Shannon Spann said these words of farewell: "Semper Fi, my love." Shannon is with us tonight.

Shannon, I assure you and all who have lost a loved one that our cause is just, and our country will never forget the debt we owe Michael and all who gave their lives for freedom.

Our cause is just, and it continues. Our discoveries in Afghanistan confirmed our worst fears, and showed us the true scope of the task ahead. We have seen the depth of our enemies' hatred in videos, where they laugh about the loss of innocent life. And the depth of their hatred is equaled by the madness of the destruction they design. We have found diagrams of American nuclear power plants and public water facilities, detailed instructions for making chemical weapons, surveillance maps of American cities, and thorough descriptions of landmarks in America and throughout the world.

What we have found in Afghanistan confirms that, far from ending there, our war against terror is only beginning. Most of the 19 men who hijacked planes on September the 11th were trained in Afghanistan's camps, and so were tens of thousands of others. Thousands of dangerous killers, schooled in the methods of murder, often supported by outlaw regimes, are now spread throughout the world like ticking time bombs, set to go off without warning.

Thanks to the work of our law enforcement officials and coalition partners, hundreds of terrorists have been arrested. Yet, tens of thousands of trained terrorists are still at large. These enemies view the entire world as a battlefield, and we must pursue them wherever they are. So long as training camps operate, so long as nations harbor terrorists, freedom is at risk. And America and our allies must not, and will not, allow it.

Our nation will continue to be steadfast and patient and persistent in the pursuit of two great objectives. First, we will shut down terrorist camps, disrupt terrorist plans, and bring terrorists to justice. And, second, we must prevent the terrorists and regimes who seek chemical, biological or nuclear weapons from threatening the United States and the world.

Our military has put the terror training camps of Afghanistan out of business, yet camps still exist in at

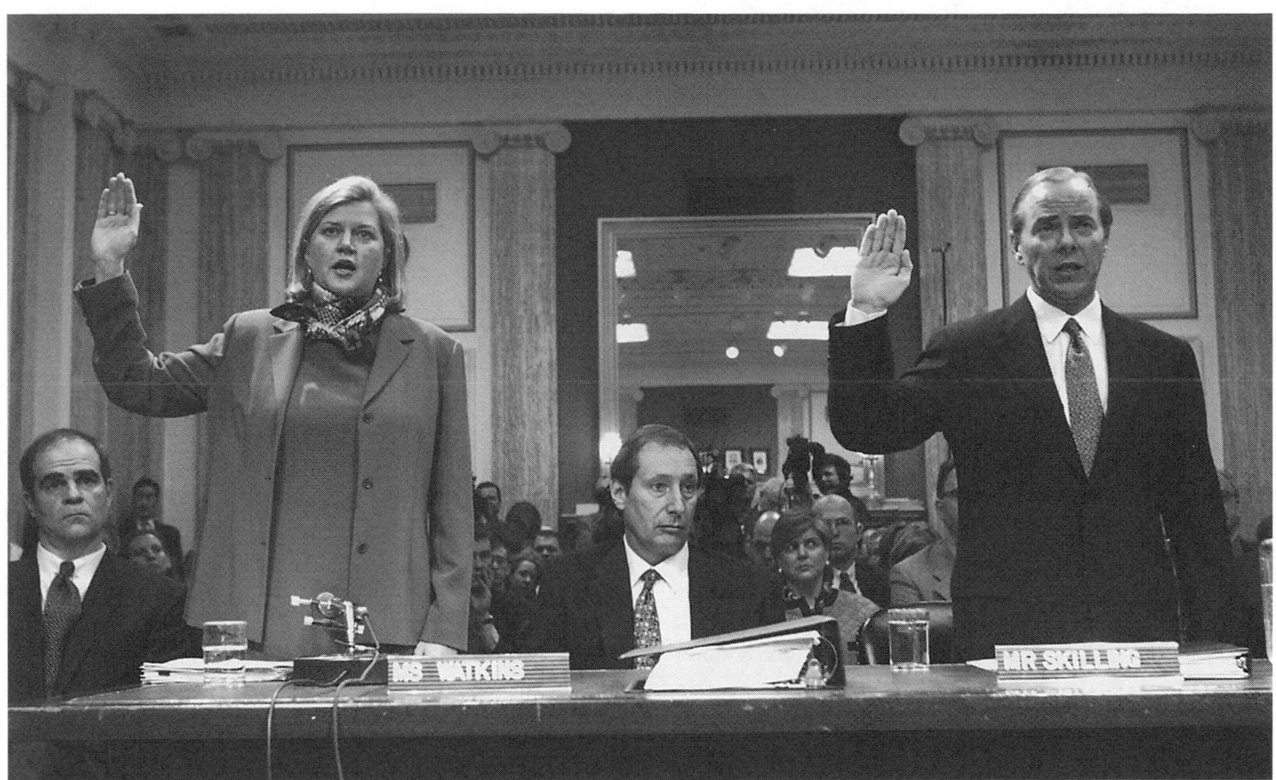

Enron vice president Sherron Watkins (left) and former chief executive officer Jeffrey Skilling are sworn in with their attorneys prior to testifying before the Senate Commerce Committee hearing on the collapse of the energy corporation. AP/WIDE WORLD PHOTOS

least a dozen countries. A terrorist underworld—including groups like Hamas, Hezbollah, Islamic Jihad, Jaish-i-Mohammed—operates in remote jungles and deserts, and hides in the centers of large cities.

While the most visible military action is in Afghanistan, America is acting elsewhere. We now have troops in the Philippines, helping to train that country's armed forces to go after terrorist cells that have executed an American, and still hold hostages. Our soldiers, working with the Bosnian government, seized terrorists who were plotting to bomb our embassy. Our Navy is patrolling the coast of Africa to block the shipment of weapons and the establishment of terrorist camps in Somalia.

My hope is that all nations will heed our call, and eliminate the terrorist parasites who threaten their countries and our own. Many nations are acting forcefully. Pakistan is now cracking down on terror, and I admire the strong leadership of President Musharraf.

But some governments will be timid in the face of terror. And make no mistake about it: If they do not act, America will.

Our second goal is to prevent regimes that sponsor terror from threatening America or our friends and allies with weapons of mass destruction. Some of these regimes have been pretty quiet since September the 11th. But we know their true nature. North Korea is a regime arming with missiles and weapons of mass destruction, while starving its citizens.

Iran aggressively pursues these weapons and exports terror, while an unelected few repress the Iranian people's hope for freedom.

Iraq continues to flaunt its hostility toward America and to support terror. The Iraqi regime has plotted to develop anthrax, and nerve gas, and nuclear weapons for over a decade. This is a regime that has already used poison gas to murder thousands of its own citizens—leaving the bodies of mothers huddled over their dead children. This is a regime that agreed to international inspections—then kicked out the inspectors. This is a regime that has something to hide from the civilized world.

States like these, and their terrorist allies, constitute an axis of evil, arming to threaten the peace of the world. By seeking weapons of mass destruction, these regimes pose a grave and growing danger. They could provide these arms to terrorists, giving them the means to match their hatred. They could attack our allies or attempt to blackmail the United States. In any of these cases, the price of indifference would be catastrophic.

We will work closely with our coalition to deny terrorists and their state sponsors the materials, technology, and expertise to make and deliver weapons of mass destruction. We will develop and deploy effective missile defenses to protect America and our allies from sudden attack. And all nations should know: America will do what is necessary to ensure our nation's security.

We'll be deliberate, yet time is not on our side. I will not wait on events, while dangers gather. I will not stand by, as peril draws closer and closer. The United States of America will not permit the world's most dangerous regimes to threaten us with the world's most destructive weapons.

Our war on terror is well begun, but it is only begun. This campaign may not be finished on our watch—yet it must be and it will be waged on our watch.

We can't stop short. If we stop now—leaving terror camps intact and terror states unchecked—our sense of security would be false and temporary. History has called America and our allies to action, and it is both our responsibility and our privilege to fight freedom's fight.

Our first priority must always be the security of our nation, and that will be reflected in the budget I send to Congress. My budget supports three great goals for America: We will win this war; we'll protect our homeland; and we will revive our economy.

September the 11th brought out the best in America, and the best in this Congress. And I join the American people in applauding your unity and resolve. Now Americans deserve to have this same spirit directed toward addressing problems here at home. I'm a proud member of my party—yet as we act to win the war, protect our people, and create jobs in America, we must act, first and foremost, not as Republicans, not as Democrats, but as Americans.

It costs a lot to fight this war. We have spent more than a billion dollars a month—over $30 million a day—and we must be prepared for future operations. Afghanistan proved that expensive precision weapons defeat the enemy and spare innocent lives, and we need more of them. We need to replace aging aircraft and make our military more agile, to put our troops anywhere in the world quickly and safely. Our men and women in uniform deserve the best weapons, the best equipment, the best training—and they also deserve another pay raise.

My budget includes the largest increase in defense spending in two decades—because while the price of freedom and security is high, it is never too high. Whatever it costs to defend our country, we will pay.

The next priority of my budget is to do everything possible to protect our citizens and strengthen our nation against the ongoing threat of another attack. Time and distance from the events of September the 11th will not make us safer unless we act on its lessons. America is no longer protected by vast oceans. We are protected from attack only by vigorous action abroad, and increased vigilance at home.

My budget nearly doubles funding for a sustained strategy of homeland security, focused on four key areas: bioterrorism, emergency response, airport and border security, and improved intelligence. We will develop vaccines to fight anthrax and other deadly diseases. We'll increase funding to help states and communities train and equip our heroic police and firefighters. We will improve intelligence collection and sharing, expand patrols at our borders, strengthen the security of air travel, and use technology to track the arrivals and departures of visitors to the United States.

Homeland security will make America not only stronger, but, in many ways, better. Knowledge gained from bioterrorism research will improve public health. Stronger police and fire departments will mean safer neighborhoods. Stricter border enforcement will help combat illegal drugs. And as government works to better secure our homeland, America will continue to depend on the eyes and ears of alert citizens.

A few days before Christmas, an airline flight attendant spotted a passenger lighting a match. The crew and passengers quickly subdued the man, who had been trained by al Qaeda and was armed with explosives. The people on that plane were alert and, as a result, likely saved nearly 200 lives. And tonight we welcome and thank flight attendants Hermis Moutardier and Christina Jones.

Once we have funded our national security and our homeland security, the final great priority of my budget is economic security for the American people. To achieve these great national objectives—to win the war, protect the homeland, and revitalize our economy—our budget will run a deficit that will be small and short-term, so long as Congress restrains spending and acts in a fiscally responsible manner. We have clear priorities and we must act at home with the same purpose and resolve we have shown overseas: We'll prevail in the war, and we will defeat this recession.

Americans who have lost their jobs need our help and I support extending unemployment benefits and direct assistance for health care coverage. Yet, American workers want more than unemployment checks—they want a steady paycheck. When America works, America prospers, so my economic security plan can be summed up in one word: jobs.

Good jobs begin with good schools, and here we've made a fine start. Republicans and Democrats worked together to achieve historic education reform so that no child is left behind.... There is more to do. We need to prepare our children to read and succeed in school with improved Head Start and early childhood development programs.

Good jobs also depend on reliable and affordable energy. This Congress must act to encourage conservation, promote technology, build infrastructure, and it must act to increase energy production at home so America is less dependent on foreign oil.....

The way out of this recession, the way to create jobs, is to grow the economy by encouraging investment in factories and equipment, and by speeding up tax relief so people have more money to spend. For the sake of American workers, let's pass a stimulus package.....

Americans know economic security can vanish in an instant without health security. I ask Congress to join me this year to enact a patients' bill of rights—(applause)—to give uninsured workers credits to help buy health coverage—(applause)—to approve an historic increase in the spending for veterans' health—(applause)—and to give seniors a sound and modern Medicare system that includes coverage for prescription drugs.

A good job should lead to security in retirement. I ask Congress to enact new safeguards for 401K and pension plans. Employees who have worked hard and saved all their lives should not have to risk losing everything if their company fails. Through stricter accounting standards and tougher disclosure requirements, corporate America must be made more accountable to employees and shareholders and held to the highest standards of conduct.

Retirement security also depends upon keeping the commitments of Social Security, and we will. We must make Social Security financially stable and allow personal retirement accounts for younger workers who choose them.....

During these last few months, I've been humbled and privileged to see the true character of this country in a time of testing. Our enemies believed America was weak and materialistic, that we would splinter in fear and selfishness. They were as wrong as they are evil.

The American people have responded magnificently, with courage and compassion, strength and resolve. As I have met the heroes, hugged the families, and looked into the tired faces of rescuers, I have stood in awe of the American people.

And I hope you will join me—I hope you will join me in expressing thanks to one American for the strength and calm and comfort she brings to our nation in crisis, our First Lady, Laura Bush.

None of us would ever wish the evil that was done on September the 11th. Yet after America was attacked, it was as if our entire country looked into a mirror and saw our better selves. We were reminded that we are citizens, with obligations to each other, to our country, and to history. We began to think less of the goods we can accumulate, and more about the good we can do.

For too long our culture has said, "If it feels good, do it." Now America is embracing a new ethic and a new creed: "Let's roll." In the sacrifice of soldiers, the fierce brotherhood of firefighters, and the bravery and generosity of ordinary citizens, we have glimpsed what a new culture of responsibility could look like. We want to be a nation that serves goals larger than self. We've been offered a unique opportunity, and we must not let this moment pass.

My call tonight is for every American to commit at least two years—4,000 hours over the rest of your lifetime—to the service of your neighbors and your nation. Many are already serving, and I thank you. If you aren't sure how to help, I've got a good place to start. To sustain and extend the best that has emerged in America, I invite you to join the new USA Freedom Corps. The Freedom Corps will focus on three areas of need: responding in case of crisis at home; rebuilding our communities; and extending American compassion throughout the world.

One purpose of the USA Freedom Corps will be homeland security. America needs retired doctors and nurses who can be mobilized in major emergencies; volunteers to help police and fire departments; transportation and utility workers well-trained in spotting danger....

This time of adversity offers a unique moment of opportunity—a moment we must seize to change our culture. Through the gathering momentum of millions of acts of service and decency and kindness, I know we can overcome evil with greater good. And we have a great opportunity during this time of war to lead the world toward the values that will bring lasting peace.

If anyone doubts this, let them look to Afghanistan, where the Islamic "street" greeted the fall of tyranny with song and celebration. Let the skeptics look to Islam's own rich history, with its centuries of learning, and tolerance and progress. America will lead by defending liberty and justice because they are right and true and unchanging for all people everywhere.

No nation owns these aspirations, and no nation is exempt from them. We have no intention of imposing our culture. But America will always stand firm for the non-negotiable demands of human dignity: the rule of law; limits on the power of the state; respect for women; private property; free speech; equal justice; and religious tolerance.

America will take the side of brave men and women who advocate these values around the world, including the Islamic world, because we have a greater objective than eliminating threats and containing resentment. We seek a just and peaceful world beyond the war on terror.

In this moment of opportunity, a common danger is erasing old rivalries. America is working with Russia and China and India, in ways we have never before, to achieve peace and prosperity. In every region, free markets and free trade and free societies are proving their power to lift lives. Together with friends and allies from Europe to Asia, and Africa to Latin America, we will demonstrate that the forces of terror cannot stop the momentum of freedom.

The last time I spoke here, I expressed the hope that life would return to normal. In some ways, it has. In others, it never will. Those of us who have lived through these challenging times have been changed by them. We've come to know truths that we will never question: evil is real, and it must be opposed. Beyond all differences of race or creed, we are one country, mourning together and facing danger together. Deep in the American character, there is honor, and it is stronger than cynicism. And many have discovered again that even in tragedy—especially in tragedy—God is near.

In a single instant, we realized that this will be a decisive decade in the history of liberty, that we've been called to a unique role in human events. Rarely has the world faced a choice more clear or consequential.

Our enemies send other people's children on missions of suicide and murder. They embrace tyranny and death as a cause and a creed. We stand for a different choice, made long ago, on the day of our founding. We affirm it again today. We choose freedom and the dignity of every life.

Steadfast in our purpose, we now press on. We have known freedom's price. We have shown freedom's power. And in this great conflict, my fellow Americans, we will see freedom's victory.

Thank you all. May God bless.

SOURCE: Text from White House website, available at http://www.whitehouse.gov/news/releases/2002/01/20020129-11.html

List of Contributors to the Second Edition

James Bergquist, Villanova University

Gretchen Boger, Princeton University

Lila Corwin Berman, Yale University

Marc Gallichio, Villanova University

Michael Jo, Yale University

Robert D. Johnston, Yale University

Russell Lawson, Bacone College

Michael Mullins, Yale University

Paul Rosier, Villanova University

John Wills, University of Bristol

Index

*Numbers in **boldface** indicate years; each year is followed by a colon and the corresponding page number. Example: Adams, Ansel, **1984:**617. Page numbers referring to non-chronology items—colonial history, sidebars, overviews, and primary source documents—also appear in **boldface.** When the subject is the focus of a non-chronology item, the item type is indicated as well in **boldface.** Example: Emancipation Proclamation, Lincoln draft, **primary source document: 222.** Page numbers in italics indicate illustrations. See separate index for more direct access to primary source documents.*

A

Volume 1: pp. 1–326; Volume 2: pp. 327–698

Volume 1: pp. 1–326; Volume 2: pp. 327–698

Volume 1: pp. 1–326; Volume 2: pp. 327–698

Volume 1: pp. 1–326; Volume 2: pp. 327–698

Volume 1: pp. 1–326; Volume 2: pp. 327–698

Volume 1: pp. 1–326; Volume 2: pp. 327–698

Volume 1: pp. 1–326; Volume 2: pp. 327–698

B

Volume 1: pp. 1–326; Volume 2: pp. 327–698

Volume 1: pp. 1–326; Volume 2: pp. 327–698

Volume 1: pp. 1–326; Volume 2: pp. 327–698

Volume 1: pp. 1–326; Volume 2: pp. 327–698

Volume 1: pp. 1–326; Volume 2: pp. 327–698

Volume 1: pp. 1–326; Volume 2: pp. 327–698

Volume 1: pp. 1–326; Volume 2: pp. 327–698

C

Volume 1: pp. 1–326; Volume 2: pp. 327–698

Volume 1: pp. 1–326; Volume 2: pp. 327–698

Volume 1: pp. 1–326; Volume 2: pp. 327–698

Volume 1: pp. 1–326; Volume 2: pp. 327–698

Volume 1: pp. 1–326; Volume 2: pp. 327–698

Volume 1: pp. 1–326; Volume 2: pp. 327–698

D

Volume 1: pp. 1–326; Volume 2: pp. 327–698

Volume 1: pp. 1–326; Volume 2: pp. 327–698

E

Volume 1: pp. 1–326; Volume 2: pp. 327–698

Volume 1: pp. 1–326; Volume 2: pp. 327–698

F

Volume 1: pp. 1–326; Volume 2: pp. 327–698

Volume 1: pp. 1–326; Volume 2: pp. 327–698

Volume 1: pp. 1–326; Volume 2: pp. 327–698

Volume 1: pp. 1–326; Volume 2: pp. 327–698

Volume 1: pp. 1–326; Volume 2: pp. 327–698

Volume 1: pp. 1–326; Volume 2: pp. 327–698

G

Volume 1: pp. 1–326; Volume 2: pp. 327–698

Volume 1: pp. 1–326; Volume 2: pp. 327–698

Volume 1: pp. 1–326; Volume 2: pp. 327–698

Volume 1: pp. 1–326; Volume 2: pp. 327–698

Volume 1: pp. 1–326; Volume 2: pp. 327–698

H

Volume 1: pp. 1–326; Volume 2: pp. 327–698

Volume 1: pp. 1–326; Volume 2: pp. 327–698

Volume 1: pp. 1–326; Volume 2: pp. 327–698

Volume 1: pp. 1–326; Volume 2: pp. 327–698

Volume 1: pp. 1–326; Volume 2: pp. 327–698

I

Volume 1: pp. 1–326; Volume 2: pp. 327–698

Volume 1: pp. 1–326; Volume 2: pp. 327–698

J

K

L

Volume 1: pp. 1–326; Volume 2: pp. 327–698

Volume 1: pp. 1–326; Volume 2: pp. 327–698

Volume 1: pp. 1–326; Volume 2: pp. 327–698

Volume 1: pp. 1–326; Volume 2: pp. 327–698

Volume 1: pp. 1–326; Volume 2: pp. 327–698

M

Volume 1: pp. 1–326; Volume 2: pp. 327–698

Volume 1: pp. 1–326; Volume 2: pp. 327–698

Volume 1: pp. 1–326; Volume 2: pp. 327–698

Volume 1: pp. 1–326; Volume 2: pp. 327–698

Volume 1: pp. 1–326; Volume 2: pp. 327–698

Volume 1: pp. 1–326; Volume 2: pp. 327–698

Volume 1: pp. 1–326; Volume 2: pp. 327–698

Volume 1: pp. 1–326; Volume 2: pp. 327–698

Volume 1: pp. 1–326; Volume 2: pp. 327–698

Volume 1: pp. 1–326; Volume 2: pp. 327–698

Volume 1: pp. 1–326; Volume 2: pp. 327–698

Volume 1: pp. 1–326; Volume 2: pp. 327–698

O

Volume 1: pp. 1–326; Volume 2: pp. 327–698

Volume 1: pp. 1–326; Volume 2: pp. 327–698

P

Volume 1: pp. 1–326; Volume 2: pp. 327–698

Volume 1: pp. 1–326; Volume 2: pp. 327–698

Volume 1: pp. 1–326; Volume 2: pp. 327–698

Volume 1: pp. 1–326; Volume 2: pp. 327–698

Volume 1: pp. 1–326; Volume 2: pp. 327–698

Volume 1: pp. 1–326; Volume 2: pp. 327–698

Volume 1: pp. 1–326; Volume 2: pp. 327–698

Q

R

Volume 1: pp. 1–326; Volume 2: pp. 327–698

S

Volume 1: pp. 1–326; Volume 2: pp. 327–698

Volume 1: pp. 1–326; Volume 2: pp. 327–698

Volume 1: pp. 1–326; Volume 2: pp. 327–698

Volume 1: pp. 1–326; Volume 2: pp. 327–698

Volume 1: pp. 1–326; Volume 2: pp. 327–698

Volume 1: pp. 1–326; Volume 2: pp. 327–698

Volume 1: pp. 1–326; Volume 2: pp. 327–698

T

Volume 1: pp. 1–326; Volume 2: pp. 327–698

Volume 1: pp. 1–326; Volume 2: pp. 327–698

Volume 1: pp. 1–326; Volume 2: pp. 327–698

Volume 1: pp. 1–326; Volume 2: pp. 327–698

Volume 1: pp. 1–326; Volume 2: pp. 327–698

Volume 1: pp. 1–326; Volume 2: pp. 327–698

Volume 1: pp. 1–326; Volume 2: pp. 327–698

V

W

Volume 1: pp. 1–326; Volume 2: pp. 327–698

Volume 1: pp. 1–326; Volume 2: pp. 327–698

Volume 1: pp. 1–326; Volume 2: pp. 327–698

Volume 1: pp. 1–326; Volume 2: pp. 327–698

X

Y

Volume 1: pp. 1–326; Volume 2: pp. 327–698

Z

Volume 1: pp. 1–326; Volume 2: pp. 327–698

Primary Source Document Index

This index provides access exclusively to primary source documents. For coverage outside of the primary source documents, see separate index.

Volume 1: pp. 1–326; Volume 2: pp. 327–698

Volume 1: pp. 1–326; Volume 2: pp. 327–698